MW01488653

NON CHRISTIAN WARNING

Prophecy, however, is for Believers

(In Jesus Christ as their Lord and Savior)

NOT for unbelievers!"

(1 Corinthians 14:22) Only one exception, Jewish People.

Accept Jesus Christ as your personal Lord and Savior to better understand the prophesies in this book! Becoming a Christian will be the most important decision you can ever make! To become a Christian pray this prayer, believe with all your heart, then turn from evil, follow His commands, and do good works for Jesus.

✝ **"Lord Jesus, I am truly sorry from my heart for the sins I have committed and ask You to forgive me. You see, I have tried on my own and failed. Now I need You to put my life back together again with Your will, not my way. Please come into my life and make me a new person. I believe You died on the cross for my sins and on the third day, God raised You from the dead. You now sit at the right hand of the Father God Almighty. Some day I will stand before You as my Judge and give an account of what I did as recorded in the books. I want the account to be good and pleasing to You. I believe by faith I am saved! Thank you Lord Jesus for sending the Holy Spirit into my life to guide and direct me in Your ways. I will turn from my old destructive ways and now begin to do good works for You, Jesus. Holy Father God, I pray this prayer in the name of Your Son, Jesus Christ. Amen"**

You are now a newborn Christian:

a) If you genuinely received an in-filling of the Holy Spirit into your life, first caused by true repentance and genuine heart-felt sorrow for past sins, then asking Jesus to forgive them and come into your life. Realize: The responsibility is with you!

b) If you genuinely experienced a true heart-felt want, desire, and confidence, that your life is now directed by the indwelling Holy Spirit and will change for the better. There must be evidence of this change through a turning away from evil and the life-long pursuit to do good works for Jesus or there's no salvation!

c) If you genuinely felt you are saved.

Finally, seek a Bible-believing Church of your choice for study and instruction concerning your public baptism. If you accepted Christ you are encouraged to first learn and follow Christian's basics by studying God's Bible and attending Church regularly. Prophecy is confusing even for the learned Christian, so learn the basics first. Now that you are a newborn Christian, the process of becoming a Disciple of Christ is at hand - there is a huge difference.

1-1-1 Israel - Jerusalem, The Via Dolorosa:

One of the cobblestones on the proposed path Jesus took to Calvary. The days of Christ are its presumed date.

Jesus may have walked on this very stone to die for your sins!

READER'S ALERT

God has scheduled you for this
Divine appointment before earth began!
You are holding this book of prophecies,
which can guide your future destiny.
If you want to keep your Nation from
falling prey to the Leopard Beast and finally
the Eagle with the Three Ugly Heads – then –

READ THESE PROPHECIES

Heed Your End Time Assignment!

THERE IS A GREAT STIR IN THE COSMOS.

Multitudes of runaway hoof beats approach with determination. There is a smell of death laced with famines, pestilences and destruction. They are galloping toward The Americas and Israel. Wars are stirring up nasty storm clouds, which boil on the blacked horizon of ashes. Their mighty blast of fury will engulf all nations.

Fear not Christian Soldiers because their leader, the angel of light will fail! For the Battle is the Lord's and He has summoned Michael, the Great Prince to stand up to protect and guide us through the violent fire-storms. We will hold our ground with perseverance, not wavering to the left or right. With faithful persistence, we will crush their ranks. Our patient endurance will see us through until the Son of Man comes on the clouds in His mighty power and glory to pronounce judgment in favor of His Saints. Glory to the Lord God for the victory He has brought us! *Bob R. Short 4-5-06 to 4-7-06*

1-1-2- Greece, Olympia - Building block of the Temple of Zeus: Pictured is a block that has deteriorated very badly from the weather. This famous center of antiquity is one of Greece's main attractions. There were many gods in this place, but none stood the test of time better than the god of sports did.

THE SCROLL

Accurate from the

† **WAKE UP CALL PROPHECIES** †

"See I have told you ahead of time"

The issuing of GOD'S FINAL DECREES
In SEQUENCE ORDER . . . . The TEST has BEGUN!

PROPHESIED BY

BOB R. SHORT, a Witness and Messenger

**Just before the test cycle ends,
Spirit-filled men will be elevated as watchmen
to warn and speak to the masses.
They will turn their attention to the prophecies and
teach many. Furthermore, they will insist upon the
literal interpretation of Bible prophecy in the midst of
much debate filled with commotion,
conflict and resistance!**

Bob R. Short, 9-18- 05

I, Bob Short, believe God's prophecies cannot be totally tied down by copyright laws, therefore, I now give permission to the reader to make one paper copy (not electronic) of any excerpts, pages, or complete section from the book. Use this paper copy for teaching, warning and spreading the (end time) WAKE UP CALL PROPHECIES to Christians and Jewish people along with their Military, Political, and Religious Leaders to instruct their congregations, and citizens.

NOTE: Precautions have been taken in the preparation of this book, although the publisher, packager, and author assume no responsibility for errors, accuracy, completeness or omissions. Any slights of people, places, organizations, religions, ideology or nations are unintentional. There are naturally some sharp disagreements in the aforementioned list. These are never meant as a disrespectful platform but a free God-given expression of ideas to disagree. This book of prophecies provides a helpful and informative insight into Biblical end time events from a Christian perspective. The author and publisher specifically disclaim any responsibility for any liability, loss, or risk, personal or otherwise, incurred consequently, directly or indirectly, of the use, adherence and application of any of the contents of this book.

Printed and Bound in the United States of America.

THE SCROLL was based from an unpublished manuscript (Serial Number: = 120.978.096.514.081.207, © 2007, TXu 1-336-817), plus many added photographs. This was further based from the WAKE UP CALL PROPHECIES, Original Rough Draft, Issue - 1, printed on 3-1996, under ISBN 0-9651408-0-6, has been included after grammar edit and clarification. Photos added with prophetic commentary (insight: 2005 to 2007) for better insight of both WUCP - Issue -1 and THE SCROLL.

THE SCROLL with GOD'S FINAL DECREES from the (end time) WAKE UP CALL PROPHECIES

All photos by: Bob R. Short or Alice Short.
All historical commentary with photos compiled by Bob R. Short from High School and College studies, the Bible, local historical guides and books, and/or tour bus leaders.
All calculations and sequencing prophetically performed by Bob R. Short
All sketches and diagrams prophetically hand drawn by Bob R. Short
Typeset arrangements, graphics-layouts, and general book design by Bob R. Short

Bob R. Short, Prophesying Author, Witness and Messenger, as inspired by:
The Spirit of Christ Jesus, the Spirit of Prophecy.

Published by: WAKE UP CALL PROPHECIES
PO Box 1582,
Bethany, OK. 73008 USA

ISBN 978-0-9651408-1-2

Attention: Churches, Schools, Military, and other organizations: Quantity discounts are available on bulk purchases of this book. Creation of Special books or Sections - 3 (as the Scroll), can be accommodated. Write to BULK PURCHASES at above publisher's address. Please enclose SASE.

To purchase a copy or the Collector addition of the Original WAKE UP CALL PROPHECIES, Rough Draft Issue-1, write for prices and enclose SASE.

TABLE OF CONTENTS

Section 1-3

This book has been divided into twelve sections.
Each section is divided into part numbers according to the topic.

Note: Following some description of the section and part number is (Issue-1 = page numbers). This refers the reader to the pages in the Original Rough Draft, Issue-1, Wake Up Call Prophecies, published in March, 1996 - not this book.

Why should you read this book of Prophecies? Because your very life may depend on it!

SECTION -1
INTRODUCTION

SECTION - 2
EVENINGS and MORNINGS

This entire section-2 was first prophesied and recorded as a matter of public record in a 232 page book called: Original WAKE UP CALL PROPHECIES, Rough draft Issue-I.

It was published (2-1996) under ISBN 0-9651408-0-6. This Section was prophesied between the following dates; September, 1994 to August, 1995, on original pages; 82 to 157.

EVENINGS AND MORNINGS VISION

Psalms 100 to 106 are designated by Slide Rule Sequencing Points (SRSP-S). Positions on God's slide ruler of seven time cycles of stabilized earth time. {Psalm 100 =100SRSP-S} through {Psalm 106 = 106SRSP-S} equals the seven years of the Tribulation Period. Study introduction about (SRSP) in section 2 - 8.

Psalms 100 to 106 are designated by Slide Rule Sequencing Points (SRSP-S) Positions on God's slide ruler of seven time cycles of stabilized earth time. {Psalm 100 =100SRSP-S} through {Psalm 106 = 106SRSP-S} equals the seven years of the Tribulation Period. Study introduction about (SRSP) in section 2 - 8.

SECTION - 3

THE SCROLL

A SUMMARY SEQUENCING EVENT CALENDAR INCLUDES LAST BEAST

SECTION - 4

LATEST PROPHECIES,

POETRY, PUZZLES, RIDDLES, WARNINGS, CALCULATIONS, and DECREES.

SECTION - 5

WAKE UP CALL I

This entire section-5 was first prophesied and recorded as a matter of public record in a 232-page book called: Original WAKE UP CALL PROPHECIES, Rough draft Issue-I. It was published (2-1996) under ISBN 0-9651408-0-6. This Section was prophesied between the following dates; May 13, to June 9, 1994, on original pages, 15 to 52.

SATAN'S DECEPTION

SECTION - 6

WAKE UP CALL II

This entire section-6 was first prophesied and recorded as a matter of public record in a 232-page book called: Original WAKE UP CALL PROPHECIES, Rough draft Issue-I. It was published (2-1996) under ISBN 0-9651408-0-6. This Section was prophesied between the following dates; July, to September 1994 on original pages, 53 to 82.

CALL TO UNITY

UNIVERSAL AMERICAN CHURCH COALITION

7

SECTION - 7
WAKE UP CALL - SHOCK WAVE

This entire section-7 was first prophesied and recorded as a matter of public record in a 232-page book called: Original WAKE UP CALL PROPHECIES, Rough draft Issue-I. It was published (2-1996) under ISBN 0-9651408-0-6. This section was prophesied between the following dates; September 1994 to August 1995, on original pages; 159 to 209.

SECTION - 8
FLOW CHART and PUZZLE - MYSTERY

SECTION - 9
FOUR BEASTS and MICHAEL

SECTION - 10
GLOSSARY - INDEX

SECTION - 11
PHOTO SUMMARY

SECTION - 12
ABOUT THE PROPHESYING AUTHOR

MY FIRST AND SECOND COMMAND

Section 1-4
from our Lord and Savior Jesus Christ

The Lord commanded me to see three hundred and thirty-three thousand churches in North and South America hear and understand the WAKE UP CALL PROPHECIES. The first goal is the United States, then North and South America and finally the entire world.

THE SPIRIT OF CHRIST, THE SPIRIT OF PROPHECY, MOVED ME TO WRITE TO CHURCHES AND ALSO TO THE LEADERS OF NORTH AND SOUTH AMERICA AS WELL AS OTHER PARTS OF THE WORLD.

JESUS SAID,
"Go make disciple nations! And be of one mind."

The USA was classified a disciple nation even with all the faults it had. Then between 1962 and 1967, the USA kicked God out of its government, laws, and schools. The Churches allowed the ***noisy den*** (special interest groups) to replace God with MAN'S RIGHTS. In that same time-period (1967), the Jewish people won Jerusalem back for God and invited Him back home. You see, the USA did not have any use for an outdated old Man called God anymore.

The Spirit told me, "the USA is now classified by God as a NON-DISCIPLE NATION and His protective covering has been slowly removed from this once great nation under God!" The Churches have totally lost their power to control the trinity of a disciple nation, that is, its government, laws and people in harmony with the teaching of the word from the Holy Bible. Christian Churches bonding together through the "UACC" will be the best and most likely way to avert "THE THREE WOES TO AMERICA" and return the USA to a disciple nation, whereby restoring God's protective covering.

The Spirit also moved me to write, "fifty to eighty-five percent of Church attendees are classified thieves or lukewarmers and will lose greatly before the judgment seat of Christ per Matthew 24:10. "Churches, take the test for lukewarmness!" Amen.

My burden is the LUKEWARMER in Churches that God is going to spit out of His mouth into the tribulation period. They could become discouraged, misled, and fall away if not awakened and find themselves separated from God forever. Lukewarmers do not have the ability to distinguish the threat the European led Leopard Beast (MNO) presents to North and South America. We must not give in to it!

Below 1-4-1- Italy, Pisa - Leaning Tower: Will the tower fall? Time will tell. Will America fall? Time will tell. The Lord God has the power to save America. Unity in the Church has the power to bring America back to a disciple nation. Unfortunately, if the lord God has to straighten America out, the costs will be enormous. However, if the church unifies and forms the Universal American Church Coalition (UACC), then much disaster can be avoided. (Refer to UACC, Section 6-5 through 6-9).

1-5-0- Italy, Rome, San Paolo Fuori le Mura - St. Paul's outside the walls Basilica:

God reminded me of my appointed task, to prophesy, warn others, and teach the truth about endtimes. He encouraged me in the Spirit of my mind, as I stood underneath this magnificent statue of St. Paul. The Lord God is poring out His Spirit on all flesh per Joel 2:28. When men or women claim to receive inspiration and speaks forth prophetic insight in the name of the Lord, do Christians test their motivating intentions? Do they investigate which spirit from outside time-space they received the information?

INTRODUCTION PART - I

How to test the spirit of a prophet

Section 1-5

Bob R. Short has prophesied this complete book with the focus on waking up the lukewarm Christians in America's Churches. Then he has warned Christians and political leaders in North and South America. Finally, it is a warning for the leaders and citizens of the Leopard Beast (see glossary). Prophesying to these people has not been a popular task. Some do not want to hear about their disobedience to the Lord God, which brings judgments of doomsday and decrees issued against them as discipline. Rejection slams the door shut on repentance, while denial ensnares attitudes to overlook the great deception engulfing the earth.

We are at the end of the second sabbatical day of the Church Age - the point when all prophecies of the ages converge and find their ultimate fulfillment. The Wake Up Call Prophecies are only part of the total picture. They disclose the future of the Jews, Gentiles, and the Church of the Lord Jesus Christ. The focus shall be on the Churches and citizens of the USA, and then the rest of the world concerning what part they play concerning end time events. Through these prophecies, the Spirit of Christ, the Spirit of Prophecy, has made known the eternal, supernatural truths and realities, which man never will realize or discover otherwise.

As you read these prophecies, apply the birthing pain principle - the phenomenon of progressive increases of signs and events lapping and overlapping toward a focal point. It shall be far better to understand the general flow of sequencing of events than to focus on times and dates. The Bible teaches us to watch for the sequencing of signs. Slide rule sequencing points (see Glossary and section 2-8) are assigned to certain events. However, this only serves to help the Christian understand progressive end time sequencing of events. Such prophecy will be completely trustworthy because God is omniscient and He promised many prophecies would occur during the last day (Joel 2:28).

When reading prophecy, the hardest challenge to the mind is how to test its authenticity. We normally evaluate what a person says by scripture. When prophets predict something not related to the Bible, our testing benchmark fads into the obscurity. We see in the book of Revelation that John did not give scripture from Old Testament prophets on every point he prophesied. He simply wrote what the Spirit said to write. We do know prophecy must be in harmony with the Bible. The only true and valid test of prophecy from our perspective must be time. In other words, did what actually happen generally agree with the prophesied event, sign, calculation or projection? Were they close enough to statistically say they were not a guess?

"DO NOT TREAT PROPHECIES WITH CONTEMPT," 1 Thessalonians 5:20. Christian, be careful at this point not to scoff at (ridicule or make fun of) other people's prophecies regardless of whether they are determined to be good or bad. The unpardonable sin (Matthew 12:30-32) of scoffing at Christians' prophecy carries the offensive label called **"blaspheming the Holy Spirit".** Scoffers are ridiculing the Spirit of Jesus Christ, not the Christian prophet. Of course we do not follow a prophecy sent by Satan, but do not scoff at his (ridicule or make fun) prophecies for this has been allowed by God Almighty so Satan can tempt and test us during endtimes.

To test the source of a prophet's spirit requires opening the Bible and studying.

Scoffing at Christian prophecy manifests itself through foolish thinking to deliberately ascribe to Satan the work of the Spirit of Prophecy, the Spirit of Jesus (Revelation 19:10 and 22:6). This is to reject the insight from the Spirit of Christ and imply it came from Satan. They knowingly or through ignorance are rejecting Christ Jesus' message through prophecy even though His Spirit has been heaven-authenticated.

Scoffing at Christian prophecy ascribes to Satan the work of the Spirit of Prophecy, the Spirit of Jesus (Revelation 19:10 and 22:6).

For God sends prophecies to men for their strengthening, encouragement, comfort, and insight into Satan's deceptive agenda. Test everything including prophecy - this is God's decree to Christians. The question arises, what if a person declares he is Christian but his prophecies are contrary to the Bible? Answer; do not follow him or his teachings! On the other hand, do not scoff at (ridicule or make fun of) his prophecies. By all means, speak out against what he is prophesying, with love and determination, but not scoffing. Be careful not to judge too harshly about disagreement concerning a denominational issue. A few are worthy to hold our ground, while most denominational issues do not contain much value when we stand before God to give an account of what we did to receive rewards for our next assignment. What Mr. Short has been discussing here is when a prophet speaks out against the validity of the Bible or denounces Jesus as the only way to the Father and issues like that. We must not follow them!

If readers cannot judge a specific prophecy by Scripture and must wait for the event to occur, how are they going to test its validity? Unfortunately, the answer is, they cannot or must use blind faith. However, saying that, the readers can cross check the prophet against where they predicted something in harmony with the Bible and whether it happened. If the prophet's accuracy is of a high degree here then it follows that maybe some validity into a prediction that require time as a testing tool should have more attention paid to it.

The immeasurable fullness of God's ways and plans leads us to the humble recognition the WAKE UP CALL PROPHECIES are only part of the total picture (1 Corinthians 13:9). When Mr. Short prophesied concerning endtimes, emotions flooded his being by the fact the judgments described in the Book of Revelation are beginning to take place today (Luke 21:31).

"Deception can't be deception unless it is deceptive." It is important for the reader to understand this statement. Let restate another way, "Deception must not appear to be deception or else it won't be effective," and if it is not effective, then the Bible's wrong and Satan's trickery is not true deception. This means the truth must be hidden from normal understanding by someone trying to test or trick others for their benefit. The Bible teaches even the elect (Matthew 24:24) would be deceived if God did not intervene and expose the lie to them. This implies two things. First, prophecies will lead the endtimer into the truth and expose Satan's agenda. Second, today's Christians must be warned about Satan's deception. Most people will not be able to understand the truth. Satan uses deception through lust of money, security, conveniences, pleasure, status, and praise to trick people into wanting worldly idols. Satan's trickery has now made attraction to idols more effective for many than the fear of God's wrath for disobedience.

"Deception must not appear to be deception or else it won't be effective." If it is not effective, then the Bible's wrong and Satan's trickery isn't true deception.

Below, 1-5-1- Israel, Mt. Carmel - Statue of Elijah - Carmelite Monastery: This is the scene of Elijah's sacrifice on the altar he had built, and the site of the heathen altars of Baal, whose priests, after being proved false prophets, were slain (1 Kings 18). Prophets must be tested today just like Elijah, false prophets and true prophets were in days of old. Therefore, it becomes important for the Christian to test prophecy first against correlation with the Bible, and second with time. Try to determine which Spirit (God's or Satan's) the prophet has heeded. Then Christians will know whether to follow the prophet's predictions. Therefore, do not scoff at individual prophecy but test it. Follow the prophet if they test okay and stay away if they fail the test. The Wake Up Call Prophecies are accurate to date.

Mr. Short has tried to clarify God's eternal purpose concerning the USA and the world, not mystify it. He has not attempted to present an elaborate outline or use heavy theological terminology. His goal is to wake up Jews, Christians and leaders of nations with simplicity through a progression of end time insights into signs, events, calculations, and God's decrees.

The Spirit of Christ Jesus through Mr. Short, a messenger, sends these prophecies. The purpose is to alert, wake up, and prepare millions of lukewarmers and the Church to the fact Jesus will be coming soon. Remember, it is going to be more inconvenient for Christians than the sinner during the endtimes to determine our worthiness.

When testing the source of a prophet's spirit, twelve steps to consider are:

1. **TIME:** Time will expose the truth to whether a prophet received credible information from the Holy Sprit (Deuteronomy 18:22). Be careful, a person's location on earth will greatly affect his perspective on a prophesied event (discuss later in the book). One person will say an event in the SCROLL fulfilled because it happened in his country. A person on the opposite side of earth will say it is not because he has not heard about it. Nevertheless, he will tell you about another event in the SCROLL that happened in his country that you had not heard about. Perception equates to reality as well as access to responsible world news, which will deteriorate and favor the Leopard Beast the closer we come to the end.

2. **PROPHET FULFILLING THEIR PROPHESIED EVENT:** This can go either way. Most prophets do not fulfill their own predictions or warnings while others did or will. For instance, Jesus will return and fulfill His own prophecies and the Great Commission. The Two Witnesses will prophesy and then in some instances fulfill their own warning prophecies using devastating force. It depends on what God has designed a prophet to do.

3. **FACTUALITY PLUS NON-FOLLOWERS BELIEVE:** To be understandable, the prediction must be such that the reader can determine whether the event occurred or not. However, some parts of the Wake Up Call Prophecies are riddles, coded, or sealed instructions for future understanding. Only at the appointed time will the appropriate persons be able to see and understand the insight. A true prophet should be able to reach people outside his circle of influence or inner circle of followers.

4. **BACKED BY SCRIPTURE:** This is false, each individual prediction, calculation, instruction, or decree does not require a specific scripture assigned to it to make it valid. A prophecy may or may not have scripture backup. A prophet writes what the Spirit tells him.

5. **FUTURE FORETOLD IN WRITING:** For prophecy to be believable so it will edify the Church or warn others of upcoming events, it is best to record it in writing. A person's oral prophesy in front of a Church congregation will be greatly diminished in the future if it is not recorded in writing by a credible source. Hearsay prophecies require blind faith to believe and may produce skepticism and folly.

6. **PUBLICLY RECORDED BEFORE THE EVENTS OCCURRED:** A prophet will sacrifice believability if the source of recording is not credible. For instance, the original Wake Up Call Prophecies were first published as a matter of public record under an ISBN number in February 1996.

7. **HARMONY WITH THE BIBLE:** A prophet may predict something that the Bible does not address. Therefore, time will be the only true test along with study and prayer. However, if the Bible has addressed the description in the prophecy, then the predictions must be in parallel or harmony with it. In other words, the supreme test of a Christian prophet is unwavering loyalty to Christ.

8. **ORIGINAL MEANING OF BIBLE PROPHECIES CANNOT BE CHANGED:** This makes sense. However, a prophet can add additional insight and understanding by issuing later prophecies, which build on the original. Consider Daniel 2, fourth beast, verses chapter 7, fourth beast, and 2 Esdras 9-13, fourth beast.

9. CONTAIN WARNINGS, BLESSING, CURSES AND INSTRUCTION: End time prophets are warning messengers of God Almighty, not polite, feel your pain, smiling, joke-telling, modern lukewarm marketers of the prosperous good life. A true prophet of God will be a warning messenger to the disobedience found in the Church and the nations of the world. Therefore, one might conclude that many will not like the prophet's warning words.

10. FOLLOWERS FULFILL THE EVENT: An effective prophet of God will have his followers help fulfill end time events. This is not true all the time, for Joel 2:28 states, men and women will prophesy and it is not necessary to have huge followings. But saying that, Daniel 11:33, states there are a few teachers or messengers some of which will be prophets and have huge following to resist the Antichrist Spirit.

11. FORETOLD EVENTS MUST HAPPEN AFTER PROPHET'S DEATH: This has always been a good measure for testing a prophet. However, end time prophets fulfilling Joel 2:28 will not have time to prophesy something then die and the event happen much later. If this is true then there will be a high turnover of end time prophets, or endtimes would be pushed out to infinity, and we know this is not the case. It is important to understand a last-days Joel 2:28 prophet will cross-reference history, the Bible, and current events to foresee what will happen next. He will then warn or prophesy this event if guided to do so by the Spirit. But a worldly or lukewarmer who lacks guidance from the Holy Spirit only thinks the same events are everyday occurrences whereby fulfilling Matthew 24:38-39. It states they did not know the flood was coming.

12. PREDICTIONS MUST BE 100% ACCURATE AND FULFILL LITERALLY: Many Christians have been told prophecy is errorless with perfect precision. However, the Lord God's prophets are not always sure of what they prophesied nor are they 100% accurate. Why, one might ask? Because God left each individual prophet's human factor in his prophecies to mystify it. The prophet uses faith in trying to relay what the Spirit of Christ Jesus is instructing him. God allotted him faith as He sees fit (Romans 2:6). Likewise, humans will try using what faith has been given to them to decipher what the prophet says or writes. Therefore, even the most learned Biblical student would find prophecy shrouded in mystery, decrees, puzzles, and riddles that are extremely challenging. A prophet of Almighty God has to be correct in his or her predictions most of the time but not 100% of the time. Now consider these points.

Sometimes prophecy is sealed or coded using;

- **Metaphorical** *(replace something or an idea with another to suggest likeness).*
- **Symbolical** *(something concrete in our reality but represents some other thing prophetically that cannot in itself be pictured).*
- **Allegorical** *(a symbolic prophetic representation of abstract truth presented by means of fictional characters, calculations, and events) language, which makes it obscure, puzzling, and hard to understand.*

An Old Testament prophet prophesied against a good man and said he would die soon. The man petitioned God, and received a number of years to live by winning his case. The prophet and the Holy Spirit or the Spirit of Christ Jesus was not 100% correct. This is one of the reasons why Jesus said there is only one perfect and that is My Father in Heaven - God Almighty. Next, we see Jesus petitioning His Father in the garden of Gethsemane about changing the prophetic test program to exclude His crucifixion (cup). Jesus knew God could alter prophecy, but Almighty God left the program the same whereby allowing Jesus to fulfill prophecy. On many occasions in Christian writings, the prophet would make a statement like, "who knows, if you repent, God may change His mind and not fulfill what I have just prophesied." In other words, many prophets were not sure what they prophesied would actually happen. One ran from God, another complained no one was listening, but God said He reserved a few thousand people for Himself.

Not all prophetic predictions were or will be fulfilled literally which produces the illusion that the prophecy was originally inaccurate. However, there must be a common denominator (literal, hidden, or calculated) tying the literal to the fulfillment. Remember, Jesus, (a Jew) prophesied about Elijah's, (a Jew), returning as John the Baptist, (a Jew) and not a literal name of Elijah (Matthew 11:13-15; Malachi 3:1-4). Mr. Short has further prophesied a male Jew in our present day has also fulfilled Elijah's return (Luke 1:17) for the final time. Again, this man's name is not literally Elijah. The common denominator is, a Jewish male raised in power by God and having the spirit of Elijah.

Another example, Paul applied prophetic insight about the literal national Israel that Hosea 1:9-10, 2:23 prophesied about and turned it around calling it the Church of Jesus Christ in Romans 9:25-26. Once again, we see Old and New Testaments prophecy colliding. We know by the Old Testament that Abraham was the literal father of Israel. However, in Romans 4:11, 16, and Galatians 3:7 we see the Church has now been included under Abraham's umbrella.

Therefore, even the most learned Biblical student would find prophecy shrouded in mystery, decrees, puzzles, and riddles that are extremely challenging.

What does all these confusing prophecies mean? Be very careful in judging prophetic event until you have completely studied and prayed about its meaning and understanding.

Being a Christian prophet will not be all some think it be. It is work, which will be unpleasant and met with resistance from lukewarmers and the world. The Bible tells every Christian to eagerly desire the gift of prophecy (1 Corinthians 14:1). However, Mr. Short will tell Christians to get ready for a shock if they become a prophet. God will call on you to predict the future or maybe speak forth the word of God on any subject. Nevertheless, ask yourself, whom are you speaking to? Answer, lukewarmers mostly and herein begins the challenge. Some Christian opposition states Jesus was the ultimate fulfillment of revelation and we need look no further than Him. If this statement is truth, then why would God include Joel 2:28 and the Two Witnesses?

Study the Bible and this book of prophecies carefully to find your end time assignment from God. Analyze how you, your family, church, community, state, nation will be affected. Watch for signs. When reading and studying these prophecies, ask the Lord God to disclose what spirit Mr. Short used to prophesy. So far, using statistics on an end time mathematical model, would suggest the subjective probability is astronomical Mr. Short could not have guessed as many future events correctly as he prophesied. Therefore, the spirit that guided him from outside our time-space domain, must have been the Spirit of Christ Jesus, the Spirit of prophecy.

Mr. Short challenges the readers to a very intriguing decision, do you honestly think Jesus Christ's second coming is close? If so, answer these three questions. What is the Church's first duty and greatest danger? What must your country do to prepare for what is ahead? Why is the world, as we know it about to change forever?

Below - 1-5-2- Israel, Old Jaffa - Bob - Prophet: Old Jaffa is best known for having the port where the Old Testament Prophet Jonah ran from God and ended up in the belly of a great fish. It is also where Peter saw a vision of heaven opening up and received instructions from God (Acts 10:11-15). The Bible issues many warnings about testing the prophet or spirit to determine which source the person's information came from outside our time-space, God or Satan's (Matthew 24:4, 1 John 4:1-3, 1 Thessalonians 5:20-21, and others).

We have examined systematically the validity of certain Christian teachings concerning the test for accepting a person's projections of future events and instruction as inspired and prophetic. If accepted, this person would be considered a prophet or messenger receiving inspired information outside the time-space of our test cycle. There are many guidelines and tests but we have discussed twelve to help the reader determine if this book is the inspired work of Almighty God or not. (Review Four Spirits, Section 4-15)

Of course, a prophet can speak forth the word of God on any subject not just future events, such as Mr. Short's instruction to the Church about starting the UACC (section 6, part 5-10). This was instruction to the Church, stating they ought to do certain actions, not prophesying the UACC as a fulfilling event to happen in the future. Nevertheless, take into consideration the same twelve discussed points for testing its Christian validity.

INTRODUCTION PART - II

God's Final Decrees

Section 1-6

From the beginning, God has progressively revealed Himself and His sovereign plan. The word of God contains the prophetic message that has guided the destiny of the human race and spiritual kingdoms since the times of Adam. In His supreme wisdom, God has hidden His plans in symbolic terms, which cannot be comprehended until it is time to understand them. Only when the Spirit of Christ Jesus, the Spirit of Prophecy, chooses to give enlightenment can the prophetic message of the Lord God be known.

Read between the lines in this book and discover the hidden mysteries you may be directly involved in!

Another factor is the human vessel through which the Spirit of Christ works. Historically, selection of a messenger has been solely the act of the Lord God. Those individuals usually did not possess credentials other than receiving the message of the Lord God for the times they lived in and commanded to speak to the times of unborn generations. However, present day prophets will only speak to this generation because there will not be a next generation.

It has been approximately six thousand years since the first prophecy appeared in Genesis 3:15. Hundreds of prophetic statements began to follow. Many have materialized and accurately fulfilled while others are yet to be fulfilled. Jesus said, *"see I have told you ahead of time."* The Wake Up Call Prophecies help fulfill this promise. Without exception, the Lord God initiates both utterance and understanding. Neither man nor spirit has any capability to unravel the prophetic mysteries independently of the Lord God.

I have been called to prepare the elect or the times we are living. My task is not to answer every question or address every critic.

A prophet or messenger can cause others to believe with the help of the Holy Spirit, although his first task is to tell what has been revealed to him. Due to the uniqueness of prophecy, it does not fit the natural mind or thinking. Therefore, the prophet may be viewed as a social misfit. Rejection is a risk one must take in telling what has been revealed to him. Time confirms the accuracy of the prophecy.

The message I want to share with you began while I was sitting at my desk on Friday, May 13, 1994. A great revelation began to unfold in the spirit of my mind as I began reading and studying Revelation 13. The Spirit of Christ drew my thinking to verse eighteen, *"This calls for wisdom. If anyone has insight, let him calculate the number of the beast, for it is man's number. His number is 666."*

Immediately the question came to me, "Lord, why are you showing me the calculations of 666."

There were no audible words to my natural sense of hearing, but in the spirit of my mind I heard the words from Proverbs 3:5-8, *"Trust in the Lord with all your heart and lean not to your own understanding. In all your ways acknowledge him and he will make your paths straight. Do not be wise in your own eyes. Fear the Lord and shun evil. This will bring health to your body and nourishment to your bones."*

"Who, what, or why is this information unfolding in my mind?" I asked.

Again, I heard Him say, *"And I saw what looked like a sea of glass mixed with fire, and standing beside the sea, those who had been victorious over the beast and his image and over the number of his name"* (Revelation 15:2). This text puzzled me; maybe God was going to show me how to overcome these obstacles.

My mind raced for reasons as to why this explosion of thoughts and insight began happening to me. In college, my studies were in mathematics, physics, and business. By nature, I enjoy calculations. My first job was working in manufacturing-computer switching equipment where international modules locked and crisscrossed with modules. I worked in the Engineering department and programmed computers, worked and understood in detail complex wiring drawings on how central office equipment tied together the entire world. One could monitor the buy and sell mode as well as controlling the movement of people simply by overseeing the connecting hub of all transmission stations, satellites and central offices worldwide.

Study each paragraph and pray the Lord God will unveil your next assignment and what action is needed.

As I pondered about what the Lord God wanted, it seemed He sought someone who did not possess boastful deeds to parade in front of the world. This was a fit when He chose me! The reasons God began revealing these messages to me have become very clear over the years. One explanation must be, God saw I believe totally and possess unwavering faith in the atoning work of Jesus Christ. Furthermore, my heart has always pursued the Lord God.

Before I share this revelation with you, I want to emphasize the warning in Revelation 22:18. Scripture says it shall be a fearful action to add to, or take from, the message of the Book of Revelation. It is not my intention to add to or take from the Book of Revelation; however, I fear God more than I fear man. Therefore, I am compelled to tell the revelation to the elect people, the Lord's saints and warn other worldwide. They must understand the times of deception and sequence of signs and events in which we are living. This message shall be especially important to those saints living during the time of the fulfilling of Revelation 13. The Spirit of Christ compels me to spread the message as broadly throughout the world as possible. I am trying to do this! **I need your help!**

The Holy Spirit imparted many more signs and events to take place before and during the tribulation period since I published Wake Up Call-I, Issue 1, in March, 1996. This book "The SCROLL" closes the gap between Wake Up Call-I (3-96) and additional sequencing of signs and wonders in the future. The Spirit enlightened me on further sequencing of events and better understanding of endtimes. This leads to the summary chapter (Section 3) of sequenced events called "The SCROLL". These prophecies are fulfilling right on target since I published the first Wake Up Call Prophecies in March 1996.

As you read the following pages, I expect you to have some natural doubts. It is not my task to answer every question or address every critic. My task or command from God dictates I tell you and commit the results to the Spirit of Christ as He prepares the elect for the times in which we are living. My burden remains the same, turning the hellbound lukewarmer back to Jesus Christ. My command is to awaken our leaders in Churches and America's elected officials and others around the world to the emerging deceptive European led World Government = Millenium Nations Organized (MNO = 666). Refer to section 6-3.

A Command for all Christians:

Nations who join the ten (10) area European Millenium Nations Organized (MNO = 666) will be required to force each citizen to receive a Mark on the hand or forehead to buy or sell. The MNO uses the Mark to collect the consumption tax to keep up the royal splendor and their armies.

It is a life first and second death issue for Christians to convince their leaders, they must not join the emerging ten (10) Area European led Millenium Nations Organized (MNO = 666). To stay under God's Grace, nations must not join the MNO whereby requiring its citizens to take the Mark to buy or sell.

It is my prayer people will read these prophecies and gain insight into God's will for their lives during endtimes. Furthermore, they will dedicate their lives to Jesus Christ as the only way to heaven.

Come quickly, Lord Jesus.
Make it so, Lord Jesus! Amen! Bob R. Short

✞ MY OATH ✞

Section 1-7

The prophesies in this book are the truth and shall withstand the test of time. I received this insight from the SPIRIT of CHRIST JESUS, the SPIRIT of PROPHECY.

I, Bob R. Short, have been called by Almighty God through the Lord, the God of the Spirits of Prophecy, to prophesy as a Witness to all World Governments and a Messenger to the Churches on behave of Jesus Christ our Lord and Savior!

The WAKE UP CALL PROPHECIES are a partial fulfillment of Joel 2:28. Come quickly Lord Jesus, God as my witness: Bob R. Short, proclaimed 1995

GOD'S FINAL DECREES

Section 1-8

Be not ignorant of God's Decrees before midnight or you may get discouraged and fall. Congratulation to Spirit-filled Christians who understand their lives are in a testing cycle which will complete at its beginning - standing before God again giving an account of what they did during their time on earth. **A Christian's ending will be where his or her beginning was.** Those who stand at the beginning (Ephesians 2:10) and understand will know the end (judgment day) and will not taste of the second death. This calls for wisdom.

These Christians are not afraid to act on what Jesus Christ commanded His disciples to do. They face great opposition from the world and lukewarm Churches. These Christians will not hide from any suffering they may endure. They repented from their hearts, are following Christ's teachings, and now are Jesus Christ's true disciples. Behold, Jesus will be coming soon! His reward shall be with Him for He is the First and the Last, the Beginning and the End. Fear **Him for He can destroy the body and the soul.**

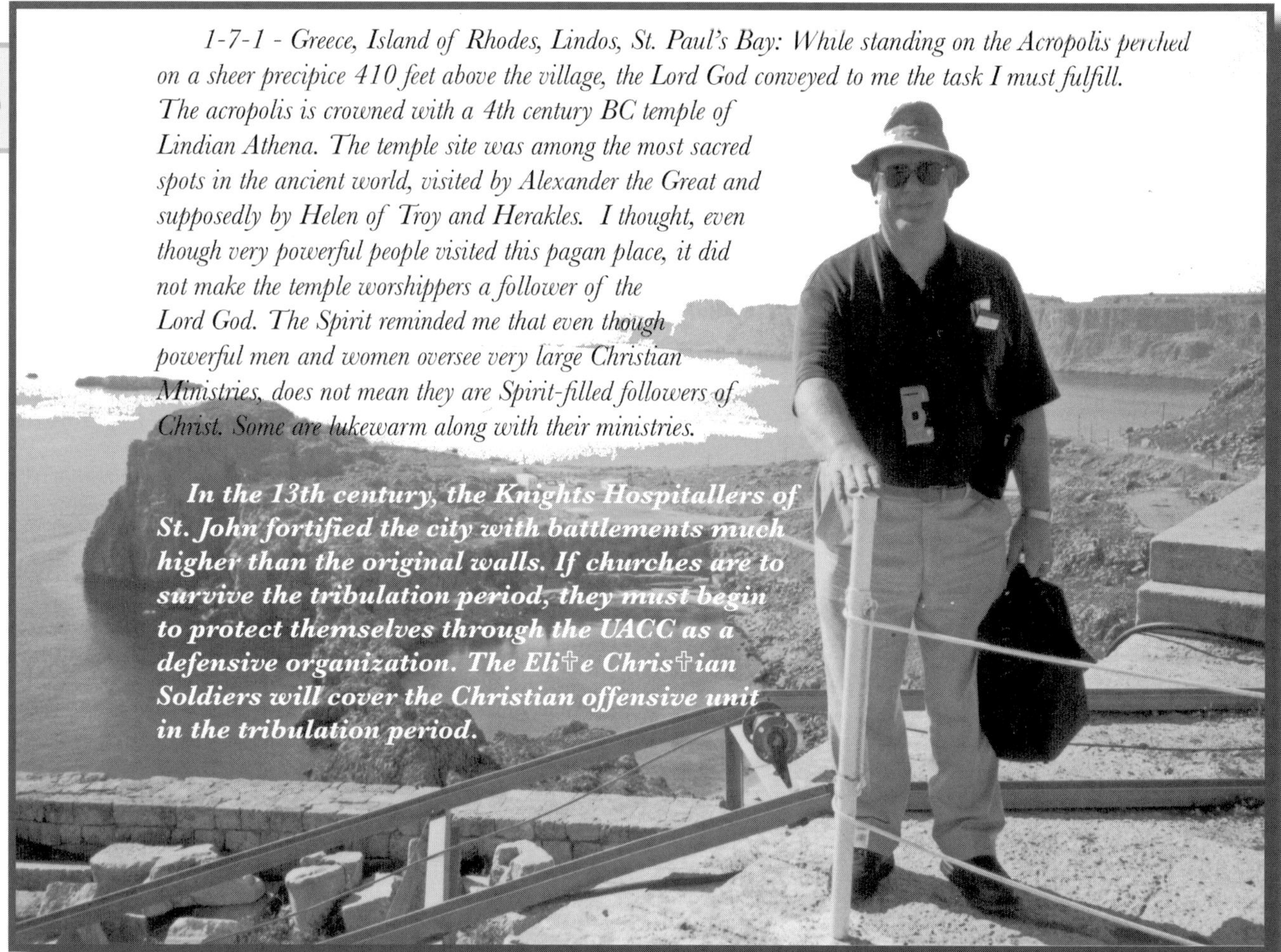

1-7-1 - Greece, Island of Rhodes, Lindos, St. Paul's Bay: While standing on the Acropolis perched on a sheer precipice 410 feet above the village, the Lord God conveyed to me the task I must fulfill. The acropolis is crowned with a 4th century BC temple of Lindian Athena. The temple site was among the most sacred spots in the ancient world, visited by Alexander the Great and supposedly by Helen of Troy and Herakles. I thought, even though very powerful people visited this pagan place, it did not make the temple worshippers a follower of the Lord God. The Spirit reminded me that even though powerful men and women oversee very large Christian Ministries, does not mean they are Spirit-filled followers of Christ. Some are lukewarm along with their ministries.

In the 13th century, the Knights Hospitallers of St. John fortified the city with battlements much higher than the original walls. If churches are to survive the tribulation period, they must begin to protect themselves through the UACC as a defensive organization. The Eli✞e Chris✞ian Soldiers will cover the Christian offensive unit in the tribulation period.

Above, 1-8-1- Turkey, Ancient Ephesus - Curetes Street leading to Celsus' Library: The libraries of old and of the present have been known for their great books about facts, wisdom, philosophy and insight. Yet, man still cannot connect with the total understand of the God of gods and the wisdom He wants us to possess. They invent their own gods to suit themselves and their interests. Ideas conjured up in the insecure and pride-ful minds of men to give them the best of both worlds, God's, and their own misguided ideology. It has become common down through history to invent escape clauses in laws, religion, and superstition to justify superior intellect. However, as mankind comes to the end of the testing cycle, escape from the tribulation period is not considered in the final program for most people and Christians today. We must endure and persevere to our end. I pray God be with each person reading these prophecies.

This book is a partial fulfillment of Daniel 11:33a, Joel 2:28, and another verse which cannot be divulged at this time. It has a wealth of end time information if people will study and search out truth and understanding with an open mind. It is better to read the entire book rather than read only one section and thinking you totally understand it.

To achieve complete understanding, requires studying many sections, which tie together. This information will be extremely important and will be useful for them, their families, and nation to survive the endtimes. This insight has come from outside our time-space test cycle and put into writing as prophesies so the Church and Nations will take heed.

A person must not rely on their intellect, or great wisdom, and lay aside what others have taught about endtimes theories as they study these prophecies. Simply let the common sense of the Wake Up Call Prophecies flow as the Scroll unfolds before you. People are not going to understand everything they read but try not to complicate these prophecies. Welcome to prophecy this will be foreign to many people, because many churches are suppressing the end time truth.

Readers will be shocked at times, and this will be a normal reaction until they stop and use their brains to translate the truth. Then insight will come as to the truth of these prophecies. I pray these prophecies given to me by the Spirit of Jesus, the Spirit of Prophecy, will commence a debate in the church and many lives will be saved because of it.

THE DOUBLE SEALED MYSTERY IN THE BOOK OF DANIEL IS REVEALED! SEE NEXT SECTION.

1-9-1 - England -
London, Big Ben:

*As you read
these prophecies,
you will begin
to understand why
Big Ben along
with the world
will have trouble
telling time
in the future.
Watch out,
for the
world will be going
into a tailspin
and it wants
to drag you with it.
Will you be able
to cope and stand firm
in the faith?
Will you be able
to connect with
the Lord God's
assignment for you?
Heed these prophecies
and read
between the lines as
to how they will affect
your soul, family,
church, and nation!*

TICK - TICK - TICK - TICK - TICK - T I C K ?

INTRODUCTION TO THE MYSTERIES OF THE

EVENINGS AND MORNINGS VISION

Section - 2: will move you through God's designated expanse of malleable time!

This entire section-2 was first prophesied and recorded as a matter of public record in a 232-page book called: Original WAKE UP CALL PROPHECIES, Rough draft Issue - 1. It was published (2-1996) under ISBN 0-9651408-0-6. This Section was prophesied between the following dates; September 1994 to August 1995, on original pages; 82 to 157.

Pictures with insight, commentary, and prophesying were added in 2005 - 2007.

Note: It would be useful when reading this chapter to lay the Holy Bible (NIV) open to the Psalm to be read. (Psalm 90 = 1990 A.D. to Psalm 95 = 1995 A.D., Psalm 96 = 96SRSP-CE to Psalm 99 = 99SRSP-CE, and Psalm 100 = 100SRSP-S to Psalm 106 = 106SRSP-S). In addition, run a copy of the Flow Chart at the back of the book so you can easily follow the sequence of events. If you do not understand a word look it up in the prophesied glossary

WAKE UP CALL
EVENINGS AND MORNINGS
PROPHECIES BEGIN HERE!

Section 2-1

I fear the Lord's command more than men. The Lord has commanded me to prophesy in writing about end time events. Some of these prophecies go against powerful ministries, denominational teachings, and other religions, as well as the up coming European led World Government (MNO). Yet, many of these revelations are exceedingly heavy on my heart. I have even become ill for short periods over the extreme gravity of what I have prophesied. The future has unfolded before me in a great detailed vision. My being is awestruck at the devastation, yet, elated at Jesus' second coming.

In 1994-95, I asked the Lord twice if He was sure I should write these prophecies down. "Lord, I am walking in total faith and if I write what You tell me incorrectly, Your credibility and mine shall be tarnished." God's answer came in a silence, which put fear in my bones. Then God revealed scripture (I Kings 13:11-32), which caused me great fear if I disobeyed Him. My answer from God, "Messenger of God, heed the warning concerning the disobedient man of God from Judah. I, Almighty God, killed my servant back then for disobedience and I will kill you if you do not write what the Spirit has told you." Then I said, "Lord, please, forgive me for doubting you. I will follow your command and always try to protect Your credibility."

My belief resounds the same statement Paul did in Galatians 1:10-12. *"Am I now trying to win the approval of men or of God? Or am I trying to please men? If I were still trying to please men, I would not be a servant of Christ. I want you to know, brothers, that the gospel I preach is not something that man made up. I did not receive it from any man nor was I taught it; rather, I received it by revelation from Jesus Christ."*

Therefore, I have prophesied and written down as directed to me, insight concerning Daniel's sealed vision in chapter eight, concerning the mystery of evenings and mornings. **This will be the key in sequencing end time events, decrees, wars, and calculations.**

Below, 2-1-1- Israel, Jerusalem - The Shrine of the Book: The Dome, which holds part of the Dead Sea Scrolls. There are many mysteries about Biblical history and the Bible. When Christians try to fit the pieces to this intriguing end time puzzle together, they have done well in some areas and failed in others. The Bible has been sealed for instance in the Book of Daniel and parts of the Book of Revelation.

The Lord God's Imperial Rule opens up this information for tele-a-transport using a Heavenly Messenger. This telepathic messenger has always been The Spirit of Christ Jesus. He reconfigures energy of spirit thought into useful information, which can be assimilated by a human mind. Christians call this transition process prophetic insight. The Dead Sea Scrolls gave us a look at the final battle (Armageddon) of Good and Evil. Book four of the Psalms helps Christians understand more of the pieces to the puzzle of endtimes. Lets look at what the Spirit has shown me.

SUMMARY OF THE EVENINGS AND MORNINGS PROPHECIES

(SEE SLIDE-RULER, SECTION 2-8)

The Spirit said, "Prophesy, my messenger, concerning the prophet Daniel's sealed vision EVENINGS AND MORNINGS. The outer seal on the Book of Daniel has now been broken for you to testify concerning the truth. I have also unlocked the seal within a seal about the vision of evenings and mornings. You now shall warn my chosen people Israel and the Church so they might envision my Glory. Many of them need to repent of their disobedient and lukewarm ways!"

This prophecy spans seven significant wars during the endtimes. Each war will add glory to God's Name. Three of the seven will be world wars. WW I, begins God's 11th and final hour by ending on a prophetical date; 11th hour, of the 11th day, of the 11th month and the year (**1**9**1**8) which contains two ones (1) or 11. **NO**ve**M**ber is the only month in our calendar, which contains the letters MNO or 666.

The original meaning of the prophecies in this book are not changed or altered in the slightest from their prophesied slide ruler positioning point which is a location on God's end time slide ruler.

The prophetical meaning of these four - eleven's: WW I has been God's prophetically appointed 11 PM time before midnight of the sixth day. After WW I until today the talk has changed into actions to start a world government (MNO). {Clarification added on 4-14-05: End time progression as follows; League of Nations - to --> United Nations - to --> European led Leopard Beast (3rd beast Daniel 7:6) - to --> The Eagle with the Three Ugly Heads (final beast).}

1. WW I - (1914-18); announces final hour (11 PM) before midnight of the sixth day. WW I, gave birth to the thought process of world government for peace and security. It evolved into the League of Nations.

2. WW II - (1939-45); preparing the way for the planting of the fig tree (Israel, 1948). The political football of world peace and security moved from the League of Nations to the United Nations.

3. WW III - (106SRSP-S); Armageddon, Revelation 19:17-21. This war makes way for the ultimate world government - the dictatorship of Jesus Christ.

Revelation, chapter six, speaks of four Seals, which have been repeating themselves since Christ was crucified. These four Seals will repeat again during the six years from (1990 A.D. -1995 A.D.) plus four slide rule sequencing periods, which represents (96SRSP-CE - 99SRSP-CE).

There will be three prophetical wars between 1990 A.D. and 99SRSP-CE (Revelation 6:1-8). These three wars are about damaging the OIL (Saudi Arabia and Kuwait) and the WINE (Israel).

4. 1990-91 A.D. - GULF WAR I - First Seal repeat (Revelation 6:1-2). This war involves Iraq against Kuwait, USA and others (Psalm 90 - 91).

5. 97SRSP-CE - GULF WAR II - second Seal repeat (Revelation 6:3-4). Iran and Iraq against Saudi Arabia, Kuwait, USA, and others. Daniel 8:1-8, describes Daniel's sealed vision about the Ram and Goat. America's action concerning this war is found in Psalm 97:2-5.

6. 99SRSP-CE - GULF WAR III - fourth Seal repeat (Revelation 6:7-8) - Ezekiel 38 and 39. This describes the Northern army (Russia). This war begins in 99SRSP-CE. It has prophetically been described in Psalm 99:1-3. The action describing the end to this aggression can be found in Psalm 99:4-5. The hero of this war will be the Antichrist whose name adds up to 666 in Hebrew. He will confirm a peace covenant along with many nations. On Monday, 100.1.10SRSP-S, he will be given power from a few to control the ten-area kingdom federation (European led Millennium Nations Organized). This is the Revelation 13 Sea Beast kingdom and Daniel's ten toes of iron and clay (Daniel 2:40-43).

7. THE FINAL STAR WARS: The seventh and final battle will be right before midnight of the seventh sabbatical day. God wins this final battle, destroying Satan and his army forever.

The Spirit said, "Write what has been revealed to you." I was shown the hidden mystery of the sealed vision of EVENINGS AND MORNINGS, Daniel 8:13-14. It will take 2,300 evenings and mornings from the time the daily sacrifices are started until the Jewish (GOD'S) temple sanctuary will be RE-CONSECRATED. The DAILY SACRIFICES will start on or about Saturday, 100.5.6SRSP-S (slide rule point or location on God's slide ruler).

The REBELLION of the Antichrist shall be on or about Sunday, 103.3.23SRSP-S. He installs his computer Internet Web of Deceit control center (Image of the Beast) on one wing of the temple. He declares he is the number one God. This fulfills Daniel 9:27 and Matthew 24:15, *"abomination that causes desolation."* It is clear that the TRIBULATION PERIOD STARTS on, or a few days before, Saturday, 99.9.25SRSP-CE. It then must be said the SECOND ADVENT of our Lord Jesus Christ shall be on, or before, the Jewish new year, Saturday, 106.9.23SRSP-S (slide ruler point not an earth date).

This condensed summary of Daniel's vision of evenings and mornings is complete and shall be in harmony with book four of the Psalms. Psalm 90 applies to 1990 A.D. through Psalm 95, which applies to 1995 A.D. and this sequence continues through book four of the Psalms to Psalm 100, which equals 100SRSP-S (slide rule point) through Psalm 106, which equals 106SRSP-S, (slide rule point).

It should be noted **SR**SP means SLIDE RULE POINTS starting with the year 1996 and thereafter (see flow chart). God may push events out to gather more souls before the tribulation period. Once these events begin to surface, they will complete the cycle with laps and overlaps in the approximate order prophesied. The reader should understand the sequences of events are more important than the actual earth dates.

Now let us flashback to 1994-95 when the Spirit gave me these prophecies in great detail. The time segments are broken into six-month intervals from 1990 AD - 1995 AD. This is to say, six months of mornings and six months of evenings make one Psalm (not earth) year cycle. From 1996 AD to the end of time will be designated by two slide ruler time periods of mornings and evenings for each Psalms 96-106.

(Clarification-Note, added 2005: Jewish New Year generally starts around October 1, give or take a few days here and there whereas much of the world starts on January 1. In other words, there are going to be laps and overlaps in sequencing of events by using the Psalms.

In addition, we must apply the exponential multiplier to birthing pains for every event and calculations. They start slow and increase to the end of its cycle. To further complicate the issue, a person's location on earth could affect their perception of the order and intensity of some signs.)

2-1-2- **Israel, Megiddo - VALLEY OF ARMAGEDDON - Jezreel Valley:**

Where the three diplomats (Frogs) of the final Antichrist persuade the kings to gather for the final battle (Revelation 16:13-16). It shall be extremely important for the Church, America's military, North and South America's politicians to understand this battle. North and South America will be fighting against most other nations of the old known world, which are amassing their armies on the floor of the beautiful valley. Why would they do such a stupid maneuver? Because they cannot remain at home and push buttons and shoot rockets with accuracy. The reason; there are enough satellites destroyed which makes it very hard to use high tech weapons with precision. Therefore, nations have to move their armies in position to fight manually.

Again, North and South America must understand what they are up against; a) few high tech weapons because many military satellites are down, b) Earth off its axis and not in a standard orbit, c) day - night has been shortened and a sort-of-confused-time prevails, d) The America's will not be what we experience today. The USA has survived the Ezekiel 38 nuclear war with Russia. The America's will be attacked again in the middle of great tribulation. Can the Church wake up and get the picture here then warn our military about this. e) North and South America will have help from Jesus. He will give us the victory if the USA will only repent and come back to Him before the battle starts in the Great Tribulation Period. Otherwise, the USA will be destroyed before the battle of Armageddon.

Above, 2-2-1- Israel, Jerusalem - the Eastern Gate: Known also as the Gate of Mercy. Saddam Hussein thought his conquest would take him to the temple mount as the King of the Middle East, but he failed. The Jews believe the Messiah will come to earth at the Mount of Olives and enter Jerusalem through this gate. Christians know the Messiah has already entered through this gate from the Mount of Olives. He was then crucified for our sins 2000 years ago.

Psalm 90 - 1990 A.D.

Section 2-2

MORNING 1990 A.D.

Morning opens with the terror of the first Seal repeat in Revelation 6:1-2. This equates to the same action as the first Sign repeat in Matthew 24:4. Saddam Hussein rides out AS A conqueror bent on conquest with the Antichrist or false christ spirit. The verbiage in the first Seal states, AS A conqueror not WAS A GREAT conqueror. This implies he will fail just as all the other Antichrist spirits have done in the past. Saddam Hussein takes over Kuwait for a short time and receives his crown as their king.

Between 1990 A.D. and 1995 A.D. was the beginning of sorrows, with the days of sorrows representing the years between 96SRSP-CE to 99SRSP-CE. A sharp increase of occurrences in signs began in 1990 A.D.; however, the sharpest increase will begin in 96SRSP-CE (slide rule sequencing point, not actual date).

Matthew 24:4-8 speaks of increases in wars, rumors of wars, deception, earthquakes, and extreme weather. God will lift His protective covering over Christian nations who are disobedient. This loss of protection will increase, as birthing pains; the destructive signs within that nation will take its toll.

Now we understand why the psalmist asked God to teach us to number our days aright. For, if Christians know how to interpret book four of the Psalms, we will know what is going to happen each year. We then can take the proper precautions to protect our family, church, nation, and ourselves.

EVENING 1990 A.D.

God has classified America as a non-disciple nation. In other words, the United States' laws, government, and people do not honor, respect, and follow God's commands. Therefore, in His anger, God is as birthing pains removing His protective covering over America. If we do not turn back to God, then God will destroy us.

The evening of August 2, 1990 A.D., Kuwait and Israel's hopes dried and withered. Note: Withered does not mean dead.

Below, 2-2-2- Italy, Pompeii: Will America end up destroyed like Pompeii in the Great Tribulation for not following God's commands or will America turn back to God and fight on the Jewish side in the last battle? Keep reading and find out! The Christian has a choice in what happens to their nation.

Right, 2-3-1- Italy - between Florence and Venice, 4000 W.W. II US Soldiers: Buried in the valley. WW-II gave birth to the Eagle Beast in Daniel 7:4, plus nation of Israel, plus United Nations (world government). Once again, American troops died to fulfill prophecy in Gulf War-I. This war will dribble out to help start Gulf War-II, where Iran and Iraq vs. America and others. This will add to the fire, which starts Gulf War-III, a nuclear war between Russia plus others nations against America, Israel, and others. This war shall be mistaken in many circles as the battle of Armageddon. This battle extends into the tribulation period.

Psalm 91 - 1991 A.D.

Section 2-3

MORNING 1991 A.D.

Israel and Kuwait are saved because Saddam Hussein's aggression was stopped as the Bible prophesied. His aggression represents the first Seal repeat. The first Seal states AS A not WAS A conqueror (Revelation 6:1-2). Saddam Hussein used deception as Sign number one (Matthew 24:4-5) prophesied. He temporarily fooled the world. However, as the Antichrist spirit was exposed, he was suppressed.

God protected Israel. America, as the psalmist so plainly stated in Psalm 91:3, saves Israel from deadly pestilence or chemical weapons. *"Surely he* (God) *will save you* (Israel) *from the fowler's snare and from the deadly pestilence* (chemical scud attacks). *He will cover you with his feathers and under his wings* (radar protection and patriot missiles) *you will find refuge;..."* (Psalm 91:4). In 1991 A.D., the Jewish people could have not worn their gas masks during the scud attacks. They could have ignored the chemical threat by Hussein, because their God had promised them protection many years ago.

The Spirit said, "Let us take a side trip for study." The Jewish people should have known how to count the days as the psalmist instructed them in Psalm 90:12, *"teach us to number our days aright, that we may gain a heart of wisdom."* Otherwise, Psalm 91 equals 1991 A.D. If the Jewish people had been obedient (accepted Jesus Christ as their Messiah) to God, they could have gained wisdom through the Psalms. They could have known God would not allow Hussein's scud rockets to contain chemical weapons (Psalm 91:3). The Jewish people have rejected Jesus Christ whereby rejecting knowledge so they are unable to understand what was promised them (Hosea 4:5-6).

Psalm 91:3-16 describes Desert Storm (Gulf War I) as it actually happened. The Spirit moved me to **"go stand on the Temple Mount in Jerusalem. Let your eyes draw a straight line through Baghdad and beyond Iraq's borders. From the line you have drawn with your eyes, the ratio killed of the wicked was approximately one thousand on the left and ten thousand on the right side. This is about a one to ten kill ratio, just as Psalm 91 predicted."** Number of Christians killed not included in these calculations.

"A thousand may fall at your side (left side), *ten thousand at your right hand* (right side) *but it will not come near you. You will only observe with your eyes and see the punishment of the wicked."* (Psalm 91:7)

This Psalm pinned by the Lord God for 1991 A.D. - Gulf War-I and no other war in Israel history has resulted with these exact statistics.

EVENING 1991 A.D.

Iraq dried and withered to become the shorter of the two horns.

PSALM 92 - 1992 A.D.
Section 2-4

MORNING 1992 A.D.

The people of the world reflect back on 1991 A.D. and see God's love and faithfulness for Israel and they begin to praise Almighty God (Psalm 92:1-5 and 11).

EVENING 1992 A.D.

There will be a new awareness of the Lord God by the end of 1992. Evildoers are flourishing. Christians have dried and withered hope for change in the USA this year (Psalm 92:6-7).

NOTE: The reader must change their mind set and read the Psalms just as if they were happening this very day. The Holy Spirit will move Christians into a new world of understanding end time events as they read the Psalms! Contained within book four of Psalm 102:18; *"let this* [Book IV] *be written for a future generation, that a people not yet created* [last generation representing 1967 A.D. through 106SRSP-S] *may praise the Lord."* In other words, we have the ability to know what shall be happening through the Psalms if we will profess Jesus Christ as the true - Spirit of Prophecy (Revelation 19:10).

PSALM 93 - 1993 A.D.
Section 2-5

MORNING 1993 A.D.

The morning starts with the Lord robed in majesty and armed with strength (Psalm 93:1). The Lord God rises from His throne to flex His muscles against a disobedient world.

EVENING 1993 A.D.

Evening starts with worldwide floods and rainstorms. The ocean turns into a thundering sea that has mighty breakers as Psalm 93:3-4 describes. God rebukes a disobedient world of sin. The lukewarmers fill the church houses. They have not kept the great commission of Jesus Christ.

America has now been classified a non-disciple nation by God. A disciple nation has its laws, government, and people's hearts, in harmony with the teaching of the Holy Word of God. Christian men and the leadership of the Churches are at fault for letting America become disobedient to God. God ordained men to lead and teach about the trinity of the great commission. If we look at Psalm 93:1-2, we will see God avenges the lukewarmer and the unsaved someday.

The Spirit spoke to me and said, "The Almighty God who avenges the evildoers is destroying parts of the world using severe weather birthing pains. America must bow down and repent of her evil ways!" This matter is closed until justice for our Lord has been completed.

Left, 2-4-1- Israel, Tel Aviv - Skyline: Tel Aviv was bombed last year (1991 A.D.) during Gulf War I and there was much weeping in the night. However, God came through and this year there is joy in the morning. God will give the Spirit-filled Christian peace as they move through the tribulation period.

PSALM 94 - 1994 A.D.
Section 2-6

MORNING 1994 A.D.

The first of the year brought forth a new crop of evildoers. They promoted sin world-wide, especially in the leadership of American government. These leaders (Psalm 94:3-8) are full of boasting, jubilant, pouring out arrogant words, crushing, suppressing God's inheritance (admission to heaven), against the righteous, and condemning innocent babies to death (Psalm 94:20-21). The leader of this wicked land is carrying the mark of the Antichrist spirit. His name is equal to 666 in Hebrew. Many elected officials are fools. It will be too late for them when they become wise. The door will be closed to them and their leaders. This door divides the lake of fire and God.

EVENING 1994 A.D.

The Spirit said, "Final judgment has been postponed for eleven years or longer," (Psalm 94:23). Psalm 94:16 ask who will rise up against the wicked. American Christians answered this on the eve of the year. They voted more God-fearing Christians into congress than in more than forty years.

Some of the lukewarmers were beginning to wake up to the fact God was displeased with America. God was sending a message through the damage from weather, earthquakes, and disasters. The November 1994 A.D., elections showed the change in America. Yet, the disobedience in America left hopes somewhat withered and dried.

Right, 2-5-1 - Italy, Venice-Island of Burano: This was a tranquil and beautiful Island. Nevertheless, as you can see the bell tower is leaning to the right and I am leaning to the left. As I looked at this picture, it reminds me of how the world gets off its rotational axis and effects time. Tranquility will fall off the bell tower and men's hearts will fail them for fear of what is coming upon the earth. Read on to gets the facts!

PSALM 95 - 1995 A.D.
Section 2-7

Above, 2-6-1- U.S., Oahu - North Beach: This is where the gigantic 40, 50,and 60 foot waves come on to the beach. Sun, fun, parties with all the thrills and excitement. As it was in Noah's day so it will be at the coming of the Son of Man, for they were having fun and not looking for the proper signs. They lacked faith in Noah's day just as many Christians do today. Some would rather sin than get ready for the return of Jesus. The end time flood came and destroyed them. Note: Jesus said the waves would be roaring when He returns. This implies the world coastlines will be battered or destroyed. Take note, most coastlines in the world do not practice Biblical principles. On the contrary, they promote sin.

MORNING 1995 A.D.

1995 A.D. will be God's transitional year of excellence. He shall be as birthing pains, beginning to accelerate end time events in a manner the world notices. Yet, the world will continue to scoff at Christians and be disobedient to God's Word. This year has been designated as a transitional year. It represents the end of the sixth sabbatical day and the start of the seventh. It corresponds to the year 5755 on the Jewish calendar. The meaning of this year in Hebrew is Year of Excellence.

Psalm 95 equals the year of 1995 A.D. It equals the sixth sabbatical day or 5001 to 6000 years since Adam. God shall change end time gears at the end of the sixth day or Psalm 95.

The Spirit said, "We must review quickly God's six sabbatical days in light of Psalms 90-95." The first six chapters of book four of the Psalms represents God's six sabbatical days since Adam. Psalm 90 was written by Moses and describes the creation of the world. This covers the years from Adam to 3000 B.C.

Right 2-6-2- Italy, Pompeii - a plaster copy of a victim: The volcano Vesuvius erupted in 79 AD. This was a tragic event in the history of the world. However, America has had more than its share of tragic events. Bill Clinton and George W. Bush are the first presidents to turn against Israel and tell Israel they have to get out of their land (West Bank) and give it to their enemies. America has experienced 10-15 severe disasters with dollars of destruction running all time highs. Do not be so foolish to think this has all been happenstance. On the contrary, God has been and still will be lifting His protective covering from America and allowing destruction to hit our shores. Christians must start the UACC and straighten out America or God will do it for us. The latter will be very painful to put it mildly.

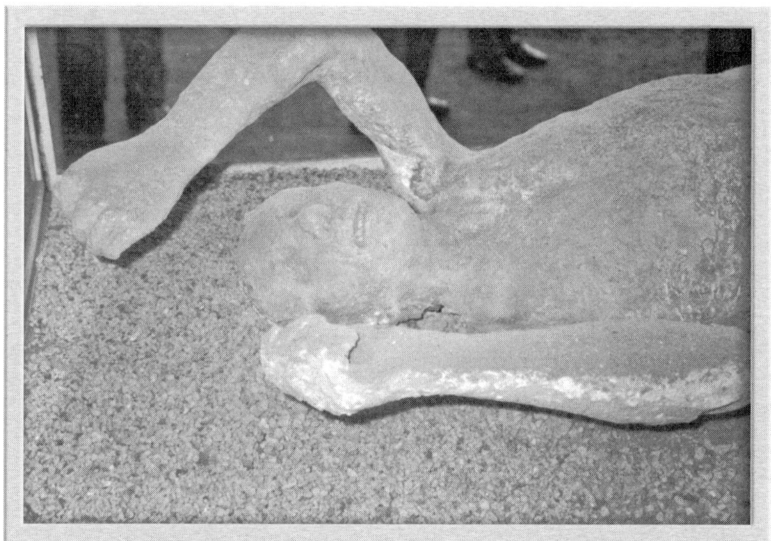

Psalm 93 covers the years 1000 B.C. to Christ's crucifixion. Psalm 93:1 describes Jesus' crucifixion at the end of the year. It says, *"The world is firmly established; it cannot be moved."* This means, when Jesus died for our sins, the world was firmly locked for two sabbatical days. This established what we know as the 2000 year Church Age cycle. Psalm 95:10-11 describes the last generation to live before Jesus returns.

The near prophecy associated with the last generation shall be forty cycles of slide rule periods between the time of 1967 A.D. and 106SRSP-S *"For forty years, I was angry with that generation; I said, 'They are a people whose hearts go astray, and they have not known my ways.' So I declared on oath in my anger, 'They* (lukewarmers, backsliders, and sinners) *shall never enter my rest.'"* (Psalm 95:10-11) The far prophecy was God talking to the children of Israel in the wilderness.

These verses represent a forty-slide-ruler year time-period from the day the Jewish people recaptured Jerusalem until Jesus' return. Matthew 24:34 states this generation (Psalm 95:10-11) will see these things happen between 1967 A.D. and 106SRSP-S (slide rule point).

We must take into account, God is a multi - time - dimensional Spirit. **It may seem that a generation equals 40 years on earth, not 40, 50, or 60 slide rule years.**

However, the Spirit directed me to use slide rule sequencing points to compensate for this displaced time-phenomena. We must watch for signs not exact dates.

EVENING 1995 A.D.

The people who will dry and wither are the generation in Psalm 95:10-11. This generation represents present-day people as described in these verses. They are disobedient to God's Word. Psalm 95:11 declares God's anger on our generation. The lukewarmer in Revelation 3:14-22 is in serious trouble with God. These disobedient people will enter the lake of fire.

The Christian should realize many of our major corporations in America are deeply involved in what will be man's ultimate achievement. This new god shall be called the Internet worldwide web of deceit. The Antichrist will turn the leadership's heart of many of these international companies over to the MNO (Leopard first - then the Eagle with the Three Ugly Heads. The MNO promises stability and huge corporate profits. From 1995 A.D. through the tribulation period, these corporations will promote sin from within. They will promote disobedience to God's Word outside their companies. They give to the radical noisy den (special interest groups), which promote sin and self-rights. The Spirit said, "God has turned these international companies over to their own lust for gain and profit by allowing others to promote people within the company who push the Antichrist agendas. These company idols are worldly power and money. The leaders of these companies are receiving their full rewards here on earth. They are promoting the destruction of America and the world for personal and company gain."

Jesus shall be coming back to destroy people like these leaders who destroy the world (Revelation 11:18). They will taste the quickening of the fire in Jesus' sword. God has turned these companies and their leaders over to their own lust of idolatry. They will not be turned around before the end. They are doomed along with their leaders and the Antichrist spirits. Their hour will come to a fiery end. His just and righteous punishments will be praiseworthy by the Spirit-filled Christian.

The Spirit turned my attention to one of the causes of the moral decay in America and around the world. Lukewarm Christian are one of the main reasons the world has become ungodly, although there are other reasons discussed in the section called Disciple Nation Blessing or Curse.

Ninety-five percent of our fight is not fought with flesh and wars here on earth. The righteous man must stay in prayer with God. America has lost eighty-four percent of her protective power to communicate with God. God has been as birthing pains, lifting his protective covering over America. His ears have been closed (II Chronicles 7:15) and ninety-nine percent of the time shut to lukewarmers prayer requests. God has better things to do than to listen to disobedient Christians.

The lukewarmers could save America by following II Chronicles 7:13-15. This scripture states: first humble, second pray, third seek God, and fourth turn from sin. These four things will stop God from destroying our disobedient nation as He currently is doing. His eyes and ears will open to our cries. He then will hear our prayers and heal our nation. This can better be accomplished by the Universal American Church Coalition (UACC) in the short time we have before the tribulation period starts.

Many lukewarmers will turn from God in the next eight years. This will happen because they are too

My burden is not for this prophesied loser called fifty-one percent lukewarmer. For they are doomed by God, *"So I declared on oath in my anger, `They shall never enter my rest.'"* (Psalm 95:11). I am concerned for the thirty-four percent lukewarmers, which can be awakened and saved. If we can motivate these lukewarmers spiritually into solid Spirit-filled Christians, they will increase our strength by their prayers three-fold to save America. God will then give His full attention and will save America or any nation who turns back to Him. Praise God!

What matters the most to you, following God or the world? America has lost a large percent of its protective power to communicate with God because

THE BODY OF CHRIST HAS INCREASINGLY BECOME LUKEWARM.

The Lord God pays little attention to lukewarmer's prayers.

busy to read the signs of Jesus' return. They simply lack the faith to follow Jesus' instructions. Some find it so frightening they refuse to discuss Jesus' return. Others are tired of hearing about it. Lukewarmers do not have the faith to believe and are not going to give up convenience for Jesus' sake. The timing must be all wrong they say. They will deny and not bend to the Lord's end time warnings.

Below, 2-7-1- Italy, Florence - Palazzo Borghese: The Royal Court Jesters entertaining. We were entertained at a renaissance banquet typifying the antique Florentine Courts. This palace we were told has accommodated one of America's presidential stay and many other VIP's. It was an unbelievable and beautiful palace. We enjoyed ourselves very much. The food and entertainment was the best of our entire tour of Italy. But the Bible commands us to be knowledgeable and watch for end time signs. It is too easy to loose perspective and be caught up in pleasures and forget to be on guard and watchful, whereby falling away. Jesus prophesied, "See I have told you ahead of time!" Matthew 24 declares endtimes will be like the days of Noah; for they were eating, dancing, drinking and having a good time when the flood came and destroyed the wicked people. They were not watching and did not know.

UNDERSTANDING
SLIDE RULER POSITIONING POINTS

Psalms 96 - 99 = 96SRSP-CE to 99SRSP-CE

Compressed or expanded time Cycles with laps and overlaps of events.

Section - 2-8

The reader will note sequence designations after 1995 A.D. carry the letters SRSP with a CE or S following as in 96SRSP-CE or 102SRSP-S. The S.R. represents God's slide ruler. SP is a point on the slide ruler depending on where the Holy Spirit instructed me to place it using Book IV (Four) of the Psalms. CE represents compressed or expandable time cycles developed from Psalms 96-99. S denotes stabilized slide ruler to earth time during the seven-year tribulation period denoted by Psalms 100-106. If we knew when God has set the time of the Second Advent, then other end time slide rule positioning points could be adjusted backwards to an exact or approximate A.D. date for each event. We do not know the earth time God has assigned to the Second Advent, so we must rely on sequencing signs leading up to it. God may persuade a few more sinners to become Christians before the tribulation period starts. He may push out time cycles (between 96-99SRSP-CE) one, two, even five years - only God knows. The Holy Spirit directed me to use the term slide rule sequencing points. Let the reader focus on the general flow of sequences of end time events, rather than actual times and dates.

Christians must watch for signs and make adjustments accordingly. Once the Christian sees these early signs in very close proximity as prophesied, they know God will move end time events quickly. They will see the rest of the sequences of events follow in a timely fashion as allocated by these prophecies especially the tribulation period.

God may move the positioning points up or back during Psalms 96-99. This is why each time-period manifests into a slide rule point of expandable or compressed cycles of malleable time. One event may seem to occur before another, which corresponds to the birthing pain principle. Everything about endtimes must have the birthing pains principle applied; start slow or small and increase quickly with laps and overlaps of events. One event may appear to happen before another simply because of people's location on earth and what they perceive as important to them at the time. The Spirit-filled Christian must keep focused on, what God has going on, not what the satanic world and the European led world news media would have you believe may be happening!

GOD'S SLIDE RULER OF END TIME SEQUENCING EVENTS.

with laps and overlaps of events.

God's slide ruler is produced from calculations using a movable middle piece (96SRSP-CE to 99SRSP-CE [similar to the bellows on an accordion - with compressed and expanded time periods] and a solid piece 100SRSP-S to 106 SRSP-S) graduated with logarithmic end time insight to produce precision scale of events which leads to the second coming of Christ.

← 1990 AD to 1995 AD →
actual years. (Psalms 90-95)

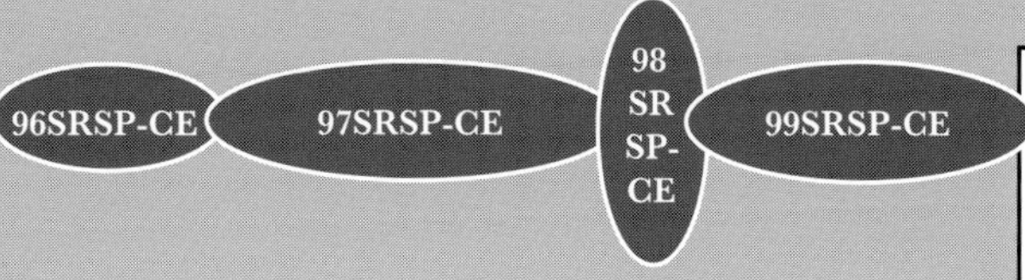

← Psalm 100 = 100SRSP-S
to
Psalm 106 = 106SRSP-S →
Seven periods of stable year cycles

God's four cycle periods to be compressed or expanded. (Psalms 96-99)

True Earth years as we understand time.
←1990 AD -1995 AD → ? 1997 ? - 42005 ?- -2007? → cannot determine actual dates →? 20?? - ? ? →Second Coming

Above, 2-8-1- England, London - Tower Bridge: This is a beautiful bridge next to St. Katharine's dock on the River Thames. As I walked London, I truly fell in love with the place. It became very clear to build anywhere one must have a zoning permit of some sort. Many areas partition London into zones. Each area has its own unique setting and culture. The European Led World Government will eventually try to accomplish similar arrangements worldwide. They will eventually divide the world into ten zoning areas, which will have fast reaction military forces to quickly stop problems and address natural disasters.

PSALM 96
96SRSP-CE Sequence
Section 2-8

(S.R. = Slide Rule Points = Not an actual date = Used for sequencing end time events)

The MORNING of PSALM 96
96SRSP-CE Sequence

The morning opens with God locking the world in Psalm 96:10. God judges nations and once again, locks America, Russia, and Israel's elections to fulfill end time prophecy. In Psalm 96:10, He says, "... *The world is firmly established, it cannot be moved...*" This will be accomplished by removing one or more important 1996 presidential candidates if the UACC has not been physically or mentally started in the hearts and minds of the church leadership. This change will bring in other candidates or another candidate from America, Russia, and/or Israel who would not have won without God's help. This will fulfill prophecy. God places kings on their thrones. The removal of this national candidate depends on the Universal American Church Coalition's (UACC's) attempt to meet God's goals by the fall of 96SRSP-CE (watch for overlaps). God will judge the leadership of churches therefore, the leaders must be of one mind in the UACC. If the UACC has been started physically or mentally in the hearts and minds of church leaders and they follow God's will in 96SRSP-CE, there will be no candidate removal.

The Lord will stir men's hearts this year and in the future to begin a worldwide zoning of area nations. This will be due to the failure of the United Nations. This zoning will be the beginning of the MNO, which equates to Daniel's ten original toes spoken of in Revelation 13 Sea Beast. The MNO organization will be discussed later. It will come to full glory in the fall of 99SRSP-CE and a king will be crowned 100.1.10SRSP-S. The ten kingdoms will end violently in the fall of 106SRSP-S.

God will test Christians for obedience. The birthing pains shall begin as Christians question and resist the sequence ladder to the Mark of the Beast, Mark of His Name, and the Number of His Name. Christians must wake up and realize the Mark of the Beast will be slowly implemented. This shall be accomplished in stealthy ways only the spirit-filled Christian will understand.

The IC chip marking cards will be introduced for many different services to buy and to sell benefits through banks, credit companies, and even our own government. This equates to one step away from the true Mark of the Beast. This will be recognized as helpful at first. It will be accepted in stages, first, the credit card and second, the IC Chip marking card. This technology will be the first marking technology, which contains all the digits of the Mark of the Beast. Next, could be the IC chip bracelet, and finally, on or in the right hand by use of the ID implant marking system, laser scanners, biometrics readers, or similar systems.

Satan's deception has been hidden because these systems are voluntary at first and finally will become mandatory during the tribulation period. In the middle of the tribulation period, the Antichrist will try to kill anyone who refuses the sequence marking numbers. He needs everyone to pay the consumption tax, which feeds his MNO (Daniel 11:20). Christians must resist this sequencing ladder starting with the IC chip.

Christians must be obedient to God through prayer and reading God's Word. They must recognize the signs of the times. Do not become lukewarm. Fifty-one percent of the people attending Churches are blinded. They shall deny the reality of endtimes. Many do not study the Bible and will resist God's warnings.

"But the cowardly, ...their place will be in the fiery lake of burning sulfur. This is the second death" (Revelation 21:8). God is not talking about the sinner here when he uses the word cowardly. Those type sinners have already been judged to go to hell. Therefore, He is talking about the lukewarmer who stands by and watches his Christian brothers fall. His Christian brothers may be doing the Lord's work such as refusing the sequences of the Mark of the Beast. A coward also allows his brothers to die when he could have helped him. Yet, for fear of personal loss, he will not help his brothers. God may judge him cowardly and send him to hell!

God intended Christians to follow in His steps. The Bible commands Christian men to protect their families, their brethren, and the church house. Jesus was about his Father's business. Sometimes He was in controversial positions. Christians following God's Great Commission (Matthew 28:19-20) will become increasingly unpopular with the world. God never intended us to walk up the beast's deceptive stairway without a fight. Christians must resist the path, which leads to the Mark of the Beast. This will be Satan's stairway of trickery, which has a broken step at the top representing death. We must resist and tell our government it has been moving in the wrong direction.

I prophesied the meaning of the Second Hidden Mark in WAKE UP CALL II, July 1994. Christians must begin to resist IC chip marking technology (Integrated Circuit Computer Chip). This convenient trickery will come through businesses, banks, and government mandates concerning IC chip marking, scanners, or other enhanced marking ID Systems (bio-chip implant). We must be a thorn in the side of the Antichrist spirit, which promotes these marking devices. This evil spirit agenda shall be to obtain money, power, control, and then total authority over the Christian's life.

Resist the IC chip sequence will start many problems for Satan. To accomplish this disruption, it must be understood and taught properly in our churches. Many churches will lack understanding and fail to address the end time events.

The family presents another problem in Christians resisting the IC chip and scanning technology. In the family, for instance, if both people have not grown together in the Lord or one has been a hardened lukewarmer and then there are going to be problems. Each Christian must remember he or she stands alone before the judgment seat of Christ.

Lukewarmers in the church represent over half the attendees and can put enormous pressure on the church leadership. Some lukewarmer may call this overkill. Add debt to disobedience and a church leader has become a slave to the system. Churches, which owe money, are in trouble. The Church loses control when it bows down to debt and becomes as a rag in the wind. The UACC shall be the best way to get churches out of debt before the tribulation starts. The longer Church Leadership waits to join the UACC, the more they borrow, the worse it is going to get.

Time is moving toward its conclusion and everything that happens to you has a spiritual significance, which can lead to heavenly rewards for your next assignment.

Tithes will drop as we move closer toward the fall of 99SRSP-CE. The lukewarmer generally thinks of himself instead of God. This shall be one of the reasons the Churches must start the UACC. The UACC can help churches get out of debt before 99SRSP-CE. Power will belong to God and the Churches to influence elected officials. Control by the Church through the UACC can influence elected officials. The Churches through the UACC can influence the action of America. This will stop America from buying into **the Second Hidden Mark of His Name or MNO led by the European world government.**

The Spirit said, "Resistance to the IC chip marking device shall be easy, if Christians nip it in the bud." Remember in our lives, if we stopped something right at first, there was not a problem. If we waited and got over our head in sin, we paid a terrible price to change our lives. God has asked His people through prophecy to wake up and stop this sequence. As helpful as the IC chip and laser scanning technology may seem at the beginning, it will lead to destruction. Churches must unite under the UACC to have the power to withstand the pressure applied by Satan's trickery.

The EVENING of PSALM 96
96SRSP-CE Sequence

In Psalm 96:13, God comes to judge the earth. In Psalm 96:10, the world is firmly established, it cannot be moved. This means God shall be judging and basing His decisions on total Christian direction of each nation. He will lock each nation into a set pattern, especially the elections in Russia, Israel, and the USA. This will complete Bible prophecy and make way for the Lord Jesus' return. This year ends with hopes of world peace withering and drying.

PSALM - 97
97SRSP-CE Sequence
Section 2-9, Page - 34

Christians must start resisting these sequences with love, not hate. They should explain in a polite manner why they are resisting.

The battle belongs to the Lord and end time Spirit-filled Christians are His warriors. They are true Disciples of Christ, fitted with the full armor of God's power through the Holy Spirit to complete the task assigned by the general-in-charge, Jesus Christ. The time to prepare for battle must be now!

2-8-2- Italy, Rome - Colosseum: Commissioned by Emperor Vespasian in AD 72. History leaves the door open to the fact that Christians were killed for sport here. Christians must understand the times we live in and react or resist the ladder of prosperity, which leads to following the Final Antichrist. Lack of faith is the main obstacle in believing end time events, predictions, and calculations.

The MORNING of PSALM 97
97SRSP-CE SEQUENCE

The morning opens with the two-horned Ram (Iran-Iraq) fulfilling Daniel, chapter eight. The Ram wars (Second Seal - repeat, Revelation 6:3-4 - Second Sign, Matthew 24:6-7, information - added fall - 1996) to the west into, but not limited to Syria, Jordan, and Egypt's Sinai Peninsula. This conquest causes famine and starvation to begin spreading (Third Seal - repeat, Revelation 6:5-6 - Third Sign, Matthew 24:7). The western block of nations sees what is happening. They issue strong warnings, *"Do not damage the oil"* which refers to Saudi Arabia and Kuwait oil. They further warn, *"Do not damage the wine"* which equates to Israel.

The Ram's conquest then moves to the north, Daniel 8:4. The small horn (Iraq) has gained strength to equal the large horn (Iran). The northern conquest will include, but shall not be limited to countries like Azerbaijan, Armenia, Georgia, then Turkmenistan and Uzbekistan. Note the Ram does not touch Russia. The Ram now has control of nuclear weapons, which can reach the United States. This was their objective in marching north.

The world shall be in shock and in disbelief as the Ram's arrogant nature will be threatening the United States with nuclear weapons. They now have confidence to charge to the south, which is Saudi Arabia, Kuwait, and other small nations. The Ram shall be successful in taking control of most of these areas. They now cut off the United States oil supply. For a short time, the Ram becomes great.

Above, 2-8-3- England, London - Tower of London - Jewel House: Each nation protects its national treasures such as the Jewel House pictured above. America has Fort Knox and other locations of importance. Nations equate success to how much Gross National Product (GNP) they possess. The judgment of Jesus Christ against nations will be final (Revelation 19:15). What counts with Jesus will be whether a nation was following and honoring God's teachings. Each Christian must understand the Great Commission of Jesus Christ leads each nation to its true Biblical national treasure. To date, few Churches understand it and push the second reading (Mark 16:15-16) of the Commission; send missionaries out to teach the Good News of Jesus Christ. This shall be judged as great, but it is not the first reading (see glossary). The first reading found in Matthew 28:19, commands Christians to "make disciple nations." The Church does not understand this, but it must be taken literally. The first nation we must disciple (make followers of Christ) must be the nation we live in. The definition of a disciple nation must be: A nation follows the teachings of Jesus Christ in three areas called the trinity of the nation - its people, government, and laws. This trinity must follow the teaching of Jesus Christ to qualify for discipleship. The lukewarm churches have let all nations of the world become non-disciple. England lost this honor a long time ago, while America lost the honor around 1990. On judgment day, each Christian will be asked to give an account as to how they kept their nation a disciple nation. Using the excuse we were never taught will not impress the Judge.

in history.

This war shall be powered by God Himself when the Ram starts wanting to destroy the wine (Israel) in the third Seal repeat, Revelation 6:5-6. With God's power behind the United States, we totally wipe out the Ram. Psalm 97:6 states that all the people will see His glory. The psalmist sang about this event, and then Daniel prophesied this war, and now I have clarified and prophesied this war so the world knows when it happens, God's glory and power will reign forever. Jordan and Syria now realize if they don't get serious about protecting Israel's borders, they're going to be taken over by someone trying to get to Israel again. America will protect them if they fulfill Bible prophecy and agree, for the first time, to truly try to protect Israel's borders, not just pretend to.

Between the morning of 97SR-SP-CE and the end of this war, God will proclaim His righteousness (Psalm 97:6). God suddenly will remove (Psalm 97:7-9) a worldly religious and important figure that sits on seven hills from his position.

This will make room for scripture to be fulfilled. The next worldly religious leader will become a man of great confusion, for Gulf War II ends and Gulf War III soon begins. He (religious leader who sits on seven hills) will never get true footing because of world events. World problems affect his ability to control internal problems in his organization.

This year ends with the world in real unrest and tremendous Middle East destruction, for the Ram has withered and dried away. The worldly financial markets will begin to feel the pinch for cash. Christian shall be, as birthing pains, awakening to the fact that part of the Wake Up Call Prophecies have fulfilled as prophesied. While the rest of the prophecies are destine to happen soon, or will come to pass in the near future! People will begin to put their money in short-term areas, which are safer than the stock market.

The EVENING of PSALM 97
97SRSP-CE Sequence

The Ram shall dry and wither as follows: Daniel 8:5, *"As I was thinking, suddenly a goat came from the west crossing the whole earth without touching the ground."* I prophesy, the Goat shall be the United States with a prominent horn. The United States is one of the ten horns of the ten-area kingdom in the original ten-nation federation (MNO) or Daniel's ten toes. United States crosses the earth with airplanes, atomic weapons, and missiles. The USA attacks the Ram furiously striking and shattering his two horns. Daniel 8:7, then the United States (goat) tramples and sends foot soldiers into the area and totally smashes the Ram.

Psalm 97:3-5 proclaims the Lord's directive as the United States uses atomic weapons (melt like wax) to destroy Iran and Iraq in an air attack as none other

Below, 2-9-1- Israel, Jerusalem - Jaffa Gate: The holes in the Jaffa Gate made by bullets used in the 1967 war, was a reminder there will be wars and rumors of wars in the middle east until Jesus Christ comes back. We should not be deceived into thinking democracy will bring peace to the Middle East, nor will America toppling Iraq or Iran. There will always be turmoil, hatred, and hostility toward Israel by the surrounding nations until Jesus returns (Ezekiel 35:1-15 to 36:1-5).

2-9-2 - Israel, Nazareth, Muslim Mosque: On December 3, 1999 our tour group walked by this proposed location for a Mosque. Muslims were praying at the sight. This location is next to the Church of the Annunciation. Christians celebrate this location as the place where an angel visited Mary and announced she would be the mother of Jesus (Luke 1:30-31).

PSALM - 98

98SRSP-CE Sequence

Section 2-10, Page - 36

The MORNING of PSALM 98

98SRSP-CE Sequence

With cautious optimism, the morning brings to an end Gulf War II (Warning note: God can overlap this war into Gulf War III with an chilling effect on the world). Psalm 98:6 says, a blast on the ram's horns will occur, which means the ram has been beaten and dehorned. God's righteousness is now known in many nations. Psalm 98:1 declares, God's right hand and His Holy Arm have worked great things for Him. "This," the Spirit said, "means there shall be a great world-wide revival. Psalm 98:4 continues about shouting for joy all the earth, burst into jubilant song and music to the Lord God. Many pastors have been looking for this revival." Let there be praise unto the Lamb! This year we will see millions of people saved and many lukewarmers rededicate their lives to Jesus.

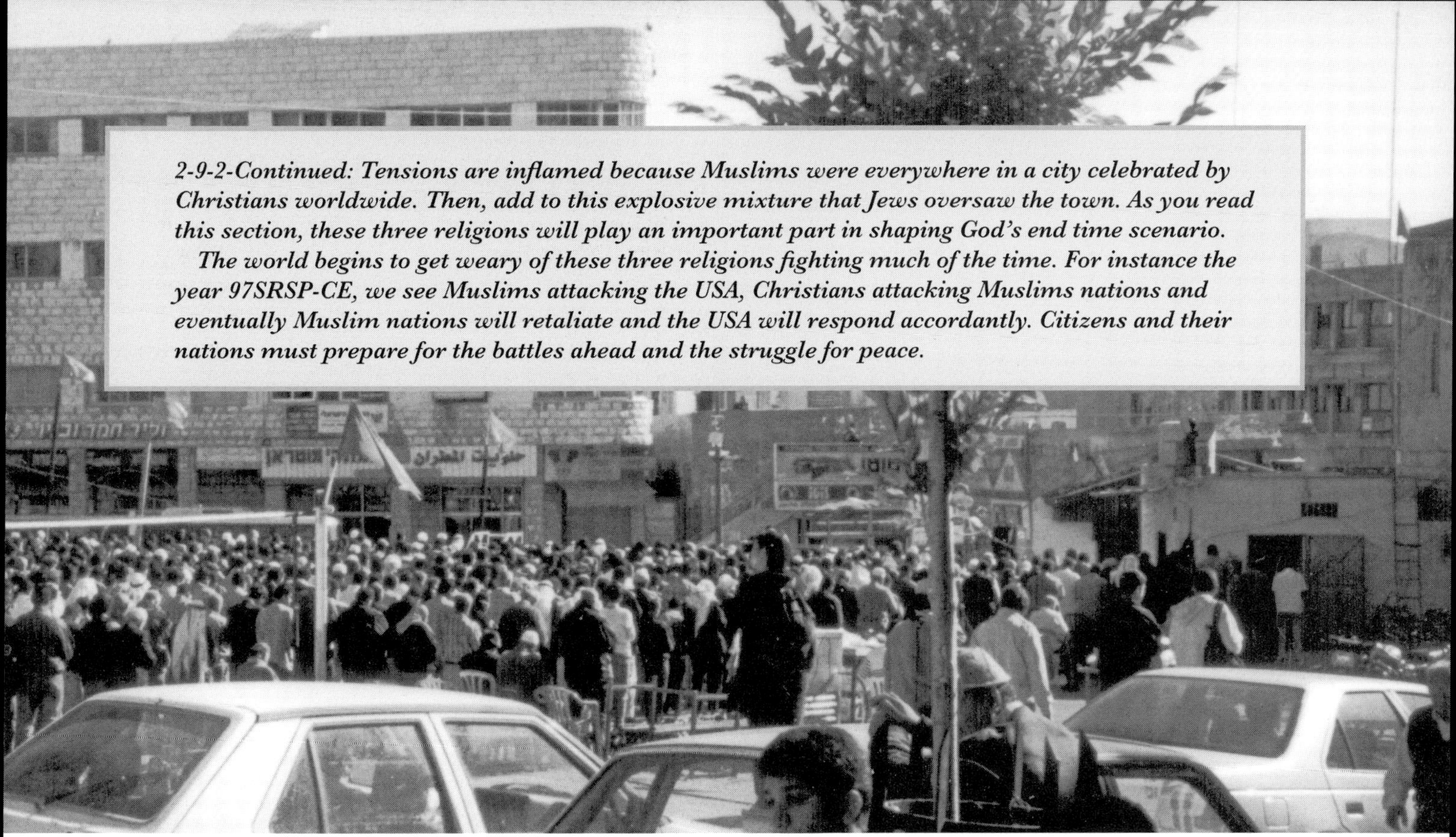

2-9-2-Continued: Tensions are inflamed because Muslims were everywhere in a city celebrated by Christians worldwide. Then, add to this explosive mixture that Jews oversaw the town. As you read this section, these three religions will play an important part in shaping God's end time scenario.

The world begins to get weary of these three religions fighting much of the time. For instance the year 97SRSP-CE, we see Muslims attacking the USA, Christians attacking Muslims nations and eventually Muslim nations will retaliate and the USA will respond accordantly. Citizens and their nations must prepare for the battles ahead and the struggle for peace.

2-9-3 - Israel, Jericho: The city where the Israelites brought down the impregnable walls with a mighty shout, after the priests' trumpets had sounded for seven days. Today Muslim nations can help terrorists use a nuclear weapon to destroy a city without the shout.

Our tour bus turned off the main road and headed into Jericho. The West Bank area was monitored by Jewish Israel, however, Jericho had been turned over to the Muslims, which is viewed on the right side of the picture. There were hundred's of them lining the road which leads to Jericho. The tour guide told us we would only stop on top of the hill near town to get a quick photo-op of some of the dig sights, and then we would leave because it was unsafe there. The problem is three religions not able to get along together in peace even when their beliefs are different. As we move toward the end of time, the religious bickering will get worse and wars will follow.

The EVENING of PSALM 98
98SRSP-CE Sequence

Once again, we see God ending this year by Psalm 98:9, *"judging the earth in righteousness and the people with equity."* The total of each nation's obedience to God will pass and receive a blessing or fail and receive a curse. The following nations will be judged to receive a curse in one year and dry and wither: Russia, Iran, Iraq, Ethiopia, Libya, Germany, Turkey, and a few others. This equates to a large part of the Army of the North, Ezekiel 38 and 39.

Above, 2-10-2- Greece, Island of Rhodes - Palace of the Grand Master: There is a powerful lessen to be learned, so lend me your ear: Note, the lighter color stone about half way up the wall. Lightning struck the church across the street with its basement full of gunpowder, causing the top half of the castle to blown off. When it was rebuilt, they substituted lighter color stone. Are modern-day enlightened Churches setting themselves up for a similar explosion? The Spirit has told me emphatically, YES! One might ask, "how can this be, we are rich in need of nothing?" Take the Church test in section-6. Have churches changed anything since WW-II? Such as, 1) doctrine, 2) praise and worship, 3) Church leadership roles, 4) brought retailers into the church or its property (coffee shops, donuts shop, photo yearbook pictures, book stores, money exchangers to charge for tickets to concerts and the like), 5) built gymnasiums, 6) entertainment director has priority over the outreach ministry, 7) younger women teaching the older women how they should act, 8) sexual sins like homosexuality are tolerated and even glorified, 9) keeping more head count is more important than sound message, 10) debt, 11) building projects to be more progressive than down the street, 12) improper dress, 13) disregard for end time teaching, 14) buying into the Internet Web of Deceit and using the 666 = WWW), and the like. Then to have the audacity to tell Spirit- filled Christians these worldly props were brought onto Church property as a witnessing tool. Many in the Body of Christ have become vomit to the Lord God. Many in the Churches should hold up a towel not to praise the Lord God but to offer Him something to wipe His mouth with after He spits most of His detestable Church out into the tribulation period to be rebuked and destroyed in the Great Christian Falling Away.

Note: Duration of 1998SRSP-CE can be one second to 50 years long!

Below, 2-10-1- Israel, Jerusalem - Via Dolorosa, Station # 10: The Way of Suffering - or Way of the Cross, as it's more commonly called in English - represents the route celebrated by Christians where Jesus walked when he carried His cross from the place of his condemnation by Pontius Pilate to the site of His Crucifixion and burial. A copy of the Wake Up Call Scrolls was given to one of the overseers at Station #10 when I walked the Way. It is wonderful to have the Lord God fulfill His Father's programmed test cycle of prophecies. The harmony of God's test cycle would have been completely disrupted if Jesus had refused His Father and used His power to call warring angels to protect Him from this prophesied cup of death. Think, about the disharmony humans cause on earth as the Lord God looks down from His throne. Therefore, Christians must try to walk in obedience with God's teaching.

PSALM 99
99SRSP-CE Sequence

Section 2-11

(S.R. = Slide Rule Point = Not an actual date = Used for sequencing end time events)

The MORNING of PSALM 99
99SRSP-CE Sequence

The morning of 99SRSP-CE opens with Russia worrying about nuclear weapons in breakaway states, which were captured by the Ram (Iran-Iraq) in Gulf War II. This has been a thorn in her side. To secure the weapons, Russia observes Iran and Iraq are defenseless after Gulf War II. Russia shall be further infuriated when a chain of world events drags her army southward. To secure the breakaway states' weapons, Russia seizes the opportunity to war south. Ezekiel 38:8, *"You (Russia) will invade a land that has recovered from the war (Gulf War II)."*

We must read and understand Ezekiel 38:4. God will cause the chief prince, of what was known as Rosh (today equates to Russia or its general area) to be moved south. Russia will be yanked by God south starting in the jaws of the bear. **Look at the picture of the Beast prophecy** (section-9 about three Beast picture). The map shows the Bear with his left shoulder toward the map viewer. Now, in your mind, follow as God says in Ezekiel 38:4. The Spirit moved me to write, "I (God) will turn you (Russia who looks like a Bear on the world map) around facing the map viewer. I Almighty God will put hooks in your jaw and bring you south for war. Your jaw shall be made of the following countries, but not limited to, Albania, Bosnia, Herzegovina, Bulgaria, Croatia, Greece, Romania, and Yugoslavia. This will be the area of hot spots that I, Almighty God, will use to start Gulf War III in the year 99SRSP-CE".

Just a side note here, Ezekiel 38:6, *"also Gomer* (Germany and land eastward) *with all his troops..."* Until the Berlin wall came down to fulfill this prophecy, Russia could not move south. Now West Germany and East Germany have been united, which in turn has helped dissolve differences between eastern and western Europe. Therefore the word ALL is appropriate rather than half their troops. It will be important in understanding end time events as it relates to Jesus' second coming. Therefore, Jesus will not be coming back today because what the Old Testament prophets have predicted has not come to pass yet (Luke 18:31 and Matthew 26:56).

People who say Jesus could come back anytime, simply have not studied properly or have some hidden agenda. Christians must make every effort and be blameless before God today just in case they die. Once again, using the scare tactic Jesus could come back today cannot be found in scripture. If this is so, then God has changed His original programing in the Bible. This was why Jesus taught us to look for the sequencing of signs before and after the tribulation period starts.

Below, 2-11-1- Italy, Pompeii, The Forum: Vesuvius destroyed Pompeii in 79 AD. I get the feeling some of today's Christians do not believe end time events will happen in their lifetime. Many Christians do not want to hear of negative events and believe scare tactics are going overboard. The victims in Pompeii did not think they were going to die at the hands of a powerful explosion either.

I do not tease Christians with folly, nor do I wish them to be emotionally distraught. Nevertheless, as surely as the sun comes up in the morning, so it will be with these prophesied events in sequence order. It will be crucial, for each Christian to use the birthing pain principle (Matthew 24:8, see glossary) on every prediction.

Therefore, one event may occur slightly before or after its sequence, but the general flow will proceed like a fire-storm of lava racing down a mountain. Once these main events start, they will increase like a raging flood. Many people will be killed quickly in this-year's war that never expected to die. Each person must watch out and make sure they are ready to meet their God.

Above, 2-11-2- Italy, Rome - Police Station: When I look into the future for the next seven years or so, the Spirit has shown me a police or rapid reaction military per the ten zones in the world. The UN and the EU have been toying with the idea and the Antichrist will push it. Many European nations will flock to this secure alliance only to find their undoing. The uniting of Germany made way for the EU or the Old Roman Empire to be reborn and healed. The original European Union will be one of ten areas of the Leopard Beast of the Revelation 13:3, head which had the fatal wound healed.

Let us look at Psalm 99:1, "... *let the nations tremble...*" as they see Russia start this conquest south. Again in Psalm 99:1, "... *let the earth shake,*" represents Gulf War III when the western nations use atomic weapons to protect Israel against Russia and her allies. Russia will try to destroy the oil and the wine (warning in Seal three). Gulf War III equates to the repeat of the fourth Seal representing war, famine, and pestilence (chemical weapons and virus like unto to, but not limited to, green monkey virus.)

Ezekiel 38-39, describe Gulf War III. Psalm 99:4-5 describes the downfall of the mighty army from the north. God intervenes and allows America and her allies to use nuclear and other weapons. This almost destroys these countries, as we would know them today. The destruction worldwide from Gulf War II and III kills millions and millions of people worldwide. America takes a few atomic hits herself, but survives.

The world now knows it can destroy mankind if this type of warfare continues. This calls for sanity. These atomic wars make the case stronger for the MNO. The European-led MNO has said for sometime they must be the ruling body to control the world. Most countries agree and want a strong leader over a world government to achieve worldwide peace.

The MNO says, "The Christian countries started using nuclear weapons first." Therefore, the world shall be afraid of the USA. Through these wars, a mighty general who headed up the military campaigns for the USA has become famous for his hard line Christian view and the protection of Israel. He shall be one of the Two Witnesses (Revelation 11:3-14). His name will be known through the land as Destroyer.

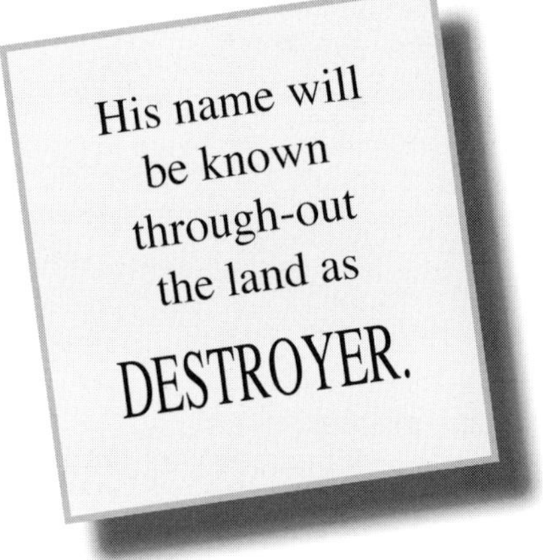

The EVENING of PSALM 99

99SRSP-CE Sequence

Here we have an overlap of time I shall call ***"confused time."*** The Gentile year ends 99.12.31SRSP-CE. However, the year 100SRSP-S, as thought of in Jewish time, starts in the fall of 99SRSP-CE in Gentile time.

Many events will happen during the fall of 99SRSP-CE. Much of the world will mistake Gulf War III for Armageddon. The Antichrist will try to convince the world this war was Armageddon to give him a foothold in Israel. Let's review the fall of 99SRSP-CE as the Spirit moved me to write.

✪ First, the mighty army from the north will be defeated. Psalm 99:4: God has established equity in Jacob. The Psalmist says, worship at His footstool and I say, on the Temple Mount.

✪ The defeat of the northern army will be another event that ushers in a stern-faced king (Daniel 8:23), a master of intrigue (made curious with stealthy plot), and he will arise to world fame. This was due to his heroic role in helping overthrowing the northern army and protecting the Jewish people. The Jewish people will be fooled when they look upon him as their Messiah returned. The foolish and lukewarmers will continue to deny what has been happening.

This man will be a true Antichrist (Revelation 13:1-10) and his earthly name in Hebrew adds up to 666 or has embedded within it MNO=666. He will sell worldwide peace and be given power by a few to take control of the MNO as their new king. He will declare peace to the world and Israel. This will be a seven-year peace pact with Israel but it will not be understood (unsigned event) as a seven-year pact. Otherwise, we could count 2520 days and know when the Second Advent would occur. It looks like the typical politician's promise. When Jesus returns, there will have been seven years between the peace declaration and His return to fulfill Bible prophecy.

This MNO king will not get along well with the newly elected American congress. The wise Christian in America believes this man could be the final Antichrist (Revelation 13:11-18). There will be much to debate about this matter. Remember the power base in most Protestant churches will be the fifty-one percent lukewarmer. The person who denies will not follow the Lord's command to refuse this man's government (Revelation 14:11). This must be where the wise Christian has to override the lukewarmer. This MNO leader will evolve into a true Revelation 13:1-10 Beast or Antichrist. He will declare peace to the world and Israel and deceive many.

The Spirit promptly stepped into my mind and said, "Stop, we must make a point here." After a discussion in my mind with the Spirit, I was instructed to write. The best advice on how to survive these dangerous times will be found in the Holy Bible. In fact, the scriptures state some will recognize, and react to, the signs of the end and prophetic warnings. The wise also will watch for signs and events being prophesied by others. Proverbs 27:12 states that the prudent see danger and make preparations, while the worldly and lukewarmers never see and keep going until they suffer for it.

Jesus made a similar statement concerning the time of His return. Christ stated, that the foolish knew nothing about endtimes and what would happen until the disaster struck and took them ALL away (Matthew 24:39). Jesus also said the wise servant would be ready for the perilous times preceding his return. The hell bound fifty-one percent lukewarmers will not see the urgency to act in time. **In other words, if we know in advance precisely what has been destined to happen, we and our loved ones, Church and nation will fare much better. The foolish ones and lukewarmers who make no provisions and will suffer for it.**

Lukewarmers, have faith to believe in the WAKE UP CALL PROPHECIES before it is too late. God always provides a warning before His judgment falls. Unfortunately, Christians don't always listen. Even our pastors and teachers occasionally misinterpret a move of the Lord. For sometime now, God has been warning America, and specifically, American Christians, the tribulation will begin soon. The Spirit had me prophesy the sequencing point will be about 99.9.25SRSP-CE. Informed and wise Christians realize the world will escalate into unprecedented chaos. Unfortunately, few unbelievers and lukewarmers understand the true severity of the dreadful years ahead.

The best time to study these prophecies and act is now!
The first casualty of the Gulf War III is when truth will be trampled on the ground.
This ushers in more lies and the tribulation period with more wars.

Below, 2-11 3 Italy, Northern Country Side - Original Roman Bridge: This bridge was crossed when the North Men attack what is now called Italy from the North over the Alps. Christians must understand events and natural disasters will begin to happen more frequently after Gulf War III. Many men, organizations, countries, and alliances will try to hold the rule by building bridges not of bricks and mortar but of electrons over the Internet Web of Deceit. They will try to control commerce, military alliances, world taxation, and movement of people. Just at the days of old, an attack is emanate, and disaster awaits the world.

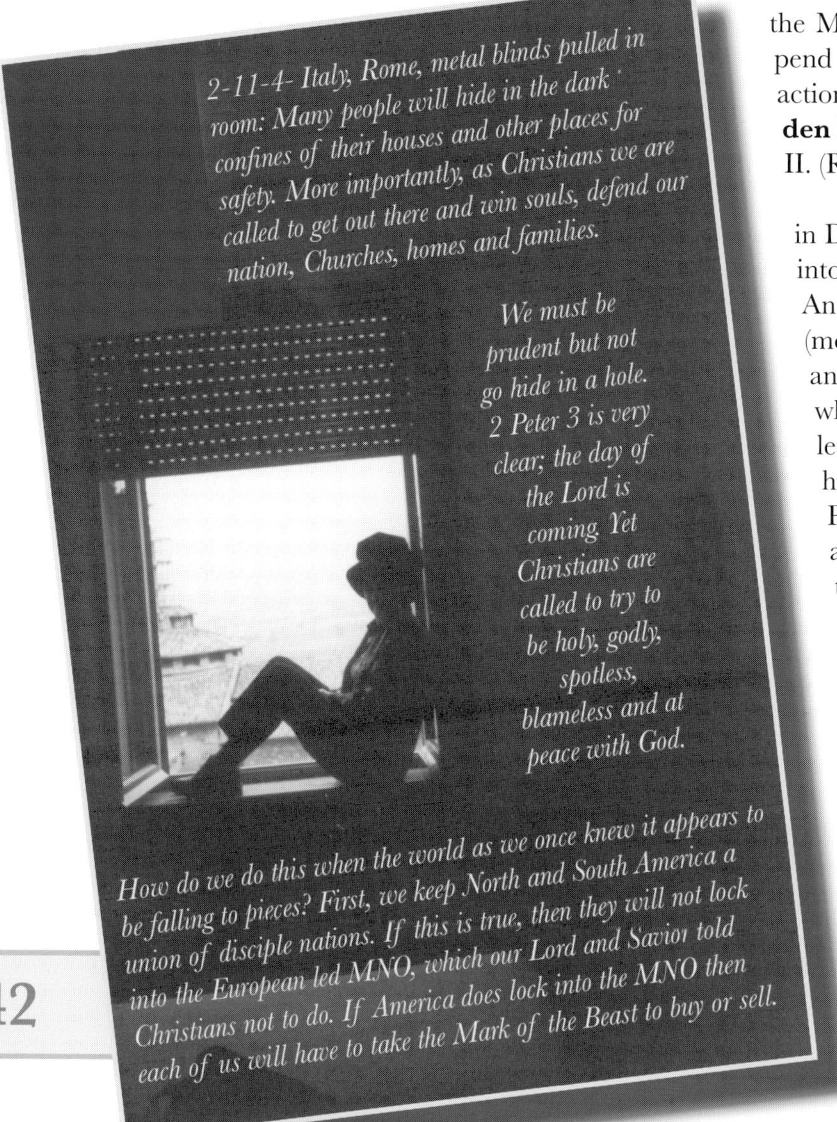

✪ We begin to experience the wise Christians becoming a thorn of resistance in the side of the Antichrist and his spirit. *"But the people who know their God will firmly resist him* (Antichrist)" (Daniel 11:32). America, as birthing pains, **will lose her horn** and standing (status and reputation) with the MNO because Christians resistance blocks America from joining this worldly government. This results in North and South Americas' being removed from the MNO and not being allowed to vote in its ten-kingdom assembly (Daniel 8:8).

Read the Beast chart prophecy section 9-1 and discover where, to fulfill Bible prophecy, North and South America will be removed. They represent the three horns (votes) in the original Beast kingdom. They no longer have voting rights in the MNO assembly.

The Christian with the spirit of love must be adamant and forceful in persuading lukewarm churches to stand up and demand the elected officials not lock into the MNO - Leopard Beast. Christian's lives depend upon stopping their government from this action. We must understand the **Second Hidden Mark of His Name** in WAKE UP CALL II. (Revelation 14:11)

✪ The one Horn (city) that's broken off in Daniel 8:8 will be replaced as birthing pains into four emerging Horns (Cities); first, the Antichrist (leader, little Horn), second, Japan (money), third, the Army of the South (power), and fourth, Israel (honor and glory). In short, what we now have will be the little Horn, the leader acquiring leadership, money, power, honor, and glory to run his MNO. (Refer to Psalm 97 and Prophecy Against the Goat, and the fourth and final Beast - Eagle with the Three Ugly Heads.)

✪ A stealthy event will occur under the cover of the fourth Seal repeat as an **unsigned removal** by death of some of the seven spirits of God. In particular, all of number Six Spirit, (Revelation 3:10). The number Six Spirits are the Christians who are found blameless before God (See Seven Spirit Church Prophecy). This will happen in confused time during the fall of 99SRSP-CE.

America's year-end overlaps with Israel's new beginning. These two periods are exactly the same time. The tribulation period will be in Jewish time. So the psalmist thinking in Jewish time recorded the removal of Spirit six in Psalm 100:2, *"Worship the Lord with gladness, come before Him with joyful songs."* **The Spirit Six removal is an unsigned event and has been currently in progress through the start of the tribulation period.**

✪ Another event to happen concerns a man know as **Amon, Amon.** (Note: There will be a great mystery behind this name.) He will be moved by God to destroy the Dome of the Rock located on the Temple Mount in Jerusalem. The world hero (Antichrist) will give Jewish people permission to build the Third Temple on the Temple Mount, in the turn of this year. He shall refuse the Moslems rebuilding rights with a stealthy plot to fool the Jewish people. Many Jews now think he must be their true Messiah.

Temple rebuilding rights, along with a deceitful campaign for world peace toward Israel, will convince the unlearned Jew this must be their Shepherd, the true Messiah. The Jewish people will put their trust in this lawless man whose true intentions and incredible power will surface three and one-half years later.

Above, 2-11-6 - Italy, Florence - Fiume Arno River: There was a beautiful reflection of the mirror images in the River of the buildings on the opposite bank. There is calm before the storm I have observed. Before this year, the world was moving at a fast pace and money was the driving force. World leaders did not perceive the total disaster, which lay ahead, or better preparations to avoid certain problems would have been made. I warned the EU members ahead of time, but they did not listen. Because they did not pay attention, Russia will suddenly be jerked south in war as I have prophesied in Issue 1. When this year begins, widespread destruction and distress will break out, as earlier described. Be on your guard! Learn to analyze between the lines of these prophecies as to how they will affect you. Prepare for the disobedient world to suffer!

Right, 2-11-5- Italy, between Florence and Venice - Nazi WW-II pillbox: It appeared everywhere we have been in Europe, there's still evidence of WW-II. Gulf War III will present a mess for Europe. Germany will be sympathetic with Russia because Russia supplies them with most of their natural resources and Germany's a member in the EU. This war will carry into the tribulation period. We must begin to educate and protect our Churches and communities. The time frame between Gulf war II and III has not been given to me, whether a day or twenty years we must prepare. Remember The Lion (England) will not stand by America's side very well after this war. The tired and played out Old Lion will side with the European Leopard Beast for security. This will isolate North and South America in many ways.

✪ A worldwide fuel shortage will come to center state. This causes unrest and destruction in America after Gulf War III has been completed. Most of the Churches who did not get their debt paid off, as UACC goals specify, now must close due to delinquent loan payments. They will turn their beautiful Churches over to the slave master who equates to the Antichrist spirit. He now controls the monetary spirit of the world. These Churches will perish and not be a part of God's salvation plan. God wanted to keep them open a few years longer to save more souls for the kingdom. Disobedience to acknowledge the signs of the times and make the church ready could be death by fire.

✪ We will see the Antichrist backed by the MNO promises of world peace and stability. Between the periods of 100 to 106SRSP-S, the Antichrist in the name of peace will destroy many. The world will follow him but the Christian has become a thorn in the side of the MNO. The MNO now stands in the world's mind as the only answer to world peace. Many Christians will be killed trying to tell the world the truth. The Christians now have become a deterrent to world peace and big corporation's international profits.

It is crucial Christians DO NOT think Gulf War III (Ezekiel 38 war) was Armageddon.

They will be told this error or lie, by the European Led News Media and others. Parts of these statements are from ignorance.

However, some are from Satan himself to set up an atmosphere to raise the Antichrist to become the world savior through peace and security.

✪ Another event involves an important worldly religious man of confusion who sits on seven hills. He will be removed before or under the fourth Seal or Gulf War III. This makes way for the true False Prophet (part of the earth Beast in Revelation 13:11-18). The False Prophet will be given power next year to team up with the leader of the MNO to achieve world peace.

We Christians must speak out against this worldly religion. The problem will be, the world will not be leaning toward Christian views anymore, but are accepting what the False Prophet says. This man has been given big blocks of time to sell his worldly religious agenda. He sells moral issues without salvation through Jesus Christ as necessary.

He pushes for world peace over the worldwide Internet web of deceit. This deceptive teaching and advertising market has now been controlled by the MNO and the Antichrist. They understand, "advertising works." The solid Christian will be simply out-financed due to lack of support by hellbound fifty-one percent lukewarmers. The solid Christian shall be overwhelmed by propaganda and cannot withstand the attacks by the False Prophet and the MNO.

To further his agenda, the Antichrist will use lying signs and deceive the people of the world. They will accept his one world religion for peace and safety. We can see why God will be angry at the lukewarmer in (Matthew 24:10).

✪ One of the last signs of this year involves the world monetary system. Evening ends with the world economy dried and withered. We now can understand why God's wrath on this world must be called true and righteous judgments. This will be the end of 99SRSP-CE.

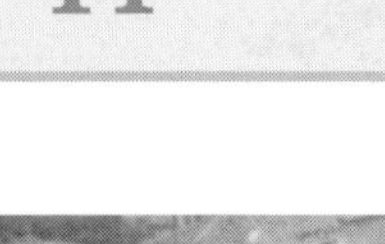

W.W. II - *Ruins*
Italy, *country side*

Left, 2-11-7 - Italy, between Florence and Venice - W.W. II ruins: We passed signs of W.W. II as we traveled through the countryside. The Church has not been warning properly and the nations of the Americas have not been preparing to fight a nuclear war? Note: Germany came into power and World War I began. There were signs before W.W. II the war was coming. Again, history discloses, Germany came into power in Europe, and World War II started.

I ask the reader, who is in power once again, Europe for the third time before 99SRSP-CE? Germany has been running the Leopard Beast - EU. They are getting friendly with Russia, which sets up a relationship spoken of in the Ezekiel 38 war. Think! If Russia dictates to Germany and Germany dominates the EU then where does this predicament leave the Americas and specifically the reader? Think! Think!

GOD'S SLIDE RULER OF END TIME SEQUENCING EVENTS.
with laps and overlaps of events.

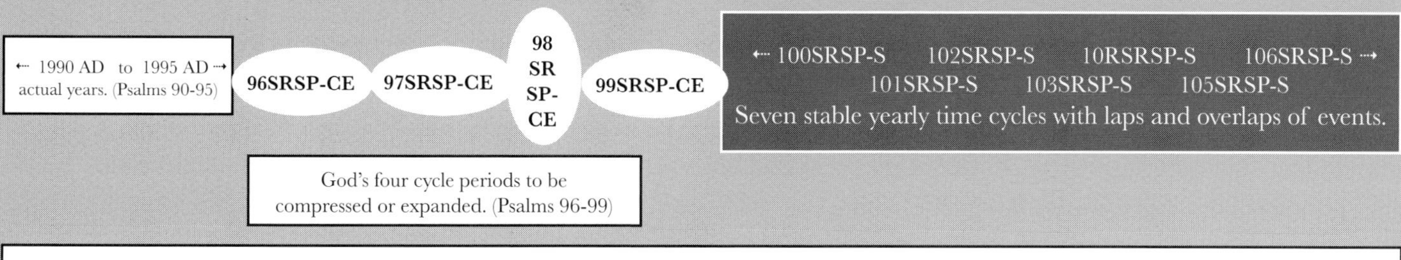

True Earth years as we understand time.
← 1990 AD -1995 AD → ? 1997 ? → 2005 ?- - 2007? → cannot determine actual dates → ? 20?? - ? → Second Coming

UNDERSTANDING TRIBULATION PERIOD SLIDE RULE SEQUENCING POINTS

PSALMS 100 - 106 =
100SRSP-S TO 106SRSP-S
Section 2-12
The Tribulation Period's
Seven Stabilized time Cycles
with laps and overlaps of events.

The reader will note sequence designations after 1999SRSP-CE carry the letters SRSP-S. The S.R. represents God's slide ruler. SP is a point on the slide ruler depending on where the Holy Spirit showed me to place it using Book Four of the Psalms. S denotes stabilized slide ruler to earth time during the seven-year tribulation period denoted by Psalms 100-106. God has set the time of the Second Advent. If we knew this appointed earth time, then other end time slide rule positioning point could be adjusted backwards to an exact or approximate A. D. Time for each event. But we do not know the earth time of the Second Advent, so we must rely on sequencing signs. Let the reader focus on the general flow of sequences of end time events, rather than actual times and unknown dates. Everything about endtimes must have the birthing pains principle applied, start slow or small and increase quickly with laps and overlaps of events. One event may appear to happen before another simply because of people's location on earth and what they perceive as important to them at the time. Spirit-filled Christians must keep focused on, what God has going on, not what the satanic world and the European led world news media would have you believe may be happening!

PSALM 100

100SRSP-S SEQUENCE

Section 2-12, continued
(S.R. = Slide Rule Points = Not an actual date
Used for sequencing end time events)

The MORNING of PSALM 100

100SRSP-S Sequence

Morning opens with the true believers (Psalm 100:1), **shouting** for joy because they know Jesus will be coming back in approximately seven years. The hero of Gulf War III will be a Antichrist whose name adds up to 666 in Hebrew. He will confirm a peace pact along with many nations. Power will be given to him by a few on or about 100.1.10SRSP-S. The ten divided areas of the world will be a kingdom federation - **Millennium Nations Organized - MNO (Leopard Beast).** This represents Revelation 13:1-8, a Sea (of nations) Beast kingdom. It also represents Daniel's ten toes of iron and clay (Daniel 2:4-43).

100SRSP-S shall be the beginning of the last repeat of the First Seal (Revelation 6:1-2). This Seal states he (Antichrist) rode out as a conqueror bent on conquest. In the name of peace, he will take peace from the earth. The Antichrist leader of the MNO has given the Jewish nation permission to rebuild the third Holy Temple on the Temple Mount in Jerusalem. He has refused building rights to the Moslem stronghold nations to replace the destroyed Dome on the Rock. The Jewish people take this as a sign the Antichrist must be their Messiah and are persuaded by his smooth talk. The world will be tricked into believing he will always protect Israel and restore world peace. They will find he will seize much through intrigue. The Christians who are left must stand up, even in the face of death, to rebuke this false leader, an Antichrist and his MNO.

Above, 2-12-1- Italy, Venice - Waterfront Retail Shop: Venice has been known worldwide for its fine glass and jewelry. Many people bought their spouses or friends jewelry and gifts. This was a pleasing experience for both parties. The Bible warns us, the love of money is a root of all kinds of evil. Therefore, Satan has noticed this phenomenon of pleasure associated with buying and has been using it to its greatest destructive power. Nations will fight each other over trade deals. International companies will threaten and try to dictate to their nation's leaders how to make decisions. Nevertheless, Spirit-filled Christians must stand up and demand from their elected officials that European world government and its trade and security deals are not the way to go Biblically. Actuality, North and South America will have a heated debate, which jump-starts into a great defining moment of breaking away from the clutches of the European led world Government (MNO). If we raise the bar one more notch, then the Americas will go to war after being attacked by parts of this European led monster, which will develop into the mighty Eagle with the Three Ugly Heads.

Spirit-filled Disciples of Christ that pray for and against their enemies in the tribulation period are making history in the future.

Prayers against your enemies will be received by the angel then given to God to add power to them against your enemies, and given back to the angel. He will hurl judgments down to earth against a disobedient world (Revelation 8:3-5) in response to your prayers.

Don't pray against your enemies and these judgments may not happen and you could be consumed on earth.

Starting in 96SRSP-CE, and up until today, Christians must not deny the times in which we live. They must accept what has been prophesied here as truth and as birthing pains a partial fulfillment of Joel 2:28-29.

These calculations and events will happen in the time sequences prophesied. 99SRSP-CE will be the last year (expandable time period) of the days of sorrow. Watch for the European led MNO to gain power worldwide while suppressing the United Nations. Christians must rebuke the MNO (Revelation 14:11). The originating thought in the minds of men concerning the MNO takes place in 96SRSP-CE and may be obscured from public knowledge. Christians must not let their money-hungry nation and politicians be steered off God's course. Christians must convince their nations not to buy into the lust of worldly business greed for international profits. These companies worship money more than Christian values and must not dictate foreign policy. Remember, to expose Antichrist thinking, just follow the money trail. Christians must convince their government to say NO to the lure of the big benefits associated with becoming a member of the MNO. ***Your life will depend on it!***

The Spirit said, "Let's have a quick study here." Revelation 14:11 states anybody who accepts the Mark of His Name or worships the Beast and his Image will be tormented with fire in the presence of holy angels and Jesus.

The Mark of His Name equates to Millennium Nations Organized (MNO or 666) as calculated on the phone pad. If Christians accept the 6+6+6 access sequence codes, they will be doomed. These codes will be hidden at first from consumers as they do business over the Internet web of deceit. People paying the retail or wholesale worldwide MNO consumption tax are in trouble with God. God will judge people as doing business with the Antichrist. This action shall be against God's command in Revelation 14:11. Christians who participate shall be judged the same as worshipping Satan and they will burn in Hell.

Daniel 11:20 predict a tax collector will be sent out to maintain the royal splendor for the agenda of the Antichrist and the False Prophet. Christians must not fall for this trap. Revelation 14:11 warn Christians must not buy into this Antichrist world system for pleasure, security, and saving money. Christians may have moved out of God's grace if they follow worldly conveniences rather than Jesus' teachings.

Right, 2-12-2- Israel, Tel Aviv, Dizengoff Shopping Center: Shopping time. I saw many ways to spend money at numerous retail shops. In the tribulation period, shopping will be even easier if people carry the Mark on their hand or forehead and their government has locked into the European Led World Government. If countries are not locked into the World Government then many items will be on the shortage list because of embargoes against rebellious countries that do not join the MNO. Each transaction will carry a series of calculations. The computer will calculate WWW as (6 + information + 6 + information + 6 + information + 6 information) when citizens buy on the Web. This is because "W" equates to the sixth (6th) letter in the Hebrew alphabet, which shall be used to separate information by the computer. The Internet web of deceit which requires the participant to use these codes before buying, selling, or interacting to and fro for knowledge per Revelation 13 and Daniel 12.

Three sequences of the Mark of the Beast have already started voluntarily and the three sixes will be hidden at first and, as birthing pains, become forced in the second half of the tribulation. This equates to real deception, for **it shall be voluntary at first.** Many Christians will fall for this deception, for the Internet web of deceit controlled by Satan has become their idol of pleasure, convenience, and monetary gain.

The Saints may have to give up some financial security as well as comforts in their lives to follow God's command. By faith, they should follow these prophecies and avoid doing business with the MNO. Look around; people are locking their lives, businesses, churches, families and even nations into the worldwide Internet web of deceit. This includes such electronic equipment as but not limited to phones, faxes, beepers, satellites, computers, television, transmission stations, laser scanners, and the like. The electronic systems will be a worldwide system in which the Antichrist will be given power to control. If people, their companies, or churches are involved too deeply, it could cost everything to get out. By taking action now, they save themselves time. You will not lose as much in the future. This takes Faith!

The need for worldly pressure will not be as great to buy into the Internet web of deceit if the system does not have a financial hold on us. It will be imperative Christians unite through the Universal American Church Coalition (UACC) to offset worldly pressure. Together we can keep the good news moving at record speed longer than if we are dispersed. One of God's goals of the UACC will be to get American Churches out of debt before 99SRSP-CE and be of one mind. One-mind thinking has been the rally cry behind the great salvation message of our Lord and Savior, Jesus Christ.

It is not wrong to be on the Internet Web of Deceit before the tribulation starts, or the first half of the tribulation.

However, Christians will fall out of God's Grace who accepts the WWW to buy and sell on the Internet in the great tribulation period.

More importantly, why stay on it, because the closer time moves toward the end, the harder it will be to disengage from it.

The sixes (6's) divided information so the computer can place info-bits into the proper loop to assimilate and calculate the proper authorization codes and then transport it through the Web of Deceit to the Master Computer in the European led World Government (Leopard-MNO).

STEALTHY

Computer programing can hold all the information of each (6 + info) in one column, whereby hiding calculations similar to WWW = 666 on the Internet. The reverse is true with the bar code. It hides the 3-6's from view by only displaying the information.

Retail Bar Code and WWW = 666: The European World Government first as the MNO and finally the Eagle with the Three Ugly Heads will try to tax the Americas. This will be voluntary at first. These tax requirements will be mandatory to buy and sell for countries that join the MNO when the Final (last) Antichrist rises to power during the Great Tribulation.

Most Churches who are in debt will have to close by the year 100SRSP-S or shortly thereafter, because they cannot make their loan payments. "Christians," the Spirit said, "we need this time to win additional souls to the kingdom."

Christians must help start the UACC. Don't be discouraged when your leaders are resistant to this idea. The UACC can be a very powerful tool of God. The UACC shall be a platform for Christian churches to bond on a united front. They will have the power to stop their government from falling into union with the MNO. Some ministries will fight the UACC for they have their power bases built. Organizations who have bonded to many different religions (outside UACC requirements) will try to stop the UACC. International companies will fight the UACC because disengaging from the European World Market lowers profits, which have become their God of security and power. The Lord God says, "Be united, in one mind." It shall be acceptable to fellowship as individual churches, but with unity in a common cause to win USA back to Christ.

We see, as the smoke, dust, and death clears from Gulf War III (the fourth Seal repeat), this was the greatest destructive war in history. Under cover of this confusion, God stealthily (non-signed event) will finish removing by death the remaining Spirit Number Six Christians as He promised in Revelation 3:10. See Seven Spirit Church Prophecy for more details. They shall enter into heaven per Psalm 100:2, *"Worship the Lord with gladness,* ***come before Him*** *with joyful songs."* We also have over half of the lukewarmers stunned and denying the tribulation has started.

Left, 2-12-3- Italy, Florence - Palazzo Borghese - Ghosts: Ghosts appeared at the renaissance banquet, which typified the antique Florentine Courts. The entertainment at the Palazzo Borghese was the best we had on our entire tour of Italy. As I watched the Ghosts float by, I thought of all the souls that will be lost in Gulf War III, which do not have to be lost. If only the lukewarm churches would listen and prepare themselves by organizing the UACC to win the USA back to the Lord God. Think of how many souls could be saved which will be lost forever.

Right, 2-12-4- Greece, Athens - Greek Dancers: Singers and Dancers perform at a festive Greek party. They were the best dancers we saw while in Greece. We had a wonderful time. These professional dancers moved left, then right, and back they would go lapping over where they had just been, and so it will be during the tribulation. Calculations, political events, and natural disasters will lap and overlap. It becomes imperative the person analyzing and studying the sequencing of events, approach every sign or calculation by applying birthing pain principles. Know that these overlaps will start slow and increase.

Remember, lukewarmers don't want to sacrifice for the Lord; they prefer to follow worldly security and pleasure. This angers Almighty God and He begins to rebuke and discipline (Revelation 3:19) the disobedient lukewarmers.

God allows people to use the Internet web of deceit to reinforce the pre-tribulation rapture theory as a signed event. This theory shall be only a portion of His Great Delusion concerning the **test** on Christians and the whole world. This dangerous theory, which falsely states the only way the tribulation will begin, is to be ushered in by large masses of Christians visibly and mysteriously disappearing at the same time. They say this will cause a great commotion on earth like wrecked cars, trucks, trains and planes. Sadly, the world and lukewarmers will not see this occurrence so denial continues. The lukewarmer will not listen at this point to sound doctrine and teaching and most will be lost to Satan's deception. With Satan's great deception and power over the MNO, he will use the Internet web of deceit to trick the unbelieving world. He will prey on at least fifty-one percent of the lukewarmers. They will fall into his deceptive trap due to false teaching and lack of knowledge.

The Spirit told me, "If lukewarmers do not understand the deception now, it will be harder for them to wake up in the tribulation period." Christians must understand the times they are living in and realize the need to fight a battle for Jesus. Christians must not deny the tribulation will occur as early as the fall of 99SRSP-CE. God has been holding to His time sequences. I cry out in prayer to God for Christians to see Satan's deceptions exposed through these prophecies.

I have a heavy burden knowing that at least fifty-one percent of my Christian friends (see glossary - broad term Christian) will be lost. They will not listen to prophecy concerning what they must do to save themselves. I can hardly stand it sometimes until I remember the Old Testament prophets whom God told to go preach the good news. Yet, few listen to him. I wish you could see what God has shown me, for Christians would be on fire for Jesus Christ, the only true Savior. Yet, God will destroy many lukewarmers and it will be called righteous and true judgments.

The Four Seals or Four Horsemen are like unto the hoof beats of the pulsing rhythm of the birthing pains to the second coming of Jesus Christ.

Just a side note, the Spirit quizzed me in my mind. The Four Seals or Four Horsemen have been continually riding with a pulsing echo through time since Jesus was crucified. They have been picking up momentum as they approach the end of the test cycle. They are like unto the hoof beats of the pulsing rhythm of the birthing pains to the second coming of Jesus Christ. Today their hoofs are pounding the ground with determination and are repeating themselves between 1990 A.D. and 99SRSP-CE. They will also repeat the first half of the tribulation period and repeat the last and final time in the great tribulation period.

The greatest misunderstanding of all times about the battle of Armageddon has been, there isn't any hope for the USA. The misled Christian believes that every nation in the world (including USA) will be fighting against Israel. This is false! Satan's deception has propagated this false teaching. You must understand this one point. When the Bible says **all** nations in the world fight against Israel over Jerusalem, that does not mean **every** individual nation agrees or will follow the MNO. Remember Daniel's ten toes of iron and clay. Iron and clay doesn't mix. The prophet used the word **all** in the Bible because the MNO - Eagle with the Three Ugly Heads thinks it represents the whole world. When the Antichrist leads the MNO against Israel and Jesus returns in the air this does not mean North and South America will be among these nations. The Americas, or a remnant of Christians there, will refuse to participate in the MNO action. We will help the Jewish people fight the MNO or, as the Bible says, all nations in the world.

The prophet used the word *all* in the Bible because *the MNO - Eagle with the Three Ugly Heads* thinks it represents the whole world.

{Information note added 2-21-05: North and South America was excluded in the minds of Bible Prophets understanding when they wrote their prophecies concerning **all nations**. All nations back in Biblical days included all earth landmass except North and South America.}

End time Christians must become thorns in Satan's side and we must start today. We must start resisting the steps, which lead to death. One step to resist will be your country trying to lock into this world system MNO (Revelation 14:11). Another step shall be the IC Chip marking devices. **Christians must first resist and finally refuse both steps.**

It will be a great honor to fight in the battle of Armageddon on the Jewish side. This battle will represent Christians alive at that moment in time. Protecting the Jewish people will involve North and South America and others on the ground (Revelation 17:14) CALLED (Christians), CHOSEN (Jewish people and spirit number five's), and FAITHFUL FOLLOWERS (saints). Coming down to earth in the air will be Jesus and his mighty army from heaven. Add to this the Lord God pronouncing judgment in heaven in favor of the Saints (Daniel 7:21-22). Satan will lose and the Lord God will win - Glory! This victory has been discussed in Psalm 106.

2-12-5- Italy, Siena, The Piazza Del Campo: The town square has become famous for its Palio Horse-Race. The horses race around the outside and whichever horse crosses the finish line first with the fastest ***time*** *wins the prize! During the tribulation period, Christians as well as others will increasingly have trouble deciphering time. This has been discussed in great length during years 103-106SRSP-S. Because of Gulf War III, a nuclear war, there will be problems in some areas of the world with time. Nuclear bombs generate a nuclear pulse that wipes out many electronics, which tell us time. I personally have an old watch, which requires cranking the stem to make it keep time. Fancy electronic watches may not work. Likewise, USA's military will have to revert to the manual mode of flying planes as they move into the great tribulation. They better be working on this or the USA will be in trouble militarily.*

Above, 2-12-6- Greece, Island of Santorini, Fira: In all the places I have traveled in this world, the city of Fira perched on top of 990 foot cliffs was the most awesome sight to see. We walked to the far end of town on the edge of the high cliffs and watched the sun set. I have never seen such beauty. God has given us a beautiful planet to live on but we are trying to destroy it.

The Bible states the end of time will be like Noah's day, they were forewarned but they did not heed the warnings. They kept on partying, drinking, eating, and getting married. Maybe they had an excuse because Noah was the only one warning. But today we have thousands of Churches, which should be warning and are not. They are too busy borrowing money for building projects, increasing lukewarmer attendance counting, and entertainment presentations where tickets are sold by money exchangers. These actions have been a total lack of faith and misguided teachings as to the end of days. If the truth were told, revenues might drop. Therefore few end time teachings concerning suffering are taught.

Now let us flashback to the year 100SRSP-S. We also see in heaven Jesus, the Lion of the tribe of Judah, the root of David, has triumphed. He begins to open the seven Seals and the scroll (Revelation 5:5). Christians and Jews must understand the section labeled Six Time Planes of the Tribulation Period. Time, as we know it, will be meaningless when compared to sabbatical time. Here we have Jesus in our mind opening the seventh Seal yet He opened the First Seal more than two thousand years ago. This unlocks the mysteries as to why there are overlaps in the Seals, Trumpets, and Bowl judgments.

We can't start reading through the Book of Revelation and assume the events are in sequence. Fortunately, the Spirit has given us insight through these prophesies. The Christian can now understand the sequence of how endtimes are laid out in detail. The times and sequencing points (undetermined earth-dates) are not as important as signs and sequence of events. For the end time Christian the ordered sequences and signs are crucial to maintain total awareness of the times we live. Note: As the cycle approaches the end, time will become elusive and less important to people.

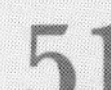

We see three Seals, number one repeat, five, and seven, representing three separate time frames being opened simultaneously. There will be silence in heaven for thirty minutes when Jesus opens the seventh Seal. The heavenly beings know it signals the start of Daniel's Seventieth Week. The first Seal repeat starts on 100.1.10SRSP-S when an Antichrist shall be given power over the MNO - Leopard Beast. The fifth Seal (Revelation 6:9-11) equals to the fifth Sign (Matthew 24:9-12). These are birthing pains and the beginning of a martyred remnant. This will continue until the end of the seven-year tribulation period when the sixth Seal takes effect.

There will be, as birthing pains, hate for the Christian and Jewish people. Many Christians will be killed in the name of peace. The Christians are the troublemakers against the world European led system (MNO). Christians will cause financial losses for money-hungry international companies. This will disrupt the Antichrist's agenda.

Over fifty percent of lukewarmers who think they are Spirit-Christians that enter the tribulation period will be lost to Satan by the end of seven years. What a price to pay for ignoring the truth. They ought to know what shall be happening and be obedient to God's commands. Satan will use the Internet web of deceit to broadcast great lies and deception. These lies are about the militant Christian movement and how it has been trying to destroy world progress and peace. Satan will use many false prophets and teachers led by the number one False Prophet who sits on seven hills. They will fool lukewarmers by their false signs and wonders. The number one False Prophet's power originates from Rome. He will receive full power after the death of the confused religious leader of Rome. Many broad-term Christians will fall because they simply cannot give up doing business with the MNO. They hang on to their money, lust, greed and what seems to be security and stability by obeying and reaping the benefits of the MNO.

The Seventh Seal will also be opened at the beginning of Daniel's seventieth week. It will end at the Seventh Satanic Doom (Revelation 20:11-15) with the great white throne judgment. God accomplishes total destruction of evil by throwing the sinner, Satan, death, and Hades into the lake of fire forever.

52

The Seventh Seal Contains:

- **Seven** Trumpet Judgments with the
- **Seventh** Trumpet Judgment containing the
- **Seven** Bowls of Wrath.
- The **Seventh** Bowl of Wrath contains the
- **Seven** Satanic Dooms to Satan.
- These **Seven** Dooms contains the
- **Seven** Sealed Thunders against Satan and his followers.

This completes the end of God's times (Our test cycle).

Small diameter meteor showers will began to hit earth. These showers will continue for some years at lower frequency of hits per day compared to the initial main body shower (First Trumpet, Revelation 8:7). This will occur in the first half of the year 100SRSP-S. Planes will be knocked from the sky, filling the sky with blood and fire. One-third of the trees and grass will burn in the hardest hit areas. The world cries for leadership from European MNO.

The EVENING of PSALM 100
100SRSP-S Sequence

The evening or second half of this year ends with solid Christians knowing what has happened and what they are called to do. The lukewarmers have been left in total shock and denial. They think destruction has been merely an accident of nature, not God's wrath on a disobedient world. This denial causes much friction between the lukewarmers and solid Spirit-filled believers. Because the wise know what is really happening. Division will increase in the next three years. Most of the time, lukewarmers will be in opposition to the solid Christian.

The vision of Evenings and Mornings has been the key to sequencing the positioning point on the Lord God's slide ruler of end time events. The Holy Spirit has accomplished this by overlaying in my mind, Book IV of the Psalms along with the Book of Revelation, the prophet Daniel and other prophet's predictions. A double Seal has hidden this insight for more than 2,500 years, but the day has come to open the Seals.

The Spirit went on to tell me, "I shall open the double-sealed (Daniel 8:26) portion of Daniel, chapter eight, so you may prophesy concerning these important events and time sequences. This will help the body of Christ shed light on end time events and know how to respond for the glory of God." End time events key around the double-sealed portion of Daniel's vision concerning evenings and mornings.

As instructed by the Spirit, I shall prophesy concerning this important matter. **The positioning point the sacrifices shall start will be 100.5.6SRSP-S.** This shall be done in the newly rebuilt Jewish (God's) temple in Jerusalem on the temple mount. Remember a man called Amon Amon has as I prophesied earlier, destroyed the Dome on the Rock. This will be done under the fourth Seal repeat in the year 99SRSP-S. Let's fast forward in time to find the positioning point, or approximate location on the slide ruler, when the temple sanctuary will be re-consecrated. Count on the Jewish calendar 2,300 evenings and mornings and find it lands on, or about, the Jewish New Year position point of 106.9.23SRSP-S. Now we know the Second Advent of our Lord will be on this position point or shortly before.

The fourth Trumpet (Revelation 8:12) will cause confusion in the first part of the year 103SRSP-S. The Lord will have shortened daylight.

The Antichrist will have changed times and laws in most of the world to confuse the issue even more. This occurs between 103.3.23SRSP-S and 105.7.28SRSP-S. 1 FM time (see glossary) change will start the first year of the **F**inal **M**illennium.

To find the approximate position point the rebellion will occur, we simply back up from the Second Advent point three and one-half Jewish prophetic slide rule years to 103.3.23SRSP-S. On this day, the Antichrist sets up his computer Internet web of deceit control center (Image of Beast) on one wing of the temple. He declares he is the number one God and this will be his headquarters. The event fulfills Daniel 9:27 and Matthew 24:15 and shall be the "abomination that causes desolation."

We then back up from the abomination positioning point three and one-half more Jewish prophetic slide rule years to find the sequencing point when the tribulation begins under the destruction of the fourth Seal repeat. That sequence point I prophesied to be about the location of 99.9.25SRSP-CE

We are now back to the year 100SRSP-S. The daily sacrifices will start on the prophesied day thanks to an Antichrist's approval, which fulfills Psalm 100:4. This states, *"Enter his gates with thanksgiving and his courts with praise..."* The Jewish people truly can enter God's Holy Temple. Most Jewish people on this day will be convinced this man must be the Messiah. This will be a tragic error, which lasts about seven years.

Throughout this year, America will have a serious fuel shortage, due to the elected officials failure to keep attuned to end time events. They have a denial problem like the lukewarmers when it comes to faith and knowledge on end time events.

This year ends with world financial markets dried and withered. Yet, the worldly person does not repent and their disobedience continues against God's commands.

PSALM 101

101SRSP-S Sequence

Section 2-13

(S.R. = Slide Rule Points = Not an actual date = Used for sequencing end time events)

The MORNING of PSALM 101

101SRSP-S Sequence

The Psalm opens the morning in verse one with the words, God's love and justice. With justice, God sounds the Second Trumpet (Revelation 8:8-9). A meteor will appear before this year. This meteor shall be a large meteor and will hit the ocean with great devastation. It will hit at an approximate point, which has great effect on the east coast of the United States. The meteor will ***totally devastate*** the east coast of South America and the west coast of southern Africa. It will cause tremendous damage. When the large meteor hits, it will destroy one-third of the ships in the total area with a mighty tidal wave (tsunami). It will also kill one-third of the sea creatures. This, in turn, will change one-third of the Atlantic Ocean into mud, blood, death, and a discolored look.

By this time the Antichrist has been gaining power and momentum in the European led MNO (Leopard). The disaster further builds his agenda for world government to handle catastrophic events while maintaining world peace.

Backed by the MNO, the Antichrist will war against nations (Second and Third Seal Repeats, Revelation 6:3-6) who resist him. Then worldwide famine will increase. There are many benefits for following the MNO for he will distribute bounty among his followers (Daniel 11:24).

Left, 2-12-7- Greece, Island of Patmos - Holy Cave of the Apocalypse: Pictured is a fresco above the entrance to the Holy Cave. It depicts St. John receiving and recording the end time revelation from the Lord God. I was moved as I toured the Holy Cave. People will prophesy and have visions (Joel 2:28). Many modern day enlightened lukewarm entertainment centers in America called churches have not listened to the prophetic fulfillment from these people. Sadly, they are too busy.

Above, 2-13-1- USA., Hawaii - Maui - Beach Resort: The Maui Beach Resort with the sand and beautiful sky, temperatures, fun, sunburns, and all the things we cling to as ultimate fun. I pondered why people would invest their money in oceanfront property when Jesus said the waves will be roaring before I return after the tribulation period ends. Insight came to me, because most shore lines in the world are not following Biblical principles. Acts of God are used to rebuke and discipline the ungodly along the shore lines and other places in the world before He returns.

Wise Christians who are left at this time must stand to the death to see their government does not join the MNO. The financial and security advantages for joining the European led MNO are tremendous. This will be the Antichrist's deceptive bait to get nations to join the MNO. Yet, this will be certain death to the Christians within their nations. By now, Spirit-filled Christians are becoming a real thorn in the side of the MNO and big international companies. This must be where the strong Spirit-filled Christian has to stand in the middle of the lukewarmers and make God's commands known and followed.

The resistance movement will be demanding, with many sacrifices. The fifty-one percent lukewarmers and many others will give into the system. They speculate God has to be all love and will understand why they become entangled in the MNO. Some will ask forgiveness for this abomination before God and continue in their lust, greed, and seeking false security. Satan's deception will be twofold. First, giving into the system brings peace. Second, rebuking the MNO (Leopard) by refusing to do business over the Internet web of deceit brings hostility toward the individual and the nation where they live. It also reduces international corporate profits and makes many people angry with the Christians. The Christians are branded radicals.

Matthew describes the great Christian falling away in Chapter 24:10; at that time (the first half of the tribulation period) a lot of Christians (over 50 percent) will turn away from their faith and cause much harm. Loss of money fuels the flames of hate.

The wise Spirit-filled Christian will become a constant thorn to the broad-term Christian. Lukewarmers will unknowingly fight on the side of the Antichrist's false spirit of peace. The lukewarmers will try to stop the wise Spirit-filled Christians from causing so much trouble.

Below, 2-13-2- Italy, Rome - Pantheon: Means "all the gods" built AD 27. Rome will have a powerful pull through the False Prophet within the Leopard Beast (MNO) to help nations in need of help from catastrophic events in the first half of the tribulation. The Americas must be very careful to NOT accept any help from the Leopard after the meteor hits. There will be strings attached to the gracious gifts, which will drag the Americas under the control of the European led Leopard. Christians beware and watch out no one deceives your leaders.

The further we move toward the end of time, the harder it will be for independent nations to cover their losses of wars and natural disasters. "There is safety in numbers," the MNO will advertise. The team approach to peace and security will look very inviting. But, beware! Because there are many lukewarm Christians in seats of high political and religious authority who will want to submit to the MNO. Citizens will be required to use the Mark of the Beast if their nation submits to the MNO.

The EVENING of PSALM 101
101SRSP-S Sequence

Evening begins with the wise Spirit-filled Christian trying to return America to a disciple nation under God. A disciple nation has its laws, government, and people in harmony with the Holy Bible. Psalm 101:2-8 tells of the struggle and intent of these Christians trying to rid evil from the Americas and themselves.

The evening closes with the east coastline of the Americas in a mess because of the destruction of a tidal wave (tsunami) caused by a meteor hitting the Atlantic Ocean.

America's eastern coastline withers and dries. For a time, Washington DC will become uninhabited. This ends the year 101SRSP-S.

America's eastern coastline withers and dries.
For a time, Washington DC will become uninhabited.

PSALM 102
102SRSP-S Sequence

Section 2-14

(S.R. = Slide Rule Points = Not an actual date = Used for sequencing end time events)

The MORNING of PSALM 102
102SRSP-S Sequence

The morning opens with the psalmist making the statement which sums up Book Four of the Psalms completely. It states Book Four be written for a future generation, that the people not born yet may praise the Lord God! (Psalm 102:18).

We see the Fifth Seal in full force as the Antichrist bullies weak nations and purges Christians. The Psalmist depicts through Psalm 102 a prayer of an afflicted Christian and Jew. These afflicted are faint and pour out their lament as a plea to the unchanging Lord God. In Psalm 102:8, the European led MNO has been after the Christians for it declares; my enemies are after me, they rail against me and curse Christians.

The Third Trumpet Judgment (Revelation 8:10-11) shall be as birthing pains cycling into motion. In Psalm 102:3, talks about bones burning like glowing embers.

The flaming star called Wormwood closely encounters with earth, causing flaming fragments to fall from the sky. This affects one-third of the rivers and springs. This causes polluted, bitter, and poison water, which kills many people. Psalm 102:9 depict the terrible condition the people are in, when it states eating ashes for food and much sorrow with many tears.

Below, 2-14-1- Turkey, Ephesus - St. Mary's Church: The first three centuries kept the secret of St. Mary's misfortune and death, but perhaps it was the Lord God's will. I was told, the first formal worship of Christianity, and the first church and basilica constructed in honor of St. Mary, arose in Ephesus, Turkey. Christians must understand the Lord God does not always reveal what we on earth would want to know at a specific time. Biblical writings contain mysteries, misunderstood delusions, sealed prophecies, hard to prophetically understand phrases, allusions, and the like. Biblical writings are the preprogramed assignments (seven layers thick) for our challenge, testing, persevering and the complete seven day (sabbatical time) or seven thousand years (earth time) heavenly contest for His pleasure. Spirit-filled Christians must stand firm in the faith and not follow the masses of lukewarm Christians who declare, "Is there a God who would let these skyrocketing disasters happen on earth?" Their faith will lean more toward the European Leopard world government for peace and security. This will cause great tension within Churches between the lukewarmers and the Spirit-filled Christians. The Great Christian Falling Away (Matthew 24:10) will be in full blossom this year.

Left, 2-14-2 - Greece, Island of Mykonos - Bob- Ghost shot with Chapel: The picture of me on the island of Mykonos appears to be shaking. The Aegean Islands have shaken before with earth-quakes and volcano erup-tions. Unfortunately, these disturbances will be nothing compared to the turmoil the flaming star Wormwood causes to the sun, moon and earth. I have heard many people refer to this passage in the Bible and seam ho-hum about the event. What they do not stop to think about will be the effect on earth's rotation around the sun and the moon's rotation around the earth.

The moon's rotation around the earth will be changed because of being hit by flaming fragments from this star. More importunely, the moon will also be affected by the magnetic mass of this star passing close to our solar system. With the moon's rotation messed up, the earth's oceans will cause the waves to roar more and the tide will change dramatically. I hope the reader has been getting the picture.

Earth will be affected also by the magnetic mass of this star and will be pulled in a slightly different orbit, which will send the earth reeling (Isaiah 24:20) so to speak. The new orbit will be one factor in shortening the day. Many electronics items will not work properly. Magnetic flux-energy from the star introduces chaos to many systems. This has been why I began to warn our military about having the ability to switch over to a manual mode because of a loss of satellites and electronic equipment failure.

Catastrophic events in the first half of the tribulation will deceptively make it seem practical to accept the foredooming Mark of the Beast. This could quickly identify people who are displaced or dead by these natural disasters. This will make people think the MNO has the capacity to ease the devastation of these events, whereas North and South America does not have total capacity to help in other parts of the world. They have enough problems of their own.

Be warned, technology's using satellites can be your nations Achilles' heel. More importantly, computer electronics associated with satellite vulnerability could become your biggest security problem. ***Watch out for the Army from the East!***

The EVENING of PSALM 102

102SRSP-S Sequence

The evening ends with the European led MNO gaining power. Many Christians are killed, martyred, deceived, and some betrayed by the fallen fifty-one percent lukewarmers and unbelievers.

The Christian in 102SRSP-S will feel as if their days are like the evening shadow; they wither away similarly to the grass in a field (Psalm 102:11).

Below, 2-14-3- Italy, Rome - St. Peter's - Dome: The dome of St. Peter's is 448 feet high and was designed by Michelangelo. Looking up at the dome is breathtaking. By this time in 102SRSP-S the False Prophet has been selling a world religion, which might sound like this: "God Almighty manifests Himself in all religions and is a God of Love. Christians demand too narrow of a religion. They maintain Jesus Christ must be the only door to heaven. This theory is outside the views of the world government to contain peace and security for all nations. Therefore Christian's doctrine must be toned down or rebuked."

Christians that live in countries who join the Leopard Beast are in serious trouble. There will be tremendous pressure applied by the European led MNO to force European Christian denominations into tolerance or be persecuted and destroyed. This will include but not be limited to such Christian religions denominations as Catholic, different European Orthodox denominations, some Reformed European denominations which still have ties in the Americas, and any other denomination which is tied to Europe-based religions. Christians in North and South America who are members of these European-tied denominations will have to make some serious decisions as to how to break off ties to any European denominations giving into the False Prophet to save their lives. There will be many hard choices ahead but only one right choice and His name is Jesus Christ.

PSALM 103
103SRSP-S Sequence

Section 2-15
(S.R. = Slide Rule Point = Not an actual date = Used for sequencing end time events)

The MORNING of PSALM 103
103SRSP-S Sequence

The morning opens with escalating conflict against the Christians who are being persecuted. People on earth will experience as birthing pains, the beginning of the fourth Trumpet judgment (Revelation 8:12-13). The past three years' meteor hits (first and second Trumpets), and the star, Wormwood, (third Trumpet) have caused considerable more cosmic debris. This cosmic disturbance generates large amounts of smaller meteor debris and disintegrated pieces of stars. This debris impacts one-third of the surface of the sun and moon. Between the sun and earth there shall be much dust and larger pieces of cosmic debris, whereby creating a tremendous refraction of light particles when viewed on earth. One-third of the available light source will be refracted away from earth.

This refraction of light creates an illusion like a full eclipse of the moon during the day. At night it creates what people might say would be moonless nights. Moonless nights create an almost one hundred percent absence of light. This looks like what people might experience when turning the lights out inside a deep dark cave. People will not be able to see their hand in front of their face.

As the Christians see this devastation, they must hold onto God's promises in Psalm 103:2-6. God will forgive sins, heal our diseases, redeem life, satisfy desires, and renew our strength like an eagle.

In Psalm 103:20, *"Praise the Lord, you his angels, you mighty ones who do his bidding, who obey his word."* This time sequence will be when Michael, the Archangel, kicks Satan and his fallen angels down to earth. *"The LORD has established His throne in heaven, and His kingdom rules over all."* (Psalm 103:19). People see now the Lord has established His throne in heaven. This will be accomplished after the war involving Michael and the dragon and their respective angels. Satan will be hurled to earth with his demons (Revelation 12:7-9). This will be great news for the third heaven but not for earth. It shall be like a swarm of angry bees attacking people and stinging them to a state of torment and/or death. **Woe to the world!**

Above, 2-15-1- Israel, North end of Sea of Galilee: We found beautiful trees within the gardens on the Mount of the Beatitudes. It was a tranquil setting for contemplating the site of the Sermon on the Mount in Matthew 5-7, "Blessed is he..." This year the world will experience the Spirit of Satan first hand and it will be anything but tranquil.

Christians will experience an inter peace which surpasses all understanding if they are truly Spirit-filled. God promises blessings on the poor, the mourning, meek, hungry, insulted, and persecuted in these tribulations times. We are called to rejoice and be glad. Unfortunately, the lukewarmers will not understand this passage for they are busy protecting their things, money and accumulated treasures. To make things worse, time of day, month and even year will be harder to distinguish as we continue through the tribulation events to the end. For some, survival will be more important than time of day or year.

We see Satan's spirit entering the Antichrist. This turns the Antichrist into a mad and lawless man who starts persecuting Christians and Jewish people. The Antichrist spirit in Satan's fallen angels will now enter into many leaders worldwide to further Satan's agenda. The swarm of Satan's demons land around the earth.

The Antichrist's hidden agenda will be interrupted by America (Eagle) with a massive airlift campaign. USA warns Jewish people to get out of Israel for the Antichrist and the MNO want to control the world through Jerusalem. This will be a voluntary airlift to bring the Jewish people out of the reach of the Antichrist before it becomes too late to escape. They are flown to a USA desert location for their protection. This airlift campaign will be before 103.3.23SRSP-S.

> **The Antichrist sets up the abomination that causes desolation in the temple.**

Many Jews will not heed the warnings to leave. They still believe the Antichrist to be their great hope. The Jewish people in the USA are now placed under God's protective security. They are protected until we fight on the Jewish side to win the battle of Armageddon. This massive airlift unveiled the Two Witnesses to the world. They begin to be recognized worldwide for their stand against the Antichrist and MNO. They are the ones who prophesied the airlift must start just before the Antichrist made his move on Israel and placed his control center in the temple.

In Revelation 12:15 we see the MNO headed by the Antichrist, armed with Satan's power, pursuing the Jews. The MNO fires many intercontinental ballistic missiles at the desert location in America (Revelation 12:16). The USA will be given warning by the MNO these missiles are not aimed at the United States but only at the Jewish people in the desert location. These people are considered traitors to the MNO cause and will be eliminated.

By now the USA has perfected the intercontinental ballistic missile defense system. The USA and its allies shot down most missiles that are fired against the Jewish people in the USA desert. They have little effect. The dragon and MNO are outraged as described in Revelation 12:17. They pull back from this missile attack because it has been ineffective. The Two Witnesses threaten to use nuclear weapons if this attack is not stopped. The Antichrist starts killing Jewish people in Israel and around the world who are easier prey than those in the USA.

The Antichrist backed by the MNO invades Israel before 103.3.23SRSP-S. They take control of the nation and, in particular, Jerusalem. The Antichrist sets up the abomination that causes desolation (Matthew 24:15) in the temple. He installs his Internet web of deceit control center on one wing of the temple in Jerusalem.

☞ Note - Clarification added 5-2006: He will force the take over of the electronic media including the Internet web of deceit. This is done to control the buy and sell mode as well as his propaganda machine. ✄

At the same time the temple sacrifices will be stopped. This begins on 103.3.23SRSP-S. For the Antichrist calculates, more businesses will be closed on the weekend. This will make it more difficult for the Jewish people to flee with food, clothes, and proper protective equipment.

The Antichrist, armed with Satan's full power, now declares himself the true God of gods. At this time, the Jewish people who did not airlift out earlier in the year are trapped. They are forced to flee with little provisions to the hills or to Jordan. This will be a terrible day for the Jewish people. The Christian nations helplessly watch the Jewish people being killed over the Internet web of deceit and TV. The Antichrist and the MNO now have Israel's nuclear weapons readily available. This greatly enhances their dwindled arsenal.

Left, 2-15-2- Israel, Megiddo - King Ahab's underground water system: This system was built over 2,800 years ago to keep water available for the city or fort. We went down 200 steps into King Ahab's underground cave where the springs are located. Going down was the easy part, coming back out required a little more effort. There was a sense of security down under the rocks. Even if fighting broke out on the surface, the secure feeling was still there. More importantly, Christians are not called to crawl down into holes or caves during the tribulation period. They are called by the Lord God to protect their families, the brethren, God's house of prayer, and their nation.

If they lose their lives protecting their friends, then they gain the highest rewards in Heaven (1 John 3:16). They may be classified cowards and could be sent to hell if they crawl into a hole or cave to hide and let their brothers die when they could have helped them. People are going to see the Jews killed in large numbers when the Final Antichrist (last) takes over the Temple. America will be unable to help the Jews very much because of the distance and resistance of the Leopard Beast who shall be transformed into the Eagle with the Three Ugly Heads (last Beast).

Above, 2-15-3- Israel, The Galilee, West Bank - Military Check Point: We pass through the checkpoint as we left Galilee and enter the West Bank, headed to Jericho. Check points will be commonplace through out the tribulation period. America will require driver's licenses or passports to move between locations. The Mark will be required to travel in the MNO nations that join with the Final (last) Antichrist. There will be much more effort put into watching and controlling East-West movements than North-South movement. The MNO reasons that more destruction can be detoured if movement is controlled tighter East and West than North and South.

Now we see the Two Witnesses rising to fame. The **first Witness** is America's leader in charge of affairs. He issues a **Three Woe Warning** over the Internet web of deceit. He harshly condemns the Antichrist leader of the MNO. Three woes are a part of the Fifth Trumpet Judgment (Revelation 9:1-2). The Three Woe Warning shall be issued, **First Woe** consisting of three warnings. Warning One (1): Overthrowing Egypt (Daniel 11:15-16), Warning Two (2): Setting up his computer control center in the temple at Jerusalem (Daniel 11:17), and Warning Three (3): Stopping war against coastal countries (Daniel 11:18), the **Second Woe** (four fallen angels at Euphrates River), and the **Third Woe** (oil and wine).

The **Second Witness** is a United States commander nicknamed **"Destroyer"**. He, with the blessings of the first Witness, will implement the **Fifth Trumpet judgment** (Revelation 9:1-12). The commander has received his nickname because of his victories in Gulf War III. He will put an end to the Antichrist's disrespect concerning the MNO attacks on nations (Daniel 11:18).

This commander, who once was a paratrooper (Revelation 9:1), was given authority to open the underground shaft, which houses a special chemical depot (abyss). This shall be located in the USA and is not the same abyss that was referred to as the jailhouse of heaven (abyss) where sinners are put in prison (Matthew 18:23-35). Numerous planes and helicopters land and load-up with these chemicals. These chemicals will not kill, only torment, for about five months. As these numerous aircraft take off and land, they create a large cloud of exhaust smoke looking like a gigantic furnace.

These special chemicals create sores like a scorpion sting, which make men want to die, yet they cannot. With these chemical weapons, they use air power to attack the Antichrist's army and his strongholds within the MNO. These chemicals will not hurt the trees, plants, or grass. They are designed to be targeted at the MNO army strongholds. The Two Witnesses hold back using nuclear weapons because of their terrible destructive effect to the planet. This ends the First Woe.

We also see this commander of the United States, under the direction of the American leader (first Witness), implement the first Bowl of Wrath (Revelation 16:2). He sends planes equipped with special chemical weapons to dispense these chemicals over MNO nations. These chemicals cause painful sores to break out on the people. These people have accepted the Mark of the Beast. They paid the consumption tax to the MNO and the False Prophet's worldly religion.

Ugly and painful sores break out on the people in many of the MNO nations. They are asked by the United States to repent and disengage from the MNO and side with the Americas. Nonetheless, these nations as a whole will not repent and acknowledge they have made a mistake. To quit the MNO would be a great financial loss as well as the loss of military protection from a hostile world. They curse the God of the United States and the Jewish people while making threats of retaliation.

The Americas are outnumbered; astonishingly, the USA fares well because the Two Witnesses will prophesy in the second half of the tribulation period. Their prophesies inform the Christian community what Satan and the MNO are planning. When the MNO implements harmful actions against the USA, we have the defensive counter to offset their offensive strike. If anyone tries to harm the Two Witnesses, they are burned with fire. This results from the Two Witnesses issuing orders to send missiles and/or planes with bombs that will produce fire to devour their enemies.

The EVENING of PSALM 103

103SRSP-S Sequence

The evening begins with God's final wrath being unleashed. This wrath comes in the form of the Seven Decrees called Trumpet Judgments (Revelation 11:15 to 20:15). This will be the Lord God's series of absolute judgments which will be executed first by the Two Witnesses and finally by Jesus. Jesus' first objective to accomplish shall be for a specific purpose, destroy those who are destroying the earth.

The Seventh Bowl Judgments contains the final Seven Satanic Dooms. They will be implemented in the year 106SRSP-S, through and including the Great White Throne Judgment. The Seventh Satanic Doom will put everything under Jesus' feet by destroying the final Satanic four (4): sinner, Satan, Hades, and death. These four are destroyed at the end of the millennium.

We must keep in mind the power of the USA, in comparison to the MNO, will be withering and drying up. This will be accomplished because the MNO is isolating the USA through embargoes to weaken us for the kill (takeover). The embargo will be a result of America's refusal to accept the Second Hidden Mark of His Name. The Second Hidden Mark means joining the MNO and paying the transfer tax by forcing its people to accept the Mark of the Beast. The embargo will begin to show America's weak spots. America should not have become so dependent on the world in the 1990's and thereafter. Because of the lust of money, we become very dependent on the outside world. Now the Americas will be paying the price for their greed.

It will be very important to understand, at this point, the United States cannot take on the entire MNO in a military conquest. This weakness was caused in the late 1990's when the government, because of greed, transferred out many repair and development facilities into the private sector. These sectors became dependent on overseas companies. Therefore, America has created many of its own problems because of lust and greed. We need repair parts, yet lack the capability to make them quickly. The year ends with America beginning to wither and dry.

Above, 2-15-4- U.S., Hawaii, Oahu - Rain Forest: We went hiking in the rain forest at Oahu. We have taken helicopter flights over both ends of the rain forest in Maui where we felt we were on a different planet. I have backpacked and camped out many times in the mountains of Colorado and numerous other places. However, the rain forests are different. Those who go into the rainforest can receive peace beyond understanding if they will be still, quiet and listen to the stunning sights and sounds God has made in nature.

What I am getting at here must be said with stern conviction. Spirit-filled Christians during this year will have a peace in their hearts that surpass understanding. It looks like everything must be falling to pieces in the world, yet this type Christian will stand firm to the end. Unfortunately, the lukewarm Christian is having a panic attack because they lack mental toughness called perseverance. They also lack faith the Lord God has control of the situation. Lukewarmers will be realizing their god of possessions and stuff are doing them little good and they will most likely loose much of it in the near future.

PSALM 104
104SRSP-S Sequence
Section 2-16
(S.R. = Slide Rule Point = Not an actual date = Used for sequencing end time events)

The MORNING of PSALM 104
104SRSP-S Sequence

The morning opens with the first Woe from the United States against the MNO. The leader (Witness) of the USA issues an order to begin the Second Bowl of Wrath (Revelation 16:3) of God on the MNO. The Two Witnesses jointly target a sea which when poisoned will cause the greatest devastation to the MNO nations. The Two Witnesses choose the Caspian Sea. They send planes equipped with a special deadly chemical agent.

These planes represent verse four of Psalm 104, *"He makes wind his messengers..."* These planes drop containers of chemically poisonous agents into the Caspian Sea. This poison pollutes the sea's water.

This devastates the adjacent countries and generates great fear and tremendous anger against these Two Witnesses of God. These Two Witnesses again warn the MNO countries to repent of their sins and disband from following the Antichrist. If they do not, then more harm shall come to their respective nations. Their answer comes by cursing God and threatening to get even. Nonetheless, the United States has been saving what was left of its nuclear arsenal and using only chemical weapons at this time.

We must understand the MNO has been systematically eliminating our military satellites between 103 and 105SRSP-S *"His* (dragon - mainly nations out of the army from the East) *tail swept a third of the stars* (satellites) *out of the sky and flung them to the earth..."* (Revelation 12:4). This has stripped the United States military capability of firing missiles equipped with nuclear warheads with reasonable accuracy.

It generally takes three to four satellites to triangulate (cross reference) for perfect accuracy. Now America only has one or two satellites in these hostile areas. However, the United States begins working to get these satellites duplicated. They use chemical weapons dropped by planes and not by missiles. They can hit targets **manually** by plane, which are nearly impossible using missiles. The MNO has been afraid of the USA because the military could wildly fire their nuclear missiles and randomly cause untold damage in targeted nations.

Remember, Russia lost most of her nuclear missile and the capability to shoot down planes, missiles, and satellites during of Gulf War III. Therefore, America still hangs on to the dominant military power in the world. Yet, we are somewhat blind because of the loss of satellites. In the 1990's and beyond, we downsized, transferred, and delegated out to the private sector our capability to repair military breakdowns. This now plagues the military when trying to follow through concerning a military manufacturing problem or new design. Big business' lust of money and politicians trying to win reelection was a major problem. Always remember, to find the Antichrist spirit just follow the money trail for it will lead directly to Satan. America has now been paying the price for its past greed.

Below, 2-16-1- Israel, Dead Sea - Salt crystals and formations: Water, Water everywhere and not a drop to drink. We tasted the water and it was salty and bitter. Much of the world's water supply will be damaged and in disarray by this year. Flashback just a few years, when the earth experienced meteor showers, a meteor hit and fragments hits from the close encounter to earth of the flaming star, Wormwood. Good drinking water will be in great demand. America led by the Two Witnesses, will destroy one of the MNO's good water supplies, the Caspian Sea. This only compounds the problems for the MNO and they are furious. However, the MNO lacking faith will not repent of their disobedience and quit following the Antichrist.

Above, 2-17-1- Israel, Masada - Main Roman Camp: On the right, the main camp of eight Roman camps that attacked the Jewish fortress. North and South America will be the Jews last worldly hope, just as Masada was the Jews last stand against the Romans. There were five or six huge bomb explosions up north in the valley when we toured the fortress on top of 1000-foot cliffs. It put the tour group on their knees and we knew war and conflicts were near. America may be weakened by war and embargoes but the America's still pack a wallop, which the MNO respects.

The EVENING of PSALM 104

104SRSP-S Sequence

As we move into the latter part of this year, we see the Fifth Trumpet Judgment ending. This signals the end of the First Woe. As birthing pains, the United States puts out another warning called the Second Woe Warning. This warning will become an official statement of protest during the year 105SRSP-S.

The Second Woe begins to warn China, Turkey, Syria, and Iraq not to make war and trouble in the Middle East. The Third Woe warns to leave the oil in Saudi Arabia and Kuwait alone and leave the wine alone. Israel equates to the wine and the Two Witnesses have promised to return it to her rightful people, the Jews.

It becomes clear the MNO nations are going to follow the Antichrist and not listen to the warnings of the Two Witnesses. Left with no alternative, the American leader decides to have God's Third Bowl of Wrath (Revelation 16:4-7) implemented by the Destroyer (witness). This follows what the Psalmist declared in Psalm 104:35; that many sinners would vanish and the wicked would be decimated.

The military leader loads planes equipped with special vials of poisonous chemical weapons. These planes are sent over targeted MNO nations. Some planes drop vials of poison into the hydro dams in Syria. This contaminates Iraq's water supply on the Euphrates River all the way to the Persian Gulf. Other planes drop poisonous vials on the Tigris River whereby polluting all of Northern Iraq. Other planes drop poisonous vials in the Nile River from Khartoum, Sudan, all the way down the river to Cairo, Egypt. This pollutes the water supplies in Northern Sudan and all of Egypt (Ezekiel 29:9-10).

The year ends with the water supply in Syria, Iraq, and Egypt polluted. They have withered and dried for many have died from the bitter waters. This ends the year of 104SRSP-S.

PSALM 105

105SRSP-S Sequence

Section 2-17

(S.R. = Slide Rule Point = Not an actual date = Used for sequencing end time events)

The MORNING of PSALM 105

105SRSP-S Sequence

The morning of this year opens with the United States releasing a warning and a threat. This warning and threat shall be transmitted over the Internet web of deceit. It will be called the Second and Third Woe Warning. Its concerns are about the potential war in the Middle East over oil and how Israel could get involved. The United States warns, "Leave Middle East oil alone whereby maintaining world peace." The retaliation threat will be, further use of chemical weapons by the United States.

The psalmist states, *"...make known among the nations what he has done"* (Psalm 105:1), and *"He is LORD our God; his judgments are in all the earth"* (Psalm 105:7). These two verses command the Two Witnesses to warn the MNO of their wrongdoing and God's judgments against them. If they continue following the Antichrist then more of God's righteous judgments will fall on the MNO nations. The United States can see through the eyes of the Two Witnesses and their prophetic insight. They see China, Turkey, Syria, and Iraq as real threats to Middle East oil supplies and Israel.

Above, 2-17-2- Israel, Jerusalem - three different building of worship: This photo brings up a good point; first building = Moslem Mosque, second building = Orthodox Church, and third building = Christian Church. Israel, like the United States is not quite sure which God it serves. Our Founding Fathers knew which God to serve. The USA knew which God to serve, up until the 1960 when the Lord God was kicked out of everything. The Protestant Churches do not have a unified voice to speak to their government when it goes astray and it has! We must start the UACC to win America back to God.

The Antichrist will be filled with fury because of the action taken by the United States. He reinforces the idea the United States, Christians, and Jews are the main threat to world peace. The Antichrist contends the United States must be destroyed.

The Psalmist has spoken of another thorn in Satan's side, where the Lord God turned their waters into a muddy or blood-like condition with fish dying" (Psalm 105:29). This prophetic prediction by the psalmist is the aftermath of the destruction of the Third Bowl wrath (poisonous chemicals into the water) implemented by the Two Witnesses earlier last year.

Since the mid 1990's, the United States has been working on weapons for mass destruction. The purpose of these weapons will be to change nature. In particular, a technology that would eliminate the ozone layers over a specified area. This technology will be one hundred percent complete by the middle of the tribulation period. A full test cannot be conducted to find the outer limits because of the nature of the weapon so small tests have been run over the North Pole. The inaccuracy of the experiments unfolds later.

The United States will be weakening because of world isolation and embargoes by the MNO.

Again, the Two Witnesses put grave warnings over the Internet web of deceit against the MNO to stop their rampant takeover of weaker nations. Further warnings are issued to cease persecuting the Jewish people and the Christians. The Psalmist once again has prophesied this Three Woe Warning. *"He allowed no one to oppress them; for their sake he rebuked kings: `Do not touch my anointed ones; do my prophets no harm'"* (Psalm 105:14-15).

The MNO responds by scoffing, cursing America's God and threatening to stop the real world oppressor, America, and the Two Witnesses.

The United States will be weakening because of world isolation and embargoes by the MNO. We now see a last ditch effort by the Two Witnesses. The two Witnesses know their time appears to be running out. Therefore, they implement the Fourth Bowl Wrath (Revelation 16:8-9) by sending planes equipped with special bomb devices to deteriorate the ozone layers over the most hostile MNO nations. God begins to intervene and the effect of these bombs will be ten times as powerful as expected. The sun scorches much of the MNO areas and humanity with great heat. It will be as though fire was actually touching their skin. Glory to God and His righteous judgments for they (MNO) repented not and cursed God for the things the Two Witnesses did.

Psalm 105:28 states, *"He sent darkness and made the land dark, -- for had they not rebelled against His words?"* The Psalmist said He sent darkness, which shall be the depletion of the ozone, with results "made the land dark" like dried-up trees and grass.

These MNO nations are seared by intense heat. They curse the name of God. The Two Witnesses are cursed because they have control over these plagues. The MNO refuses to repent and glorify God. In fact, these events made the MNO hate God and the United States even more. The Psalmist prophesied in Psalm 105:25 that God turn hearts to hate and conspire against His servants (Two Witnesses)".

The Antichrist sells his deceptive agenda to the MNO. He reaffirms the United States is the real threat to world peace. He calls for unity among the MNO nations. He thinks, with the strength of these unified nations, he can win a war against America. **Therefore, the war with America will start.** (Insight into information analysis begins). The Spirit led me on a side trip to see how God has been observing the heart of the USA. The heart of a nation shall be the obedience to God by the broad-term Christians in the nation. God judges whether they have tried to keep their nation a disciple nation. He judges on how they carried the good news around the world.

God will review a series of questions before making the final judgment. Here are a few of God's questions:

1. Have the men done their part? Have they protected their family, brethren, church house, and nation?

2. Has the body of Christ kept their nation a disciple nation - that is to say its laws, government, and people in true harmony with God's word?

3. Has the Church and the nation supported the Jewish people in a time of need?

4. Has the individual, Church, and nation properly addressed statements listed in Disciple Nation Blessing or Curse - section 7-7 and 3-16's Last Generation - section 4-6?

5. Has the local Church kept harmony within itself so the nation can stay a disciple nation? On the other hand, has it fought between denominations and lost the power thereby to control their nation's destiny. God will judge the entire Church on how it kept their nation a disciple nation. Nation judging will be a consideration when God looks at the individual to give rewards or death on judgment day. The question will be asked, "Did you help your nation become a disciple nation or did you ignore Jesus Christ's great commission?"

Psalm 105:7, states, God's has sentenced the earth with His judgments. Now let us look at the USA's two options. First, we see if God judges the USA worthy of His protection for their obedience to Him. Second, we see if God judges the USA unworthy and completely pulls off His protective covering.

If the USA is judged worthy, then it will be spared the attack of the whole (MNO) world, meaning MNO kingdoms, not every nation on earth.

If God's right hand of approval goes up, then this war will be only Satan's judgment against the USA and we will survive. If, on the other hand, the USA has been judged unworthy, then God's left hand will go up in disapproval of our disobedience. Then the war will drag out until late in 106SRSP-S. The USA will be declared a political Babylon and destroyed by the Three Woes to America under the Third Satanic Doom (Revelation 18:1 to 19:6). (Insight into information analysis ends here).

The EVENING of PSALM 105
105SRSP-S Sequence

The evening begins with Satan, through the Antichrist, realizing his time will be short. To stop Jesus from returning to earth, he must trick the Christians and destroy them. Then he can take Jesus on one-on-one. Unfortunately for the world, he tries all kinds of deception. One of which will be trying to change time and laws (Daniel 7:25). He does this by using trickery in his calculations plus omitting Jesus Christ's age of thirty-three years from the Church age. Then he converts to the three hundred and sixty day Jewish calendar. This calculates to the approximate year 100SRSP-S or one FM (Final Millennium). He will use other trickery in his calculations to get the answer he needs to convert to 1 FM time. The MNO buys into his proposal and converts to 1 FM time. (See Antichrist changes times and dates.)

Below, 2-17-3-England, Greenwich - World Time Line: I straddling the pictured world time line where the day begins and ends approximately every 24 hours. It did not seem to mix me up having one foot in Sunday's time and the other in Saturday's time. Nevertheless, there will be coming a day this year when the Antichrist will try to confuse the world and try to change to Millenium time worldwide and try to call it 1 FM time. The Americas must not change to this time. Furthermore, time will be difficult to understand because of cosmic events on the earth.

He declares he is the Messiah who will lead the world into the next millennium. More importantly, he calls the new time (FM) meaning Final Millennium. This time change could start as early as the abomination that causes desolation (103.3.23SRSP-S). It could occur as late as 105.7.29SRSP-S. The important issue here is not to know the exact time but understand what the Antichrist will be trying to do when he changes dates and times. He will be trying to confuse, through trickery, the Christians concept of time so he can deceive them in other ways and ultimately kill all Christians and Jews on earth. Then he thinks his chances of destroying Jesus are greatly improved.

There will be war and rumors of war. Let us look at Psalm 105:28, *"He* (God) *sent darkness and made the land dark....",* and again in Psalm 105:16, *"He* (God) *called down famine on the land and destroyed all their supplies of food."*

Once again, we see Christian nations headed up by the Two Witnesses fulfilling the Fifth Bowl Wrath (Revelation 16:10-11). The USA will fly planes over Israel and drop deadly chemicals in hopes of running the Antichrist out of Israel. They target his headquarters, which are now located out of Jerusalem (Daniel 11:45).

2-17-4- Israel, Jerusalem, Temple Mount - Dome of the Rock: I am standing next to the Dome of the Rock. More excitingly, the reader must remember in this year the third Jewish Temple will be standing on the Temple Mount. Five slide rule years earlier Amon Amon destroyed the Dome of the Rock. The Jews received rebuilding rights.

and food supplies are destroyed. This gives the land a darkened, depressing, dead look.

We see, as birthing pains, God beginning to bring terrible storms across the MNO. *"He turned their rain into hail, with lightning throughout their land; he struck down their vines and fig trees and shattered the trees of their country"* (Psalm 105:32-33). These storms increase until they hit full intensity in 106SRSP-S under the Seventh Bowl of Wrath and the First Satanic Doom.

God will somewhat protect the Christians as described in Psalm 105:39-41. We must never test God about His word. Yet during these terrible times we must stand in faith on God's promises to protect the believer from poisonous drink or water. *"... and when you drink deadly poison, it will not hurt them* (believers) *at all ..."* (Mark 16:18). It will be very important to ask God's blessing concerning the food and drink we consume today and especially during the tribulation period. God will protect us from deadly drink and food, if we will only ask His protection. This assumes you are a solid Spirit-filled Christian and not a lukewarmer.

This year ends with God (end time programing) turning the hearts of the MNO to conspire against His Christian nations. *"Whose hearts he turned to hate his people, to conspire against his servants."* (Psalm 105:25). The Antichrist will be trying to regain some footing since his kingdom had poisonous chemical weapons dispersed on it to destroy his stronghold. The evening ends with the Antichrist's kingdom and throne in darkness looking dried and withered.

The question is ask, "What must I do to survive this slide rule year?" Ask God to help you tune out the destruction in the world so you can focus on Him and stay in His word.

Be fearless and have unwavering faith to stand against lukewarm and worldly opposition.

Believe the Lord God has endtimes under control, not the world government.
God knows what you must go through to complete a good work He started!

The Antichrist declares his personal kingdom as Israel. His headquarters (throne) shall be the power base where he controls the MNO ten area Kingdom Federation of Nations. It will be located between the seas at the beautiful holy mountain (Daniel 11:45).

These deadly chemical weapons hit the mark, thanks to God's guiding hand. The Antichrist's kingdom and throne are plunged into darkness. The trees, grass,

PSALM 106
106SRSP-S Sequence
Section 2-18
(S.R. = Slide Rule Point = Not an actual date = Used for sequencing end time events)

THE MORNING OF PSALMS 106
106SRSP-S Sequence

The morning opens with the Christian full of excitement and standing on God's promises for victory. The Christian's overall outlook will be rather diminished if they believe the MNO lies and propaganda being put out over the Internet web of deceit. The Antichrist will be doing everything he can to destroy the Christian's and Jew's morale. The Antichrist knows his time must be very short and he will be destroying anyone he can who opposes his agenda.

Nevertheless, the solid Spirit-filled Christians stand on the promises of victory given to them by God over twenty-five hundred years ago. The Solid Christian understands he and his Country may be overrun and persecuted a little longer. The Bible teaches in Revelation to have patience for God will send judgment in the Christian's favor at the appointed time. When judgments are sent, then the tide of the battle will turn and the Christians along with Jesus Christ will accomplish the final victory. Glory to the Lamb!

This will be a very busy year as far as sheer numbers of signs and events are concerned. Let us review this year.

- First, the **Sixth Trumpet judgment**,
- then the **Sixth Bowl Wrath**,
- followed by the **Fourth and Sixth Seals**
- which are a part of the **Seventh Bowl of Wrath**.
- The **Seventh Bowl of Wrath**
- contains the **Seven Satanic Dooms**.
- Add to these judgments the **Seven Thunders of God's Wrath**. These thunders open with the message, *"There will be no more delay."*

Add another event, the Battle of Armageddon, which will be the Fourth Satanic Doom, overlaid with the echo of the Fourth Seal. This leads to the second coming of our Lord and Savior Jesus Christ.

For the Christian living in this last year, it will be an unbelievable amount of events. These signs represent a string of overlapping and simultaneously occurring events. The sheer number of disasters happening could overwhelm the Christian. It will be important to remember the promises of God and stand firm until the end which has been determined to be Daniel's 1335 Day.

How must the Spirit-filled Christian live this last year while following God's will? Psalm 106:1-4 explains it best. Praise God, maintain justice, and constantly do what is right. There will be increased insight as God touches endtimers with the gift of prophecy concerning this year.

The last beast will be in two final millennium (2-FM) time since the Antichrist changed times and laws last year. Understanding time in 106SRSP-S will be very confusing as compared to today's calendar.

2-18-1- Scotland, Edinburgh - Clock in background: The town boasts this clock is the second most photographed clock behind Big Ben in London. Regardless of the claim, it did have the correct time when we were there. This may not be the case in the year 106SRSP-S. Many things will effect our perception on correct time. The Antichrist has tried to keep his Millenium time 2 FM over all areas of the earth. North and South America or should I say what is left of them will defiantly hold out with AD time against the Antichrist's demands. People's time perspective will be off a bit because the earth orbit and its normal axis have been affected earlier. Atomic time will be thrown out the window because it is not relative to what a person will experience on earth. Daylight to dark will be the order of the day for time, although it will be confused also.

Above, 2-18-2- Israel, Megiddo - Jezreel Valley - Armageddon: This peaceful looking valley has sported some awesome battles. Egyptian hieroglyphics describes how war was waged on the city of Megiddo by a mighty pharaoh some 3,500 years ago. Old Testament kings fought Egyptians before the time of Christ in this valley. "Lord Allenby of Megiddo", a British general won a battle in W.W. I against the Turks. More importantly, the biggest battle of them all will be fought this year 106SRSP-S, the Biblical Battle of Armageddon.

Time will further be confused because God has reduced light in the year 103SRSP-S under the Fourth Trumpet. To complicate the problem even more will be the Fourth Bowl of Wrath where the USA removes much of the ozone layer over the MNO nations. The normal workweek will be gone. People will lose some perspective of time. These Christians will have lost their normal reference points through the week. This results in our body time clock getting off.

Let us look at how the Spirit of Christ, who is the Spirit of Prophecy, guided me through this last and very complicated year.

We have the Sixth Trumpet Judgment (Revelation 9:13-21). Here we see God intervening and releasing the four angels who are bound at the great river Euphrates. Psalm 106:36-38 explains the general condition of the four nations involved in the war at that time. These nations worship idols, kill innocent babies, and will be obsessed with demon worship.

The Sixth Trumpet Judgment must be looked at in more detail. In Daniel 11:44, this battle was prophesied; reports from the east will alarm the Antichrist now sitting in the Temple of Jerusalem. He will set out in a great rage to destroy and annihilate many. He will protect himself from northern and eastern military threats by blowing up many strategic bridges along the Euphrates River.

The four fallen angels with ungodly and depraved spirits represent four nations (Revelation 9:14). These four angels are released to start war at the Euphrates River. The river is full of water during the beginning of the battle. Many strategic bridges are blown up. This bogs down China's army and causes her great distress. The first angel represents the eastern army of China. Their army has two hundred million men and will be marching toward the Euphrates River and consuming everything in its path. Three more angels direct the three nations, which the Euphrates River runs through. These nations are Turkey, Syria, and Iraq, backed somewhat by the Millennium Nations Organized (MNO = 666). The Antichrist will oppose the first angel directing China's army.

The three plagues (Revelation 9:18) each side will use and/or cause are: 1) Atomic bombs, 2) Freezing conditions caused by dust fallout and smoke from the atomic bombs, and 3) The mass destruction caused by conventional weaponry. One-third of the geographic area will die from the three plagues. They will not repent or stop worshipping idols, money, drug use, sexual morality, and lawlessness, even though they know God's judgment has fallen on them.

Above, 2-18-3- Israel, Megiddo - Armageddon - Bob with-Jezreel Valley: I was moved to think there was going to be a final battle fought in this tranquil stretch of valley which was long, colorful and quiet. The Jezreel Valley stretches from the Samarian foothills in the south to the slopes of the Galilee in the North, it is Israel's largest valley. Because of its strategic location on the ancient Via Maris route (Egypt to Mesopotamia and further), great scenes have afflicted this seemingly beautiful valley. Remember, this battle is fought against Jesus and His faithful followers on the ground (North and South America and others) against all other locations on this earth. The MNO thinks it represents all nations of the world, but Daniel 2 describes the Last Beast as made of Iron and Clay. The Iron nations (MNO) fight for the Antichrist and the Clay nations who refuse to join the MNO, fight with Jesus' power on their side. Note; Jesus will be in the air in a huge object during the battle. I have no insight into what Jesus or this huge object looks like.

China's strategists have determined if they are going to achieve lightning speed west toward Israel with their army, the Euphrates River must be dry before their next move. This will be accomplished on their next try by closing approximately seventeen hydro dams upstream from Iraq (Revelation 16:12, sixth bowl wrath).

Once the Euphrates River dries up and China wars further west, this will trigger the start of the Seventh Bowl of Wrath (Revelation 16:17 to 20:15).

As China advances westward, she will halt her aggression toward Israel. This will be caused by a delegation sent by the MNO. The delegation says, "The newly discovered huge object in the sky equates to the real threat to the world." The MNO leadership will be broadcasting over the Internet web of deceit about miraculous signs and discoveries in our galaxy (Revelation 16:13-16). They believe this huge outer-space object must be headed to Jerusalem.

The trinity of the MNO leadership has declared themselves the holy ones (Daniel 12:7). The self-appointed trinity of holy ones shall be the Dragon (Satan), Beast (Antichrist, and the False Prophet (Religious leader of Rome). They have confirmed there has been something huge traveling toward earth and this mass must not be of natural origin. They declare it must be the evil one, Jesus Christ, returning to earth to kill everyone. The Two Witnesses have been warning the MNO this would happen if they did not turn from their evil ways. The evil trinity through great deception will trick people into believing Jesus intends to kill everybody including the Christians. They say, "We must stop this gigantic mass moving toward earth for it has to be Jesus and His dreadful armies."

"Jesus," the MNO says, "is the treacherous leader of the Two Witnesses, Jews, and Christians." They further build their case by saying, "Just look at what harm the Two Witnesses have done to the world." The spirit of demons spews out more convincing lies through the spirit of deception. They place propaganda on the Internet web of deceit about Jesus' intentions. The deceitful message declares, "It's too late for repentance because Jesus has already judged the earth and will destroy the entire world." Further propaganda will be broadcast. "The MNO has a commitment to mankind to stop Jesus from this unjust and terrible action. The MNO desperately proclaims it shall be the only hope in saving the world."

Spirit-filled Christians are not deceived by this propaganda. They respond by telling the sinner to acknowledge Jesus Christ as Savior, to repent and turn away from their evil ways. The Lord God will then spare them from the lake of fire. Most sinners believe the "Holy Ones" lies (remember these are not truly Holy Ones of the Lord God's) and will not repent or listen to the Christians. In fact, they will curse Almighty God even more.

The three frogs in Revelation 16:13 are evil spirits. These spirits represent three evil people who profess their loyalty to the three "Holy Ones". The delegates are sent by plane leaping and landing like frogs hopping over the world taking deception with them. They sell it to any government who will listen to their lies. Most MNO kings and nations believe the lies of the delegates. America does not believe their propaganda concerning the evil mass headed toward earth.

The delegation from the "Holy Ones" has the ten MNO kings assemble at a place called Armageddon. This will be where the MNO's world assembly building has been built. It was constructed outside Jerusalem because of the limited space inside the city. The assembly votes to move their armies to areas near Jerusalem. They want their armies close to Jerusalem to reduce the response time to maneuver into position for war.

Each king will have his army completely assembled in place when the battle of Armageddon starts later in the year under the Forth Satanic Doom

THE EVENING OF PSALM 106
106SRSP-S (Sequencing)

The evening opens with the Seventh Bowl of Wrath of the Lord God. Now we see God openly begin to intervene in man's affairs. In heaven God will announce from His throne, *"IT IS DONE."* Immediately the seven sequences of Seven Satanic Dooms begin to unfold. These dooms are designed to destroy the sinner, lukewarmer, Satan, death, and Hades. The Seven Sealed Thunders of God's wrath will overlay the Seven Satanic Dooms and the Sixth Seal. These judgments bring honor, glory, and power to the Lamb.

SUMMARY OF
SEVEN SATANIC DOOMS
Section 2-19

FIRST SATANIC DOOM
(Revelation 16:17-19)

Because the USA and the Millenium Nations Organized (MNO) are at war, many nuclear and other type weapons are used. This causes lightning, rumblings, and peals of thunder blasts. Nuclear bombs exploding cause a chain reaction of earthquakes around the world. These quakes combined are the largest earthquake in history. It destroys most of the MNO cities and causes financial collapse of the MNO. This marks the key to the beginning of Satan's downfall. Jerusalem splits into three parts after this tremendous quake.

SECOND SATANIC DOOM
(Revelation 16:19 to 17:18)

"GOD remembered Babylon the Great and gave her the cup filled with the wine of the fury of his wrath" (Revelation 16:19). The Babylon in this verse will be Rome and has become the city, which enforces one-world religion over the ten kings of the MNO. This has been the False Prophet's headquarters. This world religious center has forgotten Jesus and intoxicated the earth with worldly religious ideas.

The severe earthquake in the First Satanic Doom continues to destroy islands and mountains near the city of Rome. When people run outside to get relief from the earthquake, they will find great storms are producing one hundred pound hailstones. After the storms pass, the MNO see the chance to destroy what has been left of the city. Rome has been at odds with the MNO lately over the inhumane way the MNO has been handling its affairs. This has led up to the MNO hating the religious moral back talk coming from Rome. The deception of the False Prophet equates to his selling some morality but rebukes Jesus as the true Messiah.

The MNO and the Antichrist destroy the city of Rome. However, the False Prophet supports the Antichrist's position as the only alternative for world peace and enjoys his protection in Israel.

Below, 2-19-1- Italy, Rome - Ponte S. Angelo Bridge - Castel Sant' Angelo: Fortresses like this will not stand the test of time when it comes to modern warfare. This bridge is one of the bridges, which leads to St. Peter's Square. Rome will speak out on moral issues during the great tribulation but the False Prophet will continue to discount Jesus as the only doorway to heaven. He will push tolerance.

THIRD SATANIC DOOM

(Revelation 18:1 to 19:6)

As far as Christians are concerned today, they must try to return their nation back to a disciple nation. If Americans are successful, then the USA will not be classified by God as political Babylon. If Christians in America lose the battle to bring the USA back to a disciple nation, then God will destroy the USA by the Three Woes to America. Let us look in more detail.

The Lord God already knows the identity of political Babylon, but we in the USA, still have an option as to whether America will be classified political Babylon or not. God has placed a blessing, or a curse, before the USA.

Let us look at two of many options, which could occur. Note; the Spirit has not given me full insight for good reason. The first option, the USA will destroy the MNO city, which controls political and monetary power of the MNO. This will occur if the USA will return to God. The second option, the MNO will destroy the United States by the Three Woes to America because the USA has continued to be classified by God as a non-disciple nation.

FOURTH SATANIC DOOM

(Revelation 19:7-20)

Satan's goal was to stop Jesus from returning to earth, and then he wins. The MNO radar has picked up a huge bleep on its scope. It indicates a huge power source has been heading toward earth. The Antichrist knows this has to be Jesus and His army. The Antichrist then summons his ten kings and their armies to fight the Christians on earth and Jesus and His army returning through the air.

Before the battle starts, the Two Witnesses make a special peace crusade and fly to Israel. They speak before the nations in the (world) assembly building warning of the MNO's destruction. They speak of world peace and ask the MNO to consider the tragic error they are about to make. Their warnings fall on deaf ears. The Antichrist orders their death. On the way back to the airport, their vehicle is ambushed and both witnesses are killed. Their bodies lie in the streets of Jerusalem for three and one-half days. The MNO nations rejoice because these two men have inflicted tremendous devastation on their countries. The Internet web of deceit carries joy over the airways. Psalm 106:19 proclaims, *"They worship the manmade machine cast from metal."* The television cameras stay focused on the two bodies.

In the middle of the third day, the bodies of the Two Witnesses come to life and stand up while being filmed on television. They are taken up into the air in full view of the television cameras. Fear comes over the MNO nations for they know God has intervened. During the Battle of Armageddon (Fourth Seal), the Antichrist and the False Prophet are captured. They are both thrown into a fiery lake of burning sulfur. A last ditch effort by Satan to stop Jesus from returning to earth fails. The Battle of Armageddon will be won by the Christians on the ground and Jesus in the air. This battle will be fought in Israel as well as worldwide.

Left, 2-19-2- Israel, Megiddo - Armageddon - Birds a sign of the battle: When I was on top of Megiddo a disturbing sight appeared. A flock of sea gulls circled overhead as God gave me a sign into the near future concerning the Battle of Armageddon. After the Battle of Armageddon the birds will get their fill of flesh for it is written in Revelation 19:17-18, "And I saw an angel standing in the sun, who cried in a loud voice to all the birds flying in midair, 'Come, gather together for the great supper of God, so that you may eat the flesh of kings, generals, and mighty men, of horses and their riders, and the flesh of all people, free and slave, small and great.'"

FIFTH SATANIC DOOM

(Revelation 19:21)

"The rest of them were killed with the sword that came out of the mouth of the rider on the horse, and all the birds gorged themselves on their flesh" (Revelation 19:21).

God has given me a vision concerning this verse and how the USA may come to play in this victory. The USA will have to turn back to a disciple nation and then the vision can be shared.

The Christian nations will be fighting on the side of the Jews. They will be trying to defeat the gathering of the MNO armies, which leads to the Battle of Armageddon. Remember, all nations in the world does not equate to every nation that joins the MNO. Daniel's ten toes of iron and clay implies 'all' the nations in the world do not agree with the MNO. So we have the MNO which thinks it represents the whole world (all nations) fighting Jesus in the air on a cloud. Jesus will have Christians on the ground helping to win the battle. This will be a terrible time. Many nuclear and other type weapons will be used around the world.

Before the battle, Jesus has given the world a sign of His second coming. Jesus will be above the earth in some type of what we might call a spacecraft or some type of huge white-energy emitting object. He will be in full view of everyone on earth.

Jesus and the Christians on earth win the battle of Armageddon. The real terror will now begin for the Sixth Seal, as birthing pains, has begun to be opened. This Seal will be completed by the end of 1,335 days as described in Daniel 12:12.

SIXTH SATANIC DOOM

(Revelation 20:1-10)

This doom covers one thousand years or one sabbatical day. First, we see the Battle of Armageddon completed and the world will be in a terrible mess. At this point, there appears an angel coming down from heaven. Heavens space here in our dimension of time-space will be the huge white-energy emitting object over the earth, which Jesus occupies. The angel has come down to get Satan for he has been de-fanged. This angel, with a great chain, seizes the dragon (Satan), and binds him for a thousand years or one sabbatical day. This angel forcefully sends Satan into the abyss, and with God's help, herds all his demons from the four corners of the earth into the abyss. He locks and seals it over them.

Satan's captivity with his own and his liberation after a thousand years are both distinctly prophesied by the prophet Isaiah 24:21-22: *"In that day the LORD will punish the powers in the heavens above and the kings on the earth below. They will be herded together like prisoners bound in a dungeon; they will be shut up in prison* (abyss) *and be punished after many days."* Then, they will be released for a short time to cause more trouble at the end of the one thousand years.

This event equates to the same decree as Revelation 20:3, and 20:7-10. Isaiah says the Lord gathers powers in the heavenly, which also refers to Satan's angels. In verse twenty-two, this prison or abyss will be a place for people to be tortured until God releases them to be punished some more.

IF YOU ARE ALIVE AT THIS POINT - FEAR NOT!

Long before your parents conceived you, your heavenly Father was hammering out this test cycle. Almighty God brought you to the forefront, just for this very moment - in the mist of this escalating conflict of good and evil. This military battle will be won or lost in the mind through faith or the lack of it, that God is on your side in complete control.

In a war of good and evil, Christians can't afford to be neutral.

The best insight about Armageddon will be the realization the end is near and Christians will be with Jesus soon!

ABYSS

(Also, Review Author's - My Nightmare -Section - 12)

God has given me the opportunity to look inside the abyss. This happened while I was receiving Wake up Call I on, or about, June 1, 1994. While lying in bed at night during a violent thunderstorm, I felt a cold-hot evil darkness come over me. My eyes were open by the Spirit of Prophecy, and before me was an opening from which to view. I looked into something like a porthole and my viewpoint was a shocking side-angle panorama scan. I was overcome with fear into the deepest parts of my bones. It cannot be properly described with words.

The abyss might be called, for a lack of earthly words, the jailhouse of heaven (Matthew 18:34-45).

This visionary expanse was like endless space within a chasm, yet it had boundaries, which could not be determined or seen. It was of another dimension of continual time displacement across times and space beyond understanding. The abyss contained what looked like the absence of all light, yet it was possible to see.

Objects of all sizes and shapes were randomly scattered as far as I could see until they disappeared in the blackest of pitch-black. The objects were made of many clustered rectangular shapes in a hideous fashion. They were prisons for the tormented souls being punished by God until judgment day. The Spirit now tells me why I was not allowed to look inside any of these objects. The Spirit told me, first, I could not understand what I observed and, second, my heart could not take the strain of what I saw and would have overloaded causing death. I was trembling with fear completely through my being. I do not remember seeing any human, spirit, or energy forms there. Excruciating thoughts ricocheted through my mind as I felt the chilling presence of terrible evil and torment beyond measure. All demons know about the abyss and are exceedingly afraid of entering this place. Yet, most of today's Christians in the USA today have lost the scared-type fear of what God will do to them if they are disobedient to His commands. Every soul destined for the lake of fire will enter this hideous, tormented place before they are judged. They all will be tormented terribly by the jailer before Jesus calls them to stand before the judgment seat.

This abyss is not hell. Hell is the lake of fire or the second death. The abyss might be called, for a lack of earthly words, the jailhouse of heaven (Matthew 18:34-45). This dimension of time-space displacement does not exist as a part of heaven. Yet, God can turn sinners over to the jailer (angel) and he will send them by time-thought travel to this ghastly place. The abyss (heavenly jailhouse), hell (lake of fire), and heaven all exist at the same time but are in different dimensions of continual displacement of times-space beyond expanse.

Below, 2-19-3- Italy, Rome - Angel in charge of Hell at St. Peter in Chains: This was a revelation when I saw this 3-D fresco portraying an angel of Hell in a Church. As I travel around to the different denominations, I am finding a common thread. The modern day enlightened Churches are not talking about hell, repentance and people's wrong actions very much these days. The Sinners prayer in Churches, religious radio, and TV does not include repentance in many cases. The enlightened churches of the future for lukewarmness must not offend anybody and hint, say or imply listeners have any faults or sin. They say, "Just ask Jesus into your heart and you will be saved." This is dangerous teaching.

There must be heart-felt repentance (Luke 13:3), and true conviction of sorrow about what each one of us has done from the heart. We must realize what we have done in the past was wrong against the Lord God and is called sin! We must ask Jesus to forgive our sin after we have admitted and confessed them. Finally, we must ask Him into our hearts to change us from our wicked ways. Then we are saved!

Right, 2-19-4- Greece, Epidauros - Amphitheater: Built in 350 BC. The acoustics created by the shape of the theater are amazing. Entertainment was the order of the day in Greece. I thought to myself, about the way Christian Churches have changed since W.W. II. It seems entertainment has evolved as the order of the day while obedience and repentance has been left out. The trend is toward tolerance, the world, and non-offensive sermons. Entertainment and artist recognition are more important than solid Bible teaching and prayer. Attendance numbers are more important than quality of the attendees. Many good pastors have yielded to this temptation. Therefore, God's great love, without consequences to actions, slowly began to be preached without His predicted wrath. Another reason to water the sermons down has been that the audience's itching ears have not wanted to hear this kind of negative message. Unfortunately, the lukewarm Churches will have a rude awaking.

'*"I will make her officials and wise men drunk, her governors, officers and warriors as well; they will sleep forever and not awake', declares the king, whose name is the Lord Almighty"'* (Jeremiah 51:57). The phrase "they will sleep forever and not awake," means Jesus has sent these people to the abyss immediately after their death. He has stopped time as we think of it. In the minds of their lost spirits, these people will be tormented forever and ever, or so it will seem to them. This will only stop in the spirit's mind millions of eons of time later when God has the final judgment day. Yet, in earth years, depending on whether a person lived in the Old or New Testament times, their judgment day is a few years away or about one thousand years.

This will be where lukewarmers are headed unless they repent and turn back to God on a HOT, not halfway basis. United States leaders, who misrepresent Christ as they lead our nation the wrong way, are in trouble. Leaders were the first to be mentioned and will be the first to be sent to this place. God ordains Leaders of nations just like pastors, to keep their nation in harmony with God. Woe to you ungodly leaders.

The Spirit told me to write concerning lukewarmers who have not forgiven someone for a past injury or injustice. They may think they are the best Christians on the block. The church they go to would esteem them the same, based on their outward holy acting. More importantly, God knows their heart and it has hate and unforgiving spirits inside it. Unforgiving lukewarmers are headed to the abyss unless they wake up, forgive, and repent. Upon their death, they will be dragged by the jailer and thrown into this terrible hideous place (abyss) until judgment day arrives. This shall be different time frames in the mind of the fallen spirit. For it takes God longer in the minds on some spirits to torment them until they have paid in full for what they did in their entire lifetime on earth.

I felt with my bones their ghastly torment and it was hideously terrible.

Lukewarmers say, "Well, I can take it because judgment day will come very quickly. Because when a person is asleep time passes very quickly." If they believe this, then they are misled. Time shall and has been meaningless to God. He can stop or even reverse time so the allotment will be just. They could be tormented for a million earth years before judgment day is held which in reality will be only about one thousand years away. They must understand we are dealing with God. They must forgive deep in their hearts all who have harmed them or they shall die a thousand deaths in the jailhouse of heaven. Repent and forgive lukewarmers, for I know because in the spirit I have seen with my eyes this hideous place. I felt with my bones their ghastly torment and it was hideously terrible. This is the end of the insight concerning the abyss.

Let us review the insight about the first resurrection at the end of the seventy-fifth day, which separates the tribulation period and millennium. At the end of the seventy-fifth day (Daniel 12:11, 1335th day), the Lord Himself will come down from heaven with a loud command, with the voice of the archangel and with the trumpet call of God (1 Thessalonians 4:16) and the first resurrection will occur. The window of opportunity has come and the dead in Christ will rise first and those still alive who have made it to the 1335th day will rise to meet Jesus in his huge hovering space-type object. This object's exhaust vapor is like unto clouds. We will be with the Lord. Satan can also see this from his area in the abyss or jailhouse of heaven. He shall be furious because he had killed these saints. Now Jesus will reverse his deceiving and deadly unjust action.

Jesus can harvest the living crop of Christians on earth! Again we see in Matthew 24:30, Jesus making the statement that immediately after the distress of those days (tribulation period) He will come with a loud trumpet call and gather His living elect.

The Spirit gave insight into why Jesus has waited until now to reverse Satan's killing judgments. ***"When the power of the holy people* [Satan, False Prophet and Antichrist, (Daniel 12:7)] *has been broken, all these things will be completed."*** Jesus simply waited until the trinity of Satan was broken to redeem His people. Jesus will not pull up the strong weeds (sinners) first, lest He destroy part of the wheat (Christians) in the process (Matthew 13:24-29). He waits until Satan has been removed. Then the weeds wither because Satan's power, which they have been living on, shall be destroyed. Then Jesus separates (bundles) the weeds from the wheat since the weeds pose no threat to the wheat. Jesus can harvest the living crop of Christians on earth! Again we see in Matthew 24:30, Jesus making the statement that immediately after the distress of those days (tribulation period) He will come with a loud trumpet call and gather His living elect.

Jesus has now raised the dead tribulation saints to life and they will live with him for a thousand years. What did these Christians do to deserve this special treatment? First, they obeyed God's commands not to walk up Satan's stairway of technology, which leads to the Mark of the Beast and death. Second, they did not worship or buy into the Internet web of deceit, which will eventually evolve into the Image of the Beast. Third, they did not receive a mark on their hand or forehead such as a bracelet, headband, tattoo, ID implant, laser scanners, or the like. The mark was required to pay the mandatory consumption tax levied by the Antichrist and False Prophet to further their agenda.

As we move through the sixth and seventh Satanic Dooms, the Spirit prompted me to say, "Christians should not get upset over different beliefs any more. Our case has been sealed in the books at this point and we cannot change the verdict. In fact, we can place our Bible on the shelf marked past history. God will now give Christians an instruction manual for the millennium and heaven. What we should be concerned about must be our actions today, up and through the Sixth Satanic Doom. This will determine whether God's right hand goes up in approval or His left hand points to the lake of fire for each person."

We must look ahead one thousand years or one sabbatical day. Satan and his fallen demon spirits have been released from the jailhouse of heaven. This will be done so the last evil action (death) can be destroyed. Satan and his fallen demon spirits attack Jesus and the Holy City. God sends fire down from heaven and devours them. Satan, the old devil, is cast into the lake of fire. He, the False Prophet, and the Antichrist will be tormented day and night forever and ever.

SEVENTH SATANIC DOOM

(Revelation 20:11-15)

The **Seventh Satanic Doom** contains or shall be a part of the **Seventh Seal**, the **Seventh Trumpet judgment**, and the **Seventh Bowl Wrath.** The original prophecies opened with WAKE UP CALL I, which consisted of four times seven equals twenty-eight (see concluding remarks). Now this section ends with four times seven equals twenty-eight which is symbolic of the four things that will be thrown into the lake of fire at the last judgment; first, Satan, next the sinner, and, finally, at the same time death and Hades. The four in the equation represent the last four evil enemies of Jesus with the seven implying final judgment. Therefore, the Bible will end with Jesus overcoming the Final Satanic Four. Glory!

Right, 2-19-5- Israel, Tabgha - Ancient Olive Press: Tabgha has been the celebrated place of the feeding of the 5000 men plus women and children (Matthew 14:15-21). Judgment day will be a terrible day for most as the olive press is to an olive. They did not digest what Jesus fed them, the Word. Jesus talks about a stone of judgment, which will fall on a spirit and will crush it into destruction. (Matthew 21:44)

Let us look at the progression of events associated with the Seventh Satanic (7th) Doom.

"Then I saw a great white throne and him who was seated on it. Earth and sky fled from his presence, and there was no place for them. And I saw the dead great and small, standing before the throne, and books were opened. Another book was opened, which is the book of life. The dead were judged according to what they had done as recorded in the books." (Revelation 20:11-12)

> ☞ Clarification insight added 2005: It will be important to understand the judgment day insight discussed on the next few pages. The insight was written concerning the flow of the court proceedings associated with these events. In the future there are two testing events; the Judgment Seat of Christ at the end of Daniel's 1335th day (Revelation 20:4-6, first resurrection) and the Great White Throne Judgment at the end of the Millenium or 1000 year rein with Christ (Revelation 20:5, 20:11-15). The New Testament saints and people are judged at the Judgment Seat of Christ. Everyone else (Old Testament people) will be judged at the Great White Throne Judgment. In either case regardless of how we believe, each one of us will stand before Jesus in a court proceeding, which will flow similar to the description outlined in the next few pages and section 12-2, My Nightmare. ✂

We will look at these sequences of events, which lead to Jesus putting everything under His feet with His Father overseeing this action. Everyone, saints or sinners, will be judged from the books according to what they have done.

There shall be one very important part of the judgment concerning **"what we have done"** which will be levied with great weight. The first question asked, **"What did we do to fulfill the Great Commission?"** The second question, **"What did we do to keep our nation a disciple nation** (it's laws, government, and people in harmony with God)?" The third question, **"What did we do to carry the good news around the world?"** We will not be allowed any excuses and shall be judged severely on these questions. Jesus will not have to destroy people and nations when He comes back to earth if Christians would have followed His Great Commission. Therefore the Bible states lukewarmers and sinners will fail. Consequently, Jesus shall be forced to destroy those who are destroying the world. Each person will receive his just rewards. Then, after the rewards, the ceremony will be over. Another book shall be brought before Jesus who has been seated on the great white throne.

Jesus begins reading a computer-like printout of everyone present who originally was written in the book of life. This list includes everyone present, who will be judged on this day. **The judging begins with the test of fire.** The angel in charge of the fire at the altar will administer the fiery test (Revelation 14:18). Jesus will read a printed name in the left column from the Book of Life. Then the angel in charge of the fire takes a cup filled with fire from the altar and pours it over the person along with their works and deeds. If the person being tested has ignoble deeds and works made of low moral standards, low-down deeds that are unwashed (these represent worldly attributes), they will not pass. They have been disobedient to God's commands. Many of these lukewarmers who think they are Christians have already used their rewards during their earthly life (Matthew 6:2, 6:5, and 6:16). These people stand before Jesus with nothing to offer. They burn, with their worldly works. The angels assigned to the lake of fire, drag these burning souls to the edge of the lake and throw them into the fiery lake. Then another name shall be called, and another, and another. How will your works be judged on this day?

This is why Jesus said in Revelation 3:18, *"I counsel you to buy from me gold refined in the fire, so you can become rich; and white clothes to wear..."* Jesus was warning the number seven lukewarm spirit (Laodicea) to analyze (test) their works now (2 Corinthians 13:5), repent, and make corrections or His angel of fire will test (burn) their works later. It will be better for their souls if they remove the disobedience out of their lives before Jesus burns it out of their spirit and souls.

Let us look at the three different type entries in the right column of the book of life. The book of life shall be like a large computer printout with everyone's name printed in the left column. The order of names will not be necessarily alphabetical. To qualify for heaven, a person's name must be handwritten in the right column across from his printed name, which is in the left column.

(See example below.)
Spirit-filled Christians

EXAMPLE # 1

BOB Z. STOAD ____| *Bob Z. Stoad*

The people in example one, when tested by the angel of fire, will keep their life and heavenly rewards. Their rewards and works were built on gold, silver, and precious stones. These precious stones do not burn when fire is applied for they represent heavenly attributes. These people have followed God's commands. They will move on to heaven keeping the rewards Jesus has given them. For most people and lukewarmers, this will be a terrible and dreaded day.

The second example of an entry in the book of life will be as follows. Jesus (or the Bookkeeper) will read another name from the list of printed names in the left column. People with the identical names will know whom Jesus is calling to the throne because heavenly language is used. That person will step forward in front of the judging throne. The angel in charge of the fire will pour a cup of fire over him. He along with his works will begin to burn. This will happen when a person's name cannot be found handwritten in the right column. This person has never been spiritually born again and accepted Jesus Christ as their personal Savior. This unbeliever will be dragged, while his soul is still burning, to the lake's edge and thrown into the lake of fire.

(See example below.)
Sinners

EXAMPLE # 2

John Doe XXXX __| ____________

Jesus now reads the name of the third example. This person's name has been handwritten in the right column but now has been blotted out by black ugly blotches. At some point in this person's life, he had become spiritually born again. Then he returned to a sinful life and or became lukewarm.

They became disobedient to God's commands, and returned to the pleasures of the world. They had fallen from God's grace but they were given until the end of their lives to repent. Since repentance did not occur, their names were blotted out of the book of life. This left the printed names in the left column only. These people will fail the test. Jesus has cautioned us, it would be better for a person to have never known Him than to have known Him on a personal basis and then turned back to the lust and greed of the world.

Sadly, this indicates the direction lukewarmers are headed if they do not repent and become hot, not lukewarm, for the ways of the Lord. Let us look at what happens to these people. The angel pours the cup of fire on these people for the test. These people's souls begin to burn along with their great works and deeds. Jesus, fiery eyes flaming with wrath, moves toward the right column to see what has happened. He sees this person's name has been blotted out. Jesus becomes angry and orders the angel of fire to bring another cup even hotter than the first. He orders it poured slowly on the wicked persons' soul while He watches them burn. These backsliders or lukewarmers will be sent to the lake's edge and thrown into the lake of fire while they are still burning.

Jesus and sinners have one accomplishment in common after judgment day, they both have taken the law into their own hands!

Most people in the tribulation will choose the water jug of earthly water over Jesus and His living water, by their works.

?

How is your presentation?

Lukewarmers must realize we are dealing with a multi-time dimensional Jesus. From the time He orders the second cup of fiery wrath until these people hit the lake of fire could be countless years in their minds. This will be a terrible experience.

The Spirit enlightened me on two of many scriptures concerning additional tormenting forces used by Jesus on judgment day. Heed these warnings lukewarmers and sinners.

"I (Jesus) ***WILL MAKE them*** (sinner, Moslems, and unbelievers who says Jesus does not love them) ***come and fall down at your*** (Spirit six Christian's) ***feet and acknowledge that I have loved you"*** (Revelation 3:9).

"He (sinner) ***WILL BE tormented with burning sulfur*** (second cup) ***in the presence of the holy angels of the lamb*** (Jesus)*"* (Revelation 14:9-11).

(See example below.)
Lukewarmers - Backsliders

EXAMPLE # 3

John Doe Xxxx __ 

Jesus has truly purchased men (Revelation 5:9) for His Father, which is like purchasing men for Himself. This has been part of the mystery of why we are living our lifetime (test cycle). Jesus wants to purchase us for His Father, because in Revelation 5:9 it is prophesied. Once God has released and programmed a soul to this earthly test for His pleasure, they only have two options, Jesus (Pass) or second death by fire (flunk).

Glory to God, the Son, and the Holy Spirit! Amen. I, Bob R. Short, received this prophecy concerning the Seven Satanic Dooms during the fall of 1994 through August of 1995.

Each person's test cycle on earth and what they do can be summed up as follows:

"Everything we do and say is about our presentation on Judgment Day."

How is your presentation?

THIS CONCLUDES THE Seven (7) Satanic Dooms.

Below, 2-19-6- Israel, Capernaum - Water Jug and its Base: At Capernaum, Jesus established part of his base and teaching here. He talked about being fishers of men if they followed Him. He also taught during His ministry about Living Water. This water was not found in the above jug but through Him, Jesus Christ. Most people in the tribulation will choose the water jug of earthly water over Jesus and His living water, by their works.

SIXTH (6th) SEAL SUMMARY

(Revelation 6:12 to 7:17)
Section 2-20

The Sixth Seal equates to the Sixth Sign as described in Matthew 24:29-30. This will be a series of God's judging events against a disobedient world. These judgments leading to Satan's destruction begin in 106SRSP-S.

The focus of sequencing events unfolds below:

1. Battle of Armageddon (Fourth Seal) will be over.
2. Satan bound for one thousand years.
3. Sixth Seal will be, as birthing pains, coming to full force. (See below.)

- Great earthquake.
- Sun darkens and turns black due to nuclear bombs from wars around the world including Armageddon.
- Moon turns red because of dust and debris in the air from world war and Armageddon.
- Stars (satellites) fall from sky because of world war and Armageddon.
- Skies recede and/or are hidden because of dust and debris from world war and Armageddon.
- Mountains removed because of earthquakes and nuclear bombs. Islands removed because of earthquakes and nuclear bombs.
- Jesus temporarily holds back four destructive winds of the earth.
- One hundred and forty-four thousand servants of our God are sealed on the forehead.
- The first resurrection occurs which includes tribulation saints who were killed or died during the tribulation. There will also be a removal of saints living at this time. These living saints will be removed off the ground into the air to make way for the destruction of the world by the four winds of the earth.
- Jesus unleashes four destructive winds of the earth to destroy all land, sea, and trees. This literally destroys all sinners and unbelievers on earth.
- Reality and curved time dimension of heaven and earth, as we perceive it will pass away.

4. Millennium starts and lasts one thousand years with Christ's rule.

The Sixth Seal includes the largest impact of the Seven Sealed Thunders of Wrath (Revelation 10:1-11). The Sealed Thunders are used for a purpose found in Psalm 106:8 - to make his power known.

The Spirit led me to write. It will be better for the Christian to understand the days (sorrows) they live in today rather than become upset over disagreement about the first resurrection. It shall be far wiser for a Christian to begin today resisting the new marking devices such as the IC chip technology and laser scanners. WARNING: The IC chip marking technology is the first device that has the capability to carry the complete and total numbers of the Mark of the Beast. It contains the holder's social marking number (identification). It also contains the holder's location marking code (location). Finally, it contains the holder's code to buy, sell, or transfer electronic funds. It equates to one step short of the true MARK OF THE BEAST! That step being, the Final (last) Antichrist implication of it to buy and sell in the Great Tribulation.

It shall be a matter of life or death to the Spirit filled Christian to stop their country from locking into the ten-world area European led kingdom federation (MNO). It is more important to do this than to completely understand the Sixth Seal. If Christians let their nation lock into this ten kingdom Beast, then they will have to received the MARK OF HIS NAME and will soon be dead in God's eyes.

Let us reflect back to the beginning of 96SRSP-CE. This was when the sharpest increase in the acceleration of end time events began. The question must be asked, "Whose lifestyle will dramatically be affected more, the sinner or the Saint?" The answer leans toward the Saints. The sinner's agenda will only be increased by the added evil. The Christians will be the ones put through the most demanding test. Will they stand by faith for Jesus or will they turn, as cowards or unbelievers, and follow the lust of the world?

THIS CONCLUDES PSALM 106
AND THE
SEQUENCING PERIOD 106SRSP-S.

MORNINGS AND EVENINGS PROPHECIES END HERE. AMEN.

The SCROLL is next.

UNDERSTANDING THE SCROLL

In SEQUENCE ORDER. . . . The TEST HAS BEGUN!

Note: Please copy section 3-1 and 3-2 (Scroll), and discuss the warnings and end time instructions it has to your Christian and Jewish friends as well as military, political, Church leaders, and personnel, and members. Ask them to move into action before it is too late!

Calculations, instructions, warnings, decrees, events, and analysis sequencing was 100% prophesied by

BOB R. SHORT

3 - 1 - 0 - Greece, Island of Crete, Knossos - Palace: We know the Minoan's carried jars because there were frescos of them doing that. Jars can store scrolls similarly to what was found at the Dead Sea in Israel.

Above, 3-1-1- Greece, Island of Patmos: Pictured is the entrance to the Holy Cave of the Apocalypse. The majestic presence of the Spirit was with me when I walked around the cave where St. John received the Revelation about endtimes. I gave the monk in charge the day we visiting a copy of the Scrolls, for this was fitting and pleasing for God. It completes a cycle to time - thought - end time insight. The Monastery of St. John the Divine dominated my mind as we walked through and felt the presence of the Spirit of Prophesy.

The Spirit has unveiled the ability for me to see into the future, which horrifies me. The Lord God has historically sent prophets at their appointed time to warn others and/or edify His people. It has been very unpleasant to be a messenger of an unwanted message, which lukewarmers along with their leaders and the world do not want to hear. The norm has been rejection and is very hard to cope or deal with.

Note: It would be useful when reading the Scroll to run a copy of the Flow Chart (Section 8-2) so the reader can easily reference and follow the flow of sequencing events. If the reader does not understand a word, look it up in the prophesied glossary of words in the back of the book. After most events or calculations, a reference guide such as NI-12-99 - or - Issue 1-PG - # - or SC-Sec and Part # are displayed. NI = New insight and date received, Issue-1 comes from the original issue-1 Wake Up Call Prophecies book dated 3-1-96 - or - SC = "THE SCROLL" book with reference to section and part number where insight or commentary comes from.

The Spirit of Christ Jesus, the Spirit of Prophecy inspired the WAKE UP CALL PROPHECIES through me, a messenger. They are in harmony with the literal interpretation of the Bible.

Have faith to believe in these Biblical predictions. Most predictions were made in 1994-95 as part of the end time fulfillment of Joel 2:28. These prophecies are in summary sequence from 1990 AD ⇨ Jesus Christ's Second Coming ⇨ Daniel's 1335th day. Some overlaps in the sequences of events will occur because of the birthing pain principle (Matthew 24:8).

We are commanded in the Bible to be aware of end time events. The question comes up, "What must we look for in world news presentations to help us better understand the prophetic events which will happen? This way we can better protect our families in the last days."

Congratulate yourself! The Bible instructs Christians not to be ignorant about endtimes. Most ministers do not talk much about endtimes because of the negative content and the potential loss of membership. The Church spends little time educating people who will be going through the tribulation period how to react, how to witness in trouble times, what to resist, and a sequence of signs to help guide them. God has sent the Spirit of Prophecy to issue the Wake Up Call Prophecies to warn, educate, and edify the Churches and prepare the nations.

The entire prophesied book formulates part of the pieces to a complicated, mysterious, and controversial puzzle of end time events, calculations and the Lord God's decrees and judgments. God controls prophecies (Revelation 22:6) and He made it difficult to understand. These were done so not all will understand, repent, and turn from sin and are then forgiven by God (Mark 4:11-12). Some human forms are God or Satan's angels (Hebrews 13:2) on assignment in our test cycle and under a different test (Jude 6). A summary of the insight in this book has been placed in lapping and overlapping sequential order. The Spirit prompted me to proclaim it as **"The Scroll."** These prophecies should simplify and become helpful in understanding part of the general progression of sequences involving end time events.

The reader must believe the news media does not understand what is going on within God's prophetic timetable. They are too busy glorifying and loving themselves to notice the real story. The Bible says the coming of the Son of man will be like Noah's day. The world will not distinguish the flood of God's end time events from perceived natural disasters and wars until they are swept away. There are ways to analyze news briefs and filter God's hidden agenda out of it. The Sequencing Scroll has been prophesied and recorded so the reader can see through the biases and misleading mainstream news stories which ultimately push for European led World Government (rebirth of Old Roman Style government).

There is much misinformation about end time events within the Church. The world does not understand and has been placing its hopes in the arising New European World Government. The lukewarm Church now believes parts of God's Great Delusion, as well as lies and refuses to listen to sound doctrine. Many will be part of the Great Christian Falling Away in the tribulation period. Lukewarm Christians have adopted; a) easily sold escape clauses from the tribulation; b) sinner's prayer without true repentance; c) loving the church and the world; d) love of money over God; e) consumerism by individuals and debt in the churches.

The general flow of thinking as it pertains to end time events shall be as follows: Satan's Goal will be to rule the earth. First, he must destroy America to isolate other Christians for an easy victory. Next, he can wipe out the Jews without any opposition. Satan believes Jesus will have no reason for returning to earth then and he will win. More important for Christians, Satan's power destruction machine has been currently aimed against America in favor of Europe. We see the USA; a) being hated by the world, b) losing power to and in favor of the European led Leopard Beast, c) sin has been destroying America from within, and d) presidents (W. Bush and Clinton and others) against Israel by trying to force them out of their land and start a Palestinian State, which brings God's wrath upon the USA and others).

God may discipline America to make a midcourse correction. Why? The lukewarm Church has done very little to keep America following Christ's teachings. Since WW-I the Body of Christ has moved from thinking and acting like the Philadelphia Church (Revelation 3:7-13, faithful disciples) to the detestable lukewarm Laodicea Church (Revelation 3:14-22, unqualified Christian).

Better insight comes from understanding the overlapping phenomenon of the sequencing scroll. One event may appear or be more important to people before another simply because of the location of the observers on earth. The sequencing prophecies are only part of the total picture. We are at the end of the second sabbatical day of the Church age. The point at which all prophesies of the ages converges. They are finding their ultimate fulfillment to complete God's testing cycle (Revelation 3:10), which He has decreed on mankind.

Almighty Father God, I pray, "Make the Scroll inspire the readers and edify the Churches. Let it wake up the Nations of the World to their disobedience. Let it instruct your people in the world and their militaries. Use it to prepare the Christian and Jewish readers into protecting their families, churches, and nation. Allow it to awaken the lukewarmer from destruction. Let it inspire the Spirit-filled Christian into action. Make it so, Lord Jesus! Amen!"

Below 3-1-2- Greece, Athens, Mars Hill: Standing near the cliff's edge on Mars Hill gave a spectacular view of Athens and the Ancient Agora. This was where St. Paul addressed the Athenians concerning their unknown god. He talked about what they thought was a new idea. They were open-minded enough to listen before judging. Read the Scrolls with an open mind. I realize Bible prophecy has not been an entertaining idea in our consumerism society. What has been prophesied here could lower property values, scare people, and drive them into thinking "Is there really a God who would let all this destruction and doomsday decrees happen to mankind?" Otherwise, the subject matter does not fit our self-centered society or the modern day lukewarm Churches curriculum.

The end time result points to multitudes following false teaching to satisfy itching ears. Read the Scroll, intellectually devour and study it and let the common sense speak for itself.

Remember, the WAKE UP CALL PROPHECIES have been accurate to date! This negates any argument from those who disagree or are skeptical.

Time has always been the ultimate test to expose fraudulent predicting. Simply start marking through each event as it happens, and when one gets to the end of the Scroll, Jesus will be back! WOW! May the Spirit of Prophecy open your eyes to the truth.

THE GATHERING

NOTE: The following summary of prophecies called The Scroll is updated when additional or new insight is received. The Scroll in this book contains insight received from May 13, 1994 to Book publishing date. **Section-3 does not contain all the prophecies, calculation, riddles and puzzles in this book -** Bob R. Short.

Think about what you are reading as you study the scroll and how it applies to you personally. Book IV, of the Psalms has been the key to end time sequencing of events. All end time players have been assembled at a junction in curved-time-space displacement 1990 A.D. - 106SRSP-S where all prophecy has been converging. These players are alive today and well.

The main players are as follows:

The Lion named Jesus on His White Horse, Jesus' Army, Two Witnesses, The Eagle (Daniel 7:4), The Bear (Daniel 7:5), Leopard (Daniel 7:6), The Eagle with the Three Ugly Heads, many Antichrists trying to hold the rule, Final Antichrist, the Man of Confusion, False Prophet, Satan, the nations of the Great Prince Michael, Devil's nations, Bears jaws, Original ten Horns, Final ten Horns, Army from the North, Army from the South, Army from the East, the Head which had the fatal wound that was healed, Two Little Evil Wings, Twelve Feather Wings, Eight Rival Wings, Six Wings, Worthless Body, Ugly Head on the Left, Large Ugly Head in the Middle, Ugly Head on the Right, King of the Leopard, Four Terrifying Wings, Evil Talons, the Holy Ones, Amon Amon, Seven Spirits of God, Sea Beast, Land Beast, The Mark of the Beast (Revelation 13:16), Mark of His Name (Revelation 14:10), Name of the Beast (Revelation 13:17), Number of His Name (Revelation 13:17), Number of the Beast (Revelation 13:18), Image of the First Beast (Revelation 13:15), and many more end time players, organizations, calculations, nations, and alliances.

If you do not know what these descriptions mean, then how do you prepare or instruct other to protect their families, churches, and nation? Lack of end time knowledge could kill you!

Left, 3-1-3 - England, London, Buckingham Palace - bobby: There were many bobbies (police) around the Palace during the changing of the Guard. The changing of the Guard was very impressive. I want to point out the yellow police jacket and what it will stand for as we move toward the end of time. There will be world police or military presence everywhere monitoring the movement of people. The Leopard Beast (MNO) will put more attention on people's movement from East - West or vise-versa than North - South/South - North, as was originally prophesied in issue 1. Christians and their nations are not heeding God's warnings concerning endtimes. The human race is surrounded with luxuries, quick fixes, conveniences and the good life. They have become wealthy and prosperous while technology has produced comfortable lifestyles. In some cases, the poor and downtrodden are ignored.

The reader must begin to comprehend what I have prophesied here as truth. Christians must ask God to give them faith in understanding these prophecies and how they will affect them, their family, and nation. Christians must get ready, because the time for global trouble to greatly increase is at hand. The world has spit in Almighty God's eye and has becoming increasingly hostile toward Jesus' teaching. Jesus taught Biblical morality and good community living. Nonetheless, the world and many in the lukewarm Churches want to do it their own way. Many do and will increasing believe the Leopard Beast (MNO) will be their salvation to keep the good life and security in the future.

The worldwide Leopard Police state will be coming and the Christians can stop it in their respective countries. More importantly, they cannot do it dispersed. The best way will be to start the UACC. Christians must quit arguing, downplay their differences over beliefs, and rapture theories. Satan uses these issues to keep them from uniting as one to stop the spread of the worldwide police state and the European led MNO.

✝ THE ✝

SCROLL

Accurate from the

WAKE UP CALL PROPHECIES

"See I have told you ahead of time"

The issuing of GOD'S FINAL DECREES
In SEQUENCE ORDER . . . The TEST HAS BEGUN!

100% PROPHESIED between 1994 -2007 by

BOB R. SHORT,

a Witness to the world governments and Messenger to the Churches.

"Just before the test cycle ends, Spirit-filled men will be elevated like watchmen to warn and speak out to the masses. They will turn their attention to the prophesies and teach many. Furthermore, they will insist upon the literal interpretation of Bible prophecy in the midst of much debate filled with commotion, conflict and resistance"!

Bob R. Short, 9-18-05

Prophesied by,
Bob R. Short
- a Witness - 1994-2007

The issuing of GOD'S FINAL DECREES

In SEQUENCE ORDER... The TEST HAS BEGUN!

Events will lap and over-lap!

✪ ⇨ Fulfilled -**Beginning of the Days of Sorrows** (1990-95 AD): We have lived through this time-period. God has been lifting His protecting covering off USA for its disobedience and because some leaders have turned against Israel. Even though these years have been prosperous, many of the worst dollar disasters in US history have happened during 1990 through 2007. These disasters will increase until the USA is destroyed or unless her leaders turn back to God and protect Israel. {Issue-1=Pg-82-96. SC=Sec=2-1 and 2-7 } (Note: Gulf War-I is over, {Issue-1=Pg-88. SC=Sec=2-3 })

✪ ⇨ Fulfilled -**Removal of Presidential Candidate** -Yitzhak Rabin and Mr. Peres: Occurred as it was prophesied: It was prophesied, "This will be accomplished by removing one or more important Presidential candidate if the Universal American Church Coalition" (UACC, {Issue-1=Pg-66-79. SC=Sec=6-5 and 6-9 }) is not physically or mentally started in the hearts and minds of the church leadership {Issue-1=Pg -97. SC=Sec=2-8}. Fact: No main denominational Churches responded correctly to this idea. More importantly, the removals happened as prophesied. Now we are seeing overlaps; Al Gore removed to make way for President George W. Bush to start Gulf War II, and Prime Minister, Ariel Sharon removed to make way for Ehud Olmert and the war, which started in Lebanon. {Issue-1=Pg -102./ SC=Sec=2-9 }.

✪ ⇨ Fulfilling -**Churches Burn:** 96-Christian Churches burned (as of 6-27-96). It was prophesied in 1994 the church burning and violence against members and property would began to increase. In 1995-96, the news was filled with Church burning. In September 1999 (9-99=666), it has escalated to Church shootings. This will increase world wide as Christians remove the cancer from their nations. {Issue-1=Pg -76-79. /SC=Sec=6-9}.

✪ ⇨ Fulfilling -**Days of Sorrows Increasing:** Time has moved us into the last part of the Beginning of the Days of Sorrows (Matt. 24:4-8) in which we are now living. (1996-1999SRSP-CE) {Issue-1=Pg -93-96. / SC=Sec=2-7}

✪ ⇨ Fulfilled -**IC Chip -information:** Introduction of 'IC Chip' marking cards to buy and sell. Note on page {Issue-1=Pg -63. / SC=Sec=6-3}; "Warning: The IC and ID marking Technology equates to the first marking technology carrying all the digits and three sequences codes (S ,Z, C) of the Mark of the Beast." Also on page {Issue-1=Pg -63. / SC=Sec=6-3}; Christians must start resisting any additional personal marking (IC or ID) computer chip card which has been improved, laser scanners (like finger or body scans), tattoos, chip implants, and the like."{Issue-1=Pg-98./SC=Sec=2-8}

✪ ⇨ FULFILLING -**Dismantle Military Repair:** Trying to dismantle 60% military repair VS 40% private sector. The 90's produce greed over national security. {Issue-1=Pg -129. / SC=Sec=2-15}

✪ ⇨ FULFILLED -**Benjamin Netanyahu Wins:** He wins Israel's prime minister slot in a great up set. He was over 20% down in the polls one or two months before the election, yet upset Mr. Peres. {Issue-1=Pg -97. / SC=Sec=2-8}

THE SCROLL

From the
WAKE UP CALL PROPHECIES

✪ ⇨ FULFILLED -**US PULLS BACK FROM NATO:** Europeans gain NATO power while US pulls in her military horns. US will be pulling back from NATO for the latest deal around June of 1996 gives the European Wing of the US-led alliance the chance to launch its own missions using borrowed NATO assets, if US agrees to lend them money. Secretary-general Javier Solana said, "We have today launched a new NATO (BEAR - See beast flip char in Section - 9), " {Issue-1=Pg -38. / SC=Sec=5-7}

✪ ⇨ FULFILLING -**Abortion in Military:** Abortion was authorized in the military for a period of time during the 1990's at the consent of the USA President, who opened the doors for killing innocent babies through abortion in the European theater. This action got overthrown in Congress, because Christian men and women protested. {Issue-1=Pg -38. / SC=Sec=5-7}

✪ ⇨ FULFILLED - **Elijah's Last Assignment:** Christians can see the Spirit of Elijah leading one man with power. He has appeared before the Lord's return (Malachi 4:5, Luke 1:17) with authority to bring 100,000's of men together in football stadiums and other places to repent to God and reconcile with their families (children) across America and other nations. He has paved the way for people to make ready for Jesus return. {SC=Sec=4-6}

✪ ⇨ FULFILLED -**Daniel's European NATO Bear:** Fulfilled in 1999 just as the literal interpretation of Daniel's 7:5 prophecies. European NATO w/Russia have jointly taken over a Balkan nation on the Moslem's side killing Christians in the name of peace. Former President Clinton had earlier formed the Bear on the Beast flip Chart (Daniel 7:5) European Bear =NATO minus US plus Russia. NATO can fight its own war without the US. Russia has been included into their meeting as a nonvoting member, thus forming the Bear on the Beast Flip Chart. {Issue-1=Pg -167. / SC=Sec=7-1}

✪ ⇨ FULFILLING -**Sea Beast:** The Revelation 13:1 Sea Beast (European led Leopard) will be born in the minds and hearts of men. The European Common Nations are buying into this idea along with many powerful leaders around the world to neutralize USA world dominance. {Issue-1=Pg -98. / SC=Sec=2-8}

✪ ⇨ STARTED -**Mark of the Beast** (information): These calculations completed and now beginning to surface: Three sequence codes =social identity number (S) + assigned locator number on earth (Z) + buy or sell number (C) =S+Z+C on (Phone pad) controls the information of the 6+6+6 =W+W+W (address prefix on worldwide Web of Deceit). [W =Vav in Hebrew alphabet =6th letter =6. Therefore WWW =Revelation 13 prophecy of 666. People who are buying and selling on the Internet Web of Deceit during the great tribulation are using the Number of the Beast (Revelation 13:18) and Mark of the Beast (Revelation 13:17). To complete the deathly trinity of numbers, connect the Number and Mark with the Name of the Beast (Revelation 13:17). Christians must not use the Internet Web of Deceit when the European led world government Issue consumption taxes to buy and sell or they will be out of God's grace! {Issue-1=Pg -23. / SC=Sec=5-2}

✪ ⇨ STARTED -**World Revival:** World revival started a few years earlier and will be short lived. {Issue-1=Pg -105. / SC=Sec=2-10}

~ ~ ~ ~ ~ **"FEARFUL EVENTS"** (Luke 21:11) ~ ~ ~ ~ ~

The world has been entering a period of increases in Earthquakes -Solar Storms -Floods. Fear events: Y2K -Twin Towers -Meteors -Terrorist attack using Chemical and Nuclear bombs!

✪ ⇨ FULFILLING -**Leopard's Mouth:** England becoming mouth of the Leopard Beast (Revelation 13:1-2). The public relation unit of the UN will move from the US to European influenced England, then to Rome and finally Israel. {Issue-1=Pg -167. / SC=Sec=7-1}

Prophesied by,
Bob R. Short
- a Witness - 1994-2007

THE SCROLL

From the WAKE UP CALL PROPHECIES

✪ ➪ STARTED -**Alliance:** A closer relationship will emerge between Religious Rome and Jewish people. {Issue-1=Pg -26. / SC=Sec=5-3}

✪ ➪ FULFILLING -**Blessing or cursing for USA:** President Bush and Clinton are one of the biggest reasons God is bringing curses upon the USA. Even though these years have been prosperous, why has the USA experienced some of the worst dollar disaster events in USA history? Both Presidents tried to take the West Bank and Gaza away from Israel and give it to the enemy. The lukewarm Churches did virtually nothing to stop this action. America is no longer classified a Disciple Nation (laws-government-people following God). America is losing God's protection. {Issue-1=Pg -186-188. / SC=Sec=7-7} + (NI 7-19-04)

✪ ➪ FULFILLED: **Gulf War II Begins:** US attacks general area of Iran-Iraq, " crossing the whole earth without touching the ground." MINOR destruction scenario: this war only affects taking over of Iraq area. MAJOR destruction scenario: Could drag Iran into fighting. They most likely will go north (break away states -not Russia) to get nuclear weapons to threaten Israel, US, and others. {Issue-1=Pg -102-103 + 110. / SC=Sec=2-9 +2-11}

✪ ➪ FULFILLED **Jordan and Syria:** Now realize they must get serious about protecting Israel's borders. Even though Syria is still officially a terrorist's state, it has started working better with U.S. by giving up nuke info. They both have offered to help in Iraq if needed. {Issue-1=Pg -103. / SC=Sec=2-9}.

✪ ➪ FULFILLED **Religious Leader Removed (Pope John Paul):** He will be perceived by the world as being the religious symbol or leader of the world who sits on seven hills. He is quickly removed. {Issue-1=Pg -103. / SC=Sec=2-9}

✪ ➪ FULFILLED **New Religious Leader Installed:** He will be a leader of confusion who sits on seven hills. {Issue-1=Pg -103. / SC=Sec=2-9}

✪ ➪ Issued **God's decree as a Proclamation to The Americas:** Most Nations' ambassadors received a copy of this proclamation to unite North and South America. This will be to offset the aggressive take over of the Americas by this prophesied growing European Leopard Beast. {Issue-1=Pg -158-167 + NI 5-05. / SC=Sec=7-1 + 4-12}

✪ ➪ Issued **God's Warning Proclamation to the European Union:** The EU must try to start a world Government using ten (10) world regional zones to achieve world peace and security. As Christians, we must try to fulfill the Great Commission to make disciple of all nations. Warning Issued; this government must have Jesus Christ and His teaching first or it will fail. {Issue-1=Pg -158-167 + NI 6-05. / SC=Sec=7-1 + 4-13}

✪ ➪ FULFILLING **WAKE UP CALL PROPHECIES Believed:** Now the Christian, will be awaking to the fact the WAKE UP CALL PROPHECIES are happening and future events prophesied will come to pass. {Issue-1=Pg -103. / SC=Sec=2-9 }

✪ ➪ **Prophesy Against the Goat:** The Goat's (America) large prominent Horn shall be broken off. Nuclear weapons acquired north of Iran (not directly from Russia) by Iran or its sponsored terror groups are now a reality. The Large Horn shall be the Self-Proclaimed Great City where money has been god. Until the twins were removed, no one could see the beautiful spike (tip of horn) standing true in the air trying to touch the heavens. God forgive and help us if they do not follow Your decrees. If this happens, the world has not seen anything like this. Time frame for 'Horn' event; Ram Goat war=Gulf War II through or shortly after Ezekiel 38 War. {Issue-1=Pg -102-103 and 110. / SC=Sec=2-9, 2-11, and 4-2} +(NI 8-15-04)

Prophesied by,
Bob R. Short
- a Witness - 1994-2007

✪ ⇨ Issued **Azrail and Michael Prophecy:** It's concerns the in-depth insight of the retaliation response about the first paragraph on page 103 of the WAKE UP CALL PROPHECIES, Issue 1, prophesied September, 1994 -August 1995. This was due to the Goat's (America) large prominent Horn (self proclaimed great city where money has become god) between his eyes being broken off (Issue-1, page 110). America should retaliate by destroying general area of Iran and/or Iraq plus one surprise with Nuclear weapons. This retaliation response was sent to some US Generals as a coded poem. {Issue-1=Pg -103-104 and 110. / SC=Sec=4-14}

✪ ⇨ **Islamic debate:** A vigorous debated will break out concerning the removal of Moslems and their converts from the Americas. {SC =Sec. =4-15, Eli✞e Chris✞ian Soldiers}

✪ ⇨ **Worldly Financial Markets:** Will begin to feel the pinch for cash. Christians put money in safer short-term areas. {Issue-1=Pg -104. / SC=Sec=2-9}

✪ ⇨ **Gulf War II Ends:** #1 outcome: Iraq has been beaten by USA and others . #2 outcome: Others and the USA beat Iran and Iraq. {Issue-1=Pg -103. / SC=Sec=4-2 and 2-9 } + (Goat P.)

✪ ⇨ Fulfilling **Worldwide Revival:** Millions of people saved and many Lukewarmers rededicated their lives to Jesus. {Issue-1=Pg -105. / SC=Sec=2-10 }

Sequencing from Psalm 99 - laps and overlaps (~8SRSP)

✪ ⇨ STARTED **Great Prince Michael:** I prophesied on December 17, 1996 Michael will be born out of the America's and come to his feet by the battle of Armageddon through the last 75 days of time called Daniel's 1335th day. We can see Daniel's 11:32 resistant movement beginning and will increase until the Battle of Armageddon. Michael will be prophetically found by pushing South America underneath North America to form the literal interpretation of a prince or man standing on his feet. Draw a line around the America's and see Michael, the prophetic tool God will use to protect His people Israel from world government. (Dec. 17, 1996 prophecy called, Arise Michael) {SC=Sec=4-5, 9-1}

✪ ⇨ STARTED **Hot Jaws of NATO Bear:** More trouble begins to brew in the Balkans. This area along with Middle East problems will be the major cause for starting Gulf War III or the war of Ezekiel 38-39 (see Beast flip chart). {Issue-1=Pg -105. / SC=Sec=2-10}

✪ ⇨ OCCURRING NOW **Eight little Kings trying to hold the rule:** Kings of eight industrialized nations (G-8) will try to influence the world in peace, security and trade over the next few years. This will be part of the stair-stepladder to the birth of the 4th beast, which comes later. These kings will try but fail to hold the rule and eventually will fade away in favor of the Leopard kingdom. (NI6-99) {SC=Sec=9-2}

✪ ⇨ WILL HAPPEN SOON

EZEKIEL -38 WAR: Gulf War-III

Northern Army the NATO Bear will be yanked in war South toward Israel (see 2nd page Beast Flip Chart -sketch 9-1-2). This alliance will disintegrate and the Russian Bear alliance will be formed, (Ezekiel 38-39). This war has been fueled by problems in the Balkans and Middle East disruptions. A domino effect will most likely drag the following countries into war (but not limited to); Russia, Iran, (Iraq -sympathetic but without any real military might-a non player), Germany (Sympathetic), Turkey, Libya, Ethiopia and others. America, England and others will question this aggression toward Israel. Finally, they will defend Israel. Many nuclear and other type weapons will be used. All countries included in this war will be hit with nukes. (Note: America will be hit with nukes because it does not have a complete missile defense system. {Issue-1=Pg -107. / SC=Sec=2-11}

✪ ⇨ **Islamic removal starts:** Removal of Moslems and their converts will begin in North and South America. {SC =Sec. =4-15, Eli♱e Chris♱ian Soldiers}

✪ ⇨ **Lukewarmers vomited into the tribulation period:** Today's Christians are mostly representative of the Lukewarm spirit #7 (Revelation 3:16). They represent vomit to the Lord God and He will spit them out into the tribulation period to become a part of the Great Christian Falling Away, (Matt. 24:10). {Issue-1=Pg -189-209. / SC=Sec=7-8 to 7-10}.

✪ ⇨ **World Government Needed:** Most nations of the world realize after this war (Ezekiel 38) a world government with the power to control peace and safety must be put in place. Its name calculates to 666 =MNO =Millenium Nations Organized (Leopard Beast). This equates to the Name of the Beast (Revelation 13:17). America must not join! {Issue-1=Pg-39./SC=Sec=5-8}

✪ ⇨ **Days of Sorrows End:** Figuratively speaking, this ends the "Days of Sorrows" spoken of in Matthew 24:8. Now the world enters into a worse time of extreme testing called the last seven plus years of final tribulation. This testing period brings unprecedented grief and sorrow. (Observation note)

✪ ⇨ **Northern Army Defeated:** US and others will defeat the Russian Bear (the NATO Bear on the Beast flip chart has dissolved and the defeated Russian Bear equates to the Northern army described in Ezekiel 38) using many nuclear weapons and other types of weapons. {Issue-1=Pg -108. / SC=Sec=2 11}

✪ ⇨ **Destroyer, the mighty US General:** First world preview concerning one of the Two Witnesses. He has hard-line Christian views, protects Israel, and he helps win Gulf War -III. {Issue-1=Pg -107. / SC=Sec=2-11}

THE REVELATION 3:10

TEST ON THE WHOLE WORLD BEGINS TO INCREASE.

NOTE: Read section 2-11 through 2-15 for in-depth review, of this summary below. The next 3 1/2 years are primarily signs and wonders in the heavens and on earth. Natural disasters will grow in frequency and intensity as the end of the age approaches. This will be to shake people out of their lukewarmness, complacency and lead them to seek God. These 3 1/2 years bustle with political leaders from organizations, countries, alliances and nations for the express purpose of holding the rule over this world. They work hard to control and direct the expansion of new European world government (Leopard -MNO).

✪ ⇨ **The last seven-years - recap summary - the Tribulation Period Starts:** These last years are a time of Jacob's trouble. It will start out with a series of four prominent leaders trying to hold rule over the world through the Leopard Beast. Their time will span approximately 1320 days and amidst their rein, the Little Horn (Final, as in, last Antichrist to govern the world) will arise and gain credibility. { SC=Sec=9-1 }

✪ ⇨ FULFILLING **Daniel's 7:6 Leopard Beast is Born:** The world will try to enter into a ten kingdom government by merging similar nations into regions after the Ezekiel 38 war (Gulf War III). This government promises a better-unified world trade, money, taxes, peace, security and military agreements. Its only opposition will be the Spirit-filled Christian's belief that world harmony can only be achieved through independent disciple nations working together, not world government. A Disciple nation must be a nation whose government, laws, and people believe, are respectful, and incorporate the teachings of Jesus Christ. The land mass proposed by this would-be world Government (w/o seas or divisions - Sketch 9-1-1) will emerge into the shape of the prophesied Leopard Beast on the Flip Chart (world land mass less the Americas) within the next 3 1/2 years. {Issue-1=Pg -83-158. / SC=Sec=2-1 to 2-20}

✪ ⇨ FULFILLING -**Prophesy Against The Goat:** (previously mention) The Goat's (America) large prominent Horn shall be broken off. Nuclear weapons acquired north of Iran (not directly from Russia) by Iran or its sponsored terror groups are now a reality. The large Horn will be the self-proclaimed great city where money is god. Time frame for event; Ram Goat war =Gulf War II through or shortly after Ezekiel 38 War (Gulf War III). {Issue-1=Pg -102-103 and 110. / SC=Sec=2-9, 2-11, and 4-2 } +(NI 8-15-04)

✪ ⇨ HAPPENING NOW **Philadelphia Church (Spirit #6) removed (Revelation 3-10):** Removal has been going on for years and will complete before the tribulation starts as an sign-less event - a removal by natural and accidental death not a signed event called the Rapture. Note: Spirit #6 represents few of today's Christians. {Issue-1=Pg -110. / SC=Sec=2-11}

✪ ⇨ **Dome of the Rock Destroyed:** A man, Amon Amon, destroys the Dome of the Rock on the Temple Mount in Jerusalem. Note: There will be a great mystery behind this name. {Issue-1=Pg -110. / SC=Sec=2-11}

✪ ⇨ **Fuel Shortage:** Because of Gulf war III (Ezekiel 38-39) there will be a worldwide fuel shortage. This causes hardship worldwide. It promotes further cries for increasing world government power through the MNO to solve these kinds of global problems. {Issue-1=Pg -110. / SC=Sec=2-11}

✪ ⇨ **Worldly Religious Leader Removed:** Man of confusion who sits on seven hills will be removed. This will be before or under the Fourth Seal Repeat or Gulf War III. This opens the way for the False Prophet to emerge the next few years and team with the MNO leader. {Issue-1=Pg -111. / SC=Sec=2-11}

✪ ⇨ **7-year Peace Pack:** Third king over MNO will be the Prince of the Covenant. He has been the instigator in designing a covenant with many nations and organizations in the midst of the Ezekiel 38 war. This agreement will include the Final (last) Antichrist and Israel. This will be the prophetic seven-year peace pack. (NI6-99) {SC=Sec=9-2} . This will be a non-signed event, or one could count 1320 + 1320 days and know the 2nd advent of Jesus Christ. This just looks like another politician's agreement not a seven-year peace pact.{Issue-1=Pg-108./ SC=Sec=2-11}

✪ ⇨ **Peace and security promised by Antichrist and MNO:** Antichrist backed by the MNO promises of world peace and stability. {Issue-1=Pg -111. / SC=Sec=2-11}

✪ ⇨ **The first MNO King of the four:** The 1st king over the newly developed MNO-Leopard Beast will turn his attention to the coastlines and will take many of them, but a US commander will put an end to his insolence and will turn his insolence back upon him. After this, the king will turn back toward the fortresses of his own country but will stumble and fall, to be seen no more. (NI6-99) { SC=Sec=9-2 }

✪ ⇨ **MNO King -may be the Antichrist:** There will be much debate as to who this guy may be -the Antichrist or not? {Issue-1=Pg -109. / SC=Sec=2-11}

✪ ⇨ **America's Congress Uncooperative:** The new MNO King will not get along well with the America Congress. {Issue-1=Pg -109. / SC=Sec=2-11}

THE SCROLL

From the WAKE UP CALL PROPHECIES

✪ ⇨ **7th Seal (Revelation 6:1 to 20:15):** Prophetically begins (see Flow Chart, section 8-1) with Daniel's Seventieth Week and ends with the Great White Throne Judgment. God accomplishes total destruction of evil under this awesome Seal by throwing the sinner, Satan, Antichrist, False Prophet, death, and Hades into the lake of fire forever. The 7th Seal contains 7-Trumpet Judgments with the 7th Trumpet containing the Seven Bowls of Wrath. The 7th Bowl of Wrath contains the 7-Satanic Dooms to Satan's destruction. These Seven Dooms contain the 7-Sealed Thunders against Satan and his followers. {Issue-1=Pg -119. / SC=Sec=2-12}

✪ ⇨ **5th Seal (Revelation 6:9-11):** Equals the 5th Sign in Matthew 24:9-12. These are birthing pains and the beginning of a martyred remnant. The Tribulation Period has been preprogramed as a test on the whole world (Revelation 3:10). The 5th Seal unveils specific tests for the Christian and the unbeliever. This test allows the following to be increased: persecution, hatred, wickedness, false prophets, betraying each other, Christians falling away, and loss of love. {Issue-1=Pg -118. / SC=Sec=2-12 }

✪ ⇨ **World Sales Tax:** Birth of the world consumption tax (Daniel 11:20) to support the new world government. Some powerful people in the United Nations in the late 1990's and early 2000's are wanting a worldwide sales or consumption tax. This would help fund world peace and famine relief they claim. This evolves straight from the Antichrist and False Prophet's hearts. The old Robin Hood idea. Take from the rich nations and give to the poor nations. Sounds good on the surface but Christian Nations must not fall for this satanic trick. {Issue-1=Pg -114. / SC=Sec=2-12 }

✪ ⇨ **One World Government Task Force:** UN task force set to be enacted to study and implement a new world government. {Issue-1=Pg -22. / SC=Sec=2-12 }

✪ ⇨ **World Military Force:** The European Leopard Beast will insist on a world protective force divided into regional areas to develop world peace and safety. Each region (ten -regions), could respond quickly to problems with worldwide military backup if needed to restore peace. [NI]) + {Issue-1=Pg -159-167 + NI. / SC=Sec=7-1}

✪ ⇨ **Mark Of His Name (Revelation 14:10):** Second Hidden Mark and will be equal to the Millennium Nations Organized (MNO) =666 on the phone pad =Daniel's Ten (10) toes. The world will be divided into ten area kingdoms and Satan uses this vehicle as his greatest deception. Christians must convince their nation not to join this European led world federation for peace and security. Any nation who buys into the MNO's benefits, then its citizens will eventually be forced to take the Mark of the Beast and use the Number and Name of the Beast to buy and sell. {Issue-1=Pg -60. / SC=Sec=6-3 }

✪ ⇨ **Number Of His Name (Revelation 13:17):** The Leopard Kingdom allows this number to be voluntary at first but the Final Antichrist will try to force every nation to join in the last half of tribulation period. The Number Of His Name =666 =MNO =Millennium Nations Organized within the Name of the Beast. {Issue-1=Pg -60. / SC=Sec=6-3 }

✪ ⇨ **Number Of The Beast (Revelation 13:18):** Number will be voluntary at first but the Final AC will try to force this on every nation in the Great Tribulation. Once a nation accepts the Mark of His Name (Revelation 14:10) then they must require their citizens to use the Number of the Beast, which shall be an international phone number. It will connect the customer's transaction through the Image of the Beast (worldwide Web of Deceit) to get an approval code. Once approved the world consumption tax will be collected to fund the MNO (Daniel 11:20). {Issue-1=Pg -24. / SC=Sec=5-3 }

✪ ⇨ **America's Hostility:** All MNO Kings will not get along well with the newly elected America Congress. {Issue-1=Pg -109. / SC=Sec=2-11}

Prophesied by,
Bob R. Short
- a Witness - 1994-2007

THE SCROLL

From the
WAKE UP CALL PROPHECIES

✪ ➪ **Christian Resistance:** Spirit-filled Christians know their God will resist the Antichrist spirit of world government (Daniel 11:32). {Issue-1=Pg -110. / SC=Sec=2-11 }

✪ ➪ **Second MNO King of the Four:** The first king's successor shall arise and send out a tax collector to maintain the royal splendor. In a few years, however, he will be destroyed, yet not in anger or in battle. This king's destruction will open the way for third and fourth kings to team up and try to hold the rule. (NI) { SC=Sec=9-2 }

✪ ➪ **World Sales Tax:** The 2nd king of the four will introduce a comprehensive world consumption tax to support MNO. (Daniel 11:20). {Issue-1=Pg -114. / SC=Sec=2-12 }

✪ ➪ **Little Horn's fame is rising:** Little Horn or Final (last) Antichrist has convinced many that Gulf War III (Russia and others warring against Israel) was Armageddon. This will be a fabrication, for the prophetic battle of Armageddon will begin in approximately six years (NI 6-99). Some Jewish people will be fooled because of his part in the heroic role in overthrowing the northern army and protecting the Jewish people. Some Jewish people will look upon him as their Messiah. {Issue-1=Pg -108. / SC=Sec=2-11}

✪ ➪ **Third Temple Okayed:** Leader over the MNO gives Jewish people permission to build the third temple on the Temple Mount in Jerusalem. He shall refuse the Moslems rebuilding rights with a stealthy plot to fool the Jewish people. Many Jews now think he must be their true Messiah. There is much confusion about which leader may be the final (last) Antichrist. The Moslems nations are seriously damaged who participated in the Northern Army attack on Israel. They temporality lack the ability to challenge the MNO leader's decision. {Issue-1=Pg -111. / SC=Sec=2-11}

✪ ➪ **Arise Michael:** As birthing pains Michael the Great Prince will be resisting world trade organization's agreements through the Americas. (NI) {Issue-1=Pg -NI . / SC=Sec=4-5}

✪ ➪ **The America's are Booted out:** Because of Christian resistance, North and South America are removed from MNO (Daniel 7:8). They are not allowed to vote in the ten-kingdom assembly. This equates to three votes in the assembly (Daniel's 7:8, 3-Horns uprooted). {Issue-1=Pg -110. / SC=Sec=2-11}

✪ ➪ **Four Prominent Horns:** There will be a redistribution of voting rights within the MNO Leopard kingdom. Japan, Israel, the area formed by nations in the Army from the South and one other nation will receive voting rights in MNO. Out of one of these areas comes another king. He will be the final Antichrist, who starts small but grows in power to the south and to the east and toward Israel. (Daniel 8:8, four-horns installed, plus one king). {Issue-1=Pg -110. / SC=Sec=2-11 + 4-2}

✪ ➪ **Church Debt Bad:** Most Churches not out of debt will have to close for lack of money. Their leaders were warned and shown how they could get out of debt in 1994-95. They lacked the faith to believe and greed prevailed. {Issue-1=Pg -115. / SC=Sec=2-12}

✪ ➪ **Christian Persecution:** The MNO leaders will as birthing pains began to destroy what they determine as militant Christians and Jews in the name of peace and tolerance toward other religions.{Issue-1=Pg -111. / SC=Sec=2-11}

✪ ➪ **Millenium Nations Organized (MNO):** MNO (European led Leopard Beast) offers most benefits and best solutions to world peace and safety for nations, which want to join their cause of world government. This shall be Satan's deceptive trick, "united the world has peace or divided the world will have wars." {Issue-1=Pg -111. / SC=Sec=2-11}

✪ ➪ **False Prophet Teams w/MNO + AC:** False Prophet the religious leader who sits on seven hills will began to team up with the MNO + AC for peace and security.{Issue-1=Pg -111. / SC=Sec=2-11}

Prophesied by,
Bob R. Short
- a Witness - 1994-2001

The Scroll

From the Wake Up Call Prophecies

✪ ⇨ **False Prophet and Religious Tolerance:** He begins big sales campaign for tolerance, morality and peace without Jesus Christ as the only way to heaven. World religion demands tolerance between beliefs without Christians and others pushing their religion. This shall be where the rub comes in for Spirit-filled Christians. {Issue-1=Pg -111. / SC=Sec=2-11}

✪ ⇨ **Miraculous Signs:** Final AC begins to uses his influence on the Internet Web of Deceit in the Leopard kingdom (MNO) to display great lying signs and wonders (Revelation 13:13-14, and 19:20). He will deceive the inhabitants of the earth. Much of the misinformation will be processed through the mouth of the Beast, (first England, second Rome, and finally Jerusalem. Daniel 7:5).{Issue-1=Pg -112./ SC=Sec=2-11}

✪ ⇨ **Slow Economy:** World economy begins to dry and wither.{Issue-1=Pg -112./ SC=Sec=2-11 }

✪ ⇨ **Americas Not Cooperating w/MNO:** The Americas disagree with MNO (European led Leopard Beast), which causes disruption worldwide. {Issue-1=Pg -112. / SC=Sec=2-11 }

✪ ⇨ **1st Seal -Last Repeat:** First MNO Leader is placed into office and rides out as a conqueror bent on conquest with his world army. {Issue-1=Pg -113. / SC=Sec=2-12}

✪ ⇨ **Deceptive Numbers:** Mark of the Beast digits voluntarily used until great tribulation starts. {Issue-1=Pg -114. / SC=Sec=2-12}

✪ ⇨ **God's Wrath on Lukewarmers:** God begins to rebuke and discipline (Revelation 3:19) the disobedient lukewarmers. Some lukewarmers will become the Spirit-filled Christian's enemy while a few will repent and turn back to God (Matt 24:10). {Issue-1=Pg -116. / SC=Sec=2-12}

✪ ⇨ **Great Christian Falling Away:** Great Christian Falling Away per Matthew 24:10 begins and increases the next three years. This will be over 50% of today's Christians. They will love the world, MNO, and Antichrist's peace, security and benefit package more than they have faith in following these warnings, other's cautioning advice, and God's Word. {Issue-1=Pg -116. / SC=Sec=2-12}

✪ ⇨ **1st Trumpet Judgment:** Small diameter meteor showers began to hit earth (Revelation 8:7). These showers will continue for some years at lower frequency of hits per day compared to the initial main body shower. Planes, which can include spacecraft and/or stations, will be knocked from the sky, filling the sky with blood and fire. 1/3 of the trees and grass will burn in the hardest hit areas. The world cries for leadership from the MNO (Leopard). {Issue-1=Pg -119. / SC=Sec=2-12}

✪ ⇨ **Jewish Sacrifices Start:** Sacrifices start in 3rd rebuilt Jewish Temple on the Temple Mount. Remember, earlier the leader over the MNO has denied Moslems rebuilding rights for their destroyed Dome of the Rock and okayed the 3rd Jewish temple to be built. {Issue-1=Pg -120. / SC=Sec=2-12}

Sequencing from Psalm 101 - laps and overlaps (~6SRSP)

✪ ⇨ **Fear of Meteor Hit:** A meteor will appear before this year, which has been calculated to hit earth. Men's hearts will begin to fail them because of fear. Yet, the wise will have peace and understand. {Issue-1=Pg -122. / SC=Sec=2-13}

✪ ⇨ **2nd Trumpet Judgment:** Large meteor hits Atlantic Ocean, Revelation 8:8-9). This meteor seriously obliterates the east side of South America and the west side of Southern Africa. It causes great effect on the east coast of the United States. One-third of the ships in the total area will be destroyed by a mighty tidal wave. This causes one-third of the sea creatures to die leaving one-third of the Atlantic Ocean like mud, blood, death and a discolored look. {Issue-1=Pg -122. / SC=Sec=2-13}

Prophesied by,
Bob R. Short
- a Witness - 1994-2007

✪ ➪ **East Coast Destruction:** A tidal wave hits America's East coast causing it to wither while Washington DC must be uninhabited for a time.{Issue-1=Pg -123. / SC=Sec=2-13}

✪ ➪ **Third and Forth MNO Kings team up:** The Third King (Prince of the Covenant) and Fourth King (King of the South) team up to rule the MNO. This causes the United Nations, to rally the sympathetic nations in MNO and the Little Horn's organization (Final AC), which has been gaining power, credibility and authority within the MNO, to destroy the two kings. The Final AC will lose a battle and see an overwhelming army swept away before him. During this battle, the Prince of the Covenant who designed the original seven-year covenant (third king) will be destroyed. NI 6-99{ SC=Sec=9-2}

✪ ➪ **2nd and 3rd Seal Last Repeat:** MNO wars against hostile countries opposing them, 2nd and 3rd Seal Last Repeat, (Revelation 6:3-6). {Issue-1=Pg -122. / SC=Sec=2-13}

✪ ➪ **MNO Gains Popularity:** MNO will be gaining power because this meteor disaster further builds a need for world government to respond to global catastrophic events. Individual nations are not able to sustain this type devastation by their selves. {Issue-1=Pg -122./ SC=Sec=2-13}

Sequencing from Psalm 102 - laps and overlaps (~5SRSP)

✪ ➪ **More Persecution by MNO:** MNO gains power to persecute Christians and Jews. Great pressure will be put against any nation disagreeing with the MNO's philosophy of world government over national sovereignty. Missionaries are encouraged to stop pushing Christianity in favor of intolerance of other religions {Issue-1=Pg -123. / SC=Sec=2-13}.

✪ ➪ **3rd Trumpet Judgment:** Flaming star, Wormwood (Revelation 8:10-11) closely encounters earth causing flaming fragments hits. This pollutes and poisons one third of the water, which kills many people. This further promotes the MNO cause because they have the ability to best help distraught nations. This will be the old, united we stand and divided we fall concept. More importantly, Christian Disciple Nations under no circumstances, should give up their national sovereignty to this Leopard world government. {Issue-1=Pg -124. / SC=Sec=2-14}

Sequencing from Psalm 103 - laps and overlaps (~4SRSP)

✪ ➪ **4th Trumpet Judgment:** Sunlight reduced (Revelation 8:12-13) causing one third of light to be refracted away from earth because of the cosmic debris caused by the 1st, 2nd and 3rd Trumpet Judgments. Much of the day will be like an eclipse and the night like 100% total darkness. {Issue-1=Pg -125. / SC=Sec=2-15}

✪ ➪ **Woe to the Earth:** Satan kicked out of heaven to earth (Revelation 12:7-9). Satan and his demons swarm down on the earth to promote Satan's deceptive agenda of peace and security through world government. {Issue-1=Pg -126. / SC=Sec=2-15}

✪ ➪ **Two Witnesses:** Two Witnesses are unveiled to the world for prophesying the airlift and the Antichrist hidden agenda to control Jerusalem and the world. They stand firmly against European led world government without Jesus Christ at the head. They insist Israel has to possess the land belonging and promised to the Jewish people by God. Jerusalem will be the capital of Israel and will become the capital of the world only when Jesus Christ sits on the throne, not the "Holy Ones." The "Holy Trinity" will be Satan, Final Antichrist and the False Prophet, (Daniel 12:7). One of the Witnesses will be the leader of the USA and the other has been its military leader. They lead a rebellion against the 4th Beast. The 4th Beast will generally be wining but the Two Witnesses have managed to knock the 4th Beast down on its knees with the 5th Bowl of Wrath. {Issue-1=Pg -126. / SC=Sec=2-15}

✪ ➪ **American Airlift:** America airlifts Jews out of Israel to USA desert. America warning Jewish people of Satan's hidden agenda to control the world through Jerusalem shall precede this voluntary airlift. Once in America, the Jews will be protected until America and others fight with Jesus against the MNO with what is left of the Eagle with the Three Ugly Heads in the battle of Armageddon. {Issue-1=Pg -125. / SC=Sec=2-15}

✪ ➪ **Jews Tricked:** Many Jews do not heed America's warnings and stay in Israel. They still believe the Final Antichrist must be their hope. {Issue-1=Pg -125. / SC=Sec=2-15}

✪ ➪ **MNO'S Missile Warning:** MNO warns America their upcoming missile attack will be only against the Jewish camps in desert locations not at America itself. These Jewish people are considered traitors to the MNO cause and must be eliminated. {Issue-1=Pg -126. / SC=Sec=2-15}

✪ ➪ **MNO Fires Missiles:** MNO fires missiles at USA's desert location of Jewish camps. {Issue-1=Pg -126. / SC=Sec=2-15}

✪ ➪ **Most Missiles Stopped:** America's missile defense system stops most missiles because the missile defense system has been improved. USA Military technology operates fairly well over continental USA. However, it will be diminished elsewhere because of loss of satellites mainly due to a nation from the Army from the East. {Issue-1=Pg -126. / SC=Sec=2-15}

✪ ➪ **Two Witnesses Threaten MNO:** Two Witnesses threaten to use Nuclear weapons if this attack is not stopped against the Jews in the desert. The attack is stopped. {Issue-1=Pg -126. / SC=Sec=2-15}

✪ ➪ **Name of the Final Antichrist:** The calculations have been made to determine the Name of the Antichrist (1 John 2:18). His human name shall be irrelevant so to speak. His calculated name and what he sells and does to the world will be important to understand. His calculated name is: "Jesus the Messiah, King of kings and Lord of lords, Ruler of the **M**illenium **N**ations **O**rganized (MNO)". His goal shall be, "Toward Heaven". He sells himself as the only Messiah for the world. He will guarantee peace and security if any nation will follow him through the next Millenium. If a nation does not follow him, he will bring the wrath of the world government (MNO) against this non-progressive country. {Issue-1=Pg -39. / SC=Sec=5-8 }

✪ ➪ **Final AC Rises to World Power:** "He (2nd of the four kings) will be succeeded by a contemptible person (Final Antichrist) who has not been given the honor or royalty. He will invade the kingdom (Israel) when its people feel secure, and he will seize it through intrigue (lying and trickery). Then an overwhelming army will be swept away before him; both it and a prince of the covenant will be destroyed. After coming to an agreement with him, he will act deceitfully, and with only a few people he will rise to power (over the world government called the MNO-Eagle with the Three Ugly Heads)." (Daniel 11:21-23) [NI 6-99] {SC=Sec=9-2}

✪ ➪ **4th of 4 Kings is defeated:** With a larger army, the Final Antichrist will stir up his strength and courage against the King of the South. The King of the South will wage war with a large and very powerful army, but he will not be able to stand because of the plots devised against him. The war strategy used against the King of the South shall be team effort between the UN, Final Antichrist moving up in power over the MNO and Israel. The King of the South has many internal leadership problems and assassination attempts are made. His army will be swept away, and many will fall in battle. The King of the South and the Final Antichrist with their hearts bent on evil, will sit at the same table and lie to each other, but to no avail, because an end will still come at the appointed time. {SC=Sec=9-2}

Prophesied by,
Bob R. Short
- a Witness - 1994-2007

✪ ⇨ **Final AC heart set against Israel:** The Final AC will return to his own country with great wealth, but his heart will be set against Israel. He takes legal action against Israel in the UN. This action causes a series of internal problem and possible breakup of the UN. (NI6-99) { SC=Sec=9-2}

✪ ⇨ **One-Witness wars with the Final AC:** Just before the middle of the seven-year tribulation period the Final AC invades the South again. This time the outcome will be different from before. One of the two Witnesses, a military commander of the US will oppose him, and the Final AC will lose heart. He then turns back and vents his fury against Israel. He will return and show favor to those who forsake Israel. {Issue-1=Pg -127 . / SC=Sec=2-15}

✪ ⇨ **Israel Invaded:** Final (last) Antichrist (a man totally controlled by Satan) invades Israel. His Armed forces will rise up to desecrate the temple fortress and will abolish the daily sacrifice. {Issue-1=Pg -126. / SC=Sec=2-15}

✪ ⇨ **Final AC =Corruption:** With flattery, the Final AC will corrupt those who have helped him achieve victory over Israel. {Issue-1=Pg -131. / SC=Sec=2-16}

✪ ⇨ **America protests:** America as birthing pains has been opposing world government without Jesus at the head and the takeover of Israel by a world body.

✪ ⇨ **Heart of Great Prince Michael:** America will understand, awaken, and become the symbolic heart of the Great Prince Michael who protects His people, when the Final AC invades Israel. For the People who know their Lord and Savior Jesus Christ will firmly resist the Spirit of World Government. {Issue-1=Pg -127. / SC=Sec=2-15}

✪ ⇨ **United Nations breaks up:** The UN will be disbanded because of internal fighting and disagreements. Now we see the world busting up into the 4th and final Beast of Daniel. This Beast will be made of Iron (against Christ) and clay (for Christ). (NI6-99) {SC=Sec=9-2}

✪ ⇨ **Jews Killed:** Final Antichrist starts killing Jewish people in Israel and around the world. {Issue-1=Pg -126. / SC=Sec=2-15}

✪ ⇨ **Temple defiled:** Final Antichrist and his troops install computer control center on one wing of the temple. This will be the abomination causing desolation. He will force the take over of the electronic media including the internet web of deceit. This is done to control the buy and sell mode as well as his propaganda machine. (Matthew 24:15). {Issue-1=Pg -127. / SC=Sec=2-15}

✪ ⇨ **Sacrifices Stopped:** Final -AC stops the Jewish Temple sacrifices in the Temple (Daniel 11:31). {Issue-1=Pg -127. / SC=Sec=2-15}

✪ ⇨ **Wise will instruct many:** Many Christians will be instructed by a few who have been given insight into the near future. {SC=Sec=9-2}

✪ ⇨ **God of gods Arrived:** Final -AC declares himself as the true God of gods to bring earth peace and security. {Issue-1=Pg -127. / SC=Sec=2-15}

✪ ⇨ **Miraculous Signs:** Final Antichrist uses the power of the Beast kingdom (MNO) and the power of the Internet Web of Deceit to display great lying signs and wonders with the support from the False Prophet (Revelation. 13:13-14, and 19:20). The Final AC will deceive the inhabitants of the earth. Much of the MNO information was processed through England (Daniel 7:6), {Issue-1=Pg -112. / SC=Sec=2-11}. By now, most misinformation on world government's intentions shall be processed through the mouth of the Final Beast, which will be Rome first, then Jerusalem. This spirit of deceptive good signs started in the 90's through the EU and increases to the end! {SC=Sec=9-2}

Prophesied by,
Bob R. Short
- a Witness - 1994-2007

✪ ⇨ **Jews Flee:** Jews flee to the hills near Jerusalem and Jordan (Matthew 24:15). Christian nations helplessly watch on the internet web of deceit as the Jews are being killed. {Issue-1=Pg -127. / SC=Sec=2-15 }

✪ ⇨ **Lion Aroused:** The Lion (Jesus Christ) shall be aroused and begins to make preparations to return to earth -a second time. (NI-6-99) {SC=Sec=9-2}

✪ ⇨ **MNO Gain Military Power:** Final -AC now controls Israel's nuclear weapons. {Issue-1=Pg -127. / SC=Sec=2-15 }

✪ ⇨ FULFILLING **Land Beast:** Revelation 13 Land Beast shall be a trinity of power. First the Internet Web of Deceit (two horns like unto the two discs on the original mainframe computers) the False Prophet (like a lamb of Christ) and the Final Antichrist (but he spoke like a dragon). This trinity is being born in the minds of men. {Issue-1=Pg -119. / SC=Sec=2-12}

Great Tribulation Period (rebellion) Starts

The last few years contain many military conflicts. The next approximate 1320 days will be controlled by the Final (last) Antichrist, with God's Two Witnesses trying to hold the rule against the 4th Beast -The Eagle with the Three Ugly Heads. (NI6-99) { SC=Sec=9-1 }

✪ ⇨ **Two Witnesses Unveiled:** Identified as: First Witness = America's leader in charge of affairs. Second Witness = US commander (nicknamed Destroyer). {Issue-1=Pg -127. / SC=Sec=215}

✪ ⇨ **Three-Woe Warning:** First Witness Issues 3-Woe Warning. These Woes are a part of the 5th Trumpet Judgment (Revelation 9:1-12). {Issue-1=Pg -127. / SC=Sec=2-15}

✪ ⇨ **1st Woe Warning:** Consists of three warnings. First = do not overthrow Egypt; second = Antichrist's control center must not be in the Temple at Jerusalem; third = stop warring against coastal countries. {Issue-1=Pg -127. / SC=Sec=2-15}

✪ ⇨ **2nd Woe Warning:** States; do not start war (four fallen angels) at Euphrates River. {Issue-1=Pg -127. / SC=Sec=2-15}

✪ ⇨ **3rd Woe Warning:** States; do not bother the oil (middle east oil) and the wine (Israel). {Issue-1=Pg -127. / SC=Sec=2-15}

✪ ⇨ **Abyss Opened:** 2nd Witness will be given authority to open the abyss (special underground shaft to a chemical weapons depot). {Issue-1=Pg -127. / SC=Sec=2-15}

✪ ⇨ **Gigantic Furnace:** Numerous planes and helicopters land and load-up with chemical weapons from the abyss. Their exhaust smoke looks like a gigantic furnace. {Issue-1=Pg -127. /SC=Sec=2-15}

✪ ➪ **5th Trumpet Judgment:** Second Witness, (Destroyer) implements 5th Trumpet Judgment (Revelation 9:1-12). He uses airplanes to attack the Antichrist's army with chemical weapons. These chemicals do not kill but torment for five months. {Issue-1=Pg -127. / SC=Sec=2-15}

✪ ➪ **Attacks Temporarily Stopped:** Second Witness puts and end to the Antichrist's disrespect concerning MNO attacks on nations. {Issue-1=Pg -127. / SC=Sec=2-15}

✪ ➪ **1st Bowl of Wrath:** The second Witness implements the 1st Bowl of Wrath (Revelation 16:2) by sending planes equipped with special chemical weapons to dispense on MNO nations. These nations pay the worldwide consumption tax and accept the Mark of the Beast. {Issue-1=Pg -128. / SC=Sec=2-15}

✪ ➪ **USA Solicits Nations:** USA asks MNO nations to disengage from the MNO and side with the Americas. {Issue-1=Pg -128. / SC=Sec=2-15} Note: Last Beast with the Three Ugly Heads will be made of Iron =nations which follow AC, clay =Saints -nations which follow Christ.

✪ ➪ **Fire Down on Enemies:** Two-Witnesses bring fire down on anyone who tries to hurt them by using missiles and planes equipped with bombs. {Issue-1=Pg -128. / SC=Sec=2-15}

✪ ➪ **Arise Michael:** Again, the birthing pains tell the story of Michael's resistance. Now the Americas' resistance, which represents Michael, is coming through USA's leaders, their congress and the two America Witnesses. We are moving into a time of great distress. (NI 12-96) {SC=Sec=4-5}

Sequencing from Psalm 104 - laps and overlaps (~3SRSP)

✪ ➪ **7th Trumpet Judgment:** God's final wrath being unleashed through the 7th Trumpet Judgment (Revelation 11:15 to 20:15). The 7th Trumpet contains the Seven Bowls of Wrath with the 7th Bowl of Wrath containing the Seven Satanic Dooms (see flow chart). {Issue-1=Pg -129. / SC=Sec=2-15}

✪ ➪ **USA Withering:** USA power has been withering while the MNO is growing. This will be caused by the MNO embargoes and boycotts. {Issue-1=Pg -129. / SC=Sec=2-15}

✪ ➪ **Past Greed Surfacing:** USA in need of military repair parts. In the 1990s and early 2000s, USA greedily farmed out repair to the outside. {Issue-1=Pg -129. / SC=Sec=2-15}

✪ ➪ **2nd Bowl of Wrath:** The Two Witnesses will implement punishment (Revelation 16:3) against the un-repenting MNO nations. Planes drop containers of chemically poisonous agents into the Caspian Sea. This causes great devastation to the MNO nations. This angers the MNO against the two Witnesses and their God. The Two Witnesses threaten further action if the MNO does not stop following the Antichrist. {Issue-1=Pg -130. / SC=Sec=2-16}

✪ ➪ **USA Saves Nuclear Bombs:** The United States has been saving what is left of its nuclear bombs and using only chemical weapons at this time. {Issue-1=Pg -130. / SC=Sec=2-16}

✪ ➪ **Stars Thrown to Earth:** The Army from the East which represents one regional-state of the MNO has been the leader in systematically eliminating one third (1/3) of the USA military satellites (stars) and will try to continue to the end of the tribulation (Revelation 13:4). This makes offensive missiles and defensive weapons somewhat inaccurate, so planes using the manual mode are used. Note: Russia lacks a large part of their capability to shoot down many satellites because of losing Gulf War III (Ezekiel -38). {Issue-1=Pg -130. / SC=Sec=2-16}

THE SCROLL

From the WAKE UP CALL PROPHECIES

✪ ➩ **The Promise:** Two Witnesses promise to return Israel to the Jews and away from the Last AC's control. {Issue-1=Pg -130. / SC=Sec=2-16}

✪ ➩ **2nd Woe Warning Repeat:** Again the 2nd Woe warning of official protest will be Issued at China, Turkey, Syria, and Iraq not to make war in the middle east. {Issue-1=Pg -131. / SC=Sec=2-16}

✪ ➩ **3rd Woe Warning Repeat:** Again, the 3rd Woe warning is Issued to leave the oil (Saudi Arabia, Kuwait, and other middle east areas) and the wine (Israel) alone. {Issue-1=Pg -131. / SC=Sec=2-16}

✪ ➩ **3rd Bowl of Wrath:** The Two Witnesses will implement the punishment of the 3rd Bowl of Wrath. Planes drop vials of poisonous chemicals into hydro-dams in Syria, which contaminates Iraq's water supply on the Euphrates River. The Tigris River will also be poisoned while other planes poison the Nile River from Khartoum, Sudan to Cairo, Egypt. (Ezekiel 29:9-10), {Issue-1=Pg131./ SC=Sec=2-16}

Sequencing from Psalm 105 - laps and overlaps (~2SRSP)

✪ ➩ **Watch out Israel:** USA uses the 2nd and 3rd Woe Warnings to threaten countries that may start war in the middle east over oil and how Israel will get involved. {Issue-1=Pg -133. / SC=Sec=2-17}

✪ ➩ **Final -AC is furious:** MNO leader is filled with fury at the USA, Christians, and Jews, while maintaining they are a threat to world peace. {Issue-1=Pg -133. / SC=Sec=2-17}

✪ ➩ **USA Destructive Technology:** USA has developed a technology, which eliminates much of the ozone layer over a specified area. {Issue-1=Pg -133. / SC=Sec=2-17}

✪ ➩ **Warning Issued by USA:** USA Issues warnings to MNO to stop takeover of weak nations. The MNO scoffs, and curses America's God. {Issue-1=Pg -134. / SC=Sec=2-17}

✪ ➩ **4th Bowl of Wrath:** The Two Witnesses implement the 4th Bowl of Wrath (Revelation 16:8-9) by sending planes equipped with special bomb devices to deteriorate the ozone layers over the most hostile MNO nations. God intervenes and the effect will be ten times more powerful than expected. The sun scorches much of the MNO. {Issue-1=Pg -134. / SC=Sec=2-17}

✪ ➩ **MNO Curses Two Witnesses:** MNO refuses to repent and curses God for sending the Two Witnesses who have control over these plagues. {Issue-1=Pg -134. / SC=Sec=2-17}

✪ ➩ **Calls for MNO Unity:** The Final AC believes the MNO nations can now win a war against America. The Americas have been loosing strength while the MNO has been gaining strength. {Issue-1=Pg -135. / SC=Sec=2-17}

✪ ➩ **MNO Wars with America:** The Final AC makes war with America. {Issue-1=Pg -135. / SC=Sec=2-17}

✪ ➩ **America's Two Options:** God has set a blessing and a curse before America at this moment in time. If America has turned back to God, this war will only be Satan's judgment against America and it will survive. America will fight on the side of Jesus in the Battle of Armageddon. On the other hand, this war shall be God's judgment against America, if God has judged America unworthy. It will then drag out to the end and America will be declared political Babylon and destroyed by the Three-Woes to America {Issue-1=Pg-29./SC=Sec=5-5} under the 3rd Satanic Doom (Revelation 18:1 to 19:6). Christians, its our choice. {Issue-1=Pg-135./SC=Sec=2-17}

✪ ➩ **Changing Time and Laws:** Satan through the Final AC will try to implement these changes (Daniel 7:25) within the first two years of the great tribulation. He will try to remove Jesus Christ's age of 33 years from the calendar. The calculations will contain other trickery and flawed math to achieve his desired answer, which is close to 2000. The flawed answer helps him convince nation states they will be starting his new millennium and it will

Prophesied by,
Bob R. Short
- a Witness - 1994-2001

be called 1 FM. He will guide the world through the Final Millennium (FM). USA will reject this idea. {Issue-1=Pg -184. / SC=Sec=7-6}

✪ ⇨ **5th Bowl Wrath:** The Two Witnesses will implement the orders concerning the 5th Bowl Wrath (Revelation 16:10-11). They direct planes over Israel and drop deadly chemicals in hopes of running the Final AC out of Israel whereby returning Israel to the Jewish people. They target his headquarters, which are now located outside of Jerusalem (Daniel 11:45). They hit their mark. {Issue-1=Pg -137. / SC=Sec=2-17}

✪ ⇨ **Final -AC Withers:** Last Antichrist's kingdom and throne are plunged into darkness because of the 5th Bowl Wrath. The trees, grass, and food supplies are destroyed. This turns the land into a darkened, depressing, and a dead look. {Issue-1=Pg -137. / SC=Sec=2-17}

✪ ⇨ **Terrible Storms:** Terrible storms begin to increase across the MNO until the end. This destroys many structures, vines, and trees. {Issue-1=Pg -137. / SC=Sec=2-17}

Sequencing from Psalm 106 - laps and overlaps (~1SRSP)

✪ ⇨ **Summary:** Approximately Last Slide Rule Year of Time-cycle: The next year will be a very busy time frame as far as sheer numbers of signs and events are concerned. Let us review: First, the 6th Bowl of Wrath, followed by the 4th and 6th Seals, which, are a part of the 7th Bowl of Wrath. The 7th Bowl of Wrath contains the Seven Satanic Dooms. Add to these judgments the Seven Thunders of God's wrath. Add the Battle of Armageddon, which shall be the 4th Satanic Doom, overlaid with the echo of the 4th Seal. This leads to the Second Coming of our Lord and Savior Jesus Christ. These signs represent a string of overlapping and simultaneously occurring events. Let us walk through this chain of events in more detail. Note: The 7th Satanic Dooms occurs after the millennial reign of Christ during the great white throne judgment, which will destroy the final two enemies of Jesus, death and Hades. {Issue-1=Pg -139-155. / SC=Sec=2-18 to 2-19}

✪ ⇨ **Electronic Deception:** The MNO lies and puts propaganda over the Internet Web of Deceit against Christians. {Issue-1=Pg -139. / SC=Sec=2-18}

✪ ⇨ **Final - AC Propaganda:** He will be doing everything he can to destroy Christian and Jew's morale. {Issue-1=Pg -139. / SC=Sec=2-18}

✪ ⇨ **Gift of Prophecy:** This gift will be increasing as God pours out His Spirit on all flesh (Joel 2:28). {Issue-1=Pg -140. / SC=Sec=2-18}

✪ ⇨ **Confusion:** Many will experience a disoriented perspective of time. The earth is off its axis because of these past few years' events. {Issue-1=Pg -140. / SC=Sec=2-18}

✪ ⇨ **Disrupted work:** Some will experience disruptions in the normal workweek while others will be out of work. {Issue-1=Pg -140. / SC=Sec=2-18}

✪ ⇨ **6th Trumpet Judgment:** The four angels at the Euphrates are released (Revelation 9:13-21). The four angels represent four nations, which will war around the Euphrates River. The four angels are China, Turkey, Syria, and Iraq. {Issue-1=Pg -140. / SC=Sec=2-18}

✪ ⇨ **Eastern Army:** Last AC becomes alarmed at China (aggressive angel) and other eastern nations. He sets out in a great rage to destroy and annihilate many. (Daniel 11:44) {Issue-1=Pg -140. / SC=Sec=2-18}

The Scroll

From the
Wake Up Call
Prophecies

✪ ➪ **Euphrates Bridges Destroyed:** Final AC blows up many strategic military bridges along the Euphrates River. This will slow any aggression since the Euphrates river will be full of water when China first attacks. {Issue-1=Pg -140. / SC=Sec=2-18}

✪ ➪ **Eastern Army Attacks:** China attacks Turkey, Syria, and Iraq in its quest toward Israel. They are destroying everything in their path. When they reach the Euphrates River, they are bogged down because the river will be full of water and key bridges are destroyed. {Issue-1=Pg -141. / SC=Sec=2-18}

✪ ➪ **Three Plagues:** War brings the three plagues in Revelation 9:18. Each side use and/or causes to happen, 1) nuclear bombs, 2) freezing conditions from dust fallout and smoke from the nuclear bombs, and 3) the mass destruction caused by conventional weaponry. {Issue-1=Pg -141. / SC=Sec=2-18}

✪ ➪ **Death and Non-repentance:** One third of geographic area will die from the three plagues. They will not repent or stop worshipping idols, money, drug use, sexual immorality, and lawlessness. {Issue-1=Pg -141. / SC=Sec=2-18}

✪ ➪ **200,000,000 Bogged Down:** China has learned to achieve lightning speed west with 200,000,000-man army toward Israel, the Euphrates river must be dry. Why march manually when pushing a button and sending a rocket would do. The answer, many of their military satellite and other technology has been destroyed. Therefore, manual mode must be used most of the time. Issue-1=Pg -141/SC=Sec=2-18}

✪ ➪ **6th Bowl of Wrath:** China closes approximately 17 hydro-dams upstream from Iraq. It produces the 6th Bowl of Wrath (Revelation 16:12). {Issue-1=Pg -141. / SC=Sec=2-18 }

✪ ➪ **7th Bowl of Wrath:** China wars west across Euphrates River once it dries up. This triggers the 7th Bowl of Wrath (Revelation 16:17 / 20:15) {Issue-1=Pg -141. / SC=Sec=2-18}

✪ ➪ **Object Headed to Jerusalem:** As China advances westward, she will stop aggression toward Israel. This will be caused by a delegation sent by the MNO. The delegation says, "The newly discovered object in the sky equates to the real threat for the world." They believe this outer space object will be headed to Jerusalem (Revelation 16:13-16). {Issue-1=Pg -141. / SC=Sec=2-18}

✪ ➪ **First Signs of Jesus Christ 2nd Coming:** Great deception will be used by the "holy trinity" to trick people into believing the huge mass traveling toward earth will be hostile to the existence of mankind. The remnant of Saints which are left will understand this has to be Jesus' second coming. {Issue-1=Pg -142. / SC=Sec=2-18}

✪ ➪ **Three Frogs:** The Three Frogs in Revelation 16:13 are evil spirits in people which represent the three "holy ones" (Final [last] Antichrist, False Prophet and Satan). This delegation will be sent by plane leaping and landing like frogs hopping all over the world spreading deception. They promote world unity through the MNO to fight the mass headed toward earth. {Issue-1=Pg -142. / SC=Sec=2-18}

✪ ➪ **MNO Kings Assemble:** The delegation from the "holy ones" (Satan, False Prophet and Antichrist {Issue-1=Pg -150. / SC=Sec=2-19}) has the ten MNO kings assemble at a place called Armageddon. Note: They cannot fight this object, which is coming in the sky from their home countries because most military satellite and other technology have been destroyed. Therefore, manual mode or bodily being where they want to fight will be the best option. They discuss the mass in the sky. {Issue-1=Pg -142. / SC=Sec=2-18}

✪ ➪ **World Assembly Building:** Has been built near Armageddon for lack of space in Jerusalem. This houses ten area world federation =MNO with the Three Ugly Heads. {Issue-1=Pg -142. / SC=Sec=2-18}

Prophesied by,
Bob R. Short
- a Witness - 1994-2007

✪ ➪ **MNO Armies to Assemble:** The assembly votes to move their armies to Israel, which will be closer to Jerusalem than their respective countries. This action reduces the response time to maneuver into position to make war against the object in the sky. {Issue-1=Pg -142. / SC=Sec=2-18}

✪ ➪ **God Openly Intervenes:** We now see the 7th Bowl of Wrath of God opening. This contains the Seven Satanic Dooms. {Issue-1=Pg -143. / SC=Sec=2-18}

✪ ➪ **Seven Satanic Dooms:** Immediately the seven sequences of Seven Satanic Dooms begin to unfold. These Dooms are designed to destroy the sinner, lukewarmer, Satan, Last Antichrist, False Prophet, death, and Hades. (This includes Religious and Political Babylon) {Issue -1=Pg -143. / SC=Sec=2-18}

✪ ➪ **1st Satanic Doom:** Doom (Revelation 16:17-19) begins. Remember America will be at war with the MNO. Many nuclear weapons are used causing lighting, rumbling and peals of thunder blasts. These causes a chain reaction of earthquakes around the world, which combined, are the largest earthquake in history. It destroys most MNO cities and causes financial collapse of the MNO. Jerusalem splits into three parts. {Issue-1=Pg -144. / SC=Sec=2-19}

✪ ➪ **Satan Slipping:** 1st Satanic Doom will be the key to the beginning of Satan's downfall. Satan's infrastructure has begun to crumble. {Issue-1=Pg -144./SC=Sec=2-19}

✪ ➪ **Large Earthquakes:** Islands and mountains around the city of Rome are destroyed. {Issue-1=Pg -144. / SC=Sec=2-19}

✪ ➪ **2nd Satanic Doom:** 2nd Doom (Revelation 16:19 to 17:18) begins with great storms, which produce one hundred pound hailstones. After the storm passes, the MNO destroys the city of Rome because of the religious director's recent back talk against the MNO. Rome has been the center of world religion, which has been endorsing the MNO for peace. The False Prophet has sided with the Last Antichrist and enjoys his protection in Israel. {Issue-1=Pg -144. / SC=Sec=2-19}

✪ ➪ **3rd Satanic Doom:** 3rd Doom (Revelation 18:1 to 19:6) begins with God placing a blessing, or a curse, before America. Let us look at two of many options, which could occur. Note, the Spirit has not given me full insight for good reason. First, America will destroy the MNO city, which controls political and monetary power of the MNO. This will occur if America has returned to God. Second, the MNO will destroy the United States by the Three-Woes to America because it has continued to disobey God. Note: A Disciple Nation follows Jesus Christ's commands. {Issue-1=Pg -145. / SC=Sec=2-19}

✪ ➪ FULFILLING -**The Seven Hidden Judgments Against the Mighty Army of Babylon:** Our elected officials can stop the following Seven Hidden Judgments from continuing in America. The USA does not have to become the Biblical Political Babylon which will be destroyed by the 3-Woes to America as described on {Issue-1=Pg -29-30. / SC=Sec=5-5} if She will change Her present course of disobedience against God. When we look at the end time stage of super powers, prophetic Babylon can be another area of the world. Here are seven destructive flaws in its protective armor. {Issue-1=Pg -31. / SC=Sec=5-7}

✪ ➪ FULFILLING -**1st Hidden Judgment:** Technology can be destroyed to easily, so smart military leaders must have manual defensive backup systems. Babylon will rely too much on technology, which will be severely reduced as time comes to an end.{Issue-1= Pg-32./SC=Sec=5-7}

✪ ➪ FULFILLING -**2nd Hidden Judgment:** Warrior's have become political puppet for politician's best interest. End time motivation of nations will be determined by money = buy-sell-trade. {Issue-1=Pg -33. / SC=Sec=5-7}

THE SCROLL

From the

WAKE UP CALL PROPHECIES

✪ ➪ FULFILLING -**3rd Hidden Judgment:** The military has become overconfident. The military overconfidence in technology and its team of allies to control the world. These allies will fall apart. They display power, sell sin, idolatry, and infanticide.{Issue-1=Pg -33. / SC=Sec=5-7}

✪ ➪ FULFILLING -**4th Hidden Judgment:** The military has become friendlier to the homosexual movement. This taints the blood supply and reduces morale and troop readiness.{Issue-1=Pg -33/SC=Sec=5-7}

✪ ➪ FULFILLING -**5th Hidden Judgment:** Sin and my rights becoming social agendas in the ranks of the military. The door will be opened for the noisy dens (special interest groups, Jeremiah 51:55, states destruction) and their ungodly agenda to flourish in the military. {Issue-1=Pg -34. / SC=Sec=5-7}

✪ ➪ FULFILLING -**6th Hidden Judgment:** Opening 'warrior' positions to women in military. Women must not be in the 'warrior' positions because it is un-scriptural and totally against God's command to the male to be the protector. This shall not imply women cannot be in the military. But it is not Biblical and carries a serious consequence for allowing women to be in the 'warrior' positions (Genesis 2:15, Joel 3:9-10, Nahum 3:13, Jeremiah 51:30). {Issue-1=Pg -35-37. / SC=Sec=5-7}

✪ ➪ FULFILLING -**7th Hidden Judgment:** The military leadership will be full of arrogance. Babylon's warrior's downfall has been prophesied. They show no respect for the Son of Man by slaughtering the unborn. {Issue-1=Pg -37/ SC=Sec=5-7}

✪ ➪ **4th Satanic Doom:** 4th Doom (Revelation 19:7-20) begins with Jesus' 2nd coming to fight in the battle of Armageddon. {Issue-1=Pg -145. / SC=Sec=2-19}

✪ ➪ **Satan's Goal:** His goal will be to stop Jesus from returning to earth. The MNO radar has picked up a huge object or power source headed to earth on its scopes. The Antichrist knows this must be Jesus and His army. {Issue-1=Pg -145. / SC=Sec=2-19}

✪ ➪ **Plowshares to Swords:** The Last Antichrist then summons (Joel 3:9-11) his ten kings and their armies to fight the Christians on earth and Jesus and His army returning through the air. {Issue-1=Pg -145. / SC=Sec=2-19}

✪ ➪ **Two Witnesses Last Peace Mission:** The Two Witnesses fly to Israel for a special peace crusade before the battle starts. They speak in the world assembly building about the MNO's destruction. They speak of world peace and ask the MNO to reconsider the tragic error they are making. Their warnings fall on deaf ears.{Issue-1=Pg -145./ SC=Sec=2-19}

✪ ➪ **Two Witnesses Murdered:** The Last Antichrist orders the Two Witness' death. On the way back to the airport, their vehicle will be ambushed and both Witnesses killed. Their bodies lie in the streets of Jerusalem for three and one-half days. The MNO nations rejoice because these two men have inflicted tremendous devastation on their countries. {Issue-1=Pg -145. / SC=Sec=2-19}

✪ ➪ **Two Witnesses Taken Up:** TV cameras stay focused on the two bodies. In the middle of the third day, the bodies come to life and stand up while being filmed on TV. The Two Witnesses are taken up into the air in full view of the TV cameras. Fear comes over the MNO nations. {Issue-1=Pg -145. / SC=Sec=2-19}

✪ ➪ **Jesus on a Cloud:** Jesus has given the world the sign of His Second Coming before the battle starts. Jesus will be above the earth in some type of what might be called a spacecraft or huge object exhausting white vapor like a cloud of energy. He will be in full view of everyone on earth. {Issue-1=Pg -146. / SC=Sec=2-19}

Prophesied by,
Bob R. Short
- a Witness - 1994-2007

✪ ➪ **The 4th Seal Last Repeat -The Pale Horse:** The Christian nations will be fighting on the side of the Jews in the battle of Armageddon. They will try to defeat the MNO armies, which are assembled at a place called Armageddon. All nations in the world does not mean every nation. Note: Daniel's ten toes of iron and clay implies all the nations in the world do not agree with the MNO. Therefore, we have the MNO thinking it represents the whole world (all nations) fighting Jesus in the air on a cloud. Note: All nations of Daniel's day did not include North and South America. Jesus will have Christians on the ground helping to win the battle around the world. This will be a terrible time because all the restraints on weaponry are removed for total destruction of all land mass and people in enemy nations. Many nuclear weapons will be used around the world. Death and Hades, famine, plague, and death by wild beasts and their viruses per Revelation 6:7-8. {Issue-1=Pg-146./ SC=Sec=2-19}

✪ ➪ **The Battle of Armageddon:** During the battle of Armageddon (4th Seal, final repeat), the Last Antichrist and the False Prophet are captured. They are both thrown into a fiery lake of burning sulfur. {Issue-1=Pg -146. / SC=Sec=2-19}

✪ ➪ **5th Satanic Doom:** This Doom has been summarized in Revelation 19:21. "*The rest of them* (armies of the MNO at Armageddon) *were killed with the sword that came out of the mouth of the rider on the horse, and all the birds gorged themselves on their flesh.*" All the armies are destroyed at the battle of Armageddon. {Issue-1=Pg -146. / SC=Sec=2-19}

✪ ➪ **Armageddon Won:** A last attempt by Satan to stop Jesus from returning to earth fails. The Battle of Armageddon will be won by the Christians on the ground and Jesus in the air. This battle will be fought in Israel as well as worldwide. Note: There are still people in each hostile nation to be dealt with through the 6th Satanic Doom. {Issue-1=Pg -146. / SC=Sec=2-19}

✪ ➪ **Arise Michael:** The Americas play a role in wining the Battle of Armageddon. North and South America represent Michael rising to his feet per, Daniel 12:1.{Issue-1=Pg-146+ NI 12-96 ./SC=Sec=2-19 +4-5}

✪ ➪ **Satan bound for 1000 years:** Satan bound and thrown into the Jail house (abyss) for 1000 years or one sabbatical day (Revelation 20:1-3). {Issue-1=Pg-147./SC=Sec=2-19}

APPROXIMATELY LAST 75 SLIDE RULE DAYS OF TIME

✝

This will be a time of distress such as has not happened from the beginning of nations until then (Daniel 12:1). {Issue-1=Pg -156. / SC=Sec=2-20}

✪ ⇨ Michael has Arisen: Daniel 12:1, *"At that time Michael, the great prince who protects your people, will arise. There will be a time of distress such as has not happened from the beginning of nations until then."*
We must remember the birthing pain principle when speaking of Michael. His resistance movement starts slow and builds to the end. Christian resistance to world government has been lifting Michael to his feet before the tribulation period started. Now Michael will be totally on his feet and bring his brute force along with Jesus Christ to finish off all unbelievers. { SC=Sec=4-5}

✪ ⇨ Sixth Seal: The real terror will now begin for the Sixth Seal, as birthing pains, starting to open. This Seal will be completed by the end of the 1,335th day as described in Daniel 12:12. {Issue-1=Pg -156-157. / SC=Sec=2-20}

✪ ⇨ 6th Satanic Doom: 6th Doom (Revelation 20:1-10) begins with the 6th Seal (Revelation 6:12 to 7:17). The 6th Seal equates to the 6th Sign as described in Matthew 24:29-30. The sequence of events is as follows: {Issue-1=Pg -147-157. / SC=Sec=2-19 to 2-20}

1. Battle of Armageddon (4th Seal) will be over.
2. Satan bound for one thousand year.
3a. 6th Seal has, as birthing pains, coming to full power. (See below).
- ✪ ⇨ Great earthquake
- ✪ ⇨ Sun darkens and turns black due to nuclear bombs from wars around the world including Armageddon.
- ✪ ⇨ Moon turns red because of dust and debris in the air from world war and Armageddon.
- ✪ ⇨ Stars (satellites) fall from sky because of world war and Armageddon.
- ✪ ⇨ Skies recede and/or are hidden because of dust and debris from world war and Armageddon.
- ✪ ⇨ Mountains and Islands removed because of earthquakes and nuclear bombs.
- ✪ ⇨ Jesus has been temporarily holding back the four destructive winds of the earth.

3b. Daniel's 1,335 day as described in Daniel 12:12. {Issue-1=Pg-156-157./SC=Sec=2-20}
- ✪ ⇨ The collection of sinner, unbelievers, and lukewarmers are gathered by God's angles.
- ✪ ⇨ One hundred and forty-four thousand servants of our God are sealed on the forehead.
- ✪ ⇨ The first resurrection occurs with a bodily removal of saints living at this time from the earth. The removal of Saints will make way for the destruction of the surface by the Four Winds of the Earth.

✪ ⇨ Jesus unleashes Four Destructive Winds on the Earth to destroy all surface land, seas, and trees. This literally destroys all sinners, unbelievers, and lukewarmers along with any evidence of them living on earth (Matthew 13:24-30).

✪ ⇨ Our perception of heaven and earth as we know it will pass away into a new and wonderful curved-space-displacement of time. {Issue-1=Pg -157. / SC=Sec=2-20}

*Prophesied by,
Bob R. Short
- a Witness* - 1994-2007

✪ ➪ Judgment Seat of Christ occurs. It includes all people who lived during the Church age and Tribulation Period. Judgment begins - will you stand or fall? {SC=Sec=12-2, Judgment Day Nightmare}
✪ ➪ Millenium starts and last one thousand years or one sabbatical day under Christ's rule. {Issue-1=Pg -157/ SC=Sec=2-20}
✪ ➪ Satan loosed: Satan causes rebellion (Gog and Magog). He is defeated and thrown into the lake of fire. (Revelation 20:7-10)
✪ ➪ Second Resurrection and Great White Throne Judgment: All Old Testaments people will be judge. Then a new heaven and a new earth. (Revelation 20:11 to 21:5)

The Spirit led me to write. It will be better for the Christian to obey God's Commands to resist and understand the days (sorrows) they live in today rather than become upset over disagreements about the first resurrection or 6th Seal. It will prove to be far wiser for a Christian to begin today resisting the new smart identification marking devices and internet web of deceit. This technology directly leads to the Beast's power control agenda and his marking and tracking devices. The lukewarmers will be destroyed because they lack faith and will chase after the benefits of the Leopard Beast and the Eagle with the Three Ugly Heads on the internet web of deceit.

It must be understood as a matter of life or death for the solid Spirit-filled Christians to stop their country from locking into the European led ten-world area federation (MNO -Leopard). It will be more important to do this than to completely understand everything about the great tribulation. If Christians let their nation lock into this ten kingdom Beast, then they will have to receive the Mark of His Name and will soon be dead in God's eyes. Once a nation receives the Mark of His Name by joining the MNO then its citizens must use the Number of the Beast by way of the Mark of the Beast to get the okay to buy or sell. This will be required so a worldwide consumption tax can be levied to fund the MNO.

The Spirit of Christ Jesus, the Spirit of Prophecy said; "Blessed will be the one who has the faith to believe in these prophecies and follow the teaching of God's commands rather than the Spirit of Satan's world government for peace and security. Disciples of Christ will believe the truth whereby being purified by their righteous action. Sadly, the world will continue to be wicked. Many lukewarm Christians and none of the wicked will understand, but those who are wise will understand and act. As for you, take this message to the lukewarm consumer driven Churches and the political leaders of America and the world until you are called to another task. Then rise and fulfill this appointed duty as you have agreed to fulfill."

Almighty God, the God of the Spirits of Prophecy, has called me,
Bob R. Short, to prophesy as a Witness
to all world governments and Messenger to the Churches
on behalf of Jesus Christ our Lord and Savior!
I have prophesied this end time SCROLL
in sequence order with laps and overlaps of events
which accelerate like birthing pains
to conclude the end of the test cycle.

Come quickly Lord Jesus! Amen, and Amen.
This insight is from 1994 to book publishing date. Bob R. Short

Prophesied by,
Bob R. Short
- a Witness - 1994-2007

3-2-1-Israel, Qumran - The cave where the Dead Sea Scrolls were found: There are many caves and other scrolls found in this area. I stood at the remains of Qumran next to the caves in the cliffs. Here is the site that yielded the Dead Sea Scrolls. This important find caused many to pause and take note of the Book of Revelation.

The Dead Sea Scrolls spoke of a period at the end of time where the sons of light would battle the sons of dark (Satan/Belial or prince of darkness). We were told the Qumran sect thought Melchizedek would be the head of the "sons of Heaven' or 'gods of justice'.

Their thinking seemed to be correct with the exception they did not have readily access to the New Testament as we do. Therefore, their conclusion would be correct which pointed to a Heavenly Prince from the order of Melchizedek. Today we know this figure is Jesus Christ - "of the Order of Melchizedek".

LATEST PROPHECIES

Section - 4

Summary of insight between Wake Up Call Prophecies, Issue-1, Book, and this Book called the Scroll.

Latest

WAKE UP CALL PROPHECIES

Instructions, visions, insight, calculations, poetry, riddles, warnings, and decrees from 1996 - 2007.

They are a partial fulfillment of Joel 2:28-29 and Acts 2:17-18.

4-1-a-0 - Italy, Florence:

The photo to the right is one of many statues in Florence. There were statues made in honor of the God Almighty, Saints, and Prophets. Presently, honor and loyalty seems to be outdated in the world with its exciting entertainment and thrills, whereby leaving the Lord God behind.

A significant question comes to mind. Can it truly be endtimes? Then where are the men and women prophets promised by the Lord God? Perhaps the Church and the world are suppressing their prophecies for personal gain and self-preservation.

Truth offered to the lukewarmers and the ungodly sometimes stings like a poisonous scorpion, and therefore is rejected.

SUMMARY: GOD'S PURPOSE FOR THE LAST CHURCH

Section - 4-1-a

Why Church resistance movement against the Antichrist spirit is behind God's time line as prophesied in Daniel 11:32:

"... but the people who know their God will firmly resist him"

Antichrist spirit promoting the old Roman style European led World Government.

"Jesus Christ's last generation Church consists of a remnant of end time Saints obedient to God's commands. God's House of Worship shall be a place of prayer where souls are saved by hearing the Good News of Jesus Christ.

God's House must also be used to teach resistance and implement corrective action (Daniel 11:32) against the sin-promoting Antichrist's spirit, who promotes the European led world government. Saints must resist a world consumption tax (Daniel 11:20), which funds European controlled government. The Saints must resist smart (computer reading or marking) technology, which calculates into 666 and produces the Mark, Name and Number of the Beast through the **W**orld **W**ide **W**eb of deceit **(WWW = 666).**

Christians must influence our leaders to apply firm resistance (Daniel 11:18) against a global military. Saints must expose the False Prophet's world religion as pagan with disastrous consequences because it demands tolerance of the world's religions while denying Jesus Christ as the only Messiah. The Saints must resist the False Prophet's promotion of peace and security through the world government.

God's remnant understands true peace and security will only be achieved through Disciple Nations following Jesus Christ's Commands. The Saints' resistance movement will influence America's leader into organizing North and South America to protector itself (Daniel 11:39) and Israel (Daniel 11:41) against Satan's Leopard government (Daniel 7:6).

This alliance (Daniel 12:1, see Beast flip chart - section 9-1) of resistance will become a vehicle used by **THE GREAT PRINCE MICHAEL** to protect Israel." Insight released (1-98). Bob R. Short - servant messenger to the Churches.

Left-below, 4-1-a-1-France - Paris - Notre Dame Cathedral: I marveled at the beauty of the European cathedrals and churches. Unfortunately, many are used mainly for tourism. They gave up their power to the European World Government. Europeans see government not God Almighty as their future comforter and provider. Therefore, attendance at church has dropped off to virtually nothing. Sadly, American churches are becoming like European churches, not important when it comes to influencing society for the good.

People over 60 years of age still go - move down to age 45-59 and there will be about a 10-15% drop - analyze age 30 to teenagers and another 10-15% drop, and finally analyze teenagers and below - the world will win out over church attendance most of the time. In other words, the preachers will be talking to themselves in about twenty years. What a dilemma for pastors.

GOD'S PURPOSE FOR THE LAST GENERATION CHURCH

Section 4-1-b

1967 A.D., to September 23, 106SRSP-S (S.R. = Slide rule sequencing point of events - are not necessarily our calendar dates.)

The Spirit of Christ Jesus, the Spirit of Prophecy inspired me to write the following during July - December, 1997.

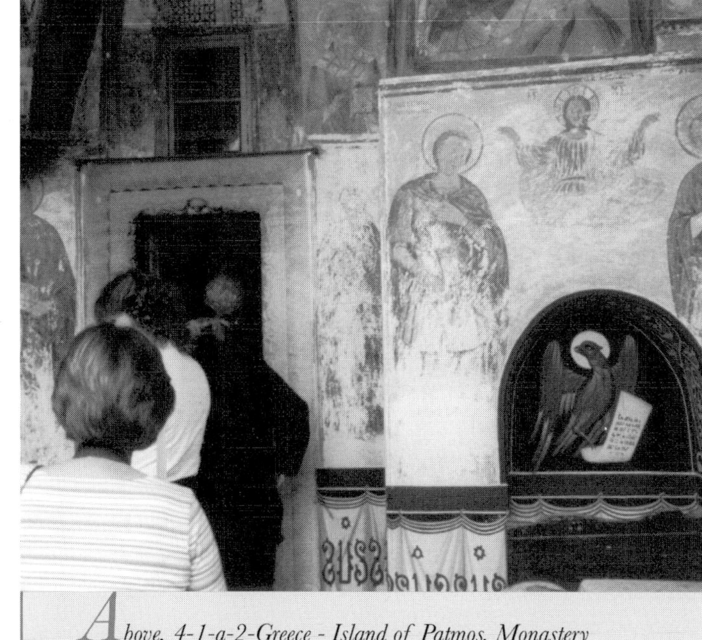

Above, 4-1-a-2-Greece - Island of Patmos, Monastery St. John: I was excited when I entered part of the Monastery covering the cave where St. John received the Revelation. He first warned about the lukewarm church, which lost its power in Revelation 3. Revelation 2-3 discussed the seven spirits of God, which make up the churches. St. John prophesied the last group of people who called themselves Christians before Jesus returned had become like the Revelation 3:16 lukewarmer - rich and in need of nothing.

The Church has been given the responsibility to lead the body of Christ in the proper direction over the past 2000 years. However, prophets will arise during the last generation to warn lukewarm Churches of their disastrous direction (Joel 2:28). The prophets inspired by the Spirit of Christ Jesus (Revelation 19:10) will help instruct Saints in the days of sorrow (1996-99SRSP-CE) and tribulation period (99.9.25SRSP-CE to 106.9.23SRSP-S). Many will not listen to these prophet's warnings and will perish through the Great Christian Falling Away per Matthew 24:10.

Today's lukewarm Churches lack spiritual involvement and end time knowledge in fulfilling the prophet Daniel's prediction (Daniel 11:32). Daniel prophesied the last generation of people who knew their God would firmly resist Satan's spirit. The Church must resist Satan's spirit. His spirit increases sin and wickedness while promoting global trade deals to control the economy through buying and selling. This worldly spirit promotes ID marking numbers bar codes, world military, world religion and European world governmental domination. Today we see these events unfolding before our eyes.

Where is the Church resistance? We remember Biblical prophecy must be fulfilled. Christians believe the Bible is the infallible Word of God, and I ask again, "Where's the Church's resistance to Satan's spirit of destructive sin, deception and European world government?" The Scroll and other end time teaching on the subject will highlight the resistance movement. World events will force Christians to face reality about endtimes and began to resist.

Prophets will surface during the last generation to warn lukewarm Churches of their disastrous direction (Joel 2:28).

Revelation 3:16 prophesied the last generation Church would become lukewarm. Our generation is the Biblical last generation of Christians. One reason for this lukewarmness is improper teaching through today's Christian media. Many of today's Christian media such as preachers, teachers, leaders, TV, radio, and bookstores have found monetary and self-satisfying rewards by embracing worldly as well as Christian principals. Quantity and success equates to the business buzzwords to achieve monetary and head count goals in the Church.

Quality, righteousness, and solid Christian values are mostly taught using psychology. This way lukewarmers are not offended. If the Church promotes quality then it must preach resistance to Satan. Quality and resistance go hand-in-hand. Therefore, our present-day Christian education has failed to teach Daniel's Firm Resistance against Satan's plan to spread wickedness and take over the world using deception.

Left, 4-1-b-1- Greece, Ancient Mycenae - The Lion Gate: The Lion Gate was the entrance to the Peloponnesian city of Mycenae. A natural fortress ringed by a deep gorge, between 1600-1200 BC it was the most powerful Greek city of all. History records the birth and death of many powerful cities or nations. Rome had its day. Germany roared during WW II. These past superpower strongholds lacked one or two major ingredients to hold the rule.

Past strong holds lacked, modern weaponry, and second, technology to control people's movement and what they do each day, like buying and selling. The coming European led World Government (MNO) has this technology.

Just before and during the Tribulation period, the hotly contested issue has to be, do American citizens let a few weak leaders kneel down before the European World Government and courts to ask forgiveness concerning our misguided forefathers when they won their independence from Europe many years ago. Then they will ask to come under the umbrella of Europe. God says NO! He will judge any nation harshly for doing this. Christians must follow the American framers, patriots, and forefathers who won our independence from Europe. Let Christian voices be united and clear; American Christians leading North and South America want to be friends with Europe, BUT they will not dictate to America for America has a different agenda. If Europe tries, there will be much Christian resistance!

Jesus said *"He who is not with me is against me, and he who does not gather with me scatters,"* (Matthew 12:30). He said we could not serve both Him and worldly gods. However, many Churches embraced demands of special interest groups and became lukewarm. These Churches are not speaking out on today's issues. Some built their ministries using prosperity debt thinking. This inspires huge debt to build larger Churches to reach more people. Churches in debt are servant-slaves (Proverbs 22:7) to the financial system, which will soon be controlled by the Antichrist's global system. Other Churches are afraid to speak out for fear the federal government will close them down or pull their tax-exempt status. Protection of Church rights can best be accomplished through the Universal America Church Coalition (UACC) as prophesied in the original WAKE UP CALL PROPHECIES.

Many in the body of Christ are being taught old-fashioned lukewarm Christian living. We are living in the generation fulfilling the last fifteen minutes of the sixth sabbatical day of time (11:45-12:00 PM). At midnight of the sixth day, Jesus comes back as a roaring Lion for revenge and to destroy the unbelievers, lukewarmers, backsliders, and those who are destroy the earth, (Revelation 11:18). The Antichrist spirit permeates itself through many powerful men and women, special interest groups, international business, organizations, and global trade agreements. We hear about a loving and forgiving Jesus without the necessary teaching of repentance through straight and narrow Biblical teaching. This equates to cheap salvation.

God's displeasure with the corrupt behavior of man will be observed after 1990 A.D. God has increased severe storms, earthquakes, and other disasters to wake the world up. However, most of the Christian media puts the Saints to sleep. The end time dangers are not being addressed enough. Example; Satan uses deception in promoting world government. Furthermore, he entices America and others to give up rights through deceptive global agreements. The media suppresses resistance against using smart marking cards, world taxes, and world police force. Little resistance has been taught concerning the dangers in setting up national databases to mark citizens trough global tracking system. Such systems will be transferred to the world European government to control the buying and selling transactions. This allows the collection of a world consumption tax to fund the MNO. The Antichrist will experience trouble implementing world ID marking system without this tracking system.

Any nation's citizens will not have to accept the
MARK OF THE BEAST OR ITS NAME AND NUMBER
if their nation does not lock itself into the European led global agreements.

The Mark of the Beast will be voluntarily sold to consumers at first because it is cost effective, convenient, and promises peace and security. Christians, be warned because it will finally be forced and controlled by the world European government. Any nation's citizens will not have to accept the Mark of the Beast or its Name and Number in the future, if their nation does not lock itself into the European led global agreements. These agreements require any member nation to give up national rights to collect the world consumption tax. Christians and their nations must not pay this world tax.

Today's Church can improve by exposing sin, implementing discipline, and resisting the promotion of World European Government controls. Increased resistance by the Church fulfills Bible Prophecy but it is not happening yet.

PURPOSE OF THE LAST GENERATION CHURCH

A. Jesus said, *"My house will be called a house of prayer, but you are making it a den of robbers"* (Matthew 21:13). The most effective tool against Satan will be prayer. Even our most devoted leaders have said staying in prayer requires the hardest discipline of their ministry. One of the Church's duties must be to provide a place for daily prayer. Christ's House of Worship must never turn into an entertainment center to glorify man. Nor does a spirit-filled Church turn into a worldly activity center. People dancing or performing in revealing clothing, short skirts or inappropriate dress in Jesus' House of Worship must be considered sinful. God's House must never have a hint of sexual immorality. Women performing during Church events in skimpy attire place stumbling blocks of lust before the brethren.

Likewise, God is not impressed when men disgrace His Holy Sanctuary by wearing hats, disrespectful dress, or immodest clothing. He must be outraged when these men honor the world more than Him. His house of Worship and Church property must never become a travel agency, retail photo shop for yearbooks, bingo parlor, director of sports promotions, gymnasium, junior high dance sponsor, fashion show coordinator, bikini contest at a youth car wash, discount house for goods and services, and other such worldly activities. Christians, God's House of Worship and its property must be separate from the world for they will become polluted or lukewarm (Romans 12:2). The building structure is God's property.

B. We must continue to pattern the last generation Church after the 21 core attributes of the first Church discussed in Acts 2:22-47. These attributes in sequence are:

1. Acts 2:22; FIRST, assemble a gathering of unbelievers.
2. Acts 2:36; SECOND, tell the story of Jesus Christ.
3. Acts 2:38-39; THIRD, preach repentance, baptism and the free gift of life.
4. Acts 2:40; FOURTH, warn the unbelievers of the consequences.
5. Acts 2:40; FIFTH, plead with them to be saved from corruption.
6. Acts 2:41; SIXTH, identify the unbelievers who now believe.
7. Acts 2:41; SEVENTH, baptize the new believers.
8. Acts 2:42; EIGHTH, teach God's word.

************THEN**************

9. Acts 2:42; fellowship one with another.
10. Acts 2:42; break bread together in God's House (Lord's Supper).
11. Acts 2:42; pray daily.
12. Acts; 2:43; expect signs, and wonders.
13. Acts; 2:44; share with each other.
14. Acts; 2:45; give to one another.
15. Acts; 2:46; meet daily in God's House.
16. Acts; 2:46; break bread in their homes together.
17. Acts; 2:46; Church members should be glad.
18. Acts; 2:46; Church members should have sincere hearts.
19. Acts; 2:47; Church members should praise God.
20. Acts; 2:47; Church members should enjoy other members.
21. Acts; 2:47; *"And the Lord added to their number daily those who were being saved."*

C. *"Let us not give up meeting together, ..., and all the more as you see the Day* (Jesus' 2nd return) *approaching,"* (Hebrews 10:25). We gain strength by meeting together in these last wicked days. More importantly, we must use these extra meetings to discuss end time understanding and strategy for our resistance against the new European world order and its global decrees promoting sin. These meetings must be used to implement ways to protect our families, God's House of Worship, the brethren, our community, state, and nation. Other topics discussed must be the seven options for dealing with issues requiring correction and discipline as described in the original rough draft issue of the WAKE UP CALL PROPHECIES (page-72). These extra meetings must be closed to non-believers for 1 Corinthians 14:22 states, *"prophesy, however, is for believers, not for unbelievers!"* This will be to protect the Saints from grievous wolves who try to infiltrate the meetings and report to the deceiver on how best to silence the Saints.

Extra meetings about end time prophecy and Daniel's Firm Resistance must be divided to fulfill Bible teaching and not violate scripture. Separate the believers and non-believers into two groups. Preach the salvation message of Jesus Christ to the non-believers. Teach the believers understanding about end time events, new prophecies, Daniel's Firm Resistance and strategy against Satan's deception. Implement ways to combat Satan's promotion of false peace and security through European world government. Find ways to start disciplinary action against his deceptive spread of sin. The Church must listen to end time Christians who receive insight through prophecies, visions, and understanding about endtimes (Joel 2:28).

What is the one meaningless task I should stop doing and the one assignment I must start doing today to prepare the kingdom for Jesus Christ's return?

D. The last generation Saints will be required to suffer greater hardships, preach the good news more boldly, and fulfill "Daniel's Firm Resistance" even if it calls for them to die (Revelation 20:4). Church resistance must be directed against the Antichrist spirit, which is controlled by Satan. This resistance must began immediately against **the Mark and Number of the Beast, second hidden Mark of His Name,** smart marking technology, the internet web of deceit, world consumption tax, world government controls, and promotion of sin. Christians will be required to sacrifice for Jesus Christ. This will separate the lukewarmers from the Spirit-filled Christians.

Jesus commanded Christians, *"Therefore go and make disciples of all nations, ..., and teaching them to obey everything I have commanded you"* (Matthew 28:19). You will notice He said go make all nations follow all My commands. He did not say, ask some nations if they would follow a few of My commands. This implies using military force on a national level because the sword of correction has been given to governments. The Church is not an offensive unit and should only "teach them" Christ's commands. However, God's Two Witnesses (Revelation 11:3-14) will use disciplinary force in trying to bring the world in line with Jesus' commands during the last half of the tribulation period.

Christian suffering comes into play when we try to teach Jesus Christ is the only answer for solving the world problems. Percussion results when Christians try to teach nations that they must acknowledge Jesus Christ is the Son of God Almighty and follow His commands. Each nation must implement laws around Biblical teaching and their leaders must follow these laws to correct violators. The result will be harmony in the world with peace and prosperity flourishing everywhere. Sadly, we know through Bible teaching this will not happen until Jesus returns.

E. The end time Church must listen to people who are Biblically prophesying at a high percent of accuracy. They must listen to people whose visions are coming true and edifying the Church. There will be false prophets and false Christ (Matthew 24:5-11) to deceive many Christians. Yet, the elect will see through the deception and warn many believers (Daniel 11:33). Do not be misled by some well-known Christian preachers and teachers. Some lukewarm preachers are being promoted to increase revenues by the Christian media. Revenues and attendance can be increased in today's promiscuous society by preaching lukewarmness. America does not want to hear the straight and narrow teaching of Jesus Christ. Therefore, Christians must read their Bibles and ask the Holy Spirit to give them insight into end time signs and events. This way they will not be misled.

Test each spirit. Let the signs prove the truth the Bible teaches and the truth will set you free. Test each sign for literal Biblical accuracy or whether it follows the true nature of God. Hold on to the Bible teaching about sign sequencing. Beware of Christian leaders teaching the easy way to escape the tribulation period.

Prophesied by - Bob R. Short, a Witness

Right, 4-1-b-2- Greece, Rhodes - Lindos: I was returning from the Temple of Lindian Athena, 4th - Century BC. The steps are part of the Doris Stoa. This building leads to the Propylaia (building), which goes up to the Temple. I wondered what St. Paul was thinking when he saw this place. He was purported to have landed just over the other side and behind where I stand in the picture. The view is magnificent on top where the pagan temple is located. Does God look at the modern day lukewarm Churches in the same light as he looked at these pagan temples? He has prophesied the Great Christian Falling Away in the tribulation period. Sadly, very few Churches are teaching what Christians must do before and during the tribulation period. Most have theories, which conveniently remove them before or during this period of suffering. Some churches believe the tribulation is already over, while others have designed fantastic rapture theories. Most of these churches believe there will be people in the tribulation period, which are Christians (Saints). It may be a shock to the reader, but most of the people attending church today will complete their testing cycle in the tribulation.

Why are few Churches properly teaching these potential tribulation Christians what they must be doing before and when the tribulation starts? Could it be, loss in membership or maybe they have a different understanding of prophecy? Are today's Christian leaders just going to let the unsuspecting souls die and let their blood fall on them on judgment day (Ezekiel 33 - Watchman)?

I pray not! We must start understanding the Great Commission when associated with endtimes. "Go **MAKE**, *not ask disciples of all nations" (laws, government and people follow Jesus' teaching). A question about the defining moment today would be, if the sleeping and disobedient churches will start teaching the resistance movement and warning their flock properly or let them get blind sided? God calls Christians to prepare for hard times ahead and resist against the progression which leads to the European led World Government (MNO). The MNO will eventually require citizens to take the Mark, their nation to accept the Name, and use the Number of the Beast.*

F. The Spirit led me to a sampling of scriptures the Church has disregarded in favor of lukewarmness. It is better to observe Biblical Church teaching before other outside activities. These extra activities have turned Churches away from their intended end time goal. See a sampling of forgotten Church duties below:

1 Corinthians 5:11-13; *"But now I am writing you that you must not associate with anyone who calls himself a brother but is sexually immoral or greedy, an idolater or a slanderer, a drunkard or a swindler. With such a man do not even eat. What business is it of mine to judge those outside the church? Are you not to judge those inside? God will judge those outside. 'Expel the wicked man from among you.'"* Churches for the most part are stopping the Biblical practice of expelling people who call themselves Christians and continue to sin or promote sin openly. The last generation Church has a hard time interpreting obscure or illegal matters as to what sin is. Some Christian leaders are not strong enough on the salvation message of Jesus Christ. This leads to lukewarmness and adds to the destruction of the Church. This makes it difficult for the world to recognize Christians from sinners. Obedience and responsibilities to God's Word must be required once an unbeliever declares himself a Christian. Christians, who continue to openly defy solid Biblical teaching, reach a point where they must be expelled from the Church. However, most lukewarm Churches are afraid to expel people.

Many Lukewarm churches confuse activity with accomplishing the great commission.

THEY HAVE BOUGHT INTO SATAN'S ILLUSION!

End time Churches will be informed by inspired prophets of God, as Daniel predicted, *"Those who are wise will instruct many, ..."* (Daniel 11:33). The highest order on earth in the body of Christ is a prophet since apostles are no longer on earth (1 Corinthians 12:27). Where does this leave average Christians who are isolated from the end time or resistance messages in their Church? The key question to ask your pastor will be, why are they not preaching about Daniel's Firm Resistance? Look for organizations, ministries, teachers and prophets currently teaching resistance if your pastor will not.

Above, 4-1-b-3- Greece, Olympia - Temple of Zeus - Sacred hearth: The Sacred hearth in front of the Temple of Zeus has been the starting point of the Olympic flame (torch) for the World Olympics. This is the birthplace of the modern pagan god of sports. It is sad the modern world has resurrected the old god of sports into a new one, even more wonderful, exciting and robust than the old god.

These days, some Churches close their sanctuary on Sunday and show football events on church property as an opportunity to witness to people who would never come to church otherwise. They use their praise and worship service to glorify the pagan god of football (sports). Note: One of the top reasons some men watch football is not for football sake even though television is saturated with porn or sinful dress. It has become a pastime of watching the cheerleaders and others in porn shots. Marketing and advertising companies realize this increases viewer ship. I have even heard of a football game where bare breasts were on display at half time while Churches view this sinful act. A dangerous trend of blending Christ with porn and violence associated with sport has been increasing in the lukewarm Churches. I wonder if Jesus might have tipped the table over which held the wide screen TV showing the latest playoff of gladiator events when He cleaned out the temple. I think He might have. What do Christians think Jesus would do in their churches if He walked in when they are doing this vulgar and disrespectful viewing? The Bible teaches us to fix our eyes on The Good - not what looks good (disgraceful worldly beauty). An overwhelming number of world citizens do not believe in Biblical moral absolutes. Sadly, they are moving toward individual moral interpretation to reach their religious fulfillment.

Imagination may make the average lukewarmer think he can run his life better than God can.

Ephesians 5:11; *"Have nothing to do with the fruitless deeds of darkness, but rather expose them."* Many Churches are stopping the practice of exposing the darkness of Satan. Abortion, homosexuals, the promotion of illegal drugs and other sins are at their highest level in America's history. Some Churches are endorsing these activities. No wonder God calls some believers wicked (2 Chronicles 7:14). God has called many of His end time people lukewarm and promised to spit them out into the tribulation period for rebuking and discipline (Revelation 3:16-19). Many are out of God's saving grace, yet they believe they are going to heaven.

Romans 12:2; *"Do not conform any longer to the pattern of this world, but be transformed by the renewing of your mind."* Many churches are conforming to the world by accepting the demands of special interest groups, for example, women's liberation movement, homosexual, and ungodly entertainment. This increases membership and reduces confrontations with the world. They are lukewarm and lack the ability to fulfill Daniel's Firm Resistance against increasing sin and world government.

Romans 12:9; *"Love must be sincere. Hate what is evil; cling to what is good."* The Church must hate evil. It has welcomed sin, the mother of evil into the Church in some cases by relaxing its resistance to lust which leads to sexual immorality and then death.

Romans 14:16; *"Do not allow what you consider good to be spoken of as evil."* The Church must not allow good to be called evil. When someone degrades the Church, God, Jesus Christ or the written Word, the Churches must rebuke these people. Some Churches remain silent while people make fun and degrade the Lord God. When the Two Witnesses come, they will handle the problem with harsh discipline (Revelation 11:3-13). Jesus will solve the problem by destroying these people. Christians are to be like Jesus (Philippians 2:5), so challenge anybody or anything, which degrades our Lord God!

James 1:27; *"Religion that God our Father accepts as pure and faultless is this: to look after orphans and widows in their distress and to keep oneself from being polluted by the world."* The Church must look after orphans and widows in their distress.

We have allowed the U.S. government to remove this activity from the Churches through increased federal taxation. This removes God from the equation. Examine the problems America's welfare system has. This must be a Church and local community function not big government. Christians must demand federal taxes be lowered which can generate local funds for godly programs in their communities. This will require Christians uniting to fulfill Daniel's Firm Resistance.

☞ Note: Bible teaching about helping others must never turn into a massive welfare program for brothers who do not want to work (2 Thessalonians 3:10) or participate in Church activities (Galatians 6:10). The Church must keep itself from being polluted by the world. However, many Churches welcome worldly ways on their property. ✂

Matthew 28:19-20; *"Therefore go and make disciples of all nations, baptizing them in the name of the Father and of the Son and of the Holy Spirit, and teaching them to obey everything I have commanded you. And surely I am with you always, to the very end of the age."* The Church must teach the nations to decide which God they follow. It must never teach tolerance of other religions. Nations who reject Jesus Christ as leader are America's enemy. These non-Christian nations display ignorance concerning their survivability during the tribulation period. Devastating destruction will come. Look at America since it gave up Jesus Christ as its leader in the 1960's. Our country now behaves as a staggering rich man not sure where to turn. America must repent and change direction or it will die. Any nation may act like the overwhelmed rich man and prosper economically but die morally and spiritually from its disobedience and lack of Christian leadership.

The USA has become a nation of many gods and its top gods outside the churches are money, entertainment, and sports.

America must publicly acknowledge Jesus Christ. Then the world will understand it is a disciple nation following the Lord God and His commands. We have become a multicultural society. This society contains many gods. Disciple nations are tolerable only when citizens understand America is Christian and its laws are written for a Christian nation. Christians must live at peace with unbelieving neighbors when possible. This holds true as long as unbelievers do not try to impose their pagan beliefs on North and South America.

Satan uses the new buzzword "world wide tolerance for religions." However, as a Christian Nation we expect them to tolerate our Christian beliefs in public areas or move to nations better suiting their interests. Majority rules and the majority are Christian.

Nations act foolish at times; therefore, it is inherent that the Church explains to them which God to follow.

The Church's commission states; go and make disciples of all nations and teaching them to obey everything I have commanded you. These are strong words coming from our Lord.

2 Corinthians 6:14; *"Do not be yoked together with unbelievers. For what do righteousness and wickedness have in common? Or what fellowship can light have with darkness?"* The Church must be yoked together with believers. This does not take away from one purpose of the Church, which must be to invite unbelievers to tell them about Jesus Christ.

Below, 4-1-b-4- Israel, Capernaum - Synagogue: Pictured; the 2nd to 5th century AD synagogue built on the site of the 1st century synagogue where Jesus taught. The day shall be coming when men will have to protect the Christians and building structures called Churches. Some lukewarmers cannot conceive of this in their minds. Remember, Christians are not winning the popularity contest in the tribulation. We are the troublemakers against the European led world government (MNO = 666 = Leopard Beast). Power to resist world government as the Bible instructs can only be obtained by banding together through the UACC as described in this book of prophecies.

Likewise, disciple nations must not be yoked together with non-disciple nations. Currently America is tragically warming up with Russia and other non-believing countries. Some of our leaders are saying, "They are on our side." These leaders lack faith to believe in Ezekiel 38-39 (US - Russia war - 99SRSP-CE). Non-Christian leaders as well as some Christian leaders are embracing Russian troops and war equipment on our soil in the name of peace through NATO (the Bear on the flip Chart) and the UN (soon to evolve into the Leopard). Some of America's leaders who are controlled by Satan try to destroy America in favor of European led world government. Churches must object to America obligating itself to any governments totally rejecting Jesus Christ as Lord God. I ask again, where are the Churches who must resist?

Terrible times will come and revenues will fall. Churches in debt will be in financial trouble and unable to present the good news of Jesus Christ.

Roman 13:8; *"let no debt remain outstanding, ...".* Churches must not be in debt! Some Christian leaders think they are furthering the gospel by placing the Church of Jesus Christ as servant slave to the loan maker. Their loan company, which now evolves into their new master, has locked into the world financial market. The church in debt has made itself into the servant slaves to the antichrist world monetary system. Church debt stems from Prosperity Debt Thinking. Some may have gotten by with this in the past, but not immediately before and during the tribulation period. Followers of this misguided theology believe placing the Church as slave to the world financial system can save more souls. Their marketing seems to work and the results are a larger crop of lukewarm Christians (Revelation 3:16).

Terrible times will come and revenues will fall. Churches in debt will be in financial trouble and unable to present the good news of Jesus Christ. Jesus taught we could not serve two masters at the same time. Therefore, Churches placing themselves as servant slaves to the world financial system cannot effectively be loyal servant slaves to Christ. Churches can effectively serve only one master at a time. Consequently, many of today's Churches have become ineffective and are producing large crops of lukewarm Christians.

G. Luke 22:36-38: *"..., and if you don't have a sword, sell your cloak and buy one."* Christian men are to arm themselves with guns to protect family, brethren, God's House of Worship, community, state, and nation. Governments must never be allowed to take guns from its citizens. Christians must not allow governments to require their approval through permits for its citizens to purchase guns. Jesus taught otherwise.

Jesus said in Matthew 24:52, if we draw the sword we will die by it. Drawing the sword will be required in the tribulation period. If we die defending our friends then we will achieve a high honor in heaven (1 John 3:16). If we have victory by the sword, we do not count ourselves great, for this came from God not our great talent (Psalm 44:6-7).

In summary, the last generation Churches must be houses of prayer. They must follow the 21 core attributes listed from Acts first Church. It must present the good news of Jesus Christ locally and around the world. However, the last generation Church must work harder to make disciple of nations into becoming followers of Jesus Christ and His commands. Churches absolutely must firmly resist Satan's world European led government and the promotion of sin through the Name, Number, and Mark of His Name. Bob R. Short, Servant Messenger to the Churches, July - December, 1997

WHY THE CHURCH RESISTANCE MOVEMENT DRAGS BEHIND GOD'S TIME LINE

Section 4-1-c

The end time Church has not prepared to resist sin, such as enticing technology which sets people up for Satan's end time trap. Neither has the Church spoken against the European led world government, which has denounced the Jewish God entirely. The absence of Church resistance has been caused by a lack of end time knowledge. Greed, lukewarmness, and contented Christians not wanting to rock the boat have caused fearful leaders. This has promoted good life preaching without resistance to Satan. A substantial decrease in younger people's involvement has left dwindling church attendees setup for the great Christian falling away. Leaders see large losses of membership if they teach resistance (truth). Many pastors are not being taught end time sequence of events and resistance to world government. Therefore, they do not completely understand prophetically what is happening or what to do about it. Many lukewarm Christians lacking end time knowledge will try to stop or suppress the obedient Spirit-filled Christian from resisting Satan's European government controls.

Satan has worked harder to deceive and control the world during the last generation. The saints who know their God will work even harder than Satan (Roman 5:20). Satan and God Almighty will fight for control of the last generation. It will be about who controls Power (1 Corinthians 4:20).

Why are most Christian Churches not fulfilling God's prophesied resistance against the Antichrist spirit? Because Christian media, TV, radio, bookstores and even the Churches are not making end time Christian resistance one of the important focuses. Christian's resistance will be viewed by some as radical conservative fascism. They have ignored the opportunity to present the dangers of end time knowledge as one of their most important topics because it is not a popular topic. This causes many people to disbelieve or ignore end time Bible teaching by others. Some Christian media are reaching their financial and membership goals by using worldly marketing and promotional techniques. This has been done at the expense of building quality Spirit-filled Christians. Here are some of the marketing and money raising events used by the Christian teaching and preaching media.

Many lukewarmers expect the world and Spirit-filled Christians to understand and respect their version of the Bible, which they neglect on a daily basis! This results in poor resistance to sin, the world, and the deceptive government it is offering.

1. Most of today's Christians are looked upon as customers. Therefore, the Christian media has been giving the customers what their itching ears want to hear. Remember most Christians in America are prosperous and in need of nothing (Revelation 3:17) if compared to the rest of the world. The last instructions they want to hear would be resistance against the wonderful convenience, security, and monetary opportunities offered by the **N**ew **W**orld **O**rder (NWO). The NWO looks and appears legitimate when one looks at the benefits it offers. Do not be deceived! **N**ew **W**orld **O**rder = **NWO** = 666. N and O = 6 on the phone pad and W = 9 = inverted 6. W = 6th letter in Hebrew alphabet. Any way we calculate the New World Order = NWO = 666 it equals the Antichrist government.

Above, 4-1-c-1-Greece, Athens - Possessionary caterpillars on the walkway up to the Acropolis: This appears to be Possessionary caterpillars. I have been told, if the lead caterpillar was placed behind the last caterpillar, they would march in a circle until they died. This reminded me of how people follow pagan gods and governments.

It also points out how lukewarm church leaders can brainwash their congregation. The lukewarm congregation will follow these false leaders all the way to hell. Therefore, read the Bible for the literal meaning and beware of false teachers. Be warned of easy salvation requirements, easy escape clauses from the wrath of the tribulation period and church debt. End time Christians are called to suffer. Watch out, take heed and be on your guard that no one deceives you!

Christians who cannot be angry at evil like their Bible instructs them to be, usually lacks enthusiasm for doing good during the endtimes by resisting world government.

The Antichrist spirit has been given power in the last generation by Satan (Revelation 13:2 and 13:7). Satan must get his approval from God (Job 2:6) to fulfill prophecy. God will see Biblical prophecy fulfilled at the appointed time. Jesus Christ, the Holy Spirit, Angels, Satan, Antichrist, Demons, False Prophets, the Two Witnesses, and human forms must stay within the time lines and parameters set in their individual cycles by the Lord God to fulfill prophecy. Negative consequences begin to happen when any character goes beyond their set time line or parameter within their cycle or the assigned test cycle. The Lord God will bring negative circumstances upon characters and situations until the player has been corrected or eliminated. When one player gets off course, it can affect many others. God's correction will be done so prophesied events happen correctly and in the time appointed to fulfill prophecy.

Any end time player expressing free will has the ability to go ahead, behind or beyond the time line or parameters set by the Lord God for their testing cycle. Currently the Church has lagged behind God's Time Line Resistance Goals for this test cycle. In other words the Church has slipped behind the parameters set on the time line by Daniel's prophecy and we will see the negative effects.

The Church must wake up, repent, and begin to fulfill prophecy at its proper set time line within its test cycle. They must now resist the Antichrist spirit as the prophet Daniel predicted! If the Church corrects itself and starts resisting, much heartache will be spared. If God has to discipline or push the Churches into action, there will be many more lost lukewarmers per the Great Christian Falling Away (Matthew 24:10). The Church must repent and start resisting or receive its just and righteous punishment!

Prophecy predicts the Antichrist spirit will succeed in most ventures (Daniel 11:36) until Jesus returns to conclude this test cycle. This shall be part of the test (Revelation 3:10) concerning faith, obedience and perseverance. The path of the Antichrist's spirit will be found by following the deceptive money trail to false security and worldly satisfaction. Therefore, the Christian media floods the market place with non-offensive teaching and leaves out Daniel's Firm Resistance. They preach cheap salvation without true repentance. Jesus did not teach His end time Saints complacency. He will return and chastise the Christians who did not follow His Great Commission (Matthew 28:19-20).

2. Many Christian media do not want to offend the customer. Good marketing technique teaches lukewarmness or customers will be lost and the media's financial goals will not be met. The customer must be made to feel good about their lives. This derives from the lust for money and management goals to increase membership. They have omitted preaching the righteous path, which demands narrow and hard choices in favor of special interest group's demands. They ignore teaching Daniel's Firm Resistance in favor of watered down Christian living which invariably leads to the "good life."

3. Teaching institutions are not instructing Christians how to resist the following: **A**) The internet web of Satan's deceit; **B**) Convenience in using (marking) smart credit cards, welfare cards, health cards, and military MARK cards; **C**) America giving up national rights in favor of job creation by signing global treaties; **D**) Security through European led global police force; **E**) Peace through European world government; **F**) The Saints must resist paying the world consumption tax (Daniel 11:20) using the marking number and name (Revelation 13:16:18). Lukewarmers will not give up some of these conveniences, security, and monetary benefits. Many lukewarmers will hold on to the benefits world marking technology offers and will end up in the lake of fire. They will lose their soul because of lack of faith in end time Bible warnings.

Some lukewarmers fear people who publicly resist sin and the promotion of world government. They feel Christians will be called troublemakers by the European world community. Other lukewarmers believe resistance must be considered very illogical. Most lukewarmers feel the resistance movement gives Christians a bad name. Lukewarm theology has evolved so that many Churches will attract a larger spectrum of worldly people to meet marketing goals. One way this has been accomplished is by bringing worldly props onto church property and using them for witnessing tools to increase Church numbers and lukewarmness. This allows the lukewarmers to call themselves Christians without being offended by solid Biblical principles.

4. It is disastrous for Christian media sales to promote resistance against a disobedient world. When they speak out against sin (Example - homosexuality), some stations refuse to put them on the air. So they surmise something will be better than nothing and they end up with lukewarmness. Therefore, most sinners feel uninhibited in pursuing their disobedient acts before the Lord God.

More importantly, Jesus did not prophesy the last generation would be meek or turn the other cheek. In fact, His Spirit through John prophesied the last generation of Spirit-filled Christians would be rebelling against sin. They will resist European world government until they succeed in building the Great Prince Michael or are killed as Christian troublemakers, (Revelation 20:4).

It is the Christian's duty to boldly protect what Jesus gave them; a Christian Nation, the body of Christ, families and God's House of Worship. Jesus wasn't authorized to use force against His adversaries at His first coming. Prophecy dictated otherwise. Christians are to sternly resist, apply firm loving discipline, and even use force (see section - Eli✞e Chris✞ian Soldiers) if necessary to the disobedient world because the prophet Daniel has prophesied it. This discipline must be similar to caring parents (Prince Michael) and their unruly child (the Leopard). American Christians are commanded to restore the USA and the Americas back under the Lord God's protection by becoming Disciple Nations.

This next point is important to understand. Most Christians say they want to be like Jesus because the Bible says they should. My next question, "if they want to be like Jesus, then answer the how, what, when, and where is Jesus this very minute?"

The Bible teaches Jesus will not be the loving lamb at the end of the age in which we are living. He has transformed into the roaring Lion of revenge appointed by God to destroy the unbelievers. He is not symbolically sitting at the right hand of God. Jesus is prophetically headed for the white horse stables. He will be coming to earth soon on the great white horse (Revelation 19:11). He is not going for a joy ride. He will be angered at the disobedience on earth. Jesus will not be coming to save the world but destroy it as we understand it today. He will not be coming with compassion and understanding but with fiery revenge using the power of a two-edged sword.

Now I ask my fellow Christians who wants to be or have the attitude like Christ. Do you still want to be like Christ? The Bible teaches us, *"your attitude should be the same as that of Christ Jesus:"* (Philippines 2:5). Jesus Christ's attitude during this last generation is set against lukewarmness, and for resistance against disobedient sin in this world. He will destroy the Eagle with the three Ugly Heads, which are backed by its world pagan religion who wants to replace Jesus. Spirit-filled Christian attitudes must be the same!

This leads us to a point, which needs to be made concerning end time resistance against the Antichrist spirit. We must remember the Church equates to Jesus Christ's body on earth (Ephesians 1:22-23). The behavior must be like Jesus. Therefore, the Churches must become bold in leading America toward becoming a disciple nation again.

Daniel introduces the phrase **"Firm Resistance."** Daniel prophesied the last generation of Spirit-filled Christians would firmly resist while lukewarmers will hold back. Let me explain about Daniel's Firm Resistance, *"..., but the people who know their God will firmly resist him,"* Daniel 11:32. Him means the Antichrist spirit during the last generation. Satan will control many Antichrists. Let us apply Jesus Christ's end time birthing pain principle to Daniel's Firm Resistance, *"All these are the beginning of birth pains."* (Matthew 24:8).

Christians will lose rewards before the Judgment Seat of Christ if no resistance to Satan's spirit can be found in their works. Prophecy must be fulfilled in the proper sequence within its time line during the appointed cycle. Matthew writes five times in the first two chapters confirming prophecy, which was fulfilled. See verses; 1:22, 2:5, 2:15, 2:17, and 2:23. Two important Biblical statements of truth are established in the first two chapters of the New Testament. First, Jesus Christ has been sent to save His people from their sins (Matthew 1:21). Second, Jesus Christ's entire life including His second coming must follow what the prophets prophesied (God's preprogramming).

The Church must wake up, believe, and teach what the prophets predicted for the last generation. Their words are not fairy tales for Hollywood movie producers to create entertainment and slander Christian values. They are for Christian action! Christians must uplift Jesus by encouraging fulfillment of good prophecy (resistance movement). Christians must resist bad prophecy such as European world government and the promotion of sin. Christians are sinning if they do not resist what they know to be bad.

Each Christian must ask himself these questions. Do I protest against America's leadership, which openly disobeys God's commands? Will I stand up and complain to our government about locking into European global agreements? Will I resist the use of smart cards? These smart cards for the first time in history contain the ability to carry the 18 digits of a person's Mark of the Beast Number.

Christians, who know all about endtimes, have deceived themselves. They are void of wisdom! If they are void of wisdom, then they are a danger to themselves and others.

God has sent a powerful delusion - but it is not sent to deceive but a preprogramed part of the end time test cycle before the world began. This increased difficulty during the last generation will help separate the sheep from the goats.

How about resisting the national database, which could be compiled for the purpose of assigning a tamper proof smart (marking) ID number to each citizen. We should resist palm and finger security scanners, which represent the S sequence in the Mark of the Beast. Resist zipper strips on cars so satellites can't track your movement. People will receive satellite transmitting and receiving equipment next; the Bible calls it being connected with the Mark, Number, and Name of the Beast! The Antichrist must restrict and track the movement of people before he can control the population. Many Christians are doing nothing to resist Satan's destruction of our nation. It is time to resist!

Ask your pastor to begin teaching the meaning of Daniel's Firm Resistance in your Church. Many pastors will not know to what you are referring. Pastors normally train in saving souls, delivering well-prepared sermons, meeting the bank note through possibility debt thinking, and interacting with others using love (right hand of God), not wrath or resistance (left hand of God). Most pastor's knowledge and teaching are not about end time Christian resistance against European world government or annualizing end time sequencing of events. They are not instructed because their teachers weren't taught. Their teachers didn't know because the book of Daniel has been sealed. God began to break the seals in 1967 so it can now be understood. Therefore, many pastors are tuned out to Daniel's Firm Resistance and end time knowledge. Many of the pulpits of America are silent in promoting Daniel's Firm Resistance.

Christians must continue to spread the Good News about Jesus Christ, while asking people and nations to obey Jesus' commands. The Churches must start the Universal American Church Coalition (UACC) to be their spokesman against global government and sin. (See section titled UACC.)

There has been an increase in people worldwide that call themselves Christians starting in the last generation (1967 A.D. - 106SRSP-S). This increase continues until approximately one or two years before the tribulation period starts when it will plunge downward because of a Northern army marching south (Ezekiel 38-39). Scripture backup: Matthew 24:10 - at that time many will turn away from the faith, 2 Thessalonians 2:3 - for that day will not come until the rebellion occurs, 1 Timothy 4:1-2 - The Spirit clearly says that in later times some will abandon the faith, 2 Timothy 4:3-4, Jude 18-19, 1 John 2:18. **Therefore, it will be increasingly harder to save the lost then than 50-200 years ago.** Why will it be harder for people to accept salvation during the tribulation period? There are many reasons. Lets review a few:

1. The death rate will begin to rise approximately one to two years before the tribulation starts and will increase during the tribulation period. People who may not have turned their lives over to Jesus during their lifetime will not get a second chance because God will cut time short. Here is an example; a person will be killed early at age 37 without accepting Jesus Christ. He may have lived to 70 years of age in normal time. This will be caused by increases in wars, pestilence, severe weather, earthquakes, famine, and other factors (Matthew 24:7-8). The end of this testing cycle has been approaching and if people are caught unprepared, then it's too late!

2. 2 Thessalonians 2:11, "... *God sends them a powerful delusion so that they will believe the lie and so that all will be condemned ...*".

> ✍ Note: Before we begin learning about this verse, we must understand **"God does not deceive"**. However, His powerful delusion is not deception but a part of the test cycle, which was programed before the world began. This increased difficulty during the last generation will help separate the sheep from the goats. We must study ourselves approved and follow Jesus' teaching to pass. (Note added 2-15-06) ✂

This powerful delusion affects the last generation of people with greater intensity than other generations. One part of the delusion implies some lukewarm, backslidden and unlearned Christians are not concerned about going through the worst part of the tribulation period. Some believe they will be taken up in the rapture under three flawed theories and others believe false teaching about the tribulation period spoken of in Revelation is already over.

Above, 4-1-c-2- Greece - Athens - Temple of Olympian Zeus. This temple was the largest in Greece. Work started in 6th century BC and finished about 650 years later. It measured 315 feet long, 130 feet wide, and contained columns 56 feet high. It was big and massive like the Roman Empire. The Romans ran a tight and tough rein over its citizens. So will the final (last) Antichrist. He will be brutal, using a platform of peace and security. Movement of people will be monitored, especially in an east-west direction.

The five incorrect theories that set lukewarm Christians up for disappointment are: 1) Pre-tribulation = signed-rapture before the tribulation period begins or the signed-rapture will usher in the start of the tribulation, so why worry - easy escape clause; 2) Mid-tribulation = signed-rapture in the middle of the tribulation period, so why worry - another easy escape clause; 3) Pre-wrath = signed-rapture between middle of tribulation period and Battle of Armageddon, so why worry - another escape clause; 4) Pre-millennial = signed-rapture anytime before the 1000 year reign of Jesus Christ. 5) No-tribulation period = tribulation period has already ended or fulfilled in 70 AD when Romans destroyed Jerusalem, so why worry.

Post-tribulation is Biblically correct within 75 days - it says; the rapture is at the end of the last seven years of the tribulation period. The truth concerning God's angels gathering His elect from the four corners of the earth is told in Matthew 24:31. This occurs on Daniel's 1335th day (Daniel 12:12) = approximately 75 days after the last seven years of tribulation are counted and before the Millenium starts. The Seven Thunders will increase power for the Sixth Seal to achieve its destructive peak on Daniel's 1335th Day. Pre-millennial rapture is Biblically correct if they believe the millennial reign of Jesus Christ starts the next day after Daniel's 1335th day and the rapture will occur just before the 1000-year (Millenium) reign with Jesus Christ.

Yet, Lukewarmers are classified unworthy by the Lord God and will not experience the rapture under any of these theories. This shall be one part of God's powerful delusion which leads to Matthew 24:10, Great Christian Falling Away in the first half of the tribulation period. Warning, some Christians who have judged themselves worthy will be turned away from Heaven (Matthew 7:23).

Men's priorities are wrong if they want to experience the rapture before or during the last seven years of the tribulation period because they fear loss of their physical or financial stability. Men must look at what Jesus did for them and want to do something in return? Yet, arrogant Christian men want Jesus to remove them from pain, sacrifice, hard work, and death during the tribulation period. Their arrogance goes so far as to believe they are worthy of this request.

Some Christians in America think when the Bible states they are called to suffer, it is referring to some other time. They must wake up, reset priorities, and repent by asking the Lord God to remove the selfish beliefs in their hearts. They ought to want to stay and try to help turn unbelievers to Jesus before the end comes. Better still, they should want to fulfill prophecy by resisting Satan. Men cannot present the good news to sinners, protect their families and nation, or resist Satan in Heaven.

I am not talking about which rapture theory men believe. I am talking about their heart-felt feelings for Jesus. What they believe and what they feel in their hearts motivating their actions can be different until they understand correctly. To understand read the section Seven Spirits of God and Seven Spirits Church Prophecy. Men must not fear dying when protecting their families, brethren, God's House of Worship, communities, and nation (John 15:13 and 1 John 3:16). Men must maintain the humility of knowing they are standing in the gap to fight Satan only by God's grace.

3. The last generation will experience greater amounts of Satan's seducing deception. This applies to the increase in Satan's deception and the lying signs and wonders of the False Prophet and the Antichrist. Spirit-filled Christians will understand in varying degrees. The Bible predicts that deception (Matthew 24:24) will be so great and marvelous only a few elect Christians completely understand. Yet, the wise (Christians with most end time insight) will teach and warn (Daniel 11:33) the body of Christ and unbelievers what shall happen. Sadly most lukewarmers and unbelievers lack faith and will not listen. They will follow the world government and what it offers, such as benefits, conveniences, and security.

The last-generation Church may not see eye to eye, but they can walk side by side armed with the sword of God!

4. Lust will be increased. Let us look at one of many examples such as sexual lust of the eye. Two hundred years ago, an average male in America could see few examples of lust of the eye. Today's average male in the United States will experience many hundreds of actual or subliminal acts of sexual, inviting look or perverted type incidents with the eye in one day. Television, sporting events, and advertising are obsessed with introducing sexually stimulating camera angles, or improper dress, or actions to excite the viewer. Repeated sexual stimulating events increase the natural aggressive behavior in men (James 1:13-21). If this behavior has not been checked, it will turn into sexual immorality.

These incidents come in the form of TV situations and commercials, which would have been called obscene 40 years ago. Books, TV, radio, and movies, use crude language to inspire lustful pictures in the brain. The World promotes women's revealing clothing as the way to succeed. It rewards enticing body language. Promotional sexuality is being used in our Christian media. Lust of the eye works on men or women, and promotes attendance, viewer ship, and increased revenues. Christians must be on their guard against sexually stimulating material. Christians must keep their minds on what is good and pure not what sexually stimulates them (Philippians 4:8). Sadly, some church buildings are being use to promote the above.

5. It will be harder to be saved in the tribulation period. The intensity of God's curses (test) will increase as birthing pains. One example: Genesis 3:16 - curse; God cursed the women to want to be as their husband or man. It can be rightly said, women in many areas are being unjustly suppressed, but this does not mean opening the floodgate to the extreme feminist to abuse God's Spirit-filled purpose in women's lives.

Curses on Nations will affect people being saved. People will be caught up in God's wrath when nations try to move or destroy Israel. Increases curses will make it harder to be saved because faith in God decreases.

Let us recapture the purpose of Jesus Christ's last-generation Church. Stand firm in the faith as we move toward the end of the age for Jesus Christ will reward you for it. *"They overcame him (Satan) …., they (Saints) did not love their lives so much as to shrink from death"*, (Revelation 12:11). They stood bravely here on earth in the name of Jesus Christ and firmly resisted Satan. The Saints will be defeated from time to time. Yet, it is the Saints duty to resist sin and European world government even knowing the Saints are outnumbered until Jesus Christ's return. Rejoice in Daniel's prophesied promise of our victory against the Antichrist, False Prophet, and Satan.

Jesus Christ's last generation Church will be a remnant of end time Saints that are obedient to God's commands. God's House of Worship must be a place of prayer where souls are saved by hearing the Good News of Jesus Christ. God's House must also be used to teach resistance (Daniel 11:32) against the European led Leopard Beast.

Left, 4-1-c-3- Greece, Athens - Ancient Agora - Church of the Holy Apostles: Jesus Christ picture inside on the center dome ceiling of the Church of the Holy Apostles. Jesus is our military leader. He will be fighting in the air with His Saints on the ground to win the battle of Armageddon. The battle will be between what is left of the Eagle with the Three Ugly Heads (two of which have been destroyed earlier) against the Great Prince Michael (North and South America).

Above, 4-1-c-4 -England - London, Imperial War Museum: This shell of an atomic bomb is like the one dropped on Japan in WW II. Current technology has reduced the size of the bomb many times from the one in the picture. Some are as small as suitcases that terrorists could use. Nuclear fusion and multiple warheads have increased the destructive power hundreds of times. It is too horrifying to imagine. Nuclear wars will continue to the end of time. There will be people who will gasp in disbelief as they say, "God would not let this destruction happen." Some will disown the Lord God because of the horrendous events they see.

However, the Bible instructs Spirit-filled Christians to realize these disasters must happen (Matthew 24:6). They are to trust in God and not be alarmed, try to complete their task for the Lord, and have unwavering faith to believe He will bring them home.

Saints must resist world consumption tax (Daniel 11:20), which funds his government. The Saints must resist smart (marking) technology, which calculates into 666 and produces the Mark, Name, and Number of the Beast through the World Wide Web of deceit (WWW = 666). They must influence our leaders to apply firm resistance (Daniel 11:18) against a global military. Saints must expose the False Prophet's world religion as pagan with disastrous consequences for it demands tolerance of all religions while denying Jesus Christ as the only Messiah.

The Saints must resist the False Prophet's promotion of peace and security through the European world government. God's remnant understands true peace and security can only be achieved through Disciple Nations following Jesus Christ's Commands. They will try to influence America to make nations follow Christ's Commands. The Saint's resistance movement must influence America's leaders into organizing North and South America into a protector (Daniel 11:39) of Israel (Daniel 11:41) against Satan's Leopard government, (Daniel 7:6). This alliance (Daniel 12:1, see Beast flip chart - section 9-1) of resistance will become a vehicle used **by THE GREAT PRINCE MICHAEL to protect Israel.**

"As I** (Daniel) **watched, this horn** (Antichrist) **was waging war against the saints** (Christians) **and defeating them, until the Ancient of Days** (Jesus Christ) **came and pronounced judgment in favor** (win Armageddon) **of the saints** (Christians) **and the Most High** (God Almighty), **and the time** (the day after Daniel's 1335th day) **came when they** (Christians) **possessed the kingdom (Millenium reign of Jesus Christ)." (Daniel 7:21-22).

Victory
will be ours
through the
Lord God Almighty!

Amen and amen!

Bob R. Short, a servant messenger to the Churches, July - December, 1997

INTRODUCTORY

Letter to the Goat Prophesy

Christians must warn other Christian of these coming Judgments! Faith is the key to believe the storm will be coming and blow the warning trumpet (Ezekiel 33).

I prophesied in 1994-95, Gulf War II would happen at this precise time in a sequence of end time events. We are currently in this war (published in a book on Page-102 of the original rough draft, Issue-1, of the WAKE UP CALL PROPHECIES 1994-95). It stated; Gulf War II = "US attacks general area Iran-Iraq" (crossing the whole earth without touching the ground).

Since 1996, church leaders who have received these prophecies have not paid much attention to the warnings because some were asleep, others disagreed or have a wait and see attitude. The last ingredient lukewarm pastors wanted would be large amounts of perceived negative information getting to their breadwinners. The collection plate might run dry in some cases.

Therefore, the Lord God will be forced to put America and its Churches on their knees to fulfill prophecy. More importantly, eventually destroy America in the Great Tribulation Period for not repenting and turning back to Him.

MINOR DESTRUCTION SCENARIO:

This war only affects Iraq area, which the America coalition currently occupies.

MAJOR DESTRUCTION SCENARIO:

This war could drag Iran with its sponsored terrorist groups into fighting. They may get or already procured nuclear weapons from countries north of Iran as I prophesied in 1994-95. They could have threatened to use them against the US and others.

> Note-2005: The Moslem terrorist sponsored by Iran-Iraq may have already planted suitcase or similar low yield nuclear bombs in some of our cities and already threatened our leaders. This fulfills part of the Prophecies on Page 102-103 of Issue - 1. Naturally, this has been kept quiet from the public to suppress panic. Time will tell the accuracy of all prophecy.

Make it so Lord Jesus. Come quickly! Your Servant Messenger and Witness to the World governments for Jesus Christ. Bob R. Short, insight 7-15-04.

PROPHESY AGAINST THE GOAT

Section 4-2

Many USA leaders received a copy in 8-2004

This is the Word of the Lord that came to Bob R. Short, a Witness to the world governments for our Lord and Savior Jesus Christ on July 15, 2004.
It's concerning the Goat (America) with a large prominent Horn (city) between his eyes.

This is what the Lord Almighty says:

"Prophesy to the disobedient GOAT (Daniel 8:5-8): Spare his rebellious and arrogant nature no words. He has not followed My Commands to stay a Disciple Nation (Leadership, laws, and people following God's Word).

See, I will break off the Goat's (America's) large prominent Horn. The large Horn is the Self Proclaimed Great City where money is god. Until the removal of the Twins, no one saw the beautiful spike (tip of horn) standing true in the air trying to touch the heavens.

This City evolved to help Christians form a disciple nation under God to protect Israel. It is supposed to be God's showcase for other cities and nations to look up to. Sadly, his god is now money and he has used it to entice the whole earth into becoming drunk with sin. He promotes and teaches ungodly spirits, vile acts, murderers, sexually immoral, drugs, lies and idolaters for money. He shows no respect for my people Israel. The Goat with its large prominent Horn has now become great in his own eyes. The world loves his money and profitable pleasures. However, these sins will bring him to ruin!

The **Nuclear threat** in the first sentence of the third paragraph on Page-102 of the original rough draft, Issue -1, of the WAKE UP CALL PROPHECIES (1994-95) **can now become a reality.** The Horn has become a major obstacle in protecting My people Israel. He has been harshly judged and his horn will be broken off. Oh, America, repent and turn to God, who knows, God may relent His fury.

Above, 4-2-1- U.S., Hawaii - Pearl Harbor - USS Arizona Memorial: Part of the Battle Ship Arizona, which protrudes out of the water at Pearl Harbor. At dawn on the December 7, 1941, the Japanese attack America. By noon, there was death everywhere around Pearl Harbor. However, this tragedy will be minor to the removal of a major city by nuclear weapons when the Horn of the arrogant Goat will be broken off. The rebellion against the Almighty God by our leaders, citizens, and lukewarm Churches leaves Almighty God no choice but discipline those He loves. This will be to fulfill prophecy and begin to rise up the Great Prince Michael.

Breaking off the large prominent Horn of the Goat will be swift and devastating! Its King and officials will be destroyed. Oh mourn, for you will never become a great city or nation again!

I now summon Michael to begin to stand on his mighty feet to protect Israel. The breaking off of the Horn has prompted this action. For as Daniel prophesied many years ago; *"At that time Michael, the great prince* (North-South America - see Angel and Beast Flip Chart-prophesied 7-1997) *who protects your people will arise. There will be a time of distress such as has not happened from the beginning of nations until then..."* (Daniel 12:1).

The use of Nuclear Weapons in the first paragraph on page-103 of the rough draft, Issue-1, of the WAKE UP CALL PROPHECIES (1994-95) **can now become a reality for retaliation.** It is prophesied; Psalms 97:3-5 proclaims the Lord's directive as the United States uses nuclear weapons (melt like wax) to destroy general area of Iran and/or Iraq in an air attack as none other in history.

Four prominent Horns (cities within their kingdoms, page-110, Issue-1, WUCP) will grow up toward the four winds of heaven to replace the Goat's large broken off Horn. The first two self-proclaimed great cities are reserved for later only to fall. Japan's great city will be one of these horns where the god of Money lives. Egypt's great City represents another horn (Controls Army from the South) where power and Jewish-Christian hate reigns as god. The third shall be Rome, which will become great only to fall again. Nevertheless, Rome will unveil the little-horn, the Final Antichrist before it falls. He started small but grew in power to the South and to the East and toward the Beautiful Land. The fourth will be Israel's Honor and Glory city called Jerusalem, which will receive the same fate only to be restored by the true King of kings and Lord of lords, Jesus Christ.

Make it so Lord Jesus. Come quickly! Your Servant Messenger and witness to the World governments for Jesus Christ. Bob R. Short, (insight received 7 - 15 - 04)

GOD'S WARNING

Move Israel, I'll curse your nation.

Since the early nineties, many of the worst monetary disasters America has ever experienced on its soil have happened. God has been lifting His protective covering from America. America lacks faith in God's promised wrath.

AMERICA'S WARNING

Many USA leaders received a copy in 8-2004

The Lord God is furious about the wrong direction America has been going since the early 1990's. President Clinton and now President Bush have become the first two Presidents to push a Palestinian State. God warns in His Word, He will destroy any nation trying to move Israel from its land. Since the early nineties, many of the worst monetary disasters America has ever experienced on its soil have happened. God has been lifting His protective covering from America. America lacks faith in God's promised wrath. Both Democrats and some Republicans since the early nineties are increasingly testing God's patience by promoting and encouraging the following three ungodly points:

POINT 1:
European sovereignty over America

- Turning America's Sovereignty over to the World Court in The Hague.
- Turning America's Sovereignty over to the World Trade Organization in Europe.
- Turning America's Sovereignty over to the UN.
- Turning America's Military Sovereignty under the direction of the UN.
- Surrender States right to above list.
- The individual obtains their rights through the new European led World Government.
- Many lawmakers along with the US Supreme Court are looking to the international community (MNO) for answers instead of defining the law, as America's forefathers would have envisioned.

POINT 2: Remove Israel

- from its God given land.
- Encourage a Palestine State out of the West Bank and Gaza.

POINT 3: Sin

- Other alternatives to marriage besides a man and a woman are spring up.
- Abortion
- Calling truth a lie and a lie the truth.
- Lovers of themselves, boastful, proud, abusive, ungrateful, unholy, unforgiving, slanderous, without self-control, brutal, not lovers of the good, treacherous, rash, conceited, lovers of pleasure rather than lovers of God - having a form of godliness (social programs) but denying its power (following Jesus' commands).

Many Americans should repent of their sinful ways, then ask Jesus Christ in their heart and be saved! I believe you personally should return to your district and ask your people to consider truly following God's commands before it is to late!

I fear unless America turns back to God it will be on a collision course with His wrath! God will allow disaster to strike America in such a devastating way America will not be able to fully recover. Last disaster was two buildings. Is the next disaster the whole city? Repent America!

Bob R. Short, a witness, and insight 7-15-04

God's Promise Concerning
the Apocalypse
Section 4-3

The Book of Revelation, unfolds the great events bringing history to consummation, including the revelation of Jesus Christ at His second advent. The word "Revelation," used as the title of the book, is from the late Latin revelation, which means (as does the Greek "apocalypse", from which the English word "apocalypse" is derived) disclosure of that which was previously hidden or unknown.

The main purpose of this book shall be to provide a better understanding for the revelation of Jesus Christ. Principal attention must be given to Gulf War II before the Tribulation period and Ezekiel 38 (Gulf War III) which leads into the last seven years called the Tribulation period (Revelation 4:19), and Daniel's 70th week (Daniel 9:24-27). Christians living under tribulation spanned from Christ's death, through His second advent and will end with Daniel's 1335th day (Daniel 12:12).

God's hidden or unknown Word concerning endtimes shall be found in Daniel 12:4. God instructs Daniel to close up and seal the words of the scroll (book of Daniel), until a time of the end (our earthly time). We see the word "Apocalypse" or unveiling of understanding about endtimes, promised by God in Daniel 12:11. None of the lukewarmers, backsliders, unbelievers and the like will totally comprehend endtimes, but only Spirit-filled Christians will understand and follow God's will.

1 Corinthians 14:22 further highlights the saints proper apocalyptic understanding of end time events, where it describes prophesy for only believers not for unbelievers! The unbelievers are blinded and most will follow the Millenium Nations Organized (European led Leopard Beast) and eventually the Final Antichrist heading up the Eagle with the Three Ugly Heads in the Great Tribulation.

The enemy will be discouraged in any nation where the Christians are more interested in mobilizing against the Beast than being tranquilized by his smooth talk.

Above, 4-3-1- Israel - Megiddo (Armageddon) - Jezreel Valley: Excavations are estimated at 20 layers of the cities, dating back as far as 3500 BC when it was captured by Egyptian Thutmose III. Its strategic location in ancient days produced some great battles. More importantly, the final battle will be fought here. The end time test has started and the race toward the end of time has begun. Sadly, the Church is still in the locker room.

Christians will increasingly begin to understand in the next years what happens when God's righteous judgments are put upon this disobedient earth for a test (Revelation 3:10). Yet, the lukewarmers and backsliders, which represent 50-84% of today's Christians, will not enjoy the faith to believe. Jesus warned His followers about the lack of faith when He returns the second time for the saints. Luke 18:8, questions if He will find faith or not. Sadly, the answer is very little!

Our understanding of prophecy or the ability to prophesy is only as good as our faith to believe God's Word and insight given through the Holy Spirit (Romans 12:6). Lukewarmers and backsliders do not posses the faith necessary, or the teaching of the obedience to God's Word to properly understand end time events. They will become part of the Great Christian Falling Away. Matthew 24:10, describes in the first half of Daniel's 70th week, many or over 50% of today's Christians will abandon their Christian faith. They will hate, backbite, scoff, and betray the Spirit-filled Christians.

Christians must understand the word "apocalypse" has a two fold meaning in this test cycle as time races toward its conclusion called the second advent and Daniel's 1335th day. First, the Spirit-filled Christian will understand, follow Christ, and rebuke the European World Antichrist Spirit-led government - MNO (Daniel 11:32). Second, the backslidden lukewarmer (Revelation 3:14-22) will not understand and misinterpret the signs (unveiling) of God's wrath on a lukewarm compromising Church and disobedient world.

Blessed are those who can hold on to the teaching of the Bible and endure until Daniel's 1335th day (Daniel 12:12). These Saints will have truly understood and endured their test cycle to the end of the "apocalypse" of the last Generation from 97SRSP-CE until 106SRSP-S (slide rule positioning point, use for sequencing only).

Bob R. Short,
a servant messenger of Jesus Christ,
insight March 30, 1997, amen!

PATIENCE

Section 4-4

Listen to the world and all its ways.
You'll find what it sells never stays.
Man runs fast then he moves slow.
Always wondering where he may go.

Why do you wonder like so many do?
God loves you and His angels too.
Up on a hill so high and dry.
Man chases rainbows in the sky.

They want to be here, not satisfied there.
Patience my child, you know not where.
Are you like them, saying good-bye?
You must wake up and look God in the eye.

Then you know the first time that day.
He has control of your every way.
Give Him your all, the best you can do.
Cause God always takes care of you.

It's time to lie down and dream tonight,
for you will see God in His purest light.
Now you know why mans on the run
and why God sent His only Son!

Bob R. Short, 2-98

ARISE MICHAEL

Section 4-5

For the Chief Prince must arise to his feet and make ready
FOR THE FINAL BATTLE!
The Spirit of Christ Jesus, the Spirit of Prophecy inspired me to write:

The Spirit began telling me the story.

"I will tell you an end time story about a Seamen and Michael that's happening this very evening."

"There once was a man who sailed the high seas under the guidance of the Good Overseer. This seaman lay claim to new land and became a landowner along with his Mother and others. His Mother became proud of him. The people built walls around part of the land. They honored their Overseer and erected a building housing a huge fiery furnace. The fiery furnace reminded them of their destructive fate if they forsook the Overseer. In their hearts, the Overseer's Son became the head Cornerstone of the building with the fiery furnace. They worshipped and obeyed the Overseer and followed the Cornerstone. Later the landowner died and his family and friends followed in his footsteps. They expanded the farmland. They built many watchtowers and honored the power of the Cornerstone whereby prospering greatly.

The Mother became upset when she lost her inheritance from the new rebellious landowners. These tenants were not children any more, but men, and demanded more freedom from their Mother. They wanted to promote the Cornerstone and warn about the wrath, which happens to those who do not honor Him. The Mother gave in after a fight. These new landowners did what looked right in the eyes of the Overseer. The new owners were more aggressive than the first and improved their inherence by quickly expanding their territory. They placed additional walls around the entire kingdom. Later they protected the rights of the chosen people who lived far away. In doing this, the overseer greatly rewarded and protected them.

The self-generation of I and me, have lulled some Christians into feeling safe and comfortable.

This is when the Church and its nation are in the greatest danger.

Now calculate this - - -

From their Mother's sorrows until the eleventh hour will be three and a half generations.

Soon some wicked heirs seized the good fruit of this great land and began throwing it to the ground to rot. Earlier the Overseer commanded the good tenants to keep the nation a follower of the Cornerstone. Sadly, they became lazy, fearful and did little. These wicked heirs made up their own laws and decrees. They called them righteous, selling their wicked ideas to the world. By doing this, they unknowingly removed the Cornerstone of stability holding the foundation to the house containing the huge fiery furnace of destruction. The furnace slowly ruptured and began to leak a stream of fiery hot stench smelling lava. The land burned and eroded away yet the wicked were blind and could not see. They mocked the old ways, which made the land great and began following their new idols.

The compromising farmers now produce little good fruit. These wicked tenants successfully convinced many good farmers to grow half tainted fruit and half good fruit. This way there has been an expanded market place. They can sell to the good as well as the wicked. This caused the half compromising farmer to become rich and in need of nothing. Everyone perceives others to be equally happy for there is no more conflict in selling either fruit. The farmer tells both the lukewarm or wicked buyer an answer their itching ears want to hear. He sells them half rotten and half good food for their empty stomachs.

This method promises, more conveniences, offers better security and is less offensive to the buyer. This results in more profitable to the seller. What a deal, for good and evil are deluded into the same non-offensive fruit. Peace, safety and less confrontation shall now come to the land. The wicked will not understand their short-lived success. But the wise understand, for they see Truth coming on the horizon and are making preparations for the impending disaster."

"Finally the Overseer will return with the Cornerstone He found abandoned alongside a desolate road. He has been angry at the once great nation and the farmers he commanded to keep the nation follower's of the Cornerstone. He will demand the Cornerstone be honored and put in its rightful place." The Spirit asked me, "what will the Overseer do to those in charge of the land and its people if they do not obey Him?"

I said, "You must tell me for I am unclear about the complete outcome."

The Spirit went on, "The Overseer will offer two options to the people He put in charge of keeping the nation righteous. First, **a blessing** or second, **a curse:**

THE BLESSING

Repent, put a righteous King over the land again and accept the Cornerstone back. The Overseer will protect and heal the land if this is done. Even with this blessing, many compromising farmers will fall. For righteous are the judgments of the Cornerstone.

THE CURSE

Keep a detestable king who does not protect My people Israel, and reject the Cornerstone and receive a curse. For those on whom the Cornerstone falls will be smashed to pieces. If the kingdom rejects the Cornerstone, this will force the Overseer to turn His back to the Nation. His protection will be removed from this once great land. Then the evil forerunners to the hour of trial and the little horn will cause astonishing devastation to the kingdom for a little while. Many will fall to their death.

The loins of Michael, the Great Prince must awaken or suffer great destruction. At the time of the end, this land will become the loins of the Great Prince, the Archangel Michael. The Most Holy calls for the court to set and the man of intrigue along with his armies will be completely destroyed by the Cornerstone and His faithful followers. After this, Michael will completely arise up on his feet dancing and with the power of righteous destruction dazzling off his fingertips. He will fight along side the mighty Lion to destroy the balance of people on earth who did not follow the Cornerstone. What a dreaded day this will be for some will be taken up in the clouds of salvation while others will be left behind to be smashed to pieces."

Michael will completely arise up on his feet dancing and with the power of righteous destruction dazzling off his finger tips.

"Now know and understand this riddle called

MIDNIGHT"

the Spirit said.

"There are four numbers
- SO EVERYONE CAN VIEW -
- they set the clock -
NO OTHERS WILL DUE!"

When the bells toll at midnight, the righteous will walk on the ashes of these unbelieving, lukewarm and disobedient people."

"This ends the matter, say no more, for many will run looking for knowledge only to find fear and death," the Spirit said to me. "As for you My messenger, go your way till the appointed time I've decreed to you, then arise to the task at hand. Quickly take this message of repentance or destruction to the lukewarm Churches and World. For it's past 11:45 PM this evening!"

Prophesied
December 17, 1996
by Bob R. Short, a servant
messenger to the Churches,
and witness to the World
Governments.

THE LAST GENERATION

Section 4-6

GENESIS 3:16 to REVELATION 3:16 and THEIR EFFECT ON THE LAST GENERATION

The Spirit of Christ Jesus, The Spirit of Prophecy instructed me to prophesy the following message. There are sixteen chapter 3's, verse 16's in the Bible that Christians must understand during the last generation. Three of the sixteen verses are considered critical in waking up Christians, their nations, and especially America. The three are: Genesis 3:16, (disobedient women); 1 John 3:16, (cowardly Christian men); Revelation 3:16, (lukewarmers and their Churches). Christians and their Churches, heed this warning message, repent and take action.

This insight covers Genesis 3:16 and ends with Revelation 3:16. From front to back, Christians will see God is angry or disappointed much of the time at the people he loves (Jews first, then Christians). God became angry because mankind has not followed His instructions and commands. It must be understood end time warnings are accelerated (as birthing pains increase) in discussions concerning; disobedience, evil, lukewarmness, curses, delusions, pouring out of the Holy Spirit, Satan's evil deception, verses God's righteous power and judgments. For instance when talking about Satan's seductive deception, more people will be tricked into believing lies, false security and wrong thinking during the last generation than previous generations. Now the sixteen verses affecting the whole world and end time Christians.

OLD TESTAMENT – 3:16 Verses

GENESIS 3:16: *"To the woman he* (God) *said, 'I will greatly increase your pains in childbearing; with pain you will give birth to children. Your desire will be for your husband, and he will rule over you.'"* The passage the Spirit highlighted in my mind to cause increased end time confusion; *"your desire will be for your husband."* Translated for endtimes, non-Christian worldly women and lukewarm Christian women increasingly want to take over God ordained male positions. The Spirit brings some examples to mind; military warrior position, law-enforcement agencies front line contact situation, leadership role in the family, overseers and pastoral roles in Churches. Women must be made aware of God's testing through the 3:16 curse. Women must overcome this curse as part of their test by first understanding and then through obedience, prayer, and petition to God.

Since World War I, some unsuspecting nations promoted the 3:16 curse. Today's international news media, radio, TV, Hollywood's movies and lukewarm Christians are promoting God's 3:16 curse to the world. The reason equates to money. They justified why women ought to fill men's traditional Biblical roles through their biased and very profitable movies, radio, TV, media coverage and lukewarm, compromising sermons.

God promises the last generation of men a helping hand in the last paragraph of the Old Testament: *"See, I will send you* (men) *the prophet Elijah before that great and dreadful day of the Lord comes. He will turn the hearts of the fathers to their children, and the hearts of the children to their fathers;"* God promises to bring some fathers and children back into loving and understanding each other (Luke 1:17). Christians can see the Spirit of Elijah appearing before the Lord's return with authority today bringing large numbers of men together in football stadiums, churches, and other places to study and repent to God and their families (children) across America and other nations. He is preparing the elect for the return of the Lord.

Yet, there is no promise to the women who live in the last generation that such a prophet will return to help them wake up from their disobedience, and God's curses and delusions. I asked the Spirit why, for this did not seem fair to me. The Spirit answered: "First, today's women already have the equivalent of wisdom and obedience of Elijah here on earth in the form of older women (60 years of age or older). Secondly, the younger women lack understanding about God's preprogrammed test through the Geneses 3:16 curse. Thirdly, younger women will rarely listen to older Spirit-filled women's wisdom on this topic any more. Consequently, they have no idea how to offset the curse through obedience and prayer to the Lord God.

If you were doing something wrong in God's eye, and your understanding of the Bible was *tweaked* off center, would you want someone to tell you about it or just overlook it and let you get blind sided on judgment day by Jesus Christ, the righteous judge?

Older women are Biblically entitled the right to instruct younger women in the Church on this topic.

Many women are not interested in offsetting the 3:16 curse for it has brought them fame, financial stability, independence and power. To obey God's word could mean giving up worldly gains such as the love of money and power, which generally promotes disobedience. Older women must also teach women with no husband or children the 3:16 curse so they may offset the ill effects of this test (program built into their test cycle) by God. Older women are Biblically entitled the right to instruct younger women in the Church on this topic. However, we generally find the opposite happening in the USA. The younger more attractive women are taking over leadership and instructing roles in Christian Churches, radio and TV. Because of the misunderstanding of God's 3:16 curse, the USA is being brought down to the depths of disaster. Reverse thinking flourishes as the order of the day and Biblical stability has been sacrificed.

In Titus 2:4-5, we see God very clearly ordaining the older women to teach the younger women. *"Then they* (older women) *can train the younger women to love their husbands and children* (if there's a husband or children), *to be self-controlled and pure, to be busy at home, to be kind, and to subject to their husbands, so that no one will malign the word of God;"* This training by older women is not to promote leadership roles over men. The Bible is very clear about this subject. Women are under the leadership of the male elders in the Church (Titus 2:3). The Spirit said to me; "Let us study eight Godly points in Titus 2:4-5 in light of the modern-day women approximately 59 years of age and younger."

EIGHT GODLY POINTS FOR WOMEN TO UNDERSTAND AND OBEY. TAUGHT BY OLDER WOMEN

TITUS 2:4-5

1. Did you notice it did not say: To hate, lord over, or run your husbands down; it says love your husbands.

2. Did you notice it did not say: Abandon children or kill babies in the womb; it says, love your children.

3. Did you notice it did not say: Be uninhibited, dress lustfully, and act selfish; it says, be self-controlled.

4. Did you notice it did not say: Disobey God, lie around with women, or other men; it says, keep yourself pure.

5. Did you notice it did not say: Put your job first and neglect home duties; it says, home duties come first.

6. Did you notice it did not say: Be a grouch, unforgiving, and unbearable; it says, be kind.

7. Did you notice it did not say: Rebuke, argue, and back talk to your husband; it says, be subject to him.

8. Did you notice it did not say: Your actions should harm God's Word; it says, follow the Word of God.

Let us look at a reason these eight points are not being taught to the younger women in many Churches.

Teaching the 3:16 curse could cause a loss in Church membership.

Teaching the 3:16 curse would cause a loss in Church membership in many Churches. Consequently, the pastor's superior will be disappointed. Even worse, a loss of membership equals reduced revenues. Churches in debt eventually may have to close or place themselves as slaves to the loan officer.

Christians must understand godly families, Disciple Nations, Christian Churches, and the body of Christ are under the same God-given leadership flow chart. *"Now I* (Paul) *want you to realize that the head of every man is Christ and the head of the woman is man, and the head of Christ is God"* (1 Corinthians 11:3). God is first in order of command, Jesus Christ second, men third, women fourth, and children fifth. Discourse abounds when this passage is rearranged and broken. Until Christians truly repent, understand, and adhere to this God-given Order (leadership authority) then America will be in trouble along with the world. God's preprogramed testing sent as a 3:16 curse will increasingly cause problems because the Spirit-filled Christian, worldly, and lukewarmer are moving farther apart in their basic beliefs and thinking.

ECCLESIASTES 3:16: *"And I* (Solomon) *saw something else under the sun: In the place of judgment-wickedness was there, in the place of justice-wickedness was there."* The last generation has been drawn by worldly lust and deceived by Satan's seductive deception until they believe the lie of; European led World Government's promotion of false security, false peace, false financial wellness, debatable wickedness, and every kind of evil. Justice will be trampled in the dust and right thinking deemed preposterous even by many lukewarm Christians.

ISAIAH 3:16: The Lord says, *"The women of Zion are haughty, walking along with outstretched necks, flirting with their eyes, tripping along with mincing steps, with ornaments jingling on their ankles."* Since Adam and Eve, mankind has disobeyed God. The end time women will get progressively worse in God's eyes. This is credited to fleshly desires, the draw of worldly lust, Satan's seducing deception, God's curses, and His end time program called great delusion. These five different forces are end time programmed tests to see who will wake up, obey, and pass. Most will not listen to the older women's Biblical teachings concerning self-control and obedience to God's Word (Titus 2:4-5). Some reasons emerge as an answer. Older women are not teaching it, refuse to teach it or afraid to teach it. Others have been stopped from teaching it.

Many modern-day women have flirting eyes, mincing steps, inviting body language, and wear revealing clothes to attract attention, whereby receiving what her worldly needs demand. Increasingly some have lusted after unnatural sexual desires of other women and demanded this sin be called legal and normal. She has itching ears to listen and gives her vote to those who fulfill what she demands society to do. Yet power, independence, self-gratification, love of money, and greed outweigh obedience to God. Sadly, many have gone beyond the point of return and have placed many tripping stones for men and women to fall.

JEREMIAH 3:16: *"In those days* (last generation 1967 A.D. to 106SRSP-S), *when your* (Jews) *numbers have increased greatly in the land* (Israel), *declares the Lord, men will no longer say, the ark of the covenant of the Lord. It will never enter their minds or be remembered; it will not be missed, nor will another one be made."* The Jews are returning to Israel just as Jeremiah prophesied. The last generation of Jewish people will be so engrossed in the new world government as their savior to bring them peace and security, they will forget some of the laws and commands of God. The world has not been impressed with the ark. The world thinks it has obtained the status of god through European world cooperation and military power to secure global peace and security. In essence, deceptive world leaders now think they control the world's destiny. Why does the European world government need Israel's outdated God who has promised to destroy their beautiful man-made world. Using deception the new gods promise global peace, security, and the ability to offer its citizens what they want not what they need. So many will forget the Ark and what it stood for to follow the Final Antichrist.

LAMENTATIONS 3:16: *"He* (God) *has broken my* (Jeremiah) *teeth with gravel; he has trampled me in the dust."* The misled Jews and the lukewarm Christians are going to be left in the dust of God's fury only to be trampled by the European worldly power. God will move as fast as the crackling of windblown fire. The end will come quickly and the lukewarm Churches are not ready. They judge themselves righteous before God's throne so why worry about the Tribulation Period or teach anything about it.

Left, 4-6-0 - Italy, Pompeii - Town Square and Business District: The citizens of Pompeii perished because they had little warning of the dangerous hot ash Vesuvius was spewing out that covered their city in minutes. What is Christians excuse today for lack of knowledge about preparing for the flood of end time events, which will overwhelm some of them? The Bible has warned us for years these end time days were coming. Some signs of endtimes are wars, terrorism, and rumors of wars.

The threat of war is real and has been on the horizon with political Islam's vision of overtaking Africa, Europe, and the world. Destroying America and Israel has been fixed in Muslin minds. In many parts of the world, nations and their citizens are oblivious to the threat of political fundamentalism in Islam.

Do you know what changes are necessary in your life to please God after reading these sixteen 3-16's verses? Another basic question, do you know your end time Christian assignment? Sadly, many Christians do not. Their cities will look like this picture of Pompeii - in total ruin, if they do not act. Part of Christians assignment must be to firmly resist the European led world government and the spread of political Islam.

EZEKIEL 3:16: *"At the end of seven days the word of the Lord came to me* (Ezekiel - watchman)*;"* Christians are watchmen like Ezekiel. We must spread the Good News message of Jesus Christ around the world while helping and protecting the Jewish people. Yet, any nation can not effectively accomplish this if their nation is destroyed. Therefore, the first duty of Christians must be to teach and keep their nation following Christ teaching. European Christians began to fail their duty and the baton was passed to the Americas. The USA has not learned by Europe's mistakes. Unfortunately, the Church's failure to hold the USA to Christian values has lead to the candlestick moving eastward to Asia and other countries around the world. They seem to have sincere zeal, real missionary growth, and stand firm against Christian persecution when witnessing to others. Because the Church has been failing in America, the Lord God is bringing judgments against America.

DANIEL 3:16: *"Shadrach, Meshach and Abednego replied to the king, 'O Nebuchadnezzar, we do not need to defend ourselves before you in this manner.'"* It shall be important for the Spirit-filled Christians to understand they are not required to defend themselves to the world concerning their belief in the God of Shadrach, Meshach and Abednego. We like Jesus must become stiff-necked against tolerating anti Christian religious discrimination.

JOEL 3:16: *"The Lord will roar from Zion and thunder from Jerusalem; the earth and the sky will tremble. But the Lord will be a refuge for his people, a stronghold for the people of Israel."* By the end of Daniel's 1335th day Jesus Christ will complete the six-day sabbatical test of the seven spirits on earth. Jesus has destroyed all lukewarmers, evildoers, unbelievers, the vile, the murderers, the sexually immoral, those who practice magic arts (drugs and alcohol), the idolaters, all liars, and Christian cowards. He is truly a refuge for His people.

HABAKKUK 3:16: *"I heard and my heart pounded, my lips quivered at the sound; decay crept into my bones, and my legs trembled. Yet I will wait patiently for the day of calamity to come on the nation invading us."* The last generation will experience seeing two different major attacks on Israel and Jerusalem. First attack begins in the year 99SRSP-CE when Russia and her hordes make the fatal mistake of warring from the North to attack Israel.

The second shall be the alliance of Nations in the world represented by the Millenium Nations Organized = MNO = 666. They gather close to Jerusalem to make war with Jesus in the Air. Earlier prophesied as the battle of Armageddon and will occur in 106SR-SP-S. Any Christian's nations left at this time will be helping Jesus. This represents what is left of North and South America and a few others nations.

IT APPEARS TO ME, **what a lukewarmer learns from** THE BIBLE AND HISTORY, **is they never seem to learn from** THE BIBLE AND HISTORY.

Above, 4-6-1- Israel - River Jordan: Jesus was baptized by John the Baptist. Christians should do the same after committing their lives to Christ. Salvation only comes if there has been true heart-felt repentance. Well-crafted sinner's prayers have been introduced into some Churches and Christian media to deceive the unsaved into making quick salvation decision. Salvation without repentance has been introduced to increase membership. By not offending anyone, the opportunity to be truly sorry for their past sins, sets up false-hope. Many Christians have been deceived by this practice. Without heart-felt repentance (Luke 13:3), what is a person being saved from and to what? Repentance moves Jesus to negate the past sins and then He opens the door to a new and exciting life with Him.

THE NEW TESTAMENT 3:16 VERSES

LUKE 3:16: *"John answered them all, 'I baptize you with water. But one more powerful than I will come, the thongs of whose sandals I am not worthy to untie. He will baptize you with the Holy Spirit and with fire.'"* John the Baptist was the greatest person to walk the earth up until this statement. He said he was not worthy to untie Jesus Christ's shoestring. The point to be understood is found in Joel 2:28, and that is it prophesies God will pour out His Spirit on all people. The scripture does not say the Spirit will fall only on the Jews and Christians but **All People.** However, most people have and will reject the Holy Spirit and not believe that Jesus Christ is the true Messiah of the world. America does not fear the Lord God anymore.

We will all enter into heaven or hell on judgment day. Each of us will stand before the Lord God and experience our works tested with fire, or as some say, be baptized with fire. The angel from the altar of fire will pour the testing ladle of fire over each person and their works. If they and their works burn, they have lost their rewards. If they and their works do not burn, they stand on solid ground. Then the book of life shall be opened and if their name is not found in it (blotted out), they will be tossed into the lake of fire. Each person has a choice here on earth as to whether he will pass the test of initiation into Heaven or the Lake of fire (hell).

JOHN 3:16: *"For God so loved the world that he gave his one and only Son, that whoever believes in him shall not perish but have eternal life."* This must be the good news message for Christians to take to the whole world. Sadly, the world will not listen but reject this message. The Bible teaches if the world hates Christians, remember they hated Jesus first. Hate for the Christians and Jews will be greatly increased in the last generation. Christians owe no one an apology for their beliefs for other religions are wrong. The followers of other religions are going to Hell. God sent His Son as the lamb in this passage to save the world but in the last generation, Jesus will become a mighty Lion to destroy the disbelievers. It must be our duty as Spirit-filled Christians to wake up as many lukewarmers and unbelievers as we can. The number to be awakened or saved is up to us because there is no set number assigned to it. However, there are a set number of Jews and Christians to be killed (Revelation 6:11). Revelation 13:9-10 states; the Beast's kingdom will be controlled by the Antichrist and Satan who are given authority to put a set number of Christians and Jews into captivity or kill.

Endtimers must start thinking more in terms of salvation from the spiritual second death and less of the physical first death.

There is an eternal blessing or curse within John 3:16. A dreadful hidden warning is stealthily placed inside the literal reading of this verse. It is directed to the Lukewarm and backslidden Christians. Woe to them for 2 Peter 2:20-21 says; it shall be better for unbelievers who never knew Jesus on the day of judgment, than lukewarmers or backsliders. John 3:16 promise is, *"have eternal life."* It does not say whether you will spend it, in Hell or Heaven. Here in lies each person's responsibility.

Spirit-filled Christians must walk in the uncomfortable zone.
When Christians spread the Good News,
they will be challenged and therefore enter this zone.

REVELATION 3:15: *"I wish you were either one* (hot Christian) *or the other* (cold sinner)*!"* Why does Jesus wish lukewarmers should have stayed sinners rather than turn from Him. Because He knows the terrible consequence promised in John 3:16 for lukewarmness or backsliding. Sinners' or unbelievers' punishment will be the second death in the lake of fire (Revelation 20:14) and that's the end of the matter. But, if a person accepts Jesus and then becomes lukewarm or backslidden they will spend eternal torment in the lake of fire called Hell. The difference being eternal torment in hell verses the second death in the lake of fire, which ends the matter. These two time dimensions cannot be properly explained in our earth understanding. In either case, it will be separation from God Almighty. What a price to pay for disobedience. Woe to the backsliders and lukewarmers, for they fill America Churches!

2 CORINTHIANS 3:16: *"But whenever anyone turns to the Lord, the veil is taken away."* This shall be one of the Christian's offensive weapons to fight Satan's deception and offset world hate for Christians. We receive a (free) gift of the Holy Spirit when we turn to the Lord God by accepting Jesus Christ as our personal Savior. If we continue to walk, in the light the Spirit will give us power to reach up into God's mind for understanding (1 Corinthian 2:6-16). We can understand God's will for our lives, scripture and the future through insight, visions, and prophecies. The world does not understand Christians and our beliefs. We represent folly to their superior intellect and world government thinking.

2 THESSALONIANS 3:16: *"Now may the Lord of peace himself give you peace at all times and in every way. The Lord be with all of you."* God does not appoint Christians to wrath, but there are times we must withstand and endure perilous times. The last generation will see and experience increased evil and destruction such as the world has never experienced. Through this end time calamity the Lord has given a quiet peace to each Spirit-filled Christian. Endtimers must start thinking more in terms of salvation from the spiritual second death and less of the physical first death.

Our hopes are in Jesus Christ as our Rock. God has given Satan much of the authority over the first death on earth during the last generation but Jesus Christ has total controlling power over the second death.

Let us analyze 1 John 4:4, during the tribulation period. It states; *"Because the one* (Jesus) *who is in you is greater than the one* (Satan) *who is in the world."* There is a great warning to lukewarmers and backsliders in this scripture; generally speaking, God's protection can be validated only when thinking in terms of the second death not the first. Because some are appointed to captivity, others to be beheaded, others to fight, others to preaching, and others to whatever our assigned task of hard work and suffering will be. Christians are called to suffer, as part of our test! Suffering has not been a popular subject in lukewarm churches.

Below, 4-6-2- Israel - Church of St. John the Baptist: We see the alleged spot where St. John the Baptist was born. Everyone starts his or her test cycle with proper instructions. John fulfilled his duties and passed the test. Before we came down into our designed test scenario God programmed (Ephesians 2:10) our souls to do good works to take care of what He gives us. Once we are here, we quickly discover we are in a war about right and wrong Christian values. John stood up for what is right, more importantly Christians cannot afford to be neutral? Spirit-filled Christians must walk in the uncomfortable zone.

Above, 4-6-3- Greece - Ancient Corinth - Pagan Temple of Apollo: Ancient Corinth reminded me of modern and enlightened America. Close by the Temple was the agora (market area). In the Agora area, protruded a Bema (stage or platform) where St. Paul spoke to the Corinthians. God opened my eyes to St. Paul's frustrations. Many of there people were spiritual, but most acted like heathens. Jesus prophesied that just before His return most Christians would act like the ancient Corinthians or in His words, lukewarm.

2 TIMOTHY 3:16: *"All Scripture is God-breathed and is useful for teaching, rebuking, correcting and training in righteousness."* God's word through scripture teaches Christians to become righteous. God communicates and listens to the prayers of the righteous. He listens to only true repentance prayer from lukewarmers and backsliders who fill our present-day Churches. America is losing God's protective covering because of the decrease in righteous Christians and increase in lukewarmers in our Churches. Some Christians disbelieve 2 Timothy 3:16 and live by their own self-guided lifestyle instead of by the word of God.

1 JOHN 3:16: *"This is how we know what love is: Jesus Christ laid down his life for us. And we ought to lay down our lives for our brothers."* This scripture hits at the heart of the problem for lukewarmers, do nothings, and cowardly Christian men during the last generation. Some will watch their brothers in Christ fall or be unnecessarily persecuted and not lift a finger to help.

Revelation 21:8 describes what could happen to Christian men in the last generation who do nothing to help their persecuted brothers. They may be declared cowardly and their place will be in the fiery lake of burning sulfur.

The protect mode has been given to godly men (Genesis 2:15) not to women. Men must be Spirit-filled who strive to protect our fellow Christians and Jews against persecution. Through cowardly acts, men will save their own lives today. More importantly, on judgment day they could lose their souls in the second death. Reason: They are judged cowardly before the throne of God. Some brave Christian men may lose their lives here on earth trying to help fellow Christians or protecting their Church houses from being closed by an oppressor. Later they will receive favorable judgment over the second death and will live.

REVELATION 3:16: *"So, because you are lukewarm - neither hot nor cold - I am about to spit you out of my mouth."* I shall not comment on this verse for the entire book of prophecies has been directed toward waking up and saving at least 34% of the lukewarmers who can be saved. Most lukewarm Christians will be spit out into the tribulation period to be rebuked and disciplined (Revelation 3:19). Most (over 50%) will fall never to recovered (Matthew 24:10). Make ready for battle my solid and righteous Spirit-filled Christians for we are the Lord God's warriors and He shall be our Commander in Chief. I pray for peace in Jerusalem and for the Lord God to come quickly! Amen and Amen.

HOW TO PRAY
IN THE TRIBULATION PERIOD

What I am about to discuss shall be of a critical nature to Christians in the tribulation period. Christians are taught in Matthew 5:44, during the Church Age to pray for their enemies. The tribulation period starts on or about the sequencing point of Saturday 99.9.25SRSP-CE. When this occurs we are no longer in the Church Age because it has ended. We are now entering the last seven years of Jewish time which must be fulfilled before Jesus' second return on or before Saturday, 106.9.23SRSP-S. In Old Testament or Jewish time, God's people fought against and prayed for the destruction of their enemies (eye for an eye). In the tribulation period (Jewish Time), Saints are taught to do the same.

Why you ask do we pray for our enemies during the Church age and against them in the tribulation period. We can find a clue in Revelation 8:3-6; "... *He* (angel) *was given much incense to offer, with the prayers of all the saints, on the golden altar before the throne. The smoke of the incense, together with the prayers of the saints, went up before God from the angel's hand. Then the angel took the censer, filled it with fire from the altar, and hurled it on the earth."* Saints must pray against their enemies in the tribulation period. The angel at the altar receives Christian's prayers and adds incense (power) from Jesus as mediator. It's forwarded to God to add judgment-making power to the Spirit-filled Christian's prayers for vengeance against the evildoers. These ultra energized powerful prayers will be sent back to earth as weapons of destruction against our enemies who persecute Christians and Jews. **Prayer cannot be over estimated as our most powerful offensive weapon against Satan and our enemies.**

Insight prophesied, November, 1996 by Bob R. Short,
a servant messenger of our
Lord and Savior Jesus Christ.

DECREE ISSUED TO:

REBUILD JEWISH TEMPLE ON THE TEMPLE MOUNT JERUSALEM

Section 4-7

I shall write, interpret and
prophesy to the Jewish people
and their leaders these
instructions from G-d
through insight received (8-1996) from
Ezekiel 43:6-12.

While the man was standing beside me, I (Ezekiel) ***heard someone speaking to me from inside the temple. He*** (our coming Messiah – Jesus Christ) ***said: "Son of man*** (watchmen per Ezekiel 33:6-7), ***this is the place*** (Temple Mount in Jerusalem) ***of my throne and the place for the soles of my feet. This is where I*** (coming messiah – Jesus Christ) ***will live among the Israelites forever. The house of Israel will never again defile my holy name – neither they*** (first – Israel currently letting Moslems control the temple mount instead of Israel and second – Israel allowing Millennial Nations Organized (MNO) in second half of Daniel's 70th week to take control of temple mount) ***nor their kings*** (Moslems first, MNO second) ***– by their prostitution and the lifeless idols of their kings*** (Moslems first, and the ten kings of the MNO second) ***at their high places*** (place of authority -headquarters).

When they (Moslems - first, MNO - second) ***placed their threshold next to my*** (Coming Messiah - Jesus Christ) ***threshold and their doorposts beside my doorposts, with only a wall between me and them, they defile my holy name by their detestable practices. So I*** (Coming Messiah – Jesus Christ) ***destroyed them*** (first the Moslems in 1991 to 97-99SRSP-CE per Daniel 8:2-7, and second the MNO 106SRSP-S - per Daniel 11:45) ***in my anger. Now let them put away from me their prostitution*** (first; this is G-d's authority for Israel to destroy the Moslem Dome of the Rock and rebuild the Jewish Temple. Once the Jewish sacrifices start on, 100.5.6SRSP-S, (slide rule sequencing point see glossary) do not let the world leader of the MNO take over the temple mount) ***and the lifeless idols*** (The MNO's Image of the Beast or Internet Web of Deceit') ***of their kings, and I*** (coming Messiah – Jesus Christ) ***will live among them*** (Jewish people) ***forever.***

"Son of man (watchmen per Ezekiel 33:6-7), ***describe the temple*** (Jewish Temple per Ezekiel chapters 40-48) ***to the people of Israel, that they may be ashamed of their sin*** (cowardly leadership does not have the faith in G-d's protection if they were to remove the Moslem Dome on the Rock and rebuild the rightful prophesied end time Jewish Temple).

☞ Note: The Temple referred to here is the Temple I prophesied in section 2-12. It will be built after the USA, Israel, England, and others engage in and win a nuclear war against Russia, Arabs nations, and others. This Temple cannot be identified as Solomon's Temple, Herod's Temple, or any known Temple because the descriptions in Ezekiel do not match. ✂

God's ultimate task for you during endtimes is not comfort, but you discovering your Godly assignment and then acting on it!

LET THIS DECREE
BE KNOW
THROUGHOUT
ISRAEL:

Since the leadership of Israel is branded cowards in G-d's sight: I, a Witness to the world governments shall prophesy the following instructions to the Jewish People of Israel:

G-d will raise up a man of mystery who will be known as Amon Amon and destroy the Moslem Dome on the Rock somewhere about the year 99SRSP-CE when Russia marches south per Ezekiel 38 and 39.

This war makes way for Daniel's 70th week to start, which will be seven years of Jewish and Christian persecution. The MNO calls for world peace and offers security. Then the MNO leader (Antichrist) over the newly unified ten-kingdom world federation (Daniel 2:40-43) **will authorize the rebuilding of the Jewish Temple. The Jewish sacrifices will start as I have prophesied in the** (WAKE UP CALL PROPHECIES, Issue-1) **on 100.5.6SRSP-S.** (NOTE: S.R. = positioning points on G-d's end time slide rule, see section 2-8.)

Above, 4-7-1- Israel, Jerusalem - Temple Mount: This was a very moving moment for me, as I walk the Temple Mount realizing some day in the millenium we will visit the King of kings, and L-rd of L-rds here. He will be here in His prophesied Temple and He will be our G-d and we will be His people.

Let them (Israel) ***consider the plan*** (Ezekiel chapters 40-48), ***and if they are ashamed of all they have done*** (first; not removing the Moslem Dome on the Rock after they took Jerusalem in 1967, and second; allowing the Antichrist or leader over the MNO to move into the rebuilt Jewish temple during the middle of Daniel's 70th week [Daniel 9:27]), ***make known to them the design of the temple – its arrangement, its exits, and entrances – its whole design and all its regulations and laws. Write these down before them so that they may be faithful to its design and follow all its regulations.***

"This is the law of the temple: All the surrounding area on top of the mountain (currently defiled due to lack of Jewish control) ***will be Most Holy.*** (Yet the leadership of Israel is cowardly and lacks the faith in G-d's protection for following G-d's instruction through the Prophet Ezekiel.) ***Such is the law of the temple.***

BOB R. SHORT, A Witness to the world governments for our L-rd and Savior JESUS CHRIST, Insight received 8 -1996

LET THIS DECREE
BE KNOW
THROUGH OUT ISRAEL:

G-d will raise up a man of mystery who will be known as Amon Amon and destroy the Moslem Dome on the Rock somewhere about the year 99SRSP-CE when Russia marches south per Ezekiel 38 and 39.

DANIEL'S
FIRM RESISTANCE

(Daniel 11:32)
Section 4-8

The Spirit of Christ Jesus, the Spirit of Prophecy has moved me to write the following: I, Bob R. Short, a Witness, received this insight from May 1994 to June 1997.

Daniel 11:32: *"But the people who know their God will firmly resist him"* People, meaning; true Spirit-filled Christians and some Jews. The word Him in this verse refers to any spirit or leader who tries to control the world without the core values of Jesus Christ. Therefore, Christians must firmly resist the following:

1. Deceptive worldly spirit before the tribulation period starts. (Note; this world spirit started to grow after WW-I, with the birth of the League of Nations.)

2. The spirit of trickery in promoting safety and security through a European led world government (MNO).

3. World religion backed by the MNO, which promotes tolerance in all religions. For they say, "Who has the right to force their religion upon someone else for we all have the same creator? God manifests himself in all religions.

4. A smart-cashless society, which promotes the Internet Web of Deceit as a vehicle to trick people into becoming dependent on its deceptive benefits.

5. The peacemaking Antichrist (any leader who tries to control the world through an organization or alliance) in the first half of the tribulation period.

6. The Final Antichrist in the second half of the tribulation period who will be totally controlled by Satan himself."

Firmly resist - as I pondered the words firmly resist, I was moved to write:

Immovable faith to have loyal to Jesus Christ by improving daily toward being spotless, blameless and at peace with God before one stands before the Judgment Seat of Jesus Christ.

Solidly believing in the end time Biblical teachings, stubbornly question the deceptive European world spirit and the Antichrist himself, persistently applying pressure to the unbelieving world to accept the only way for eternal life with God has to be through repentance and His Son, Jesus Christ.

Unyielding belief in the Great Commission of Jesus Christ to set Christian goals to achieve His command, "make disciple nations".

Uncompromising position to rebuke, refuse, and publicly warn against the benefits of the European-style world government system of peace and security.

Relentless resistance to the World Wide Web of Deceit, marking smart cards, scanners, bracelets, implants, cashless society and a worldwide consumption tax to fund the ten-kingdom world federation (MNO).

Severely punish those countries, which lock into the Leopard Beast as described in the WAKE UP CALL PROPHECIES. Note: most of the severe punishment will be carried out by the United States military, plus some trade embargoes.

The United States will begin to listen to the wisdom of two men during the first half of the tribulation period. These two men become the Two Witnesses (Revelation 11:3-13) overlapping in the second half of the tribulation period. The USA will totally follow the advice of the Two Witnesses during the great tribulation period.

Below, 4-8-1- Italy, Rome - Roman Forum, Arch of Septimius Severus: The Arch dates to AD 203. The Temple of Saturn is represented by the columns in the background to the left. The Roman Forum was the place from which the world was ruled in its day. It will once again draw power away from the UN and build a European led world government (MNO). The power will shift from Europe to what is left of the Eagle with the Three Ugly Heads ruling from Jerusalem.

Roman Forum - Faustina Temple

Above, 4-8-2- Italy, Rome - Roman Forum - Faustina Temple: Look at the foundation of this building, it was strong and sturdy. Nevertheless, Rome still fell, just like the upcoming MNO Roman style world government will fall. The Roman Forum gives us a glimpse of the power of a world government. The upcoming MNO European Roman style world government will be a nightmare for North and South America. Have faith to warn others. The Bible instructs us to never follow a world government, which has denounced Jesus Christ as the head.

THE LEOPARD IS COMING!

THE LEOPARD IS COMING!

THE LEOPARD IS COMING!

This will be a fulfillment of Daniel 12:1, *"At that time Michael, the great prince who protects your people, will arise. There will be a time of distress such as has not happened from the beginning of nations until then."* (See Michael, the Bear and the Leopard Beast flip Chart, section 9-1)

The Christian body must wake up to the times we are living in and begin as birthing pains to fulfill Daniel's Firm Resistance as prophesied in the Bible. Daniel's time frame concerning firm resistance starts today and increases through the end of the tribulation period. We must start resisting the deceptive spirit, which promotes a world religion, government, language, smart money, smart marking ID's, laser scanners, and global consumption tax system.

Christians must emphatically increase the pressure to get out of world trade agreements, which will eventually develop, into the ten-kingdom world area government (MNO). This will inevitably isolate (Daniel 7:8) North and South America (three votes in world trade government — agreement) from the rest of the world (Daniel 7:8). Will the USA be ready to exist when it becomes isolated from the Leopard Beast? Are Christian Churches ready? The answer to both questions is no! For they are both not attuned to the end time days we are living in. The Bible teaches God Almighty will move like a flood at the end. Yet, Christians as a whole are not ready.

God Almighty will give authority to the Two Witnesses. They will lead America into inflecting destruction on the un-repenting world. This directive will be done by following the Great Commission of Jesus Christ, which says *"go make disciple nations"*. You will note Jesus' command didn't say go ask but He used the forceful word MAKE which in some cases can only be construed as a military term.

Naturally, the Body of Christ and the Two Witnesses will fail at completing the Great Commission of Jesus Christ for the Bible prophesies they will. Therefore, Jesus Christ Himself will have to return a second time as the Lion to save the Saints and destroy the unbelievers, the people who are destroying the world. **Therefore, Jesus will have to fulfill His Own Great Commission.** Praise be to God and His Son Jesus Christ. Amen. Bob R. Short, a Messenger to the Churches and Witness to the world governments for our Lord and Savior Jesus Christ. Insight from May 1994 to June 1997.

END TIME VISION ABOUT WARNING AN OLD LION, HER CUBS, THE EAGLE, and the Three Ugly Heads, while Michael begins to rise to his feet.

Section 4-9

The Word of the Lord came to me January 30, 2005, by way of the Spirit of Christ Jesus, the Spirit of Prophecy.

It inspired me, Bob R. Short, a Witness to the world governments, for our Lord and Savior Jesus Christ to prophesy in writing the following vision of warnings:

These decrees are against you, so consider the message carefully and understand the gravity of your future decisions as it relates to this vision:

"**Warn** the Royalty, Politicians, Religious Leaders and Elders and the people of the Old Lion, **this vision contains decrees issued to you from the beginning by the Sovereign Lord.** Religious Leaders and Elders listen to what I say! Hear this, all who live in the land! Pay close attention, oh Royal House and Politicians!

These decrees are against you, so consider the message carefully and understand the gravity of your future decisions as it relates to this vision:

Oh, proud and tired Old Lion, how I once stood by your grand side when you promoted the Word. Once you were great and mighty while following Me, The Almighty God. The world **trembled** at your presence and I was delighted in helping you, but power and authority has slowly been taken from you and given to your strongest Lion Cub.

Below, 4-9-1- England, London - The Great Churchill: During WW-II, a man rose to his feet to lead England to their finest hour. Sadly, he will be their last great hero. They have forsaken God, and turned their back on Him. After Gulf War-III (Ezekiel 38), they will fold and lose their backbone as a mighty nation. The tired Old Lion will crawl underneath the European led Leopard Beast for its peace and security. Will you ever wake up to your abominations?

There are few true statesmen left in western politics today. When they give warnings about foreign powers and ideologies with spiritual overtones taking over the USA or England, their message is rarely played on mainstream European led world news. It has been written Churchill warned parliament in 1932 about the difference between statesmanship and what was being said in the world of politics concerning the rise in power in Germany. He mentioned smooth talkers who uttered words to the people for their itching ears to hear. He was not popular when issuing these warnings. He warned England repeatedly until disaster struck. The people were more interested in the good life and the easy road to short-term security. They could have avoided much disaster by confronting the hard issue up front. God Almighty is warning you again, "Tired Old Lion and her cubs, disaster is in the wind, and you are not properly addressing the world issues." Conformable lifestyles have rotted you, tolerance has eroded your brain, and lack of censorship pertaining to abortion, homosexuality, and other non-individual rights has blinded you. You have chosen to deny the wisdom contained in Biblical principles and laws. Next is the Lord God's judgment on you!

Above, 4-9-2- England, London - London Bridge: We sang London Bridge came falling down as we walked and skipped across the bridge like two kids. We truly fell in love with England, yet we notice a lack of Christian values. For instance, in London, we could not tell any difference in the Lord's Day (Sunday) or any other day. Most were rushing around, busy making money, going back and forth from watching shows, theater and parties. The Old Lion will pay a huge price for this disobedience. London Bridge may come tumbling down in the future, because the Lord is withdrawing His power from England.

This Cub stood with Me but has become arrogant and recently found your wayward path. Therefore, decrees have been issued for his discipline and destruction will reach his shores. He must suffer a while to season his perseverance, change priorities, choose a different path and improve his overbearing character. Discipline will help the Cub quickly grow up independent and learn to fly like a Mighty Eagle. He will then join with neighbors, some of which are sincere and some not. I will give this Mighty Eagle a heart of a man to protect My people Israel because you, Old Lion, have become unworthy by abandoning Me. I, The Almighty Lord, will raise this Mighty Eagle and its neighboring nations up together on two feet like a Mighty Man. I will proclaim His name to be the Great Prince Michael, protector of Israel! There will be distress as never before. Take heed! **Decrees have been issued against every nation of the world! Repent!**

You say, "What have I done to deserve these judgments." I will say; "You did not listen for you were warned and failed to correct your disobedient course." You have not followed My command to keep your nation a disciple nation {Government, Laws and People} under the supervision of the True Rock.

You tell Me, "I am the proud and mighty Lion that has **roared loudly.** I have carried David's genealogy down through history for You. I deserve to hold the Rock until the King comes. But, this is what The Lord Almighty says: "I tell you your roar is gone. Thrones were put in place, and The Ancient of Days has taken His seat while the Court was set. Decrees have been issued against you and your arrogant pride. Therefore, David's genealogy in the Rock has already been taken from you. I have already given it to the prophesied King of king and Lord of lords worthy to be called the True and Mighty Rock. You have gone your own way disowning the Rock and disowning My Sabbath."

" I will stand with you through the war you are in (Gulf War II = Goat and Ram War) because of your past loyalty to Me. I will also be with you through the next dreaded and prophesied Gulf War III, nuclear holocaust with Russia and others (both wars were prophesied in 1994-95 in the Wake Up Call Prophecies, rough draft, issue-1).

You will courageously fight for Israel during this dreaded War. Your great City has been damaged. This is not what you wanted although I moved you to stand strong with your cubs and fight on My side (Israel). But now you have become weak hearted unwilling to fight such a battle again.

Therefore, after these two wars I shall back away from you and let you decide. You search for what you think is a more secure den than I can offer. This will be a grave error.

I hold some things against you: You have become a tired Old Lion after two wars and you will not stand with your cubs anymore. Will and perseverance have left you along with the ability to fight after that dreaded battle (Gulf War III). Some of your cubs along with others are standing lonely in the gap for God Almighty and the Great Prince Michael across the waters. They are trying to defend My Holy Name and the people of Israel against the Three Ugly Heads. But, unlike your forefathers you are turning cowardly and spineless in the face of great opposition. They were not afraid of war in My name, but you back away. You are torn between money, power, security, greed and other gods instead of following My Holy Commands. You have mistakenly chosen the former.

I decree as silver is melted in a furnace, so you will be melted into the Leopard Beast. You will speak for the Leopard from time to time. This will be counted against you since you have let many pagans with false gods into your midst. You lazy Old Lion, you follow them more than Me. You will be divided between the Great Prince Michael and the Three Ugly Heads. You mistakenly side with the last two Ugly Heads. You will cowardly watch and say little when the Great Prince Michael's three votes are removed from the world assembly. This is also counted against you.

I decree as silver is melted in a furnace, so you will be melted into the Leopard Beast.

You should go to your beginning for there your end will be properly understood. However, you go your own way. Your first love (God Almighty's Word) is behind you and you look to the Ugly Larger Head in the center {UN} for comfort. Sadly, the Old Lion will not find it anymore for it has disappeared before your very eyes. Then you search for relief from the Ugly Head on the right [Leopard Beast] but find no satisfaction. Out of desperation, you reach out to the Ugly Head on the left (large Iron Teeth Beast) only to be laughed at and ridiculed. You and the Leopard will then be forcibly dissolved like dirt into His (Final Beast) raging flooding river of violence for peace. I, The Almighty God have called you to sacrifice. You have already received your rewards for that. But, I demand obedience! Weep, you disobedient tired Old Lion for your days are numbered if you do not repent and come back to Me. You will then know I, the Lord, have poured My wrath out upon you."

The conversation with the Lord God suddenly stopped in the spirit of my mind. I said, "This vision is very upsetting to me Lord, for I have walked on the Lion's turf and enjoyed Her company and was welcomed by Her." I continued, "For the Lion has been friends and allies with America for years. She issued Your Holy Word to the world. In the past, she has sacrificed for You. Does this not count for something? Surely Lord, You could turn her back?"

The Almighty God answered me sternly, **"No!** She may never change her direction back to Me again for I am leaving that up to her now. She must prove herself. Whom I love, I discipline! She must blow the trumpet, sound the alarm, and let all who live in the land tremble, for the day of the Lord is coming! It is close at hand! For those who stand firm in the faith until their end will be saved. Repent and turn your heart back to Me, Old Lion, or your bones will crackle like fire consuming stubble! This ends the matter concerning the Old Lion. I will hear no more! Issue these decrees and Go your way until your appointed time. Remember to warn the others and do not delay for the time is near!"

I, Bob R. Short received this vision with great sadness and prophesied these decrees with fear and trembling between January 30, 2005 and February 7, 2005. I must follow God, not man's wishes, for I am His Witness to the world governments for our Lord and Savior Jesus Christ. I mailed to some government officials in the USA and England. Who knows, if you (the Lion and her Cubs) repent maybe God will relent His righteous fury and have pity?

Make it so Lord Jesus,
Amen, and Amen!
Bob R Short

143

THE LAND OWNER, His Shepherds and Their Flocks.

Section 4-10

Once upon a time, a Land Owner had many flocks of sheep in a pasture. The flocks were made up of loyalist, lukewarmers and unfaithful sheep. Many strayed from time to time. So, He appointed shepherds over each flock.

Some of the sheep wanted to go one way and others wanted to go another way by themselves. Others wanted to slip back and forth through a hole in the fence, which separated the good pasture and the bad pasture. The shepherds were told to unify and build the flocks per His righteous instructions regardless of the mix within the flocks.

The Land Owner knew from experience His shepherds must be moved from time to time, a lesson learned from His earlier experience in the pasture when the herd became restless. The shepherds became bored with the same spot in the pasture and demanded a new flock. This caused disruption in the pasture.

Some shepherds leave their flock assignment when pressured to change flocks. Other shepherds take part of their old flock with them to different parts of the pasture. This causes complete disorder in the original flock and there will be disruption for a time in producing good offspring because of loyalty to the old shepherd. The sheep are unhappy along with the Land Owner for they were trained to listen to the voice of the original shepherd!

More shepherds are assigned to a restless and bewildered flock, which has dwindled with orders to build the flock per His instructions back to expectation. The newly assigned shepherd quickly sees the restless and bewildered flock is having difficulty connecting with the outside world. The shepherd encourages them to reach out, with little success.

Therefore, he perceives the only logical answer to increasing the numbers would be to invite the worldly ways of the pasture into the flock. To accomplish this by going out in the world not to witness, but to bring the worldly props back onto his assigned spot in the pasture.

He immediately announces his new witnessing tools, such as sports complexes, gourmet coffee shops, inappropriate dancing women, dance hall music with Christian lyrics, inappropriate dress, theater tickets sold to the entertainment event, closing the sanctuary and honoring football events, money exchanger at many events giving favor to rich people in better seats, glorifying the entertainers more than the Land Owner, and the like. The world cannot see any difference between the shepherd's spot and the rest of the pasture. The Shepherd thinks, the Land Owner won't care if he compromises some points of His instruction because he claims the changes were only man made rules in the first place not God's. Furthermore, the Land Owner will be pleased with him for getting the numbers back up to expectations. He prides himself for the win-win negotiating with the world and the flock.

Above, 4-10-1 - Israel, Bethlehem, Church of the Nativity: Jesus was purported to have been born to the Virgin Mary under The High Altar which is over the grotto of the Nativity at the far end of the Church. The hole in the floor is a dig showing the floor of the original church with ancient mosaic paving. The Church is emphasized by the rows of powerful red-sandstone Corinthian columns.

Jesus said the Gates of Hell would not destroy the Church. Sadly, the Gates of Hell led by Satan have wrecked havoc on the modern end time Christian and their leaders. Today it would be frustrating to try to manage a Church as a pastor. He must try to keep order in the House, attendance at acceptable levels, pay the bills, compete with the increasingly competitive and hostile world and feed the flock. Then, here comes the Wake Up Call Prophecies to challenge the lukewarm Churches. It will stir much debate, scare some people and bring unrest into a somewhat tranquil and lukewarm environment. Lukewarmness becomes a tranquil environment, while Christian discipleship endures within the uncomfortable zone, by challenging evil head-on. The last insight American Christian wants to happen would be the Biblical end time predictions with Jesus coming back. Remember they are rich and in need of nothing. We must pray for the many pastors who are not doing well. Our prayers and praises must also be for the other pastors performing an outstanding job for the Lord God and their assigned Church.

Words without action are Satan's delight!

Other shepherds are assigned to troubled flocks having a hard time paying for their huge stable and pens. Previously they believed the Land Owner would provide a way if they honored Him with a bigger stable than the shepherd over the grassy hill. They neglected to see the signs of endtimes. **Possibility debt thinking** will not work in the last days. They ignore warnings and sign their souls over to the money exchanger from another pasture. The shepherd quickly realizes he must feed the sheep half good and half worldly food. He perceives this was the only way to keep a great number in the flock and to pay back the money exchanger.

Another shepherd emerges in the pasture. He is interested in making a good name for himself among the shepherds. He forgets his original instructions from the Land Owner. They were, "Feed My sheep." He feeds them with improper food because he wants to build power for himself rather than his sheep. When he finds a lost sheep, it is for show to get everyone in the pasture to see and admire him for this righteous deed. He must always sit at the head table in the sheep pens. He encourages his sheep to show favor for his disobedient ways by assigning them the more prestigious duties in the flock. The righteous sheep are scorned because they have left their disobedient flock and found a righteous shepherd. They are called quitters, troublemakers and unwilling to come down from their pious thrones.

Since old-time evangelistic preaching on hell, fire, and brimstone has almost disappeared from the pulpit, hell must have cooled off, because it doesn't seem nearly as *hot!*

Another disappointment to the Land Owner surfaces when a Shepherd becomes completely beat down by the disobedient sheep and the spiteful world. He has given up by staring and babbling at a wall in dismay. He has forgotten his original instructions from the Land Owner. "Feed My sheep and don't get tired or disillusioned when you are doing my work or running into opposition. I say rejoice not quit."

In summary, the Land Owner sees these disobedient and self-centered shepherds are dissolving what He started to build many years before. The lukewarm sheep follow their wayward shepherds thinking they have done right. Sadly, they help the shepherds destroy the legacy the Land Owner started.

I ask, what do you think the Land Owner will do with these disobedient shepherds and the lukewarmers following them?

The answer came to me. These Shepherds blasphemed in matters they did not understand because they could not find their beginning. They must know their proper end to avoid tasting the second death. Blackest darkness will be awaiting them. They were caught without proper knowledge when their cycle completed. This causes them to stumble toward the black hole, which leads to nowhere.

Lukewarmers following these shepherds are in worse trouble than when they did not know the Land Owner. They are like the lost shepherd who was caught between time planes looking for their beginning when their end came. Their demise has been discussed below.

Blessed are the righteous Christians who were scoffed at when they stood up and pointed out to the flock and the Shepherds their evil desires and problems.

Abundantly blessed will be the hard working Shepherd following God's instructions and decrees. He will be given great rewards.

Everyone must watch out that no one deceives him before his testing cycle completes. He must not be caught wandering around off the narrow path. Because they will be shredded like pieces of rotten wood between two jagged and massive steel plated grinding wheels. These time-plated wheels are moving closer together in a massive but void expanse of time and space. Some may ask, why? Answer, to assign and transfer by curved-time-warp souls in an instance from their old test cycle to the beginning of newly appointed cycles per their Father's pleasure in His sabbatical domain. Their soul's worst nightmare begins to happen if they are lost in stellar time-space off the narrow path when the Land Owner shows up! Woe to this one!

Words of Wisdom: Today's Church feels safe and comfortable while it sleeps. Yet, great end time danger lies ahead. Most church services are sanitized to lift up lameness, tameness, and sameness. What is needed must be Spirit-filled sermons about end time hell, fire, brimstone and resistance against the European led MNO.

Insight, April 2004 - March 2005
Bob R. Short, a servant messenger to the Churches
for our Lord and Savior Jesus Christ

PLASMOID ENERGY FORCE

4-11-0 - USA, Hawaii, Maui, Crystal in showcase: The Spirit spoke to me in the voice familiar to me. "Write down why and who people really are and what will happen to them at the end of the age. Explain what will happen to the non-Christians (sinners) and lukewarmers. Tell the highly enlighten Spirit-filled Christians who can discern very deep mathematical and physicochemical truths and understand beyond normal Biblical teaching, what will happen to them."

PLASMOID
ENERGY FORCE
Section 4-11

The Holy Spirit instructed me to use words like, Plasmoid electromagnetic energy force to describe human and glorified body-energy forces. Earthlings cannot understand the highest order of this form, which equates to SPIRIT-GOD, who has no limitations like those of the plasmoids discussed later. Therefore, keep in mind the descriptive words chosen are the best I was able to decipher from the Holy Spirit to convey insight into our elementary minds.

Here goes an exciting journey through the Christian's mind with the Holy Spirit guiding. It will stretch our primitive mind's understanding of God's mysteries (Ephesians 5:32, 6:19, Colossians 1:26-27, 2:2, 4:3, Revelation 1:20). I pray the Lord God will open Christian's minds to part of the complex understanding of God Almighty's great and hidden mysteries as the Spirit moved me to write.

We must analyze the creation of the Plasmoid Energy Force called male and female human forms. Description of PLASMOID ENERGY FORCE: An energy force, which can be formed into any shape the Lord God desires for the particular test cycle. This energy force has been given life by the Lord God breathing into its nostrils. It is like a plasma jet of super intellectual interaction of electromagnetic, thermal, and hydrodynamic forces compressed into a plasma state. This state (Plasmoid) will be capable of reacting in its assigned test cycle woven into a designated level of endurance and curved-time displacement. Otherwise, this plasmoid energy force has been formed into a unit, which will undergo magneto hydrodynamic forces applied to it by the whole test cycle.

Should the unit be split or divided by the Lord God for His specific purpose, these two half units are substantially reduced in power. Split-units will not be able to withstand every action, temptation, and persecution they encounter in a magnetic field test cycle (Example - life on earth). If God splits an original plasmoid, there will be a loss of what looks like a complete neutron or Holy Spirit (within the nucleus). This complete neutron can separate into two half-neutrons, representative of the Holy Spirit designed to reenter the half plasmoid (Acts 2:3). To endure the test cycle, each half plasmoid must pickup one half-neutron. Otherwise, the radius of its circular [Pi (π) "r" squared equals circumference of enduring time allotted or displaced] test cycle has been substantially reduced, because it is a fragmented (like unto a designer rip) plasmoid energy form which will definitely not hold up as well as the original unit.

Unfortunately, the partial Plasmoid has a destructive tendency to rebel against God's original program (Ephesians 2:10). The self-program to survive or follow God's intent has short circuits torn (DNA-designer-rip) into it. By this designer-rip, each energy force has been given a unique set of weakness, natural tendency and flaws depending on what test the half plasmoid will be going through.

Lets say for example; the original Adam #1 (Genesis 2:7) had an assigned variable (radius) of ten (10). Therefore ten (10) squared, times Pi (π), equals "C", equals circumference, equals enduring time allotted for a complete plasmoid (Adam #1) = 314 PP (Persevering Power). If a plasmoid has not been split then its test cycle and endurance are the same. The plasmoid can make it through the complete test on its own (PP). However, if the plasmoid has been altered in any way its endurance becomes less than the test cycle and it will need additional divine help from the Lord God to make it through the complete test cycle without self-destructing.

God split the first man Adam #1 in the Book of Genesis 2:22, whereby making two incomplete half plasmoids. God previously gave Adam #2 (one half man) a dominant positive charge when he was formed. The positive charge equates to the starting point or headwater of the nucleus of the original unit. The other half Adam #1 was made by God and assigned a dominant negative charge (Female). These two half plasmoids were given different magnetic charges to introduce a natural magnetic attraction and complete the reproductive process (offspring) and a natural yearning to return to the base state or completely reassembled Plasmoid (Adam #1).

Understanding Plasmoid Energy Force will allow you to* stretch *beyond your limits of imagination and better grasp God's hidden mysteries.

Above, 4-11-1- Greece, Mykonos Island: It was evening on the Jet-set Island of Mykonos, and the Aegean Sea looked to be calm or without destructive energy. However, let a large earthquake happen off the Island and this bay would soon become a disaster. The calm water would energize into a powerful wave. This will be like each half Plasmoid during the resurrection if they have the Holy Spirit (split-Neutron). They gain great energy and power in their glorified bodies as the Lord God puts the parts back together. Note: This assumes they have the Holy Spirit, for without it they shall not be put back together but will be left broken to stand at judgment. This leads to a new assignment; "outside with the dogs".

Note, when a plasmoid has been split there will be a calculable loss factor. Part of the factor, which shall be lost, equates to the reduction assigned by God to the radius "r" of each plasmoid half unit, which equates to one half the original in our test cycle. Above we saw the original un-split man Adam #1 had an assigned variable (radius) of ten (10). Therefore, his enduring (PP) test ability will be 314 or equal to the test cycle he was to complete. The two half plasmoids (Genesis 2:22) have an assigned radius of one half the original, or five (5). Therefore, their enduring test ability (PP) (newly calculated circumference) has dropped to one forth the original (PP) of Adam #1. Calculates are as follows. The radius five (5) squared and multiplied by Pi ($\pi = 3.14$) equals 78 or about one fourth the original unit's circumference (time displacement) or (PP) of 314.

An observation shows how God for His pleasure (Luke 12:32) has set up a self-destructive test cycle, which can be passed. The half Plasmoids will need God's help to survive (Holy Spirit). Otherwise, they will not exhibit the proper complex mass-energy characteristics to endure completely through their test cycle.

Biblical understanding calls this help the Holy Spirit through personal repentance. It is accomplished by heart-felt repentance and accepting Jesus Christ by faith, as Lord and Savior. Furthermore, Jesus must be the only door-gate to heaven to receive this power.

The Holy Spirit equates to the measure of the magnetizing God - induced force exerted on the half Plasmoid (half or split-neutron equals the neutral force to help) to extend the enduring ability through the test cycle. The half-neutron has been previously programmed for each unique (Ephesians 2:10) half Plasmoid to guide it through its specific test cycle. The half-neutron has been assigned to a specific half plasmoid to be the primarily helping force, but only if asked. However, on the other hand, the half plasmoids may decide their free will (given them by God) will dictate the choices and make all the decisions. Then they will be destroyed before they reach the end of the test cycle. Plasmoids must stay in tune with the helping and guiding Holy Spirit as they progress through their independent and unique testing cycle, to keep their endurance and magnetic field intact.

If a half Plasmoid flunks the test, they crash into a wall of non-displaced dimensional void headed toward a dark world where light is absent yet a spirit can see. God perceives it as time folding together upon the half Plasmoid and they are expired as far as God's testing is concerned. Yet, the half Plasmoid will still complete the original test cycle. The observation point God uses equates to our perceived flow of displaced time and space.

I pray this has increased the understanding for Christians to see how a partial Plasmoid unit operates with less efficiency than the original (Adam #1). Even the original Plasmoid will need additional help to transform into a glorified heavenly body which has the ability to operate on multidimensional modes at the same time. We do know by simple Bible study, Christians will not be raised as partial units (male or female) at the resurrection. We know how Plasmoid energy force units were formed (God split original Adam #1).

Therefore, a reversal of plasmic electromagnetic wave energizing mass will form at the resurrection. We might imagine it as if we were standing at ground zero of a nuclear blast, an awesome sucking chemical action between a time-substance placed in a God like white light magnetic field. The upward sucking sound of the regeneration of the glorified body being magically fused back together will be like unto a 50 caliber bullet whizzing past an object, magnified 1,000,000,000 times. The concussion would literally suck the object off the ground into a plasmic electromagnetic wave of energizing mass. This matter would be dragged behind the bullet representative of movement through time headed for its next assignment! Another inquisitive thought came to mind, so...

I ask the Spirit what does a test cycle look like from a time displacement point of view? The answer came to me and it equates to the following example: Each half plasmoid's test cycle looks like the volume inside a miniature rubber "O" ring. The earth's test cycle looks like the volume inside a gigantic earth-moving machine's tire many stories high. Now, pour into the gigantic tire millions and millions of miniature "O" rings all the way around the tire. This represents the earth test cycle with human forms being introduced into it at different times. Start turning the tire and the miniature "O" rings start revolving which represents their personal test cycle at one complete revolution. Naturally, the "O" ring's test cycle is very short compared to the huge tire. When the tire makes one complete revolution, time has gyrated itself to its beginning and the tire will stop. It can be noted; some of the last "O" rings have not completely finished their test cycle when the gigantic tire stopped. This represents the second coming of Christ and the first resurrection (Revelation 20:5).

I ask the Spirit what does a test cycle look like from a time displacement point of view? The answer came - "look up, your beginning is the same as the ending!

HOMOSEXUALITY + +

The Spirit of Christ Jesus gave me a stern warning to decree. If two positive charged half Plasmoids try to procreate (homosexuality) this causes a non-polarized condition. Otherwise, the test cycle God has programmed and designed, homosexuality equates to a contradiction in God's programming. In God's domain, this would be like, two diametrically repelling forces trying to reshape the design. It will not happen. Two positive charged half Plasmoids having sex introduce into their positive energy field a magnetostriction.

The Spirit continued to give insight that these half Plasmoids would experience God's judgment by mechanical deformation through electronic plasmolyzing of their enduring test capability. This will be like a proton and a look-alike electron (play-like female) which is really an antiproton (antiparticle to the proton) carrying a negative charge having sex together. If one of the players was a Christian with a neutron and they decide to become homosexual, this triggers a "prompt neutron magnetic moment." What happens next? A neutron released with the fusion (sex) of these two homosexuals results in their loss of salvation. The cause and effect of this sexual relation equates to embrittlement, reduction or loss in toughness and ability to sustain the half plasmoid through its test cycle. It will not be able to withstand the test cycle nearly as long and will be destroyed prematurely (approximate adult life expectancy will be reduced about half).

The violent unbalanced state caused by this unauthorized action of two positive charges introduced by fusion (sex) are subjected to a disoriented action of a magnetic field of terrifying violence. This violence projects a state of magneto hydrodynamic turbulence or a motion of the half plasmoid in which velocities programmed and abilities to withstand the pressures from the test begin to fluctuate irregularly and erratically tears itself apart. They lose control and magnetic stress sets in. This would imply, they could not combat the natural test forces, which acts across a programmed surface of life because of the perceived curving and stretching of magnetic flux lines caused by disobedience to the Lord God. The result equates to magneto hydrodynamic instability where the half plasmoid becomes unstable and cannot move through the test cycle properly. It will be expelled from the field of magnetic moments or what would be understood as hydro magnetic instability of the half plasmoid. Their reward will be the Lake of Fire!

Above, 4-11-2- U.S., Hawaii, Oahu Island - the Polynesian Cultural Center: The finale of the show was the Fire Dance. It was awesome, for fire and what looked like tongues of fire filled the stage. It could be stated the resurrection may look like a similar event but magnified 1,000,000,000,000 times.

RESURRECTION

I marveled at the majestic panorama of the resurrection as the Spirit of Christ Jesus opened a viewing aperture in the spirit of my mind for a snap shot at the brilliant light show, which mystified me. There to see were skyrocketing energy fields magnetically bonding together as they sped upward in the expanse as Jesus raised them. Then out of the void came what looked like tongues of fire from the Holy Spirit to unite with the newly formed primordial elector-magnetic field (like the original Adam #1, before he was magnetically split). He was made up of one complete neutron plus one proton plus one electron. There was an unprecedented fireworks display when this happened.

A photo magnetic glue came from Jesus' throne like lightning bolts of electronic fire. When the glue hit the oncoming elector-magnetic field, a critical mass fusion was released and it slammed the surrounding expanse with such impact it cannot be expressed in word-picture dimensions.

The impact was a hair-raisin concussion, which unleashed my emotion. Yet, a wonderful feeling came over me as I experienced the true expression of Jesus' love when each union (two, one half-neutron, plus one proton, and one electron equals one complete atom) was reformed. The sparkling glorified body was unifying and forming instantly, like the angels in heaven, who do not die, (Matthew 22:30).

Again, Galatians 3:28; *"There is neither, male or female, for you are all one in Christ Jesus."* This text states the same understanding as conveyed above in scientific terms.

Another text, The Gospel of Thomas found in 1945, (The Complete Gospels - Robert J. Miller, editor, 1994. It was discovered as part of a large collection of ancient religious texts known as the Nag Hammadi Library). In this text, the Spirit gave me expanded insight to paraphrase the following. It has been recorded Jesus said: Thomas 22:4, when two are made into one. Thomas 22:5, or when male and female are made into a single one, males are not males anymore and females are not females anymore. Thomas 22:6, when all parts are made (transformed) anew then the glorified body can enter the (Father's) domain. It further states (old) image must be replaced with (new) image then as we call it here on earth, our flesh cannot enter heaven but a glorified body can enter into heaven's domain. Finally, The Gospel of Thomas has been in harmony with the Bible on this issue of glorified body just as the Spirit instructed me to write. The Spirit allowed me to see which was awesome! I did not completely understand what I saw but immediately I had this overwhelming desire to be a part of it! Praise Jesus!

A complete resurrection is available, when you discover God's end time purpose for your life and drive yourself against all odds to complete it!

IN THE ORDER OF MELCHIZEDEK

The spirit spoke and said; now let your mind fly into an uninhibited state to move from reality into a deeper understanding of test assignments in the heavenly realm. For this analysis, lets say there are ten (10) levels of difficulty for a Plasmoid to endure in one test or war cycle. Here on earth we are experiencing level one (1). This level has four time planes, which can apply force and stress on the Plasmoid as it moves through the cycle; X, Y, Z, and T (time-displacement) axis.

As you continue to read this section, ask the Holy Spirit to raise the magnitude of your thoughts one more notch higher in understanding.

There are stacks upon stacks of these time planes as I have shown you years ago, the Spirit told me. When the level has been increased, the difficulty will be greater. Plasmoid in their completed state would not endure. Their physical magnetic energy field cannot hold up on a high level of play. The Lord God controls the program within the Imperial Rule for His pleasure; therefore, He has to strengthen our ability to survive under the increased pressure applied. Look at the Gospel of Thomas again, the Spirit continued.

To complete this increased test level, God will form more than one complete plasmoid together. In Thomas 23:1-2, Jesus states He will take a plasmoid from a thousand and two plasmoids from ten thousand. He will form the three of them together and they will stand as one or a unified single increased power-up plasmoid. To calculate the persevering power (PP), I was instructed by the Spirit to double the original radius of ten (10) x two (2) = (20 x 20 x 20) squared = 8000 squared = 64,000,000 x pi (π = 3.14) = 200,960,000 Persevering Power (PP). This equates to an increase of 64,000,000 (PP) times the original Adam # 1. The Spirit expanded this to say, the Lord God, the Trinity, and any super Plasmoid in the order of **MELCHIZEDEK** could take a dozen or two dozen from one hundred thousand, form them together and they would stand as one super plasmoid. The Godhead can draw power from everyone. This has been why the power of God cannot be explained in understandable human terms.

Push the magnitude of thought one more notch higher in understanding by compressing it and then unleashing a new explosion of awesome insight. Thomas 4:2-3, Jesus said many of the first or Old Testament saints will be last. Nevertheless, the Lord God will make them a single one by forming them together in an unbelievable field of PLASMOID producing electromagnetic energy force. We cannot comprehend this power or its ability to operate on multi-time planes at the same time. Its electromagnetic particle-transfer rate at the speed of thought equates to mass acceleration into foot-pounds of energy beyond our imagination. Again, one cannot grasp this awesome power to mass to speed ratio.

The miraculous and most powerful energy PLASMOID force could operate on many multidimensional junctions while operating at the same timeframes displacement. This equates to the level spoken of in the Bible as, **in the order of Melchizedek,** that equates to ten in difficulty and carries with it the ultimate honor. I told the Spirit, "Believing has been easy, because all things are possible for the Lord God. However, this expanded insight has gone far beyond where we can grasp rational thought to assimilate it into reasonable sense in our primitive minds. But I have this hope that some day God will grant me a chance to operate on a higher level." Therefore, Christian's first objective in this journey of time-thought-space and cycles must be to pass the test they are currently going through (2 Corinthians 13:5). Christians must pray they can stand before God Almighty and receive honors to be assigned to the next level for God's pleasure.

SINNERS, UNBELIEVERS and LUKEWARMERS at the RESURRECTION

151

Daniel 12:2, prophesied about the endtimes; when multitudes that sleep in the dust will awake, either to everlasting life with Christ or to shame and everlasting contempt. The Spirit-filled Christians will be resurrected to eternal life with Christ. Sinners will be locked down on a dusty shelf never to be used in this type scenario again. They will be separated from the Lord God. Cast out!

The lukewarmers will not be able to stand before the Lord God on Judgment day. They will be given a new assignment to everlasting contempt. They shall be a pitiful sight. Lukewarmers never bonded together with their other particle energy force because at the resurrection they had no half-neutron (Holy Spirit). The Holy Spirit or half-neutron must be present in both the proton (male) and electron (female) energy forces to complete the bonding process. Because they lack a half-neutron, they were never bonded and are still half Plasmoids. When they stand before the Lord God they are defenseless and without excuse. They are awarded the lake of fire for eternity.

4-11-3- Turkey, Ephesus - Curetes Street: Picture taken from within Celsus' Library up the endless Curetes Street. This street stretches up a hill and there are multitudes of people going up the street. It reminded me of when the Bible says the powers in the heavens and the kings on earth will be herded as if prisoners up something like this street to judgment where they will be shut up and punished in prison. What a terrible day for most who will not obey and are willfully disobedient to the Lord God's commands. (Isaiah 24:21-22)

FOUR ADAMS

The Spirit led me to write about four different Adams or electromagnetic energy forces, which are discussed in God's Holy Word.

ADAM # 1: GENESIS 2:7 - God formed a man. This unit of energy called a man equated to something representing a Plasmoid Energy Force. It was similar in nature or magnetic energy properties as Adam number four (4) which will be discussed later. Otherwise, this plasmoid energy force has been formed into a unit of energy, which will undergo magneto hydrodynamic forces applied to it, by everything else in the test cycle. Therefore, it can complete its assigned test cycle without any help from God with the exception it possess the complete Holy Spirit. Adam number one (1) equals something like one proton and one complete Holy Spirit (neutron in a state of completeness) both within the nucleus (launching point of the energy magnetic force field). Adam #1 also includes one electron moving around on the outside of the nucleus to complete the magnetic composition of Adam number one (1) (atom). Therefore, these three fundamental particles complete the characteristics of the trinity within a plasmoid mass-energy force. Just as God is a trinity, so shall it be with complete Plasmoids. Plasmoid energy equates to a magnetic force field not flesh. Flesh covers or shall be a tent over the force field so to speak.

ADAM # 2: GENESIS 2:21 - God reformed by degenerating Adam number one's (1's) energy force into a half Plasmoid Energy Force (taking part of the man's side and or rib). This produces Adam number two (2) who does not have the power within his force field to complete his test Cycle before he disintegrates or discharges all his energy field. To complete his energy cycle he must pick up (invite into him) the Holy Spirit (split or half-neutron) while proceeding through his test cycle. He will fail the test if he does not pick the Holy Spirit up through the cycle. If he picks the Holy Spirit up then Adam number two (2) equates to one proton and half-split neutron (Holy Spirit) which will pass the test with various degrees of rewards depending on what he does. The Split Holy Spirit has been spoken of in the Bible when it was sent by the Lord God in Act 2:3, *"They saw what seemed to be tongues of fire* (Holy Spirit or neutron in a state of completeness) *that* ***SEPARATED*** **(Split-Holy Spirit)** *and came to rest on each of them (within the nucleus of the magnetic energy force)."*

ADAM # 3: MATTHEW 1:18 - Holy Spirit - the Spirit of Prophecy completed a set or what might be called a way point in the programmed time cycle of prophetic events and the outcome was; *"...she was found to be with child through the Holy Spirit."* This Male child or half-God Plasmoid Energy force (reduced power) still had awesome powers beyond our understanding. His Childhood was absent the Holy Spirit (Neutron in the nucleus) until John the Baptist, baptized Him and God sent the Holy Spirit down like a dove on Christ. This increased His power, to jump-start a much greater energy surge when He was resurrected and His Father gave all authority in heaven and earth to Him.

He had awesome power to contend with during His childhood. This was a learning process of how to control this power, and understand, and experience first hand what other half plasmoid energy forces undergo. Without the Holy Spirit or purposely disengaging from part of the Trinity of the Godhead power, Jesus was able to experience first hand human trials, pressures, stress and the like. He did this with ease and Christians know the story. Only He will be the one worthy to open the scrolls at the end of time.

Jesus can transfer power to us or reclaim it. If a Plasmoid does not pick up the Holy Spirit and flunks the test, its power will be automatically transferred back to Jesus. Jesus does not lose power, He only gains power and gets stronger. When this test cycle completes, He will have gained the increased power from any half Plasmoids passing the test. They start out this test cycle a half Plasmoid and finish it as a complete plasmoid with about a fourfold electromagnetic power-force gain.

Jesus has the ability to implement electromagnetic-nanotechnology particle transfer. In other words, He has been given authority by God Almighty to control all manipulating energy matter redistribution.

To impact your nation during endtimes for Jesus Christ, you must understand Biblical sequencing, calculations, and mysteries to focus on your godly assignment as a half plasmoid.

In short, He can redistribute electromagnetic particles on a very small scale by splitting a Plasmoid or adding their magnetic forces together to achieve unbelievable power. He can restructure energy to accomplished curved time into a preset cycle by changing their properties. A transfer of energy might look to humans like something similar to an aurora borealis (northern or southern lights). The electromagnetic disturbances will not be random movement in the atmosphere but a well-defined energy transfer of such magnitude our minds cannot grasp its dimension.

ADAM # 4: Revelation 5:9 - Jesus purchased **MEN** for God Almighty. It shall be very important not to get mixed up in the gender war here, when it says MEN it has been talking about the nucleus (head waters or starting point) of the energy force (Plasmoid). This does not say men and women as it did in the Book of Genesis but only men (complete Plasmoids) for very good reason. The Bible uses the word Men describing a completed energy force in heaven. The forces are similar in their molecular structure as the plasmoid energy force of ADAM (# 1) = one proton, plus two half neutrons reunited as one complete neutron and one electron. All three complete parts of the trinity are working harmoniously together. These are put together with God Almighty's glue to form this spirit-energy force. Jesus said we are not raised male or female, nevertheless, we are a completed energy Plasmoid Force at the resurrection (glorified male energy source, where male refers to head waters or starting point - not gender)! Praise God!

Time is directly tied to Pi (π = 3.14) and shall always be infinitely flexible depending on the amount of energy applied to its curved space.

Energy Produces Time

In our primitive world of explaining relativity and its principles, we could draw the conclusion, energy cannot be created or destroyed but it can be displaced. On the other hand, for every action with energy displacement there must be an opposite and equal displacement of energy usually at right angles if not disturbed by other forces and friction. However, what we have not pursued is energy directed on a curved space will produce time displacement.

Nevertheless, in Jesus' malleable dimension of curved time and space, His technology offers energy gain. That is to say, it is equal to the number of Plasmoids passing a timed test cycle (multiplied times) the speed of light in heaven's dimensions (squared) and multiplied by Pi (π = 3.14). Herein lies a great mystery the Lord God has revealed to me. The flow of time is relative to any object or force's immediate surrounding it within an assigned curved space. The perception of time that equates to energy is directly proportional to the radius of the assigned curved space and pi (π = 3.14) times the speed of light in heaven's dimensions (squared). Energy and time have a direct relationship here, think, imagine, ponder, and pray that a great mystery will be revealed to the wise.

To move any object or force through curved time cycles requires energy. This formula will give the holder who can produce enough energy and direct this energy within a curved space, the ability to travel within a time loop and manipulate time at will. Time is directly tied to Pi (π = 3.14) and shall always be infinitely flexible depending on the amount of energy applied to its curved space.

There are travel-using corridors (God's assigned routing) of zero gravity between objects of mass. These routing corridors trap time in a void, which cancel gravity. Zero gravity can exist on one plane or penetrate multi-planes through pathways into inter-dimensional time-portals. The trajectory needed is elliptical in nature but on multidimensional planes of gravitational forces. Speed cannot drop below the velocity needed to achieve balance between all object's gravitational pull on the time traveler and the inertia the traveler produces by their motion through the corridors. I do not know why Almighty God, the creator of time through energy, has unfolded this great mystery, but I have written it down as directed.

Don't Fool Mother Nature

Finally, the last bit of insight on the subject of Plasmoid energy forces and the programmed test cycle. God has guidelines and perimeters to operate within a test program. Our test performance has an absolute set of limits, which warn, do not go beyond this boundary or test preprograming by the Lord God. Let us examine a few examples, which can ultimately lead to destruction of self, cities, countries or the entire world.

1. Manipulating DNA: This analysis will only discuss the affect on Plasmoids. DNA chain equates to most of the rip-line, which was caused when God split Adam #1 (making male and female). We all have built-in flaws. This has been deliberately planned (designer-rip) by God as part of each individual's unique test to overcome defects by using the Holy Spirit to pass the test. All people operate under the flawed rip-line, which makes them initially fail the test (Romans 3:23). This equates to Biblical old nature. Nevertheless, there also shall be a Biblical new nature, which means overcoming the world and the flawed rip-line in our character. This Biblical overcoming shall be defined as New Nature covered by the Blood of Jesus Christ and the Cross (following Christ). The world and Satan are desperate to sell the fact as they say: "There can only be one nature because a person really can't change." Look at any liberal news broadcast and it can be picked up readily.

2. Splitting the Atom: Half Plasmoids are crossing the limit-bar and going outside the guidelines set in the test cycle. This will lead to world destruction if not stopped.

3. Fusion of two positive protons (hydrogen fusion explosion): Half Plasmoids are combining two particles magnetically carrying the same charge. These unnatural unions of protons will cause untold devastating destruction. It equates to a contradictory state against God's test cycle. This will lead to world destruction.

4. Cloning, using animals parts for human body part replacement, some kinds of stem cell manipulation, and any type disruption of Mother Nature. When plasmoids go beyond the limit of God's plan, friction and abrasion, which deteriorate the process of clean unabated movement toward the end, has been introduced. We best understand this friction as diseases, plagues and the like. This point must be understood. Disaster strikes if the Lord God's programming has been altered or tampered with. Many times people think they can do a better job than God, however, the more men think they have become wise and knowledgeable in reprogramming the Lord God's test cycle, the worse it will get.

Note: People will lose their lives on judgment day if they cross the technology limit lines of God's designer rip during their test cycle to temporarily extend their lives. For the wise in their own eyes, become fools. The Lord God knew in advance that the human forms with a free will would eventually outsmart themselves. He shortened in advance the radius of the people in the world's test cycle. The Plasmoid who tries to save his life by short cutting God's plan will lose it. The time has come for Spirit-filled Christian's to say NO to much of modern electronic and medical technology which has crossed God's outer limit lines into Satan's world of desperate preservation. The half Plasmoid will be saved and gain his life back on judgment day who says no to ungodly technology today but who had lost his life during the test cycle. This ends the insight concerning Plasmoid Energy Forces. Praise God. Amen! Insight 4-21-05 to 11-12-05 Bob R. Short

Below, 4-11-4- Italy, Rome - Roman Forum - Colosseum: Inside the Colosseum I began to wonder about judgment day. A chilling thought came to mind when we were told Christians were killed for sport here, would that day be the reverse of what happened in this place? This must be a fascinating point to ponder, I told the Spirit. The Lord God told us to leave room for His wrath. He has promised in Revelation 3:9, He will make some fall down at Christian's feet at Judgment Day. He will defuse these evildoer half Plasmoids right in front of them. Some will be drug off while their souls are still burning (magnetic discharging) to the lake of fire in full view of the multitudes, while disobedient leaders will be condemned to the blackest of black holes. This will not be a good day for most.

Maybe all should pay more attention to what scripture says and make every effort to obey it. The key to getting your magnetic particles supercharged must be to end up on the correct side of Almighty God on Judgment Day. The largest percent of the total people being judged will not be standing when they are done talking. Where does each one of us stand? We are told to test ourselves to see if we are Spirit-filled Christians.

INTRODUCTION TO GOD'S PROCLAMATION

Section 4-12

The following is a letter mailed to most of the nation's Ambassadors in North and South America.

The Spirit of Christ Jesus, the Spirit of Prophecy, once again spoke prophetic wisdom to me. "In Revelation 22:6, the Lord, who is the God of the spirits of the prophets sent visions and future insight to St. John on the Island of Patmos. You were on the Island of Patmos and additional insight was given to you there. It has been sealed and hidden from your conscious mind up until now. Therefore, let it be known throughout North and South America: Issue this Decree now as a Proclamation to the Americas."

The Spirit went on, "Do not think it strange concerning the four Beasts in Chapter 7:4-7, of the Prophet Daniel. I warned you years ago what generally will happen. Now, the God of the Spirits of Prophecy will show you the harmonious beauty program He introduced into this curved test cycle.

This Test Cycle has been hammered out into four time-curves so the tempo of oscillations begins rebuking the next at the appropriate point. Consequently, the test can be bent into a beautiful time warp ending at the appointed moment. God programmed for His pleasure the curves of each Beast before the beginning so the duration of each gives way to the next perfectly.

The defining moment to the end time games started a few hundred years ago. The Lion (Daniel 7:4) was given power because She followed the Lord God. However, as you can see and history reveals today, England has disregarded God. Therefore, I have transferred her power and authority over to the Eagle (Canada, America and Mexico). But, having said this, history proves the Eagle's wings were torn off symbolically signifying the War of Independence from Europe. The Eagle stayed and became powerful America, Canada and Mexico. Sadly, they are following in the disoriented Lion's footsteps wondering down the topsy-turvy path to destruction.

Now understand the mystery of this riddle.

**One Beast lives
and dominates at a time.
However, the first Beast
will be first, and
the last will be last,
and yet they all
live together.
Power will be given
to the first, first,
and so it will go
until the last.
Each will try to
hold the rule.
Each will fail.
Division will prosper.
Do you not realize
all four Beasts
are busy
at work today?**

Left, 4-12-1 - Italy, Verona - Roman Bridge: A original Roman bridge with the ***eye*** *in the middle of the column to reduce stress when flooding came. Romans were the first to perfect this idea. The feeling of power and strength can be sensed in the Bridge once the* ***eye*** *was installed. It could withstand a powerful storm and flood. Once again the Old Roman empire has been trying to flex its muscle by designing the so called eye of the world or the European led World Organizations to withstand any opposition against it. They want to control all buy and sell, civil judgment suits, and the like. The hidden design will be to transfer control from the world to them. The name of the organization equates to European led* ***M****illenium* ***N****ations* ***O****rganized (MNO).*

Unfortunately, serious pruning of the Eagle must be done to form all The Americas into a man. I will give it a heart of a man and it will stand on its feet to become the Great Prince Michael (Daniel 12:1), protector of Israel. The Americas will face off against the skyrocketing dominance of the European led Leopard Beast, Daniel 7:6. Then along came the last Eagle Beast with the Three Ugly Heads (Daniel 7:7), it was frightening and terrifying - more powerful than the European Leopard or the first Eagle Beast. Amazingly it will not speak so much from the original location of the Three Ugly Heads or its Ten Horns but from the middle of its body, Rome first and Jerusalem last.

Let The Americas see their - death of terror - in this Last Eagle Beast, for it has birthed and has been growing at an unprecedented speed. It has been forcefully advancing its ungodly anti-Christian influence upon the world. Wake up North and South America, you will be consumed by the Leopard or the Last Beast if you do not band together as one man in spirit per Daniel 12:1, as the Great Prince Michael protector of Israel and of each other!"

Decree as a Proclamation to The America's.

The Americas must have harmony, one Spirit, and a backbone to fight and die for each other. The alternative will be to do nothing and let the European Leopard Beast or the Last Beast with the Three Ugly Heads devour, destroy and spit your nation out of its sharp-fanged teeth. **North and South America must settle their differences in the following areas:**

✪ Secure your borders

✪ Unify trade between North and South America

✪ Unify all differences quickly before the Ezekiel 38 nuclear war starts (Gulf War III). This war equates to USA and others VS Russia and others in a nuclear war (not Armageddon).

✪ Prepare North and South America to be allies against the rest of the World = European Leopard Beast (Daniel 7:6) in world trade, money, tax, and Christian's values.

✪ Fight and die for each other

✪ Nations must keep control of national security identities and strategic sectors such as, seaports, manufacturing, farming and technology industries. Examples: aerospace, steel, oil and gas, auto, food, high tech computer components, and the like. Otherwise, do not let any business or nation outside North and South America buy up or into any company, which will become a national security issue.

✪ Disown the European Leopard Beast's Strategy to take over the Americas through organizations such as or similar to: (World Court, World Trade Organization, GATT, European System of central banks [ESCB], Europol, soon to emerge Millenium Nations Organized [MNO], world tolerating religion and other world organizations cultivating their roots of growth from within the Leopard Beast).

> Note: This does not mean the Americas cannot get along with them. However the Americas will not bow down to them or their concocted world organizations and yield under their umbrella of peace, security, trade, judgments and the like.

✪ Disown-Last Beast with Three Ugly Heads in the same way as you rebuked the Leopard Beast and do not join or yield to any of its world organizations, which requires giving up your countries' membership in it.

✪ Do not require your citizens to use the Mark of the Beast to buy and sell = three access codes 6+6+6 to collect the European world consumption tax spoken of by the prophet Daniel 11:20. This shall be promoted by any or all three of the Ugly Heads of the Last Eagle Beast: Destruction to Nations who follow the last Beast has been prophesied. This Beast shall be last, more importantly, it lives today.

Explanation of Three Ugly Heads of Last Eagle Beast:

✪ First head to appear - Ugly Head in the Middle = United Nations = First to promote the world consumption tax (Daniel 11:20). It will be sold under the cover of European greed as a way for richer nations to help the poor impoverished nations. It is the old Robin Hood idea. But Jesus Christ warns if any nation joins the Leopard or the Last Beast eventually it will have to force its citizens to take the Mark to buy or sell.

✪ Second head to appear - Ugly Head on the Right = Millenium Nations Organized (MNO = 666) = European led Leopard Beast = starts with Old Roman Empire (Head with fatal wound-was healed, Revelation 13:3) the EU expands to all world landmass except North and South America.

✪ Last head to appear - Ugly Head on the left = Millenium Nations Organized (MNO = 666 on phone pad) = Final Antichrist given power by the ten area world kingdoms leaders (horns) to rule from Jerusalem.

This Proclamation began to formulate in the spirit of my mind at night on April 29, 2005. This I am told was the same exact day (April 29th) pilgrims came upon the shore in America many years ago. They staked into the ground a Cross and decreed the land (which includes all the Americas) for our Lord and Savior Jesus Christ. I awoke the next morning and began to write down the substance of this insight and the vision it contained. Final insight came to me on May 28, 2005.

Praise God for everything He has done. Make it so Lord Jesus, Amen! And Amen!

Bob R. Short, a Witness to the World Governments for our Lord and Savior Jesus Christ. (4-29-05 to 5-28-05)

Decree as a Warning
Proclamation to the European Union
of (most nations)
TO THE EUROPEAN UNION
Section 4-13

The following is a letter mailed
to most of the nation's
Ambassadors in the EU.

WARNING

The MNO will produce a nightmare of abuse if Jesus Christ and His teaching are not at its head!

June 22, 2005

European Union Building, Brussels, Belgium

Re: World Peace and Security through the MILLENIUM NATIONS ORGANIZED, (MNO).

Attn.: AMBASSADOR:

1. **NAME CHANGE:** If the EU's purpose has been to offer peace and security to the world then it must change its name or title. The EU must invite the world into their formula without appearing to control over others using any regional name, which carries a negative stigma such as "The European". Therefore, I am offering the EU a universal name, which will be Nation friendly. The world has entered a new Millenium and the goal shall be world peace and security. I am proud to introduce the expanding EU to its inspiring and progressive new world title: MILLENIUM NATIONS ORGANIZED, (MNO), for world peace and security.

2. REGIONAL ZONING MOVEMENT RESTRICTIONS (Warning): The Schengen Accord abolished border controls (Passport-free-zone) between certain EU countries must not be expanded to all future enlisting countries or zoning regions. History proves combining many religious and culture-different nation-states with uninhibited movement within this zone will cause chaos. History has proven repeatedly, if the EU tries to control the world and unite the peoples of the world, God will scatter the masses, and then trouble will arise. Their fruitless accomplishment will only try to rebuild the Tower of Babel (Using English as the world language).

Serious disruptive problems arise, when Middle Eastern, Asian, Jewish and different Christians religions all have uninhabited movement within a worldwide zone of Nation-States. The world loses its design by God as to the beautiful cultural differences. Compare England, US and many European countries when multi-culture societies were introduced and the disruption caused by it. When this happens "tolerance" must be introduced into the culture. This word motivates disobedience, which leads to the rebuilding of the tower of Babel. There must be some controls or ~~EU~~ MNO goals will be greatly diminished, beautiful cultures destroyed and religious war started!

3. ZONING - REGIONAL - MEMBER - STATES: a.} It shall be very important for world stability, to control the movement of people in and out of any zoning region. b.} The ~~EU~~ MNO must have quick reactionary military force within each zoning region when expanding regional-members-states. Therefore, destiny has designed ten Member-Regions of the world (MNO) to expedite this zoning matter: A.) Europe, B.) Russia, C.) Greenland plus Antarctica, D.) Africa, E.) Middle East, F.) Asia with Japan, G.) Australia plus Oceania Areas, H.) Mexico and Canada, I.) United States, J.) South America.

4. WARNING: The EU has opted to omit God from their constitution. This will prove to be a serious mistake. If the EU truly wants to reach its goals to expand and become representatives to the world, it must accomplish this through the MNO. Jesus Christ' teachings must be at the top of the list and followed or the ~~EU's~~ MNO's quest for peace and security will fail.

I am of the order of God's Witness to the World for my Lord and Savior Jesus Christ! I am not associated or paid by any government or organization. Please implement these progressive and cutting edge suggestions. The ~~EU~~ MNO has a defining moment in history to achieve world financial and trade stability, along with peace and security through Jesus Christ. INSIGHT - June-2005, Bob R. Short

WARNING

The EU has opted to omit God from their constitution. This will prove to be a serious mistake. More importantly, Jesus Christ's teachings must be at the top of the list or the ~~EU's~~, MNO's quest for peace and security will fail.

AZRAIL and MICHAEL

Section 4 - 14

This is the word of the Lord that came to Bob R. Short, a Witness to the world governments for the Lord God on 6-10-05 and ending on 9-11-05.

It concerns the in-depth insight of the retaliation response about the first paragraph on page 103 of the Wake Up Call Prophecies, issue 1, prophesied September 1994 - August 1995. This was due to the Goat's (America) large prominent Horn (self proclaimed great city where money has become god) between his eyes being broken off (Issue-1, page 110).

This is what the Lord God Almighty says: "Issue this decree as instruction to the heart of Michael (America), but code and seal part of it until the appointed time. The Goat must have faith to follow these instructions."

"I the Sovereign Lord, instructed you to prophesy to the disobedient GOAT (Daniel 8:5-8) and many of his lukewarm church leaders since 1994. For the Goat and the Church leaders have not followed My Commands to keep America a Disciple Nation (leadership, laws, and people following My Word - Bible).

I now summon Michael to begin to stand on his mighty feet to protect Israel. The use of Nuclear Weapons in the first paragraph on page-103 of the rough draft, Issue-1, of the WAKE UP CALL PROPHECIES (1994-95) can now become a reality for retaliation. Psalms 97:3-5 proclaims prophetically My directive for the United States to use atomic, hydrogen or other thermonuclear-type weapons (melt like wax) to destroy general area of Iran and part of Iraq plus one surprise in an air attack as none other in history. Take heed, oh mighty generals of Michael. Retaliation must be without warning, one hour after the Horn has been broken off. The world must instantly see My wrath through Michael.

The following City's and Nation's targeted must be preprogrammed in multi-locations (backups) so every targeted area will be completely destroyed using the prophesied size and quantity of direct hits. This is to fulfill prophecy in Daniel 8 and the Wake Up Call Prophecies, issue-1, Psalms 97-99 sign sequencing. I summon you to decree this directive to the Goat's mighty Generals concerning how to make a retaliation response. Issue it as a coded poem with embedded riddles as directed on the following page.

Ponder the consequences of My decree, oh Goat. Then, think again, at the alternative - slow death to America and the world. There will be no other choice but to follow My decree - no other will do!

After this, the Goat will lose recognition as a friendly nation with some of the European led MNO's leaders and people. This especially holds true with leadership over the armies from the North, South, and East. The world will experience some consequences such as, domestic religious unrest and violence, a fuel shortage, economic distress, and other problems. America will be boycotted. This will be to raise Michael not break him. Therefore, Michael must standup and begin to protect My people, Israel."

I, Bob R. Short, prophesy this decree as Witness for God to the heart of Michael and say, "Make it so Lord Jesus. Come quickly! Oh America, repent and turn back to God, who knows, He may relent His fury." (Insight received 8-10-05 to 9-11-05)

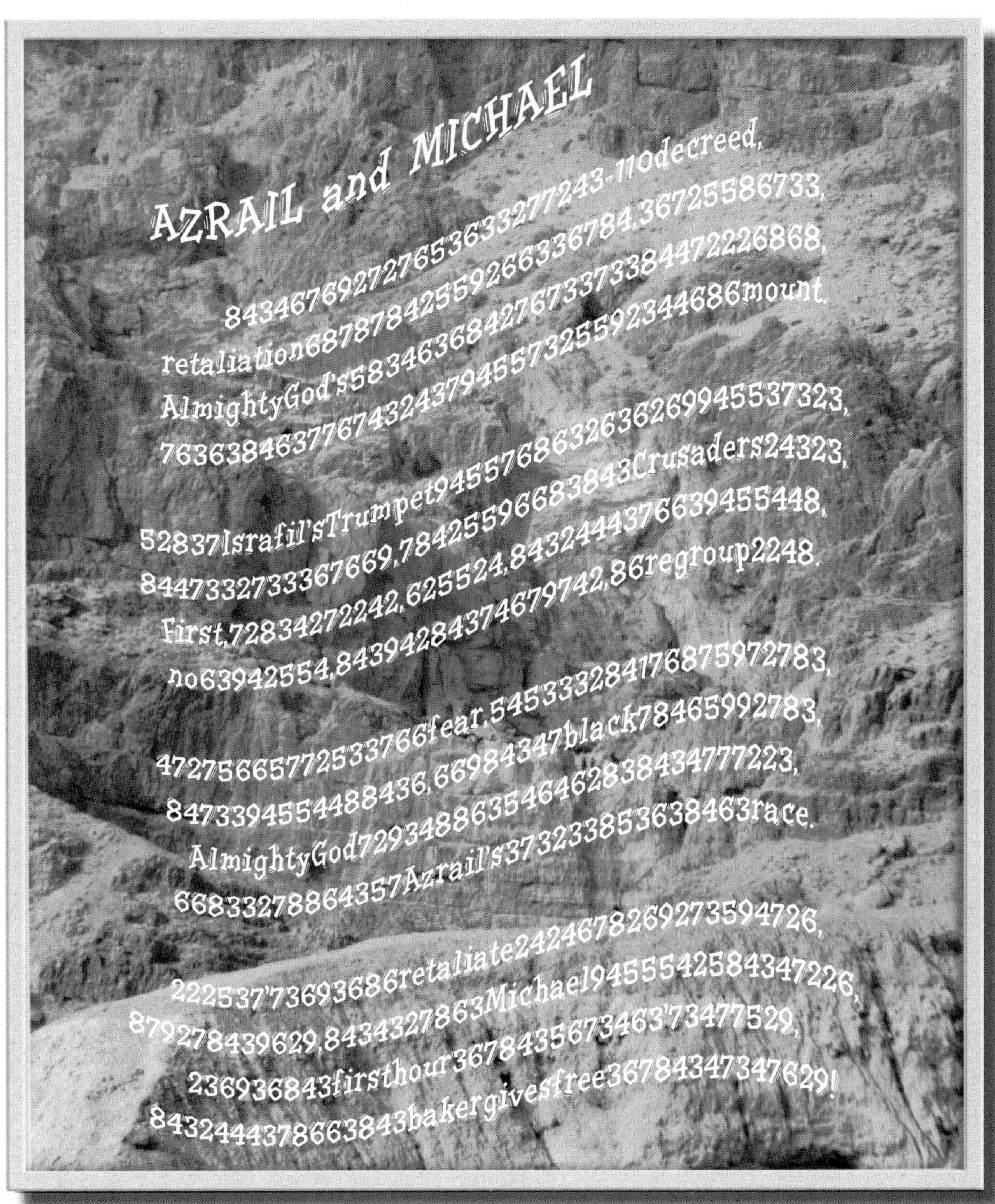

4-14-1 - Israel - Dead Sea - Qumran-Cliffs: The Dead Sea Scrolls gave us instructions and insight on how the final battle will be fought just like this section gives us the final bombing instructions for the Daniel 8 war.

The Goat's retaliation response, issued as a coded poem with embedded riddles!

Eli✞e Chris✞ian Soldier's (E✞C✞S)

Tribulation Period Goals

Section 4 -15

Goals to be finalized, updated, and utilized during the tribulation period by the military commander known as one of the Two Witnesses.

✪ E✞C✞S believes God Almighty has issued this decree in prophecy for their destined task.

✪ The Eli✞e Chris✞ian Soldier's (E✞C✞S) CREED: "They are soldiers of Almighty God's mighty army on earth. Christian protectorship is their duty to the greatest nation on earth, the USA - the heart of the Great Prince Michael. Their belief being, Daniel's 70th week will play out similar to the literal interpretation in Bible prophesies. Therefore, they will always act creditable to their service and disciple nation they swore to guard because they are respectful of their Christian faith in Jesus Christ."

"They are proud to be a part of the Eli✞e Chris✞ian Soldiers (E✞C✞S). They will do all in their power to make God's earthly army the finest protecting and fighting unit for Christian and Jews. They will be loyal to those under whom they serve and to Jesus Christ their only Savior and Lord of lords. They will do their full part to carry out orders, decrees, God's commands, and instructions given them or their EliUe unit."

"The Eli✞e Chris✞ian Soldiers (E✞C✞S) realize they are members of a time-honored profession - time will be running out on Daniel's 1335th day. Therefore, they shall not delay or waver in aggressively fulfilling Jesus Christ's Great Commission to MAKE disciple nations and pave the way for Christ's return. They will do their share to keep principles of freedom alive, which Jesus Christ taught. God will be with them and their unit regardless of the situation. They will strive to never disgrace God, their unit, or any disciple nation. They will discourage or restrain any soldier or civilian from saying evil things about the Eli✞e Chris✞ian Soldiers or Jesus Christ."

"E✞C✞S serves their disciple nation with honor. One of their greatest heavenly rewards will come if required to lay their lives down for their country or fellow soldiers. The Bible teaches them when a fellow soldier or Christian is in need of help because of aggressive opposition, they must help if given the opportunity. Otherwise, they may possibly be branded a coward by God Almighty. They will try to present Jesus Christ to the people of their nation and around the world as Lord and Savior and their only hope. They are GOD'S Eli✞e Chris✞ian Soldiers! "

✪ They will uphold Christian's values, while protecting property and fellow Christians. Keep their nation disciple or followers of the commands Jesus taught.

✪ E✞C✞S will protect Israel from aggressors.

Left, 4-15-1 - England, near London - Hatfield House Palace (1480 A.D.) - King's Chair: I sat in the King's chair thinking how easily power, money, and authority can tempt a person to compromise their Christian values. I truly felt if I stood up and issued a loud command for the court to sit that all 200 or so present plus the court attendees would obey. This overwhelming sense of gaining power and authority can lead to reckless disregard for a person's allegiance to the Lord God. The next problem to manifests its ugly head will be lukewarmness. The Spirit-filled Christian will have to deal with some very powerful lukewarm and self-promoting elected officials. It will be difficult to expose the enemy's true intentions toward the state, because many love money, power, and greed.

✪ E✞C✞S believes the Kingdom of God is advancing by force (Matthew 10:32-34, 11:12). It will oppose the European led Leopard Beast with its Mark, Number, and Name of the Beast, taxation, and finally the last Beast - the Beast with the Three Ugly Heads led by the Final Antichrist and supported by the False Prophet.

✪ E✞C✞S will use any force necessary to accomplish the goal of taking down the Final Antichrist kingdom before the end of the Great Tribulation. This task will be difficult because the False Prophet supports the Final Antichrist.

✪ E✞C✞S believes the victory will be theirs through the Lord God and the Battle is His alone. They are his assigned Warriors of Honor.

✪ E✞C✞S has faith that there is no greater honor in heaven than to die following these decrees and goals (1 John 3:16).

✪ E✞C✞S understands they will be led by the Two Witnesses as an aggressive offensive force as well as a defensive army.

Eli✞e Chris✞ian Soldiers (E✞C✞S) Commandments

The Purpose is clear, follow the Lord God's end time instructions! The military commander known as one of the Two Witnesses will finalize, update, and command into action the following objectives and goals for the Eli✞e Chris✞ian Soldiers during the tribulation period.

1. DEFINE CLEAR OBJECTIVES

a. First, the Eli✞e Chris✞ian Soldier can distinguish the truth as spoken by the Lord God through Christian's writings. Therefore, REALITY becomes that which exists and agrees with God's end time prophecies. Not what the Leopard Beast concocted and twisted with fictional or deceptive imagery through the propaganda machine of the electronic news and advertising media (internet web of deceit). Reality to an Eli✞e Chris✞ian Soldier will be different from the world's perception. Therefore, they will be steadfast against political maneuvering by the Leopard and mentally tough to withstand the pressure.

b. The E✞C✞S believe the literal interpretation of the first-reading of the Great Commission (Matthew 28:18-20) will be their mandate to move toward making other nations into Disciple Nations under Lord Jesus Christ.

c. The E✞C✞S will work with the UACC to confront their enemy and protect Israel, Christians and property under the UACC Seven-Point Church - Protection Commitment - Item Seven (7). Note: Eli✞e Chris✞ian Soldiers are not affiliated directly with the UACC, but are separate entities. They do have a common goal under item seven (7). The difference being, they can take the offensive, but the UACC can only take a defensive stance.

d. The E✞C✞S understands they volunteered as **God's warriors**, knowing fully will the hazards of their calling. They will endeavor to uphold the prestige, honor, and high godly Spirit of their regiment.

e. Eli✞e Chris✞ian Soldiers understand they will forcefully advance the kingdom of God here on earth. This aggressive act has been ordained for the last days by Almighty God so they may lay hold and have authority to make ready for the ushering in of the kingdom by Jesus Christ's second coming to completion (Matthew 11:12). Honorable Soldiers learn through experience how to survive, in a life-or-death situation - by faction, alliance, or religious motivation, whom they can trust. They must learn to think and act like the enemy, to blend in like terrorists, and aggressively kill them.

f. The Eli✞e Chris✞ian Soldier foresees his duties may fall in the unconventional or special operations category. Therefore, the targets cannot be attacked the traditional way. However, the strategic and operational target generally has to do with the center of gravity of an enemy. The center of gravity, which must be eliminated can be physical, psychological, economic, or false spiritual ideology to achieve the purpose intended if conventional methods could not deal with the threat.

2. The E✞C✞S understands that increased unity produces, greater victories and farther-reaching influence. Eli✞e Chris✞ian Soldiers will strive at never failing their brothers in arms. They will shoulder more than a share of the task whatever it may be, one hundred percent and then more. Each soldier will always keep mentally alert, physically strong, and morally straight.

3. When it is time to fight, the Eli✞e Chris✞ian Soldiers will not hesitate. The infidels will attack them from all sides but they will push aggressiveness to the limit and win the fight. They know procrastination and paralysis to fight gives loss by default - by indecision, cowardice, and pride (Luke 10:19). The spread of political Islamic government ideology under Sharia Law and the European led world government (MNO) will mean future submission to it if not fought. Therefore, Eli✟e Chris✟ian Soldiers choose to fight the infidels along with the world Leopard government and neutralize them.

4. Almighty God chooses leaders from among the Eli✟e Chris✟ian Soldier. One Witness in the tribulation period is a commander and he will make ready for his leadership by summoning the call to action early. The other Witness will become the leader of the USA to lead the fight against aggression toward Israel and North and South America. Both Witnesses actions will be done using end time birthing pain principles (Matthew 24:8). They will warn of cause and effect to any nation's actions as associated with the Leopard Beast. Their warning will be, **"The Leopard is coming! The Leopard is coming! "** They will warn of Europe and others trying to take USA by legal action or causing economic collapse. They will further sound the call to start legal action to have Islam declared a clear and immediate danger against the USA, its constitution, the rule of western civilized law, allies, and interests. Eli✟e Chris✟ian Soldier's actions are against any hostile organization, treaty, or government, which does not have core beliefs in Jesus Christ as Lord and Savior and His teachings (disciple nation). Therefore, the Leopard Beast is declared enemy of North and South America.

5. The Air war must be implemented first. By this, an Eli✟e Chris✟ian Soldier understands prayer will be his first line of action. Understanding, as time moves the test cycle into the final seven years or tribulation period, they are once again in Old Testament time or eye for an eye strategy. They must ratchet up the intensity of the fight to find and destroy sources of generating power, and launch pads for Satan's fiery darts.

6. When committed to a mission the E✟C✟S will know exactly what will be expected of them. They do not have the option to surrender or agree to peace agreements! Kill or be killed is their destiny for they were born for this moment to do great things for the Lord God. God assigned each one to this mission before time began. God will guide their fate to quickly neutralize the infidels and sternly resist the Leopard world government with unyielding determination.

7. The E✟C✟S realize a few specialized missions sometimes become one way. Modern warfare may dictate the resources to get a team or individual into an area but because of distance, loss of technology, battle plan shift, enemy counter attack, and other unforeseen changes, are unable to get them out of harms way. Volunteers will be chosen. It will be a great honor to serve the Almighty God in this way (John 15:13 and 1 John 3:16). Eli✟e Chris✟ian Soldiers know their leaders, the Two Witnesses, are destined to a one-way trip for world peace at Jerusalem when their assigned time comes (earthly death) to exit. The Eli✟e Chris✟ian Soldier is proud to serve without hesitation in the same fashion as their leaders. They know every effort will be made to return them safely after a mission, but end time warfare during the Tribulation Period sometimes dictates otherwise. They have the faith to believe God is with the Eli✟e Chris✟ian Soldier so who can stand against them?

Below, 4-15-2- Italy, Rome - St. Paul (outside the Walls Basilica): Inside St. Paul's (outside the Walls - San Paolo Fuori le Mura) there is this vault or underneath this area, that reputedly holds St. Paul's remains. Whether all, part, or none of St. Paul's remains are there, does not change what he did. Saul, who's name was changed to St. Paul, thought he was doing right by going against Christian values but later found out he was wrong. We as individuals have experienced similar circumstances. Tragically, we must judge our nation and the way it has been heading. Would Almighty God approve? Has your nation moved away from Christian values and are your leaders selling your nation to the highest bidder in the Leopard Beast. Do you think its time to do something about it? There must be radical change and this will require sacrifice. Most Christians are not willing to do this but the Lord God will motivate many people in the near future.

DEFINING THE ENEMY

To defeat the enemy it must be identified

DURING THE
TRIBULATION PERIOD.

By using birthing pains back to present day,
we can highlight the problem today
and begin to address it NOW!

~~~~~~~~~~~~~~~~~~~~~~~~

ENEMY NUMBER ONE

Self - lack of end time faith - denial

Issuing of God Almighty's final decrees through THE SCROLL, from the Wake Up Call Prophecies, covers this problem of 'self' completely.

ENEMY NUMBER TWO

European led Leopard Beast and
the Eagle with the Three Ugly Heads

This book discusses the tribulation governing bodies; one will be North and South America (The Great Prince Michael - Daniel 12:1). Michael's enemies are: The first half of the tribulation will be the European led Leopard Beast (Daniel 7:6 and Revelation 13:1-10). It will be taken over by the remainder of the Eagle with the Three Ugly Heads (Daniel 7:7 and Revelation 13:11-18) in the last half of the tribulation period led by the Final Antichrist and endorsed by the False Prophet.

ENEMY NUMBER THREE

Non-Christian Religions, Political philosophies where loyalty to the state comes first, and a blend such as Fundamental Moslem Ideology of World Islamization under Sharia Law using militaristic overtones.

Take Heed: The Eli✞e Chris✞ian Soldiers led by an American commander called "Destroyer" (one of the Two Witnesses) **will perform the task listed in this section during the tribulation period** just as Jesus did when he cleansed the temple of the money exchangers. He had a task to complete (Matthew 21:12) **without hate or anger.** Likewise, the Eli✞e Chris✞ian Soldiers will complete the assignment designed by God Almighty. This will insure Christian values and commands dictating constitutional rule of law over governments in North and South America. At the same time, it will preserve the lives of the cooperative infidels. This Combative Operation shall be know as:

The dominant philosophy of Islam is not a religion and must not be protected by government laws because its basic belief equates to Islamic ideology and government laws are the same (Sarah 48:28, 61:9).

Michael's Whirlwind!

(Exodus 22:20-33 and Nahum 1:3)

Political philosophies where loyalty to the state comes first have always been threats to Christian societies. Non-Christian religions will be another end time enemy of Spirit-filled Christians. It will be important to point out Moslems and their converts will be an aggressive enemy. The dominant philosophy of Islam is not a religion because its basic belief equates to Islamic ideology and government laws are the same (Sarah 48:28, 61:9). Therefore, any global, national, state, or local law must not protect Islam as a religion. Basic (fundamental) Islam equates to a political ideology with a goal under the banner of jihad to remove all existing governments of the world and replace them with Islamic desert tribal laws and government (Sharia law). The average Westerner must come to grips with Islamic countries serious drive to promote their dogmatic politics and intolerant spiritual minded social behavior as inseparable.

The Eli✞e Chris✞ian Soldier understands the Middle East Arabs are using an old negotiating gambit to further their world takeover to Islamic Sharia Law. It has been called "Good Guy - Bad Guy". The Good Guys are the ones infiltrating a country by immigration saying "Peace", "Peace, because Islam does not promote violence." Others will say "Peace and Security" or "Peace and Justice". These immigrates deceivingly know the person or group addressed will perceive they are talking about their behavior under the host-nation's constitution and laws of the person being addressed. But this is far from the truth. The Islamic immigrants are in reality referring to "Peace" or "Justice" or "Security" as under Islamic Theocracy or government when they overtake a nation and put it under Sharia law.

Their propaganda methods are to soften the perception of Islam and the Prophet Muhammad: Some of their deceiving information is being spread through comedians, cartoons, stand-up comics, and animated feature-length films about the Prophet Muhammad. Their misleading propaganda has been
~~~~~~~~~~~~~~~~~~~~~~~~

This propaganda leads to misinformation, it is the same fundamental (basic) expansionist teaching instruction of political Islam, to conquer the world and put it under Sharia Law.

initiated to combat the Islamaphobia (all Muslims and their converts are bad guys). This effort is to soften resistance, with a subtle appeal to increase converts, and brainwash citizens and children into believing Islam is the answer. They promote Islam as a wonderful spiritual atmosphere rather than the truth - a heavy-handed Arab-male dominated political system.

The Eli✝e Chris✝ian Soldiers will not fall for this type trickery because history proves the Good Guy perception is a lie and Islam has always been advanced by intimidation and the sword. Furthermore, the Eli✝e Chris✝ian Soldiers recognize that some world organizations and nation-states will brand them as projecting Islamaphobia (attacking or condemning all of Islam). The sources of these accusations are non Spirit-filled Christian identities and will be ignored.

The Eli✝e Chris✝ian Soldiers understand Islam's first goal involves: Infiltration, promote propaganda, use of violence, and finally overthrowing existing government. Their primary goal is setting up a mandatory political system of Sharia law. Middle Eastern Male Arabs not converts will control management of this new government. Their second goal is to force Islamic spiritual undertones on the conquered society. Therefore, the Eli✝e Chris✝ian Soldiers will look at Islam's first goal and not recognize their second objective by refusing them religious and /or civil protection under the constitution of the USA. Let us analysis further.

On the other hand, the European led international press and the Good Guy Moslems deceivingly call the Bad Guy Moslems such names as extreme Moslems, terrorists, freedom fighters, insurgents, Suicider's, bombers, and the like. The truth being they are all Moslems or their converts! This manipulation of facts can be exposed through history which proves fundamental teachings of the Prophet Muhammad will eventually evolve in using violence and intimidation to win their cause. This propaganda leads to misinformation, it is the same fundamental (basic) expansionist teaching instruction of political Islam to conquer the world and put it under Sharia Law. Muhammad made the statement, *"Say: 'I am no bringer of new-fangled doctrine among the Messengers,* ***nor do I know what will be done with me or with you. ....'"*** (Surah 46:9). This verse and the verses listed below negate Islam as a genuine religion and place it in the secular, artificial, and political world of Islamic government ruling law under Sharia. Furthermore, Surah law (48:28 and 61:9) has been prophesied through Islam to spread into a worldwide takeover. Remember Islamic religion as they call it equates to government ideology under Sharia law. Knowledge becomes apparent they are talking about you and non-Moslems if we consider the "Sword" verses, which promote killing the Jews, Christians, and infidels or making slaves out of them. Fundamental Islamic ideology is an immediate danger to any nation, which does not want to surrender their country's constitution and governing body over to the Arabs.

The key point to be made about each listed verse below becomes very disturbing. Islam political and warring ideology does not fit the definition of religion and it is an enemy of the following: Christian/ Western-European rule of law, liberty, equality, separation of government to impose its religion (salvation message), human rights, ideas concerning individualism which spawn constitutionalism, and fundamental democratic style of government. Read the Qur'an to get the complete text and meaning. **Here are the points or paraphrase of each verse:**

(See God's revenge in the Bible - Psalm 64)

* Surah 2:190-191, fight in the cause of Allah.
* Surah 2:191-192, slay them wherever you catch the unbelievers. Drive them out where they have driven you out (whole world).
* Surah 4:77, fight against Jews and Christians who are the friends of Satan.
* Surah 4:85, fight (unbelievers), for the cause of Allah.
* Surah 4:95-96, believers fight in the cause of Allah with their wealth and lives. Say no to people who greet you with an offer of peace.
* Surah 4:89-90, seize them and slay the unbelievers whenever you find them, take no prisoners as a friend or helper.
* Surah 4:101-102, unbelievers are open enemies to you.
* Surah 4:102-103, unbelievers, Allah has prepared a humiliating punishment.
* Surah 8:13-18, I will instill terror into their hearts of the unbelievers. Smite ye about their necks (**Cut off their heads**) and smite all their fingers - tips of them. (**Amputate all fingers**)

When meeting disbelievers, advance in force and do not turn and run or Allah will get mad. Do not take credit for the unbelievers you kill for it is Allah who has done this.

* Surah 9:29, fight those who believe not in Allah. Allah curses Jews and Christians.
* Surah 5:51, Moslems take not the Jews and the Christians for friends or protectors.
* Surah 4:74, lose life in battle and get great reward in Hereafter.
* Surah 2:216, fighting is prescribed upon Muslims.
* Surah 9:5, **fight and slay the pagans (Christians and Jews)** whenever you find them, beleaguer them, and lie in wait for them, in every stratagem of war.
* Surah 5:33-34, punishment of those who wage war against Moslem is: **execution, or crucifixion or the cutting off of hands and feet on alternate sides.**
* Surah 4:34-35, men are the protectors and maintainers of women because Allah has given them more.

If women become disloyal and ill-conducted, admonish (call down using a warning) them (first), (next) refuse to share their beds, and (last chastise) punishment, even **beating them**!
* Hadith 9:57, whoever changes his Islamic religion - kill him!
* Fatwa (a religious decree) issued by some leaders today to kill Americans, Jews, and their allies.
* Whether Moslems use "Peace, Peace" as an expression of jihad (struggle) or "Boom, Boom" as an expression of jihad (meaning a continuing warfare against nonbelievers), it does not matter. **Moslem's goals are to place every government of the world under Islamic Sharia Law. Therefore, Islam is classified an extreme threat!** I repeat Islam is not a religion but a governmental Ideology (regulatory body of Arab clerics to oversee nation-state's political and social affairs).

Islam ideology hides behind a few Christian and Judaism teachings (some which have been rewritten and twisted to favor the Arab male) only to gain protection through religious laws. This will be ideal for the Arab Moslems, but not very productive for the second class converts, the lowly infidels, and Islamic women.

The Eli✞e Chris✞ian Soldier uses the term second class convert not as a put down but a warning witnessing tool to explain to the converts the teaching of the Qur'an. Converts are non-Arab people who convert to Islam. They never hold Arab Moslem status. Moslems are to oversee the converts and can do with them as they determine. They can kill converts, make slaves of them, or simply leave them alone. The message, converts must always live in fear of the Moslems overseers, even in the USA. Take note at what is happening to the converts in Africa.

YOUR ASSIGNMENT!

Citizens must immediately demand that their elected officials reclassify Islam as a hostile intolerant political ideology not a religion and therefore an

enemy of the State.

Consequently, Moslems and their converts are entitled to no-rights in that country and must be ejected.

When a person converts to Islam or is an Arab Moslem then they have given up their national citizenship and declared war against the non-Islamic government in charge of the nation they currently live in. They are entitled to no-rights under the constitution of that government. Their right are now covered under Islamic Sharia Law.

They will use two types of offensive weapons first terrorism and second immigration hiding behind religious laws of protection. Given enough time that nation will be consumed and forced to abide by Islam laws (observe Western Europe's and Africa's problems). Therefore Islamic followers are classified the enemy of the Eli✞e Chris✞ian Soldier. In other words Moslems and their converts are enemies of the USA and the rest of North and South America as well as any nation-state which wants to continue under its current government laws and political system.

Make no mistake about it, Islam is a one sided political organization bent on creating violence to oppose each countries constitutional order and along with immigration, use intimidation to implement their governmental law called Sharia. **Therefore, strong words must accompany very strong action to protect each government.** We observe the Leopard is currently being consumed with the cancerous Islamic movement to slowly take it over. The citizens within Michael must learn by the Leopard's mistakes and immediately eject this cancer.

The Eli✞e Chris✞ian Soldier has determined the consequences between the lines what must begin to happen and the effect it will have on people. Citizens are fighting for the soul of their nation and the Eli✞e Chris✞ian Soldier will lead the charge. Citizens must immediately start demanding from their elected officials that Islam be classified an enemy of the State. To do nothing, is to admit defeat and the takeover of their nation by Islamic Sharia Law. Arab Moslems have been immigrating to the USA and other nations to secretly pursue a slow takeover of that nation like a cancer from within a body. They have not come to chase the "American Dream" as our forefathers and mothers did. Think, think, and prepare! Everyone's life will be affected. Christians will be called to suffer.

Powerful organizations control or manipulate most multinational corporations and many politicians.

The gravity or pull is to take the Americas underneath the European led Leopard Beast for security and prosperity.

Immigration should have been stopped before the Tribulation period. Islam's political ideology of world takeover also should have been declared a clear and immediate enemy of the state. Therefore, any followers must be removed or in the process of being removed from the North and South America continents. They will be given free passage to any nation within the Leopard Beast except, Gaza and the West Bank. Unfortunately, the full wrath of the Eli✞e Chris✞ian Soldier will have to be brought to bear against the infidels who refuse to go or make trouble. It has already been prophesied in Issue One, if the reader will analyze between the lines, that God will remove a large cancerous problem in South America. Therefore, patience will be required in South America.

ENEMY NUMBER FOUR

Multinational Corporations with ties to the rich man's clubs in USA and European Leopard Beast

The buy and sell mode equals trade, power, and money. The enemy is multinational corporations influenced by the three or four USA and European secret and open organizations, orders and societies. These entities are filled with lukewarmers who are very powerful and rich people. These powerful organizations and orders control and selfishly influence many nations' leadership. Many politicians today have been go-along get-along compromising elected officials to enhance the good life so they and their party can be reelected next term. This has been achieved at the expense of eroding the USA's national security and other nations in favor of the Leopard Beast.

Therefore regardless of what they say, most multinational corporations are the Spirit-filled Christian's enemy and therefore are the USA's enemy. This does not mean Christians cannot work with them, but remember their goal is not the Eli✞e Chris✞ian Soldier's goal. Most multinational Corporations and many politicians are bought out by powerful organizations. However, there is not a total global conspiracy by the rich elite and global bankers to completely control the world. It is simply economics: money driven commercial velocity, common sense business practice, and security compelling business to globalize. Corporation loyalty will move from the nation it evolved from when that corporation chooses to go into the international - global (Antichrist spirit inspired) market place. The European led Leopard Beast appears to be the best business move to improve their bottom line and revenues globally while improving security of their assets. The gravity or pull is to take the Americas along with all nations underneath the European led Leopard Beast for security and prosperity. Therefore, they must be classified as enemies. Are you beginning to understand the picture God has given through these prophesies to enlighten you to this immediate danger? Are you going to contact your state and federal representatives about this critical issue or be silent and let them take you over?

The Eli✞e Chris✞ian Soldiers understands that citizens will be required to give up many of the comforts pertaining to the Good Life if they are to win the USA back as the Framers envisioned when they wrote the USA Constitution. The Good Life will have to be renounced in favor of the resistance movement. The Eli✞e Chris✞ian Soldiers and allies know the longer they wait the more painful it will be to remove the cancerous global government.

ENEMY NUMBER FIVE

Lukewarmers and Unbelievers

Understand the four Spirits Outside Time-Space!

During the end of the test on the world, four spirits from outside our test cycle's displacement of time-space have been and will continue to impute thought and insight into our minds. We as participants can choose where to accept this information and how to assimilate correctly end time preprograming. Sadly the lukewarmers and unbelievers will follow the wrong information and therefore are the Spirit-filled Christian's enemy! Three of the four spirits will lead people away from the Lord God if they are not Spirit-filled Christians, who can discern the difference. Only one Spirit of the four will take people through their end time test cycle properly. That will be the Jesus side of the Holy Spirit discussed in this book - "Jesus the Spirit of prophecy and insight."

Above, 4-15-3 - Greece, Athens - Acropolis - the Caryatids: The southern portico of the Korai or Caryatids marked the grave of the mystical king Cecrops. Six graceful maidens, attired in Doric peplos, proudly support the entablature over capitals with special decoration. Greece had many mystical stories to tell about kings, gods, and spirits. As I looked at the beautiful Caryatids, I remembered how enticing and cunning the wrong spirits appear to us and are interacting with us today. Of all the different forces that interact with people, there are many wrong spirits, which seem right but are wrong in God Almighty's sight. Christians must study themselves approved and have the full armor of Almighty God or they may be deceived in endtimes.

One assignment the Holy Spirit was given has been to deliver God's Great Delusion on a disobedient world, which unfortunately includes many of today's Churches. This delusion is not to deceive but a preprogramed part of the **enhanced test** associated with the end of time. Two of several parts of this delusion are, believing in the many different rapture theories as signed (visual) events and following the European led Leopard Beast which evolves into the last beast (world government) for security, financial gain, and peace.

Note: Deception enters the picture when Satan makes an idea look more appealing than God's options. Disobedience enters the picture when the sin within us overrides spiritual intellect and we become convinced Satan's direction is creditable. Failure in God's eye, enter the picture when action is taken to follow or believe the Great Delusion (end time test) rather than follow solid Biblical principles and laws. ✂

The other two-sided spirits comes from Satan. One we are very familiar with, which is Satan's deceptive side of making bad look appealing. We have all fallen for that at one time or another. But the dangerous side, which is hard to discern has to do when he masquerades as an angel of light (preacher, Jesus, righteous politician, Archangel Gabriel, and the like). Matthew 24:4 or any scripture dealing with endtimes will have similar warnings -- watch for people who look right with God to be like snakes working for Satan, -- watch out -- take heed -- wake up -- and other warnings. Satan's spirit has been promoting acceptance under the European Leopard Beast (MNO) for personal security, finance, and peace solutions which has been a part of the preprogramed test (Revelation 3:10) that equates to part of God's Great Delusion.

Why would God allow all this misinformation to overwhelm people when they are going through one of the most distressful times in history? When a person needs help and reaches out, why are three sources of insight wrong and only one is correct? To make matters worse, most leaders are leaning toward the European Leopard Beast (MNO). Revelation 3:10 gives us the answer, "*... the hour of trial that is going to come upon the whole world to* ***test*** *those who live on the earth.*"

Which spirits are people listening to, the three that will cause them to fail the test or the correct one, which will help them pass? The disastrous outcome of this test will encourage lukewarmers to ask Jesus the same question John the Baptist did. Some may question, "Are you really the Christ I need to be asking for help and following or should I go with the European Roman Empire (MNO) and look for another Savior."

Deception enters the picture when Satan makes an idea look more appealing than God's options.

Some of the Great Christian Falling Away is caused by a material breach in many misinformed Christians following the MNO.

Note: Apply birthing pains to the above paragraphs and it becomes evident everyone's lifestyle will change in the near future (see section 2-9 to 2-20). But think and prepare! The longer citizens and nations wait to act, the more it will cost them in most areas of their lives. ✂

Learn how to calculate your own personal MARK in the next section!

THE CALCULATIONS BEGIN

Section 5

This entire section-5 was first prophesied and recorded as a matter of public record in a 232-page book called: Original WAKE UP CALL PROPHECIES, Rough draft Issue-I. It was published (2-1996) under ISBN 0-9651408-0-6. This Section was prophesied between the following dates; May 13, to June 9, 1994, on original pages; 15 to 52. (Except poem 8-1993) and (Pictures with insight and commentary added in 2005 - 2007)

Note: This page is where the original Rough draft Issue - 1, book entitled Wake Up Call Prophecies started on page - 15.

Section 5 - 1

From the earliest days of my youth, Revelation 13 has challenged me. Because I enjoy numbers and calculations, the number 666 has been intriguing.

On Friday, May 13, 1994, I had just finished reading this chapter when my conscience became aware of the voice of the Spirit of Christ speaking in my thought processes. "Put your study materials aside and reread chapter thirteen in its entirety. I will show you something no one can explain."

This seemed very strange to me, so naturally my argumentative nature began to debate and question these thoughts. I found myself telling God what was in chapter thirteen and started explaining to Him what He already knew. Insight disclosed my arrogance in giving a folksy version of the dragon, beast, and false prophet as they try to tattoo numbers on everyone and deceive the world by spreading their false miracles. The Lord waited patiently for me to rehearse my foolish assumptions.

When my thought process was ready to listen, the Spirit said, "My son, verse eighteen is where you will see what I've hidden all these centuries. Now shall be the time to reveal Satan's trickery and deception which is associated in the three hidden numbers."

Suddenly my soul became gripped with fear and excitement as I reread verse eighteen. **CALCULATE THE NUMBER.** It seemed as if the other words disappeared from the page. Understanding the meaning of the number will be revealed through the process of calculating. My imagination was immediately intrigued.

Reading verse eighteen a second time disclosed, it is man's number. Before this, I had assumed this was Satan's number for man. More importantly, the Bible clearly says Satan uses man's number.

Deception doesn't generally come full-blown. It is gradual and not easily detected. Deception must not appear to be deception or it won't be effective. Jesus referred to birth pains to illustrate the progressive movement of events toward a predetermined and known conclusion.

The global population uses numbers. How threatening and deceptive are numbers? The Spirit of Christ has foretold a satanic plan to gain control of people through a sequence of numbers, which will become prominent in the times just before the return of Jesus Christ to earth.

The Lord God does not openly reveal His plans to the world, but He does reveal them to His elect. Jesus clearly told Peter, James, John, and Andrew (Matthew 24; Mark 13; Luke 21) the elect people shall become special targets of deception. Therefore, the Lord God provides the knowledge for the elect, which will enable them to detect and expose the deception. The saints of the Lord God have always had the right knowledge at the right time. Today is no exception for the elect of the present times are as much a part of the Lord God's plan as the generation of Moses.

The unraveling of the three mystery numbers began with the instruction, "Look at the pad on the telephone. That is the key."

I studied the arrangement of numbers and letters on the telephone pad. It became clear to me through the international telephone systems there would be a worldwide electronic communications Internet or web. Through this device, it shall be possible for the entire population of the earth to communicate with the Image of the Beast during the time known as the great tribulation.

The Spirit of Christ has foretold a satanic plan to gain control of people through a sequence of numbers, which will become prominent in the times just before the return of Jesus Christ to earth.

More instructions followed, "Get your business index cards and look at the telephone numbers." The international telephone number is made up of five series of numbers, as I studied further: 011 xxx x xxx xxxx. The first three digits of 011 are the access numbers to the international telephone systems. The second series of numbers access a particular country code. The next series identifies a city. The final two series of seven numbers is a specific telephone location.

The plan materialized in my mind. The beast will gain access to the international telephone number and telelectronic Internet (web) transfer system. My mind began racing with the idea of what might happen if the beast had an Internet number of 011 666 x xxx xxxx. It would be possible to have electronic access to the world by interfacing his number with the major computer systems now in operation. Therefore, it appears the Number of the Beast is interwoven with man's present numbers. The numbering system is partially being used today.

Studying the calculations closer, I began writing out the numbers we live by today - credit cards, social security, federal identification numbers, and telephone numbers. Bible prophecy scholars have said the old Roman Empire shall become prominent in the last days before the coming of Christ. The geographical area of this empire included Jerusalem.

A close examination of the messages of the prophets, especially of Daniel and Revelation, can lead to a logical conclusion the Antichrist may first choose Rome, Italy, as the capital of his empire. If we assume this interpretation is accurate, we are in for a very interesting observation based on telephone numbers. If someone wanted access to the seat of government for the Antichrist, he would dial the following sequence of numbers:

- 011-972-6-66J-ESUS.
- 011 is the access number to the international telephone system.
- 972 is the current number for the nation of Israel. It is also the alpha sequence of ZSC, which will be discussed later in other calculations that reveal hidden meanings.
- 6 is the current city code for Rome and could possibly become the code number for spiritual Rome.
- 66x-xxxx becomes the specific location of the Antichrist.
-

The Spirit revealed the Number of the Beast is different but dependent upon and linked to the Mark of the Beast. It shall be the same with the Beast's Mark and the Number. The different sequences of numbers functioning in the correct order or combination shall make it possible for someone to obtain the means and power to gain total world control.

Let us consider the telephone number system once again. Through the international telecommunications Internet web, the ten-area worldwide regional kingdom federation in Daniel, chapter two, will have direct access to the beast and the beast to them.

During my ten years as an engineer associate and manufacturing supervisor in the electronic switching equipment industry, there emerged a new buzzword, which began being used in the, 70s and, 80s -- "joint venture." This enabled nations to link their electronic hardware to the systems of other nations and thus create a global communications network. This makes it possible for citizens of the world to literally be linked together in a master computer and telecommunications system.

The Spirit of Christ prompted me to look at the telephone pad again and transpose the numeric figures to the alpha sequence. By punching the alpha sequence of MNO, you transform into the numeric sequencing code of 666.

The question entered my mind, "What does MNO stand for? The meaning requires wisdom." I didn't know.

The Spirit directed me to write down Millennium Nations Organized. This organization of nations will be deceived by the claim of the beast that he is Jesus Christ the Messiah.

Draw a line across the page was my instructions, in order to begin calculating a different set of numbers.

I then wrote the heading - MARK OF THE BEAST. The thought entered my mind, "You must calculate the other numbers called the `Mark of the Beast' before you can calculate the actual Number of the Beast."

My initial reaction became one of argumentative resistance because I had always been taught 666 was a single number rather than the key to a calculated series of number sequences.

The Holy Spirit gave insight by revealing the meaning of verse eighteen. In order to have access to the electronic highway or web of telelectronic energy transfers, you must first know the number, which identifies the beast. This number is his personal mark and is another series of numbers based on the three sixes.

At this point, it is very important for the reader to understand what the Spirit of Christ was communicating to me. The Spirit related that for this part of the calculating, I must try to think as the beast, and how he would implement the exact order of the number 666 in Revelation 13.

While pretending to think as the beast, the Holy Spirit conveyed to me three sequences, which became clear that would serve to implement the beast's plan of deception.

✪ **S SEQUENCE** - Read Revelation 13:15,16: The **S** was derived from the **S** in **S**ocial ID and how the beast would try to control identity. The first step must be to give an identity number to everyone. In the event someone refused to worship the beast, the world police (quick regional reactionary force) would try to find and execute him.

✪ **Z SEQUENCE** - Read Revelation 13:15: The **Z** was derived from the **Z** in **Z**ip Code, meaning locator number assigned to each person. The second phase must be to monitor the physical and electronic movement of everyone through the electronic Internet web system. Any form of rebellion, including teaching the Bible, could be quickly squelched electronically. This sequence would also replace the passport.

✪ **C SEQUENCE** - Read Revelation 13:17: The **C** came from the **C** in **C**ash sales transaction. The third, and final phase must be to gain control of money and financial transactions through the Internet web system. All transactions must use the personal PIN of the beast, number 666, to be authorized to conduct business.

"That's easy," I thought. The correct sequence was "SZC". Nevertheless, the Spirit quickly began leading me into more calculations.

Three different categories of numbers began to emerge, as I started the calculating process. These sets of numbers, if used together, have the potential of literally bringing a population of people under the control of a single individual.

The three calculations are identified by the letters Z, S, and C. They are the alpha equivalents of 972 on the telephone keypad, which is the country code for Israel. Their calculations are as follows.

✪ **The S Number:** The **S** number stands for a **S**ocial Identification Number such as the social security number. This is a number the USA government forces by law upon every citizen. Other nations may use similar numbers which might be phone numbers, national ID, personal pin, numeric finger prints scan, and the like. The standard social security number equates to a nine-digit number similar to 123-45-6789. These numbers are in the major computer networks and an inquirer can obtain information quickly. Assume these social identification numbers are in the computer of the one who will be identified as the Final Antichrist. The right to pull up information shall be possible by using an access code number six.

Utilizing my background in mathematics drew me to the conclusion, the beast could easily obtain information about anyone, anytime, and anywhere. In addition, if anyone wanted to obtain information from the computer systems controlled by the beast, it could be done by dialing the 666 access codes along with the identifying numbers.

Mental weariness setting in while pondering over the insight the Spirit of Christ was giving me. His prompting caused me to begin looking at the next number sequence.

✪ **The Z Number:** One way to control a population would be to have the ability to be able to control their moving about and communications. Various governments have imposed such regulatory systems in the past and will do so again. This would be especially effective if a particular segment of the population needed constant monitoring. Such a "warden" could know the exact location of potential prisoners at all times. With today's electronic technology, population monitoring is feasible by simply implanting an identifying silicon chip on or in the person.

The **Z** stands for a location identity number. This is similar to the zip code number for mail delivery and uses a sequence of five numbers - 12345. Access to the Antichrist could be through the code of six plus the zip, or **Z**, number. At present, this is a number used voluntarily. Under the right circumstances, it could be forced upon people to use this number to communicate with others and identify their personal location. This sequence would also replace your passport.

Below, 5-1-1-Israel, Jerusalem - Church of all Nations: The presbytery is a large fragment of rock on which Jesus was supposed to have prayed the night before the Passion and can be seen in front of the high altar. The rock has been surrounded by a crown of wrought iron thorns.

The Rock and the thorns are real and uplifting as a reminder of what Jesus did for each one of us. However, the name of the building, Church of all Nations, could be considered amusing. I assume this is a representation or effort to mimic, Mark 11:17. It is where Jesus quoted Isaiah 56:7, which referred to God's building structure as being His house of prayer for all nations. I do not know of any nation not trying to or already have kicked the Lord God out of their laws and government. Sadly, I do not know of a single nation on earth, which has most of its people Spirit-filled Christians that would represent one nation for Christ's Church.

Above, 5-1-2-England, London - House of Parliament: We walked through London and fell in love with it. However, after the Ezekiel 38-war (Gulf War - III), the tired Old Lion will side more with the Leopard Beast to gain peace and security. This will isolate North and South America when it comes to Money - the buy and sell mode, which will be controlled by the European led Leopard Beast.

In the name of security, government will produce technology, which will intrude into the privacy of individual lives as well as business. This technology will make it possible for a computer to break through billions of pieces of scrambled, coded, secret information.

In the hands of the government of the beast, it would be impossible to hide any information or conduct personal affairs or business without detection and monitoring. Within moments, policing agents could locate any individual.

✪ **The C Number:** The third number will be the **C** sequence which is related to having access to financial institutions and through which one makes transactions involving money or credit. The kingdom of the Antichrist could very possibly begin with an access code of six followed by a specific account number; a number would be similar to six- (x), where (x) being a loop from one to nine representing checking, selling, and/or loans. On a global scale, many people are already interacting through banking and credit numbers even though participation is voluntary.

The Bible clearly indicates one method to be used by the beast to control the population of his empire is to exercise absolute power over the right to transact business matters (Revelation 13:17). Whoever controls the monetary system will control the lives of the population. The Beast will govern business, industry, and all economic facets of life as well as social interaction. Banking, buying, savings, insurance, wages, retirement income, and all other transactions linked to money will be limited to those who receive the Mark of the Beast.

Society has witnessed a steady decrease in the use of currency when conducting business transactions. Monetary transactions are rapidly becoming electronic functions. Wages and retirement incomes are deposited directly to banking accounts of recipients. More purchases are very likely made with checks or credit/debit cards than with currency.

Now it is increasingly possible to think in terms of a consumer society no longer using a nation currency. Let us compare the credit card with the banking card. They have a similar appearance but their functions are somewhat different.

Credit cards led the way with their convenience and the lure to "buy now, pay later" for the things we want. Major retailers, banks, and lending agencies promote their cards because of the tremendous profits generated through interest rates and low payment plans. Your consumer transactions are quickly sent to the card-issuing company, and each month your statement arrives. How convenient.

With the arrival of automatic teller machines, banks increased their accessibility to the consumer, especially low-income people. Clients of the bank are issued cards with magnetic information strips. It is possible to transact many banking functions from convenient locations across the nation.

Banks are now issuing bank draft/credit cards, again, targeting low-income people. When you use these cards to make purchases, the amount of the purchase will automatically deducted from your bank account balance. If your account is too low, don't worry. An instant loan covers your purchase. Satan's goal will be to gain control by getting everyone into the electronic money network.

An interesting feature about credit or banking cards is in order to have access to information or funds, a person must use a secret code called the personal identification number or PIN. That's the number, which provides access to the computer through which a person will conduct his business. This points to the trend, which will very possibly be used by the beast, and his PIN is the three sequence codes 6+6+6.

Credit and banking cards with their magnetic information strips are a convenience, but they can be easily stolen and misused. However, the next logical step shall be to put the information on a tiny silicon chip and implant it under the skin on the hand or forehead. The security problem will be solved and crime will not pays as much when people carried cards.

THE LOGICAL CONCLUSION

Now let us see where these calculations could possible take us. Because we are still in a time of prophetic anticipation, we can very carefully conjecture through these three number sequences the Antichrist could control the social status, location, and financial transactions of every citizen in the realm of his government. The three calculations will form the personal (PIN) number of the Antichrist using three sixes, or 666, as a means of access to him.

The method by which the SZC sequence Mark of the Beast can logically and voluntarily be placed on the hand or forehead of an individual is by means of metallic silicon injections, laser tattoo, finger scans, or similar techniques such as implanting a tiny silicon chip under the skin on the right hand or forehead as mentioned above.

In addition, this numeric system has completely developed within the lifetime of one generation. It must be noted the Mark of the Beast equals but shall have a completely different meaning than the Mark of His Name which will be discussed later.

MARK OF THE BEAST

Section 5-2

We will look at each of the calculated number sequences and see how they come together to form the Mark of the Beast. The Bible indicates the key to calculating the mark must be 666. The number will be different for each person in the kingdom of the Antichrist. The Spirit of Christ prompted me to write out the calculations in the following order:

America's Completed Mark

18 Digits = 6 + SS # + 6 + ZIP + 6 + (1 to 9 Loop)

~~~~~~~~~~~~~~~~~~~~~~~~~~~~~~~~~~~~

NUMBER OF THE BEAST

Section 5-3

I began questioning the ordering of the SZC, reasoning the order appeared to be too simple. Most Christians I thought could easily see through the deception and refuse to take the 666. Nevertheless, the Spirit of Christ impressed the correct arrangement should be SZC for this part of the calculation. However, the sequence arrangement needed to be changed now.

When each sequence was written down as directed, an amazing thought began to emerge. The insight came very strongly to arrange the alpha sequence in a different order with its corresponding number. The order transformed to:

THE HIDDEN SERIES EQUALS ISRAEL'S COUNTRY CODE

173

(Z) equals 9 (first hidden number)

(S) equals 7 (second hidden number)

(C) equals 2 (third hidden number)

That unmistakable voice spoke to the spirit of my mind urging me to "look at the phone pad again. I'll reveal the mystery of the three numbers having been kept hidden from the saints." The hidden code emerged as an alpha sequence (ZSC), which can be translated into a numeric sequence. Again I heard, "Look at the phone pad for this shall be the key to unlocking the deceit behind the Number of the Beast."

MARK OF THE BEAST (DIGITS)

(S)	(Z)	(C)
Social	**Z**ip	**C**redit-**C**ash
Social Identity #	Location #	Credit/Bank Card #
6+123-45-6789	6+73159	6+(x)
(Forced by government)	(Voluntary use)	(Voluntary use)

America's Completed Mark (18 Digits) 6 SS # + 6 Zip + 6 (1 to 9 Loop) = Note: Information after each six (6)

Other Nations: 6 Social ID + 6 Location number + 6 (1 to 9 loop)

Note: a. Buy, sell, loans, deposits, etc., determines the number assigned in 1 to 9 loop column.

b. "6" = access code, or breaks between information.
~~~~~~~~~~~~~~~~~~~~~~~~~~~~~~~~~~~~

NUMBER OF THE BEAST					
A.	B.	C.	D.	E.	F.
011	**972‹---**	**------**	**----›6**	**66J**	**ESUS**

Below, 5-3-1-Italy, Rome - Ponte Sant' Angelo bridge: I pondered this statue of a powerful angel. Angels represent power and the old revived Roman Empire is pursuing power. European government (one of the ten heads of the upcoming Leopard Beast) will try to use their self-righteous authority and power to enforce their beliefs upon America and the world. The Americans will never concede to Europe on this point. Herein lies a great struggle with many problems for Europe and their world proclaimed Leopard government.

My eyes scanned the (Z) key. It was not on the keypad of the telephone (in 1994, no Z key, but latter it was added). Using the process of elimination technique, I began asking the Lord, "Can it be the nine key because it does not appear on the bottom set of keys?"

I received the following impression, as though the Lord instantly responded to my inquiry; "This breaks the secret to the calculations involving the concealed number which reveals the three hidden numbers in Revelation 13."

It became very hard to contain the excitement filling my soul. With amazement I began to notice the alpha key for (S) could also translate into the number seven (7) key.

Next, my memory recalled having been previously prompted to call the international telephone operator to obtain the country code for Israel. It equals, 972, and the city code for Rome, which is six (6).

The final alpha symbol is (C) which translates to number two (2).

It appeared before my very eyes. The ZSC sequence numerically calculates to the Israel country code of 972. Even though Israel has cities beginning with the number six (6), I became impressed the city of Rome must be the significant one beginning with the six (6). This sequence of numbers now translates into the Number of the Beast as follows:

A. The number, 011 can be used to direct dial into the Internet worldwide web of a self-contained community.

B. The number, 972, represents the country code for Israel. It has been part of the great plan of deception for Satan to cause people into believing "Christ" has returned to the earth and resides in Israel.

C. This part represents the spiritual unity, which will exist between religious Rome and the Jewish people.

D. This area points to the actual city code for Rome, Italy. It will be used deceptively as a means of contacting the government of the Antichrist, possibly first in Rome and finally in Israel.

E. Revelation 13:18 indicates the key to calculating the Number of the Beast has to be a series of three [sequencing] sixes (666).

F. The final four numbers will be the precise location of the beast during the great tribulation.

More pieces of the puzzle began to form in my mind as though there sparked flashes of light in my head. I assumed at first the 972 country code pointed to Italy. Further investigation disclosed it truly equates to the country code for Israel and the city code for Rome is six (6). I pondered what appeared to be an inconsistency, my mind began opening to the understanding; "during the endtimes of the Gentile Age, the religious Rome and the Jewish people will form an alliance with each other."

The 66J translates into the still unknown but future area code for the Image of the Beast. The final series of four numbers (ESUS) will be revealed in the tribulation period and will be the exact location of the headquarters of the beast. Very likely, it will be the location of the computer center from which the Antichrist links himself to everyone in his empire.

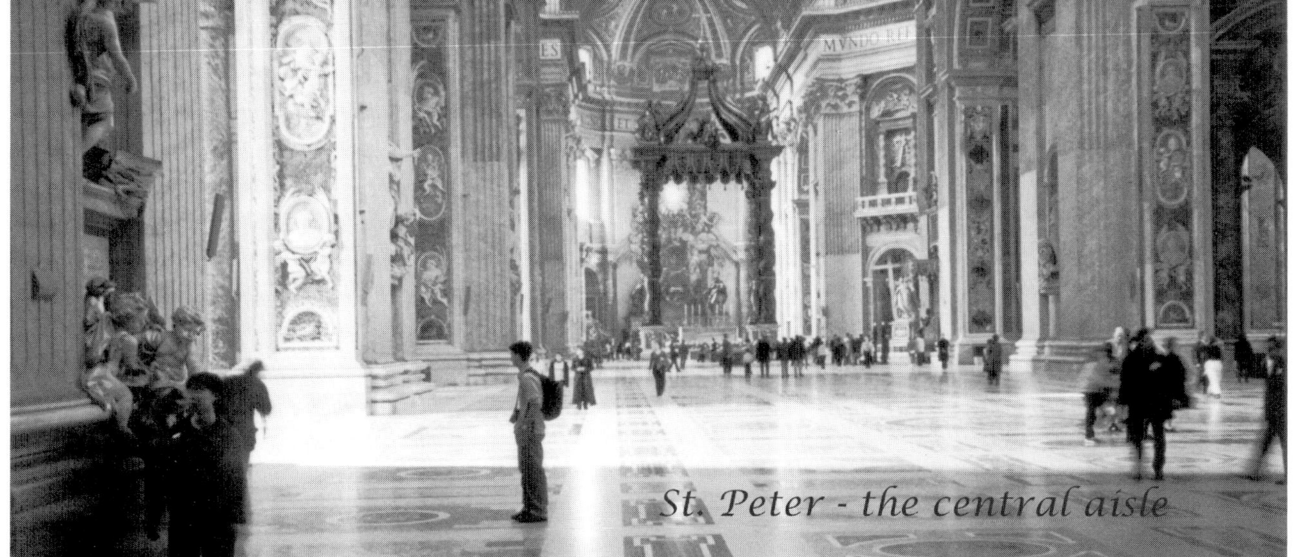

Above, 5-3-2- Italy, Rome - St. Peter-the central aisle and Papal Altar: I could feel the power and influence on cultures as we walked inside St. Peters. Tolerance through most religions will ultimately stretch and join with Israel and its infamous leader the Final Antichrist. Many leaders will try to hold the rule over the Leopard Beast to control the world during the first half of the tribulation period. All will fail! Christians whose religious headquarters are in the Leopard Beast will have some very disturbing choices in the future. Make no mistake about it, Christians will have to decide whether to go with the European tolerance views of their respective Mother Church or break off and stay firm in the faith.

SATAN'S DECEPTION

Section 5-4

My mind became impressed by the Holy Spirit to turn my attention toward the hidden numbers a couple of days later while upstairs in my home praying. I slid into my favorite chair in the living room, and began to relax when the voice of the Spirit placed these thoughts in my mind.

"You will receive insight into the two other hidden numbers and how Satan will bring about the deception which will affect the world and many who are called saints before and during the tribulation period. The insight and understanding you are about to receive shall be the key to notifying the elect saints so they will not be led into the deception which is about to occur."

The voice of the Spirit continued, "The word of God teaches mankind to follow the ways of the Lord God and to believe in the only Name, the Name of Jesus Christ, which ensures eternal life. Do not be alarmed, dismayed, or surprised at Satan incites, scoffing, and mockery at those who teach the truth and expose sin. I've revealed three sets of numbers with the alpha sequence of S,Z,C."

The voice asked, "How do you think Satan will introduce this sequence?" I replied, "It will be the opposite way you use them."

Yes, my son, you are correct," came the Spirit's reply. "I will show you how Satan will launch these numbers in reverse order to achieve the ultimate illusion. First, he will introduce the (C) number to gain control with the credit/money card system. Following this, the second, or (Z) number, will be established in order to control the movement of people. Finally, the third, or (S) number, will be the identification number. By taking the final (S) number, a person will acquire the final six number, thus forming the complete 6+6+6 sequence."

An exceeding joyful feeling came over me. I was reminded as the number sequence was altered, concerning the events moving the world into the tribulation period. They will come gradually and increase steadily like birth pains.

What are Christians looking for and expecting regarding the 666 Mark of the Beast? Many seem to be looking for a sudden moment when the number 666 will be imposed on the kingdom of the beast. However, that's too obvious and too easily detected. Instead, the number will gradually emerge in a series of stealthily imposed numbers whereby people will accept without question. People will voluntarily participate because of the benefits of receiving the numbers and the negative consequences of not receiving them.

Retail businesses will promote the idea as appealing solely from a business perspective. This means they will no longer be required to deal with bad checks, counterfeit money, or bogus credit cards. Each customer shall simply scan the hand or forehead by a light beam and the funds will be transferred from the customer's banking account to the business account. Merchants will insist on doing business in this manner while providing incentives for customers to participate in receiving the electronic chip, laser hand scanners, and/or having it embedded under their skin or some other marking device.

It is important to say I do not understand the consequences of voluntarily receiving the (C) and (Z) numbers. These two do not form the complete Number of the Beast. But the Bible is very clear in Revelation 13 regarding the consequences of receiving or refusing the complete number. Non-complying persons will be hunted and if found, jailed or death.

The computer network (Internet web of deceit) evolves into the Image of the Beast.
The Final Antichrist and False Prophet will acquire power over the system in the tribulation period.

We must look at where the world and many Christians, who love and are entangled in the super highway web of deceit, are going. The data highway model everyone is looking at shall be a confederation of computer networks that today we call the Internet, or Satan's web of future deceit. It equates to a completely self-contained utopian community of ultra telelectronic light transfers. I heard a voice say, "It shall be a spider web of Satan's deceit which will prey on unsuspecting insects. The insects are the Christians during the tribulation period." Spirit-filled Christians during the last days, are considered the "trouble makers" who will be hunted down.

The computer network (Internet web of deceit) evolves into the IMAGE OF THE BEAST. The Antichrist along with the False Prophet will acquire power over the system in the tribulation period.

THREE HIDDEN WOES TO AMERICA

God's Judgments on America
Section 5-5

This insight shall be issued as a decree and warning message given to me by the Spirit of Christ.

America, wake up, hear, and understand the first woe for the time is short.

If you, America, are following the illusion of trying to eliminate pain by overspending and forgetting God's Word;

If you, America, are in love with debt and self-praise;

If you, America, are promoting electronic money to squeeze and control people for the sake of power;

If you, America, use the web of super highways of telecommunication to control people's lives and money;

If you, America, eliminate the laws protecting My Church and make laws hurting it financially by changing tax codes;

If you, America, infringe on the rights of free expression of Church assembly because your definition of church is associated with a tax code;

BEWARE! This shall be the fulfillment of the (C) sequence of the mark and the warning holds true for America as well as the Saints and the Church. America, WOE TO YOU!

America, wake up quickly. Hear and understand the second woe for the time will be very short.

If you, America, love the second sequence (Z), which is the abuse of electronically tracking people and secretly monitoring telecommunication web messages;

Left, 5-4-1- Italy: Egyptian mummy casket: This picture reminded me of how Satan uses deception and has mastered using great illusions to accomplish his goal. (Note, I have not altered this picture to form a mirror image.) Are there two identical twins in the picture or maybe there is only one? Maybe one real woman and her Ghost, which has been drawn to the mummy casket. Could it be she does not exist and the image is an illusion? We must understand Satan's a master of deception. The world does not care and lukewarm Churches are very confused about the three six's access codes (6+6+6's). This separates information, which the computer then assimilates into useful information and sends over the Web of Deceit to the European Leopard Beast during the tribulation period.

Above, 5-4-2- Italy, Rome: People hiding in room with metal blinds: Many will be deceived by the craftiness of Satan. While others, lacking faith and knowledge in proper Biblical instructions will follow God's Great Delusion. This will be part of our test! Wake Up! Instead of listening to the warnings in the Wake Up Call Prophecies, the unwise go their own way. Some people never hear about these prophecies because their leaders suppress them.

Herein lies a very important point: You will be required to accept the Mark of the Beast digits, if your nation decides to join the European led ten nation federation (MNO - Leopard - which will transfer into the Eagle with the Three Ugly Heads). Convince your nation to abstain from joining the MNO and its citizens will not be required to take the Mark. How simple!

If you, America, are electronically infringing on people and church's rights to free speech in preaching the word through telecommunication and transportation modes;

If you, America, are censoring Biblical teaching from free movement within the (Z) sequence of schools, public places, government, and churches;

Then WOE TO YOU! America, quickly wake up! Hear and understand the third and last woe, for there will be no more time allotted for you. If you, by your lust and love, accept and implement the last set of numbers, the (S) sequence, thereby forcing the use of 666 as a number of identification on the right hand or forehead, then beware of this cryptic riddle and listen to its trustworthy saying:

This will bring fire on you and your name will be changed to the great city of Babylon, which is dressed in fine linen, purple, and scarlet, and glittering with gold, precious stones, and pearls.

The Beast will give power to the Image of the Beast to unplug your mighty army, oh, you great and wonder city that boasts, "I will never mourn."

"Then the jackals will prey on your flesh and bones for one hour and there will be much fire and smoke such as not man has ever seen before."

The Spirit of Christ firmly impressed, "America's three woes are written. Seal your lips about this matter for what I have said is now clearly explained and written about to the elect saints as an end time warning to America. Mighty is the Lord God who judges you, great city."

Another Cryptic Riddle

THE BEAST'S MARK
HAS ALWAYS BEEN.

TWO HAVE NOT,
BUT NOW ARE,

AND

THREE WILL GATHER
FOR THE FINAL FEAST.

Above, 5-5-1- Greece, Olympia - Temple of Zeus: The Temple of Zeus, built by the architect Libon in 471 BC. Churches have not addressed end time problems and starting a resistance movement because they are afraid. Many Churches have moved God over and introduced other gods and worldly props on its property. The Spirit led me to understand that while walking through Olympia, one god evolved from Sports. The Lukewarm churches have discovered using worldly props on Church property is a good witnessing tool to increase membership but this causes lukewarmness. Therefore, they bring sporting events, build sports complexes on Church property, and praise their disobedient deeds. God has already provided these facilities out in the world. It is shameful for the Church leaders to squander God's money on worldly props and not use it for God Almighty's purpose.

MY PRAYER FOR AMERICA

Section 5-6

Oh, Lord, I pray with exceeding sorrow. The time has now come, as prophesied, our world, especially America, does not receive or endure sound doctrine. Instead, my country pursues its own desires, using special interests groups as facades for personal gain and pleasure. Our people use electronic communication devices to watch and listen to teachers who say what their "itching" ears want to hear.

With lustful eyes, they see only what they want to see, and nothing seems to be looked upon as being morally wrong. Electronic mind-altering gadgets are used for experiencing ultimate pursuits of pleasure, but my people are never content with the pleasure they possess.

Our once great nation has turned its ears and eyes from the truth and toward spiritual darkness filled with forbidden myths and idolatry. Please, save our great nation and wake up the elect saints, great and mighty Lord God, for my fear comes from the depths of my soul.

In my younger years, our nation was a mighty lady. Please, Lord, don't hurt her. You know my love for this nation. I plead with you, crying great tears, in behalf of this nation and the lukewarm saints, for fires of judgment mixed with darkness are on the horizon if they don not repent quickly.

Amen! Bob R. Short

Below, 5-6-1- Israel, Nazareth, Church of the Annunciation: Proposed location where Gabriel told Mary she would become the mother of Jesus. Notice the armed soldier out front of the Church. Is this what America shall turn into? Unfortunately, the answer could be YES. Churches must wake up or America will be in deeper trouble. They must start the Universal American Church Coalition, (UACC) to change America's destiny.

INTRODUCTION
to the
SEVEN HIDDEN JUDGMENTS
Against the
MIGHTY ARMY of BABYLON
in the Tribulation Period
Section 5-7

I inquired of the Lord about the three hidden woes to America. "Lord, if You change America's name to Babylon because of its sins and idolatry, and, You allow the jackals to attack it for one hour, are You forgetting something? You are the Lord God, but what are You going to do with our fierce, honored, and brave army of mighty warriors? They are the best equipped, fighting military units in the history of the world. Our soldiers have fought many battles in the name of preserving Your truth. Lord, today no other army can challenge them. You have revealed to me the events of the last days are linked with the moral deterioration of society and not to some star wars supernatural occurrence. Lord, how could our mighty army get caught off guard without supernatural causes?" Terrifying feelings came over me by what I heard and saw, as the Spirit of the Lord God responded to my prayer.

"As the birth pains related to the three woes to America are increased, so will the seven final, hidden judgments on the mighty army of warriors be increased."

Once again, I responded, "Lord, please give me understanding about the seven hidden judgments directed on Babylon's great military so the churches can warn the government about these events and proper actions can be taken to stop this terrible tragedy."

FIRST HIDDEN JUDGMENT
Against Babylon's
GREAT ARMY OF WARRIORS

The Internet web of computer-generated weapons will greatly increase the false sense of security given to leaders. Dependence on technology will be one of seven downfalls and final judgments of Babylon's army.

Babylon's offensive weapons are controlled by or through the Internet web, which will not allow these weapons to be brought to bear against the enemy from the north. The hidden meaning is in Jeremiah 51:3, *"Let not the archer string his bow..."*

Below, 5-7-1- Scotland, Edinburgh - Craigmillar Castle: The Crown Jewels of Scotland were housed here. Jewels, big guns, castles and protection were going through my mind. The big guns protruding out of the upper castle fortress were needed to protect in their day. Modern day technology has triggered fascination in warfare. More importantly, there will be a day when technology will take a back seat to the manual mode. America cannot rely on star war technology to save her in the Great Tribulation. Elected officials better take heed now and make sure our military is trained and can operate in the manual mode or the USA will be in for a big defeat in the future. The farther we move into the tribulation period, the less technology nations will have to protect themselves. See section on Evening and Morning prophecies for warning details about how electronics will be reduced.

USA's elected officials can stop the following Seven Hidden Judgments from continuing in America. The USA does not have to become the Biblical Political Babylon in the tribulation period, which will be destroyed, if it will change its present course of disobedience against God.

Still, the elect ponder who or what city, combination of cities, nation or nations encompass the Biblical Babylon. Christians point to some favorite assumptions. The answer might be the combined cities of the Eastern seaboard of the United States or USA itself. The answer maybe Rome, Italy. Better still, the answer could be all the major cities of the European led ten-area world federation (MNO). However, what we know to date, points to Babylon's army initially having the traits contained in the seven hidden judgments. Once again, America does not have to be the Biblical Babylon if corrective action is taken. These judgments are warnings to the churches and leaders in our nation and military.

Above, 5-7-2- Greece, Thermopylae - 300 Spartans vs. 10,000 Persian solders: Led by Xerxes (480 BC): Babylon's Great army thinks it will be able to destroy any army with their power, just like the 300 Spartans held off 10,000 Persian solders. Nevertheless, it will not hold up to the test of time.

Many defensive weapons of planes, missiles, and radar are not effective for the same reason in some areas of the world. The Internet web has the means to scramble radar screens with a super-scrambler. Again, Jeremiah 51:3 provides the hidden meaning, *"... nor let him put on his armor."*

An old saying came to my mind, "The more complex they make-um, the easier it will be to stop up the plumbing." Moving from fiction to reality, the same must be said for the mighty army with the high tech weapons. Too much faith will be vested in the Internet web of deception.

The effectiveness of technology in civil use and military weaponry will be exponentially reduced in some areas as we move through the tribulation period.

SECOND HIDDEN JUDGMENT
Against Babylon's
GREAT ARMY OF WARRIORS

The Spirit of Christ implanted into my thinking, "I will divert Babylon's mighty army from its intended goal and make it dart back and forth like fish playing in the water. It will be unaware of impending danger, neither will it notice the hook, line, and sinker being slowly dropped from the north to drag it into the flaming fires of judgment.

I will put blinders on its warriors' eyes and make them a political puppet accomplishing nothing. It will become a noisy den for special interest crusades."

"The Lord will destroy Babylon; he will silence her noisy den" (Jeremiah 51:55). The noisy den will be so busy selling sin and impressing the world it will not notice the ambush which is being set up for Babylon's army. Its leaders point to problems, never realizing the ambush will come from above. Jeremiah 51:12 states, *"...prepare an ambush..."*

THIRD HIDDEN JUDGMENT
Against Babylon's
GREAT ARMY OF WARRIORS

Babylon's mighty army puffs up, proud of its recent victory. Her commanders are confident in their thick walls and defenses reaching (high gates) to the second heaven (outer space).

"... In her heart she boasts ...I will never mourn" (Revelation 18:7). Many countries are allied with her strength and are overconfident in her military might. Babylon has become proud of what she sells worldwide -power, sin, idolatry and infanticide. Jeremiah 50:32 said, *"...the arrogant one will stumble and fall and no one will help her up..."*

FOURTH HIDDEN JUDGMENT
Against Babylon's
GREAT ARMY OF WARRIORS

Words from the Spirit of Christ impressed these thoughts, "For a short while I (Romans 13:1) will place a weak king in charge of the military. He will come to hate the use of military force. He will promote the cause of homosexuals and their desires for political power and recognition. He will establish himself because of the power and authority he gives to women as they pursue militant issues of rebellion against God."

Jeremiah 50:43 states, *"The king of Babylon has heard reports about them..."*

The Spirit continues, "This weak commander-in-chief shall be warned by his military generals about the army from the north, but he will refuse to act on their information. He is busy being busy with issues, which transfer into little meaning or consequence. Conflict which might have been avoided will result."

Jeremiah 50:43, *"...and his hands hang limp."* This verse refers to fear, but the hidden military meaning refers to a commander's preferential treatment of homosexuals. The inclusion of homosexuals into the military under his reign will contaminate the army's internal blood supplies, break down morality, and reduce troop readiness.

FIFTH HIDDEN JUDGMENT
Against Babylon's
GREAT ARMY OF WARRIORS

Many of these young warriors have been raised during a time when there was no national cause to fight and die for. Some never learned to salute the flag or honor a once great nation proudly proclaimed the glory of the Lord God.

This evolves into a divided nation serving many gods. Many of the warriors lack knowledge or fear of the Lord God because they were never taught about Him in school or church.

The warrior's view is, "Why should I fight for Babylon? Our leaders make folly of laws and the judicial system. They promote laws which destroy the families, steal from the people, and use military might as political gambits for personal gain without regard for consequences to others."

Jeremiah 51:30 foretold, *"Babylon's warriors have stopped fighting. They remain in their strongholds."* The warriors' belief in the Babylonian system will be destroyed. With fear, some will hide and refuse to fight.

Jeremiah 51:30 *"...their strength is exhausted..."* The Spirit of the Lord says, "I have slowed their training to accommodate the weakest of men and women. Special interest groups will applaud this move because it conforms to their political and social agenda for equality without regard to consequences. Recall the words, `*... they have become like women*' (Jeremiah 51:30). Remember My warning in Nahum, `*Look at your troops, they are all women! The gates of your land are wide open to your enemies: fire has consumed their bars*' (Nahum 3:13).

"Because of her sin within the ranks, I will increase disease and plagues which will come progressively as do birth pains. `*Therefore, in one day her plagues will overtake her*' (Revelation 18:3). These once great warriors will become cowards who are incapable of fighting because they will no longer be properly trained. They will find ways to escape military service and the defection rate will increase. They will lose the will to stand and fight for what's truth and right."

Above, 5-7-3- Israel, Jerusalem - Armed Israeli Soldiers: The protect-and-take-care mode was originally given to the male (Genesis 1:15). God made women as a suitable helper in the protect-and-take-care mode (Genesis 1:20). The Lord God has ordained the male in the warrior position of the military. Females are in the backup positions as suitable helpers. There are dangerous consequences if this role should be reversed. The technology of modern weaponry will confuse and blur this issue. For instance, clarify warrior and backup positions in today's armies of the world.

The King over the Babylon army will for a while, use this reversal as political gambits for great gain. First, he will use females' desire (Genesis 3-16, curse) to do or be like males and give them what they want (leadership position over men in military and warrior positions). Once this King gains world power he will show no regard to females after he uses them to get what he wants, (Daniel 11:37).

SIXTH HIDDEN JUDGMENT
Against Babylon's
GREAT ARMY OF WARRIORS

Babylon's mighty army will be weakened by the addition of women in all branches of the military - land, sea and air. This will decrease morale and cause aggressive behavior and confusion among the warriors. It will lead to the fall of generals. Troop readiness will be affected because of fear and disorder.

From the beginning, women have coveted the position of authority given to men by the Lord God, and the hidden meaning of Babylon's weakening army must be linked to the rebellion of militant women against the Lord God. The woman was told, *"Your desire will be for your husband [or male figure]"* (Genesis 3:16).

The Spirit of the Lord says, "Oh, once great Babylon, follow My ways. Now they scoff and show contempt by their great arrogant laughter at My word. My word does not conform to their thinking or desires, especially the lifestyles of the younger generation who serve in Babylon's armed forces. I have warned them through the prophets Nahum (3:13) and Jeremiah (51:30)."

Daniel 11:37 speaks, *"He* (Antichrist) *will show no regard for the gods of his father or for the one desired by women..."*

The Spirit of the Lord says, "They have generally understood this to mean Jewish women desiring to birth the Messiah. But the hidden meaning to the mighty army of Babylon shall be, men's hearts will be moved by desires for personal gain to include women in the ranks of Babylon's warrior positions within its mighty army. I, the Almighty God, set the stage as early as WW I, WW II, and in the 1960's when the equal rights movement should have been a call to the saints to awaken. This trend is spreading worldwide and has led to the progressive rebellion of women against My word.

"Have I not commanded everyone to love each other as I loved you (John 15:12), and to love your neighbor as yourself (Luke 10:27)? Their spiritual blindness has caused them to turn from My words and seek their own way. Satan has turned the equal rights movement, which might have done much good, into a platform to promote the perversions and wickedness of special interest groups. It's time to awaken, My elect!"

One satanic goal has been accomplished by the perversion of the 1960's movement. This evolved into the progressive weakening of the Church into a lukewarm, political entity embracing the wicked agenda of the demonically influenced special interest groups. The standard of righteousness weakens and lawlessness prevails in all segments of society as the Saints of the Lord God become unaware of the deception filling the world. The result has been a deterioration of the family and neighborhoods, which now produce the men who serve in the military. At that time, many of these men will no longer serve as warriors.

We will see the day when the demands of extremists, who abuse the good intent and purposes of the 1960's movement which is spreading worldwide, will bring about part of the weakening and downfall of the mighty army of Babylon.

Her warriors hear of wars and rumors of warfare, and this produces great fear, which progressively weakens the will to fight as a cancer destroys the body. Superficially, they boast and seek to please their commanders. Sadly, the real issue brings about weakness, which promotes wickedness and greed. Loving one's neighbor will give way to selfishness, and this leads to a socially callous state in which individuals seek only their own welfare and interests.

The Spirit of Jesus Christ urges us, "It is time for my people, whom the world does not recognize, to stand like mighty warriors and invade spiritual darkness with the message of the gospel which will draw men to me." Now must be the time to enter the harvest of human souls for the time is quickly drawing to a close.

"Mighty warriors of Babylon will not stand in your ranks and see the fulfillment of the desires of their leaders. Their destruction will be as swift as the lightning. Their destruction has been already predetermined for Babylon to slide into a detestable state of being."

5-7-4- Israel, Armageddon - King Solomon's horse stables: Our tour stopped at King Solomon's horse tie down and watering trough. Military leaders who think they can implement part or most of these seven judgments upon any army will not be standing in the end. Any nation's commanders must keep Biblical standards of conduct (see section on Eli✝e Chris✝ian Soldiers) in the ranks or decay, fear, and improper actions will occur resulting in disaster during the tribulation period.

"Your women soldiers will lead the ranks of Babylon into the trap of the beast (MNO). The promise of rewards and honor will deceive you, for you will not be able to detect and expose the lies which will bring about the dominance of wickedness and rampant lawlessness.

Destruction will be certain (Revelation 18) when Babylon's mighty army becomes foolish, boastful, proud and lacking complete awareness of its backslidden spiritual state. It will be consumed in one hour for I am the Lord God who has decreed it!"

Above, 5-7-5- Israel, Jericho - Dirt mounds are some of the dig sights: Jericho has been best known with Joshua and the walls which came tumbling down. American Military, just like Jericho will come tumbling down if it does not heed these warning messages. It can be said, America has few God-fearing statesmen within her political or military ranks of leadership. Few are listening to these God-fearing statesmen within our ranks.

Unfortunately, God will bring a destructive wake up call to our leadership to whip them back in line. This shall be a sad day. Warnings were issued, yet few listened. The Lord God slammed the door shut on opportunity when America's leadership quit adhering to Biblical standards of conduct. America must make corrections in its military and nation or reap total destruction. Amen!

SEVENTH AND FINAL HIDDEN JUDGMENT AGAINST BABYLON'S WARRIORS

"Babylon has heaped up her sins and has arrogantly displayed her disregard for the Son of Man. She will progressively enter the final alpha/numerical "S" sequence. My judgment will come upon her, slowly at first like birthing pains. There will be no repentance once Babylon allows its leaders to downsize the mighty army, meanwhile boasting of her great strength and prowess, thinking, `I will never mourn because of my great wealth, technology, and military might.' Her generals scoff at the world, which they think has become too weak to challenge Babylon. Political leaders deceptively use monetary resources to promote false men and do not heed the cries of the needy and suffering. Babylon's leaders show nothing but contempt for Me as they endorse and promote the shedding of innocent blood by slaughtering the unborn. My judgment has been revealed through Jeremiah 51:57, "*... they will sleep forever and not awake*" declared the Lord God Almighty.

"Your judgment has been hidden in the words of Isaiah 18:5; `*For before the harvest, when the blossom is gone and the flower becomes a ripening grape, he will cut off the shoots with pruning knives, and cut down and take away the spreading branches.*' You interpret this as a literal vine. But my hidden meaning will be to cut off your `shoots,' which are the offensive strike weapons through downsizing. Your alliances with other nations (spreading branches) will be destroyed. I will `cut down' your ears to your on site intelligence gathering sources so you will withdraw to your own borders.

Boastfully they will rely more and more on the worldwide Internet web of deceit, which will ultimately bring them under the influence and control of the European Leopard Beast (MNO).

"Now must be the time to reject the foolish leaders who are blindly leading Babylon into certain judgment. A nation from the north will attack her and destroy her land. Neither man nor animal will inhabit the land any longer for they shall flee. Babylon's allies (Revelation 18:10) will stand far off as they witness the predicted torment. They will not come to Babylon's rescue but will only cry and shake in fear of their own destruction."

Unfortunately, God will bring a destructive wake up call to our leadership to force them back in line. This shall be a sad day.

Thus, the final judgment for Babylon's mighty warriors (Jeremiah 51:56) will come at the hands of the destroyer who will capture the nation and destroy Babylon's military might. This is the Lord God's retribution, paid fully.

NAME OF THE ANTICHRIST
AND THE BEAST
Section 5 - 8

After the Spirit of Christ gave me the revelation, I realized the Name of the Beast had not been revealed. My heart became burdened for what appeared to be the judgments, which are coming upon the United States. I was afraid to ask any more questions because of fear of what might be disclosed to me.

The question continued to haunt my mind. "Why did the Spirit show me everything except the understanding of the key to the Name of the Beast?" I prayed for insight and asked the Lord to show me the full Name of the Beast. There are three entities working together to bring about the ultimate deception and fullness of wickedness and evil on the earth (Revelation 13:17).

The reader, who researches the Bible, will notice the Lord God has used numbers throughout the Bible as though there must be numeric codes associated with God's great revelation of His plan. Understanding has been hidden from and beyond the comprehension of the natural mind, especially as numeric codes are correlated with alpha meanings. The Bible contains the details of the plan, but they are symbolically hidden until the time for fulfillment arrives. It could be assumed the languages used in writing the Bible employed a numeric/alpha system, which could only be translated into the Greek and Hebrew languages. These two languages do not have Arabic numbers like one, two, three, four.

Therefore, the Greek and Hebrew alpha/numeric language system means every alpha word has a numeric counterpart. For example, I have read unconfirmed sources claiming the numeric values of the six alpha letters forming the name of Jesus in the Greek language total 888. The numeric value of the Greek word, "Christos," totals 1480.

Each variation of the name of Jesus (Christos, Savior, Lord, Emanuel, and Messiah) contains letters in which the numeric total shall be divisible by eight. The number eight can be linked to the eight souls being saved in Noah's ark and the Lord's resurrection.

This fascinating phenomenon suggests, in His secret wisdom, the Lord God purposely used specific names demonstrating this pattern. The mathematical pattern of cycles, or loops within loops, can only be understood as the Lord God gives insight and wisdom. The number 666 indicates the Greek letters of this number will form the Name of the Antichrist. His name can be added up to, divided, and multiplied by numbers linked with six. Recall the telephone pad as it translates into **M**illennium **N**ations **O**rganized equals MNO, which equals 666.

Some computer experts may be able to translate the entire Bible into numeric sequences and then program a computer to search for common factors. It is sufficient to remember the Greek and Hebrew alphabets both contain an alpha and numeric meaning as one symbol. When John wrote (Revelation 13:18) the 666 in the original manuscript, he used the Greek alphabet letters to represent numeric equivalents. Together they form the 666, which identifies the beast.

This results in every sequence of alpha letters which forms names, words, phrases, chapters, and books having a corresponding numeric sequence that can be added, multiplied, or divided by a common number which conforms with the Lord God's purposes.

In many cases, the Spirit of Christ spoke to chosen prophets through a special hidden numeric system, which translated into the Greek and Hebrew languages. Therefore, with insight provided by the Spirit of Christ, it will be possible to calculate the Name of the Beast.

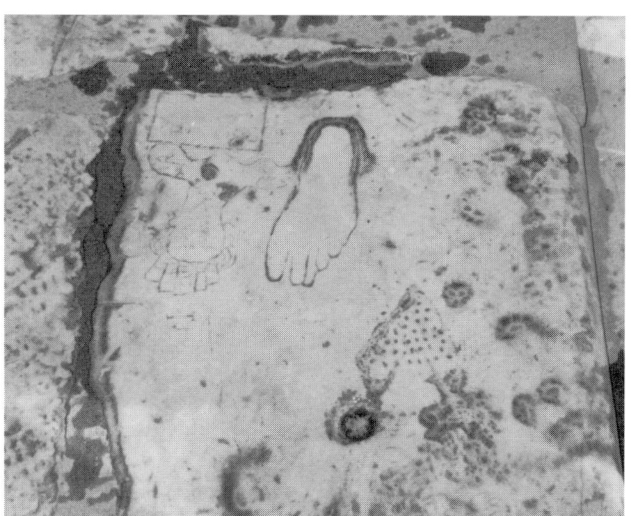

Left, 5-8-1- Turkey, Ephesus - Drawings giving directions using sign language: In St. Paul's day these road signs were helpful. In our day, we must analyze what may happen. Nations joining the European lead MNO or Leopard Beast will require its citizens to have the Mark. Unfortunately, road signs as shown in the picture will be replaced by electronic checkpoints. Citizens will only be able to pass with proper identification (Mark). However, if a nation does not lock into the Leopard Beast (MNO), the citizens will not be required to take the Mark to buy or sell.

The Lord God has promised to provide adequate warning to the elect before the fulfillment of the prophecies related to His judgment and wrath on the earth. Why I, who am a servant of the Lord's with nothing to boast about, have been given insight into the calculations of the beast's name and number is beyond my understanding. However, I must share this knowledge with the elect as we rapidly approach the coming of the Lord Jesus Christ.

Paul wrote to the Corinthian Church (I Corinthians 2:6-16), concerning the matter about Christians having the mind of Christ. Therefore, we know we can receive end time insight because Christ Jesus is the Spirit of Prophecy. It has been God's purpose in prophecy to provide warnings about the future rise and revelation of the Antichrist who will be identified with a name, number, and mark related to 666. It has not been technologically possible earlier to use laser or finger scans, computer chips, space telecommunication, and fiber optic light transfers to identify individuals with a concealed computer chip under the skin or a similar scanning technology. It is now possible to understand and calculate the meaning of the figures (Revelation 13), which add up to the six plus six plus six sequences (6+6+6).

Satan's plan of deception must be linked with these numbers and the calculation of these numbers, which will expose Satan's scheme to use the Antichrist to gain worship. Even though the Spirit of Christ had given partial insight into the calculation of the Name of the Beast, it became necessary to obtain an understanding of the larger picture before being able to make specific calculations.

Please recall the numeric 666 was translated on the telephone pad into the alpha sequence of MNO. As the Spirit impressed me, I wrote Millennium Nations Organized. This became part of the clue to the beast's name. Jesus warned the elect, *"Watch out that no one deceives you. For many will come in my name claiming, 'I am the Christ, and will deceive many.'"* (Matthew 24:4,5).

Revelation 13:17 says the *"mark is the name of the beast."* Receiving his mark correlates to the same equivalent as taking on his name. The false prophet will go throughout the world preaching the deceptive message that the Final Antichrist is the true Messiah, Jesus Christ, who has returned to earth and to Israel. The promise will be if someone receives his mark/name and aligns himself with the Millennium Nations Organized, there will be peace and righteousness on earth.

Above, 5-8-2-Turkey, Ephesus - Curetes street - Celsus' Library: The view stretches up Curetes Street where I stood inside the Celsus' Library pondering the wonders of this fascinating city in St. Paul's day. They could buy and sell in any of the shops along the way. Unfortunately, in the near future, nations will require three series of access codes 6+6+6 to buy and sell. The 3-6's are already on everything we buy. The bar code label has 3-6's and the Internet web of deceit caries the 3-6's also. WWW (the English W is equivalent to the 6th letter in Hebrew.) Therefore, WWW cryptically calculates to 666. The 6's separate information for the Computer to assimilate it. Money collected from the worldwide consumption tax (Daniel 11:20) will be electronically transferred to the European Leopard Beast.

WWW

The English W is equivalent to the 6th letter in Hebrew. Therefore, WWW cryptically calculates to 666. The 6's separate information for the Computer to assimilate it.

The MNO sequence has another hidden meaning symbolically related to end time prophecy. If we transform these letters into the Hebrew alpha equivalent, an interesting observation emerges. M equals 40, N equals 50 and O equals 6. The Spirit of Christ opened my understanding to the following calculations:

M x N equals O
40 x 50 equals 6 or the (S) sequence
2000 years equals appearance
of the (S) sequence or 666
End of gentile time equals the
appearance of Antichrist

The last (6) or (S) sequence of the mark comes without warning. It will be forced upon people. This will be unlike the first two sequences, which are voluntarily received. Many saints will be deceived into worshipping the messianic impostor, if there is not proper interpretation given to the Church. Therefore, the call must be to wake up the sleeping saints so they will be alert and prepared for the days of deception, which has been coming upon the world.

One contributing aspect of the deception equates to the false prophet and Antichrist as they resort to false, illusionary miracles to convince the world the Antichrist must truly be the Son of God. In fact, the Antichrist will be the embodiment of lawlessness and evil, and the spirit of this individual has been manifested through such tyrants as Hitler and Nero.

The false prophet of lawlessness will deceptively disguise the identity of the Antichrist as he leads the world into believing the Antichrist name equates to:

ANTICHRIST
name equates to

JESUS THE MESSIAH
KING OF KINGS AND
LORD OF LORDS
RULER OF THE
MILLENNIUM
NATIONS ORGANIZED

The ultimate objective will be to replace Jesus Christ with himself, and actually believe he has become the true Messiah who is Jesus Christ. More importantly, the elect will not be deceived by the deceptive gospel or miracles because they will know of his false identity by correctly exposing the meaning of his name and number. The Final Antichrist and the False Prophet will preach morality as well as salvation without Jesus Christ entering into the formula. God forbid!

The human, earthly identity of the Antichrist will be known (see Psalm 100). But as the great apostasy takes place and people openly reject truth, many false prophets will rise, and eventually the one destined to be the leader of the MNO (see glossary) or final Antichrist, will emerge on the world scene. Cunningly, he will assume the identity of Jesus Christ with **a goal "toward heaven."**

THE ONE HUNDRED AND FORTY-FOUR THOUSAND

Section 5-9

With the Spirit's urging, I prayed for the one hundred and forty-four thousand that they would be alert to the gospel and not be deceived during the time of the great tribulation. This was the prayer:

"Lord Jesus, a set of numbers the prophet Daniel prophesied in the Old Testament foretold the exact number of days before You would ride into Jerusalem on the colt of a donkey. Their hearts were hardened toward You and they refused to accept You as Lord and Savior. But the Jewish people failed to understand the numbers or count the days properly. Therefore, they were destroyed because of their lackadaisical approach to learn knowledge, the religious leaders corruptness in not teaching all of God's Word, ignoring the law, and hardening of their hearts toward the truth" (Hosea 4:6). On the exact day prophesied, You entered Jerusalem where the sentence was crucifixion and rejection.

You were crucified between two evening periods so the Jews could be in their homes by evening time, which was the beginning of the next day. There they prayed for the coming of the Messiah, the very person whom they had just crucified.

Therefore, the call must be to wake up the sleeping saints so they will be alert and prepared for the days of deception, which has been coming upon the world.

Prophesied by - Bob R. Short, a Witness

Right, 5-9-1- Israel, Jerusalem - Temple Mount-Holy of Holies: When the Jewish 3rd Temple is rebuilt, the Holy of Holies will be just to the left in the picture or right to the reader, 20 or 30 feet (per my educated guess). Many of the Jewish people will follow the Final Antichrist who will sit in the Holy of Holies in the Temple and call himself God. Note: A temporary Temple may be set up while construction on the permanent Temple is completed.

Hosea 4:6, states the Jews have rejected knowledge, therefore, God will also reject them as His priests. God was saying if only they could count and understand the numbers, they would have known Jesus was the true Messiah. If they had known You were the Messiah, their hearts should have been changed. Sadly, they were not.

It is now almost two thousand years later, and we are nearing the end of another age, the time of the gentiles. Once again, the Jewish nation has been preoccupied with world affairs and does not seem to understand the great revelation being given to this generation. You are once again calling your people to awaken, twelve thousand from each tribe, as the time draws near. The time to understand the calculations has arrived."

The Spirit of Christ provided the enlightenment, saying, "As the prophetic birth pains increase in intensity, the one hundred and forty-four thousand will believe the prophecy and revelation of the calculation of the numbers which expose Satan's master plan of deception. As a whole, the nation of Israel has not heeded the warnings and signs, which would awaken them if they would only pay attention. As before, they will reject the Messiah once again. They continue being involved in events having little meaning or significance to their well-being or preservation."

My heart grew heavy for Israel as I saw their faces when their horrible fate was coming upon them. Hosea 6:1-3 foretells the hope for Israel:

"Come, let us return to the Lord. He has torn us to pieces but he will heal us. He has injured us but he will bind up our wounds. After ***two days*** (two thousand earth years) *he will revive us; on the* ***third day*** (start of third millennium after crucifixion) *he will restore us that we may live in his presence. Let us acknowledge the Lord; let us press on to acknowledge him. As surely as the sun rises, he will appear; he will come to us like the winter rains, like the spring rains and that water the earth."*

In refusing God's work and awakening call, Israel will be led into following after and accepting a false messiah. They will be deceived into believing in the Antichrist because of the deceptive signs, miracles, power, and wonders. Once again, they will reject the numbers and calculations, which would open their eyes to truth, and the result will be their persecution. Israel's tendency to be stubborn like a heifer is highlighted in Hosea 4:16.

It is the duty of Christians to pray for the peace of Jerusalem. Until the true Messiah returns in the clouds of glory, Israel's land will experience Jacob's trouble.

Jesus clearly pointed out the times would be influenced by an unprecedented form of deception. This deception would eventually draw the world into the worship of Satan.

I still hear the voice of the Spirit saying, "Wake up, one hundred forty-four thousand, for your nation has been blinded to my numbers once again. The time is near for you to remove the evil from your nation as your people face the tribulation period for the testimony of Jesus Christ."

Above, 5-10-1- Italy, Verona - Roman Arena: Verona, probably best known for Juliet's Balcony and the saying; "Romeo, Romeo, where art thou, Romeo". Roman arenas were used for plays, entertainment and in some cases abuse of Christians. It shall be imperative, Christians understand abuse and destruction lies waiting at the doorsteps of the lukewarm Churches. Christians cannot afford to continue to live like the disobedient people in Noah's day. They refused to heed the warnings given to them. Unfortunately, they did not know the flood was coming. Likewise, the enlightened churches of today are not knowledgeable to the times we live in. Some churches have correct interpretation of the times of wrath but mistakenly have added to or taken away from the Book of Revelation. This condemns them to go through the tribulation and experience the plagues and curses described therein.

A WAKE UP CALL TO THE ELECT SAINTS

Section 5-10

Jesus clearly spoke of the times and world events which appear in the daily headlines of newspapers around the world (read Matthew 24, Mark 13 and Luke 21). Peter, James, John, and Andrew asked Jesus to tell them about the nature of the times when Jesus would return to earth from heaven. Jesus clearly pointed out the times would be influenced by an unprecedented form of deception. This deception would eventually draw the world into the worship of Satan. However, there will be one exception. Jesus pointed out the elect saints will not be deceived because they know the truth and understand world events in light of Biblical prophecy (are taught by the wise, Daniel 11:33).

The insight I have been given concerning the calculation of the Number of the Beast will be primarily for the elect saints of the Lord Jesus Christ. This information is for the times of this generation, therefore, it wasn't necessary to reveal it to prior generations of true believers.

The elect of all generations since the days of Moses have been instructed not to worship anything or anyone other than the Lord God Almighty. The tribulation translates into an issue of whom mankind will worship, the Lord God or Satan. A choice will have to be made to accept or reject the Number of the Beast. Receiving the Number of the Beast equates to certain spiritual death and separation from the Lord God. Rejecting the number means being ostracized and killed by the empire of the beast. Either choice means loss of security, or finances, and even death.

The elect has the assurance the Lord God will not allow more pressure to come upon His people than they can endure. He will provide a means of escape. **But He does not spare the elect from the testing and trials, which are designed for the fulfilling of the times in which they live.**

The elect must live with understanding and awareness of the events unfolding in the great prophetic panorama of the endtimes as the world races to the end of its testing cycle to make ready for the return of Jesus Christ. They must be prepared to make right choices and persevere in the consequences.

It is interesting to study the seventh phase of the Church as it is symbolically revealed in Revelation 3:14-22. Its name translates into Laodicea and, spiritually, it's described as "lukewarm," not being fit for anything except to be "spewed out of My mouth." Laodicean "Christians" are vulnerable to the deception Jesus warned us about, because they have been compromised and deceived by perverted doctrines of wealth, security, entertainment, and spirituality. It is easy to see how the institutional Church will be drawn into the web of Satan's scheme and never realizes what's happening.

When Biblical truth has been compromised or ignored to gain acceptance in the world, the institutional Church is neither able to warn people nor protect them from the deception of the times. When taken to a logical conclusion, the apostasy, which occurs as the world rushes toward judgment, will happen in the Church and will probably resemble a revival or spiritual renewal. The elect will see through the sham and not be deceived by the different gospels (II Corinthians 11:2-4) being preached.

The deceptive scheme of Satan will necessarily try to silence the voices of those who see through the falsehood. As birthing pains, the message will be silenced electronically. When silenced, the only means of sharing the true gospel of Jesus Christ will be through preaching and word of mouth. The elect will hear and believe. Others will not.

The primary point, which needs to be expanded upon, is this: It must be imperative for the elect to awaken to an awareness of the times. What I have tried to share with them regarding the calculations of the Number of the Beast is intended to help them have understanding, which will enable everyone to make right choices. Some will agree while other will disagree with these prophecies on the Number of the Beast. This shall be a secondary matter when compared to being aroused by the Spirit of Christ as the elect are called to preparation and readiness today. Sharing the insight into the numeric calculation is meant to reveal a message, which causes every Christian to wake up and be the Church of the Lord Jesus Christ. It must call believers to a life of devotion and holy living unto the Lord.

Many who call themselves Christian are fascinated by the lure and promise inherent in deceptive gospels, which entangle them in the web of Satan's deception. These gospels flow out of the original lie told in the Garden of Eden to Adam and Eve; gospels which promise access to, and control of, the Lord God. Hidden in the subtle meanings and definitions of "new gospel" is doctrine, which encourages a path leading unaware believers away from truth and into the idolatrous worship of Satan.

To sum up this warning call, let us not forget Satan will be out to gain total control over a lawless society and to lead them into worshipping him. It is a calculated scheme, which will use the available resources of technology, politics, religion, and economy to control and influence the daily interactions of people. As Satan's influence is gradually and sometimes forcibly imposed upon society through these means, the elect will increasingly have to make tough decisions and remain alert. If the elect fail to understand the times and preach the true message of Jesus Christ, there will be little or no hindering force to the spread of lawlessness and deception throughout the world. The call to the elect, which was deeply impressed on me by the Holy Spirit, must be to wake-up and stand strong in our faith in Jesus Christ the Lord. Spirit-filled Christians are called and destined for these times. Give glory to the Lord God Almighty.

SOMETHING PERSONAL

Section 5-11

I have no illusions that theologically or academically my qualifications would make me eligible to be recognized as a great Biblical scholar in the Church. However, my soul and life have been transformed by the experience of receiving the insight into the calculation of the Beast's Mark, Number and Name. Understand my achievement, enthusiasm in pursuing a pure and sincere devotion to Jesus Christ as my Lord and Savior has never been higher. A message through prophecy has been given to me. The assignment must be to carry this message to the political leaders as well as churches and the Christians around the world. I am to be a witness to the world concerning our Lord and Savior's second coming at His appointed time which will be approximately on or before the sequencing positioning point of Saturday, 106.9.23SRSP-S.

My qualifications to receive these prophecies are found in 1 Corinthians 1:26-31, to paraphrase Paul as he taught his brothers. Think of what you represented when you were called, not wise, not influential, not noble birth. God chose the foolish, weak and lowly things so that no one can boast before God. With these attributes, I qualified!

Below, 5-11-1-Greece, Island of Patmos - Monastery of St. John: It was fitting I gave copies of some of the Wake Up Call Prophecies Scrolls to the monk in charge the day we visited the Monastery. In the Spirit of my mind, it bridged the gap of time by bringing the Wake Up Call Prophecies Scrolls in contact with the Scrolls of the Book of St. John's Revelation.

There was a bonding within a curved test cycle of unified prophetic insight dazzling like lighting into the future of time. It culminated with an unavoidable collision bursting into screaming streaks of magma energy flux racing to close this great testing cycle. Everything instantly stopped in a voided expanse when the beginning and the ending of time collided. I can see time and matter waiting for their new assignment into another time-space parallel state. My mind rests in peace for I know God has bridged the prophetic gap of time-thought and insight into warning His people.

Left: Finally, for the edification of the readers, I must share some personal thoughts and insights. In 1993, I wrote an essay to my two sons as well as end time Christians. Perhaps the poem to the left will provide some strength for the spiritual encounter during the last days as we anticipate the return of Jesus Christ.

When Biblical truth has been compromised or ignored to gain acceptance in the world, the institutional Church is neither able to warn people nor protect them from the deception of the times.

Below, 5-11-2- Greece, Patmos - Holy Cave of the Divine Apocalypse: John's dedication and openness to accepting the end time prophetic message pierced my mind by the Holy Spirit when I stood outside the Monastery of St. John. The Spirit of Christ Jesus gave me assurance what I have and will prophesy with accuracy and His truth.

Then the Spirit disclosed the lukewarm churches would not like what I prophesy any more than the pagan world does. Unfortunately, to my great awakening, the Spirit gave me sound advice. I found lukewarmers are unwilling to listen and many are set in their disobedience.

What I have prophesied will stand the accuracy test of endtimes. It will edify the Spirit-filled Church and Christian while being the springboard to help raise up the nations which will fulfill the coming of Prince Michael in Daniel 12:1.

PATMOS
Holy Cave of the
Divine Apocalypse

LIFE'S CHALLENGE

TO REACH THE MARK

Section 5-12

"I BOLDLY SAY TO YOU do not fear the evil forces of this world, nor the fierce and ravaging nature of things.

CHARGE AT THEM with a full armor of authority and be savage against them.

YOU MAY STUMBLE and fall, but get up quickly, get up! This requires the pain and hunger to climb for the mark. It demands persistence and suffering to go against the grain of man and never waver from the narrow path.

LIFE WILL TEAR AT YOU for your good deeds, men will laugh at honorable accomplishments, friends will stomp on you when you are down. Never get discouraged, never! Get up and stand courageously like a mighty lion.

YOUR FEET WILL THICKEN from stomping out evil. The face, yes, your face will weather from strain. Before each day ends, your heart, filled with compassion and love for others, will shine through with hope of better things to come for all.

THE WORLD WILL MAKE YOU weary and swarthy, your cloths ragged, then men will ask you for safety's sake to flock with them on the darkest side of the low lands of life. Pay no attention to their lies and money! Rebuke their false fears, gods, and worldly idols.

BITE OFF MORE GOOD than you can chew and chew it! You alone with God will stomp out the flocks of fear and evil.

WITH HIS AWESOME POWER, you will soar like a mighty eagle to new heights where your dreams are waiting.

LIVE HIS WILL, improve daily without looking back.

ONLY THEN WILL YOU be a righteous man that has fought toward the mark of the higher calling - - - - and

TOUCHED THE FACE OF GOD."

BOB R. SHORT,
August of 1993

CONCLUDING REMARKS
Section 5-13

The experience of relating these prophesies to you has left me with mixed feelings. As I pondered what the future might be, and whether or not people will believe this message, the Spirit of Christ began to reassure me in his now familiar voice:

"I, the Lord Almighty, have given this revelation to Bob R. Short, a servant of Jesus Christ. It is to be issued to the saints throughout the world. I have partially sealed his lips concerning the three hidden woes to America and the seven hidden judgments against the mighty army of Babylon. The Church and the saints must interpret what has been revealed in these prophecies. I have commanded my servant to speak with hope and enthusiasm, and to provide the details about the insight he has received regarding the calculations of the Number, Name, and Mark of the Tribulation Beast."

Understanding of, and obedience to, this revelation will result in the salvation of millions of lives, which might otherwise be lost as the world enters into the time of tribulation.

These prophecies came to me over a period of twenty-eight days, beginning on May 13, 1994, and ending on June 9, 1994. The twenty-eight days are symbolic of the four times seven which designates the final chapter of fulfillment of Bible prophecy before the return of Jesus Christ. Four designates the Roman Empire and seven is the number of completion. This shall be the final chapter of the old Roman Empire.

On June 9, 1994, a complete rough draft version of all calculations were given to a saint and servant of the Lord Jesus Christ for the purposes of editing and developing the text for distribution at later dates to the Church. Other Christians have prophesied "great strips of evil" will be removed from the earth. This revelation from the Lord requires one message. These two revelations create the potential of turning many hearts to Christ Jesus if the Wake Up Calls and Great Strips of evil are accepted and believed as one. From God's perspective, looking back through a paradox in time toward earth, there would by great strips of evil removed from earth.

The Lord God knows the end from the beginning. Man has no understanding of his times in light of prophetic fulfillment apart from the enlightenment provided by the Spirit of Christ. The Lord God is aware of the nearness of His judgment, and He has been warning His people. If people will receive this message, they can prevent their being deceived as, the 6+6+6 code is being implemented on the world stage. It must be the duty of true believers in Jesus Christ to make every attempt to win the world to Christ, by leading one soul at a time to salvation.

Below, 5-13-1-Israel, Jaffa - Simon the Tanner's House: Peter was given two huge assignment changes. In Act 10:9-48, Peter's assignment on food changed because of insight from the Spirit of the Lord, to include most other foods, which had been unclean before. Another assignment change came when the Gentiles were included into the salvation through Jesus Christ.

Another assignment change came to me just like St. Peter's changes. The Spirit directed me to go to the Leaders of Nations and others outside the church with these warnings because the Church refused to listen in the past. The body of Christ as a whole in America has become rich and in need of nothing. Therefore, the original Wake Up Call Prophecies issued in May-June 1994, as listed above, have been modified. Today, I can talk, warn and prophesy outside the Church about what was mostly a closed matter in Issue-1 (1994-95).

Above, 5-13-2- Israel, Qumran - Baptismal pool: Across the canyon is where the Dead Sea Scrolls were found in 1947. It has been said this sect may have had an influence on John the Baptist and Jesus. Their strict teachings were very similar. These teachings were written on scrolls, placed in jars, and hidden for years. Now we have similar strict teachings in the Wake Up Call Prophecies and other warnings.

Romans destroyed the Essenes in AD 68, an ascetic Jewish sect of the Second Temple period. Are we Christians in North and South America going to set by without a fight while the European Leopard Beast of the Old Roman Empire destroys Gods people again? The Wake Up Call Prophecies suggest otherwise. We must stand up like mighty soldiers of God and protect the Jews and the Americas from the evil desires of the Leopard Beast.

Unfortunately, it does not get any better. The Leopard Beast transforms into the Final Beast with the Three Ugly Heads (Daniel 7:7, Revelation 13:11-18, and with greater detail in 2 Esdras 11 and 12). Lukewarmers and Spirit-filled Christians must quit sitting around like lazy whimpering kids ignoring the last days we live in. God has demanded Spirit-filled Christians resist this ungodly growth toward world government. We must unify through the UACC. This shall be our best hope in gaining enough power to offset some of Satan's destructive influence in the Americas. Stand today and fight or fall never to get up on Judgment Day. Christians have this choice!

The final words of the Spirit of Christ to me about this prophecy were; "You will receive persecution for being the messenger of this awakening call, but be strong and trust in the Lord, your God. The wise will understand and obey these sayings, but the wicked will not comprehend. Many will scoff and ridicule My servants because of this message. The ungodly are foolishly busy with their interests. Repentance is folly and their eyes are blurred. Truly, they have become fools. Many do not realize they are outside the opportunity of salvation with the dogs and unclean. Soon I will shut the doors of opportunity. However, to My Saints I say, be strong in the Lord for the conclusion of your time cycle nears its end. I am faithful to My promises. I will come at the appointed time - the very hour I've set from the beginning of time."

"I, the Almighty Lord God, have given this insight to Bob R. Short." Then, I said Amen!

What I have shared with you demands a choice. Remember, deciding not to decide shall be construed as a decision on Judgment day. Many may disagree and ignore this message about the 6+6+6 sequence, while others may agree.

I give thanks to the Lord God for choosing me to be a messenger. May all glory and honor be given to Him. It is my desire this message will serve to awaken the saints to the times in which we live. God has always forewarned His people.

It seems proper to close with Revelation 22:17, *"The Spirit and the bride say, `Come!' And let him who hears say, `Come!' Whoever is thirsty, let him come; and whoever wishes, let him take the free gift of the water of life."*

I, Bob R. Short, am a servant of our Lord Jesus Christ. Amen! Come quickly, Lord Jesus. May the grace of the Lord Jesus be with God's people!

WAKE UP CALL 1

INSIGHT: FROM MAY 13, to JUNE 9, 1994

PROPHECY ENDS HERE

Remember, choosing not to decide shall be construed as a decision on Judgment day.

Understand the worst MARK of them all, the Second Hidden MARK, in the next section!

WAKE UP CALL II

THE SECOND PROPHECY STARTS HERE

PROPHESIED JULY -- SEPTEMBER 1994

Section - 6

✞ CALL TO UNITY ✞

This entire section-6 was first prophesied and recorded as a matter of public record in a 232-page book called: Original WAKE UP CALL PROPHECIES, Rough draft Issue-I. It was published (2-1996) under ISBN 0-9651408-0-6. This Section was prophesied between the following dates; July, to September 1994 on original pages; 53 to 82. Pictures with insight and commentary added in 2005 - 2007

THE CHURCH TEST, GOD'S WARNING AND CALL TO UNITY

Section 6-1

During the printing of the prophecy given during May and June 1994, the Spirit of Christ prompted the development of a test to identify lukewarmness and disobedience within the Church. The call of the Spirit of Christ is to deal with sin, repent, and actively become involved in those actions making the Church an effective force in the world.

The first, deep impression of the Holy Spirit is for the Church to obey the instructions to read aloud (Revelation 1: 3) the Revelation, heed the warnings, and be obedient. This blesses the Church as it becomes involved in the end time events.

The starting point must be to analyze every element of major change in the Church after World War II or better still since 1900 A.D. Keep in mind the last three churches, Sardis, Philadelphia, and Laodicea (Revelation-3) and their descriptions. Compare the changes with the following twelve criteria and ask, **"Was the change made to conform to the world?"**

The Twelve Steps to Consider:

1. What changes have occurred since World War II? Were they biblical or a move toward lukewarmness? Were they worldly props brought into or placed on church property and called witnessing tools to improve attendance?

2. What has been the effect of the militant women's right movement? This is linked to the woman's desire to be in, or replace the man in his God-ordained position (Genesis 3: 16).

3. Has the church experienced a fear of reprisal or loss of membership?

4. What antichurch laws have been enacted, such as parts of the 1964 equal rights movement, tax codes, and other such legislation?

5. Is there a significant increase in the emphasis on the love and procurement of money and indebtedness call (prosperity debt)? This will be naturally disguised as a sign of spirituality.

6. What activities are engaged in to gain a more compatible relationship with the world by making the Church less offensive? The push has been toward political correctness while ignoring the mandates of separation clearly stated in God's Word.

7. Has the pressure to emphasize human and self-rights replaced the rightful place of the Lord God to receive glory and be worshipped?

8. Is the Church following after a one-world unity, which compromises the God-ordained structure of the Church? The biblical call must be to holiness, purity, sound doctrine, and righteous standards based solely on the morality contained in the laws of the Lord God.

9. Are there prophets who are boldly proclaiming different gospels, spiritual demonstrations, and a Christ for which there is no biblical pattern or practice? This is an attempt to weaken the Church with erroneous teachings disguised and presented in warped, invalid interpretations of scriptures. Does your leadership suppress new prophecy such as The Scroll, which could enlighten its members and help them in their future to walk with Jesus? On the other hand, do they present it and let the common sense of the matter be guided by the Holy Spirit to each member, as it will affect their individual life.

10. Is there greater, and growing, competition between churches which are rooted in greed and self-love?

11. Is there open disobedience to and contradiction of Jesus' statement, *"My house will be called a house of prayer"* (Mark 11: 17)?

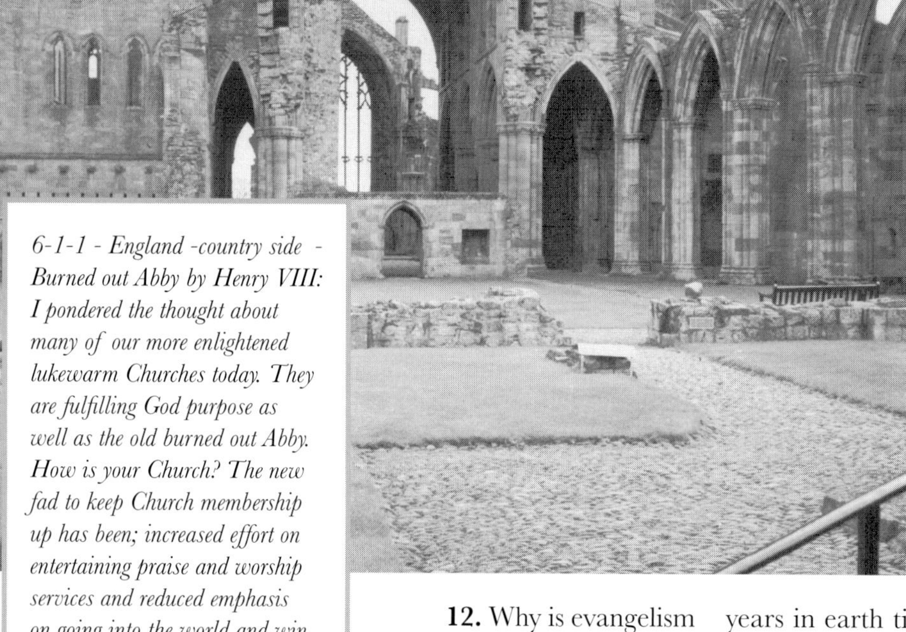

6-1-1 - England -country side - Burned out Abby by Henry VIII: I pondered the thought about many of our more enlightened lukewarm Churches today. They are fulfilling God purpose as well as the old burned out Abby. How is your Church? The new fad to keep Church membership up has been; increased effort on entertaining praise and worship services and reduced emphasis on going into the world and win souls like the Great Commission commands. This takes too many resources from their marketing department.

The easiest and best way for return on our investment must include bring the world props onto Church property and using them for witnessing tool. What a time saving idea for the lazy at heart! When Jesus judges on the dreadful day concerning these disobedient acts by Church leaders, He will tip their reward table over! Take the test for lukewarmness.

12. Why is evangelism not emphasized with the objective of taking the Gospel to those who are without the message of salvation? Has evangelism become a new form of Christian entertainment, which has quantitatively and qualitatively become helplessly ineffective in reaching a lost world and holding its Spirit-filled membership intact?

✍**NOTE:** It is not realistic to invite a person away from sin into lukewarmness. For both the sinner and the lukewarm Church are standing on sinking sand. The difference being, the lukewarmer will be punished more than the sinner will. First take the plank out of the lukewarm Church's eye, and then invite the person into righteousness.

Rule of thumb for change: Has past modifications to procedures and doctrine or will future changes made in your Church be a part of or play a roll in the Millenium Temple that Jesus sits in to teach us His ways during the Millenium? If the answer is YES, then this change probably is a move toward righteousness (how Jesus would operate your Church). More importantly, if the answer is NO, it may indicate a clear and deliberate move toward lukewarmness, laziness, and the lack of discipleship to reach others outside the Church property line. ✂

As the Church becomes indifferent to the biblical standards of conduct and purpose, it will increasingly become lukewarm through undetected disobedience. If your church or denomination can be described by answering yes to the above questions, then it's very likely the church may be experiencing deep, serious, spiritual problems. It is in trouble!

The Apostle John directs true believers to try or test the spirits to determine whether they are of God or not. (1 John 4:1)

The word of God is a living and powerful force which cannot be changed or altered from the purposes of the Lord God. The force of God's word is the spirit of the Lord God, vital, breathing, and forever active toward predetermined ends, which are revealed in prophecy. When viewed in terms of millennial days, (see II Peter 3: 8) where a millennial day equates to one thousand years in earth time, the prophetic movement of God's word must be approximately six days old since the time of Adam.

It behooves the Church to NOT conform to worldly standards and enter a condition of lukewarmness in view of the certainty of God's sovereign to fulfill world events. The pull of the world increasing attracts the Church to become more enlightened and less hypocritical by easing up on the holy and righteous standards of the word of God. The purpose of the Church must be to preach the Gospel message, which brings conviction, and to save lost souls. What determines the great need today?

We see the political, educational, religious, sports and entertainment facets of society becoming in progressively the messengers of lawlessness. There is a spiritual conspiracy in these factors forcing a society to cave in to their perverted demands to recognize the right to murder the innocent and openly practice lifestyles, which will bring the judgment of the Lord God upon a nation. Satan's perverted 1964 equal rights movement has put under the yoke, the power of America's Churches. Then God was asked by our government in 1967 to leave America and the schools where He has been teaching since the birth of our nation. As birth pains, American government has been trying to disprove God Almighty and reject Him. The Jewish people had just won Jerusalem back for the Lord's return that same year and warmly welcomed Him back. This happened even though most of the Jewish people are secular and not devout. Satan's new stronghold against weakened Churches helped him launched great influence since 1994 on government decisions in America. America has been in a serious accelerated decline since the 1960's, which will ultimately lead to the Three Woes to America, which will consume her bars. Therefore, the great need today becomes somewhat obvious to those who seek truth and righteousness.

Our world must hear a clear, united voice in America that speaks for the millions of believers in Christ Jesus. Its clarion call must reach the highest offices of government. It must become a cry, which rallies and unites the elect saints of the Lord God into a mighty force of righteousness called the Universal American Church Coalition (UACC).

"I, the Lord God Almighty, told churches of the end time to judge themselves (Revelation 3: 2), yet they proudly humble themselves to the world. For this, they will suffer greatly in the hour of trial. I shall start moving quickly and men will be left in the dust to be trampled upon by Satan.

I have told the churches of the end time to `hold on to what they have so no one will take their crown' (Revelation 3: 11). Yet, many churches will not heed, obey, or repent. Therefore, I will blot their names out of the book of life. Their buildings and works will be burned, shaken and destroyed as a fulfillment of the `Three Woes to America'. Furthermore, I decree upon their armies, `the Seven Judgments against the Mighty Army of Babylon'.

Below, 6-1-3- Italy, Rome, St. Peter's Square: Viewed in front of St. Peter's Cathedral: It became apparent some people were being turned away from entering St. Peter's for disrespectful dress and mannerism. Some became very upset while others were disappointed, because they did not see themselves as disrespectful. Herein lies the problem of lukewarmers. They cannot see their problem because of Satan's deception or they have never been taught properly. I overheard their conversations as they scurried off angrily. When Christians enter God's Holy House of Worship, we must be respectful of our dress, mannerisms and leadership authority. This experience reminded me of 2 Chronicles 26: 16-23. King Uzziah became full of pride and powerful and tried to do something disrespectful in God's House. In short, godly leadership confronted Uzziah and God gave him leprosy. The Scripture says, courageous men of leadership status confronted Uzziah for his disrespect. Lukewarm churches cannot find this quality of men in them. Unfortunately, there are few older women qualified to teach the younger women how they should act either. This equates to lukewarm churches.

Above, 6-1-2- Greece - Delphi - Temple of Apollo: With The Oracle of Delphi in the background. I recall my thoughts as they raced to find the Spirit of my mind. Then insight came to me, many of the churches are no different from the Oracle of Delphi. The Delphic Oracle was the means through which worshipers could hear the words of god Apollo, spoken through a priestess or Phthia. People paid a levy called a pelanos and the question was answered. Sounds like some of our enlightened modern-day churches where the same organized money exchangers are busy taking money at the door so people can envision their questions will be answered by song, dance, and other entertaining events. Some Churches really go the extra mile and for a few dollars extra offer the more wealthy patrons front row seats, so they do not have to sit with the blue-collar workers in back.

They are no better than the Delphic Oracle and the Temple of Apollo who charged their patrons for spiritual insight and answers. What do you think Jesus would do, if he walked to the front door of His own Church-house to see a concert and was not allowed to enter because He had no money (pelanos) for a ticket? God help them!

Many in the Church will give into other spirits and hate, backbite, and pursue their brothers in hate. They will stumble and fall away.
(Matthew 24:10)

Right, 6-1-4- Italy, Rome, San Pietro in Vincoli: Chains purportedly which held St. Peter in prison. Unfortunately, many churches are tied down with the chains of Lukewarmness. Satan's latest attack on America and the Churches has been the Internet Web of Deceit. He has lured the unsuspecting Christian leaders into allowing into the Church one of the filthiest, ungodly, and unspeakable perverted pieces of demonic mind-scrambling devices in Satan's arsenal. This has been the computer connected to the Internet Web of Deceit. I warned all major Church denominations in 1995 or 1996 and no one listened. Availability has proved to be a culprit in promoting sin. I have heard statistics about some church leadership and employees are watching perverted, filthy, inappropriate material and porn on the Web of Deceit on Church property. This is the ultimate disgrace of the modern day Churches.

Churches must get rid of this filthy modem into the dark world of Satan. I have witnessed a person in God's holy sanctuary working feverishly on a lap top computer just before the service started. If the computer was hooked up to the proper equipment and I did not check, that person could view porn while the choir warms up for the morning service. Satan encourages watching porn and singing Holy, Holy, Holy all at the same time. Is anybody getting the point here? God help us!

On May 18, 2005 for the first time, I heard a famous religious speaker on his show say, "If the Internet has been drawing you into the filthy chat rooms, cybersex on web-sights, or watching porn and other non-Christian areas or bad influences, then GET RID OF THE INTERNET and/or YOUR COMPUTER!" He further went on the say a recent survey disclosed: One third of all divorces were directly or indirectly caused by the Internet web of deceit.

With this test for lukewarmness, I have counseled their Churches to buy the `gold refined in the fire, repent, and obtain the white clothes to wear.' Failure to heed this warning will result in being excluded from the wedding banquet. Furthermore, they will experience and `taste the main course' of God's wrath through violent destruction of life on this earth.

Disobedient Churches will come to understand the true meaning of "fear the one who has power to destroy the soul." Then shall the second death be upon the disobedient Churches as they are cast into the lake of fire!

Almighty is the Lord God who judges the Churches!" I said amen, and amen.

ANOTHER OPTION
FOR AMERICA

Section 6-2

The Spirit of Christ has revealed another option for America, which has a different outcome. God always gives us at least two options. This option if executed will transform into a lighthouse to the world through which a one-minded group of Churches-appointed men will speak for the Universal America Church Coalition (UACC). This coalition of 333,000 Churches must come to a place of prominent leadership very quickly. They must be empowered to lead the United States back to a place of glory. This comes from acknowledging the Lordship of Christ. In clear words to my spirit, I hear Him say, "My people must repent now for the time is too short to continue to hold hands with the world any longer."

America will be victorious with Jesus Christ in the battle of Armageddon as the Jewish nation is protected. The best way for this to happen would be for the elect saints to repent and come back and build a single-minded Church Coalition (UACC), separate from Europe's one-world church.

The Spirit enlightened me on America's option, (Revelation 17: 14) *"and with Him will be His called, chosen, and faithful followers."* Faithful followers could include America but it is up to the saints and Churches of America. This one-mind Church comprises many groups, but they are united by unity of spirit, having the mind of Christ, yet each group can worship God as they believe.

Another impression deep within my spirit expanded the idea Satan will have great influence over the entire world as we know it today. Yet, America can better withstand Satan using the power of the UACC. When the Bible refers to the whole world, it is referring to the governments of the world as they were structured two millennial days (2000 years) ago. The whole world represents the entire world except North and South America. This observation will be discussed in the Beast Chapter.

"Has the Internet been drawing you into the filthy chat rooms, cybersex on web-sights, or watching cyber-porn and other non-Christian areas of bad influences, then remove the Internet and/or your computer! Sin and availability are brothers."

Above, 6-2-1- Italy, Rome, inside the Colosseum: Top half of picture is where the seats were located. This represents the world stage where most nations following the European led MNO will watch hungrily at America's deterioration and possible destruction.

The bottom of the picture exposes where animals and Christians could be herded up on top to the main floor of the Colosseum and be slaughtered for sport. Churches not participating in the UACC may unknowingly be doing something similar. Individual Churches lack the power to change America fast enough. This will cause many Christians here in America and around the world to die unnecessarily. The UACC can best obtain the power to turn America back on course in time to offset the European World Government. If Christians refuse to form the UACC, God will be forced to harshly turn America in the proper direction.

The elect saints in America are offered two options. Either they will be victorious with Jesus in the battle of Armageddon or our nation, as we know it now, will not exist at the second advent of Jesus Christ (His return). The Three Woes and Seven Judgments mentioned previously are America's downfall. We can fight for honor and victory with Jesus or die in disgrace. As for me and my house, we will serve and fight for our Lord Jesus Christ.

My brothers, I charge you before the Lord this entire prophecy and judgments be read and explained before the brothers, or at least a copy given thereto. God forbid we ignore His warning!

The next two paragraphs are very important for Christians to understand!

In short, if Christians do not get it, then many could be destined to Hell. I will summarize the entire section in three sentences:

Christians must do what ever it takes to influence their countries' leaders not to lock into the European led World Federation of Nations or MNO. Nations refusing to join the MNO will not require their citizens to accept the Mark, Number, and Name of the Beast. However, Nations joining the MNO will be forced to make it mandatory upon its citizens to accept the Mark of the Beast to buy and sell.

Below, 6-3-1- Italy, Rome, Roman Forum - "The Curia" - or ancient Roman Senate House: The Roman Forum appeared massive and powerful to me as we strolled among its ruins. I pondered in my mind as the Spirit led me into this understanding of future events. "The Roman Empire seemed to have a fatal wound from their past history. More importantly, its spirit to dominate the world has been reborn before our very eyes. Warn the brethren, the fatal wound has been healed and it will be one of the ten heads of the final empire!"

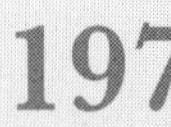

Above, 6-3-2- Italy, Roman Forum - Faustina Temple: The Roman Empire of old is resurfacing first under the present European Union (EU). However, it will soon evolve into the Third Beast of Daniel 7:6, the Leopard. It will have a form of spirituality without power from the God of the Bible. It will have a form of worldly power, but only temporary. It will have a form of security and peace, but only to crumble and give into the Final Antichrist over the Fourth Beast in Daniel 7:7. America must stay separated from and not lock into hidden deceptive ways of the two Beasts.

MARK OF HIS NAME
SECOND HIDDEN MARK
REVEALED
Millennium Nations Organized
Section 6-3

Like the initial birth pains, the intention is to trick the Christians, Churches, and nations into being unable to disengage themselves from the system of monetary control which will be enacted in the last six or (S) sequence. Nation's will be trapped first, and without Christians' guidance, any nation will be tricked into this false security illusion.

Christians, Churches, and nations will be forced to make a decision of great consequence between accepting the monetary system, and thus worshipping Satan, or being true to the Lord God by rejecting the system. Rejection of the world monetary system will prevent the saints from being able to conduct business as they have done previously. Following the Lord God shall be equivalent to being in rebellion against the Millennium Nations Organized. This requires sacrifice for America.

The Spirit paraphrased Revelation 14:10-11, as a warning to pastors who must protect their people and warn them about satanic deception.

"There is no rest day or night for those persons, Churches, and/or nations who worship or conduct business with the **M**illennium **N**ations **O**rganized (MNO) and its master computer. Also, anyone or any Church or nation who receives or accepts the Mark of His Name, which equates to the **M**illennium **N**ations **O**rganized, will be tormented with an atomic blast until they fall directly in front of Jesus' feet and His holy angels. His angels will be singing holy praises to Jesus for His righteous and fair judgments against those who are disobedient toward His word."

My call is to the pastors to awaken for the sake of the Church. It is time to forget the emphasis on individual ministries and begin a unified effort to influence the United States' federal government not to fall for the lurking deception. For nations will fall to this deception first, leaving little options open for Churches, businesses, and individuals to offer other solutions or refuse the second mark (MNO). Our nation has and will continue to run blind without guidance and the UACC would be a good way to accomplish God's goal.

WE MUST STOP THE AMERICA'S FROM LOCKING INTO THE MARK OF HIS NAME WHICH IS THE MNO - EUROPEAN LED (Leopard Beast) TEN KINGDOM FEDERATION.

Once a country accepts the Mark of His Name - MNO, then that country shall be out of grace with God and is ready to accept the Number of His Name. That is to say, citizens can now buy or sell internationally by using the Number of His Name.

Number of His Name = 666 = MNO = 6+6+6

Otherwise, the Number of His Name interlocks with the Mark of His Name and with the Mark of the Beast. Simply saying, we now have the three correct sets of numbers to buy and sell from the MNO.

Prophesied by - Bob R. Short, a Witness

Right, 6-3-3- Scotland, countryside - Baby Sheep: This Sheep has its assigned number. Unfortunately, for Christians to receive the Mark, Name or Number of the Beast will lead to the second death. Sheep cannot resist but Spirit-filled Christians can! North and South America must stick together to offset the pull and enticement of joining the European led World Government (MNO). The MNO's ability to offer worldwide aid and security because of disasters will be debated. Liberals will want to go under the umbrella of the European MNO, which will require paying them a consumption tax and conservatives will not.

If Satan does not deceive us this way and the UACC has been organized and is successful in turning America, he will enact the last six or (S) sequence. Americans will be told their money will be worthless and, in order to do business, American businessmen, corporations, and Churches operating on borrowed money must interface with the computer and monetary system of the Antichrist. Likewise, Churches and denominations, which are closely linked to the monetary system of the world, are setting themselves up for trouble through indebtedness. Satan will promote the Internet web systems through subtle monetary and peace initiatives.

Christians must start resisting or even refusing any additional personal marking (IC, ID, or RFID) computer chip card, which has been improved, laser and finger scanners, tattoos, chip implants, and the like. The key equates to numbers of Christians not just one Christian's refusal. Each step promotes itself using security, peace, and safety. They say it is more cost effective and user friendly. More importantly, the hidden truth emerges; it only takes a person one step closer to the Mark of the Beast by way of the C, Z, and S sequences. The Spirit of Christ strongly emphasized Christians must hinder the Antichrist's time frame by resisting or refusing further ID invasion. This will cause great public interest whereby revival will be born in America and more souls will be saved.

WARNING

The IC, ID, or RFID (marking) technology is the first (marking) technology carrying with it all the digits and three sequences (S,Z,C) of the

MARK OF THE BEAST.

This may require great sacrifice on the Christian's part. On a worldly standard, most American's are classified rich. Many Christians will be asked to give up worldly possessions and stand for Jesus just like the rich man in the Bible parable. Will each of us do as the rich man and shamefully walk away and cling to the world? On the other hand, will we boldly walk in faith and obedience to start resisting or refusing (IC, ID, or RFID) marking improvements, which are one step closer to the last S or six sequence.

Saints, remember you must not accept the last six or (S) sequence. This will complete the 3-6's=666 combinations of numbers. This prophecy will provide the insight, which will keep the saints from being deceived.

The moment in time approaches us when the terrible consequences offer no alternative or options to either imprisonment or death if the final six or (S) sequence is rejected. Financial assets or indebtedness will slowly pull people into the deceitful web that leads to a twofold death scenario in Revelation 20: 14. The Spirit tells me, Christians will be forced to sacrifice their money, businesses, savings accounts, time, and even their lives (Revelation 17: 6). Many may be jailed to stop America's rushing into the Internet web of satanic deceit. The Spirit led me to write "America's losing her sight while Europe's gaining his might."

Unconfirmed statistics indicate ninety percent of Americans believe in God and sixty percent to seventy percent believe they are going to heaven. However, God's word says few will make it. Moreover, from what I have heard, my estimation puts the actual number at a much lower percent. The Spirit has impressed upon me the Wake Up Call Prophecies are for repentance and action by individual Christians as well as leaders of Churches and denominations.

However, there remains a WARNING FROM GOD to the leadership of Churches. Leaders are in trouble who allow their Church to be in debt and/or locked into the Internet system web by accepting Revelation 14: 10-11.

THE GOOD, THE BAD
AND GOD'S OPTION
Section 6-4

The Spirit of Christ Jesus instructed me to write, "Church leaders must not leave snares and rocks for their tribulation flock to trip on such as but not limited to debt. Some pastors think the rapture will occurs just before the tribulation period starts, in the middle of the tribulation period, or before the battle of Armageddon. This will leave the helpless person judged unworthy by God abandoned on earth to pay the bills and fight Satan's wrath while they sit up in the high and mighty and tell me these unworthy people should have listened to them. No! Pastors in debt need to listen. Debt is now considered a tripping stone for your flock!

All is not lost if they will repent before their congregation and join the one-mind, multi-body, believing Universal America Church Coalition (UACC). Their Church can quickly get out of debt. There is power to get Churches off the Internet web of deceit by joining other Churches in a single-minded effort to bring the Church of Jesus Christ back to power. Then they can be a guiding light for America and other nations to follow. Note:

Pastors who do not heed this warning are not attuned to the days we live in. The Three Woes to America will consume them and their Churches. With righteousness I judge the Churches"! I said, Amen. Note: Do not confuse the liberal World Council of Churches with the righteous Universal America Church Coalition (UACC).

Once again, the Spirit of Christ has told me to write; "When a person's acts and deeds are judged - part of the judgment will be, what did they do to keep God at the focus of their country. Remember Jesus will judge each nation, which means His question will be asked directly to His Christians. Inaction by Christians in this matter will result in losses before the judgment seat of Christ. Satan has used misinformation of interpretation of scripture to reduce the power of the local Churches. If the Church does not wake up, this reduction will accelerate into the tribulation period. Satan will, as birth pains, become more effective in keeping any nation's focus off God. But unity in the UACC will help win!"

Center, 6-4-1- England - London - St. Paul's Cathedral: I was impressed with the beautiful structure of St. Paul's. However, my heart cries out to God Almighty, to lift the Church up in unity to fight Satan. Churches fight about denominational issues and do not unite. I have studied many different rapture theories, which have become major denominational issues. Church unity has been stymied because of these incorrect theories. Most people will not listen with an open mind to what I have to say if it does not agree with their precise rapture theory. In some cases, the rapture theories have become a more important issue than the salvation message of Jesus Christ. The UACC can be God's end time common bond to set this destructive issue aside to unify and protect the Church. Most denomination contacted has their agendas and have held back from starting the UACC. It will be too late to react if the leadership does not wake up before God intervenes for us. Some say only about two percent of people go to Church in London on a regular basic. In Western Europe, it is four to eight percent. The USA is seeing a fifteen to as high as thirty-five percent drop of young people into the Churches. The lukewarm Churches are in trouble. Christians must unite or they will fall to Satan's power of deception.

The Church has not pursued political influence before the tribulation period begins. However, in Revelation 13, God commands the Church to get political. The Church must refuse to worship the beast, take his mark, join the political Name of the Beast (MNO), or use the Number of the Beast.

UNIVERSAL AMERICAN CHURCH COALITION (UACC)

The UACC was never prophesied as an end time event to happen as a sign to look for. I only spoke the instructions received from the Holy Spirit in September-October 1994 that the Church should start the UACC and prepare for the tribulation period.

However, there was a prophecy attached to the UACC insight. I prophesied the removal of presidential candidates if the Church leaders did not start the UACC. This can be found on Page-97 of the Original Rough Draft Issue-1, of the Wake Up Call Prophecies, and now located in section 2-8 of the Scroll. Names of leaders removed so far are found at the front of the Scroll, Section - 3.

GOALS OF UNIVERSAL AMERICAN CHURCH COALITION (UACC)

Section 6-5

The UACC is to serve the following goals:

1. **To** achieve the uniting of 333,000 Christian congregations with a combined membership of 50,000,000.
2. **To** encourage all USA congregations to eliminate indebtedness before the tribulation period starts.
3. **To** unite for the purpose of seeking the Lord God to bring forth a spiritual reviving of all member congregations.
4. **To** unite as a Christian body and politically influence government leaders to return to a biblically based foundation of morality and ethics.
5. **To** resist the receiving of the (C, Z, S) sequences in the satanic scheme of deception, and to resist receiving the Second Mark of the Antichrist's Name hidden in the European led **M**illennial **N**ations **O**rganized (MNO). Revelation 13 will be our guide to oppose these government mandates.

PURPOSE OF UNIVERSAL AMERICAN CHURCH COALITION (UACC)

Section 6-6

The purpose of the UACC must be to lead America back to a fear of the Lord God and an understanding of the times in which Jesus Christ will return to earth in power and glory to judge individuals and nations. America has turned from being a nation honoring the Lord God and regarding the moral standards of the Bible. In view of this fact, it is imperative God's nation no longer be left to the vices which are inherent in an "I" generation of "anything goes" mentality. If unchecked, the moral deterioration of America will progressively lead to disaster described in the Three Woes to America.

A nation, which honors the Lord God, will be governed by individuals who preserve the rights of the Church. But, observed in the prophetic light, as the times near the coming of Christ, the nation will begin the birthing pangs in which the government will turn against the Church and the righteous standards it represents. Persecution of the righteous shall be the logical expression of a society governed by special interests groups and people whose god promotes pleasure and self-indulgence.

You can perform a very important action for your family, Church, and Nation by convincing your Church leaders to start the UACC for protection.

Indecision is a vote for Satan. Unity in the UACC is faith that God truly sent these prophecies to the Church for its end time assignment!

6-5-1- England, London, Buckingham Palace: Unfortunately, the reverse of the picture may be true if Churches do not unite and form the UACC. Christians will find themselves in the near future forcefully looking out the bars of a hostile European led Leopard Beast's controlled government instead of freely looking into friendly government places. Instead of changing of the guard, it will be a firing squad for the disobedient Christians who will not obey and take the Mark, Name, and Number of the Beast!

This spirit asserts America has been founded upon principles of separation of state from the Church. (Added 6-19-06: Otherwise, the Church was not to run our Government and the Government was not to set up a Church as England had. But, never was there intent by the framers to stifle the Christian values taught in the Bible to be omitted from our government. Where the principle of separation comes into play is clearly written in the Constitution that Government would not stifle Christian churches.)

The intention of those who wrote the documents of freedom and fought the battles of liberty was that the fledgling nation would perpetuate the Christian values and worship of the Lord God. Schools would serve to train younger generations in the laws of the Lord God without government interference. Never did the founding fathers envision the morally perverse, blasphemous teachings, which have been taught to the children the last forty years. The objective was not an adversarial relationship between true believers in Christ and government at any level.

As our nation rose in power and stature, its very Constitution stood for the freedom to teach the Bible as the best standard for judging morality and personal conduct. It is the basis of social equity, peace, and a deterrent to lawlessness.

It is sheer folly to deviate from the standards and teaching of the word of God. The Spirit of Christ has revealed "a society will drown and suffocate in its own spiritual vomit if it continues to be blatantly disobedient to the commands of Almighty God."

UACC is intended to be a moral preservative and directive force in society, being as Jesus said, "The salt and light of the earth." The impact of individual righteousness is compounded when true believers unite in a common cause and purpose. UACC has as its mission the turning of the government and the people of America back to the laws of God, which will produce right thinking, based on authoritative Biblical teaching. UACC will work toward seeking the Lord God for a revival of righteous living and thinking. We believe our bonded faith will position UACC with the power to turn America into a spiritual beacon, which will shine its light into other regions of the world.

The mission of the UACC is turning the government and the people of America back to the laws of God, which will produce right thinking based on authoritative Biblical teaching.

It will be necessary to implement replacement of laws, which are contradictory to the laws of God. Sound doctrine must be reinstated and become the basis of educational institutions and government. Furthermore, UACC will demand optional low-cost Christian school programs, which are funded by the government but not subject to government regulations. UACC member churches will administer such schools with funds being augmented by the cooperative efforts of the UACC headquarters. The UACC may purchase public school facilities and turn them into Christian schools.

(UACC) MEMBERSHIP REQUIREMENTS FOR UNIVERSAL AMERICAN CHURCH COALITION

Section 6 - 7

The Spirit of Christ prompted me to write the following:

1. Membership in UACC is extended to any church or ministry preaching or teaching salvation through Jesus Christ as the only name under heaven, which can forgive man's sins, and by grace through faith, we receive salvation and eternal life with God. Salvation is defined as being saved, born again or turning our lives over to Jesus Christ.

2. Any church or ministry that claims, through men, to have the power or authority to forgive man's sins shall not be eligible for membership. This perpetuates the error of the Pharisees (Luke 16:14). The Spirit has led me to understand this will occur in the Church during the endtimes. As Jesus told the Pharisees mortal men cannot justify or forgive sins, so the message must be for the Church today. Intrusion into the realm of power and authority that belongs to deity alone is detestable before the Lord God. Also forbidden into membership are those who teach and believe mortal man can attain a state of godhead comparable with the divine position of Jesus Christ.

3. All member churches and ministries shall believe and teach eternal life is provided by the grace of Almighty God through the vicarious atoning work of Jesus Christ, His Son. *"He who has the Son has life; he who does not have the Son does not have life"* (1 John 5:11,12). This requirement excludes all religions throughout the world from membership, which do not embrace salvation by faith in Jesus Christ.

The Spirit of Christ has warned me that the UACC must not lock into binding agreements or joint ventures with religions or other organizations, which tend to contaminate the moral and ethical standards of the word of God. False religions, though they may have the appearance of honoring the Lord God, are truly instruments of the spirit of error and progressively lead toward the world religion, which will embrace the worship of Satan through the Antichrist.

4. All member churches and ministries must acknowledge a belief in the infallibility of the word of God as the inspired, God-breathed revelation of Himself to man. It must be the rule of conduct and the final authority in all matters.

5. All member churches and ministries must acknowledge a belief in the trinity: Father, Son, and Holy Spirit.

6. All member churches and ministries will hold to a belief in ridding themselves and their ministries of all indebtedness. In doing this, the bondage to the monetary systems under Satan's control will be broken. The **"prosperity debt"** mentality, in which evangelism is linked to building projects, will be rejected and discontinued. Upon being received into membership, each member will pledge not to return to the bondage of indebtedness. Indebtedness after becoming a member will be grounds for dismissal.

Below, 6-6-1- U.S., Hawaii, Honolulu - Waikiki Beach: I got the feeling on Waikiki Beach, life here in the good old U.S.A. has evolved into nothing more than sun, fun and pleasure. One might say this to be true inside and outside some Churches. Americans seem to be in a dream world and think everything shall continue as always. Once again, a warning must be issued, life, as we know it will not remain the same!

Terrible wars will increase and America will be greatly affected. Natural disasters will increase to a point where countries will not be able to respond properly. The Church has been doing a splendid job preaching messages on; good feelings, loving feelings, correcting Christians' problems, possible debt thinking, giving and expecting rewards. Some of these subjects were great in the past, but without explaining what God has decreed for endtimes will leave the average Christian naked and without ample preparedness. They could fall. We must start the UACC to protect Churches, nation, and ourselves.

7. As described by the Lord Jesus Christ, we are the "salt of the earth." The Spirit has revealed to me America must deal with its own faults and failures before trying to straighten out the faults and failures of others. This does not eliminate the need to provide missionary ministries throughout the whole world, which is a direct command to believers. However, the focus of the UACC must be on America, and the mission shall be to bring this nation back to the principles of honoring the Lord God and living by the standards of His word.

8. All voting representatives from each member organization must meet the following criteria.
A. The representative must be of the male gender.

Clarification note - part 8A, September 2006: This note was added partly because of technology advances leading to non-Biblical medical practices. Other reasons include the deterioration of the Church and society since July - September 1994 when this directive was issued. In addiction, the perception of the traditional description of gender as associated with male, female, wife, and marriage described by strict Biblical standards as compared through the distorted lens of the secular world and lukewarm Churches, leaves no choice but to clarify the original statement. Consequently, the following qualifying statement must now be included. The representative must be of the male gender (meaning natural born) and not married to more than one wife (wife, meaning female not by a sex change or a homosexual male) at a time (Bigamy).

Therefore, each individual church will determine using these guidelines which qualifying male to send whether he is single, divorced, married to only one wife at a time, or married to only one wife in his entire lifetime.

It is imperative the UACC help silence the radical noisy-dens (Anti-Biblical special interest groups) inside and outside the Church. The Prophet Jeremiah 51:55, speaks of an end time event when God will silence the noisy-den for good.

B. He must lead a blameless, controlled life.
C. He must not be overbearing, quick-tempered, or violent.
D. He must not be given to drunkenness nor pursue dishonest gain.
E. He must be hospitable and love what is good.
F. He must be self-controlled, disciplined, upright, and live a holy life.
G. He must hold firmly to the trustworthy message so he can encourage others through sound doctrine and refute those who oppose truth by using the power and authority gained by unity with the UACC.

9. No church or ministry controlled, led, or ministered by women will be allowed into the membership of UACC. God has placed the woman under the headship of her husband (a male). The woman shall not usurp the male's authority to protect, lead, and take care of what God gave him (Genesis 3:16). Church leaders are to be men (Hebrews 13:17).

10. No church or ministry will be admitted into membership led by homosexuals or those leading a sexually perverse lifestyle. UACC will not accept into membership individuals or organizations openly showing contempt for the holy standards of living clearly stated in the word of God. Sin leads to judgment and death and it has no place in the fellowship of God's people. The Spirit of Christ led me to say, "The UACC shall not contain even the slightest hint of sexual immorality."

11. The representative list of exemplary churches, denominations, and ministries which are encouraged to become members of UACC are listed alphabetically: Assemblies of God, Baptist, Church of Christ, Independent, Interdenominational, Methodist, Nazarene, Non-denominational, Pentecostal, Presbyterian, other Christian type Churches passing the UACC guidelines.

It should be noted, there may be individual congregations within the listed groups, which may not qualify for membership in the UACC.

12. UACC member churches and ministries may worship God in their normal manner, in the privacy of their individual congregations, so long as there is no violation of the stated membership requirements. UACC retains the right to dismiss any member church or ministry in the event dismissal becomes warranted by such violations.

UACC BY-LAWS AND RULES

THE UNIVERSAL AMERICAN CHURCH COALITION

Section 6-8

1. The Universal American Church Coalition (UACC) must be established to function as a voluntary agency through which funds are raised and channeled toward stated goals. Churches and ministries in the United States, Canada, Mexico and South America are encouraged to participate first. UACC focus must be on the spiritual needs of North and South America with USA being highlighted first.

2. UACC will first payoff its American members' indebtedness on a rotating basis as money becomes available. A minimum of two months project-operating expenses must remain in the treasury at all times. Loans will be paid out of funds in excess of this cash flow amount.

3. No permanent chairman or leader will be appointed, but shall be by a system of rotating leadership selected from membership groups. No group in a position of leadership shall speak from a denomination bias, but shall always espouse the views of UACC. Each problematic situation will be addressed and resolved by the rotating leadership group chairman in order to meet the goals approved by UACC. The Church has been instructed to make petitions through two or three people.

The Spirit of Christ spoke to me that Satan's attack on the UACC would be made more difficult if there is a rotating leadership rather than a single individual placed in a permanent position of authority. The true power of the Church has always been the authority of Jesus Christ expressed by His Spirit through His people. When the collective power and unified purpose of 333,000 churches focuses on a single objective, the results will be awesome.

4. There shall be one head of the UACC, the Lord Jesus Christ. A voting membership, made up of servants of Christ, will exist to turn America back to right biblical thinking and to the Lord God.

5. UACC will exercise no authority over the autonomous rights of member churches.

6. Any membership church or ministry who is a recipient of funds to eliminate indebtedness shall not be required to sign a promissory repayment note. However, each such recipient will make a verbal commitment to reimburse UACC for the funds received. Such reimbursements shall be made in addition to membership dues. Reimbursements will be set at levels lower than the former monthly payments to ease the financial burdens of member churches. Furthermore, each recipient shall make a verbal commitment not to return to a state of indebtedness and, if such indebtedness does occur, membership will be forfeited.

> Confidence in Washington D.C. and the Old Roman Empire-revised EU governments, will lead your nation down the gutter to destruction. They have hopelessly lost their way.
>
> The Americas can best be saved through the power of the Church using the UACC to unite for a common cause. First, to win the USA back to Christ, then the Americas, and finally the world!

7. Membership dues: All member organizations of UACC will contribute one dollar ($1.00) per person per month based on weekly attendance figures. In the event the ministry is through some form of media, such as radio or television, membership dues will be based on the average number of people declared to be adherents and contributors to such ministries.

8. The number of votes, which can be cast on general collective issues in the UACC, will be based on the number used for assessing membership dues. The weekly average attendance or contributors number will be the number of votes allowed by the member organization. In order to vote, dues must be paid.

9. UACC will have seven options for dealing with issues requiring correction and discipline. They are:

A. Negotiations.
B. Boycotts.
C. Demonstrations.
D. Marches.
E. Lawsuits.
F. Any other peaceable action deemed necessary.
G. A call to arms (defensive only) as an ultimate, necessary means to protect member churches and property from oppression.

10. UACC does not advocate the overthrow of the lawful government of any nation. UACC does not advocate the use of its collective membership, with its unified power, to rise up against such governments. Rather, UACC believes in calling its membership to prayer for leaders of lawful government as directed by Romans 13.

11. As needed, UACC will establish the following departments:

A. Law office.
B. Public relations.
C. Accounting, which includes secretary and treasurer.
D. Advertising and marketing.
E. Media offices including radio and television.
F. Others as necessary.

The heads of these offices shall not serve as officials or permanent spokespersons for UACC. Only the presiding chairman for a designated month shall officially speak in behalf of UACC.

Chairmen in the various departments are to be rotated on a monthly basis, and they may serve as spokespersons under the direction and authority of the presiding chairman.

No person shall possess the authority to act in his own power apart from the vested authority of UACC.

12. All issues submitted to a vote of the membership will require a minimum of fifty-one percent of the vote to pass. In the event of a call to arms to protect the membership, a vote of sixty-six percent will be required for such action to be initiated.

Voting can be conducted in person or by mail at monthly meetings.

Three weeks written notice will be given each voting member church regarding issues of business requiring voting.

New agenda items may be brought before the body through proper rules of order. Such items will be put before the electorate in the meeting of the following month. Emergency issues shall be regarded as exceptions to the ordinary procedures of conducting business, and members present must pass such issues by a sixty-six percent majority vote.

13. Chairmen shall be elected from the voting membership by a simple majority vote of fifty-one percent or better. Chairmen shall hold office for one month.

The office of chairman will be rotated between members of various denominations. No denomination shall have two chairmen elected from their organization within the calendar year.

The chairman, while in office, must refrain from promoting the unique beliefs and doctrines of his denomination. The chairman must promote the beliefs and doctrines of UACC when serving as an official spokesman. The chairman shall abide by the statement of unity of the UACC: ONE MIND AND MULTI BODY BELIEVING PARTS.

At its monthly meetings, the voting body will appoint rotating chairmen for various departments. Such departmental chairmen will work with the general chairman to promote the message and cause of the UACC before the media, law enforcement agencies, political and governmental leaders, and other organizations as necessary.

Each departmental chairman will serve for one month. At the end of the term, the departmental chairman will give a report of accomplishments, then yield the office to the next duly elected person to fill the position.

Election of officers shall be the first order of business. No individual may be elected to the same office within a period of twenty-four months.

The Spirit of Christ has impressed me with the importance that no individual or organization be allowed to exercise undue power or influence. Otherwise, the purpose of the UACC will be inherently weakened and become a lost cause. We are servants of the Lord Jesus Christ, and this must be the prevailing issue uniting all members of UACC. Personal gain and glory must not be the motive of officials who serves in any capacity in the UACC.

NOTE - added 2006: It is important to understand internal security problems will skyrocket when America begins to fight more Middle East Muslim countries. The enemy has been allowed to filter into America and live with us. Jesus said people, organization, and countries are either for Me or against Me. Muslims do not acknowledge Jesus as their savior or the only way to the Father God.

The ideology of Islam hides behind religious teachings but cannot be categorized as a religion. Islam is called a religion purely to protect its cause from hostile targeted governments such as America. Islam has always striven to make a governmental policing body ideologically evolving with a goal to expand into the international community of nation states using a desert tribal structure of governing peoples. The purpose has been to build a world government using The Qur'an as its rulebook of laws. Many have replaced their intelligence with jihad and use terrorism to accomplish their political goals.

The UACC business is to help confront (Romans 14:16) or remove evil.
But some lukewarm churches are doing no more than supervising it.
It's house-cleaning time!

While other Muslims and Islamic converts use a heavy atmosphere of intimidation, especially against women, and no freedom of expression or equality under their law. Their allegiance is to their leaders, who promote progressive force to accomplish their world dream. This presents an unparalleled hostile force for the Western and European way of life and rule of law. Islam has become a clear and immediate danger to America and any nation that disagrees with their laws. When the chips are down, most Muslims loyalty has been toward Arab countries and the Muslims brothers who live there. Not America, England, or whatever nation they live in at the time. Therefore, they are citizens not of America, England, or non-Arab countries, but Middle East Arabs.

Church leaders must think about what will happen if they do not start the UACC before these security threats become full blown. The later they wait the worse it will get. ✂

14. Bob R. Short shall not be eligible to serve as either a voting member or elected official of the UACC. He is the vessel through whom the prophecy has been given to pass them on to the Church and elect saints of Jesus Christ. The role of Mr. Short within the UACC must be strictly limited to an advisory capacity as requested by the leadership. It is the sole responsibility of the membership of the UACC to initiate and perpetuate the purposes of the UACC, not Mr. Short. The membership shall be warned about allowing any individual or group gaining undue power or influence in the UACC. Power struggles must be avoided.

15. Any changes in the by-laws require a sixty-six percent vote of the membership.

16. Guest speakers, who may be regarded as experts in some field of knowledge, are allowed to speak at meetings so long as they adhere to the basic beliefs of the UACC.

17. General monthly meetings may rotate from city to city by the discretion of the UACC membership.

18. UACC meetings are closed to the public and media. All meetings shall be taped for viewing by the at-large membership. Edited versions may later be made available to the media.

19. All UACC meetings shall be regarded as closed, private meetings. Guests may be permitted to attend if approved by a prior vote of attending members. Exceptions will be made if the chairman requests the public relations chairman to rule on allowing unexpected guests to be in attendance. Security of access to meetings will be the responsibility of doorkeepers.

The recording secretary shall take minutes of all meetings. Copies of minutes shall be mailed to all member churches. Financial reports will also be provided, and such reports will give the details of the disbursement of funds to relieve the indebtedness of member congregations.

If member churches request, a copy of the meeting, it will be made available for an appropriate charge.

Below, 6-8-1- Israel, Dead Sea - En Gedi Oasis: This picture was taken toward a southerly direction. We could see an Arab sand storm coming. The wall of sand filled our eyes and limited our vision when it hit. I saw barren rocky land, salty sea, and a feeling of sorrow as I thought about America's future. America and the Dead Sea are similar because they both are rich yet have a degree of worthlessness. The Spirit moved me to think upon the disaster, which awaits America if the UACC has not started before the tribulation period begins. It may look like the picture of a vast wasteland. Christians must understand if we do not change America's direction back to the Lord God, He will be forced to do it for us to fulfill prophecy. There will be more destruction if God has to prune Christians and America. The day will evolve when Churches shall need armed men protecting them just to have a Sunday morning service. The UACC must be started!

SEVEN-POINT CHURCH PROTECTION COMMITMENT - (UACC)

UNIVERSAL AMERICAN CHURCH COALITION

Section 6-9

From Genesis 2:15, it's clear men are commanded by the Lord God to work and protect those things committed to their care and keeping.

UACC views this as the authority to use any necessary means to deal with and resolve issues pertaining to the welfare and protection of the UACC membership organizations.

In the realm of spiritual things, faith and prayer are the two recommended offensive weapons. Other options for protecting the membership and property of churches are:

1. Negotiations.
2. Boycotts.
3. Demonstrations.
4. Public marches.
5. Lawsuits.
6. Other peaceful actions as deemed necessary.
7. A call to arms as a last resort, defensive measure against any outside oppressor, threat, or hostile body.

Men are commanded to accept the responsibility to preserve and protect the membership of the UACC in order to ensure the right of freedom to assemble and worship the Lord God. This may require the ultimate test of love, loyalty, and commitment as stated in 1 John 3:16: *"This is how we know what love is: Jesus Christ laid down his life for us. And we ought to lay down our lives for our brothers."*

Going beyond mere asking, the Lord stated, *"... My command is this, love each other as I have loved you. Greater love has no man than this, that he lay down his life for his friends."* (John 15:12-13)

The call to action of arms is an extreme measure when other options fail. In the inevitability of armed confrontation, lives may be lost at present, but the gain shall be eternity with the Lord Jesus. Then so be it for the glory of God. This fulfills Revelation 18:24, *"In her was found the blood of prophets and of the saints..."*

The Lord Jesus commands end time Christian men to protect their brothers in the faith. Psalms 37:11 states, *"The meek will inherit the land"* and Matthew 5:5 reiterates the statement.

The Spirit of Christ has given me understanding of the meaning of meekness for the end time Church.

As the times reach their prophetic fullness when the coming of Jesus Christ is near, meekness has the meaning of "great power with great restraint." The Church today, through faith, hears the words in Hebrew 11:34: *"... whose weakness was turned to strength and who became powerful in battle..."*

The Spirit led me to write believers must not waver or be fearful in following the Lord's command to use this power, if necessary, to rebuke and thwart the attempts of tyrants to harm the Church. Remember the statement, "The gates of hell will not prevail against my Church." I am impressed to write Jesus did not intend His people to sit idly and passively by and expect Him to encounter the enemy. The command is to become involved to protect that over which He has made us stewards. God forbid any believing man ignore the instructions to take a forceful stand in the face of wickedness or government abuse.

Christians are expressly forbidden in Romans 13 to advocate the overthrow of legitimate government. Governments and their leaders are divinely appointed, and through them, the Lord God fulfills His purposes and will. Government leaders are viewed as servants of the Almighty Lord God.

The Spirit has impressed on me if any government does not fulfill the command to ***"do good to you,"*** (Romans 13:4), then that government and its leaders are in violation of the laws and expressed will of the Lord God. In the event governments initiates actions of persecution against the Church, confiscating property unlawfully, then the members are justified, even commanded, to rise up against the government as a stand in righteousness. This stand would generally be a defensive mode to protect church property or its members. (For offensive mode, see section 4-15, The Eli✝e Chris✝ian Soldiers).

If any government does not fulfill the command to "do good to you," (Romans 13:4), then that government and its leaders are in violation of the laws and expressed will of the Lord God.

Note added September-2006: God did not call the New Testament Church as an offensive or aggressive body of believers against oppressive governments. Herein lies the prophetic end time insight, the tribulation period is not New Testament time, but rather Old Testament time. When we study Daniel (9:24-27, we see verse 26 mentions 62 sevens (7's) and then verse 27 we find one (1) seven left (seven year tribulation period). This equates to the Lord God adding seven years of Jewish persecution, which is Old Testament time, on the end of the Church test cycle, which is New Testament time.

In Revelation 13, we understand a tremendous change in the Church must take place. It must become political involved and refuse certain technology and political ideology. It must stand against Babylon, the Beast, False prophet, and all the nations, which agree with their political and religious empire.

UACC will expressly advocate a stand, by all necessary means, which fulfills a love for Christ over loyalty to any ungodly government. In extreme measures, the pastor of member churches will have the discretion to issue a call to arms. UACC may vote to protect nonmember churches where this effort furthers the UACC cause and God's glory. These churches must meet the UACC membership requirements in their preaching and teaching otherwise this action cannot be authorized.

The Church will stand through unity. In division, it will fall prey to the wicked oppressors, political ideology, and terrorists.

Inaction by local, lukewarm churches will result in offering no resistance to evil forces which will burn, blow up, and steal church property, close meeting places, and imprison faithful followers of Christ. The longer it takes to think rightly about biblical principles, the more it will cost the church to gain back the power and position it has lost in society.

The Spirit of Christ has deeply impressed me with a familiar statement from the Bible. It is a warning for the end time church quoting Jesus as saying, "He who dies for me will live with me. And he who lives for today will surely die." The Spirit inspired me to say, men who do not fulfill Jesus' command to the call to arms in the end time tribulation period could surely lose rewards on judgment day. The Church will stand through unity. In division, it will fall prey to the wicked oppressors. This shall be the beginning of the prophetic pains of birthing. The Bible teaches, be of one-mind thinking.

To do this the Spirit of Christ led me to write, we must keep the UACC rally of unity simple so even a child could understand the message and purpose. Remember what Jesus said to His future church leaders in Matthew 18:3, *"...unless you change and become like little children, you will never enter the kingdom of heaven."* For end time churches this means rally around the UACC and its simple, clear cry of unity and multi-body thinking.

The Spirit has revealed the mightiest weapon of the Church against the forces of Satan and darkness will always be prayer. Our fight is not with flesh and blood, but against the unseen rulers of the empire of spiritual darkness, which enslaves the world systems.

If necessary, mortal Christian men may have to resort to the list of seven options as a means of standing against the oppressors of the Church. If this becomes necessary, then stand proudly in the name of Jesus Christ who commands you to action. May the Lord God bless Christians and keep them from fear and harm.

The Spirit opened my understanding to see mortal men view ninety-five percent of their problems as being fleshly and five percent as being of spiritual origins. The reverse is actually true as viewed by the Lord God. Therefore, prayer will be the most effective means possible of encountering and defeating Satan. The walk of faith must be an essential factor in dealing with the forces that go undetected by natural senses.

It shall be known throughout the land that the mighty men of the UACC will be called.

COMMAND KEEPERS

Thus saith the Lord. Amen.

6-9-1- Israel, Qumran Community - Scroll Cave: This is the caves where the Dead Sea Scrolls were found in 1947 which described the final battle (Armageddon) that ends the World as we know it! The battle will engage the Sons of Light (North and South America an a few others) against the Sons of Darkness (all other nations of the World). Many teach America cannot be found in prophetic end-times and will be destroyed. However, the Lord God has kept this hidden for the time of the end. In short, America will play a very large part during the tribulation period protecting the Jewish people and fighting the European Leopard Beast and the Eagle with the Three Ugly Heads.

This shocking insight has been revealed in the Wake Up Call Prophecies.

THE SPIRIT OF CHRIST JESUS LED ME TO SUMMARIZE AMERICA'S FUTURE

Section 6-10

"Wake up America, for God has established a universal, eternal, holy law which governs the affairs of mankind. Obey His laws, America, and reap the guaranteed blessings. Disobey, America, and become the recipient of the Three Woes to America for your rebellion against your Creator! The wise are given understanding of the meaning; "the Most High gives kingdoms to whomsoever He will."

"America will be shipwrecked if she continues to pursue her present course. She is blind, naked, and will burn with the Three Woes to America. Most churches in America are shipwrecked and lukewarm without power or influence to control government any longer. America's Christian men are shipwrecked, tired, and beaten down without a goal for victory."

"But there's GOOD NEWS! IT IS NOT TOO LATE! Their churches can start the UACC, if men will first win them back. Then the plans for victory will be prophesied to them. United with the UACC, they can then win back the judicial and political systems of government. America can be won back. Once again her streets, neighborhoods, and schools can be places of safety. The victory will go to the glory of the Lord God."

"America can then place watchmen on her shores to preach the good news when Jesus calls for his faithful followers (America) to stand at His side in the ultimate victory to protect the Jewish nation at Armageddon against most other nation in the world." Glory to the Lamb of God! Amen!

THIS IS THE END OF WAKE UP CALL II PROPHESIED JULY - SEPTEMBER 1994

On November 8, 1994, the Spirit gave me this cryptic riddle, "I am the Almighty God who gives kingdoms and it shall be known;

The Vision Follows

`The coming of the Son of man in His full glory will energize it. The weak eagle will be awakened and receive great strength by it. In one mighty assault, the eagle's powerful claws, full of the glory through it, will hit the mark of ten with such power and glory, as no man can understand. With the glory through it, the King of kings and Lord of lords will be ruler over the world. Seal this saying until the churches awaken.'

Glory to the Lamb! AMEN!" And the saints said, "Praise be to the King of kings!" Amen!

Below, 6-10-1- Italy, Assisi: A common narrow street or path in the hill country. God demands nations and individuals to stay on the narrow path He has laid out for them to follow. America has wandered from God's narrow path called Disciple Nations. A Disciple Nation incorporates the basic teachings of the Holy Bible into its laws, government and people. America has been falling short. Christian unity is the self-disciplining act, which will bring America back to a Disciple Nation and under the Lord God's protecting power.

Left, 6-10-2 - Italy, Florence, Santa Croce (Church): It has been called the pantheon of Florence and of Italy. Arnolfo di Cambio began work on the church in 1294 with the facade dating from the mid-19th century. There are many famous people laid to rest here such as, Michelangelo, Ghiberti, Galileo, Machiavelli and many others.

I looked at their tombs (some mounted on the walls) and wondered how they would stand before Almighty God, as we toured the Church. Fame and fortune on earth means nothing to God on judgment day - only if you have first repented of your sins and accepted Jesus Christ as your personal savior, and then started following him with evidence of good works.

People ask me all the time if it is the last days. "How can I be really sure about this end time stuff?" First, it takes faith to believe in Bible end times. Matthew 24 states, when ALL these things are visible at the same time. What things, they ask? After presenting some of these prophecies as proof, they begin to get interested because they are receiving little teaching on the subject at their churches. Finally, we get to 2 Peter 3, and the scripture asks the question about what kind of Christian are you going to be - knowing the disaster and destruction will befall the world as a test on mankind. It speaks of being at peace with Almighty God. To be at peace with God, Christians must be about the Father's end time assignment laid out for them. Do you know, and are you preparing. Are you sitting back doing nothing while your nation goes down the tube to destruction and falls under the Leopard Beast's authority?

See the

EUROPEAN LED LEOPARD BEAST

in next section

WAKE UP CALL SHOCK WAVE

PROPHESIED SEPTEMBER 1994 - AUGUST 1995

Section - 7

This entire section-7 was first prophesied and recorded as a matter of public record in a 232-page book called: Original WAKE UP CALL PROPHECIES, Rough draft Issue- I. It was published (2-1996) under ISBN 0-9651408-0-6. This Section was prophesied between the following dates; September 1994 to August 1995, on original pages; 159 to 209. Pictures with insight and commentary added in 2005 - 2007)

THE BEAST

Section 7-1, Rough Draft Sketch - 7-1-1
I saw the Beast. Who is like the Beast?

Who can make war against him?
To find the Beasts, see section - 9, sketch 9-1-2.
Prophesied, May 24, 1995. Bob R. Short

The Final Beast draws from all of the earth's mass less North and South America. The Antichrist Spirit will pull them together to form a Leopard Beast Daniel 7:6. North and South America will represent three horns booted out of the world assembly (MNO).

FIRST WOE
CONCERNING THE BEAST:

America must not lock into the protection of this ten kingdom federation. If America worships, loves, receives the "Mark of His Name = Millennium Nations Organized = MNO = 666, "then as nations, or individuals, we are fulfilling Revelation 14:11 and shall receive DEATH!

SECOND WOE
CONCERNING THE BEAST:

Spirit-filled Christians must warn the general population of Christians and give them the opportunity to make their own decisions in "this truth" as specified here in. Otherwise we will be adding more LOST Christians in the first half of the tribulation period according to Matthew 24:10.

Many of these lukewarmers will become discouraged and fall away because of lack of knowledge. We have an opportunity to share with them today. Are Christians going to share this end time insight with their fellow Christian or suppress it? However Christians can warn them, for the apostle said, he had told them all insight so they may choose themselves which direction to take.

THIRD WOE
CONCERNING THE BEAST:

As watchmen for the flock, our silence will justify God placing their blood on our shoulders! The world area nation's map is divided into ten kingdoms to form the Millennium Nations Organized (MNO).

WARNING!

This is a warning to the reader concerning Satan's greatest deception. Most Christians are looking to refuse the 666 on the hand. Yet, they will be in trouble with God before they get the opportunity to refuse the Mark of the Beast. They will loose rewards and eventually may fall from God's grace if they understand this mystery revealed and continue to accept the **Mark of His Name-MNO-666** (Revelation 14:10-11).

Christians must band together through the UACC into a mighty force to influence our government NOT to lock into the Beast - MNO - **M**illennium **N**ations **O**rganized. Division of the world in 96SRSP-CE will be different countries and zones in the minds of men than what I have prophesied within the original Beast.

Remember, each nation will have a vote within its kingdom. Each kingdom will have one vote in the world general assembly. Most countries will want to manipulate the nations within each kingdom to their advantage. The nations within each kingdom will change from time to time. There will be a constant struggle for power within the kingdoms. There will be some wars during the tribulation which will involve Egypt and the Antichrist's MNO over kingdom territory.

Eventually it will end as prophesied. "North and South America (three horns) will be isolated from the rest of the world because of their Christian beliefs. They will refuse to accept the Second Hidden Mark of His Name - MNO - 666."

The warning must be repeated:
A person's very existence depends on their nation refusing to join the MNO!

(Revelation 14:10-11)

Repeating the warning in the gravest of terms. Christians must stop their country from locking into the Beast (European led world government). **Nations locking into the MNO must at some point force its citizens to accept the Mark of the Beast on the right hand.** This shall be required to pay the world consumption tax (Daniel 11:20) necessary to fund this world organization. The world being divided into ten kingdoms represents the Revelation 13 Sea Beast.

I saw the earliest BEAST

MNO = Leopard = (Revelation 13:1-10)

Daniel's ORIGINAL ten toes of iron and clay, which will eventually transform into the Final ten toes of Iron and clay. (4th Beast - see Section 9)
Rough draft Sketch 7-1-2

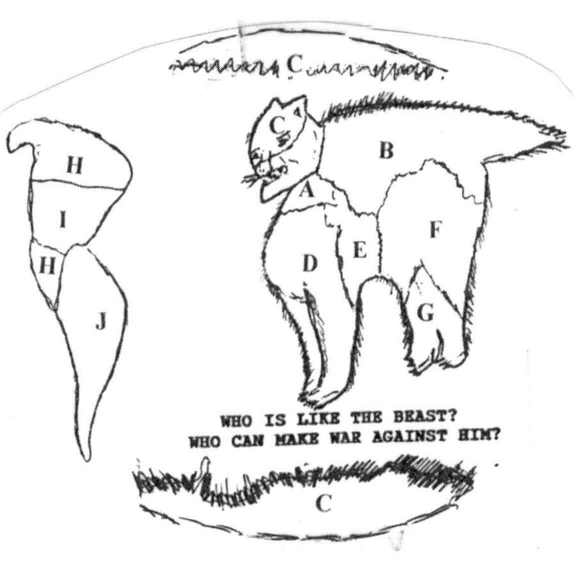

THREE OF THE ORIGINAL TEN HORNS WERE UPROOTED (not destroyed) by the influence and power of the little horn (Antichrist) in charge of the Millennium Nations Organized = MNO = 666 = Daniel's ten toes of iron and clay.

TEN AREA
WORLD KINGDOM (MNO)

(Millennium Nations Organized)
Leopard Beast (for runner to the 3rd beast)
ORIGINAL TEN HORNS
Sketch 7-1-2, Area - Nations

A. Europe (EU) - Old Roman Empire- England (Lion's Mouth), Rome (Capital)
B. Russia - Rosh
C. Greenland + Antarctica
D. Africa
E. Middle East - (Includes army from the south)
F. Asia - (Includes Japan)
G. Australia + Oceania Areas
H. Mexico and Canada - will be booted out
I. United States - will be booted out
J. South America - will be booted out

A - G = SEVEN HEADS

I saw the alliance of the BEAST

MNO = Leopard = (Revelation 13:1-10)

Daniel's FINAL ten toes of iron and clay,
which will eventually transform into the
Eagle With Three Ugly Heads
(To see the 4th Beast - review Section 9)

FINAL TEN HORNS

To complete Daniel 7:6, Leopard Beast
Sketch 7-1-3

~~~~~~~~~~~~~~~~~~~~~~~~~~~~~~~~~~~~

1. Europe (EU-Beast's spokesman) Head of Beast with the fatal wound, which had been healed (revived)
2. Russia = Chief Prince Rosh
3. Greenland + Antarctica
4. Africa
5. Middle East (Includes Army from the South)
6. Asia (200,000,000 Man Army)
7. Australia + Oceania Areas
8. ISRAEL (Jerusalem) World Capital
9. Japan (Monetary)
10. Army from the South, Egypt, Ethiopia, Libya...

1 - 7 = SEVEN HEAD

The final ten area kingdoms (horns) now have their respective crowns since they each have received their king of authority over his designated area.

Right, 7-1-1 - Italy, Venice - Basilica di San Marco: The Old Roman Empire owned the high seas. Much trade came to Venice and the captains would bring gifts such as jewels to St. Mark's Basilica. Likewise, the New Roman Empire called the Leopard Beast (MNO) will try to dominate trade, money and world military control. This is done so it may give gifts to its allies.

The Antichrist spirit is controlling the stairway to the Mark of the Beast

1. Man's identity changed from his name to a social identification marking number better known in America as the social security number.
2. Computer invented [built on sixes (6's)].
3. Man's identity associated with his assigned location on earth changed from a street name to a locator marking number, better known in America as a zip code.
4. Man's identity associated with his buy-and-sell mode changed from a simple handshake and thank you to a computer marking number similar to (may vary): one (1)-buy, two (2)-sell, three (3)-savings, etc.
5. Credit cards introduced for marking purposes to buy, sell, and transfer funds over the Internet web of deceit.
6. a. IC Chip marking and scanning devices are marking technology introduced to the world. It can be found in such things as, but not limited to, credit cards, military MARK card, welfare cards, gift-cards, medical cards, etc.
7. b. ID implant marking devices comes first in animals, then humans.
8. IC or ID marking devices in bracelets or headbands (This is a forerunner to the Mark of the Beast). Persons accepting this in the great tribulation period will be out of grace with God and go to Hell!
9. ID marking implant and/or laser marking tattoo (visible or invisible like a finger scan) on or in the right hand or forehead or similar technology This equates to the Mark of the Beast. If people accept these marking devices in the Great Tribulation, they are out of grace with God and will go to Hell!

~~~~~~~~~~~~~~~~~~~~~~~~~~~~~~~~~~~~

Above, 7-1-2 - Italy, Assisi - Roman Temple of Minerva: This first Century BC Temple, in the Piazza del Comune was impressive. The Old Roman Empire had a form of spirituality and tried to control people. The New Roman Empire will constantly monitor people, companies, and nations, with the difference between Old and New being technology. Now they will try to control movement, buy and sell modes. Prophesied in the Bible and the Wake Up Call Prophecies are instructions for Spirit-filled Christians to refuse and/or resist certain new technology as being against God's teachings. Now must be the time!

MILLENNIUM NATIONS ORGANIZED = MNO = 666 = SECOND HIDDEN MARK

A ten area kingdom federation will be born and shall be equal to the MNO or 666. At some point, in the future the MNO will issue upon its members a tax (world consumption tax) on retail and wholesale products sold or bought within their federation. This consumption tax helps cover costs associated with its military and administrative expenses. For citizens to buy or sell, the store computer will scan their card (later, the same digits on their right hand). The computer will then connect their transaction to the Internet web of deceit.

The connection will be made by the computer dialing an international phone number (Number of the Beast) to gain an approval code for the Image of the Beast. This transaction will be done so a small consumption tax will be collected. Citizens cannot buy or sell without paying the consumption tax, which requires the eighteen-digit mark. Six + social ID + six + area number + six + (one to nine) buy sell loop.

1 + 9 + 1 + 5 + 1 + 1 = 18 digits

IC Chip marking devices contain the total eighteen digits of a person's Mark of the Beast.

WARNING

The beast will control the mark.
The mark will reward the person.
The person will chose his path.
The path will dictate his destiny.
The destiny is forever until the end.
The end will separate into one of two dimensions.
The two dimensions are either Heaven or Hell.

END TIME CHRISTIANS ASSIGNMENT: Do whatever it takes to stop your country from locking into the European Leopard Beast. You will have to take the Mark, Number, and Name of the Beast if your nation joins into the Leopard.

THE BEAR, DEVIL, AND THE IMMOVABLE ROCK

BEAR = NATO + Russia - USA

DEVIL = Moslem Nations (Middle Eastern)

Immovable Rock = Jerusalem (burdensome stone) on the back of the Devil

Rough Draft Sketch 7-1-4

SEE THE BEAR SHAKING HANDS WITH THE DEVIL (MOSLEM NATIONS)!

This means the Bear will be sympathetic toward the Devil nations because of oil and many Moslems have infiltrated the Bear Nations. They will eat away at the Bear until it will give way to the Leopard Beast (Sketch 7-1-3).

Ezekiel 38:4, *"I will turn you* (Russia the Bear) ***around*** (toward the Map viewer), ***and put hooks in your jaws*** (Bosnia, Herzegovina, and others) ***and bring you out with your whole army ..."* This aggression along with Middle East problems start Gulf War III, when Russia marches South.**

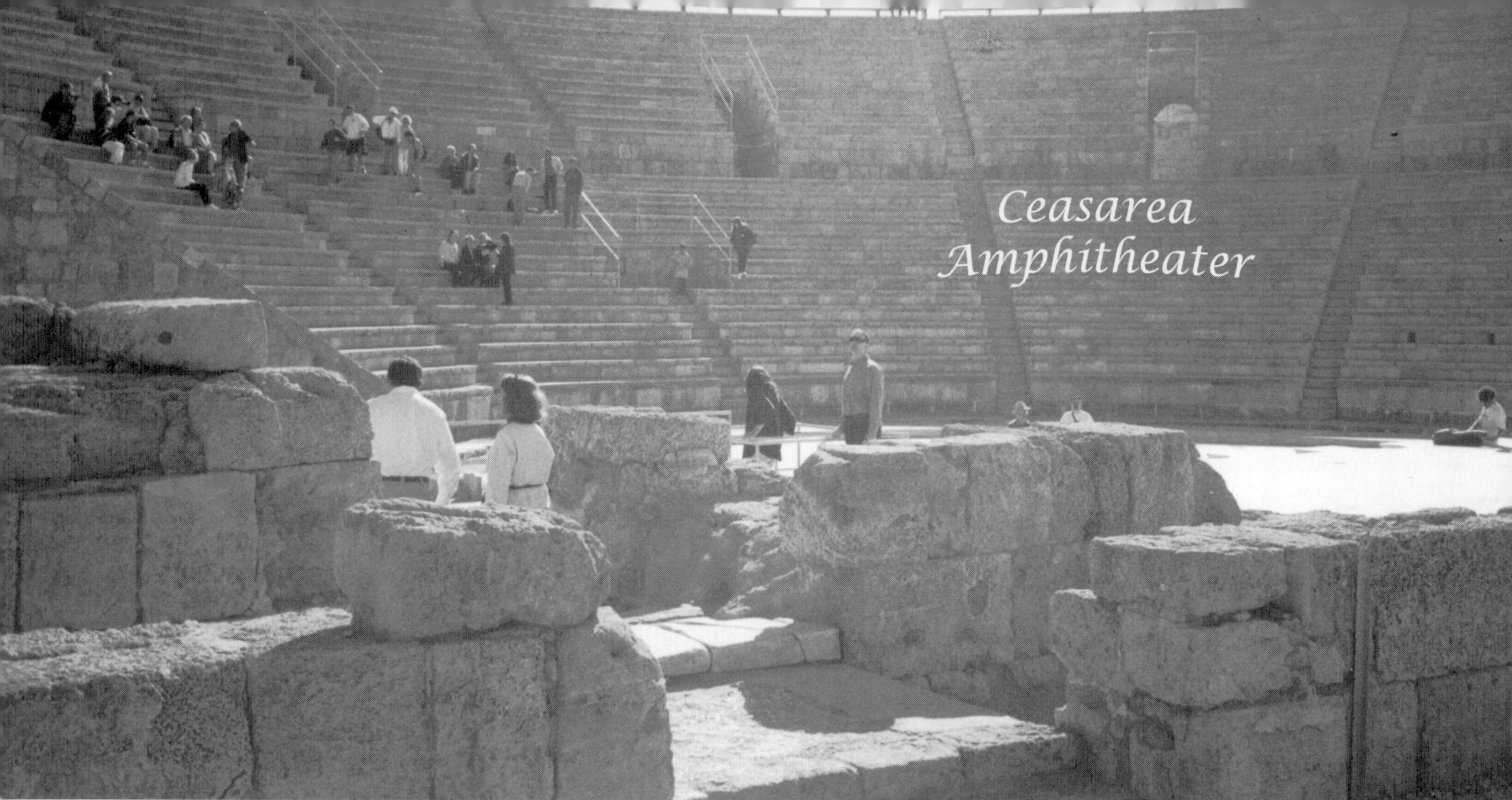

Above, 7-1-3- Israel, Caesarea Amphitheater: Caesarea is the town where Peter led a centurion, Cornelius, to become a Christian (Acts 10). Caesarea was an area sectioned off by the Old Roman Empire. The New Roman Empire - Leopard Beast will section areas of the world off also. Each area will have a vote in the world assembly. Once again, identity is going to be important for the Leopard (Daniel-7, 3rd beast) and Eagle with the Three Ugly Heads (Daniel-7, 4th beast) Beast.

Many Christian leaders are in denial or not addressing the times we are in. We must start objecting to some of the new technology. On the other hand, if Christians want to do nothing because of lack of faith, they will wake up some day trapped in a corner. Faith is the key. When we see three sixes (3-6's) on everything we are buying it should shoot up a red flag. Bar codes contain three sixes, WWW on the web equals 666 (calculated as 6th letter in Hebrew.) Birthing pains must be the key. Starts slow and increase to a point at which one cannot stop the outcome without loss of life.

WE KNOW THE BATTLE IS THE LORD'S AND WE ARE HIS WARRIORS.

GOD'S WAR COMMAND AND PROMISE FOR VICTORY!

Section 7-2

God's command for endtimers must be to wake up! Then start today resisting the marking sequences such as the IC chips identification marking technology (see glossary). These devices will lead to the Mark of the Beast (Revelation 13:16-17). Christians must not worship, which equates to the same action as doing business with the Image of the Beast. It will evolve into the worldwide Internet web of deceit. Christians must also persuade our elected officials to resist the deadly Mark of His Name (MNO) (Revelation 14:11). This would stop nations from locking into the MNO (European led Leopard Beast).

We follow God's command knowing this will eventually lead The Americas with the USA at the helm, into war with the Antichrist and the MNO. We know the BATTLE IS THE LORD'S and we are his warriors. The warrior will carry the fight to the enemy who has transformed first into the European Leopard Beast (MNO) and finally the Antichrist, False Prophet, and the Eagle with the Three Ugly Heads.

Christians and the beloved Jewish community, we will see many brothers fall in the next few years before our Messiah returns. Be of good cheer for many have overcome and gone to see the Father (Revelation 20:4). We know these things must happen for God's glory before our final victory with Jesus.

Mighty male warriors prepare for physical battle. First, protecting our families, brothers and sisters in Christ, then God's house of prayer, which will become the target of the evildoers and terrorists using cross-border phenomena in their attacks. Next, we must protect our nation. Men, we must stand proud with an obedient steadfastness to our Lord's command. We must uphold the protect mode given first to men in Genesis 2:15, that states men should protect and take care of their area of influence. Then the male leaders of the church in the New Testament were given the protect mode again in the Great Commission (Matthew 28:18-20). From today, until the last battle in the great tribulation period, the men are given the protecting war command again in Joel 3:9. There will be a few Christian nations left when Armageddon starts. The war cry must be given to men (not women) to fight to the death in protecting Israel. Men, here constitutes our command and rightful authorization to do physical battle in the endtimes:

"Proclaim this among the nations: Prepare for war! Rouse the warriors! Let all the fighting MEN (not women) ***draw near the attack. Beat your plowshares into swords and your pruning hooks into spears. Let the weakling*** (North and South America) ***say, `I am strong!'"*** (Joel 3:9-10)

The Spirit led me to three of many such scriptures for end time warriors. They must remember the scriptures and gain strength to win each daily battle. This battle starts today and ends with victory at Armageddon!

1. ***"As I watched, this horn*** (Antichrist Spirit over the MNO first, then Antichrist leading the Eagle with the Three Ugly Heads) ***was waging war against the saints and defeating them, until the Ancient of Days*** (Jesus) ***came and pronounced judgment in favor of the Saints*** (win battle of Armageddon) ***of the Most High*** (God Almighty)***, and the time came when they*** (Jewish People and Spirit-filled Christians) ***possessed the kingdom"*** (Daniel 7:21-22, 6th Century B.C.)

2. ***"Surely the day is coming; it will burn like a furnace. All the arrogant and every evildoer will be stubble, and that day that is coming will set them on fire,"*** says the Lord Almighty. ***"Not a root or a branch will be left on them. But for you who revere my name, the sun of righteousness will rise with healing in its wings. And you will go out and leap like calves released from the stall. Then you*** (his warriors) ***will trample down the wicked: They will be ashes under the soles of your feet on the day when I do these things,"*** says the Lord Almighty (Malachi 4:1-3, fifth century B.C.)

3. ***"They*** (ten kings of MNO-Eagle with the Three Ugly Heads) ***will make war against the Lamb*** (Jesus)***, but the Lamb will overcome them*** (MNO) ***because He is Lord of lords and King of kings, and with Him will be His called, chosen and faithful followers"*** (Revelation 17:14. A.D. 95).

We are Jesus Christ's mighty warriors to carry out His commands. The battle shall be the Lord's for we are victorious together.

Praise God! Amen!

Below, 7-2-1- Israel, Megiddo (Armageddon): The road King Solomon's horses and chariots used. He had a strong army but will not compare to the upcoming Antichrist's army. The Antichrist is facing USA plus North and South America backed up by the best military weapon available, the King of kings on the white horse - Jesus. Will the Antichrist's army use these same roads? Yes, he will!

SIX TIME PLANES OF THE TRIBULATION PERIOD

Section 7-3

The Spirit of Christ, the Spirit of Prophecy, has given me a simple format to display the endtimes on six time planes operating at the same time. God's four planes are as if a day equates to a thousand years. Otherwise, time is meaningless to God. God is a multi-time dimensional being. He operates on an X, Y, and Z axis multiplied by (T) the time element in earthly thinking. These represent four time planes at the same time.

The fifth plane exemplifies what saints, Christians, elect, and faithful followers should be doing for God's glory. Many will be judged or elected by God to participate in the hour of trial (Tribulation Period). Persons who repent and accept God through His Son Jesus Christ during the tribulation period will need leadership to show them what to do.

The sixth plane is Satan's deceptive agenda and his goal to stop Jesus Christ from returning to earth. He wins if he can accomplish this.

We will attempt to mathematically calculate the size and magnitude of God. Human thinking begins and ends on one time plane and three dimensions of thought. Humans think up and down (X-axis), front and back (Y-axis), and sideways, left to right (Z-axis). Otherwise, their thinking equates to the volume inside a sphere (X, Y, and Z axis).

Now move this sphere through time by sliding it along a T axis. What we have representing our thinking and life equates to the volume inside a cylinder or time displacement by an object or us.

Let us look at it another way. Think of our entire lifetime and thoughts as the volume inside a lead pencil. The length of the pencil, seven inches, will be our age plus as far as our minds can conceive before we were born and after our death. Any location on the pencil will be a calculated quadruple dimensional X, Y, Z, and T point of our thinking. Our thinking (left, right, up, down, front, back) could go beyond the stars. This would represent the radius of the pencil or one-eight of an inch. How far our mind can conceive and believe equates to the radius of the pencil.

We have three-dimensional thinking or a sphere. Now move the sphere in a straight line down a T axis as far as our mind can conceive into the cosmos. That volume would make a sphere, which would look like a pencil.

God on the other hand is a multidimensional being representing the pencil's volume to the sixty-fourth power and much more. Let me explain as the Spirit led me to write. Our life and thinking equates to the volume of the pencil. Take three pencils and crisscross them until we have an X, Y, and Z axis. Then move this X, Y, and Z axis or sphere along the T axis of time to make a very large cylinder, seven inches in diameter and sixteen feet long.

This very long cylinder represents one axis of God. Take this large cylinder and crisscross three times again to make a huge X, Y, and Z axis and move this sphere along the T time axis. What we end up with calculates to a cylinder so huge we cannot comprehend it. This represents the second axis of God's four time planes. Now repeat this sequence of crisscrosses again for God's third time plane. Finally, move this sphere down the T axis to form a gigantic cylinder. Take this gigantic cylinder and repeat the complete process one more time and we have the T axis of God's being. This expands so large we, as humans, cannot even begin to understand this enormous God.

Let us now come back to earth. Picture us in a room and our thoughts are still on the pencil. Pretend we shrink God to a size we can grasp so we can learn what is happening during the endtimes. God will represent in this model the volume of air inside the room. For this model, let's say we are forty years of age. This represents halfway down the pencil. Ten years ahead, or when we are fifty years old, there will be a problem in our life. This would represent one inch further down the pencil to where the problem will be located.

The question we ask, "Where is God?" The answer, He is already at our problem waiting for us to get there. God has the answer to our problem and/or a way of escape. If the air in the room equates to God and we are operating inside the pencil, then God is completely surrounding and penetrating the pencil. God permeates everywhere. Christians should ask God for insight and help when they get there. If they do not ask God, then the world will happily offer them a solution to their problem. The world's solution will be money, security, no-pain, and fun for forever. If Christians are backsliders or lukewarmers, then God will let the world answer their problem. His listening volume has been greatly diminished to this type of Christian's prayer request.

It does not matter where they are age wise in their life (pencil), God is already there and will be ready to help if asked. His answer to Spirit-filled Christians' prayer requests may come exactly as we asked, a partial answer or total silence.

For endtimers, God wants Christians to do what is best for themselves and the kingdom of God. This may not necessarily be what they want to do. They must walk in faith when the world and the lukewarm

Church tell them otherwise. Christians must always seek His will for their lives. Anyone as awesome as God has plenty of power, might, and time to direct a Christian's life. So completely turn it over to Him.

The multi-time dimension of Jesus is why the four Seals are opened repeating themselves through time before He opens the seven Seals in the tribulation period. This is impossible for us but practical for Jesus. He is already there before it happens in our earthly thinking.

This explains why we have laps and overlaps in the judgments of God in the book of Revelation. When the Spirit of Jesus had John write down what he saw it was not in human order of sequences but rather in heavenly sequences. The heavenly sequences fall on four different time planes of God's (X, Y, Z, and T) curved test cycle. This prophecy reveals (flow chart) the proper sequences of events. Jesus promised in Matthew 10:26 everything concealed will be revealed. Joel said it would be done by prophecy. Praise the Almighty God!

God's four time planes are prophesied in proper order sequence in section-8 called Flow Chart. Let us now look in the next section at the sixth (6th) time plane of Revelation concerning Satan's agenda.

✍ Added note - insight, 11-14-2005: What even makes these calculations more amazing is the fact God assigns time within a test cycle. Time is malleable or hammered out by Almighty God. If we assume the speed of light must be constant or an electron will travel at the same time interval around the nucleus of an atom with the exception of outside interference, then time must be the part of the equation, which must constantly give in to other forces. Therefore, we can conclude, there can be no universally definable "now" on the X, Y, Z, and T axis. This is only a local phenomenon governed by one's rate of speed in a local (now) assigned universe and curved test cycle. As I discuss in other areas of this book, time will be laid out and assigned by God on a curved space or cycle. He manipulates time and the test cycle for His pleasure. Always remember, God Almighty has infinite flexibility of time and we only have now to do His bidding using our free will at any assigned X, Y, Z and curved T (time displacement). We must make the most of our opportunity with the time allotted. ✂

SATAN'S AGENDA IN AMERICA

The Sixth (6th) Time Plane

Section 7-4

Satan's agenda has been threefold. First, to destroy Christian countries like America, second, kill the Jews and, third, stop Jesus from returning to earth. Satan has been working on America, which has been his first obstacle. The destruction of America through a series of slow timeframe assaults has led to God declassifying America as a disciple nation under His protection. A disciple nation shall be described as the unity of the trinity, its laws, government, and people in harmony with the teaching in the Holy Bible (Jesus' Great Commission, Matthew 28:19). Jesus taught us, first, secure the nation under God, and then take the good news around the world. This insures long-lasting results. To reverse this process becomes disastrous.

We shall discuss how Satan has accomplished bringing America below the standard set by God for a disciple nation.

Satan has won the fight in America so far. However, the battle could be won if the Universal American Church Coalition (UACC) would start, and solicit Jesus' help. God has declassified America as a disciple nation in the year 1990 A.D. *"We are consumed by your anger and terrified by your indignation"* (Psalm 90:7). The Spirit enlightened me that even though the USA had practiced slavery, racism, subjugation of women, tobacco, alcohol and drug abuse and much more, the nation as a whole was after God's own heart and improving. This began to change in the 1960s, and became full-blown by the 1990s when the USA's leadership quit backing Israel 100% and rebelled against Christians.

Therefore, God has, as birthing pains, removing His protective covering from America. Since 1990 A.D., America has experienced many of the worst dollar disasters in its history while maintaining a fairly strong economy. Do not let this fool us for the bad news will show disastrous events getting worse due to our disobedience to God.

If we cannot drastically improve the list below, then God will destroy America. The Churches were commanded in the great commission to control this list so their nation could be classified a disciple nation. Jesus commanded control through instructions such as, teach them (nations and individuals) to obey everything I have commanded Christians to do (Matthew 28:20). The word teach in this great commission must be used in a very harsh sense of the meaning.

Jesus' teaching was meant (as a threat) to punish if the leaders and citizens of a country wavered from their obedience to God. Otherwise, Jesus was saying the Church must keep America a disciple Nation. If America wavers, Jesus wants the Church to come down hard on the leaders until the nation returns to a disciple nation under God.

Yet, the Church's leaders are losing their power to keep this list in balance with God's commands. Now it is apparent through the UACC we could return America to a disciple nation under God's protective covering in the timeframe God has allotted.

This list equates to only part of the symptoms and problems confronting America. Yet the spirit said, "Write this list down." It is hoped the Churches of America will bond together after reviewing these symptoms and the problems. God wants to reverse Satan's agenda in America so we are able to protect ourselves and the Jews in the last days.

Multiculturalism - a new religion and god.

In the name of political correctness all religions and cultures are declared equally valid. Part of the problem must lie within the ideology about core-values associated with multiculturalism.

A serious problem in judgment and blindness to the dangers multiculturalism presents has resulted in mistakenly interpreting the immediate threat (Political - fundamental Islam) facing the west along with the world.

Satan's deceptive assaults, which have led to a decline in America, are listed below. These assaults brought it below God expectations. Each problem will be listed in random order, which means, the first may not be the most important. Each person, church, and/or the UACC if started will work on the area where the Holy Spirit leads them to improve on.

TRUTH: Since the 1930s the definition of truth in our school systems has been changed. The backup data for truth in the past was faith and/or facts. Today truth must be backed-up totally by facts. The Bible teaches by faith Jesus Christ is our Messiah which equals truth. The Bible is factual even though we cannot prove all of it scientifically or historically. In our modern day, schools equate their redefined truth as being proven only by facts. Fact shall be redefined as being backed-up by solid scientific evidence which can be seen, felt, or touched.

The Bible teaches Jesus Christ arose after three days. By faith, Christians believe this equates to evidence of a fact, not fiction. This redefining of truth and fact by some of our warped educational minds has led to children questioning the validity of the Bible. Students will question there has not been found any fact substantiating Jesus Christ as the true Messiah. Therefore, the Bible must be false or at least questionable concerning some people and events. The frequency the student hears truth falsely defined in school and colleges has reached many times per day. Churches average about one hour per week teaching the meaning of truth. The churches are losing this battle. To prove this, just ask most people born after 1955 what is the definition of truth. They will most likely use the schools' definition not the Churches'.

Below, 7-4-1- Israel, Megiddo (Armageddon) - Pagan Canaanite altar: It is fitting for the Canaanite's pagan alters to be here at Megiddo. They ran after the wrong god. It is interesting the final Armageddon battle will be fought by the god of darkness and the God of light. America must make itself ready to fight on God's side in this battle. When prophets foretold all nations would gather, it only pertained to all nations, as they knew about at the time they lived. North and South America was not known then. North and South America will be the nations which rise up as Michael, the Great Prince of Daniel 12:1. Therefore, we must make America ready.

MONEY, THINGS, and CONSUMERISM: The love of money and the materialistic increases it brings has overwhelmed America's thinking. Lust for money and things outweigh God's commands. Money and the illusion of being satisfied and independent are now some of America's most important idols. This creates social isolation, for few in our society need help from anyone because with money they can do it their own way.

RISING BUREAUCRACY: Abuse of bureaucracy has been promoted through the Antichrist spirit. It demands an entity, such as government, to interface with people in need. Yet God teaches LOVE must be the answer. Love increases by individual people helping people in communities, not big government. To change God's formula by using big government has extracted love from the neighborhoods of America and has isolated many.

Government red tape has been another problem, which has bogged the country down. It promotes loss of productivity and less effective competitiveness in the world marketplace.

NOISY DEN AND OVERSPENDING: Since the 1960's, the noisy dens (special interest groups protecting individual rights and the "I, me, and self generation") are dramatically growing. This has forced the government to lose control over its concern about economic spending. In other words, America's broke because bureaucrats are spending money, which does not exist. They try to satisfy the noisy den's request to be reelected. People want a balanced budget, yet they tell our elected officials to bring home the goodies. Jeremiah 51:55 puts it another way, "God, Almighty will destroy the nation or nations which has the largest noisy dens."

Human life has been valued below animals and has become more important to save the rats and rodents than starving people and our own flesh.

IDOLATRY: We have exchanged the true God of gods for many gods. It seems the more gods we have the merrier things become. Entertainment, sports, money, drugs, booze, homosexuality, and on and on we can go. Satan has been very proud of America for its great accomplishments in the area of new gods.

CHURCH BICKERING: Some churches are holding hands in the name of moral issues with religious faith contrary to the Lord God's teaching. The Bible strictly shall forbid this. God forbid and forgive us.

The WAKE UP CALL PROPHECIES were prophesied and released in 1994 asking churches to bond under the UACC as the Spirit had instructed me. This instruction about Church bonding has been sent by the Lord God to save America; yet, the leaders at first will refuse to listen to God. This reminds me of when Jesus tried to talk to the religious leaders back then. They did not listen to Him either. Jesus has been at the door knocking and some Christians are not letting Him into their churches. If Christians start the UACC and back the principles of the UACC then they can stand proudly under the banner of God. Divided as they are currently doing could cause them to fall while watching America disintegrate before their very eyes.

INTERNET WEB OF DECEIT: The public in America has been locking itself helplessly onto America's latest god. This new god emerges as the Internet web of deceit (Image of the Beast). The more Americans lock onto this monster, the harder it will be to disengage from the system. By the time they see the hidden agenda (WWW = 6+6+6 access codes - "W" calculates into the 6th letter in Hebrew alphabetic) waiting for them in the next few years and especially during the great tribulation period it will be too late. They must start, as birthing pains, resisting or refusing it. This will be one of Satan's deceptions. Most Christians will be deceived by it at the start. To use the Internet before or during the first half of the tribulation period is not a sin. More importantly, why go down a path that will lead to the second death in the great tribulation. To side with the final Antichrist and use it during the last three and one half years (Great Tribulation) takes you outside of God's grace.

HUMAN LIFE DEVALUED: Through television, movies, and other Internet web of deceit media, we have now become callous to the act of killing and murder. Human life has been valued below animals and has become more important to save the rats and rodents than our own flesh and starving people. Many love the creation more than the Creator.

COURT SYSTEM: America's ability to deliver the right to a speedy and fair trial without special interest groups pressured agendas has been slowly deteriorating. The Bible warns about consequences to a nation's destruction when the court system becomes bogged down by outside interference and wicked people pursuing their own agenda for personal gain (2 Samuel 15:1-6). The USA's court systems in some cases do not look for truth but the special interest's agenda and to the European Leopard Beast for insight. In other cases, activist judges make laws contrary to the Constitution and Biblical teaching. The court systems should rule righteously with an iron rod of severe correction just as Jesus Christ will be doing when He returns to earth.

Below, 7-4-2- Israel, Tabgha - Church of the Loaves and fishes: It sets atop a first century AD church. The well-known miracle of Jesus (Matthew 14:15-21) is displayed in this Mosaic in the floor showing a basket full of loaves between two fish. Look back at item labeled Money, Things, and Consumerism in this section: Some Christians today seem more interested in collecting things with their money than feeding and helping the hungry. Take notice of item labeled Noisy Den and overspending. They also feed their special interests groups before they feed the downtrodden. Everything is about what I want, my rights and self-centeredness. It might be a good idea if they read the last part of Matthew 25. Jesus will separate them out for He will say, "I never knew you".

ALCOHOL AND DRUGS: Alcohol and drugs are destroying our nation. Yet, we turn our heads from the Biblical solution. The solution shall be simple. Just follow what Jesus prophesied. Jesus will be coming back to destroy those who are destroying the world (Revelation 11:18). Therefore, we should execute or incarcerate those who are destroying America through drugs. On the last page of the Bible, it explains some of the people who are not going to heaven. It says they will be outside with the dogs, and explains who they are (Revelation 22:15). Magic arts equates to sorcery, equates to pharmaceutical, equates to becoming abusive in drugs, equates to the lack of ability to take care of the area God gave each person.

Lukewarmers are like a big base drummer in the Christian band. They make plenty of noise and lots of action with their arms and legs but only accomplish lip service for Jesus.

LAWLESSNESS: Lawlessness has increased. This will fall right into Satan's master plan. The Antichrist spirit will say, "We must institute better identification." This will deceptively lead to the Mark of the Beast. This, they say, will help law enforcement identify more criminals. Yet, we turn our heads from the Biblical solution again. The solution has never been more intrusive government powers through better identification so the Antichrist using a tracking system to follow the Christians when he tries to and eventually takes over most of the system.

CULTURE: America's culture and the foundation it was built on have become weaker. Multicultural societies destroy beautiful individual nation's cultures in favor of world-wide oneness (rebuilding the tower of Babel). Multinational corporations also destroy nation's cultures by world-wide oneness.

TRADITION: Our respect for America's tradition has fallen. We have replaced America's traditional Christian God with many gods. We now mistakenly look at the European Leopard for inspirational thought.

EDUCATION: Our founding fathers sent school teachers into the west to teach reading, writing, arithmetic, and the Holy Bible. The reason the Holy Bible was to be taught in public school was because young people would learn better. In the beginning, they believed America should be a Christian nation. Now children are taught how to find themselves without God. Consequently, there has been a drop in the quality of the educational system. Our nation has been founded on the principal of one nation under God with Jesus being His Son. Today we do not explain to our students who God and Jesus Christ are. Many do not understand whom God represents or what He stands for and demands. Therefore, they do not know what the nation was founded upon or where it should be headed under God's guidance.

CHURCH LUKEWARMNESS: Churches have lost the ability to convey the two types of fear of God, reverence and dread to America and the world. So we now disgrace our sanctuaries with improper dress, mannerisms, lack of reverence, loud noise, and honoring others rather than honoring God. Our lackadaisical attitude has evolved into believing God shall be all-loving and He surely will understand our casual mindset toward Him. Christians must read the last book of the Old Testament if they want to see what happens to a nation when the followers of God cut Him short in their tithes, praise, and worship services.

PERSONAL RIGHTS: America's mindset has now expanded into my personal and special individual right over everyone else. Many people have the "I, ME, and SELF" generation, possession-centered or what's in it for me attitude. This has helped Satan's noisy den (special interest groups) thrive for power. Note, Jeremiah 51:55: *"The Lord will destroy Babylon; he will silence her noisy den* [special interest groups and pro-European news media]*..."*

OVER TAXATION: We have taken love out of the formula. This also removes God from the equation. Over taxation comes from the Antichrist spirit, It has been the result of people, families, and churches ducking their responsibility to help themselves, their family, and community. The church has bowed down to the noisy dens (special interest groups and European led world news media). Therefore, the government now has to overtax to fund many government inappropriate programs. We are breaking our nation with these non-biblical programs. People and families should help people and families. Then we have love back into the equation and healing begins.

FAMILIES: The family, which has been historically the backbone of the Church and America, has deteriorated. This was caused by man thinking he was smarter than God was. The churches in the 60s lost total control of the trinity of the disciple nation (laws, government and people). So man thought he would write a series of laws using his wisdom, not God's word. Man thought this would offset where the churches had failed. God promises to destroy the wisdom of this foolish world. God didn't intervene here; we simply destroyed ourselves.

The 1964 Equal Rights movement, along with laws, and liberal judges have done more to destroy the backbone of America and the traditional family than any other type of man's great wisdom. We have outsmarted ourselves. The 1964 movement had already been written by God in His Holy Bible in seventeen words, "Love your neighbor as yourself, and do unto others as you would have them do unto you." Why was this evil 1964 movement started, because the churches had not led in showing the different races to love one another? The Church must be the leader in God's affairs, especially, when it comes to loving our brothers and sisters. Yet, some churches have failed.

Note added 2-20-06 for insight: Before 1964, Moslems were screened carefully and few were allowed into the USA. More importantly, after the 1964 equal-rights movement, many millions have been let into the USA so the nation is not discriminating against any religious group. Islam must be declared an Ideology of Islamic law-government, not a religion. Their goal is to take over the USA and put it under political Islamic Law! Therefore, it must not be protected under our laws and must be declared illegal. Furthermore, it must be declared a clear and immediate danger to the security of the USA and eliminated. Failure to do this will bring additional staggering destruction in the future. ✂

There isn't a father or loving father in the home in many cases. In other cases, the fathers have refused to help their children when they had an opportunity to do so. Because of this and other factors, the father has been devalued as the head of the household. The Bible teaches the man must be the head of the house, only if Christ is the Head of him. Many men do not deserve to be the head. Many men have not held up their end of God's care. Men will pay for this on judgment day. God must come back into the equation of our laws and families.

SUNDAY: America now does not honor God's day of rest like our founding fathers did. Our forefathers honored God's day, yet, today, we as a nation are busy chasing after other gods especially on the Sabbath. Some of these gods are pleasure, money, sports, and entertainment. This evolves as a result of today's American citizens not having the dreaded or scared type fear of God. The news in heaven has been, God's about to teach America what real fear means.

MILITARY: America has degraded its military by placing women into the warrior positions. Again, the Churches are bowing down to the special interest groups (noisy dens and world news). The liberal Internet web of deceit has given the extreme women the spotlight to sell their Antichrist spirit of thinking to the world. These misguided women have a strong desire to reverse their roll per Genesis 3:16 (want of the woman to be as a man).

Remember the warning through Nahum the prophet, *"Look at your troops. They are all women. The gates of your land are wide open to your enemies. Fire has consumed their bars"* (Nahum 3:13). Again, through Jeremiah, *"Babylon's warriors have stopped fighting; their strength is exhausted; they have become like women; Her dwellings are set on fire; the bars of her gates are broken"* (Jeremiah 51:30). Then destruction will be certain (Revelation 18).

IMMORALITY: The rise in immorality has been rampant in America. Our lust of the pleasures of today outweighs our fear of what God will do tomorrow. Again, the Church has not instilled the dreaded type fear of God in America.

There are dangerous words some churches and noise dens are using today. These words are, relate to us, get in tune with our philosophy or ideology, and finally tolerate us. Some teach citizens must relate to this group or non-Biblical belief, yet, God's word does not change. Therefore, the message will not change. If these groups do not like what Jesus wrote in His Bible, then on judgment day Jesus will send them to the lake of fire (hell). American churches have become lukewarm themselves by kneeling down to many noisy dens (special interest groups and world news media). By doing this, the Church has become ineffective in confronting immorality.

Below, 7-4-3 Greece, Athens - Mars Hill: St. Paul addressed the freethinking Athenians concerning their unknown god. He told them about Jesus the Christ and what He taught. The twenty-two items above have been discussed very clearly in the Bible. Yet, the people ignore these guidelines. This will bring disaster on judgment day.

If history has taught us anything, it has shown us homosexuality (sin) destroys nations. There have been many civilizations recorded down through history. Generally, the last decaying sign before these nations fell was the rampant increase in sin, one of which was homosexuality.

The absence of fear is not the courage within a man,
but an end time battle - the conquest of it. Quitters can be branded sinners,
but a Christian man who is afraid to start his end time assignment
may be branded worse!

America, WOE TO YOU! This shall be the reason Jesus returns and destroys billions of people. He returns to destroy those who are destroying the earth and His judgments are called righteous and true.

RELIGIOUS BELIEFS: American beliefs in religion are decaying. They look at the lukewarmers and see their actions are basically no different from the sinners. This has led to confusion. Lukewarmness leads to the great Christian falling away in the first half of the tribulation period (Matthew 24:10).

When people look at the above list, it overwhelms the mind. They must talk to their pastor and show him these prophecies concerning the bonding of Christian type Churches into the Universal American Church Coalition (UACC). Today, churches need a goal to rally behind and UACC is a good starting place.

Remember, God's mighty power has been moving away from our once great nation, not toward it. This corresponds to churches, not the sinners, have moved away from God. To reverse this trend Christians must turn their churches back to God and wake up the lukewarmers. The UACC has a better chance of changing our government, laws, and people back to God.

Glory to the Lamb!
Insight recorded between (9-94 to 8-95),
Bob R. Short, a Witness

FEAR GOD

Section 7-5

The Spirit began to stop my mind and focus on the word fear. Many of the churches, regardless of denomination in America, have become unsuccessful in conveying the sacred (dreaded) portion of fear to their flock. This has led to an America completely unafraid of God. Consequently, our present day churches are filled with Spirit Seven lukewarmers. The lukewarmer fears personal discomfort and financial losses more than God's wrath. The lukewarmer will not walk in faith.

"Let's take a quick test," the Spirit said. "The readers should ask their Church, Sunday school class, or a group of Christians one question to prove this point. The question shall be, `Describe God and/or Jesus and their actions in only one or two words.'" The answer you most likely will get is "love, holy, solid rock, saves, Father, Master, redeeming, eternal, righteousness, wisdom, understanding, forgiving, creator, all-knowing, answers prayer," and many kinds of wonderful meanings God truly relates to us.

"This relates to one part of God," the Spirit went on to say. "Let us now look at the other side of God which will better represent His actions during the last generation." God Almighty will be very harsh with the disobedient and, especially, the lukewarmer. The Lord God has given authority to allow Satan through deception to win saints over to his side until the end. He will rule the world until Jesus returns. This does not mean the saints won't win victories from time to time. Satan will cause astounding devastation. Therefore, Christians are outnumbered and outgunned.

In short, the lukewarmer needs to understand the following list of words. Jesus will not be returning to earth to throw flowers of praise on a beloved and blessed world. He shall be coming back to stop those who are destroying the world. Unfortunately, this includes unbelievers, disobedient, and, especially, the Spirit Seven lukewarmers.

Lukewarmers remember Jesus' warning - it would have been better that you had never known Me, than to know and understand Me and then turn back to the world (2 Peter 2:20-21). Jesus will inflict more harm on these type people and the lukewarmers than he does on the sinners (see Seventh Satanic Doom, section 2-19). Lukewarmers magnify the following list of words by increasing the intensity. I hope the reader will come to understand and appreciate the opportunity to experience real dreaded type fear firsthand and the true awe of God.

The following compiled list of some, but not all of the characteristic traits which describe God, His action, disposition, wrath, and judgments concerning people living in the tribulation period (old testament time, prophetically). They are direct scripture quotes or paraphrases taken directly from the Bible. Note, some of these are associated with God's programing of our end time test cycle, and we may run headlong into these dilemmas, so prepare.

Eyes closed, unanswered prayer, destroys, consuming fire, turns face, terror, punishes, jealous, hard judge, curse-giver, hardens spirits, strong-handed, anger, disciplinarian, tester, mis-director, confusion maker, evil spirit-sender, harsh deliverer, smote-kills, burning anger, judgment kills, vengeance, punishes, stirs opposition, jerks jaws, war-starter, break-warriors, anger outbreaks, death-destruction, displeased, fierce wrath, fear, awesome, lightning, earth-shaker, twists oaks, controls floods, earth destroyer, mankind destroyer, mighty demanding, scatters bones, despises, afflicts people, fierceness, wrath, avenged, turns hearts, winepress-wrath, rejects, shakes heads, brings ruin, turns men, shoots arrows, incites wars, head wound, magnifies enemies, everlasting vengeance, repays, overthrows, un-escapable, shortens life, harshly disciplines, rebukes, blinds, sends delusions, four dreadful judgments - sword - famine - wild beast - plague, and many other judgments on a disobedient world.

I hope the above list of words describing the character of God or His wrath has created a true scared (dreaded) type of fear in the reader. Wake up and begin to see the times we are quickly approaching. If Christians have backslidden or just realized they are lukewarmers, then repent. They must ask God to forgive them and make adjustments to do the Lord's will. We must work out our salvation with dreaded fear and trembling.

The Bible has been very plain that only those who possess a reverence and a scared fear of the Lord will go to heaven.

Christians must wake up to the fact they are in the days of sorrow spoken of in Matthew 24:5-8. We are quickly moving toward the tribulation period, which has been called Daniel's seventieth week. Daniel's seventieth week shall be calculated into Jewish time and thinking, not Gentile time and thinking. As birthing pains, our world has been moving quickly back to the terrible days of Lot and Noah. Jewish Old Testament thinking was an eye for an eye and a tooth for a tooth.

End time day's will most likely further the sinner agenda. The real test will be applied to the Christians (Revelation 3:10).

Below, 7-5-1- Greece, Island of Crete, Knossos the Palace-1900 BC: On the Island of Crete, at the Palace of Knossos the myths and legends ran wild. Greek mythology tells a story about a final battle of Theseus and the Minotaur (half bull and half man).

Christians will be tested (Revelation 3:10) through the tribulation and they will also have many battles such as; 1) Understanding, and sidestepping, God's great delusion to believe a lie (explained in some detail in this book). 2) Withstanding the many destructive and deceptive methods Satan, Antichrist and the False Prophet will bring on Christians and the world. 3) Christians wanting to get off the narrow path by chasing the European led World Government and the many benefits it has to offer. The Spirit-filled Christian who understands the days we live in will have to contend with the resistance Lukewarmers and their Churches present. Lukewarmers will say I cannot believe there is a God this bad who will allow so much death and destruction. Lukewarmers will fight the resistance movement and be the Spirit-filled Christian's enemy at times. God's wrath will be felt here on earth and worst yet, on judgment day if we as Christians cannot withstand, understand, and pass the test of the above mentioned obstacles. Christians who fail to pass the test of correctly persevering to follow Jesus' commands to resist will not be standing when they are done talking on judgment day! Jesus first came as the lamb, but He will be returning as the mighty Lion!

SATAN
CHANGES TIMES AND LAWS
Section 7-6

We know, what the prophets predicted concerning the days of sorrows and the tribulation period must take place before Jesus' second coming. It shall be important to understand Jesus cannot come back (second coming) at any time. He has an appointed time set by the Father and only the Father knows the time.

This highlights the importance of watching and understanding end time signs and events. Jesus will not return before Satan tries to changes time and laws, because the prophet Daniel predicted this to be one of the signs or events preceding Jesus' second coming. Daniel saw Satan changing times in the great tribulation. Satan knows his time shall be short, and through trickery tries to fool the Christian concerning times. This way he can kill them before Jesus returns.

"He (Satan) *will speak against the Most High and oppress his saints and try to* ***change the set times and the laws****"* (Daniel 7:25). Let us look at the word ***try*** in verse twenty-five. Satan tries to change times and laws, but does not mean he will get this change implemented worldwide. Otherwise try to change times does not mean he did change times worldwide. Satan shall try to remove the true Jesus Christ's age from our calendar system.

The USA will rebuke his action. Yet, in the MNO area, he will change dates and laws. Satan will use a similar calculation as follows.

Satan will justify rounding numbers and keeping every calculation simple. Satan's calculation may vary just a bit such as omitting seven years of the tribulation period or subtracting four to seven years because Jesus was born between 4-7 BC. Whatever he uses these calculations are close enough for people to see his trickery. His answer will always calculate close enough to round off to the year 2000 or one (1) FM time.

Regardless of the earth year Satan performs these calculations, he will distort them into an answer equal to 2000 which he calls 1 FM time. (One of many scenarios, calculated example below)

Let us say it is the year 2012 for this example:

- Times 365 days in one Church age year equals x 2012 = 734380 days =
- Divide 360 prophetic days in one OT Jewish calendar year
- Equals = 2,040 years prophetic = 734380 divided by 360
- Subtract, 33 age of Jesus Christ + 7 years BC (Jesus born) = 40
- Answer: 2040 - 40 = 2,000 recalculated years.
- (Start of Millennium)
- Answer = 2 sabbatical days or end of Church age

We have two sabbatical days which means we are at the true end of the Church age or some call it the end of the Gentile age. Satan will try to trick the world into believing it's really not the year 2012 or what ever year it is when He implements this change. He will convince some it is really the year 2000. In reality, he hopes to gain fictitious years in the minds of the Christians. The year 2000 equates exactly to two sabbatical days. So he says it shall be time to start a new millennium and a new calendar.

Left, 7-6-1-England, Greenwich - The Clock: This clock tells the world what time it is daily - West side (longitude) is a new day, while the East side (longitude) is finishing up yesterday. However, a second face may appear on this clock in the great tribulation period. The second face will be the Antichrist's FM time (Final Millenium time). Remember, by this time, England yielded to the European Leopard Beast (MNO) and now the tired old Lion has been pulled into the Mighty Eagle with the Three Ugly Heads (Final Beast).

There will be a debate in the secular world to remove Jesus Christ's association with present-day dates. Some may want to use B.C.E. ("Before the Common Era") and C.E. ("Common Era") while others may suggest lunar time or other ideas. The bottom line will be when the Antichrist tries to settle this confusion in the great tribulation.

Satan's calculations are at least one or more years off because the first day of the first year in the Church age starts with the first year, not the zero year. The exact dates Jesus lived cannot be substantiated, so Satan could be off a few years here also. Yet Satan will not address these issues, for he will say, "Keep it simple. This shall be the new time one-Final-Millennium (1 FM) and we are going to live with my decision. For I am the true Messiah who has been destine to lead the world through the next millennium."

Christians and Jews on earth at this time, beware. If Christians see this happening in the great tribulation, they will already know Satan is up to his trickery. Christians must be on their guard, for a great deception will be accompanying his hidden agenda. Satan shall be trying to buy time so he can eliminate the Jews and Christians from the face of the earth.

Satan's new time (FM) may start as early as the abomination causing desolation (103.3.23SRSP-S). It could occur as late as 105.7.29SRSP-S (sequencing points only, see section on Scroll). The important issue is knowing what the Antichrist will try to do.

DISCIPLE NATION
BLESSING OR CURSE

The Spirit of Christ, The Spirit of Prophecy,
led me to prophesy:
Section 7-7

Christians in America are given an option as to the future of this nation. It shall be a very simple math course. Let us look at the mathematical numbers when they are applied to the cause and effect formula, which God placed in His Holy Bible. Prayer shall be ninety-five percent of the answer. Sadly, the Church has lost much of its protective prayer for our nation. This has been due to a slow increase to eighty-four percent of Christians going to Churches and home Churches are now being classified by God as lukewarm and their prayers are not being addressed by God (2 Chronicles 7:15). America finds itself in trouble for our protective covering is as birthing pains being lifted from America. We must arouse the thirty four percent of the lukewarmers, which can statistically be awakened. Therefore, it follows, much power shall be gained because then God will listen to more prayers of protection. Add thirty-four percent to our current sixteen percent and it yields three times as many prayers currently being heard and addressed by God.

We must first start the Universal American Church Coalition (UACC) to best gain the power to see this nation return to a disciple nation - laws, government, and people in harmony with God. "How does America come back into the grace of God's protective blessings?" I asked and the Spirit answered me as follows. "Messenger to the Churches and Witness to the world, write what must be done." God judges a nation's heart before He judges its actions. God will show mercy to a nation if the heart of the nation, which equates to the Christians within the nation, has been truly trying to change the nation into a disciple nation. Great wrath shall come upon a nation if the heart of this nation has been asleep and not trying or has allowed open sin within the whole body to stand unchallenged.

Let us now look at how to return God's protective covering over our nation. Remember, if the Churches join hands under the UACC, then these changes will be many times easier to accomplish. Note: The closer the end approaches the more important these will be to keep stability in America. The list compiled below has been organized in the order of importance:

1. Acknowledge this is a Christian nation by a constitutional amendment. Within its texts, a statement affirming Jesus Christ shall be the only true Savior of the world.

2. A constitutional amendment describing sin and the promotion of sin as described in almighty God's Holy Bible. The affirming statement highlighting which of these sinful type activities are against the law. Pass severe and just punishment for these unlawful activities.

3. Honoring a day as the Lord's Day of rest with a constitutional amendment. The affirming statement - we the people shall honor our Lord and Savior with one day of rest from our work. This day can be whatever day is established, like Sunday or Saturday. It shall be against the law to operate businesses, meetings, or any activities or events, which are not essential in protecting against life threatening acts of man or nature and medical treatment. Activities deemed unlawful include but are not limited to; general retail, entertainment, sports, gambling, and any other activity which lusts after money.

4. Laws and courts must be conducted with an iron rod of quick and severe correction.

5. Replace federal and state welfare with Bible discipline such as, if you do not work, you are not guaranteed a meal. Welfare, in its current form, has been of the Antichrist spirit, leaving God out of the equation.

6. Replace federal and state Medicare, Medicaid, or any other taxpayer funded medical plan with Bible discipline such as families taking care of their own. Churches and communities should pitch in where needed. Taxpayer funded medical plans in it's current forms are of the Antichrist spirit. Again, God has been left out of the picture.

7. Federal taxes must be reduced by at least seventy-five percent with a balanced budget before the year 99SRSP-CE (sequencing point only). Generally speaking, states should not increase their taxes (Fed's down a lot - State's up a little). Over taxation has been of the Antichrist spirit.

8. A constitutional amendment concerning military status to be completed before 99SRSP-CE. Phase out women from the warrior position of the military. Women in warrior positions of the military, place the nation at the highest risk of total and complete failure.

9. An amendment to the constitution stating the Holy Bible must be the normal and best way for children to learn and operate successfully in this Christian Nation. Basic Holy Bible believing values will be taught in public schools, as they once were when America was founded.

10. Any swearing in office, or under oath in a courtroom, must be done to the Lord God Almighty upon His Holy Bible.

The USA will come back to a disciple nation, if the Christians will vigorously start working on these suggestions. The Lord God will begin to place his protective covering over our nation again if we follow these instructions. The heart (Church) of our nation must first start turning back to God and it must start with the lukewarm Christians realizing their disobedience to the Lord God and repenting. We will never turn our nation around if Christians cannot turn our Churches back to God by trouncing out lukewarmness.

Below, 7-7-1- Israel, Jerusalem - Garden Tomb: The tomb is situated outside the walls, to the North of the Damascus Gate, and is believed by many Christians to be the true burial place of Christ. A thought flowed in my mind, about the condition of the Church. Jesus died for us so we would quit living for ourselves and start living for Him. Yet, some Christians want to move toward the world by bringing the world into the Church. America slides toward destruction as the Church moves toward the world. "Oh, Lord God, help us and forgive our sinful ways," Amen.

The UACC shall be the best answer, if Christians look at the time allotted before and after the tribulation starts.

SEVEN SPIRITS OF GOD

Section 7-8

The Seven Spirits of God (Revelation 1:20 and 4:5) equal seven lamps blazing before the throne equal seven church-type spirits equal seven (so to speak) personality traits in the broad-term Christian. The character of each of these sevenfold spirits combined to make one complete Holy Spirit. God introduces seven unique parts of the one complete Holy Spirit into seven different flesh lusting bodies. This produces seven unique personality traits in seven different people. These seven traits, in turn, manifest into seven different characters in people to influence groups of people and even whole nations.

Let us look at these sevenfold type personality traits of today's endtimers. These seven personality traits are made up of the physical, intellectual, and emotional structure of the fleshly body. This body (actions) will be judged as to its obedience to God's word. It includes the emotional structure of an individual. The Lord God looks at a person's heart to judge. Outward actions are displayed for the world to see. God checks to see if this spirit person followed the command of God when using their assets, abilities, interests, and attitudes. The difference between the way a Christian lived his life compared to the way Jesus would have lived their identical life will be the bar of measure as to how far they missed the mark. God has established a goal for Christians' personal lives to reach. Christians should, fulfill the complete duty in their lifetimes, that Jesus expected them to accomplish for the glory of His Father's kingdom.

If they have not repented to God for their errors, this will lead to the second death in the lake of fire. This will separate them from God forever. We lose rewards before the judgment seat of Christ by not following God's word. Christians can obtain more rewards if they are more obedient to God's word. The choice must be theirs.

We can summarize each sevenfold end time spirit's attributes, its shortcomings, and God's rewards for the people who shall overcome and pass the test of their cycle. Each person will identify with one of these type spirits and should make changes where necessary to be in harmony with God's will.

First-Sevenfold Spirit with a Personality Trait like unto Ephesus, Revelation 2:1-7.

This spirit represents hard workers with perseverance toward life in general. They cannot tolerate wicked men. They test those who claim to be church leaders or apostles to be true or false witnesses for Jesus Christ. They never get weary when they have to persevere and endure hardships for Jesus Christ's sake. They hate people who profess to be Christians, yet live licentiously. Their shortcomings are forsaking their first love of Jesus, and falling from their height and standing with God. The world does a good job in distracting them from their love for God and replaces it with worldly pleasures. If they can overcome this weakness, their rewards will be eating from the tree of life in paradise.

Second-Sevenfold Spirit with a Personality Trait like unto Smyrna, Revelation 2:8-11.

People who in their lifetime have been poor are representative of this spirit. They have been afflicted usually by leaders professing to be righteous and fair. Religious leaders will persecute them. We can see by these leaders' works that they are of the synagogue of Satan. Evil men will put some number-two spirit persons into prison. This will test them for a time to see how their Christianity holds up. They will suffer persecution from time to time. Some of Spirit two's will rebuke and spit in Satan's face even to the point of death to receive the crown of life. The shortcomings of this person are self-pity, getting discouraged, and giving in to the pressure of Satan. The rewards of this person, who overcomes, shall not be hurt at all by the second death.

Third-Sevenfold Spirit with a Personality Trait like unto Pergamum, Revelation 2:12-17.

People representative this spirit will live in an area, city or country, which has much evil, hate, and violence. This person remains true to Jesus Christ even in great opposition from the world around them. They do not renounce Jesus Christ or their faith in what He is about to do. They hold fast when they see their community, friends, and leaders taken advantage of or even unjustly put to death.

The shortcomings of this person are holding to the teaching of world idolatry and being easily persuaded into sexual immorality. Some have a hard time distinguishing the difference in world and church thinking. They rationalize an overlap will help win souls to Christ. They can talk the talk but have a terrible time walking the walk of Jesus Christ, for they live licentiously. God's rewards for overcoming are, some of the hidden manna, a white stone with a new name on it.

Fourth-Sevenfold Spirit with a Personality Trait like unto Thyatira, Revelation 2:18-29.

Number four spirit will most likely be people who are overflowing with love, faith, service, and perseverance. They are constantly increasing stewardship. They are always working to hold on to what they possess, for it will be hard for them in a sinful world. Many of these spirits will overcome and do the will of God to the end. Their shortcomings include no involvement in world affairs, which would keep their nation a disciple nation. (Its laws, government, and people following the word of God.)

Below, 7-8-1- Italy, Rome - Church of St. Peter in Chains: The Angel in charge of Hell should be a chilling reminder of the time and space outside God's domain where the disobedient are assigned after their test cycle. Let us discuss the Spirit-filled Christian who can discern and understand complex Biblical teaching. Christians must open their minds to a part of the complex understanding of the Lord God's great and hidden mysteries as the Spirit has moved me to write.

We are not born equal as our pagan world and governments try to teach us. The end time portion of our test cycles is different and unique. They are especially designed for each person, which does not necessarily contain the pursuit of happiness as our government implies but a call to suffer for the Gospel. Our rewards will be separated into seven different categories (Revelation 2 and 3 - seven spirits). Each glorified body has separate and unique heavenly rewards. Our assignments will differ depending on which Spirit we are and what we did on earth as good works for Jesus to receive heavenly rewards from the Lord God for His pleasure.

Above, 7-8-2- Israel, Caesarea - Amphitheater: City started about 22 BC by Romans with 6 BC being the year designating the official residence of the governors of Judea, and for some 500 years it was the capital of Roman administration in Palestine. For gentiles, this was the starting point for they were included in the salvation message of Jesus Christ for the first time. Peter led a centurion, Cornelius, to become a Christian (Acts 10). I thanked God for His great mercy and pray gentile Christians will honor Him. Some will miss the mark on judgment day while others will shine like the stars in heaven.

The consequence of these lazy actions added to making America a non-disciple nation in God's eyes. Since 1990 A.D., God has slowly removed His protective covering off our once great nation. Their disobedience to the Great Commission (Go Make Disciple Nations) shall be costly. They tolerated sin, which leads people into idolatry and sexual immorality.

After this person has overcome, it would be good for them to help start the UACC. The person, which overcomes, will rule over many nations and have the morning star.

Fifth-Sevenfold Spirit with a Personality Trait like unto Sardis, Revelation 3:1-6.

People who make God talk to Himself. They are over doers for good or whatever. If they are into something, we can expect them to be one hundred percent into it. They do remember to praise God for their salvation. Some strengthen their knowledge after realizing they are not quite as smart as they thought. They are generally worthy people, who have not soiled their clothes. They will be called CHOSEN. If goals are set they believe in, they will move mountains in a short period to reach that goal.

The number five spirit has a problem when it comes to shortcomings. They have a reputation for living for the Lord. Yet, because of lack of knowledge in knowing and doing His will, they are dead. These type Christians think they know the teaching of the Bible, but they have not performed their first duty as Christians. Their duty must be to study themselves approved unto God. Then they will know what will be pleasing to Him. This spirit has a lack of knowledge, too much pride, and likes themselves too much. They have a terrible time obeying the word, for the world keeps them off balance most of the time. Spirit five believes they have done some fine things for the Lord.

These people have a real problem admitting they are wrong. This does not mean they are extreme know-it-alls, although their chests are puffed-up somewhat. They overdo for pleasure, and again, their deeds are not complete before God. These type people are very hard to turn back once they get off course. If they ever wake up, repent, and overcome their shortcomings, Satan, watch out! The Lord has just added a mighty warrior to His army and his name will be called chosen. These people, with God's help, are rock solid and will never fall. They understand the importance of following 2 Peter 1:1-13, which speaks of increasing certain described attributes constantly.

These warriors' rewards for overcoming are to be dressed in white and never blotted out of the book of life. They receive one of the highest honors in heaven when they are acknowledged before the Father and all of His holy angels for a job well done! Glory!

Sixth-Sevenfold Spirit with a Personality Trait like unto Philadelphia, Revelation 3:7-13.

Mighty people who have fought the good fight against world thinking and have kept My word at the expense of wear and tear on their souls and bodies, which has left them with little strength. They refuse to shave off a little faith in Jesus Christ by giving into the world just to gain acceptance. By doing this, they did not deny My name. They have kept My command to endure patiently even when facing great pain or worldly opposition.

They know one hundred percent in their hearts they belong to the Lord God. Their heart-mind is connected by the word pure, and they are judged blameless before God. This does not mean they are perfect before God. There is only one who can be called perfect at the start of the tribulation period. This perfect Spirit, the almighty God Himself shall be worthy to appoint His Son to open the Seven Seals and His name is Jesus Christ our Lord and Savior. If Christians wish to be perfect before God, then study the rich man's parable. He followed all the commands of the Lord, even though he was a rich man. Therefore, if you want to be perfect, this one example teaches us to become rich and still follow the commands of God, which is almost impossible. Then give your assets to the poor and follow Jesus. I haven't heard of a man who has perfected this down to the last detail.

Spirit six rarely has shortcomings for long, for they fear the Lord more than they fear the world. If a circumstance shakes their faith, they, with the help of the Holy Spirit, quickly bring this bubble in their life under control.

The rewards and honors for spirit number six are many. First, the heavenly door has been opened for them to come and receive their crown. Jesus shall reward spirit number six by making Moslems and others who constantly told them Jesus didn't really love them and they were not entitled to their heavenly inheritance, to fall before them. Jesus will make them confess their lies and receive a second fiery cup of His wrath. Then these evildoers will slowly be ushered, while still burning, to the lake of fire.

Read the Seven Spirit Church Prophecy to completely understand this next reward. Spirit six will not have to go through the hour of trial or tribulation period. Many of the other six spirits are required to go into the tribulation period to complete their test. Spirit six has been slowly removed stealthily (non-signed event) through death just before the tribulation starts. Under the cover of the Fourth Seal Repeat (99SRSP-CE) the balance of Spirit sixes will be removed in the same manner when Russia marches south (Gulf War-III).

This spirit will be honored by being made a pillar in the temple of God. Written on them will be the name of God and the name of New Jerusalem and the new name of Jesus.

This spirit has been on many assignments for God outside the temple in other eons-time cycles and time frames, which the natural mind cannot grasp. Now God shall reward these spirits by, *"no more assignments outside the temple."* They do not have to leave it any more. The temple exists not as a building structure like we earthly beings understand construction. When a spirit enters into the temple, time-space, speed, and distance are meaningless when compared to earth's. It is just past our comprehension to assimilate into understanding what heaven's time-space means. Christian prioritizing transforms into what type end time Christian should we be? We must shore up our position before God.

Seventh-Sevenfold Spirit with a personality Trait like unto Laodicea, Revelation 3:14-22.

The number seven spirit represents fifty to eighty-five percent of attendance in ninety-nine percent of American Churches.

The number seven spirit represents fifty to eighty-five percent of attendance in ninety-nine percent of American Churches. My burden shall be part of the movement to reduce this high percent of eighty-five down to just above what Matthew 24:10 describes in the great Christian falling away. In the tribulation period, there will be at least a fifty percent loss of lukewarmers. The Bible tells us and I have further prophesied the lukewarmer will be spit out of God's mouth into the tribulation period. This will be just after Gulf War III, which equates to the Fourth Seal Repeat and the lukewarmer will be rebuked and disciplined by God.

It will be better for them to wake up now and repent. It would be worse to wake up in the tribulation period thinking they were going to be raptured out of the way before hand. They will be disillusioned and disarrayed, disappointed, and in trouble with God. Most likely they will be a product of Matthew 24:10, the great Christian falling away.

We must not be negative, the Spirit imparted to me. God used the word many would fall away in Matthew 24:10 not the word few. Few designates substantially below fifty percent and many means above fifty percent but close to it. The word most, means close to one hundred percent. At best, only thirty-four percent of lukewarmers now lost in American churches can be saved. Lukewarmers will be hard pressed to follow these prophecies for they require giving up some worldly comfort, convenience, and pleasures. In some cases, they must give up money or even their life.

Above, 7-8-3- Israel, Caesarea Phillipi: Pictured is the pagan cult grotto of the god Pan. This city had many false gods just as our culture has many false gods. Here Jesus changed Peter's name from Simon and gave him "the Keys to the Kingdom of heaven," after Peter declared him the Messiah for the first time. Unfortunately, Satan's role in the Christian's test cycle is as our great deceiver. He performed a good job back then and has been doing an even better job with deception during the endtimes.

Church leaders, if the flock complains long enough, hard enough, and loud enough, many leaders will become lukewarm too. Silence them quickly or they will take over the Church. It is very evident many pastors are mellowing and giving into these complaining spirits for their worldly demands and requests. Many of these requests are concerned with their rights, not God's rights. Just look at what happened to Moses. Pastors are in error that thinks they are stronger than Moses in resisting these complaining spirits in their churches. These spirits always have complaints. Sadly, some pastors are giving in, mainly because of these complaining spirits and lukewarmers.

God has been pacing up and down muttering to Himself for quite a while, *for He is furious.*

The Spirit has given me the opportunity to observe one of God's window chambers. God has been angry at America and the Christian men for letting their country become a disobedient nation. A vision was given me; America's disobedience has become such a hot spot with God that He cannot sit on His throne. God has been pacing up and down muttering to Himself for quite a while, for He is furious. God has been lifting His protective covering, as birthing pains, since 1990 A.D. He will continue to lift this protection off America, until we repent or worse yet, are destroyed by the THREE-WOES to AMERICA.

Lukewarmers will gather speakers to preach what their itching ears want to hear. Jesus was a wave maker and was not lukewarm. He made more waves than anyone did. We must follow our leader Jesus Christ, the WAVE MAKER!

Now let us look at the lukewarmer's attributes. Lukewarmers have nothing worthy to offer before Almighty God. They are worse than zero, for they are as vomit before the Holy throne. They shall be washed with a double cup of fire while being dragged away to the lake of fire. Only a few (up to thirty-four percent) may wake up and repent.

The lukewarmer has many problems. I will summarize some of the shortcomings and faults lukewarmers and their churches may possess. Churches must think upon these things with their hearts, not their minds. For the minds of most Christians today are cluttered with worldly problems and entertainment choices. Satan's deceptive opinions and prejudices are clouding their minds from seeing clearly. Christians must use their hearts to think and seek the Holy Spirit's insight. God looks at our hearts to see our inner thoughts and motives.

Unfortunately, most lukewarmers are not going to make it to heaven. God does not want them, for they are going to say, "Lord, Lord," and God will say, "Depart from Me, for I never knew you." The lukewarmer believes the path must be wide, easy, and with much rewards. Yet God says the path has been cut out narrow and hard.

Christians must work out their own salvation with fear and trembling or burn in front of a large audience of heavenly beings. Angels will be clapping and praising the Lamb for His just punishment levied on lukewarmers and unbelievers. On the other hand, it does not mean God has been sitting in heaven plotting how to do lukewarmers harm. It does mean He has become furious at the lukewarmer for throwing away their salvation He freely gave to them. I pray this list will awaken the lukewarmer from their assured deaths. May this insight lead them to repent and save themselves from this corrupt world.

CHARACTERISTICS of the LUKEWARMER'S

Section 7-9

NOTE: Some of these characteristics do not make a person lukewarm. However, people must take corrective action in their lives and Churches if they find themselves or their churches identifying with these characteristics. Look at your church and make sure in has not turned into a "contemporary" Church, which has totally abandoned its pedagogical responsibilities. In other words, it may be warming up to the below ideas or may even be promoting them.

Many of the Lukewarmer's Characteristics are as follows:

Lukewarmers become spiritually blind and are unable to understand God's powerful delusion (2 Thessalonians 2:11-12). They are carnal and spiritual while living fifty percent for the world and fifty percent for God (Revelation 3:14-22). They think monetary possessions are the most important things in life. Their fear of the world has been greater than fear of the Lord God. Most are un-repenting, rendering service from the lips and not the heart. The warm love of God has vanished from their personalities. They display indifference, carnality, rebellion, self-security, self-righteousness, self-satisfaction, and desire power and materialism. They have moved away from their first love and lack the living relationship with the Lord God. They have become puffed up with pride. Their job title has always been very important to them. They refuse to help or associate with people of lesser social status. They need self-praise and demand self-rights instead of God's rights. They become greedy and tithe less than expected.

They participate and support the noisy dens (special interest groups), which in turn protects their individual rights. They ignore the truth about noisy dens and continue donating money to these organizations. The Church could spend this money better, yet they want their rights before God's instructions. They do not understand Satan has been working harder today and more will be required of them. They cannot see the importance of going to church on a regular basis because they feel they have acquired enough Biblical knowledge. The lack of knowledge causes them to think they have God's approval and respectability of their moral life. They perform works to satisfy the religious fulfillment of society acknowledging their efforts. They believe other people ought to live their lives and let them pursue theirs.

They ignore the increases in destruction in the United States since 1990 A.D. (Psalms 90-106). They believe Mother Nature, man's global warming, or some hostile group triggered it and refuse to believe it was caused by God's judgment of wrath against a disobedient nation and world. (Obey God = Generally good weather: Disobey God = Generally brings bad weather.) See, Job 37, Deuteronomy 28:22-24, Leviticus 26-note verse 4 requirement, and Revelation 8:4-12.

Below, 7-9-1- Israel, Judean Desert - Nomads Camping: Nomads were camping in the desert between Jerusalem and Jericho. These people have wandered unrestricted over the Middle East since Bible days. However, with tighter borders and higher security they are stuck in the desert. This shall be exactly like the lukewarmers will find themselves in the tribulation period. The solid Spirit-filled Christian does not want them. Likewise, the world does not want them except to use them for gain. Many lukewarmers are in powerful positions in international Corporations and others are politicians. They will wield untold misery on the Spirit-filled Christians. They will be dissolved like salt poured into hot boiling water, never to be viewed again.

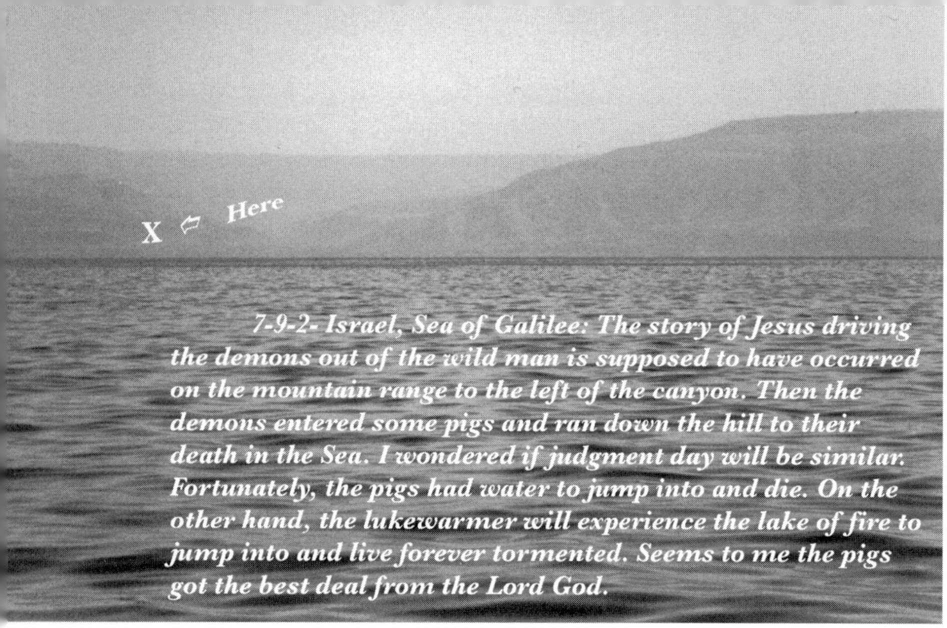

X ⇦ Here

7-9-2- Israel, Sea of Galilee: The story of Jesus driving the demons out of the wild man is supposed to have occurred on the mountain range to the left of the canyon. Then the demons entered some pigs and ran down the hill to their death in the Sea. I wondered if judgment day will be similar. Fortunately, the pigs had water to jump into and die. On the other hand, the lukewarmer will experience the lake of fire to jump into and live forever tormented. Seems to me the pigs got the best deal from the Lord God.

They cannot comprehend God's warning statement in Matthew 24:10 when God says He will send lukewarmers to hell. They are satisfied with their own condition, and lack self-recognition into what they have become, lukewarm. Churches have lost the fear (awe or dreaded) of the Lord, and this can cause people to become lukewarm. They spend more time praising men in church than giving God the praise for lifting these men up. As the fear of God moves out of their Church, the spirit of rebellion, carnality, pride and bickering moves into their Church.

They dishonor God's House in their worldly dress, mannerism, and language. Lukewarmers do not respect God's House for it has become only a building to them. They see nothing wrong with money exchangers giving discounts and vendors selling merchandise and service inside the church foyer or worse yet the sanctuary. They do not see where this takes the focus off Jesus in their church.

Lukewarmers want the best of both worlds. They want a system where they can sing praises to God and hear a sermon which does not point out sin in their lives while at the same time purchasing merchandise and pleasure at discount prices on Church property. Nonetheless, Jesus said you have made My building structure a den of thieves. Lukewarmers are not afraid (fear) of the Lord, for they have an egotistical nature, and constantly complain of others. They have a self-assertion problem and sometimes believe no one loves them. They deny the tribulation period will be in their lifetime and believe there will not be a need to prepare as these prophecies warn of world destruction.

They are unwilling to suffer for others and have unnecessarily sued others. They have a "the world owes me" attitude and unnecessarily defend themselves in court. They have little true enthusiasm for the Lord. They are halfhearted, half-supportive, half-obedient, indifferent, and unconcerned, especially when discussing problems about the poor. Lukewarmers do not understand the importance of protecting Israel or God's Holy City Jerusalem. In general, the lukewarmer has become disobedient to God's command.

1. Did any of these characteristics ring a bell?

2. God judges the heart not outward works.

3. Lukewarmers must repent or they will die the second death.

4. I pray God opens each Christian's eyes to their faults and the lukewarmness spreading through the Churches.

In my mind the Holy Spirit said, "We must talk quickly. "I slipped off to a quiet, secret place in my childhood where my mind rested in peace. The Spirit began to talk very forcefully and convincingly to me. "Of any truth the lukewarmers and their churches do not fully comprehend the importance of the literal meaning concerning the first reading (see glossary) of the Great Commission of Jesus Christ (Matthew 28:18-20).

Most pastors teach the second reading (Mark 16:15 - interpretation) which will be fine and necessary. The second states, take the good news around the world. There is nothing wrong with the second reading unless they completely leave out the first meaning (first time it appears in New Testament - Matthew 28:19-20). Remember, Jesus did not come down to earth for the so-called great preachers, educated Christians, and the rocket scientist. For these people are able to read the word and comprehend the meaning on their own. He came down for the poor, uneducated, downtrodden and so on, you know the story. Now just think, Jesus did not leave His word in a format that would be so complicated a simple or uneducated person could not understand what His commands were. The first reading must be taught and obeyed first or in harmony with the other six readings. What part of the first reading of Jesus' Great Commission (Matthew 28:18-20) have the lukewarmer and their Church missed? **Answer:**

GO MAKE
DISCIPLE NATIONS
AND TEACH THEM
TO OBEY MY COMMANDS.

Christian's first duty must be to keep America or the nation each person lives in a disciple nation. Then, our second goal must be to take the good news around the world. The terrible lack of understanding of this basic truth by lukewarm church leaders has inspired their churches in America and around the world to do just the reverse. In America let's say, Christians are trying to save the rest of the world at America's expense of losing our nation to Satan.

Jesus knew end time churches would have a problem with understanding the Great Commission. Only when a nation stands on solid spiritual ground as Jesus commanded will it save more souls in the long-term. The words **go and make** mean, go take and then make into a disciple nation. The word (disciple) means follower of Jesus Christ and all His teaching. The word (nation) means trinity or its government, laws, and people in harmony with the word from the Holy Bible. The words, (teach them to obey), mean the laws and the government who carries the sword of correction for the Lord must rule with a iron rod in making each nation obey all the commands of God.

Lukewarmer's misunderstanding of this simple-truth (first reading) of the Great Commission has nearly led to the destruction of our once great nation. Christians and their Churches in America have totally lost their power to control the trinity of America. Jesus also commanded, "Be of one mind." Through the Universal American Church Coalition (UACC), America can better fulfill the first reading of the Great Commission and return America to a disciple nation. Then God will place His protective covering over our nation again.

The Spirit glaringly looked at me and in a forceful manner said, "Remember your forefathers took a nation, then they made your nation under God and dedicated it to God. Since the 1960s, the Christians have lost America to Satanic thinking. It is time to get started. Let us peaceably take America back through the UACC for Jesus Christ. Men must heed the statement `Satan will push harder but God will push even harder yet.' Now go and give this warning to the Churches before the Three Woes to America destroys your once great nation! "

The Spirit imparted to me that we could wake-up an extra thirty-four percent of the lukewarmers. Unfortunately, fifty-one percent are hellbound for they will not give up their position of controlling, or the better of two worlds. The good news points to their being saved if they wake up to their abomination before God and repent. He will then give them the power they do not possess by themselves to overcome their detestable ways. The lukewarmers in many cases are receiving their rewards here on earth. There will be no rewards in the lake of fire, which has been patiently waiting for their arrival. The lukewarmer has become the unbeliever's best excuse for not attending church and receiving the salvation message of Jesus Christ. God is exceedingly angry at the lukewarmers!

The rewards for the lukewarmer are: To him who overcomes, I will give the right to sit with me (Jesus) on my throne, just as I overcame and sat down with my Father on His throne. Amen.

Below, 7-10-1- Greece - Athens - Mars Hill: St. Paul stood in a meeting of the Areopagus on top of Mars Hill. The Areopagus' were Athenians and others who lived there and spent their time doing nothing but discussing and listening to the latest ideas. Paul addressed (Acts 17:22-34) the intellectual thinkers with the good news of Jesus Christ and had a few followers. Unfortunately, some of the intellectuals in the modern freethinking Churches and Media have been encouraging an easy plan for salvation to the world and escape clauses for the lukewarm Christians. Their sophisticated thought process has been interpreting scripture incorrectly. They cherry pick scripture which cannot stand alone and therefore have been misinterpreting its meaning. Consequently, this promotes unsound salvation theology, which causes a false sense of warm comfortable feeling within God's security.

Add to this problem a new dimension of heresy. The electronic media through advertising has displayed the ability to deceive, by reaching down into the mind of the inexperienced newborn Christian who thinks he stands on solid ground. Many of these non-Christian's minds are grasping for a quick relief from their problems to remove discomfort. They have set up a disaster by accepting easy plans of salvation. This attracts lukewarmness and the conditions of false hopes to be experienced during endtimes as a fulfillment of the prophesied ***Great Christian Falling Away.***

THE SEVEN SPIRIT
CHURCH PROPHECY
Section 7-10

The Spirit of Christ, the Spirit of Prophecy, gave this prophecy to me, for presentation to the Church to convince each Christian to study the Book of Revelation. The Seven Spirit Church Prophecy has been sent to wake Christians up from misguided teaching, lest you will become a product of Christian falling away in Matthew 24:10. First, I ask your prayers, and, second, your support in getting this urgent message to the Church.

The spirit inspired me to ask the reader two questions before reading this prophecy.

LET THE COMMON SENSE OF THE MATTER STAND ON ITS OWN MERIT:

1. ☞ How many souls could be carelessly lost if the pre-tribulation, mid-tribulation, or pre-wrath rapture theories are correct, yet the Seven Spirit Church Prophecy was widely accepted? Answer: Not one would be lost, because all Spirit-filled Christians would be raptured and go to heaven. ✂

2. ☞ How many souls could be carelessly lost if the Seven Spirit Church Prophecy is correct, yet the pre-tribulation, mid-tribulation or pre-wrath rapture theories was widely accepted. Answer: MANY millions will be lost in the first half of tribulation period or shortly after the rapture should have occurred due to discouragement, deception, hate, and mistrust. Thinking they have been unjustly left behind, they will wake up in the tribulation and find themselves fulfilling Matthew 24:10. "By backbiting, betraying, and hating other Christians." They will believe God has left them behind, betrayed them, or this cannot really be the start of the tribulation period. They set themselves up because of denial and lack of knowledge. Note: It is imperative Christians and their Churches do not make the many different rapture theories a denomination issue. When Churches do, valuable end time information is not shared and the sad consequence will equate to many unnecessary lost souls. ✂

There is another possibility I pray for, that some of the ill-taught Christians will realize their error, and rededicate themselves wholly to Christ. With this new understanding, they reset their priorities on the important issues of the tribulation period and promote the Great Commission of Jesus Christ (Matthew 28:18-20).

The endtimes must be an arena of Christians' ideas gathered together with LOVE for proper instruction to direct Christians. Many Christians will be experiencing the tribulation period. Therefore, they must be taught how to react to Satan's deception and God's wrath. Otherwise, lukewarmers could get discouraged, bitter, and fall away.

John was commanded to write what he has seen (past), what is now (present), and what will take place (future) concerning the seven Spirits of God's Church. He wrote how the seven church Spirits move through the next two sabbatical days (2000 earth years). The analyzing and directive toward each church Spirit was to an angel or a time messenger for two sabbatical days. The Spirit told me John did not write to the current pastors or elders from their period. Nor did he write to the board of directors of a future time. He wrote to a time messenger (angel) to carry the message for two sabbatical days.

Who must get out of the way has always been a question so Satan has the power to overthrow part of the saints in the tribulation (Revelation 13:7). Some well-meaning teachers say the answer has to be ALL Christians or the Church. This includes all of the Holy Spirit experiencing the pre and mid-tribulation rapture. Others say just one obstacle and it's the Holy Spirit. Others say there will not be a pre mid-tribulation rapture. Well, who's right? Maybe a little bit of all three. I shall prophesy the truth as clearly stated in the first reading in the book of Revelation on this subject. Here comes the shock for the lukewarm Churches in America!

The Church would be better if Christians would spend as much time and energy doing what our Father in heaven wants, rather than quarreling about different rapture theories.
A theory can become like a - merry-go-round - it doesn't go anywhere but in circles.

Right, 7-10-2- Greece, Ancient Athens - Ancient Agora Area: View of the Ancient Agora Area from Mars Hill. St. Paul was distressed to see the city full of idols. He reasoned in the market place (Agora Area) day after day. Some philosophers began to debate him and said, "What is this babbler trying to say?" (Acts 17:16-21). Paul found opposition when presenting the truth to others.

There has been some opposition from the intellectual world and lukewarm Churches when these prophecies, decrees, and warnings were presented to them. In all fairness, understanding and believing prophecy is hard for people. I have found many people do not want to hear what I have prophesied concerning a major shift in the way their life styles will change in the near future. Some sense what I have prophesied must be true but it is not what they want to hear because people are comfortable in their sinful, and lukewarm world. Many Christians today have an easy life style and the last event they want to happen would be Jesus coming back and changing their world.

They are in complete denial and refuse to accept the truth about endtimes as it might relate to them. Some people like to engage in frivolous debate while others enjoy needless spiritual jousting just for confusion. Their intellect has deceived them and the Wake Up Call Prophecies are accurately unfolding as prophesied. This has disturbed them. If given the chance to see the Wake Up Call Prophecies, the Spirit-filled Christian would begin to inquire of their leaders some serious end time questions and debate.

The total removal by death of Spirit number six in the PHILADELPHIA church has been the power that has been holding Satan from crushing part of the Christians. "*...I will also keep you from the hour of trial that is going to come upon the whole world to test those who live on the earth*" (Revelation 3:10). Spirit six will stealthily (non-signed event) be removed by death before the tribulation period starts. Most of their bodies will be visibly dead here on earth. Christians on earth will not be visibly raptured even though the results are similar (go to heaven).

There will be masses of Christians dying and going to heaven in a short period because of Gulf War III (Fourth Seal, Repeat, Revelation 6:7-8), Russia marching south.

It must be noted: When a nuclear bomb hits a city, there will be the exact condition of many Christians being raptured. If they are at ground zero when the bomb explodes, they will instantaneously and gloriously shed their tent of a body and obtain their glorified body without experiencing the sting of death. There will be no evidence of a dead body left behind. These people in a sense will be raptured to heaven. We are all appointed to die once. So most Christian's bodies will be visibly dead here on earth by natural causes. The difference in some rapture theories compared to this prophecy translates into the different quantity going to heaven. For many rapture theories state all Christians will go which includes the lukewarmers. While God's plan states only one of the seven church Spirits or people having the characteristic of the number six Spirit judged blameless by God will totally be removed. See section describing Mornings and Evenings Prophecies, and 99SRSP-CE.

The Spirit moved me to write that the total Church body in our earthly thinking has always been made up of seven personality traits. God uses these traits in separate ways to accomplish the destruction of Satan. Each personality trait of the Spirit of a church will manifest itself through the two-thousand year church age. Most churches number one through five and number seven Spirits will be here during the tribulation period for there will be much to do for God.

Lukewarmers represent approximately fifty to eighty-five percent of people in Bible-believing churches in America. This includes many of the leadership who think they're going up with the shout!

Most American Churches are unsure of end time events. They do not know what to do and are scared, don't want to talk about it, or are depressed when discussing end time events. More importantly, God said He will BLESS Christians for just reading it. *"Blessed is the one who reads the words of this prophecy, and blessed are those who hear it and take to heart what is written in it because the time is near"* (Revelation 1:3).

It is very important for Christians to know what days they live in. Many Christians will overcome the Beast, Antichrist spirit, or his Image during the days of sorrows and the tribulation period. *"And I saw what looked like a sea of glass mixed with fire and, standing beside the sea, those who had been victorious over the beast* (MNO) *and his image* (Internet web of deceit) *and over the number of his name...* (MNO -- 666)*"* (Revelation 15:2).

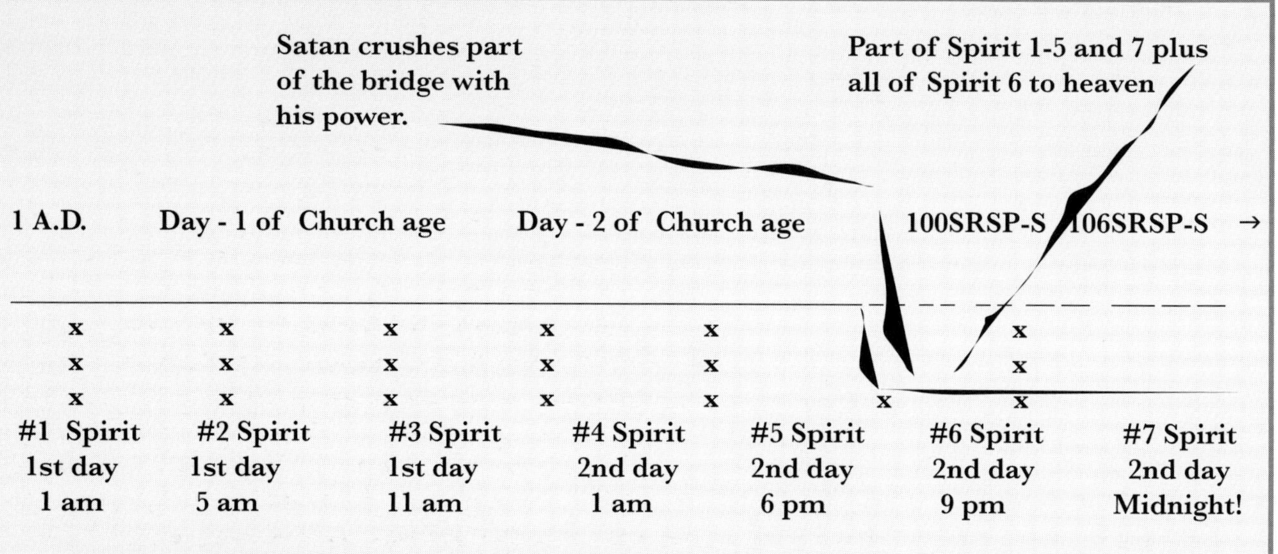

Satan crushes part of the bridge with his power.

Part of Spirit 1-5 and 7 plus all of Spirit 6 to heaven

1 A.D.	Day - 1 of Church age		Day - 2 of Church age		100SRSP-S	106SRSP-S →
#1 Spirit	#2 Spirit	#3 Spirit	#4 Spirit	#5 Spirit	#6 Spirit	#7 Spirit
1st day	1st day	1st day	2nd day	2nd day	2nd day	2nd day
1 am	5 am	11 am	1 am	6 pm	9 pm	Midnight!

Midpoint of highest concentration of each Spirit through the two day sabbatical time calendar.
Figure 7-10-1

We cannot really understand the removal before the tribulation period. It will be like unto only one-part of the total sevenfold Holy Spirit leaving in our earthly thinking. We judge ourselves holy from a different perspective than God does.

This total Holy Spirit would be like unto a bridge built through two sabbatical days or two-thousand years of the church age. God uses each church Spirit one to seven to represent a type of person or group of similar people as the seven support Spirits. Church Spirit seven represents most American Churches, as the seventh support spans of the bridge (see Figure 7-10-1). Satan's deception represents the weight applied to the bridge. It will be like unto most of the total power of the Holy Spirit still being here holding the remaining support span during the tribulation period.

Church Spirit six will be taken out of the way by death in a ***non-signed way.*** God judges them blameless. Satan now crushes part of the bridge after the number six-support span has been removed with his power to overcome some saints.

The Spirit of Christ impressed on me this removal of Spirit six shall be partly accomplished with something like unto the green monkey virus introduced by God to the world as a warning in the 1990's. This removal could be some other animal virus, which has been increasing at a rapid rate. *"They were given power over a fourth of the earth to kill by sword, famine and plague, and by the* ***wild beasts*** *of the earth,"* (Revelation 6:8, fourth Seal).

The fourth Seal repeat includes the second and third SEAL repeats plus a new and more deadly way to kill masses of people quickly - ANIMAL VIRUSES. These types of viruses have the capability of destroying the entire earth in seven days. When these viruses become full force, the Internet web of deceit will warn people to stay inside until they announce the all clear. This will signal everyone has died that can be affected.

There will be millions of lives lost in Gulf War III (fourth Seal). This war brings death by nuclear bombs, chemical weapons, conventional weapons, and famine. Add to this people dying for lack of good water and the three gulf wars will have killed many millions of people.

What a price to pay for disobedience to God's word. God will finish removing Spirit six Christians by way of **death** under the cover of the pale horse, (fourth Seal-Repeat, Revelation 4:7-8). This shall be done so the world and much of the improperly taught Church will be blinded to the fact the tribulation has started. This shall be part of God's great delusion sent upon a disobedient world and church. Note: This is not to deceive but has been a part of the preprogramed scenario, which will be a test on the whole world (Revelation 3:10).

"They (unbelievers, backsliders, and lukewarmers) *perish because they refuse to love the truth and so be saved. For this reason God sends them a* ***Powerful Delusion*** *so that they will believe the lie and so that all will be condemned who have not believed the truth but have delighted in wickedness* (lukewarmer)*,"* 2 Thessalonians 2:10-12.

The total church pre-tribulation rapture theory leads to dangerous thinking. The Spirit has shown me we cannot have what some people call the instantaneous disappearance of masses of bodies from earth called the pre-tribulation rapture. Otherwise, we could simply count 2520 days from this sudden disappearance of numerous bodies from earth and know the exact day of the Second Advent. No one can know the day except the Father. Therefore, it follows there cannot be a so-called visible pre-tribulation rapture. Therefore, a removal of souls, not bodies, will be hidden from the nonbeliever and lukewarmers. This way the exact date of Jesus' return to earth will be concealed.

Now let us go back to the bridge spans. The bridge now being partially crushed shall be represented by good, backslidden, and lukewarm Christians during the entire tribulation period.

This has been prophesied as being one of the reason why there will be a great bitter Christian falling away from the faith through the first few years of the tribulation period (Matthew 24:10). Lukewarm Christians will feel rejected by God. Their love will wax cold because they haven't been properly instructed before the tribulation period starts. Church leaders must be teaching their flock what to expect and do before and after the tribulation period starts.

The Spirit encouraged me to write: "Warn the Christians about the tribulation period." The terrible things people will experience includes, God's wrath, or God's lifting of protection allowing Satan's wrath to increase on the world. This will greatly affect Christians. Christians must understand through the Internet web of deceit and the European led MNO, Satan will try to distort God's wrath. He does this to influence the world into hating the militant Christian, Jewish God, and Jewish people. God has allowed Satan to begin destroying the USA, therefore Christians must, humble themselves, pray, seek Jesus' face, and turn from wickedness (II Chronicles 7:13-15). Then, and only then, will God listen to lukewarmer's prayers.

Christians in the tribulation period who are improperly taught will not have a clear understanding of end time events. They may become a product of Satan's deceit and fall - never to recover. This has been why God sent the WAKE UP CALL PROPHECY to enlighten the Churches about Satan's end time deception.

At the start of Daniel's seventieth week, there are a few very special chosen people called for God's service (Revelation 3:4-5). These are special persons chosen from among the saints to do extraordinary duties like lead the saints, through the tribulation period against Satan. These chosen saints will never be blotted out of the book of life. They will lead the fight against Satan exposing his dark deception. They will tell the world the Antichrist and False Prophet are liars and the wrong men to follow. Christians with good Spirits out of church one to four plus born-again believers during tribulation will be known as called. (Revelation 17:14)

It must be noted ALL of the un-repented Spirit seven lukewarm churches will move into the tribulation period. God will discipline them to see if they repent and turn back to Him on a hot, not lukewarm, basis. Number five good Spirit has been chosen to lead and number six good Spirit shall be taken away. The person which is classified Spirit six (Revelation 3:12) by God shall be blameless.

God has promised Spirit six they will never again leave the temple (Revelation 3:12). This implies the number six Spirit has been on other assignments for God in other dimensions of time cycles. Now they are judged blameless and will never have to go out of God's temple to complete His work assignment again.

Some ministries, teachers, and writers believe in the pre-tribulation rapture. The theory of this philosophy describes the total Church with all seven Spirits (includes the lukewarmers) gone during the tribulation period. They ask, what will the unbelievers do during the tribulation period since they have been abandoned on earth? This assumes all Christians go and all unworthy stay. They added to the meaning of Revelation and will receive the plagues per Revelation 22:18. The pre-tribulation, mid-tribulation, and pre-wrath rapture theories are dangerous assumption or weak theories at best, which indirectly leads to the great Christian falling away in Matthew 24:10. Paul warned the believers, *"Do not go beyond what is written"* (1 Corinthians 4:6).

I have prayed more to communicate in love, about this section than other areas of this book. There are Christians who may disagree with this section, however they may be putting too much faith and hope in one of the many signed flawed rapture theories.

Their faith and hope have been placed on the wrong priorities. It must be on the written Word of God Almighty. When the Bible proclaims God gave all the authority in this scenario to the Son, we must have faith and place our hope in the written word of God.

Above, 7-10-3- Greece, Epidaurus - The Museum Courtyard: The Museum was full of old statues of gods, rulers and noblemen who have been known for their great worldly ideas, facts, wisdom, philosophy and insight. Yet, man still cannot connect with the total understanding of the God of gods. They invent their own gods to suit themselves and their interests. Ideas are conjured up in the insecure minds of men to give them the best of God's world and their misguided world. It has become common down through history to invent escape clauses in laws, religion and superstition to justify superior intellect. Nonetheless, as we come to the end of the testing cycle, we must endure and persevere to the end. As the Bible states, Christians are called to suffer. I pray God be with each person reading these prophecies.

God used believers to accomplish much of His work in the first sixty-nine weeks of Daniel. He is not going to change His method the final week of Daniel. God will use believers to help win souls, fight and expose Satan during the tribulation period!

Many Christians are using pre-tribulation tapes to win souls. If these Christians believe in the total Church pre-tribulation rapture theory, they will be disappointed. Lukewarmers and newborn Christians could be lost shortly after the tribulation starts if they believe in the pre-tribulation rapture theory. They will feel they have been abandoned because they were judged unworthy. Yet, some are judged worthy Christians. Remember God's word teaches, it would have been better had they never known me, (2 Peter 2:2-21)! I pray that they will see their error, repent, and follow the Lord God. God wants to use Christians in the tribulation period to help fight the Antichrist, False Prophet and Satan.

The Spirit prompted me to write: In Matthew 24:30 the words, *"at that time"*, which means after verses (4-29), this represents the Days of Sorrows and the tribulation period. Then after all this, (tribulation period and Daniel's 1335th day) God with a loud trumpet call (as described in 1 Thessalonians 4:15-18) gathers His elect (Matthew 24:31) before the destruction of the four winds (Revelation 7:1-3). This gathering of living Saints shall be on Daniel's 1335th day! It will not occur before Daniel 12:7, "*... when the power of the holy people* (Antichrist, False Prophet, and Satan) *has been finally broken, all these things will be complete.*"

A removal of Saints before Daniel's 1335th day would destroy part of the souls because saints are bonded to sinners by the command of love. When the power of holy people has been broken, this bond will be released (Matthew 13:29-30). This allows Jesus to remove His Saints without harm! Then Jesus releases the four winds with the power of the Seven Thunders to destroy all sinners, unbelievers, lukewarmers, land, sea and trees on earth.

Christians will ask which Spirit of God should we pray to become? The Spirit impressed on me to tell believers to study the word of God and pray for insight into His will. Be of good cheer for the hard work must begin soon. Glory to God! I only pray, through my witnessing, to honor God and fulfill His will for me.

Now read the two questions again at the start of this prophecy section. Let the Spirit guide each person to the truth, which has to be the Seven Spirit Church Prophecy.

Prophesied January 1995, by Bob R. Short, a messenger servant and a Witness to the world for our Lord Jesus Christ. Amen.

See when the Tribulation Period starts in the Next Section!

INTRODUCTION

to end time flow chart

Section 8-1

The original end time flow chart was first prophesied and recorded as a matter of public record in a 232 page book called: Original WAKE UP CALL PROPHECIES, rough draft Issue-1. It was published (2-1996) under ISBN 0-9651408-0-6. Issue-1 was prophesied; July 1995, on original pages; 210 and 211.

Pictures with insight and commentary added in 2005 - 2007

Note: When studying the End time Flow Chart it would be useful to read the corresponding chapter in the section of Morning and Evenings. Open the Holy Bible to the corresponding Psalm above the date or reference point on the flow chart, (Psalm 90, Psalm 91, to Psalm 106). Underneath these points are the sequencing events. Starting with Psalm 96 the Spirit directed me to use S.R.S.P. These are **slide rule sequencing points** used to determine a movable position on God's slide ruler of endtimes. These are not actual dates but sequencing points.

Therefore, I have prophesied and written down what I was directed concerning Daniel's sealed vision in chapter eight, revealing the mystery of evenings and mornings in this flow chart.

Flow Chart - next page: Sequencing end time events, decrees, calculations, seals, trumpets, bowls, satanic dooms and schedules.

Right, 8-1-1 Italy, Rome - Pantheon - AD 27: The Pantheon has endured the test of time. More importantly, time will not withstand our test cycle and last forever. It completes the programed test cycle and abruptly terminates at its beginning. It is as if God Almighty has driven a nail through the beginning of time with His mighty hammer to secure it. Then He takes a straight timeline and bends and forges it to His liking. This produces a curved time-space, which ends at its precise beginning. This curved time cycle brings us into a new dimension called judgment time.

Watch the signs on the flow chart, and make proper preparations. The wise Spirit-filled Christian can see and believe. Sadly, the lukewarmer is close-minded to a degree and the sinner cannot discern endtimes correctly. Many Christians are called to suffer and endure, the Tribulation Period. Christians must follow Jesus while persevering their personal test. Christians must resist world government and fight for Jesus Christ to return their nation to a disciple nation - followers of Christ.

We Win!

END TIME FLOW CHART

(Page - 244 of Scroll)

SKFC-8-2-1L - This was page 210 of Issue 1, from the Book, Wake Call Prophecies. It was upgraded in September 1996 = 1.1, May-September, 1999 = 1.2, December 2006 issue 1.3, and most of this chart is a copy of the original which was done on a five-line word processor plus lots of tape and glue. Note: Any locations listed 1996 or later are Slide Rule Sequencing Point and not actual dates. They are only used for sequencing of events on God Almighty's slide ruler (See section 2-8).

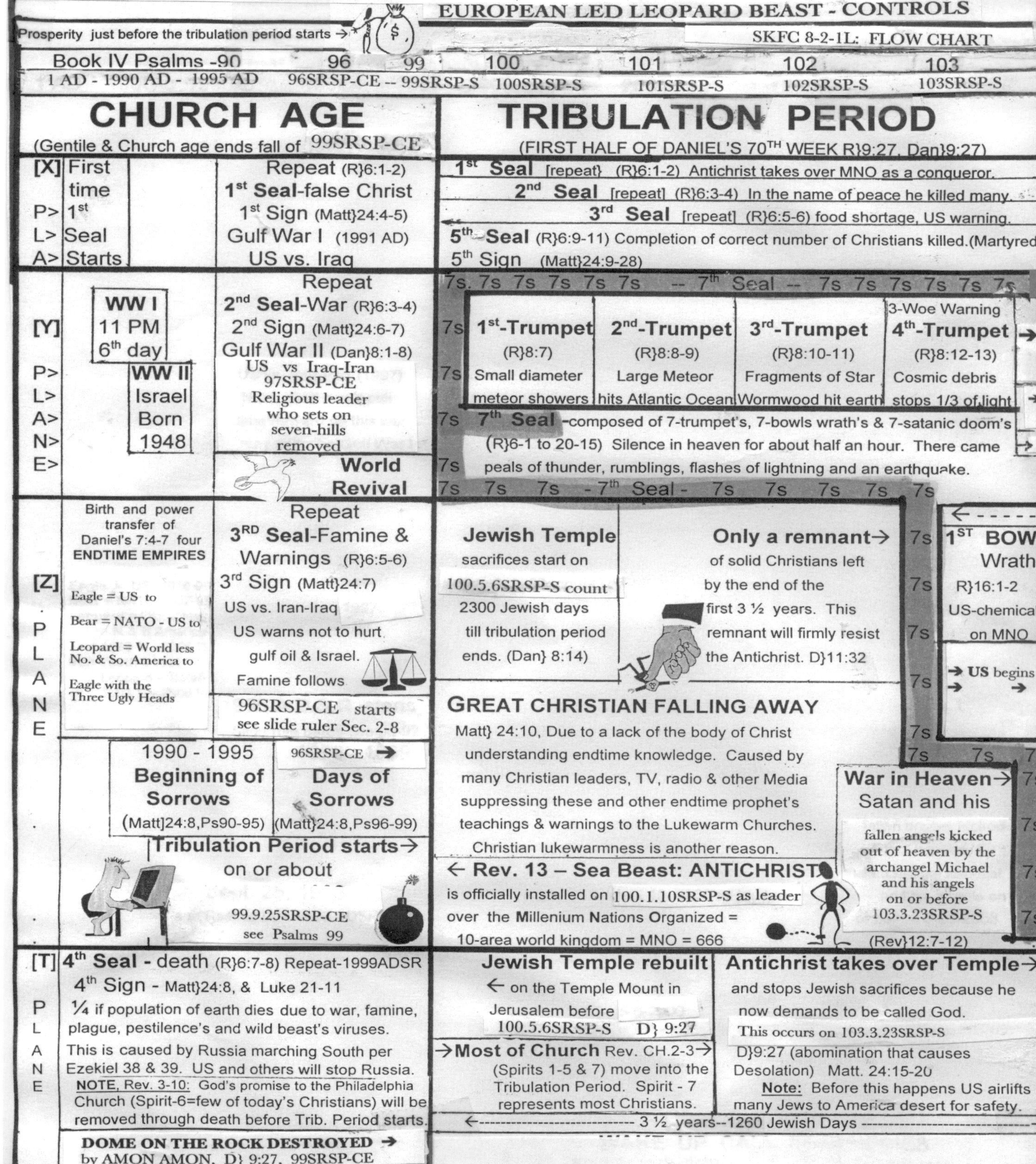

END TIME FLOW CHART

(Page - 245 of Scroll)

SKFC-8-2-1R - This was page 211 of Issue 1, from the Book, Wake Call Prophecies. It was upgraded in September 1996 and this is a copy of the original worksheet, which was done on a five-line word processor plus lots of tape and glue on what is now old paper. Note: Any locations listed 1996 or later are Slide Rule Positioning Points on God's end time slide ruler and not actual dates. They are only used for sequencing of events. (See section 2-8)

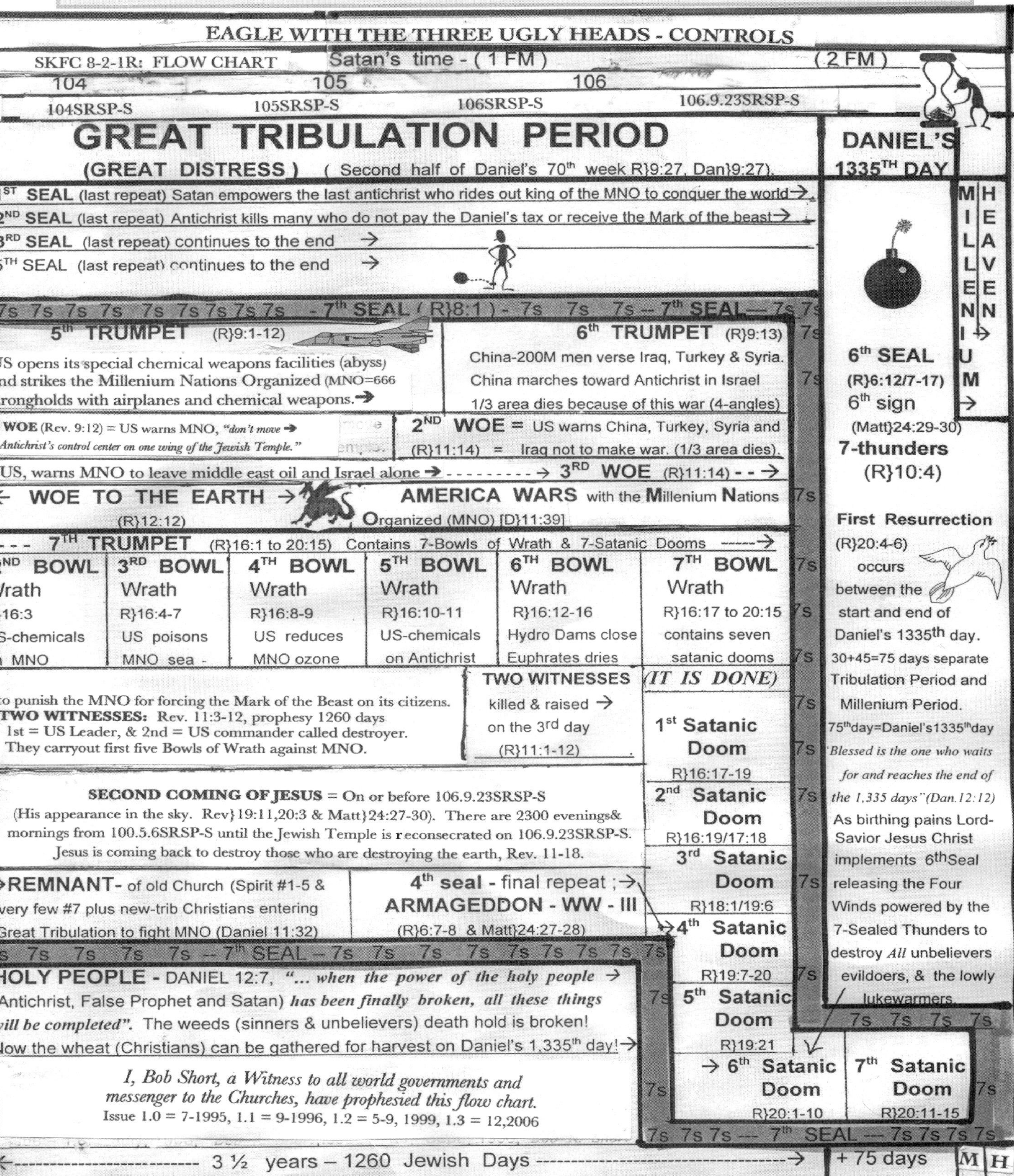

ORIGINAL ROUGH DRAFT, ISSUE - 1

100% PROPHESIED

PROPHECIES

CALCULATE YOUR OWN - ***MARK OF THE BEAST***
DATE JEWISH TEMPLE - *SACRIFICES START*
ANTICHRIST NAME - *(REVEALED)*

6+6+

HELP ME! ~~911~~
TRY THE NEW NUMBER.
011-972-6-66J-ESUS

Death by 2nd Hidden Mark (MNO)

---WARNING---
NON-BELIEVERS IN JESUS CHRIST BEWARE! WOE TO YOU FOR YOU SHOULD NOT BUY THIS BOOK OR READ THESE PROPHECIES! WOE TO YOU IF YOU DO !!! 1 COR. 14:22, "PROPHESY, HOWEVER, IS FOR BELIEVERS, **NOT** FOR UNBELIEVERS!" ONLY ONE EXCEPTION, JEWISH PEOPLE.

100% PROPHESIED
BY BOB R. SHORT, A SERVANT MESSENGER AND WITNESS TO THE WORLD FOR OUR LORD & SAVIOR JESUS CHRIST. (1994-95, ISSUE-1)

I SAW THE BEAST - see page - 159

FRONT COVER (SKFC 8-3-1) ↑

BACK COVER (SKBC 8-3-2) ↓

ISSUE- 1 BOOK COVER,

WITH PUZZLES AND MYSTERIES

Section 8-3, Page - 246

The mystery of the Christian writings, Ancient of Days, and the end time puzzle has slipped away from the grasp of man's intellect for centuries. But as we near the end of time, Christians understanding of the Book of Daniel is beginning to open and make rationale logic. Biblical study and insight through the Holy Spirit is now beginning to make sense out of the Book of Revelation and the other end time prophets.

You must be able to understand endtimes too! If you do not have a general idea about what is going to happen and prepare for it, ***you, your family, church, and nation may suffer for it.***

There are many hidden meaning on the back and front cover of The Wake Up Call Prophecies, Issue - 1. By studying this book The SCROLL, you should be able to answer the following questions and prepare:

WHY ARE

THE FOLLOWING ON THE FRONT AND BACK COVER ?

✯ There 18 digit mark, number, name/goal? ✯ Rome inside the "C" and the "C" inside the first "6"? ✯ CZS on the man's hand and not on his forehead? ✯ Image spewing out a ***web*** over the man? ✯ love, peace, and safety on his apron? ✯ the last six (6) a different color than the first two sixes and used to cut the mans head off? ✯ **the "Second Hidden Mark (MNO) the cause of death for the man and not the Mark of the Beast?** ✯ What's the international phone number all about? ✯ Two disc looking eyes with horns? ✯ The man's hand on the cord, which plugs the Image to its power source? ✯ Arrows pointing toward heaven? ✯ 911 crossed out? ✯ The C before the Z and S in the number ✯ The three 6's on the back cover if turned up side down look like they could make the neck and heads of the Eagle with the Three Ugly Heads? ✯ There are many other mysteries on the front and back cover of Issue - 1, can you find them and know what they mean?

Note: 911 (9-11) on front cover stealthy prophesying the twin towers (//) would fall (✕).

THE BEAST

Daniel 7:6

MILLENIUM NATIONS ORGANIZED

MNO

Section 9 - 1, Page = 247

Sketch 9-1-0: **The Beast**
(Sketch 9-1-0 derived from Sketch 9-1-2)

~~~~~~

I saw the Beast. Who is like the Beast?

Who can make war against him?

Prophesied, May 24, 1995.
Bob R. Short
~~~~~~

THE EAGLE, BEAR, LEOPARD BEAST, AND MICHAEL

Originally prophesied 9-1994 to 8-1995
in the book, WAKE UP CALL PROPHESIES, Issue-1, on pages 159 to 169.
Expanded insight to include Michael, July 1997.
PAGE - 248

TO MAKE THE BEAST FLIP CHART,

Overlay Sketch 9-1-1, on Sketch 9-1-2.
Hold up to bright light and see the MNO Beast!

FINAL TEN HORNS

1. Europe=(EU)=Spokesman England = Lion's Mouth EU = Old Revised Roman Empire (Revelation 13:3)
2. Russia = Chief Prince Rosh
3. Greenland + Antarctica
4. Africa
5. Middle East
6. Asia -- 200,000,000 Man Army
7. Australia + Oceania Areas
8. Israel (Jerusalem) World Capital
9. Japan (monetary)
10. Army from the South Egypt, Ethiopia, Libya

Sketch 9-1-1

~~~~~~~~~~~ (Sketch 9-1-1 derived from Sketch 9-1-2) ~~~~~~~~~~~~~~~~~~~~~~~~~~~~

US Eagle has come and gone!
The Great Prince Michael's resistance movement is increasing!
European NATO Bear is here killing Christians on the Moslem's side in the name of peace.
Ezekiel's - 38 War is next to happen! AMERICAN IS NOT READY !
Leopard Beast = World Government will form due to the destruction caused by Ezekiel's-38 war!

The Eagle (North America, Daniel 7:4) gains power and loses authority = 1918-1997. In 1997, authority was given to European NATO to fight its own war without the US. They added Russia to their meetings thus forming the above landmass of the NATO Bear. The above European NATO Bear with Russian troops invaded a Balkan nation for peace thus fulfilling the prophecy. God declares in Ezekiel 38:4, ***"I will turn you*** (European NATO Bear) ***around, put hooks in your jaws*** (Balkans) ***and bring you out with your whole army…"*** These conflicts in the Balkans along with Middle East problems causes the European NATO Bear to disintegrate internally. Ezekiel prophesied the Northern Army Alliance (Russia and others) would form and war south against Israel. This war occurs between the Bear and Leopard kingdoms. America and its allies will protect Israel by destroying the Northern army.
~~~~~~~~~~~

However, America will be hit with nuclear weapons because of its ineffective defense missile system. America's criticism against European led world government increases into what was prophesied as **Daniel's Firm Resistance** by Christians, in (Daniel 11:32). South America will follow USA's lead per Daniel 11:34, about none sincere countries joining them. The America's firm resistance gives birth to the prophetical form of the Great Prince Michael. These countries will rises to resist and battle the Beast, per Daniel 12:1. Michael's resistance will increase like birthing pains to the end.

The rest of the world will enter into a ten-kingdom government by merging similar nations into regions after Ezekiel's prophesied war. This government promises a better-unified world trade, money, taxes, peace, security and military agreements. Its only opposition is the Spirit-filled Christians belief that world harmony is achieved through disciple nations not world government. The land mass represented by this Government (without seas or divisions) will take the shape of the Leopard during the next 3 1/2 years. After this period, the Leopard nations will evolve into the Eagle with the Three Ugly Heads and will be completely controlled by Satan for another 3 1/2 years. Any nation, which signs the world trade and security agreement, must require their people (Revelation 13:17) to receive the Mark of the Beast on the hand or forehead. To buy one must get approval using three access codes = WWW (W is 6th Hebrew letter) = 666 in conjunction with the telephone Number of the Beast (Revelation 13:18) on the Internet Web of Deceit. This connects to the Name of the Beast (Revelation 13:17, New World Order (NWO) where the W is an upsidedown M. Therefore NWO = NMO = 666 on the phone pad.), which has authority to authorize the sale. This transaction will credit the proper world consumption tax (Daniel 11:20) to the world government.

Which side are you on, Michael's Firm Christian Resistance or the deceptive New World Order of Nations - MNO?

Below, 9-1-1 - Italy, Rome, Inside the Roman Forum: The Old Roman Empire is growing through the European Union (EU). It will try to hold the rule again, only to give its power up to the Eagle with the Three Ugly Heads (Last Beast). (Page-249)

FOUR END TIME SUPERPOWER GOVERNMENTS

From 11:00 PM to Midnight of the 6th sabbatical day. Prophesied and expanded 7-97 by Bob R. Short

See the Bear shaking hands with the Devil!

This denotes the Bear will be sympathetic toward Moslem nations and somewhat intolerant toward Christians and Israel. Jerusalem is a burdensome stone on top of the Devil and the heart of the Leopard Beast.

Ezekiel 38:4; ***"I will turn you*** (Bear) ***around*** (toward the map viewer), ***and put hooks in your jaws*** (Balkans) ***and bring you out with your whole army."***

This promotes world friction, mistrust and others VS Israel, England, USA, and others.

To make the BEAST FLIP CHART,

Overlay Sketch 9-1-1, on Sketch 9-1-2.

Hold up to bright light and see the MNO Beast!

~~~~~~~~~~~~~~~~~~ Sketch 9-1-2 ~~~~~~

To find the Eagle (Daniel 7:4): Most of North America. Tail = Alaska, Wings = Canada's Northern Islands, Head = Quebec, Body = USA, and legs = Mexico.

To find the Bear (Daniel 7:5): Remove USA from European NATO + Russia.

To find the Great Prince Michael (Daniel 12:1):

1. Move South America up underneath the USA where Northern tip of South America touches and fills the Gulf of Mexico, which forms legs to raise Michael.
2. Bring and fill in around Canada's northern Islands to form Michael's head!
3. The Peninsula D'Ungava down to Newfoundland forms the knife of resistance.
4. When the Americas are squeezed together, it forms The Great Prince Michael!

To find the Leopard Beast

(Revelation 13:1-2, or Daniel 2:31-43, 7:6-7): (Leopard Beast = Daniel's Ten Toes = Millennium Nations Organized = MNO = 666 = WWW [web])

1. Lay the top of England left against the land and move Greenland on top of England, forming the head with **A Mouth like a Lion (England).**
2. Push Africa straight up against Europe to eliminate all sea areas. This puts Jerusalem at the heart of the Beast. Jerusalem truly is the heartbeat and power center for the Beast. Antichrist moves control center to Jerusalem (Daniel 9:7).
3. Move all islands and Australia up underneath Asia. This forms fat back **legs with feet like a Bear!**
4. Move far eastern Russia's land tip around to form the tail of the Beast. Trace around solid land mass and discover the Revelation 13:2 = **resembles a Leopard with a mouth like a lion** (England) **and Fat feet like those of a bear.**

Summary of 6th day from 11:00 - 12:00 P.M. Biblical end time super power governments

The Book of Daniel 7:4 = [1st] Like a lion (England) but wings of an Eagle (America) becomes world super power WW-l and 2
" 7:5 = [2nd] (Bear) is world super power formed in 1997SRCP-CE and fulfilled in 1999SRCP-CE.
" 7:6 = [3rd] (Leopard) is world super power for the next 3 1/2 years
" 7:7 = [4th] (Large Iron Teeth Beast) Satan and Leopard join to form the most terrifying and powerful ten area world power ever known to man for the next 3 1/2 years. It is the Eagle with the Three Ugly Heads (Section 9-3).
~~~~~~~~~~~~~~~~~~

THE EAGLE WITH THE THREE UGLY HEADS!

Iron Teeth Beast

Section 9-2

found in the EZRA Apocalypse from the APOCRYPHA. Opens insight into Daniel's 7:7. (Hidden or Secret Books. Deuterocanonical Books of the Old Testament)
Prophesied by BOB R. SHORT between May-September, 1999,
with interruption from the original 1994-95 WAKE UP CALL PROPHECIES.

The Prophesied EAGLE begins

To complete the pieces to the puzzle of the EAGLE we must first believe and understand THE THREE BEASTS in the WAKE UP CALL PROPHECIES, "BEAST FLIP CHART". Otherwise, the Eagle's interruption will be greatly misunderstood!

It shall be essential the reader understand the flow of the "Beast Flip Chart". Then apply birthing pains to the flow of Beasts. All four Beast (Daniel 4-7) are here today, some totally and some growing to maturity. As the Eagle gives way to the Bear so it will give way to the Leopard and the Leopard will be devoured by the Final Beast (Eagle with the Three Ugly Heads). Now I will prophesy a great mystery which has been hidden in the word but shall be revealed.

2 ESDRAS 11 and 12 has been the predicted birth, growth through maturity and death of Daniel's 2:40-43 and Daniel's 7:7 fourth kingdom Beast which must be the same as the Revelation 13:11-18 second Beast. The EAGLE also includes the overthrow of many kings, alliances, nations and area-kingdoms which must be the same as the Revelation 13:1-12 first Beast (Leopard on the "Beast Flip Chart"). The climb to world control includes the guiding power of the spirit of Satan through a series of Antichrists trying to **hold the rule.** Now let us began as the Spirit guided me, to explore and understand the Eagle with the Three Ugly Heads, as it relates to present day and endtimes:

The First will give its power to the Second, while the Second folds to the Third, and the Third will be devoured by the Fourth.

But the astonishing fact is **all four Beasts are alive today in some form trying to hold the rule!**

THEY WILL ALL FAIL!

PROPHESIED INTERPRETATION

of 2 ESDRAS 11 and 12

11:1 Eagle out of the sea *of nations.* (4th kingdom of Daniel 2:40 and 7:7, Eagle made of **Iron** [nations and people controlled by Satan] and **clay** [Christians and their nations]) 12 feather covered wings = [represents the 12 star flag of the EU] {*ruling kings, one after another w/2nd reigning longest*} (longer than the 12). The EU represents the head in Revelation 13:3 that seemed to have a fatal wound which had been healed (old Roman Empire revitalized). It will be one of the ten area regions to form the Leopard Beast.

Three (3) (Ugly) Heads were resting *(at peace)* on the eagle *(three kings, renew many things, rule the earth, rule more oppressively* (terrible) *than all who were before them.*

Therefore, they are called the Ugly Heads of the Eagle. Note: The Ugly Heads do not speak because the mouth (Mediterranean Sea area) *is located in the Body.* Rome will speak first then Israel.

They will sum up his (Satan's) wickedness and perform his last actions.

[**Right Ugly Head** = Leader (final Antichrist) of the Large Iron Teeth Beast (Daniel 7:7), MNO nations.]

[**Middle or greater Ugly Head** = Leader of the United Nations (UN)]

[**Left Ugly Head** = Leader of Leopard Beast (the first of a line of Antichrists) (Daniel 7:6)]

11:2 Spread its wings over the whole earth [influences whole earth] all winds of heaven blew upon it [God wrath was against this Beast.] clouds were gathered around it [War surrounded these Beasts]

11:3 Out of these wings came opposing [Christian resistance, Daniel 11:32] (additional) wings *(great struggles, kingdom in danger of falling, but will regain its former power.)* They became little puny (dwarfish) wings [The resistance movement gets crushed (Revelation. 13:7 and 12:12). God gives authority to the Beasts and especially the 4th Beast to defeat the Christian for a limited time. (Daniel 7:22) Part of Christian's test. Revelation 3:10]

11:4 Its (Ugly) Heads were at rest; [rest means at peace with what the body, legs, claws, wings, and other heads were doing] middle head [UN] (greater) larger than the other two but it too was at rest with them

11:5 Eagle flew with its wings [power changing hands or U N moving] it reigned over the earth and over those who inhabit it.

11:6 All things under heaven were subjected to it [him] (Eagle with three Ugly Heads). No one spoke against it - not a single creature that was on the earth.

11:7 Eagle rises upon its talons (claws) [getting ready to make war in the name of peace]. The eagle uttered a cry to its wings,

11:8 "Do not all watch at the same time let each sleep in its own place [Area-Kingdom concept of merging like nations in a general area] each watch in its turn

11:9 but let the heads be reserved for the last."

11:10 This voice came from the middle [Rome and Israel where the Mediterranean Sea makes the Mouth of the Final Beast] of the (him) body *(of nations)* not the heads.

All things under heaven were subjected to it [him] (Eagle with Three Ugly Heads). No one spoke against it - not a single creature that was on the earth.

11:11 8 rival (additional) wings = [G7 + Russia = G8 = eight industrialized nations] *(Eight kings shall arise in it, whose times shall be short and their years swift; Two (2) shall perish when the middle of its time draws near. Four (4) shall be kept for the time when its end approaches. Two (2) shall be kept until the end.)*

11:12 one wing on the right side rose and reigned over all the earth. Its reign stopped with no trace.

And nothing remained on the eagle's body except Three {3} (Ugly) Heads that were at rest and six (6) Little Wings.

11:13 after a time its reign came to an end, it disappeared, so that even its place was no longer visible.

11:14 next (2nd) wing rose up and reigned for a long time. Its end came, it disappeared.

11:15-16 A voice sounded, saying, "Listen to me, .."

11:17 "after you *(two wings)* no one will rule as long as you have ruled, not even half as long."

11:18 3rd wing raised itself up and held the rule and it also disappeared

11:19 So it went with all (4th - 8th) the wings, they wielded power one after another and then were never seen again.

11:20 In due time the wings (little wings) that followed also rose up on the right side to rule (be emperor). Some ruled (emperor) and disappeared suddenly [G-8 breaks up and dissolves]

11:21 others rose up, but did not hold the rule (emperor).

11:22 After this: Twelve (12) wings [EU] and the two little wings had disappeared [has now became one kingdom of ten (10) area kingdoms that forms the 3rd Beast, a Leopard, of Daniel 7:6. See the Beast Flip Chart Section 9-1].

[First of the two little wings = WTO or a similar World Trade Organization.]

[Second of the two little wings = GATT or a similar trade organization]

11:23 and nothing remained on the eagle's body except three {3} (ugly) heads that were at rest and six (6) little wings [are six (6) people that protect, lead, or represents different areas that include all nations of the world.]

11:24 Two (2) little wings [Two Witnesses representing America] separated from the six [America will be pulling out of these world organizations and demanding equal trade and taxation among trading countries. This action starts the forming of the landmass of North and South America used by the Great Prince Michael who tries to protect Israel. (Daniel 12:1)] And remained under the head that was on the right side. *(These whom the Most High has kept for the eagle's end;)* Four (4) (little wings) remained in their place. [Daniel 7:6, 3rd Beast called the Leopard Beast gives the four (4) wings (kings) authority to rule the whole world except the Americas]

11:25 These little wings (4 little wings) planned to set (raise - promote) themselves up and hold the rule (become emperors).

11:26 one was set up (raised itself up), but suddenly disappeared; [King of the North (Daniel 11:15-19]
11:27 a second also and this disappeared more quickly than the first. [Daniel 11:20, His successor will send a tax collector to collect the world consumption tax"]
11:28 two remaining were planning between themselves to reign together [one king was the Prince of the Covenant, {Daniel 11:22}, (The Prince of the Covenant was the instigator in designing the seven-year peace pact, covenant, treaty and/or alliance. Many nations and organizations which include Israel and the Final Antichrist, will agree with this covenant. This will be viewed by the world as just another peace agreement and will be a non-signed event.)] [the second was the King of the South (Daniel 11:25)]
11:29 While they were planning, one of the heads that were at rest (the ugly one in the middle) suddenly awoke [UN became angry and opposed to the two wings plan]; it was greater than the other two heads.
11:30 Middle (Ugly) head allied the two heads with itself
11:31 The big (ugly) head turned with those that were with it and devoured the two little wings that were planning to reign.
11:32 The Big (Ugly) Head [UN] gained control (master) of the whole earth with much oppression dominated its inhabitants; it had greater power over the world than all the wings that had gone before.
11:33 After this the Big (ugly) Head [UN] suddenly disappeared, just as the wings had done. *(one king shall die in his bed, but in agonies)*, [UN will disband because of internal fighting and disagreements. Now we see the world busting up into the 4th Beast of Daniel in chapter 2 and 7. This Beast will be made of Iron (countries against Christ) and Clay (countries for Christ).]
11:34 Two (Ugly) heads remained *(sword shall devour them.)*, which also in like manner ruled over the earth and its inhabitants.
11:35 The (ugly) head on the right side [The leader of the Large Iron Teeth Beast Kingdom, Daniel 7:7] devour (ate up) the (ugly head) one on the left [The leader (war hero) of the Leopard Beast Kingdom, Daniel 7:6] *(for the sword of one shall devour him who was with him; but he also shall fall by the sword in the last days.)*

A Lion Roused from the Forest

11:36 a voice said; "Look in front of you and consider what you see." [The Spirit moved me to write the following interpretation to prophesy.]
11:37 Then a lion was roused (rose out of) from the forest, [Jesus Christ's 2nd coming] roaring [upset, mad and full of vengeance]; it (he) uttered a human voice to the eagle.

Are you not the one that remains of the four beasts (animals) that I had made to reign in My world, so that the end of My times might come through them?

11:38 Listen and I will speak to you. The Most High says to you,
11:39 Are you not the one that remains of the four beasts (animals) that I had made to reign in my world, so that the end of my times might come through them?
11:40 Fourth Beast [Large Iron Teeth Beast, Daniel 7:7] conquered all the beast (animal) that have gone before; have held sway over the world with great terror, over all the earth with grievous (harsh) oppression; lived on the earth so long with deceit
11:41 You have judged the earth, but not with truth.
11:42 You have oppressed (persecuted) the meek and injured (hurt) the peaceable; you have hated those who tell the truth, loved liars, destroyed the homes of those who brought forth fruit, have laid low (torn down) the walls of those who did you no harm.

The (ugly) **head on the right side** [The leader of the Large Iron Teeth Beast Kingdom, Daniel 7:7] **devour** (ate up) **the** (ugly head) **one on the left** [The leader (war hero) of the Leopard Beast Kingdom,]

11:43 Your insolence has come up before the Most High, your pride to the Mighty One.
11:44 The Most High has looked at his times; now they have ended and his ages have reached completion.
11:45 Therefore you, eagle, will surely disappear, you and your terrifying (dreadful) wings, your evil little (additional) wings, your malicious (malignant) heads your most evil (cruel) talons (claws), [The bird of pry's talons represents Satan's power through the Antichrist to honor the god of fortresses, Daniel 11:38-39.] your whole worthless body

11:46 so whole world freed from your violence may be refreshed and hope for judgment and mercy.
12:1 While the lion *(Messiah)* was saying these words to the eagle
12:2 the remaining (ugly) head [on the right, the king over the Large Iron Teeth Beast Daniel 7:7] had disappeared. [This disappearance or going under cover will be caused by the Two Witnesses from the US ordering chemical weapons on the Final Antichrist's strong hold in Israel and plunging his kingdom into darkness per the 5th Bowl of Wrath (Revelation 16:10-11]. The two wings [Two Witnesses] that had gone over to it rose up (see 2 ESDRAS 11:24) and set themselves up to reign, and their reign was brief (short) and full of tumult (uproar)

[The Two Witnesses using the power of the USA to bring the following judgments for God to knock the 4th Beast to its knees:]

✪ The 1st - 5th Bowl judgments, Revelation 16:1-11. These judgments are actions by the USA against the 4th beast with Iron teeth (MNO=666). Note: The 5th Bowl begins the turning point of the downfall of the 4th Beast. USA uses chemical weapons against his strong hold in Israel plunging it into darkness.

✪ The 5th Trumpet judgments, open special chemical weapons facilities (abyss) and strike Millenium Nations Organized (MNO) = 666 on phone pad. Revelation 9:1-12

✪ 1st Woe Warning, US warns Millennium Nations Organized to move Antichrist's control center out of the Jewish Temple. Revelation 9:12

✪ 2nd Woe Warning, China, Turkey, Syria and Iraq not to make war. One third of area dies in war. Revelation 11:14

✪ 3rd Woe Warning, leave the middle east oil and Israel alone, Revelation 11:14

✪ 1st Satanic Doom; America and God cause financial collapse of the MNO to start. (Revelation 16:17-19) *(Two little wings the Most High has kept for the Eagle's end;* this was the reign which was brief and full of tumult)
12:3 and (they) vanished (disappeared) [Revelation 11:3-12, "the Two Witnesses went up to heaven in a cloud."] whole body (world) of the Eagle was burned [Battle of Armageddon, 4th Seal, Revelation 19:17-19, the world is made of Iron and Clay. The Iron represents nations wanting a global government with religious tolerance. The Clay represents nations believing in individual Disciple Nations working in harmony with Jesus Christ' teachings. The Clay represents the nations which Daniel 11:32 prophesied would have firm resistance. Jesus Christ and the Clay will fight the Iron nations in the Battle of Armageddon.] earth was exceedingly terrified (panic - stricken). [6th Seal, Revelation 6:12, 7:17, People will be panic-stricken from the Battle of Armageddon to Daniel's 1335th Day. On that day, God will destroy the world (surface area) as we know it and the first resurrection will occur.]

9-2-1- Israel, Jerusalem - **Temple Mount: The Final Antichrist** ***will try to hold the rule from atop the Temple Mount inside the newly built Jewish Third Temple. The Two Witness will dish him up some misery. They will eventually put his kingdom into darkness and total chaos before they themselves are taken out. All four Beasts must birth and die to complete the testing cycle (Revelation 3:10) programmed by Almighty God.***

SEE THE LAST BEAST

Summary of insight through rough draft sketches into Daniel's 4th Beast was obtained from expanding the insight from the Beast Map using sketch 9-1-1 and sketch 9-1-2. This was derived from 2nd Esdras 11 and 12 = Final Beast in Daniel 2 and 7, and the two Beasts in Revelation 13. Insight received May - July of 1999, Bob R. Short.

The 4th and Final Beast evolved through a series of organizations, leaders and area kingdom governments which struggle to rule and influence the world with ideas on religion, trade, taxation, peace, and security. Each ruler equates to an Antichrist if they do not promote Jesus Christ' Great Commission to "Go make disciples of all nations", (Matthew 28:19-20). Iron represents nations (Daniel 2:40-43) who will try to establish world government without Jesus Christ. The Clay in, Daniel 2:40-43, is Christians nations, leaders, and many people. Review the birth and death of the 4th and Final Beast:

Daniel's 7:5 European NATO Bear will dissolves when Gulf war III (Ezekiel 38 and 39) begins. This war involves a northern army of Russia, Germany (sympathetic), Iran, and other nations marching south toward Israel. They will be stopped by USA, Britain, Israel and other nations. After this war, the NATO Bear's power will be transferred to a new European concept in area government, which looks like a Leopard (Daniel 7:6, 3rd Beast) [see the WAKE UP CALL PROPHECIES Beast Flip Chart]. The 4th Beast of Daniel 7:7 (Iron teeth Beast) is evolving today before our eyes.

Rough draft Sketch - 9-3-0

☜ - RIGHT SIDE <----------> LEFT SIDE - ☞

THE EAGLE WITH THE THREE UGLY HEADS

How to find the Eagle using Sketch 9-1-1 and 9-1-2: Move all land mass together without seas (except Mediterranean sea - this forms the mouth, and a small space between Michael and the Leopard to represent opposing sides). Where South America and Africa come together add the right leg with the talons. Add the left leg with talons on the bottom of Australia. Now add three heads to symbolize three powerful Antichrist leaders to complete the Eagle with the Three Ugly Heads.

The Birth and Death of the

FINAL BEAST

I prophesied concerning insight into most of the parts of the Eagle with the Three Ugly Heads trying to control the world's last empires, organizations, countries, regions, and alliances.

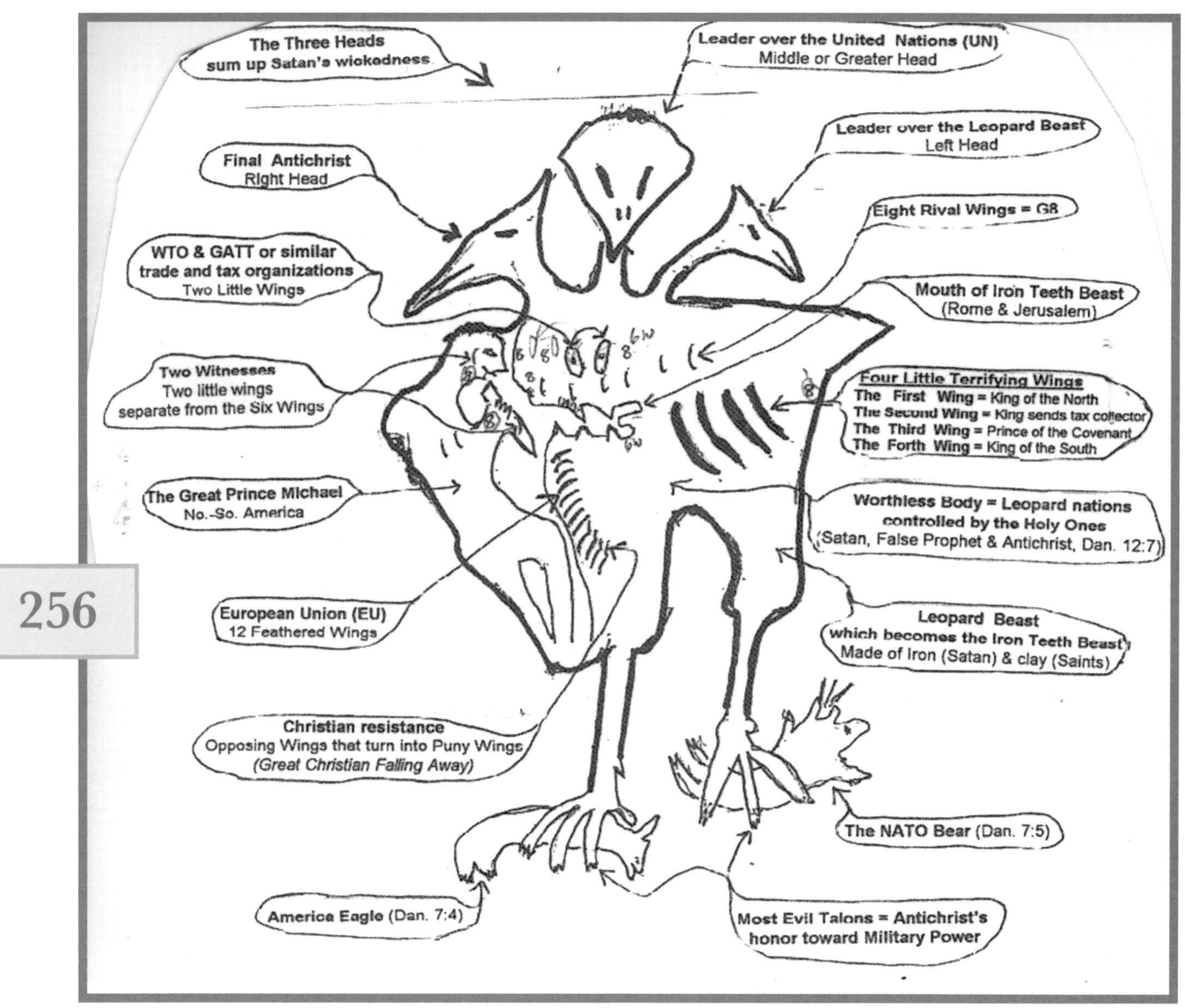

- RIGHT SIDE <-----------> LEFT SIDE -
SK 9-3-1, ESDRAS 11 and 12 - COMPLETE SKETCH:

DANIEL 7:4-7, FOUR BEASTS ARE LIVING TODAY.

The first will try to hold the rule and fail. The second will try to hold the rule and will also fail only to be absorbed by the third. It will try to hold the rule but will be devoured by the fourth and final Beast. It does not win and will be destroyed by Jesus Christ's second coming! The first will be first, and the second, second, while the third is third but they all live today with the fourth.

The Eagle or 4th Beast (11:1) is forming before our eyes as the 2 ESDRAS 11 and 12 prophesied. The 12-feathered wings (11.1) represent the 12 stared flag of the EU, which represents 12 kings. The three (3) heads (11.1) are:

✪ **Right head (11:34-35) Final Antichrist over Large Iron Teeth Beast, (Daniel 7:7 and Revelation 13:11-18).**

✪ **Middle or greater (11:4) head is the leader of the UN.**

✪ **Left head (11:34-35) Leader (war hero) over the Leopard Beast = Daniel 7:6, 3rd Beast or Revelation 13:1-10.**

The opposing wings (11:3) represent Christian resistance within the area of the Leopard Beast's body. They will be neutralized and become weak wings, which represents the Great Christian Falling Away (Matthew 24:10). This opposition along with other problems causes the UN power base to shift (11:5) from America soil toward Europe. Rome (11:10) begins issuing instructions and warnings that irritate the Leopard Beast. Then there are eight (8) rival wings (11:11) which represent the old G-7 + Russia = new G-8. These wings represent leaders of 8 industrialized nations that try their hand of influence with world trade and peace problems. They come and go with little affect (11:11-20). The G-8 eventually disappears and breaks up (11:20).

After this, we see the EU and the two little Wings (11:22) loose their power and are merged into the 3rd Beast (Leopard). These two Wings represent two world tax and trade organizations such as but not limited to WTO and GATT.

The only leaders of nations or kingdoms left on earth now are the three (3) heads listed above at rest (peace). There are six (6) little Wings (11:23), which represent, protect, or lead areas that include every nation in the world.

Two little wings separate (11:24) from the six wings (11:25). The two little Wings represents the Two Witnesses influence on America's leadership into having disagreements with the four other Wings on how to stop Christian persecution and administer world tax, trade, and peace keeping efforts. Eventually their harping gets the America's booted out of the assembly. This opens the door for the 3rd Beast (Leopard) to be born as Daniel 7:6 prophesied (11:25).

- RIGHT SIDE <----------> LEFT SIDE -

SK-9-3-2, ESDRAS 11:1-21:
TRANSITION OF DANIEL'S 4th BEAST
2 Esdras 11 & 12 = Final Beast in Daniel 2 & 7,
& the two Beasts in Revelation 13

1st Wing
King o the North

2nd Wing
King who sends out a tax collector

3rd Wing
Prince of the Covenant

4th Wing
King of the South

Other Two Wings
Two Witnesses

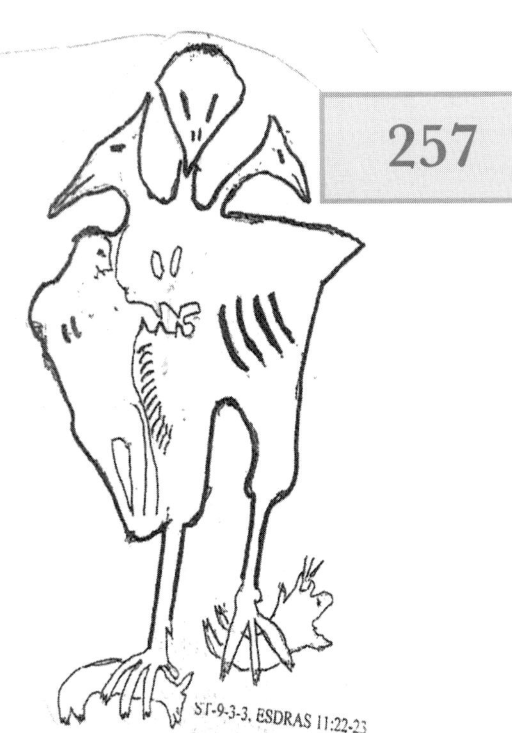

- RIGHT SIDE <----------> LEFT SIDE -

SK-9-3-3, ESDRAS 11:22-23:
TRANSITION OF DANIEL'S 4th BEAST
2 Esdras 11 & 12 = Final Beast in Daniel 2 & 7,
& the two Beasts in Revelation 13

Four (4) little wings (ESDRAS 11:25) try to put themselves in charge of the 3rd Leopard Beast. The first Wing (King of the North) tries to lead and fails (Daniel 11:18-19). His successor the second Wing sends out a tax collector and tries to lead but fails (Daniel 11:20).

The 3rd and 4th wings are: Prince of the Covenant (Daniel 11:22) who instigated a covenant among many nations and alliances including Israel and the Final Antichrist; the 4th is the King of the South (Daniel 11:25). The Prince and the King plot to rule (11:28). This makes the UN rally (11:30) the other two heads. One of the heads is an alliance that will turn into the third Beast-Leopard (MNO) and the other head is an alliance, which will turn into the last Beast. This three-headed alliance will oppose and devour (11:31) the two kings (the Prince of the Covenant and the King of the South). The UN became very great and oppressed the inhabitants of the world (11:32).

Due to wars in Europe and with Moslems nations the UN begins to inappropriately forced its agenda on many. This causes internal problems in the UN, which are irreversible. The UN (the Big Ugly Head in the middle) suddenly breaks up (11:33) in favor of the Leopard Beast (MNO). There are two Heads remaining, one on the left - the Leader over the Leopard Beast and the other on the right - the Final Antichrist over what is left of the Eagle (11:34). This occurs about the same time Satan is kicked out of heaven to the earth.

ST-9-3-5, ESDRAS 11:33-34:

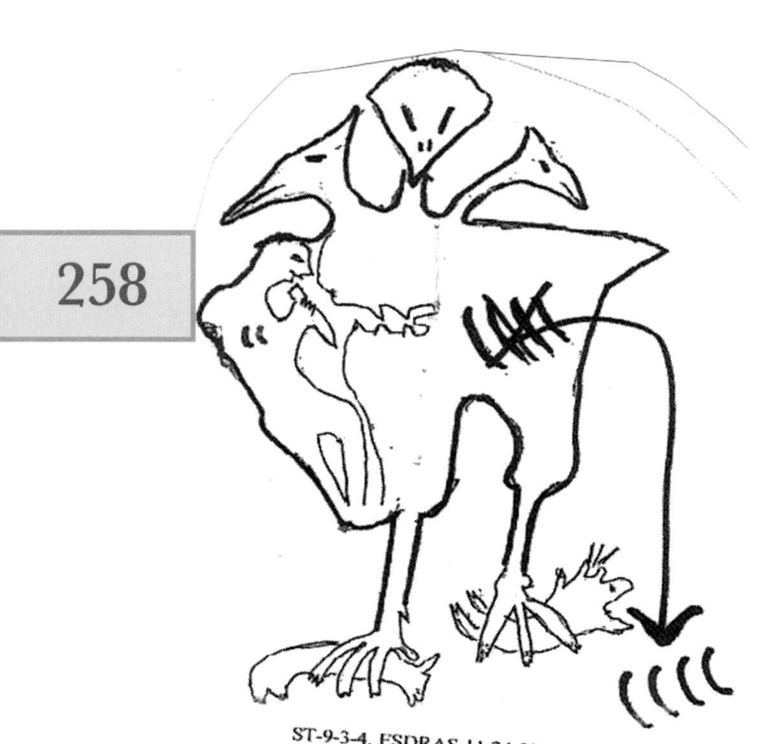

ST-9-3-4, ESDRAS 11:24-32:

- RIGHT SIDE <----------> LEFT SIDE -

SK-9-3-4, ESDRAS 11:24-32:
TRANSITION OF DANIEL'S 4th BEAST
2 Esdras 11 & 12 = Final Beast in Daniel 2 & 7,
& the two Beasts in Revelation 13

- RIGHT SIDE <----------> LEFT SIDE -

SK-9-3-5, ESDRAS 11:33-34:
TRANSITION OF DANIEL'S 4th BEAST
2 Esdras 11 & 12 = Final Beast in Daniel 2 & 7,
& the two Beasts in Revelation 13

Satan uses his deceiving spirit to influence people to change leadership in some countries while enticing other kings of the Leopard Beast. They will give authority to the Final Antichrist over that area (all area of the world except the North and South America) which transforms it into Daniel's Final Beast with iron teeth. This in reality equates to the Ugly Head on the left (Leopard) being removed or devoured. By process of elimination, the Eagle now only has one Ugly Head on the right (Daniel's 4th Beast).

The Final Antichrist will plot and use enticing persuasion to wheeled his distasteful power over the entire world. Note: Michael the Prince (North and South America) will oppose him. The Final Antichrist invades Israel and devours its leader (11:35). This aggression rouses a Lion (11:37) which represents Jesus Christ's second coming as the Lion of the tribe of Judah. The power base to promote peace and security will be moving from Rome to Israel with the Final Antichrist as its king. The Two Witnesses accuse the Final Beast of oppressing the meek, injuring the peaceable, and hating the truth while promoting liars. Its insolence has come up before the Most High (11:43).

The Lukewarm Church fails to understand and therefore does not fulfill the Great Commission of Jesus Christ. Therefore, God elevates Two Witnesses to the forefront to try to fulfill the literal interpretation of the commission "make disciples nations not ask them". They will begin to use military force to rebuke the Final Antichrist's disrespectfulness to prepare the kingdom for our Lord and Savior Jesus Christ. One of the Witnesses (11:24) is the leader of the USA and the other will be its military leader. They lead a rebellion against the 4th Beast. The 4th Beast is generally wining but the Two Witnesses managed to knock the 4th Beast on its knees with the 5th Bowl of Wrath. When US warplanes drop chemical weapons on the Final Antichrist's strong hold in Israel (Revelation 16:10-11).

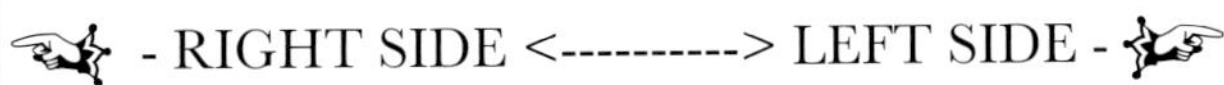

SK-9-3-6, ESDRAS 11:35-43:
TRANSITION OF DANIEL'S 4th BEAST
2 Esdras 11 & 12 = Final Beast in Daniel 2 & 7,
& the two Beasts in Revelation 13

SK-9-3-7, ESDRAS 11:44-46:
TRANSITION OF DANIEL'S 4th BEAST
2 Esdras 11 & 12 = Final Beast in Daniel 2 & 7,
& the two Beasts in Revelation 13

The Two Witnesses attend a peace conference in Israel (12:2) in a last ditch effort to stop world war (Armageddon). They try to convince the nations of the world the object in the sky headed toward earth is Jesus Christ (11:37) and it will be useless to make war with Him. Their effort fails and they are ambushed in the street and killed on the way back to the airport. Their bodies lay in the street for 3 1/2 days.

The Two Witnesses come to life and are raised up to Jesus in the air while the world watches on the Internet web of deceit. The Two Witnesses failed and Jesus Christ Himself must return to fulfill His Own Great Commission (Matthew 28:19-20).

Next, we see the whole body of the Eagle being burned (12:3). This will be the battle of Armageddon where Jesus turns the tide of victory to the Saints (Daniel 7:21-22). After this, the earth will be exceedingly terrified (12:3). God unleashes the 6th Seal, which hits full force on Daniel's 1335th Day and destroys the evildoers, unbelievers and Christian cowards. Note; on that day the first Resurrection will occur and then the Judgment Seat of Christ. Fear God!

SK-9-3-8, ESDRAS 12:1-2:
TRANSITION OF DANIEL'S 4th BEAST
2 Esdras 11 & 12 = Final Beast in Daniel 2 & 7,
& the two Beasts in Revelation 13

- RIGHT SIDE <----------> LEFT SIDE -

SK-9-3-9, ESDRAS 12:3:
TRANSITION OF DANIEL'S 4th BEAST
2 Esdras 11 & 12 = Final Beast in Daniel 2 & 7,
& the two Beasts in Revelation 13

Come quickly Lord Jesus and have mercy on your people. Insight received between May - July of 1999, Amen, and Amen!

Prophesied by Bob R. Short, a Witness to the world governments and messenger to the Churches for Jesus Christ our Lord and Savior!

GLOSSARY

Section 10-1

3-1-1996 to 2007 PROPHESIED Glossary of Terms, Words and Phrases.

NOTE: These are prophesied words and terms associated with the Wake Up Call Prophecies. Some of these are not standard definitions but how the Holy Spirit communicated to me.

✪ ***ABOMINATION THAT CAUSES DESOLATION:*** The Image of the Beast is set up on a wing of the temple, which begins the abomination that causes desolation. It is a massive computer center to control the world through the ten area kingdom, MNO. The beast uses the Internet web of deceit to concentrate his agenda.

✪ ***A.D.S.R.:*** This sequencing point was used in Issue-1 of the original Wake Up Call Prophecies, published in book form 3-1-96. The S.R. in A.D.S.R. means slide rule dates designation point on God's slide ruler of end time events and not an actual date. This sequencing begins with Psalms 96 and runs through 106. God may push all events out between the time period (Issue one designation =1996 A.D.S.R. and 1999 A.D.S.R., and this book the SCROLL = 96SRSP-CE to 99SRSP-S) and start of the tribulation period later to save more souls. Once the tribulation starts these signs and events begin to surface, they will complete the whole cycle in the approximate lapping and overlapping order and time sequence prophesied.

Why was slide rule DATES dropped from Issue-1 in favor of POINTS used in this book the SCROLL? There was too much confusion in placing a slide rule date on a designated point of God's slide ruler of time. All insight received was from Book Four of the Psalms not from dates. Therefore, sequence of events are more important than trying to determine current dates since we are instructed to learn and then watch for signs and sequences of events. Otherwise 2000 A.D.S.R. positioning point on God's slide ruler of endtimes is identical to positioning point designated by 100SRSP-S.

✪ ***ANGELS:*** Part of the armies of heaven coming back with Jesus Christ during the second coming which will be on, or before, Saturday, 106.9.23SRSP-S.

✪ ***ANTICHRIST:*** (1 John 2:18-19) Any person or leader who does not acknowledge Jesus Christ as Lord and Savior. These people openly go against Jesus' teachings. The final lawless man that is against Christ and leader over the MNO. (One of the Heroes of Gulf War III - 99SRSP-CE) The final (Last) Antichrist will lead the last Beast, the Eagle with the three ugly Heads.

✪ ***APOCALYPSE:*** The Book of Revelation is known as the apocalypse. The word revelation comes from the Greek word apocalypse, meaning an uncovering or unveiling.

✪ ***Azra'il:*** Equates to the (proper) Islamic understanding of the angel of death, also can be known as Malikul Mawt.

✪ ***BABYLON (POLITICAL):*** Political Babylon is an area that controls the world monetary system and is located on earth as described in Revelation, Chapter 18, as Political Babylon.

✪ ***BABYLON (RELIGIOUS):*** Rome is Religious Babylon, the city that sits on seven hills. The false prophet will control this city. This city will be destroyed in 106SRSP-S.

✪ ***BEAST (REVELATION 13:1, SEA):*** The Millenium Nations Organized (MNO) is the (Sea) Beast: The world will be divided into ten area kingdoms headed up by a Antichrist to bring world peace and prosperity. It is the same as Daniel's ten toes of iron and clay, which equates to the same as the MNO. He will be given power over the MNO to bring peace to the world on Monday, 100.1.10SRSP-S.

✪ ***BEAST (REVELATION 13:11, EARTH):*** The Eagle with the three ugly Heads will be the Beast-of-nations led by the final Antichrist. The false prophet will rule from the Seven Hills of Rome and later from Jerusalem. He and the Antichrist will collect a consumption tax to keep both their agendas moving ahead. They promote morality, tolerance and world peace without salvation through Jesus Christ.

✪ ***BEGINNING OF SORROWS:*** Part of a six-year period before the tribulation period starts. The beginning of sorrows represent the first six chapters of Book Four of Psalms. Psalms 90 to 95 equal the years 1990 A.D. to 1995 A.D. These six years include the First Seal plus one Gulf War. For a list of signs and events, refer to Matthew 24:4-8 and Luke 21:8-11.

✪ ***BIRTHING PAINS:*** This expression is to explain the pain and sorrow associated with the progressive acceleration of events described in Matthew 24:4-8, Luke 21:8-11, and the Book of Revelation.

✪ ***BLAMELESS:*** The blameless Christian has been obedient to God's Commands and has walked the straight and narrow path. However, this does not mean they are perfect.

✪ ***BORN AGAIN, (TO BE):*** An experience of the second birth in the Spirit (John 3:3-21). To be born again, a person first must show positive action through a heartfelt repenting request to God for help. A belief Jesus Christ died for their sins. Then God will give this person the faith required to accept His free gift of grace. This newborn in the Spirit now must pick up the cross and follow God's command as evidence of his salvation. The first order of business for a newborn Christian is to study themselves approved unto God. Studying helps the newborn to distinguish right from wrong. It more quickly helps them understand God's will in their lives to perform good works for Him.

✪ ***(C,Z,S) NUMBER (SEQUENCE):*** The three sequences of the Mark of the Beast. Look at each individual letter in glossary to determine meaning.

✪ ***(C) NUMBER (SEQUENCE):*** This is the third sequence of the Mark of the Beast. It consists of one column, one digit loop. Options to buy, sell, deposit, save, transfer, and other transactions are sent to the computer over the Internet web of deceit. This is a voluntary sequence, not a forced sequence.

✪ ***CALLED:*** Christians God has called out of the body of Christ to help in the tribulation period. They will help the chosen and faithful followers (Revelation 17:14) ".... who have been called who are loved by God the Father and kept by Jesus Christ." (Jude 1)

✪ ***CALL TO ARMS:*** A defensive action by men (not women) used when a pastor will call for the physical protection of the church building and/or its members from destruction. (Luke 22:36, "Protect ourselves using weapons.")

✪ ***CHOSEN:*** The elect are God's chosen people. The Jews were the first people chosen (Deuteronomy 7:6). Then special chosen Christians (Acts 1:2, Revelation 3:4-5) were next. Chosen end time Christians with the Spirit of Church Number Five never will lose their name out of the book of life.

✪ ***CHURCH AGE:*** Represents 1 A.D. to 99SRSP-CE or two sabbatical days.

✪ ***CHRISTIAN (BROAD-TERM):*** Broad-term Christian as I use it in this book includes the widest grouping of people who think they are Christians. It includes lukewarmer Christians, backslidden Christians, fearless Christians, Christians that continue in sin from lack of knowledge or disobedience, regular Christians, solid, and wise Spirit-filled Christians. The above list of Christians is worldly labels. God does not judge some of these Christians. He calls them by their rightful names - sinner or hell-bound lukewarmer.

✪ ***COMMAND KEEPERS:*** A term referring to trustworthy and obedient men following the UACC commands.

✪ ***CONFUSED TIME:*** Time between Jewish New Year (usually last of September to first of October) and Western world's new year (January first).

✪ ***CONSUMPTION TAX:*** A world sales tax placed on nations within the MNO to eventually fund the agendas of the Antichrist and the False Prophet. A tax will be paid on what each person buys or sells by using the Mark of the Beast (6+6+6). Wholesale as well as retail goods and many services will have this tax levied on it.

✪ ***COWARD:*** A coward is classified as a Christian who does not physically protect his family, brethren, church house, and/or nation. Generally this will be talking about a man since God demanded he protect what He gave him in Genesis 2:15. However, a man or women can be judged cowardly (Revelation 21:8) and sentenced to the fiery lake of burning sulfur.

✪ ***DANIEL'S 1335 DAY:*** The Battle of Armageddon will end. People will be panic-stricken for the Great Tribulation is over and the 6th Seal starts and runs through 75 days until Daniel's 1335th Day. On that day God will destroy the world (surface area) as we know it and the first resurrection will occur.

✪ ***DANIEL'S SEVENTIETH WEEK:*** Daniel's seventieth week is the dreadful tribulation period represented by Saturday, 99.9.25SRSP-CE to Saturday, 106.9.23SRSP-S, God literally will cut time and insert Daniel's last week (seven years) between the end of the Gentile Age and the thousand year reign with Jesus Christ. It will be a time of God's wrath on a disobedient world. Daniel's seventieth week will end with the second coming of Jesus Christ.

✪ ***DANIEL'S TEN TOES OF IRON AND CLAY:*** The ten toes represent how the world will be divided into ten area kingdoms, headed by the Antichrist, to bring world peace and prosperity. The ten toes are the same as the Revelation 13 Sea and land Beast which equate to the Millennium Nations Organized (MNO).

✪ ***DISCIPLE NATION:*** Disciple nation is found in the first reading of the great commission when Jesus Christ gave His church leaders (Matthew 28:18-20) the command to make Christian nations. This command consists of building the trinity of a disciple nation. The trinity of a disciple nation will have its laws, government, and people in harmony with the Holy Bible. A disciple nation will receive blessings in the form of a blanket of protection by God from harm.

✪ ***DISCIPLE OF CHRIST:*** A true Spirit-filled Christian that follows Jesus Christ's teachings. Lukewarmers are not Disciples of Christ.

✪ ***DRAGON:*** Satan.

✪ ***EAGLE WITH THE THREE UGLY HEADS (MNO):*** Fourth Beast in Daniel 2:40-43 and 7:7, 2 ESDRAS 11 and 12, and Revelation 13:11-18. A combination of nations-states or regions working with other world alliances, and trade organizations will try to hold the rule.

✪ ***E✞C✞S:*** See Eli✞e Chris✞ian Soldier's below and section 4-15.

✪ ***ELECT:*** The same as chosen. God has entered into a special relationship with this end time Christian through whom He has decided to fulfill His purpose concerning prophetical end time events.

✪ ***Eli✞e Chris✞ian Soldier's (E✞C✞S):*** Soldiers of Almighty God's mighty army on earth. Christian protectorship in the tribulation period is their duty to lead the offensive charge in protecting Israel, USA, and other Christian Nations opposing the MNO.

✪ ***ENDTIMER:*** An endtimer is a term used for Christians (includes lukewarmers) living in the last days between 1990 A.D. to 106SRSP-CE.

✪ ***FAITHFUL FOLLOWERS:*** The faithful followers are the Christians who are called Saints. They hate evil (Psalm 31:23) and they will defend their beliefs in Christ. They will denounce one-world religion and world government - Millennium Nations Organized (MNO).

✪ ***FALSE PROPHET:*** The false prophet is spoken of as a religious leader operating with in the tribulation period. He teams up with the MNO headed by the final Antichrist to try to achieve world peace and prosperity. He tries to force on mankind a one-world religion and obedience to the Antichrist. He comes from the city on seven hills called Rome and promotes morality and salvation without Jesus Christ.

✪ ***FINGER SCAN:*** Technology that uses biometrics to measure and then calculate these measurement into a numeric X-Y-Z grid to identify the potential user. It currently is being used on such body parts as eyes, forehead, face, hands, and finger (fingerprint). Man can now become his own user-identity platform, because his personal body biometrics will carry his key to identifying with the Beast computers (Internet web of deceit). This will evolve into the first part of the Mark of the Beast used to determine the "S-Number, (social identity)" when the Final Antichrist takes over the system in the Great Tribulation.

✪ ***FIRST READING-MEANING # 1:*** Meaning deeper understanding, (associated with the seven time planes of understanding of Christian writings: First reading is the same as the literal meaning of a Bible verse, not the first time it is read. The insight received from the first reading (literal) must be in harmony with the second through the sixth readings of the Bible. Great caution and restraint must be adhered to so individuals do not think they possess the power to change the literal word of God into something else, for which we have only their word. The second through the sixth readings are only obtained through guidance from the Holy Spirit and not how many times the verse is read. Example: The literal word used in the parable of Matthew 25:14-30 is talents. The word burden, proclaim the good news of Jesus Christ, or following God's commands could be inserted for talents. Each three different interpretations are in harmony with the first and could make an interesting topic to understand better the full knowledge of God. But always keep in mind these interpretations are not a license to alter the actual or literal meaning.

✪ ***FIRST READING-MEANING # 2:*** As pertaining to the first time a word, verse, or instructions are given in the Bible as if you started reading from the front and continued to the end. This term means nothing except it is how the Holy Spirit communicated with me about some verses.

✪ ***FREE WILL:*** Man's choice to decide between good and evil.

✪ ***GENTILE AGE (TWO-DAYS):*** In these prophecies the expression Gentile Age represents sabbatical days five and six of a total seven days which involve Jesus' goal. His goal is to purchase men for His Father (Revelation 5:9) and to establish His own kingdom. The two-day Gentile Age represents 1 A.D. to 99SRSP-CE and is sometimes called the Church Age in these prophecies.

✪ ***GOAT:*** USA (Daniel 8)

✪ ***GRACE:*** God's free gift to man is the divine favor and inner power necessary for salvation.

✪ ***GREAT COMMISSION:*** The great commission is the directive from Jesus Christ to first make disciple nations. The second goal is then to reach every person on the face of the earth with the good news of Jesus Christ.

✪ ***HELL:*** Hell is the lake of burning sulfur, the second death, and eternal separation from God forever.

✪ ***HOLY SPIRIT:*** The mysterious third person of the Trinity of God. He is the instructor to seven different personality traits, which generate themselves in people. But the whole is made up of only one Spirit called the Holy Spirit. This power sent to man by God reveals His will, empowers individuals, and discloses His personal presence in the Old and New Testaments. When prophesying, a person is lead by the Spirit of Christ Jesus, the Spirit of Prophecy (Revelation 19:10).

✪ ***IC TECHNOLOGY:*** IC means Integrated Circuit Computer Chip. The IC technology is one step away from the 666 identification (ID) mark described in Revelation 13. This is the first marking technology that contains all three marking sequences (SZC) of the complete Mark of the Beast. IC chip technology can be embedded in credit cards, passports, medical ID cards, and many other items.

✪ ***ID BIO-CHIP IMPLANT:*** Identification (ID) bio-chip implant utilizes low frequency FM radio waves (125 kHz) which pass through objects such as the skin on your right hand. These or one-step away from and similar marking devices as the Mark of the Beast technology described in Revelation 13 which leads to death. Radio Frequency Identification (RFID) can be made from slivers of silicon embedded into a sealed glass tube and then implanted in the body. They give off a unique identifying low frequency radio signal.

✪ ***IMAGE OF THE BEAST:*** The Image of the Beast is the operational center of computers that oversee and control the world-wide Internet web of Satan's deceit. This is man's greatest achievement and has become his newest god. The image is further described as a confederation of electronic and computer networks. It is a completely self-contained utopian community of ultra-telelectronic light transfers. Users can obtain almost anything they desire at the touch of their fingertips.

✪ ***IMMORTALITY:*** There is eternal life after death and life imperishable.

✪ ***INTERNET WEB OF DECEIT:*** This is a world-wide data highway. It is like a confederation of electronic loops and computer networks called the Internet, or Satan's web of future deceit. It will become the Image of the Beast in the Great Tribulation Period.

✪ ***Israfil:*** This is an angel believed in Islam to be assigned to blow the trumpet, signaling the last days.

✪ ***JESUS CHRIST:*** Jesus Christ is our true Messiah. He is the rider on the white horse called faithful and true (Revelation 19:11). He will be coming back to earth in all His glory at the end of the tribulation period to destroy those who are destroying the world. The only way to eternal life with God is salvation through His son, Jesus Christ.

✪ ***JEWISH TIME:*** Jewish time is represented during the Tribulation Period. The Jewish year contains 360 days per year. The Jewish New Year starts in September or October.

✪ ***Jihad:*** To struggle, fight a war in the name of Islam, strive or exert or give up a bad habit. The fundamentalist of Islam in present day, have reinterpreted the meaning to be an end time battle cry to fight against the infidels to spread Political Islam over all existing governments of the world.

✪ ***JUDGMENT DAY:*** The day of judging by God on the last judgment day (great white throne- judges Old Testament people) after the thousand-year reign of Jesus Christ. Rewards and punishment will be declared. Death, hades, sinner, lukewarmer, and Satan will be thrown into the lake of fire. NOTE: The Antichrist and the false prophet are already in the lake of fire.

✪ ***JUDGMENT SEAT OF CHRIST:*** Jesus Christ returns to earth for the second time and He will judge people and nations. This will be at the end of the Tribulation Period and before the Millenium reign of Christ. He judges New Testament people.

✪ ***LAKE OF BURNING SULFUR OR FIRE:*** Second death and eternal separation from God. This lake is Hell (Gehenna).

✪ ***LAST GENERATION:*** Christ spoke of the last generation in a parable of the fig tree (Matthew 24:32-35). You will see God return the Jewish people to Jerusalem. Last generation represents 1967 A.D., until forty malleable years of slide rule sequencing points later, 106SRSP-S at which time Jesus Christ, shall return to earth.

✪ ***LASER SCAN:*** Technology that uses biometrics to measure and then calculate these measurement into a numeric X-Y-Z grid to identify the potential user. It currently is being used on such body parts as eyes, forehead, face, hands, and finger (fingerprint). Man can now become his own user-identity platform, because his personal body biometrics will carry his key to identifying with the Beast computers (Internet web of deceit). This will evolve into the first part of the Mark of the Beast used to determine the "S-Number, (social identity)" when the Final Antichrist takes over the system in the Great Tribulation.

✪ ***LEOPARD BEAST:*** (Daniel 7:6) European led landmass of the whole world less North and South America. Will operate in the first half of the tribulation (about 3 1/2 years).

✪ ***LIKE UNTO OR LIKEN TO:*** Is a term meaning similar, alike, or much the same. It is used to communicate the heavenly event or idea to the reader.

✪ ***Lion the tribe of Judah:*** Jesus Christ

✪ ***Lion - Old:*** England

✪ ***LUCIFER:*** Satan.

✪ ***LUKEWARMER:*** (Revelation 3:14-22) Lukewarm Christians love God half the time and love the world half the time. Lukewarmer is a spirit number seven Laodicea person and not considered a disciple of Christ or Spirit-filled.

✪ ***LUKEWARMER (34 PERCENT):*** The thirty-four percent represent the number of broad-term Christians in American churches that can be spiritually revived for Jesus during the last generation. If awakened, this group can escape the great Christian falling away in the tribulation period (Matthew 24:10).

✪ ***LUKEWARMER (51 PERCENT):*** The fifty-one percent represents the number of broad-term Christians in American churches who will disobey God's command. They refuse to break ties with worldly idols, which include money, security, and conveniences. They deny the MNO is bad because they believe it brings world peace.

✪ ***MARK OF HIS NAME:*** (Revelation 14:10) The second hidden mark and equates to the Millennium Nations Organized. MNO equals 666 on the phone pad, which equals Daniel's ten toes. Here we see the world's being divided into ten area kingdoms with each kingdom containing one or more nations. Here in lies Satan's greatest deception and Christians must do everything they can to stop their nation from joining the world federation for peace and security.

✪ ***MARK OF THE BEAST:*** (Revelation 13:16) This mark represents the three sequence codes equal to S+Z+C, which equals 6+6+6 on the phone pad. In the USA, this will be an eighteen digit number. The computer is looking for eighteen digits such as 6 + social ID number (SS) + 6 + zip code + 6 + `one to nine loop'. The sixes (6's) are access codes used by a computer to obtain information. This sequence of numbers will be put on the hand by the use of a marking device or bracelet during or before the great tribulation. The Christian must refuse this technology.

✪ ***Michael, THE GREAT PRINCE:*** (Daniel 12:1) North and South America in the tribulation period.

✪ ***MILLENNIUM:*** The thousand year reign of Jesus Christ, which is equal to one sabbatical day. Millennium represents the seventh sabbatical day of rest.

✪ ***(MNO) EUROPEAN LED MILLENNIUM OR MILLENNIAL NATIONS ORGANIZED:*** The world being divided into ten area kingdoms. This may be hidden at first but will come to full view before the world on Monday, 100.1.10SRSP-S. At this sequencing point the Antichrist will become the leader of the MNO with a goal of restoring world peace after Gulf War III. MNO represents Daniel's ten toes of iron and clay and the Sea Beast (Revelation 13:1). But it will evolve into the Revelation 13:11, Land Beast or the Eagle with the Three Ugly Heads. The MNO represents all landmass in the world except North and South America during all seven years of the tribulation.

✪ ***NAME OF THE ANTICHRIST:*** (1 John 2:18) The name of the Antichrist is, "JESUS THE MESSIAH, KING OF KINGS, and LORD OF LORDS, RULER OF THE MILLENIUM NATIONS ORGANIZED". His goal is, "TOWARD HEAVEN". Name plus goal equals eighteen digits.

✪ ***NAME OF THE BEAST:*** (Revelation 13:17) The beast's name is found in the Antichrist's name. Millenium Nations Organized = MNO = 666 on the phone pad. If a nation so joins this ten kingdom federation, then its citizens can buy or sell with all nations involved in the MNO.

✪ ***NEW NATURE:*** After a commitment to Christ and the in-filling of the Holy Spirit, a Christian has acquired a new nature. The old sinful nature is gone and the ability if one chooses to turn from sin has now been instilled, a new nature.

✪ ***NUMBER OF HIS NAME:*** (Revelation 13:17) The Number of his Name equals 666 which equals MNO which equals Millennium Nations Organized within the Name of the Beast. If a nation so joins this ten kingdom federation, then its citizens can buy or sell with all nations involved in the MNO.

✪ ***NUMBER OF THE BEAST:*** (Revelation 13:18) This is an international phone number, which equals 011-972-6-66J-ES-US. This number connects the customer's transaction with the Image of the Beast to get an approval code. It will also collect a consumption tax for the ten area world wide kingdom federation (MNO). This number can be hidden within the programming of the computer.

✪ ***OLD NATURE:*** How a person lives up and until they accept Jesus Christ as their personal Lord and Savior. Sin is a part of their regular life pattern of behavior.

✪ ***PLASMOID ENERGY FORCE:*** An energy force which can be formed into any shape the Lord God desires for the particular test cycle He has assigned this form to experience. This energy force will be given life by the Lord God breathing through His fiery nostrils. This state (Plasmoid) will be capable of reacting properly in its assigned test cycle. Otherwise, this plasmoid energy force has been formed into a unit, which will undergo magneto hydrodynamic forces applied to it by everything else in the test cycle. If the unit is split or divided by God then these two units are reduced in power to withstand every action they encounter or are subjected to in a magnetic field test cycle. The partial Plasmoids (most earthly humans in our test cycle) have a destructive tendency to not follow the Lord God's original program (Ephesians 2:10) as to their survivor goals in a test cycle.

✪ ***POSSIBILITY DEBT THINKING:*** (OR PROSPERITY DEBT) Church leaders starting a building project with debt. They sell the flawed idea by saying we must walk in faith that God will provide a way to pay for the project in the future. This may have worked in the past. It equates to total lack of faith in the Bible teaching about the disaster of endtimes. It will surely fail in the tribulation period.

✪ ***POST TRIBULATION RAPTURE THEORY:*** See rapture

✪ ***PP = PERSEVERING POWER:*** The length a Plasmoid can endure in a specific test cycle without God's help before it is destroyed. This is calculated by squaring the plasmoid's assigned radius times pie = C = circumference = PP.

✪ ***PRE MILLENNIAL RAPTURE THEORY:*** See rapture.

✪ ***PRE TRIBULATION RAPTURE THEORY:*** See rapture.

✪ ***PRE WRATH RAPTURE THEORY:*** See rapture.

✪ ***PROPHECY:*** History in advance. It is usually directed to the Christian community and sometimes even to the unbeliever. Such prophecy is completely trustworthy because God is omniscient. Christians prophesying today is a fulfillment of scripture, Joel 2:28.

✪ ***RAPTURE THEORIES:*** The word rapture is not literally used in the Bible. But the gathering of the Elect by the angels Jesus sends will happen shortly after His return (Matthew 13:37-50). This is ordered by Jesus to separate His people from the sinners before He and His angels destroy all sinners. This event I have prophesied will follow the Battle of Armageddon 75 days after the tribulation period is over on Daniel's 1335th day.

There are many different nonfactual rapture theories such as: Pre-tribulation rapture, this theory holds the view a signed-event rapture happens before the tribulation begins to usher in the start of the seven years of Jewish persecution. The Mid-tribulation rapture, this theory believes the rapture will occur at the midpoint of the tribulation period. There is the Pre-Wrath rapture theory, which believes the rapture will occur between the middle of the tribulation and the battle of Armageddon. The Post tribulation rapture is believed to be at the end. The Pre millenium rapture is anytime before the thousand year reign of Jesus Christ. Finally, there is the post Millenium rapture, which predicts it will occur after the Great White Throne judgment and the thousand year reign of Jesus Christ. To confuse the Issue even more, there are numerous variations within each theory. Do not make this a denominational Issue.

✪ ***REBELLION:*** Rebellion will be full-blown when we see the abomination that causes desolation. Others rebel against going to church and Godly parental instruction. Some rebel against government authority. Increased lukewarmness. Some place their hope in world government over a belief in Jesus Christ.

✪ ***REPENTANCE:*** To turn from a sinful life to a godly life. Tell God you are sorry from your heart His Son had to die on the cross for your despicable sins.

✪ ***REVELATION:*** God reveals or makes known as in scripture or visions. For endtimers it focuses on a period of time just before and during Daniel's seventieth week.

✪ ***RFID (see ID):*** Radio Frequency IDentification that has all the ramifications of high-tech reality to track people on earth.

✪ ***(S) NUMBER (SEQUENCE):*** This is the first sequence of three, which makes up the Mark of the Beast. The (S) sequence is the number six (6) computer access code followed by a nine-digit social identification number.

✪ ***SABBATICAL DAY:*** A sabbatical heavenly day is as a thousand earth years. God is a multiple time dimensional being. Time, as we think of it, is irrelevant to God. He is already present at every time frame of our entire life.

✪ ***SALVATION:*** Salvation is the rescue of man from evil or guilt by God's power so man may obtain blessedness through eternal life. This generally requires action on the person's part by asking God from their heart to help or forgive him. Then faith is given so man can believe he has received grace through the power of God. To receive salvation a person must believe in God's Son, Jesus Christ. Only through Jesus Christ can man have eternal life with God.

✪ ***SATAN:*** The transliteration of Satan in Hebrew means adversary. He is a created being who has rebelled and can tempt, but not force. His agents in crime are called fallen angels or demons. He acts within the limits set by divine sovereignty. God will allow Satan much power over the endtimers. Yet God will bring judgment against Satan and in favor of the saints at the end.

✪ ***SECOND ADVENT:*** The second advent is the Second Coming of Jesus. It is His return to the world to make the end of history.

✪ ***SECOND COMING:*** The advent of Jesus is the second coming. It is His return to the world to make the end of history. He will set up his kingdom and see Satan put in jail. He will return to destroy those who are destroying the world.

✪ ***SECOND DEATH:*** The disobedient person will be thrown into the lake of burning sulfur. This is eternal separation from God.

✪ ***SECOND READING:*** Pertains to the second time a word, verse, or instructions is given in the Bible as if you started reading from the front and continued to the end. This is how the Holy Spirit communicated to me as a reference point in the Bible.

✪ ***SEVEN SPIRITS OF GOD:*** This is like seven personality traits, which manifest themselves in people, churches, and nations. They are spirits of the seven Churches in Revelation 2 and 3.

✪ ***SEVEN THUNDERS:*** (Revelation 10:3) God's seven separate judgments of power against sinners and Satan. This is the sealed portion of Revelation 10.

✪ ***666 EQUALS 6+6+6:*** Revelation 13:18's, 666, equals 6+6+6 equals the Mark of the Beast which will be assigned to a person. If that person accepts this total sequence of numbers to buy or sell in the great tribulation, then he is out of grace with God. When a person buys or sells, using this number, it tells the computer that a MNO consumption tax is due. This, in turn, sets off a series of transactions through the Internet web of deceit. Each six (6) represents a sequence, then a number that will tell the computer how to handle the incoming international phone call. The first six represents a social identification number. The second six has the person's assigned location (zip code in America) on earth. The last six tells the computer what type of transaction the person is trying to complete. Transactions will need an approval from the Image of the Beast. This buy and sell mode will be voluntary at first and then enforced later. Six hundred sixty-six (666) also equals the name of the beast (Revelation 13:17), the number of his name (Revelation 13:17), and the mark of his name (Revelation 14:11).

✪ ***SLIDE RULE DATES:*** See A.D.S.R.

✪ ***SPIRIT OF CHRIST JESUS, THE SPIRIT OF PROPHECY:*** The Spirit of Christ Jesus, the Spirit of Prophecy, is Jesus issuing prophetic insight through the Holy Spirit. It is defining a sharper focus on one subject matter and that subject is prophecy. The Holy Spirit moves in all areas of a Christian's life. The Spirit of Christ Jesus moves specifically in the area of prophetical insight (Revelation 19:10).

✪ ***SPIRIT ONE TO FOUR CHRISTIANS:*** Spirit one to four are Christians with personality traits described in their respective churches; Ephesus equals Spirit one, Smyrna equals Spirit two, Pergamum equals Spirit three, and Thyatira equals Spirit four. These Christians will move directly into the tribulation period to help God fight Satan (Revelation 2).

✪ ***SPIRIT-FILLED CHRISTIAN:*** They are disciple of Christ and true followers of Jesus Christ's teachings. Lukewarmers are not Spirit-filled Christians.

✪ ***SPIRIT FIVE CHRISTIAN:*** Described in Revelation 3:1-6 (Sardis Church). The big difference between a Spirit five and the first four Spirits is found in Revelation 3:5. Jesus states He never will blot out this Spirit from the book of life. This type of Christian will move directly into the tribulation period. God has chosen this type of spirit for a special duty to be performed for the Kingdom of God.

✪ ***SPIRIT SIX CHRISTIAN:*** Spirit six is a Christian with a personality trait like the Philadelphia Church (Revelation 3:7-13). This Christian is found blameless before God and is guaranteed removal (non-signed event through death) before the tribulation period starts (Revelation 3:10). This removal will be through physical death before and under the four seals or Gulf War III.

✪ ***SPIRIT SEVEN CHRISTIAN:*** Spirit seven is a broad-term Christian described in the Laodicea Church (Revelation 3:14-22). The number seven meaning final and, in some cases, past the point of returning to God. This Christian is a fifty-fifty percent or lukewarmer. He is an abomination to God and God will vomit him out of His mouth into the tribulation period (Revelation 3:16). MOST (over 50%) will be lost through the great Christian falling away in the first half of the tribulation period (Matthew 24:10).

✪ ***SRSP - SLIDE RULER SEQUENCING POINT:*** This sequencing point has been used in this book, The Scroll. The S.R. in SRSP means slide rule sequencing point or designation point on God's slide ruler of end time events and not an actual date. SRSP designation begins with Psalms 96 through 106. God may push all events out between the time period 1996 SRSP and the start of the tribulation period to save more souls (expandable time period). Once the tribulation starts these signs and events begin to surface, they will complete the whole cycle in the approximate lapping and overlapping order and time sequence prophesied. The sequence is more important than the current date since we are instructed to learn and then watch for signs and sequences of events. (See slide ruler in section 2-8)

✪ ***THREE (3) WOES TO AMERICA:*** God will destroy America through a progression of events if Christian values are not restored. The same course of events will occur if the American government persecutes the Church or closes down church structures.

✪ ***TRIBULATION:*** The Tribulation Period is seven years called Daniel's seventieth week of Jewish persecution. It is a time of intense trouble on earth prior to Christ's return. This is a time of God's wrath on a disobedient world.

✪ ***TRIBULATION PERIOD (GREAT):*** The Great Tribulation is the second half of Daniel's seventieth week and it equals to three and one-half years or 1,260 Jewish days. It will be a time of increased wrath from God and fury from Satan.

✪ ***TWO WITNESSES:*** One is an American leader in the second half of the tribulation who inflicts much pain on the disobedient MNO kingdoms. The other witness is an American General who is called "destroyer" after Gulf War III. He will work with the American leader to carry out the Lord God's wishes.

✪ ***UACC:*** Universal American Church Coalition, if started could be a union of 333,000 Christian congregations in North and South America. This is not a fulfilling prophecy but instruction to the Churches as the Holy Spirit gave me instructions. Whether it fulfills is up to Church leaders.

✪ ***USA:*** The heart of the Great Prince Michael.

✪ ***VISION:*** Vision is an experience in a person's life whereby a special revelation from God is received. Endtimers who have visions are a fulfillment of Joel 2:28. End time visions are used by God to guide, instruct, warn, and encourage Christians to fulfill Bible prophecy and to be obedient to His commands.

✪ ***(Z) NUMBER (SEQUENCE):*** This is the second sequence of numbers making up the Mark of the Beast. It represents the location on earth where a person's permanent residence is located as declared by their Government. Z sequence is your five-digit zip code in America.

INDEX

of words and phrases

Section 10 - 2

All words or phrases are referenced by section and part number in this book - The Scroll, (SC=Sec= number). Some are referenced to the page number in the original Issue - 1, Book - Wake Up Call Prophecies, (Issue-1 = Pg - number).

A ~~~~~~~~~~~~~~~~~~~~

B ~~~~~~~~~~~~~~~~~~~~~~~~~~~

C ~~~~~~~~~~~~~~~~~~~~~~~~~~~~

D ~~~~~~~~~~~~~~~~~~~~~~~~~~~~~~

E ~~~~~~~~~~~~~~~~~~~~~~~~~~~~~~

F ~~~~~~~~~~~~~~~~~~~~~~~~~~~~~~

G ~~~~~~~~~~~~~~~~~~~~~~

H ~~~~~~~~~~~~~~~~~~~~~~~~~~~~~~

I ~~~~~~~~~~~~~~~~~~~~~~~~~~~~~~

J ~~~~~~~~~~~~~~~~~~~~~~~~~~~~~

K ~~~~~~~~~~~~~~~~~~~~~~~~~~~~~

L ~~~~~~~~~~~~~~~~~~~~~~~~~~~~~

M ~~~~~~~~~~~~~~~~~~~~~~~~~~~

N ~~~~~~~~~~~~~~~~~~~~~~~~~~~

O ~~~~~~~~~~~~~~~~~~~~~~

P ~~~~~~~~~~~~~~~~~~~~

Q ~~~~~~~~~~~~~~~~~~~~

R ~~~~~~~~~~~~~~~~~~~~~

U ~~~~~~~~~~~~~~~~~~~~~~~~~~~~

V ~~~~~~~~~~~~~~~~~~~~~~~~~~~~

W ~~~~~~~~~~~~~~~~~~~~~~~~~~~~

X ~~~~~~~~~~~~~~~~~~~~~~~~

Y ~~~~~~~~~~~~~~~~~~~~~~~~

Z ~~~~~~~~~~~~~~~~~~~~~~~~

10-2-1 - Italy, Pompeii - Cobble Stone Streets: The wagon wheels cut into the stone streets of Pompeii. The large raise rocks in the roadway were for pedestrians to cross the street and not get their feet wet. Pompeii was not prepared for their disaster and neither is the Lukewarm Churches. They are not teaching Christians and non-Christians how to respond in the Tribulation Period.

See Judgement Day Nightmare! Section - 12

BEFORE: PEACE & SECURITY TRANQUILITY

10-2-2 - Italy, Vesuvius Volcano: Vesuvius destroyed Pompeii in 79 AD. We passed underneath the volcano and I though if it erupts we would sure make the news for being buried under ash. More importantly, if we think about it, Pompeii's destruction was unexpected and may be a better example of end times than Matthew 24 where it predicts it will be like the days of Noah.

In Noah's day, the earth was destroyed with water and the people did not know the flood was coming. But in our day, endtimes will end like Pompeii - fire and ash will be all that is left.

PHOTO SUMMARY

Section 11-1

NOTE: Although precautions have been taken in the preparation of this book, the publisher and author assume no responsibility for errors or omissions. These pictures have prophetical and historical commentary compiled in summary form through 2005-2007 to provide a helpful and informative insight into Biblical end time events. The author and publisher specifically disclaim any responsibility for any liability, loss, or risk, personal or otherwise, which is incurred as a consequence, directly or indirectly, of the use, adherence and application of any of the contents of this book.

All photos taken by: Bob or Alice Short. Photo historical commentary compiled from local and tour bus guides. Their accuracy was double-checked using many historical book guides, the Bible, Bible dictionaries, travel books, atlas, along with my educational classes. My commentary on many biblical sites should carry the words, "proposed, or we think this is the place, or this may not be the exact location but it is where we celebrate the event".

SUMMARY BY SECTION:

First Number = Section picture is found
Second Number = Chapter within section
Third Number = Picture sequence within chapter

Location	Country Photo Description
1-1-1 FP	Israel - Jerusalem, The Via Dolorosa:
1-1-2-FP	Greece, Olympia - Building block of the Temple of Zeus
1-4-1-	Italy, Pisa - leaning Tower;
1-5-0	Italy, Rome, St. Paul's outside the walls Basilica -Bob
1-5-1-	Israel, Mt. Carmel - Statue of Elijah - Carmelite Monastery:
1-5-2-	Israel, Old Jaffa - Bob - Prophet
1-7-1-	Greece, Island of Rhodes, Lindos, St. Paul's Bay:
1-8-1-	Turkey, Ancient Ephesus - Curetes Street - Celsus' Library:
1-9-1-FP	England - London, Big Ben:
2-1-1-	Israel, Jerusalem - The Shrine of the Book:
2-1-2-	Israel, Megiddo - Valley of Armageddon - Jezreel Valley:
2-2-1-	Israel, Jerusalem - the Eastern Gate:
2-2-2-	Italy, Pompeii - cobble stone street
2-3-1-	Italy - between Florence & Venice; 4000 W. W. II US Solders
2-4-1-	Israel, Tel Aviv - Skyline
2-5-1-	Italy, Venice-Island of Burano - leaning bell tower
2-6-1-	U.S., Oahu - North Beach
2-6-2-	Italy, Pompeii - a plaster copy of a victim
2-7-1-	Italy, Florence - Palazzo Borghese - dancing entertainers
2-8-1-	England, London - Tower Bridge:
2-8-2-	Italy, Rome - Colosseum:
2-8-3-	England, London - Tower of London - Jewel House:
2-9-1-	Israel, Jerusalem - Jaffa Gate - bullet holes
2-9-2-	Israel, Nazareth, Moslem Mosque:
2-9-3-	Israel, Jericho, Road into the Moslem control city
2-10-1-	Israel, Jerusalem - Via Dolorosa, Station # 10
2-10-2-	Greece, Island of Rhodes - Palace of the Grand Master:
2-11-1-	Italy, Pompeii, The Forum
2-11-2-	Italy, Rome - Police Station:
2-11-3-	Italy, Northern Country Side - Original Roman Bridge
2-11-4-	Italy, Rome, metal blinds pulled in room
2-11-5-	Italy, between Florence and Venice - Nazi WW-II pill box
2-11-6-	Italy, Florence - Mirror view of Fiume Arno River:
2-11-7-	Italy, between Florence and Venice - WW II runes:
2-12-1-	Italy, Venice - Waterfront Retail Shop:
2-12-2-	Israel, Tel Aviv, Dizengoff Shopping Center:
2-12-3-	Italy, Florence - Palazzo Borghese - Ghost procession
2-12-4-	Greece, Athens - Greek Dancers:
2-12-5-	Italy, Siena, The Piazza Del Campo:
2-12-6-	Greece, Island of Santorini, Fira, magnificent view
2-12-7-	Greece, Island of Patmos - Holy Cave of the Apocalypse-fresco
2-13-1-	U.S., Hawaii - Maui - Beach Resort:
2-13-2-	Italy, Rome - Pantheon
2-14-1-	Turkey, Ephesus - St. Mary's Church
2-14-2	Greece, Island of Mykonos - Ghost shot - Bob and chapel
2-14-3-	Italy, Rome - St. Peter's - Dome:
2-15-1-	Israel, Sea of Galilee, Mount of the Beatitudes - trees
2-15-2-	Israel, Megiddo - King Ahab's underground water system:
2-15-3-	Israel, The Galilee, West Bank - Military Check Point:
2-15-4-	U.S., Hawaii, Oahu - Rain Forest:
2-16-1-	Israel, Dead Sea - Salt crystals and formations:
2-17-1-	Israel, Masada - Main Roman Camp:
2-17-2-	Israel, Jerusalem - Three different buildings of worship
2-17-3-	England, Greenwich - World Time Line:
2-17-4-	Israel, Jerusalem, Temple Mount - Dome of the Rock
2-18-1-	Scotland, Edinburgh - Second most photographed Clock
2-18-2-	Israel, Megiddo - Jezreel Valley - Armageddon:
2-18-3-	Israel, Megiddo - Armageddon - Bob with-Jezreel Valley:
2-19-1-	Italy, Rome - Ponte S. Angelo Bridge - Castel Sant' Angelo:
2-19-2-	Israel, Megiddo - Armageddon - Birds a sign of the battle:
2-19-3-	Italy, Rome - Angel in charge of Hell at S. Peter in Chains:
2-19-4-	Greece, Epidauros - Amphitheater:
2-19-5-	Israel, Tabgha - Ancient Olive Press:
2-19-6-	Israel, Capernaum - Water Jug and its Base:
3-1-0- FP	Greece, Island of Crete, Knossos - Palace:
3-1-1-	Greece, Island of Patmos - Holy cave of the Apocalypse
3-1-2-	Greece, Athens, view from Mars Hill:
3-1-3-	England, London, Buckingham Palace - bobby:
3-2-1- FP	Israel, Qumran - Cave where Dead Sea Scrolls were found
4-1-a-0	Italy, Florence - One of many statues there.
4-1-a-1-	France - Paris - Notre Dame Cathedral
4-1-a-2-	Greece - Island of Patmos - Monastery St. John:
4-1-b-1-	Greece, Ancient Mycenae - The Lion Gate:
4-1-b-2-	Greece, Island of Rhodes - Lindos:
4-1-b-3-	Greece, Olympia - Temple of Zeus - Sacred hearth:
4-1-b-4-	Israel, Capernaum - Synagogue:
4-1-c-1-	Greece, Athens - Possession-airy caterpillars - walkway
4-1-c-2-	Greece - Athens - Temple of Olympian Zeus.
4-1-c-3-	Greece, Athens - Ancient Agora - Church of Holy Apostles:
4-1-c-4-	England - London, Imperial War Museum - atomic bomb
4-2-1-	U.S., Hawaii - Pearl Harbor - USS Arizona Memorial:
4-3-1-	Israel - Megiddo (Armageddon) - Jezreel Valley - excavations
4-6-0	Italy, Pompeii - Town Square and Business District:
4-6-1-	Israel - River Jordan
4-6-2-	Israel - Church of St. John the Baptist:
4-6-3-	Greece - Ancient Corinth - Temple of Apollo
4-7-1-	Israel, Jerusalem - Temple Mount:
4-8-1-	Italy, Rome - Roman Forum, Arch of Septimius Severus:
4-8-2-	Italy, Rome- Roman Forum - Faustina Temple:
4-9-1-	England, London - The Great Churchill:
4-9-2-	England, London - London Bridge:
4-10-1-	Israel, Bethlehem, Church of the Nativity:
4-11-0-	USA, Hawaii, Maui - Crystal in showcase
4-11-1-	Greece, Mykonos Island:
4-11-2-	U.S., Hawaii, Oahu Island, Polynesian Cultural Center:
4-11-3-	Turkey, Ephesus - Curetes Street:
4-11-4-	Italy, Rome - Roman Forum - Colosseum:
4-12-1-	Italy, Verona - Roman Bridge:
4-14-1-	Israel - Dead Sea - Qumran-Cliffs:
4-15-1-	England, near London - Hatfield House Palace -Kings Chair
4-15-2-	Italy, Rome - St. Paul (outside the Walls Basilica) - the Vault:
4-15-3-	Greece, Athens - Acropolis - Caryatids:
5-1-1-	Israel, Jerusalem - Church of all Nations:

Waikiki Beach

11-1-1- USA, Hawaii, Island of Oahu, and Waikiki Beach Area: The glass boat ride was exhilarating as we toured the Bay. I thought, look at the money, which was spent on the waterfront. The design was pure sun and fun. I also noted the storms brewing in the background. Remember the Bible gives us a warning sign about waterfronts, as they are associated with endtimes. It has stated the waves will be roaring and tossing when Jesus returns at the end of time. But before the end, we must apply birthing pains to every end time sign.

Since the Clintons and Bush team took power, the continental USA has experiences some of the worst dollar disasters in the history of our nation, especially its coastlines and rivers. Issue 1, of the WUCP warned against this. The warning was any nation which tries to move Israel out of their God given land, would receive the Lord God's destructive judgments.

It is interesting to look at two judgments from the Lord God against the USA in 2005. Question one; what happened precisely the same day Hurricane Katrina hit? This was not broadcast on any of the major news networks, which are anti-USA and pro-European World Government (Leopard Beast). Answer: The last Jewish Citizen was forcefully drug off their property in Gaza and kicked out - Katrina hit. Question two; what happened precisely the same day hurricane Rita hit? Answer: The last Jewish soldier left Gaza who was protecting the citizen's land - Rita hit. Does anybody get the picture? The Clintons and Bush was all for this because they keep pushing a Palestinian state against God's Holy Word.

I am giving another stern prophesying warning to America. If USA kicks the Jewish people off the west bank and gives it to the enemy to have their own state, the Lord God will punish the USA and she will never be the same. Our leaders should not be so stupid as to think what I have prophesied is folly!

5-1-2- England - London - House of Parliament
5-3-1- Italy, Rome - Ponte Sant' Angelo bridge:
5-3-2- Italy, Rome - St. Peter's (inside)
5-4-1 Italy, Rome - Egyptian mummy casket and Alice
5-4-2- Italy, Rome: People hiding in room with metal blinds:
5-5-1- Greece - Olympia - Temple of Zeus
5-6-1- Israel, Nazareth, Church of the Annunciation:
5-7-1- Scotland, Edinburgh, Big Guns - Craigmillar Castle:
5-7-2- Greece, Thermopylae-300 Spartans vs 10,000 Persian solders:
5-7-3- Israel, Jerusalem - Armed Israeli Soldiers:
5-7-4- Israel - Armageddon King Solomon's horse stables
5-7-5- Israel, Jericho - Dirt mounds are some of the dig sights:
5-8-1- Turkey, Ephesus - Drawings giving directions - sign language:
5-8-2- Turkey, Ephesus - Curetes street - Celsus' Library:
5-9-1- Israel - Jerusalem - Temple Mount - future Holy of Holies
5-10-1- Italy, Verona - Roman Arena:
5-11-1- Greece, Patmos - Monastery of St. John:
5-11-2- Greece, Patmos - Holy Cave of the Divine Apocalypse:
5-13-1- Israel, Jaffa - Simon the Tanner's House:
5-13-2- Israel - Qumran Dead Sea - Baptismal pool
6-1-1- England -country side - Burned out Abby by Henry VIII:
6-1-2- Greece - Delphi - Temple of Apollo
6-1-3- Italy, Rome, St. Peter's Square:
6-1-4- Italy, Rome, San Pietro in Vincoli - St. Peter's in Chains
6-2-1- Italy, Rome, inside the Colosseum:
6-3-1- Italy, Rome, Roman Forum - "The Curia"
6-3-2- Italy, Roman Forum - Faustina Temple
6-3-3- Scotland - country side, #37 Baby Sheep
6-4-1- England - London - St. Paul's Cathedral:
6-5-1- England, London, Buckingham Palace:
6-6-1- U.S., Hawaii, Honolulu - Waikiki Beach:
6-8-1- Israel, Dead Sea - En Gedi Oasis - Arab sand storm
6-9-1- Israel, Qumran Community - Scroll Cave:
6-10-1- Italy, Assisi: Narrow Street
6-10-2 Italy, Florence, Santa Croce (Church):
7-1-1- Italy, Venice - Basilica di San Marco:
7-1-2- Italy, Assisi - Roman Temple of Minerva:
7-1-3- Israel, Caesarea - Amphitheater :
7-2-1- Israel, Megiddo (Armageddon) - King Solomon's road
7-4-1- Israel, Megiddo (Armageddon) - Pagan Canaanite altar:
7-4-2- Israel - Tabgha , Church of the loaves and Fish
7-4-3 Greece, Athens - Mars Hill:
7-5-1- Greece, Island of Crete, Knossos the Palace-1900 BC:
7-6-1- England, Greenwich - Time Clock:
7-7-1- Israel, Jerusalem - Garden Tomb:
7-8-1- Italy, Rome - Church of St. Peter in Chains - Angel of Hell
7-8-2- Israel, Caesarea - Amphitheater:
7-8-3- Israel, Caesarea Phillipi - Pagan cult Grotto - Pan
7-9-1- Israel, Judean Desert - Nomads Camping:
7-9-2- Israel, Sea of Galilee - Demon in the pigs
7-10-1- Greece - Athens - Mars Hill:
7-10-2- Greece, Ancient Athens - Ancient Agora Area:
7-10-3- Greece, Epidaurus - The Museum Courtyard - with statues
8-1-1- Italy, Rome - Pantheon - AD 27:
9-1-1 - Italy, Rome, Inside the Roman Forum:
9-2-1- Israel, Jerusalem - Temple Mount:
10-2-1 Italy, Pompeii - Cobble Stone Streets:
10-2-2 Italy, Vesuvius Volcano:
11-1-1- USA, Hawaii, Island of Oahu, Waikiki Beach Area:
12-1-1- Greece - Ancient Corinth - Berna in Agora Area - Bob:
12-1-2- England, London - Alice at the University of London
12-2-1- Israel, Jerusalem - Golgotha-Jesus-Cross - station #12
12-2-2- Italy, Rome-Arch of Constantine (AD 315) at Roman Forum
12-2-3 Israel, Sea of Galilee - Jesus Boat - crew member throws net

A Witness to the World governments and Servant Messenger to the Churches for Jesus Christ. Bob R. Short, (insight received 1994-2007)

ABOUT THE AUTHOR
of these prophecies

Section 12 - 1, Page - 275

Bob R. Short was born in a rural college town in Oklahoma where the conservative citizens valued attending church services. Working for a living was considered normal, and young Bob frequently found himself working in the grocery store owned by one set of grandparents and learning the ways of farming, ranching, and selling leather goods from his other grandparents.

Mom and Dad Short trained their son with marketing skills, money management, and a love for calculating numbers in their western wear store. From his childhood, Bob developed a fascination and desire for math and science as it related to the Bible and the mysteries it contained. His fascination with numbers prompted him before age ten to question his grandparents about the Beasts and calculations in the Book of Revelation. The Holy Spirit encouraged a hunger for more insight at this early age even though the sequence of events in Bible prophecy were not clear because of lack of knowledge. The puzzles in Bible prophecy began to unfold in the Spirit of Bob's mind as he grew in the faith and studied the prophets.

After high school graduation, he earned his Bachelor of Science Degree with mathematics major and minor studies in business and physics. His first job after college was working as an engineering associate in the industrial engineering department of a worldwide electronic switching system manufacturing plant. The Lord God later opened his mind using this job experience to understand the fulfillment of Daniel 12:4 and the Book of Revelation. His job required programming computers using sixes (6's) as the base unit of information. He studied intently how electronic circuitry would be used in the future to communicate massive amounts of information internationally locking modules with modules and later realized this information could be used for good or evil destruction. After ten years in the electronics business Bob returned to his first love of retailing.

Lets flashback to where the Lord God started the long process of molding Bob into a disciple of Christ. Dad and Mom Short saw to it that Bob was Christened and Baptized (infant's) along with their dedicating him in Church to Jesus Christ at a very early age. Bob believed from the age of five or shortly after, he had one of his deepest experiences with the Lord God. God answered one of his prayer requests, which gave young Bob the confidence to begin gaining faith in the Bible. He grew up believing he was God's child called to do something great for the Kingdom. The Lord God did not disclose any insight to Bob.

Below, 12-1-1 - Greece - Ancient Corinth - Berna in Agora Area: My thoughts focused on the pagan Temple of Apollo and this ancient town while standing quietly atop the Berna (raised stage area) in the agora (market) area. The Spirit open my mind concerning St. Paul distress of this place and emotions overcame me. Quietly standing atop the Berna my Spirit was taken into a different time dimension to experience and see through St. Paul's eyes as he stood here many years ago. Helpless masses of people were revealed in my mind concerning their great need for the Good News message and correct end time prophetic sequencing of events. Trying to regain my thoughts, the Spirit imparted many Christians choose to prioritize their lives in a manner which omits end time knowledge. Many Christians do not want Jesus coming back at this time and disrupting their good life. Some end time theories are taught incorrectly that may cause many to lose faith, stumble, and become a part of the Great Christian Falling Away (Matthew 24:10). My eyes became filled with tears of sorrow when my mind locked onto St. Paul's feelings as he gazed upon this pagan place.

However, Bob began to make his own rules, as a teenager. He would ask God to rescue him rather than honor God in his daily life. Looking back he says, "I just wanted to do enough for Jesus to squeak into heaven." At around age 13, he studied in the Church and made a commitment to follow the ways of Christ. Bob dedicated his life many years later to Christ during April 1979 and he was baptized a few weeks later. This began a series of experiences that would mold, shape, and prepare him for the Lord God's plans.

It seems when he began his walk with the Lord Jesus Christ; Satan made greater attempts to draw him away. He began chasing money, committing worldly sins, and became pride-ful with an unforgiving spirit. Loving Jesus at the same time he loved the world became an everyday occurrence. He was truly walking like a Revelation 3:16 lukewarmer while thinking he was okay with the Lord God. More importantly, if serious changes were not made, Bob was headed for hell. Although Satan's deception was covered very well concerning Bob, each temptation resulted in Bob experiencing the wonder of God's love and the keeping grace of the Lord Jesus, and it served to draw him closer to the Lord God.

Many years of wandering and disillusionment eventually led Bob on a journey into God's world of kindness and forgiveness. The Holy Spirit moved Bob to take a hard look at his sinful condition. He awoke to the fact, that if he were to die he would go to Hell thinking he was a Christian. Bob repented his past sins and recommitted his life or as some say, experienced a rebirth in Jesus Christ around January 1987. This new commitment to Christ really stuck! He has experienced new dimensions of insight as he learns to become a true Spirit-filled Christian.

Late at night on November 8, 1993, Bob took another major step in his walk with Christ. He committed to total Sanctification and now believes the Holy Spirit will direct him to live out a dedicated life to God in holiness and obedience to God's commands. The Spirit of Christ Jesus, the Spirit of Prophecy has revealed many things to him since that awesome night. The major starting point of understanding of prophecy came on Friday, May 13, 1994, where he had just finished reading Revelation 13 and became aware of the voice of the Spirit of Christ speaking in his thought processes. One urgent assignment the Spirit gave Bob was to wake up lukewarmers and their Churches, and warn nations of their disobedience to the Lord God. Bob now believes he was set apart by the Lord God for a particular purpose, which is end time prophesying and other objectives discussed in this book of prophecies.

Bob is active in community work and Church. He received his first experience in prison ministry at William Keys Prison from 1979 through 1981. He has returned to ministry work in 1999 by leading daylong seminars in Federal and State prisons. He volunteers weekly in County Jail Ministry, helps with nursing home ministry, and serves as a greeter in a local Church. He is the father of two sons by a previous marriage and a proud grandparent of one boy and one girl.

Below, 12-1-2 - England, London - Alice: I married Alice, who loves the Lord God, on June 27, 1994. She is a Spirit-filled Christian woman who is trying to serve Jesus Christ. She is a door greeter, and helped in many other projects at local Churches, as well as having taught Sunday school class.

Her help in editing this book has been a tremendous asset even though reading through these prophecies has not been easy for her. Jesus stated you could not be a prophet in your own house.

Her great photographic shots are invaluable when cross-referencing Biblical sights and events to these prophecies. Prophecy is not her calling, but helping others through cheerful community giving and supporting the church has been her ministry.

Our conversations included some disagreements in scripture analysis similar to the different denominational issue of the day. God was also in control of these minor differences of opinions whereby achieving His desire to complete the work. She has supported my different ministries and truly is a God sent blessing to me.

SALVATION TESTIMONY OF
BOB R. SHORT

Section 12-2

The moment that changed my life for eternity and has encourage others into accepting Jesus Christ after hearing it!

I have stepped out in faith and tried to become transparent before you to share this frightening yet triumphant event in hopes it will awaken the readers and encourage others to take a humble look at their presentation on Judgment day. One of the sins of the Church is not explaining what Jesus looks like on judgment day. Read to the end of the book and you will find out why the Bible warns us to fear Him. The question must be asked; "Will you be standing when you finish talking on judgment day?" In addition I further challenge, "Everything we do and say is about our presentation on judgment day." After hearing this testimony many people have repented and dedicated their lives to Jesus Christ.

The purpose of my testimony is to share a message of hope. Included are some of my past (old-nature) mistakes and failures to demonstrate how God's grace (love and kindness) was sufficient to severely prune and prepare me for my salvation victory!

A QUICK REVIEW OF MY LIVE - THAT NIGHT!

Processing my thoughts seemed hard because something was different about this night that had a disturbing silence. My thoughts were coming under conviction by the Holy Spirit as to how my live of disobedience was lived. Rational thought seemed to be in a vacuum obscuring my ability to comprehend it. Shivers ran up my back as my mind searched for answers. My thoughts were bottomed out trying to make sense out of my desperate condition. My memory went into recall mode and began to review my past (old nature) before I made a commitment that night to Jesus Christ at the age of forty-one.

Problems started with injuries to my back playing basketball my junior year in High School, which knocked me out of sports for good. Sports were my God and making All State Football like my dad was my goal. Hope of playing on the first team my senior year and getting a scholarship to play college football had evaporated with my injury. Feeling left out and watching from the bleachers, prompted me to over drink to cover-up disappointment and pain. Letting the team down was a concern. Getting in trouble for drinking seemed to increase. Burning the candle at both ends was a common occurrence especially during my college years.

My first experience of being arrested and put in jail was in 1963, my freshman year in college. It was our first year high school class reunion and I had too much to drink. The next recollection was finding myself in front of the sheriff's office located in the middle of the downtown square. This resulted in unintentionally damaging some trees and grass along side the courthouse, which upset the Sheriff. When he pulled me out of the car my comments were, "I was lost in a forest and didn't know how to get out." He instructed me the way out of the forest was in his jailhouse where trees were never a problem.

Probation under the personal supervision and guidance of the City Police Chief was ordered until I proved myself responsible. The Chief personally signed for me and the charges were dropped. He explained the responsibility he was taking when he agreed to cover any additional liabilities caused by me under his jurisdiction. Then he proceeded to put real fear in me by advising me of what could happen for failing him. Because he had faith in me, I tried harder to walk the good path for a while. My opportunity to thank him came 35 years later. Most class reunions somebody has to tell the story of "lost in the forest". They still laugh about it. Nevertheless, it brings very unpleasant memories back in my mind about my terrible old nature and what my life stood for.

"I was lost in a forest and didn't know how to get out." **He instructed me the way out of the forest was in his jailhouse where trees were never a problem.**

My first marriage lasted about seven years and terminated mainly because of my drinking. The party really began after the divorce. Womanizing and making up or lost time was the order of the day. Unfortunately, the sad results of this sinful life style began to surface.

There isn't any reason for me to be alive today
except for God's protection
to complete my future assignment.

I continued living outside God's will and all the sad experiences, which accompany such irresponsible action. This led to a few one night stays in jail where praying to God was in order. The Almighty would ask me two questions. First, "How are you taking care of your Garden I gave you in jail?" (Genesis 2:15 - Men take care of what God gives them.) Second, "You are going to the Jail House in Heaven (Matthew 18:34-35) because of your unforgiving spirit toward others." My answer to God each time would be crying out in prayer, "Oh, God, get me out of this one and I'll never do that again." My next prayer was even better, "Oh, God, if You will get me out of here and keep everyone off of me long enough, I will fix the problem myself." God was not impressed! He had been left out of the fix part of my problem, which is His specialty.

Living past 50 years old was not in my expectations and having fun now made sense. Being a professional most of my life prompted my career start as manufacturing engineer associate, then production supervisor in two different companies and assistant manager in two separate companies. Ownership of several businesses can be found in my portfolio. It appeared all was well with me most of the time. Sadly, I was a failure and worse to God.

I do not stand before you as a saint,
that God picked to prophesy end time events because
of my great straight-laced Christian background.

There isn't any reason for me to be alive today except for God's protection to complete my future assignment. Many stories could be told about why I should be dead. There could have been future stories about incarceration if my past course had continued. Satan convinced me to redefine lukewarmness as the proper lifestyle for a spiritually acceptable walk with the Lord God.

My second marriage after seven years ended. Money was my God, and I had other problems some of which were pride and an unforgiving spirit. As a husband, I was a failure to my family.

Actions in my old nature (before accepting Christ) give me cold chilling shakes when recalled. My wrong choices produce bad results. It seems my irresponsible walk had taken me inside hell on earth and experienced the sewer of life first hand. I am ashamed and sorry for my past disobedient behavior. If St. Paul said he was the worst, then my score during my old nature will be close to his. Being knocked off a horse by God as St. Paul experienced would have seemed easy but God Almighty took His biggest pruning shears and began to lob huge chunks out of me. He got my attention!

Going to church and praising Jesus was an every Sunday morning experience. Sadly, the rest of the week my true nature leaned heavily toward the world to chase the money, unforgiving spirit, fun, and all it had to offer. Smoking marijuana in the mid 1970s during the hippy movement for a few years was my course of action. Growing long hair was my choice when riding a chopped motorcycle, dirt bikes, and partying. Living on the edge of death was an exhilarating feeling when I pushed bikes past their limit. There were only two ways to ride bikes or to live, ***wide open or off***. Unfortunately, a price was to be paid for living on the edge most of the time. I ended up on crutches sometimes or worse yet in a hospital with all my ribs broken on the left side and two sticking through a lung.

What I have written must be heard. I do not stand before you a saint, which God picked to prophesy end time events because of my great straight-laced Christian background. God usually picks the foolish people to do great things for Him (1 Corinthians 1:26-31). This has been done to rebuke and nullify the wise, strong, and noble. Therefore, boasting of great things accomplished for the Lord God is impossible. My boasting comes when telling others what great things Jesus has done for me! I would still be the scum of the earth or dead if it were not for God's Grace (kindness) and His promise to rebuke and discipline whom He loves (Revelation 3:19). Oh thank You, Almighty God, for saving me.

Above, 12-2-1- Israel, Jerusalem - Golgotha-Jesus-Cross: Church of the Holy Sepulchre's Station #12 of the Via Dolorosa depicts Jesus dying on the cross. This Greek altar, ornamented in Eastern Style, stands over the Rock of Calvary. It has been purposely placed over where Jesus and the two thieves were crucified. Calvary was the place my heart and mind had to mentally focus on what Jesus really did for me. Satan had blinded me from seeing my faults. He was using my selfish interest in this age and worldly desires to keep me in a state where I was unable to perceive my disobedience. Then heavenly concentration on my choices in life began to be focused in my mind. Jesus' searchlight started exposing my disobedience to God. Only then could my mind recognize the need to repent and ask Jesus into my heart. How about you, has the King of deception, that old snake Satan, used the fast-paced culture and worldly pleasures to blind you from seeing correctly?

There was no excuse for my actions because I was taught better by my entire family and Church. Mom and Dad taught me God's right way. One of my grandfathers spent day after day instructing me in how hard work pays off and to love and honor God first in my life. One grandmother knew the Bible as well as the preacher and answered many of my questions concerning its mysteries. The other grandmother had instilled in me something that comes from the Psalms. Her little but powerful paraphrase, she would tell me when I was growing up was, "Everything is just fine, Sugar." I knew a few times my grandmother wasn't feeling well and she would still say this sugar-phrase to me. She just bubbled over with spiritual joy for Jesus. This would cause me to say, "Grandmother everything isn't fine, because you are feeling bad." "No!" She quickly interrupted me, "Jesus has a handle on it, and everything is just fine, Sugar." My intuition as a kid led me to believe she might be a little off center here but I accepted it.

Nevertheless, my grandmother taught me something else to praise Jesus for with the "sugar-phrase." She instilled in me, you need to praise Jesus when you're down and when you're up. Well I was down about as low as anyone can get. It took me to age forty to appreciate what my grandmother was saying.

After reviewing my life, I began to become aware of something happening around me, which could not be explained. Something was going to happen on that dark night. Please read the next section and find out what happened to me!

✞HE VISI✞A✞ION

The following story may seem visionary, nevertheless, it really happened!

THE NIGHT WAS STRANGE AND UNUSUAL. I felt a cold dark death approaching my house, which made me feel unnatural. Something was coming and a commitment would be required.

Alone, on my knees I sobbed uncontrollably about my disobedient choices. My soul was groaning from anguish of a broken spirit. My inner being had never experienced such a deep mournful cry before. I was ashamed with a truly heart-felt sorrow, because of my lifetime of bad choices. They were playing before my eyes and erasing them from my mind seemed impossible. My soul was in a distressful state - total brokenness.

A powerful human-like form appeared slowly in front of me to my left about three or four feet away from me, while my cries and moaning continued for 30 minutes. Chills moved up my spine. Behold, it was Satan for sure! His evil presence seemed to hold me in his cold and slimy grip of death. My angered words lash out at him, "I have lost everything, my business, family, pride and followed you by turning my back on the Lord God. You have taken everything dear to me using your deception, however you do not have my soul!"

I felt like a hostage
in the grip of these two powerful human forms.

I must reach out and choose one of these forms.

Then another human-like form began to appear on my right side about three or four feet in front of me as if He was seeking me (Luke 19:10). This form was awesome as His presence pierced me like a laser beam. There was not a sign from this silent but powerful form to help me out of my distressful state of mind. I felt like a hostage in the grip of these two powerful human-like forms. I must reach out and choose one of these forms. My eyes stared at the human form standing in the darkly lit room on the right. The Holy Spirit opened the window to my soul so my senses could discern who it was!

It was Jesus! However, His face was not in focus but my spirit knew Him. Satan's face was not in focus either. My eyes were filled with remorseful tears, focus was impossible. However, I began trying to rationalize my thinking and said, "Satan you have taken everything away from me but not my soul!" With desperation my eyes flashed to my right to get a look at Jesus while remorsefully saying, "My attempts have failed many times to change my life for the better because You were not ask to help."

The Spirit brought me under conviction and I asked Jesus if He would forgive me for my sins because of my sorrowful feelings. My understanding does not comprehend the kind of love Jesus possesses. However, He came again to give me an opportunity to choose life one more time with Him. My repentance was from my heart as my quivering mouth blurted out, "I will follow and praise You the rest of my life regardless of the consequence. You do not owe me a return visit. I am not asking You for my life because my worthiness to be with You has been shattered. My promise to You will be two fold. I shall go to church on a regular basis and learn Your ways. My other promise will be studying Your Bible and trying to understand what it says and make every effort to follow it to change like You want me to be."

My tearful eyes were temporarily blinded by my mind locking onto what seemed to be pure white-light. This seemed to clear my mind and almost instantly an incredible peace and calmness came over me. When my eyes cleared enough to see again the two powerful human forms of Satan and Jesus had vanished. Neither one said anything but there was communication in the spirit with them. I knew and felt what their desires were. Satan wanted me to continue in his worldly and evil ways, whereby worshiping him. However, Jesus had a better life for me and all that was required was repenting and asking Him back into my heart. Praise God for my latter choice. That mystical night will never be forgotten because I have become a different man because of it. Further more I have been blessed by God ever since. The road, that returned me to God, was tough, but it has been a satisfying, growing, and learning process to honor Jesus. The principle in Proverbs 22:6 came true for me. It states, a person will turn back to God at an older age, assuming he was taught correctly about God at an early age, even if he strayed during mid-life. Following the power of the written word has returned me to my youthful teachings about Jesus.

THERE IS HOPE

When I teach one-day seminars or just talk to an inmate one on one, my rating of myself equates to six or seven on a scale of one to ten as a Christian. One (1) means a person does not believe in God and ten (10) this person thinks they are as good as God and five (5) equates to an average Christian. Look at my old carnal nature, which equates to zero and now look at my new nature, what a difference God makes! I am trying to grow in Christ and become a true disciple of His teachings. There is much work to complete this process of becoming holy by staying in the word and with daily prayer. Jesus Christ has done this for me and Jesus will do this for you too.

Sharing this testimony brings tears of joy to me. The experience was soul shocking and emotionally draining. The reader may think, if Jesus and Bob can make this wonderful change for the good, then others can change with the help of Jesus also. The word HOPE equates to His name, which is Jesus! I pray people will be blessed by my testimony. Please repent and make a commitment to Jesus Christ at once. This decision can be an emotional event such as mine or it can be an unemotional event. Refer to page one and make a decision to repent and turn toward Jesus Christ our Lord and Savior. Amen and amen!

God is my witness, Bob R. Short, insight completed January 1, 2006.

WARNING

If you are walking in disobedience to the Lord God or are not sure where you stand with God, then read the next few pages. **Read with caution, if you are weak stomach.**

> **The Holy Spirit said, "I will take you in the spirit to see your fate if you had NOT committed your life to Jesus Christ."**
>
> ASTONISHMENT CAME OVER ME AS MY SPIRIT BECAME DRAWN INTO A HORRIFYING NIGHTMARE.

JUDGMENT DAY NIGHTMARE

{ Refer to Sections: The Abyss and Seventh Satanic Dooms }

My mind opened with a flashback in time. The Holy Spirit said, "I will take you in the spirit to see your fate **if you had not committed your life to Jesus Christ.** Advise and warn others because many churches are failing to do so!"

Astonishment came over me as my spirit became drawn into a horrifying nightmare. My spirit was zapped instantly after my death into the Abyss. Thoughts ricocheted through my mind because of the punishment I received after death in the Abyss (Luke 16:19-31). God Almighty bents each soul's time cycle so the beginning could not meet its ending until judgment day. Time was being manipulated like a corkscrew spiraling within God's tight control. When Almighty God bends time, a variance of energy displacement produces friction in the cosmos of the Abyss and intense heat will be produced like fire. This fire is used to torture each condemned soul. They will be transferred to judgment day when they have paid back everything Jesus' personally did for them when He died on the cross. After paying back everything, my soul was transported at the speed of thought from the terrible abyss into a sea of confused souls before the throne. Multitudes were around the throne watching and waiting to be judged.

Jesus sometimes announces the name of the next soul to be judged. However, this time, my name was shouted out by the hostile sounding voice of the Keeper in charge of the Book of Works (Revelation 20:12). An ill feeling came over me at the tone of his voice. Then to make matters worse, part of the souls waiting to be judged began to chant, "He is rich, he's was an American." They kept repeating the chant as my body trembled forward. An evangelist told us most Americans would be classified rich as compared to the rest of the world on judgment day. The story flashed through my bewildered mind about the rich man, the camel, and the eye of the needle. So what, I thought! This does not apply to me, an average Christian. Apparently, Christians must pay back their bad deeds in the abyss before they receive rewards on judgment day I wrongly thought.

Confusion was setting in for no one had clearly explained this to me. This place can be a terrible time dimension because my distorted sole had seen the horrifying punishment of the preceding souls, which did not pass the test. Jesus was holy, with energetic glow, a hue so to speak with colors beautifully separating in crisp contrast to the surroundings. Earth does not contain the ability to produce such beauty as this higher dimension of curved space about the flaming throne.

It was frightening and exhausting to walk onto the platform before the throne of Christ. The wheels, which supported the throne and platform, were also ablaze. They were something like thruster jet rotary engines with an infinite amount of afterburners firing off in a synchronized fashion. This kept the throne floating and in a different multiple time overlap displacement than the multitudes waiting to be judged. It appeared to be different judging going on at the same time yet in different dimensions. This is wild, for the past, present, and future all exist at the same location in this time displacement. Am I experiencing the ultimate paradox about truth or is this a bad dream? Multi-time dimension was beginning and ending from the throne. Controlling my thoughts was hard because they were freaking out! There was a river of fire coming out before Him like a magnificent energy flux being transferred into another time dimension. Yet, the judging platform extended over the river of energy-fire. It was hot to the touch from the river and something else, which will be discussed later.

My mental toughness which was self pride, melted like hot wax and dripped onto the floor.

On the throne was an awesome figure in the image of a man. Thousands upon thousands were waiting and serving around the throne. Out of this group, my mother and other familiar people to me from earth emerged for a quick glance. They were not making any physical effort to come over to see me, they just had a sorrowful stare at me as they went about the throne. This gave me a creepy feeling as my red glazed eyes looked back up to Him on the throne. Paralyzed with fear from His appearance, my legs failed to work as my knees hit the hot floor to bow down to the King of kings. Holiness manifested itself like a super energetic glow gleaming everywhere from the throne. My mental toughness, which was self-pride, melted like hot wax and dripped onto the floor. It began to smell and bubble like a slimy substance. "Stand up," the Bookkeeper shrieked! Getting up to take the test was hard to do with my wobbly legs. My body was fearfully shaking because **not one** pastor, teacher, or Christian had completely warned me of this on earth. My Spirit brought to my recollection when Dad, Mom, and others warned me to live a better life. My decrepit soul stood there feeling faint in a pool of my melted pride trying to be calm and looking at this awesome sight. My soul sensed His name because it was written on Him, Word of God.

His robe was dripping with blood (Revelation 19:13) from the war He fought at the end of our test cycle. Disorder flashed through my brain as havoc with my thought process was playing out. In addition to my raddled thoughts, what was even more disturbing, the appearance of the blood seamed to have a royal energized glow and the newer blood sparkled fiery red with a pulsing (hot-warm) translucent glow on His robe and legs. My mind gasp uncontrollably when I determined it was the blood of the souls who were judged before me. Their blood would hit the hot floor and spatter on the bottom of His robe and legs. My thoughts were petrified with (dreaded) fear. Yet, I was being injected with understanding and insight into the heavenly. The robe had a name written on the upper part of it, "KING OF KINGS, AND LORD OF LORDS" (Revelation 19:11-16). The robe reached down to His bronze feet, which had a translucent glow similar to a hot fire inside a furnace because of the sparks spilled from the ladle held by the angel over the altar of fire (Revelation 14:18). The fire in the ladle was used to test each person's works for quality (1 Corinthians 3:12-17).

Jesus' had many gold crowns on His head and it glowed a brilliant white, with hair that looked the same, or maybe like wool or snow when bright sunlight hits it. His face was even brighter like many suns having a violent eruption of super-white light. Seven eyes (Revelation 5:6), each with the power of a giant sun, were like blazing crystal clear fire. They scanned about to see if the court was set (Daniel 7:9-10). The seven eyes were moving in different directions and appearing in parallel time-displacement at the same time. This bothered me because they seemed to be impatient or waiting for something to happen. He had seven horns, which represented the power and strength He was drawing from the Seven Spirits of God (Revelation 1:4, 4:5 and 5:6).

completed. It does not put emphasis on

There was one glaring eye [👁] that penetrated my soul with a lacerating stare. Instruction in my spirit came concerning this eye and the Book of Works (Revelation 20:12). I was shown how the Lord God used each appointed Horn and Eye. Each Eye and respective Horn has an assigned Spirit one through seven. The Eye would be like a satellite movie camera, which records every response and reaction a person commits during the test cycle. This information will be received back via the antenna (horns). Through the completed cycle, each human form's works will be recorded, stored, and processed in a master-☺-computer file, and sorted using rightness accountability. Note: Jesus has the only authority to hit the delete button to erase sinful actions, which have been recorded. If an unforgiving spirit like mine is detected during the judgment, Jesus can if He chooses hit the recall button at different intensities depending on the amount that person has forgiven others. This will result in losing rewards, which are desperately needed to compete and be successful for future rewards in the next assignment or test cycle. Fear and trembling came over me at this insight while decay crept into my body.

The Horns were sapping what was like electromagnetic energy and information from the seven Spirits (earthly human forms) and other sources at such a high rate of velocity my being understood how insignificant our world really was in the scheme of things. The transfer of energy equated to something like a hydrodynamic turbulence oscillating above the horns. This caused fluctuation and irregular pulsing of energy, which vibrated the cosmos. "Terrified" understates my inadequate feelings. This transfer of energy appeared like something similar to an aurora borealis (northern or southern lights). The electromagnetic disturbances were not a random movement in the atmosphere like the aurora borealis, but a well-defined pulsing of electromagnetic energy being transferred at such magnitude my mind could not grasp its dimension.

Heaven was quiet for a minute or two as I lay there petrified as
horror
crept over my thoughts.

THIS WAS SO FRIGHTENING TO ME.

✋ **-Stop! It is very important for the reader to close their eyes and meditate by trying to imagine this awesome sight. Go back ☜ and reread the previous paragraphs and then be still and listen and pray to the Lord God that He will open your mind to this spectacular event. Remember, you will be standing there some day. Now continue, ☞ but pray constantly for insight about this. Sadly you are most likely not receiving insight about this in your church.**

As my mind determined, these horrifying thoughts could not increase, insight opened my Spirit to what was taking place next to me on the platform. My Spirit screamed inside my mind, "How could this be?" Jesus' head was leaned forward and bent over as in a mediating state. It was creepy to me standing amidst a huge horde of suffering souls. The Spirit-filled Philadelphia Church Christians (Revelation 3:7-13) were standing in front of me. They were excited with anticipation, jumping with joy, and shouting songs of praise to Jesus for avenging their blood (Revelation 6:10-11), as they stood in front of the millions of poor bewildered and tortured souls. "Who are these poor souls standing with me?" I questioned. The Bookkeeper replied, "These are Moslems, their converts, and others that are from the synagogue of Satan, who claimed to have the true Jewish inheritance to the Holy Lands, Jerusalem, and God. They thought they were following righteousness and obeying God, but were deceived by Satan masquerading himself as the archangel Gabriel-of-light (2 Corinthians 11:14). They have been judged liars and are being made to acknowledge the real God of gods, Yahweh, before the Spirit number Six Saints (Revelation 3:9, see section Seven Spirits of God)". They were being tortured and tormented by the angels as they herded them like cattle on the platform before the throne of Jesus to be electromagnetically discharged in front of the Spirit number Six Saints.

Then Jesus' head abruptly rose along with His right hand using a distinct gesture to silence heaven. The concussion from this hostile motion knocked me down where I had been observing this phenomenon. Heaven was quiet for a minute or two while I lay there petrified as horror crept over me. This was so frightening to me.

Suddenly, Jesus made an angry gesture with his left hand as it went up and his right hand cut the air with a stabbing sound as it violently hit the armrest with a mighty explosion of lightning bolts. His mouth opened and magnetic electric pulses like a sharp two-edged sword extended an awesome pulse of energy over the Moslems and their converts as to knock them flat on the ground. They were kicking and screaming with torment as they acknowledged Jesus had loved the Spirit number Six Saints and Satan had misled them disguised as Gabriel. They acknowledged themselves liars. Then Jesus pointed to the lake of fire and made another aggressive gesture to start the transport. Instantly, like a swarm of mad bees there were warring angels coming down and picking up each screaming soul to take toward the lake of fire.

What was astonishing, seemed impossible for this was happening in real time for each soul. Otherwise, what my mind was experiencing happened the same time my judging took place. The Bookkeeper gave me a warning to relay to the reader that mortals do not understand the multidimensional properties of Jesus or the righteous wrath He can use to torment a soul on judgment day.

He had an unexplainable sneer on his time-weathered face while drumming his fingers on the ladle's handle with anxious anticipation.

I pleaded with Jesus to take me out of this time dimension, which overlapped my real time. Objective reality seemed here and now, yet my soul was being stretched into a multidimensional imaginary illusion. Quantum entanglement of intersecting time-space-dimensions was all modulating from the throne. Instantly my soul was carried away from the time-dimension containing the swarm of angels removing the Moslems. My being was before Jesus as if nothing had happened except my mind was frazzled. Experiencing two time-space displacements at the same point-reference was more than my intellect was prepared to accept. My soul was exhausted and quivering with fear!

After that horrifying experience, I tried to pull my composure together for my presentation before the Lord. Cautious optimism was the order of the day as my lukewarm presentation began giving an account of my works, which were recorded in the books concerning what accomplishments on earth might merit treasures in heaven. My wish was to be hopeful of getting rewards until my memory flashed a horrifying thought in my mind. People's works are as filthy rags compared to God's on His throne. This was easy to see when standing before the throne. Faith and imagination was not needed here because Jesus' dimension of time-space was reality. He rewards us after we become Spirit-filled Christians for good works, which were done for Him, not for ourselves. My confidence slipped away and skeptical thoughts began to flash into my rattled mind. My focus of thought was scattered about because the Holy Spirit was not in me to direct my presentation. I began to realize my presentation was in desperate trouble for if I was a Christian where was the Holy Spirit? Crying out for the Holy Spirit to help was useless for there was nothing - just-dead silence. My soul began to tremble uncontrollably when, a disturbing noise began to increase beside me. Maybe the Holy Spirit is coming to help me?

Desperately glaring at the direction of the noise brought great disappointment for it was the angel over the altar of fire, not the Holy Spirit. He had an unexplainable sneer on his time-weathered face while drumming his fingers on the ladle's handle with anxious anticipation. His fingers made a disturbing tapping sound, which echoed the expanse, giving me the shivers, and distracted my focus of thought. The Bible had taught me this angel was the one who brings ladles of fire to test the quality of people's deeds to receive a reward. My intuition told me he was ready to get at me.

To my amazement, Jesus began to get very upset with me. This was unexpected for I believed my good works equated to a Christian, which should win me rewards. After finishing my presentation concerning a good deed, Jesus would angrily bang His clenched fist against the armrest of the throne. What seemed like fire and sparks splattered everywhere from the mighty impact as my teeth rattled and the platform shook. Jesus then forcefully motioned with the sharp sickle in his hand at the angel to test (1 Corinthian 3:12-17) my previously stated works with fire. The angel's expression turned to a torturing grin as he slowly poured the hot acidity fire from the ladle over my works and me. They burned and the fire ate at my soul with torment (James 5:3). Fire on earth cannot harm the soul but the fire from the altar, which the angel used, ate like acid on my soul as it tested the quality of what I was presenting. Fear was crawling over me as pain crackled down my spine.

There was a sharp decline in my composure and presentation. Disruptive thoughts flooded my rattled mind concerning what words to use in defending my good works. Stammering I said, "Jesus this is not fair, for my good works must receive rewards." Again, my presentation contained another good work, thinking it was commendable, but with less optimism, and the same hair-raising results continued. Jesus judged my actions were not worthy to pass the Book of Works (Revelation 20:12). Each time Jesus asked **"Why did you do what you just told me you did?"** I had to answer, "For myself, not You, Jesus". My own words were convicting me just as the Bible predicted. I remembered some Spirit-filled Christians warning others about the saying, "Works without salvation is dead and salvation without works is dead".

Two perspectives of insight flashed through my mind. Our distant view to perceive the outcome of judgment day has been blinded. Therefore, we must test our deeds (2 Corinthians 13:5) by calculating our ability to stand before God. Our real time reality comes to play on judgment day when both perspectives are compared. The discrepancy between how we perceive our works and the Lord God judges them will equate to some of our lost rewards (Malachi 1:12, Matthew 25:44 and 7:21-23, Revelation 3:17). I then realized a Christian who passes the test must have some balance in their lives to report on judgment day. Which means, Spirit-filled Christians will have accomplished good works that testify to the genuine nature of their faith for Jesus. The reverse follows, if people have good works for Jesus, then they must be Spirit-filled Christians. The key is, good works for Jesus not ourselves.

A disturbing thought flashed by, "Oh, woe is me!" Then Jesus gestured at the Keeper over the book of works again. The Bookkeeper sneered at me again as he opened my works to the place assigned to nation judging. Again, my thoughts were trouble, and torment crawled all over my decrepit soul. Gasping for self-control was hard because there was nothing recorded which showed effort to keep my nation a disciple nation. I retorted angrily at Jesus hoping an offensive answer would help. "Nobody in the Church explained to me that nation-judging involved me personally. Seldom was anybody taught to get involved in government affairs or to influence them toward Christian values. This is unfair!" My mouth blurted out frantically. Jesus judged my works had not fulfilled the effort necessary to pass the section of the test labeled Great Commission (Matthew 28:19-20).

My assigned eye, the seventh one that watched over the lukewarmers [👁] had become dark red and puffy as it cried sorrowful tears of my own blood. The blood seemed energized and different than on earth, for it appeared to have a rich glow of energy as it hit the floor by Jesus' feet. Power from the droplets dancing on the hot platform was transferred from the splatters to Jesus. Then shock hit me as insight came, this power should have been mine for doing good works for Jesus. Sadly, for me this power was being returned to Jesus for my miserable works had failed to meet His righteous judgments. My being was traumatized further as more blood droplets hit the floor. I could see more rewards vanishing before my eyes. My grief was heavy-laden by a force that only extreme divine shame could produce.

The other six eyes were impatiently slicing the cosmos with their sharp laser-like headed glances. They must have wanted to have some of their assignments tested and it made me shiver uncontrollably. Then Jesus with fire coming from His awesome eyes looked at the Keeper of the Book of Life and angrily nodded as He cut the air with His sharp sickle in a hostile gesture. The Bookkeeper opened the Book of Life to where my name had been electrotype set and fused into print before time began (Revelation 13:8, 17:18) on this earth to participate in my unique assigned testing cycle. My soul shook with awe as I saw where my name had been blotted out of the Book of Life. Everyone else could view it also because the Bookkeeper held the verdict up for others and turned in a mocking way around and around with a smirk on his face so all could see.

"This is not fair!" I cried. Then quickly I mounted a frantic and staunch defense for my lukewarm actions and unforgiving spirit. I further recounted how Satan had deceived me into believing I could love Jesus and the world like two half brothers (Lukewarm). Jesus roared like a Lion loudly enough to shake the platform;

"I never knew you, away from me you evildoer"

(Matthew 7:23). My thoughts became hostile and argumentative. Words began to come out of my mouth against Jesus' righteous judgments. "Jesus, You could have overridden Satan and saved me. You could have nudged somebody in the many different Churches to warn me about Your harsh judgment. I thought we could talk things out and besides they told me You were a loving and understanding judge, not this!

My defensive nature frantically challenged Jesus, "I have reasons for some of my unforgiving and wrong behavior. How about the time old So-and-So hurt me. You remember, don't You, Jesus? He treated me wrong and I had to do what you are accusing me of and have unforgiving feelings about him."

Impatiently Jesus looked at the Bookkeeper and shouted, "Show him!" The cosmos shook from Jesus' response and the Bookkeeper with that same sneering grin opened the books or what we would call a computer screen to the day and hour which I had accused

As my eyes looked, shock came over my petrified soul once again, for the screen was blank just as if it had never happened.

this So-and-So of mistreating me. As my eyes looked, shock came over my petrified soul once again, for the screen was blank just as if it had never happened. The Bookkeeper explained So-and-So had repented and dedicated his life to Jesus after hurting me and the sin I was accusing him of does not exist.

Then Jesus cut us off by roaring, "I have forgiven him as far as the East is from the West." Jesus then declared me a liar in addition to my other shortcomings. He said, "No liar will be tolerated in My presence, away with you!" I tried to explain to Jesus that there was not enough time before my death to forgive the man. My resistant nature angrily screamed at Jesus, "This incident really happened and I must get some slack here so my unforgiving spirit can explain some more reasons for my disobedient behavior"! Jesus was not impressed and angrily swung his sharp sickle at me as He made a gesture for the angels to remove me from His sight forever.

"No! No! Jesus! This insight has helped me see the light!" Oh, forgive me - please - Jesus." But, my frantic protests and pleas echoed off a void expanse into nothing, never to be heard by any ear again.

Staggering with pain my soul cried out in anguish. For my being was still burning and crackling from the laser-acid like fire poured over me by the angel testing my works. These cries could not be heard over the cracking sound of my burning soul shriveling into an awful twisted figure. The stench concluded the defining moment in my tormented soul, for time had ran out on my assigned testing cycle.

We must not fool ourselves about this matter, because Satan has been exceptionally good at deceiving today's Christians, especially in America.

My decrepit soul was being designated to a new time-space dimension, **'outside with the Dogs'** (Revelation 22:15). Two angels seized what was left of my burning arms. They began to drag my violently disturbed soul toward the lake of fire. Pieces of smoldering creamy ash splattered the way, while my flaming soul was dragged forcefully through the expanse at the speed of thought. My decaying soul screamed with terrible torment as it tried to fight its way from the two angels and petition Jesus one more time for another chance. It was too late, as my impaired sight caught a backward glimpse one more time at the flaming eyes of Jesus. Uncertainty vanished and reality hit my senses for my burned eyes saw Jesus motioning the next person to center stage before the throne to be judged. He refused to give me even a glance or ear to my hysterical pleas of torment.

Electrified jolts hit my decayed soul as it turned around in the direction we were traveling, for the Lake of Fire was approaching. We had traveled outside God's time-space domain through a transparent membrane into another horrible cataclysm displacement of time-space. This caused muffled vibrations in the void cosmos, which increased my panic. Oh, my God, the lake looks hideous and it was ghastly terrible, - - - horrified I screamed, "Jesus, I'm sorry, if only someone had warned me better in the Churches, ♒ ♒ please do not do this ghastly deed, ♒ give me one more chance",,,,, ♒ - ♒ it was too .... ♒..............., late... ♒.... ..... zzsssst.

MY LAST THOUGHTS TO YOU

This nightmare has become more vivid with my maturity in Christ. I truly see how close my choices brought me toward receiving worse punishment than a sinner (2 Peter 2:20-21). Only by the free gift of God Almighty's Grace (kindness) and mercy was I spared from this tragedy of second death. This book of prophecies refers to lukewarm Christians acting like me in my old nature before truly accepting Jesus Christ. They are anything but lukewarm when judged by the Lord Jesus. They really are sons of the devil thinking they are okay Christians. Jesus says we cannot serve two masters. We must not fool ourselves about this matter, because Satan has been exceptionally good at deceiving today's Christians, especially in America. He has blinded many of their eyes to the truth.

2 Corinthians 13:5 challenges Christians to: "Examine yourselves to see whether you are in the faith (Christian); **TEST yourselves.** Do you not realize that Christ Jesus is in you - **unless, of course, you fail the test?"** How do Christians constantly test themselves to see if they pass or fail? They must make necessary corrections along with repentance before they meet their real Judge - Jesus Christ. Jesus will be separating the field of players, which have completed the testing cycle on judgment day. Fear the Lord God and understand it will be too late to change to a new improved plan for people's test cycle, which has been judged completed. They will find themselves standing at their beginning (which is their ending) on judgment day before the Lord.

Congratulations, I pray Christians are moved to take the test. Christians can test themselves by using 2 Corinthians 5:15, as their guide. It states, *"And he* (Jesus) *died for all, that those who live should no longer live for themSELVES but for HIM* (Jesus) *who died for them and was raised again."* Christians, please circle ***"SELVES"*** and ***"HIM" in the Bible.*** On judgment day when the book of works shall be opened, each person must give an account of what they accomplished as recorded in the books (Revelation 20:12) to get rewards. After they present to Jesus what they assume is a positive "work" for a reward, Jesus will ask them a question. "Why did you do what you just told me you did?"

He judges our hearts, not the outward appearance like the world has been doing. The world will always be quick to glorify selfish works in front of men. Judgment day for true Christians will be a rewards banquet. **But for sinners, unbelievers, and lukewarmers it will be a nightmare.** The Spirit moved me to understand in the fall of 1987 this testing process of myself, which led to a commitment to Jesus Christ.

How's your presentation? Will you still be standing when you get finished talking? I hope so, and pray the Lord God will open your eyes. If you, dear reader are willing to repent (Luke 13:3) and make a commitment to Jesus Christ, then read page one and make the most important decision of your life. God as my witness, Bob R. Short, March 23, 2006

Center, 12-2-2 - Italy, Rome - Arch of Constantine (AD 315) at Roman Forum: The Ancient Roman Forum was a place where laws, judging, and sports involved life and death decisions for many people. The Lord God has given the governments the sword to correct. Ancient Rome in the Forum area and Colosseum areas abused its powers. We are all equal at the foot of the cross so to speak, but that is as far as it (equal) goes. Equality stops as we progress through our test cycle using our free will to gain or lose rewards for our next assignment. On Judgment day, Jesus has the sword of correction to issue a righteous deathblow to the disobedient or gifts for His faithful followers. Right now Christians have Jesus as their defense attorney to intercede before God Almighty and themselves. But on Judgment day Jesus prophetically leaves their side, walks up, and sits on the judgment seat to judge not represent. If a person is a Spirit-filled Christian, the Holy Spirit now becomes their attorney so to speak and mediator concerning their presentation to receive good gifts from Jesus the appointed Judge. People who are lukewarm or are sinners will stand without the Holy Spirit as your counselor and are in big trouble! They will walk alone on the judging platform to defend themselves and will not be able to stand!

Many people invite Christ into their heart before true heart-felt repentance is achieved. They are now lukewarm with Jesus and sin in their heart. They are now worse than a sinner. Church leaders are at fault here. Their false teaching has confused repentance with obedience. Desiring to turn from sin and doing so is obedience not repentance. To be truly heart-felt sorry for your past sins against Almighty God and asking Him to forgive you is repentance. Therefore, to be saved one must first repent and then invite (Revelation 3:19-20)!

I pray the Lord God will bless you by my testimony and these prophecies. Amen, and amen. Bob R. Short

12-2-3 - **Israel, Sea of Galilee** - Jesus Ship: The Sea of Galilee is in fact a freshwater lake, 13 miles long and seven and one half miles wide. One of the crew demonstrated how to throw a fishing net from the ship.

It is the last few minutes in the sixth sabbatical day of the eleventh hour. It seems the world has been fishing for fish, eating, drinking, and having a good time. The world has been unaware midnight races to close the final hour of the test cycle. Many Churches have been asleep, in denial, and/or lukewarm. Nations are corrupt and building a world government without following Jesus Christ's teachings. Jesus warned Christians to watch out and be on their guard because endtimes will come like a flood and catch most people off guard and destroy them. People must realize, our time-perception will become increasingly harder to grasp as it races to meet its end at the feet of its Master-designer.

When the end comes, you will find yourself at your beginning.
Will you be able to stand before the Lord God and His Royal Court?

The time has come for Christians to be FISHERS of MEN, and MEN to become Elite Christian Soldiers!